# History vs. Apologetics

# History vs. Apologetics

## *The Holocaust, the Third Reich, and the Catholic Church*

David Cymet

LEXINGTON BOOKS
A division of
ROWMAN & LITTLEFIELD PUBLISHERS, INC.
*Lanham • Boulder • New York • Toronto • Plymouth, UK*

Published by Lexington Books
A division of Rowman & Littlefield Publishers, Inc.
A wholly owned subsidiary of The Rowman & Littlefield Publishing Group, Inc.
4501 Forbes Boulevard, Suite 200, Lanham, Maryland 20706
http://www.lexingtonbooks.com

Estover Road, Plymouth PL6 7PY, United Kingdom

British Library Cataloguing in Publication Information Available

**Library of Congress Cataloging-in-Publication Data**
Cymet, David, 1931–
  History vs. apologetics : the Holocaust, the Third Reich, and the Catholic Church /
David Cymet.
    p. cm.
  Includes bibliographical references and index.
  ISBN: 978-0-7391-3293-7 (cloth : alk. paper)
  eISBN: 978-0-7391-3295-1
  1. Catholic Church—Relations—Judaism. 2. Judaism—Relations—Catholic Church. 3.
Christianity and antisemitism—History. 4. Pius XII, Pope, 1876–1958—Relations with
Jews. 5. National socialism and religion. 6. Holocaust, Jewish (1939–1945) 7. World
War, 1939–1945—Religious aspects—Catholic Church. I. Title.
  BM535.C88 2010
  940.53'18—dc22                                                    2009027464

Printed in the United States of America

*And God said to Cain: Where is Abel your brother? And he said, I don't know, am I my brother's keeper? And He said: What have you done? The voice of your brother's blood cries to me from the earth.*
Genesis 9: 4-10


*Thou shall not stand idly by the blood of thy neighbor.*
Leviticus 19:16


*O earth, cover not my blood nor let my outcry come to rest!*
Job 16:18

# Contents

Contents

# Acknowledgments

This book on the Holocaust and the Catholic Church is the product of seven years of full-time research and writing. I am indebted to the many scholars who preceded me in this field whose names are mentioned in the notes. My gratitude goes to my family who inspired and encouraged me to bring this book to fruition, in particular my wife Leah and my children. Very special thanks to my daughter Sara Rachel Tenenbaum who generously gave of her time and put her professional computer skills to assist me in producing the typed manuscript.

I wish to thank editorial director of Lexington Books Julie E. Kirsch and my editors Jessica Bradfield and Paula Smith-Vanderslice, and production editor Victoria Koulakjian. My thanks to Dr. Michael Berenbaum, former director of the Research Institute of the U.S. Holocaust Memorial Museum in Washington, D.C. for his comments on the book. My thanks to the U.S. Holocaust Memorial Museum for granting permission to use the photographs included in the book. This book not only bears witness to the Holocaust but is also a reminder that we must always stay vigilant. Its final message is not of doom but of hope. I pray that my grandchildren will draw spiritual strength and inspiration from the book as they grow up.

Dr. David Cymet
Brooklyn, N. Y.
February 2009

# Preface

After the annihilation of six million Jews in Christian Europe, there were many questions to be asked and issues to be raised with the Catholic Church, but in view of the desperate situation that the Jewish people faced after the war, it seemed wiser to postpone such reckoning for better days. Throughout history, the Jewish side was never eager to get involved in controversies much less in confrontations with the Catholic Church. Even the so-called dialogues were fraught with dangers. The lessons drawn from historical experience advised against them. Neither the Second World War nor the Holocaust altered this prudent attitude rooted in historical memory. A veil of silence was drawn over the role of institutional Catholicism in the Holocaust in spite of the momentous significance of the question. History took second place at that moment.

The last thing Jewish leaders wanted after the Shoah was to engage the Church in historical reckoning and recrimination for past offenses and increase the hostility of the Church. More urgent priorities stood at that moment before a wounded people involved in a desperate struggle for survival. Many of the Holocaust survivors in the DP camps were trying to pry open the doors of Mandate Palestine, while others were desperately knocking doors asking for visas to rebuild their shattered lives in other continents. Jewish orphans left with Christian families or institutions by their parents before being sent to death were waiting to be brought back to their people and their faith. A fledgling Jewish state underway was in the midst of its painful birth pangs. Even if for no other reason than the entrenched traditional opposition of the Church to the resettlement of the Jews in the Holy Land and its age-old resistance to return Jewish children in Christian hands to the faith of their parents, it seemed wiser to postpone such reckoning for better days.

It was not a Jew but a German Christian, Rolf Hochhut, who in his youth had belonged to the Nazi *Jungvolk*, who dared to ask in 1963, seventeen years after the end of World War II and five years after Pius XII's death, the first disturbing questions on Pius XII's response to the Holocaust. His drama *Die Stellvertreter*, which was brought to the scene for the first time in Berlin on February 20, 1963, centered on the Pope's obstinate silence in the face of what Winston Churchill called the greatest crime registered in history—the systematic annihilation of the Jewish people by the Germans and their helpers. Published in book-form that year, it was translated into more than twenty languages and brought to the scene the world over.

The Pope's silence was a question of burning concern during the war long before *Die Stellvertreter* was brought to the scene. Pius XII received during the war countless heartrending appeals from European Jewish communities in peril of death, from their rabbis and lay leaders as well as from Allied leaders. These appeals to the head of the Catholic Church were not about Jews being socially discriminated and denied access to universities or exclusive country clubs, but desperate SOS life-and-death pleas of help against Christians who were exterminating every living Jew in Christian Europe for no other reason than having been born Jewish. Did Pius XII live up in face of such a crime to the moral standards that he himself set down before the Italian Ambassador Dino Alfieri, not long after he rose to the papal throne, on May 13, 1940?

> The Pope is free, and God will pass judgment on him if he does not react to evil or does not do what he believes is his duty. Mind you we will all, all, be subject to God's judgment, and earthly successes cannot save us from this terrible judgement. [1]

Hochhuth's verdict on the role played by Pius XII in the Holocaust was devastating. The refusal of Pius XII, as the leader of Christianity, to confront Germany during the war years with the enormity of its crime through a public condemnation took center stage in Hochhuth's drama. The annihilation of the Jewish people happened in the heart of Europe, the cradle and center of Christian civilization. At the zenith of his power in 1942, Hitler ruled over the largest Catholic community in the world with more than 200 million Catholics. In Germany more than 90 percent of the population identified themselves officially in 1939 as Christian and 43.1 percent as Catholic. The allies of Nazi Germany in Europe, such as Italy, Hungary, Vichy France, Slovakia, and Croatia, were overwhelmingly Catholic. So were occupied Poland and its Baltic neighbors.

The fact that the Final Solution was being carried out in Christian Europe by its governments and Christian citizens made it imperative upon the head of the Church to warn its followers publicly that they were committing a Cain act of unprecedented gravity. The minimum that could have been expected from the spiritual center of Catholicism was moral guidance during the long twelve years of unprecedented victimization of the Jewish people by Europe's Christians. Hochhuth intended to remind the Church of the responsibility—a responsibility bordering on complicity—of having remained silent while those whom the Church considered to be the bulwark of "Christian Civilization" were annihilating the Jewish people. He did not spare words in his moral indictment:

> Perhaps never in history have so many human beings paid with their lives for the passivity of a single statesman (Pius XII).[2]

Albert Schweitzer, from far-away Gabon in Africa, joined Hochhuth in his moral indictment. As a Protestant theologian deeply aware of the dismal record of his own Protestant coreligionists with respect to the Nazi annihilation of the Jews he made his voice heard in the preface he wrote to Hochhut's book:

> After all, the failure was not that of the Catholic Church alone, but thatof the Protestant Church as well. The Catholic Church bears the greater guilt for it was an organized, supra-national power in position to do something, whereas the Protestant Church was an unorganized, impotent, national power . . . To stay in the right path of history we must become aware of the great aberration of those days, and must remain aware of it, so as not to stumble further into inhumanity. It is significant, therefore that the drama "The Deputy" has made its appearance. Not only is it an indictment of an historical personality who placed upon himself the great responsibility of silence; it is also a solemn warning to our culture *admonishing us to forego our acceptance of inhumanity which leaves* us unconcerned.[3]

In carefully chosen words, Francois Mauriac (1885-1970), the 1952 French Catholic Nobel Prize laureate of literature, expressed the awesome moral responsibility involved in standing quietly aside while a whole people were being annihilated:

> A crime of this proportion redounds in no small part on all the witnesses who did not protest and on those who were responsible for their silence.

Fr. Andrew Greeley, a Catholic theologian, reminded the Church that the ancient universal moral principle that silence presumes consent is part of Catholic theology:

> The ancient principle of Catholic moral theology applied then, as it does today: silence presumes consent.[4]

Carlo Falconi formulated his condemnatory conclusions in the following words:

> Pius XII not only failed the duty of his office, but his duty to Christianity and mankind. His refusal to speak out played into the hands of evil and this grew bolder and fiercer and became more provocative. Silence amounted to complicity with iniquity.[5]

The historical record provides unmistakable clues to the meaning of the Church's obstinate silence. A closer look at the role played by the Church in the consolidation of the Hitler regime, the agreements signed or verbally established with the Nazi regime, the anti-Semitic campaign from the pulpits and the Catholic press in the pre-war years, and the Catholic frontline role in the promotion of anti-Jewish legislation in the Catholic countries of Europe was anything but neutral. It is only against the general background of its record of coincidence and collaboration with the Nazis and their helpers that the silence of the Church during the Holocaust acquires its full significance.

Hochhuth's drama resonated worldwide and brought to life a polemic that is far from over. It opened a Pandora box that could not be closed since. A far-more damning picture than Hochhuth intended surfaced as a result of the polemic. For all its merits, the drama created unwittingly the wrong impression that passive silence was the limit of the Church's wrongdoing. When the Church's responsibility went far beyond having been passive when millions of Jews were singled out for annihilation, by focusing exclusively on what the Church *failed to do* for the Jews at the moment of their greatest need, the drama unwittingly diverted attention from what the Church *did* against them. By concentrating on the Church's silence the drama eclipsed the Church's very active role in Hitler's rise to power and conquest of Europe and its frontline participation in the adoption of anti-Semitic legislation in almost every country in Fascist Europe that prepared the ground for the Final Solution. The sins of omission that Hochhuth focused on covered up the more grievous sins of commission.

The first historians who approached the question of the role of the Church during the Holocaust faced serious obstacles in their pioneering work. The Vatican had not yet made public any of its documents at the time, and then, as today, blocked open access to its archives. These pioneers had to search for alternative sources. Fortunately, some important parallel sources were becoming available at the time, such as the correspondence of the foreign diplomats accredited before the Vatican with their governments, particularly those of the German, English, and American envoys, including the personal documents of the German ambassador to the Vatican, Diego von Bergen. The documents of the German Foreign Office, captured intact by the Allies in 1945, were beginning to be published in the late 1950s and the British Foreign Office documents corresponding to the 1922-1945 period reached the end of their thirty-year secrecy limit. In addition, some German diocesan archives agreed to open their doors to the historians.

Historians Saul Friedlander, Guenter Lewy, Klaus Scholder, and Carlo Falconi were the first pioneers who made skillful use of these alternative sources very early on, and they were able to venture far beyond the limited domain of the issues raised by the Hochhuth drama. Their path-finding work has not lost its validity over time and remains a solid reference point for anyone entering this tragic chapter of history. An impressive list of competent historians and writers followed soon after. Among them were Anthony Rhodes, Gitta Sereny, Robert Katz, Sam Waagenaar, C.E. Helmreich, Randolph L. Braham, Moshe Y. Herczl, Georges Passelecq, Bernard Suchecky, Michael R. Marrus, John Cornwell, Renée Bedarida, Garry Wills, and Doris Bergen. Last but not least, Susan Zuccotti, Michael Phayer, David Kertzer, and Daniel J. Goldhagen made important contributions that have greatly increased knowledge and understanding of the subject.

In the aftermath of *The Deputy*, Pope Paul VI (1963-1978), Pius XII's trusted undersecretary of state, appointed a team of Jesuit priests—Pierre Blett, Burckhardt Schneider, Angelo Martini, and Robert A. Graham—to make a selection of the correspondence between the Vatican Secretariat of State and its representatives and Church dignitaries abroad, for the period 1922-1945. Fr. Pierre Blett has stated that the publication of the *Actes* was the Vatican's response to the polemic on the role of Pius XII during the Holocaust. The product of their selection was an eleven-volume collection of documents under the title *Actes et Documents du Saint Siege relatifs a la Seconde Guerre Mondiale* that was published between 1965 and 1981. One volume was specifically dedicated to documents related to Jews and the Holocaust. Some respected Catholic priests and scholars such as Fr. John Morley SJ, Fr. Ronald Modras, Fr. John Pawlikowski, and Fr. Pierre Blet joined the polemic with exemplary objectivity on the basis of these published Church documents.

Serious doubts were raised not long after the *Actes* were published concerning the comprehensive character of the collection when it was compared with other parallel sources available. The absence of vital major documents prompted Gitta Sereny to express "the gravest doubts as to the integrity of the Vatican publications" as early as 1973:

> Particular documents which are of the greatest possible significance in the context of establishing the extent of the Vatican's early awareness of the situation in Poland with particular reference to the extermination of the Jews have also been excluded from the *Actes et Documents du Saint Siege relatifs a la Seconde Guerre Mondiale*. This omission, in view of the purpose of the publication and the nature of these papers—all of which were highly relevant official diplomatic communications—raises the gravest doubts as to the integrity of the Vatican publications.[6]

In more recent times other historians, such as Michael Phayer, again raised the issue of the selective character of the collection and pointed out that the absence of such crucial documents as the Gerstein report, the documents on the deportation of the Jews of Rome, and part of the correspondence between Msgr. Preysing and Pius XII, among others, were indications that the selection was flawed in other areas as well.

Notwithstanding the limitations of the Vatican selection, Fr. John Morley SJ produced in 1980 an outstanding historical work on the basis of the material included in the *Actes*, which he published under the title *Vatican Diplomacy and the Jews during the Holocaust 1939-1943*.[7] His conclusions did not by any means invalidate the results of the earlier authors but, to the contrary, provided unquestionable proof from the selected material itself to many of their conclusions, beginning with the proposition that the Vatican and the Church hierarchy were very well aware of the annihilation campaign against the Jews in Europe at the time it was taking place.

In what seemed to be a hopeful sign of greater openness and cooperation in the search of truth, the Joint Historical Commission of Christians and Jews was established in December 1999 with the declared aim to "study the Vatican archives dealing with World War II to try to resolve the highly contentious issue of whether the Roman Catholic Church could have done more to avert the Holocaust."[8] When the Commission was denied access to the unpublished documents in the Vatican archives and was advised by the Vatican to limit its activities to review the material published in the *Actes*, it arrived to a conclusion not very different from the one reached by Gitta Sereny thirty years earlier:

> No serious historian could accept that the published edited volumes could put us at the end of the story.[9]

As a result the Commission decided to dissolve itself on July 23, 2000. The contention that much still remains unknown on the role of the Vatican during the Shoah is confirmed every time new independent documentary sources previously closed becomes available.[10] A request that the Vatican should open its archives was again put on the agenda in December 2006 by thirty-five Catholic and Jewish scholars who signed a petition promoted by the David Wyman Institute:

> The undersigned include representatives of a range of views on this subject. But we all agree that the Vatican should open its archives for the Holocaust period to historians, so that the role of the wartime Pope will not be subject to conjecture as to what he knew, what he did, and what he chose to say or not say about the plight of the Jews. [11]

The efforts to defend the actions of the Catholic Church during the Holocaust in apologetic terms go back to the war years, but *Die Stellvertreter* had a catalytic effect in reactivating those claims. Unlike their not-so-distant cousins—the Holocaust deniers—they did not claim that the Holocaust never happened, but rather chose to take cover behind half-truths, misrepresentations, and subtle distortions. At the margin of legitimate discussion beholden to historical truth, the defenders of all sorts aimed at derailing the discussion by creating a thick cloud of confusion and doubt. It is most unfortunate that some of their contrived arguments found their way to legitimate literature.

The aim of this study is to look critically at the polemic and present a view of the issues within the wider context of their contemporary political and ideological background. It implies confronting facts and conclusions from different sources and authors in a unified perspective that aims at separating history from apologetics. It goes without saying that this study would have been impossible without the path-finding works of the authors previously mentioned.

I acknowledge with sincere and humble gratitude the intellectual debt I owe to each of the authors mentioned.

The exhortation to face the Shoah with truth and respect for the victims made by the Speaker of the Italian Senate, Marcello Pera, at the commemoration of the sixtieth anniversary of the liberation of the Nazi concentration camps before the UN General Assembly on January 24, 2005, should show the way:

> We have an obligation to tell the truth. The Holocaust is not the product of imagination or propaganda or rhetoric. The Holocaust has been a tragic, unique, fact of history. Those who deny it, underestimate it, or try to revise it, are simply committing another crime.
>
> We have an obligation to remember and pay respect to the memory of the millions of human beings that were gassed, tortured, starved, forced to die in the most humiliating ways.
>
> We have an obligation to understand. How was it possible that Europe, at the peak of its civilization, could commit such a crime? How could Nazi Germany, Fascist Italy, collaborationist France, and many others, become responsible—in different ways and to different extents, but in any case responsible of such immense massacre? [12]

# Notes

1. *Actes et Documents. vol. I,* Audience with Italian Ambassador Dino Alfieri, 13 May 1940, 454-455.

2. Hochhuth, Rolf, *The Deputy. Sidelights on History* (New York: Grove Press: 1964).

3. Declaration of Repentance by the Roman Catholic Bishops of France issued at Drancy on September 30, 1997.

4. Richard Z. Chesnoff, *Pack of Thieves: How Hitler and Europe Plundered the Jews and Committed the Greatest Theft in History* (New York: Doubleday, 1999), 249

5. Carlo Falconi, *The Silence of Pius XII* (Boston: Little, Brown, 1970), 72-73.

6. Gitta Sereny, *Into that Darkness* (New York: McGraw Hill Book Co., 1974), 330.

7. Morley John F, *Vatican Diplomacy and the Jews During the Holocaust 1939-1943* (New York: Ktav Publishing, 1980).

8. The *Holy Sees's Commission for Religious Relations with the Jews* and the *International Jewish Committee for Interreligious Consultations* were its sponsors.

9. JCR. Letter to Cardinal Walter Kasper, president of the Vatican's Commission for Religious Relations with the Jews, July 20, 2001.

10. Hundreds of thousands of pages of FBI, CIA, and U.S. intelligence and army records related to Nazi and World War II war crimes were released under the Nazi War Crime Disclosure Act of 1998 on May 13, 2004.

11. David Wyman Institute. Petition signed on December 2006.
12. Marcello Pera. 27 January 2009. *We have an obligation*. United Nations Organization General Assembly Special Session January 24, 2005 New York www.marcellopera.it.

# Chapter 1
## Introduction

## Christian Anti-Semitism: The Seedbed of Nazism

According to Nazi ideology Jews were primarily defined as a race. In consequence, even those that converted to Christianity were classified as Jews. The Catholic Church on its part relegated the racial criterion to a second place and determined Jewish identity on the basis of religious allegiance. The Church referred to baptized converts and their descendents as non-Aryan Christians, while the Nazis referred to them simply as Jews, without generally adding any adjectives.

The rejection of Aryan racism by the Church did not imply, however, a reversal of its traditional teachings of contempt against the Jewish people. While the Church in modern times did not endorse the racial justification of anti-Semitism that the Nazis promoted, it had no problem with anti-Semitism practiced on religious, cultural, social, or economic grounds. In congruence with this position, the Church tried sometimes to protect baptized converts but otherwise was quite at ease with the persecution of Jews in general.

An authoritative modern formulation of the Church's view on anti-Semitism, contemporary to the growing Nazi movement in the late 1920s, was published by a long-life close associate of the future Pope Pius XII in Munich and later part of his inner circle in Rome, the Jesuit theologian Fr. Gustav Gundlach SJ (1892-1963) under the title *Anti-Semitismus* in the *Lexicon für Theologie und Kirche*, edited by Bishop Buchberger of Regensburg in 1930. Gundlach's formulation of Church policy carries great weight and is of value to determine the coincidences and differences between the Church and the Nazis on the subject of anti-Semitism at the time.

Gundlach distinguishes between Volkisch anti-Semitism based on racist motives and anti-Semitism promoted for general political, economic, and cultural reasons. While he rejects the first as un-Christian, he approves the second. He considers the two Austrian anti-Semitic politicians, Karl Lueger and Georg von

Schoenerer, who strongly influenced Hitler during his years in Vienna, an excellent model to follow. When referring to "global plutocracy and Bolshevism" they allegedly manifest, according to Gundlach, "dark aspects of the Jewish soul expelled from its homeland which are destructive of human society." Although he rejected the Nazi rationalization of anti-Semitism on racial grounds, he fully subscribes to the measures against the Jews advocated by them. In his article he provides the guidelines of what he considered "good" anti-Semitism:

> The first type of anti-Semitism is not Christian because it is contrary to brotherly love to oppose men solely because of the difference in their nationality, rather than because of their actions. This type necessarily also turns against Christianity on account of its internal link with the Jewish people formerly chosen by God.
>
> The second type of anti-Semitism is permissible when it combats, by moral and legal means, a truly harmful influence of the Jewish segment of the population in the areas of economy, politics, theater, cinema, the press, science, and art [liberal-libertine tendencies] . . .
>
> The Church has always protected Jews against anti-Semitic practices proceeding from false jealousy, false Christian zeal, or from economic necessity. On the other hand, it has inspired and supported measures opposing unjust and harmful influence of economic and intellectual Judaism.[1]

Presenting anti-Semitism as an act of "self-defense" against the Jews and their alleged negative influence, Fr. Gustav Gundlach was taking high moral ground to justify anti-Semitic activism in Christian society. While he maintains that natural law establishes the equality of all those "redeemed" through Christianity, he excludes those not "redeemed" (Jews) from that equality.[2] His approval to fight the "harmful" influence of the Jews in the "areas of economy, politics, theater, cinema, the press, science, and art," is not distinguishable in a practical sense from the Nazi approach.

Gundlach's underlying assumption that the Jews were on the offensive, attacking or in any way threatening Christian society in Germany and in Europe, as implied in his words, was nothing but the same classical anti-Semitic canard used to justify such crimes against the Jewish people as economic boycotts, discriminative legislation, quotas in the universities, exclusion from government and the professions, forced emigration, and pogroms. In a practical sense Gundlach and the Church were on the same wavelength as the Nazis. Their attack against the intellectual Jewish elite in Germany and Austria that included some of the most famous scientists, artists, and humanists is permeated with the same mean-spirited envy and jealousy that inspired Hitler and his followers. It is relevant in this context to quote Hitler's address to a delegation of Aryan physicians on April 6, 1933, to which Gundlach might have well-agreed on the basis of his thesis of "self-defense":

> Germany's claim to an intellectual leadership of her own race must be satisfied by a swift eradication of the majority of the Jewish intellectuals from the cultural and intellectual life of Germany. The admission of too large a percentage

in proportion to the whole nation might be interpreted as recognition of the intellectual superiority of other races, and this must absolutely be rejected.[3]

A pastoral letter published in 1935 by the bishop of Linz, Msgr. Johannes Maria Gföllner, went a step further in its support of anti-Semitism. It is representative of the Catholic approach to anti-Semitism at a time when the Jews were already subject to fierce persecution in Germany. It proves that David Kertzer stands on very solid ground when he contends, "The distinction between anti-Judaism and anti-Semitism will simply not survive historical scrutiny." The pastoral letter, which is a radicalized version of Gundlach's approach, underlines the common bond that anti-Semitism creates between Aryans and Christians. Gföllner exhorted the Catholics:

> It is beyond any doubt that many Jews, unrelated to any religious concern, exercise an extremely pernicious influence on almost all sectors of modern civilization. The economy and business . . . law and medicine, society and politics are all being infiltrated and polluted by materialistic and liberal principles that derive primarily from Judaism. Newspapers and leaflets, the theater and cinema, are full of frivolous and immoral elements that deeply poison the Christian soul, and it is in fact Judaism that, for the most part, inspires them and spreads them . . . Not only is it legitimate to combat to end Judaism's pernicious influence, it is indeed the strict duty of conscience of every informed Christian. One can only hope that Aryans and Christians will increasingly come to recognize the dangers and troubles created by the Jewish spirit and to fight them more tenaciously.[4]

Although the Catholic Church manifested its unwillingness in the twentieth century to endorse Aryan racism in its extreme Nazi version, it is nevertheless a fact that racial anti-Semitism was not alien to the Church at all in earlier times. Racial anti-Semitism was practiced for long centuries in Spain against Jews who were forcibly converted to Catholicism during the periods of mass persecution that began in 1391. Not only the converts themselves who attempted to save their lives through conversion but also their baptized descendents many generations after were the victims of fierce persecution by the Church, for no other reason than their kinship or "blood relationship." Their extraordinary advancement in every sphere of life, including the ecclesiastical ladder, awakened the jealousy and resentment of the "Old Christians" to a degree not seen before. To stem the tide of advancement of the converts and their descendants, discriminatory laws and decrees were enacted against them. Christians in Spain began to be classified according to blood kinship and categorized as "Old" or "New Christians" in terms of their ancestry.

Laws and ordinances based on blood criteria were passed, barring access to the army, universities, and religious orders to the converts and their descendents, even after many generations of their conversion under the influence of such theologians as Fray Alonso de Espina. An elaborate accounting system of blood purity was put in place to apply these discriminatory laws. Categories such as "three-quarter," "half," and "quarter" Jewish were established to rank the degree of blood purity of the New Christians. For the lack of anything better, "purity of blood" or *Limpieza de Sangre* became the only motive of pride and distinction for Old Christians—as Aryan blood later became for the Germans. Thus, to mention two examples among many, Christian descendents of converts up to the third generation were not allowed under death penalty to set foot on Spanish America, and descendents of the converts up to the fifth generation could not join the Jesuit order until the twentieth century. The fires of the Inquisition were kept burning for long centuries until the eighteenth century, depriving the descendents of the converts from their rights, wealth, freedom, and life.

As late as the end of the nineteenth century *Civiltà Cattolica*, the most authoritative Jesuit periodical published in Rome under the direct supervision of the Curia, endorsed the notion that Jews are essentially a race. Its founding editor, Giuseppe Oreglia SJ, printed an article that was cleared by the Vatican Secretariat of State, in which the notion was given sanction:

> Oh how wrong and deluded are those who think Judaism is just a religion, like Catholicism, Paganism, Protestantism, and not in fact a race, a people, and a nation! . . . For the Jews are not only Jews because of their religion . . . they are Jews also and especially because of their race. [5]

History replayed itself in Germany in the aftermath of the Napoleonic emancipation of the Jews. When Jews, who numbered less than half of 1 percent of the German population, moved rapidly ahead to prominence after the fall of the ghetto walls and produced figures of first rank in literature, music, science, medicine, philosophy, finance, and industry, traditional clerical anti-Semitism raised its ugly head in Germany and Austria as earlier in Spain. Instead of receiving the bounty of the unparalleled creativity of their Jewish citizens as a contribution and enrichment of German culture, they were perceived as dangerous competitors who were conquering the citadels of Germanic culture. Hostility was not only directed against the steadfast Jews who kept their loyalty to their millennial faith and tradition but even more against the apostates who abandoned their faith and converted to Christianity to sidestep the great obstacles that stood in their way to advancement in Christian society.

As anti-Semitism based on religious grounds alone seemed insufficient to counter the rationalistic arguments of the liberal and *Aufklerung* movements in favor of Jewish emancipation, a modernized version of the sinister concept of blood purity dressed up in pseudoscientific garb was reintroduced to stem the tide of Jewish emancipation. The reactionary *Volkish* movement that appeared in Germany in the nineteenth century revived the old concept of blood purity. The ideology of Aryan racial supremacy was put again in circulation using Darwin's then novel theory as a prop.

The *Volkish* charlatans shamelessly came forward with the claim that the Aryan race was superior to all others in human society—the only one possessing the creative genes that make civilization and culture possible, whereas the Jews were the antithesis of the Aryan race and capable only of destroying culture and civilization.[6] Assimilation and conversion to Christianity were a mere ruse to undermine the pure Germanic racial community, a deception directed at the heart of the true German *Volk*. They lamented the Jewish presence, which they claimed was the source of the "downfall" of Germany in modern times and added the accusation that the Jews were part of a conspiracy to undermine the blood purity and racial qualities inherited from the ancient Germans.

The pressure on converted and estranged Jews was worked up in Germany in the nineteenth century like in Spain to the point that many converted Jews and their descendants were terrified to be identified as having Jewish blood in their veins. Their stereotyping was so overwhelming that it translated itself into self-hatred and self-loathing among many of the assimilated converts and their descendants.

The *Volkish* ideas appealed to the German public, which took them deadly serious and "infected like rabies the social body of Germany." They penetrated the schools, history textbooks, and literature and exerted an enormous influence on the growing generations. The Jews in Germany were declared a problem and became the focus of political debate. A problem obviously demands a solution, and the anti-Semites of different persuasions began to display their ingenuity in finding "solutions" for the so-called Jewish Problem. The German term *Judenfrage*, used to refer to the Jewish Problem, became a byword in the political lexicon in Germany and Austria, and was even used by naïve Jews who did not perceive its sinister connotation. The academic underworld joined in the choir and added its own pseudoscientific mystifications. Political movements such as the Pan-Germans, and the *Antisemitn Bund* in Austria in particular, centered all their political activity around promoting "solutions" to the *Judenfrage*, which were presaging Hitler's *Endlösung*—the "Final Solution." The suggestion that Jews should be deported to remote places in Africa such as the island of Madagascar was brought forth for the first time by the notorious German anti-Semite, Paul de Lagarde in his *Deutsche Schrifften* (1866).

When parliamentary democracy was forced upon the monarchies of Europe in late nineteenth century, reactionary political parties opposed to the trend perceived the potential of anti-Semitism in its various forms as a powerful electoral weapon. Political parties, clerical and Volkish, turned to anti-Semitism as an effective vote-getting strategy to stem change. With the help of newspapers, journals, and tabloids these parties built up their popular appeal through anti-Semitism long before the Nazis. The Jews became the scapegoat and scarecrow of Europe's new parliamentary politics. "Jew hatred" acquired a new poisonous dimension.

Anti-Semitism, whether in its traditional clerical garb or in its racist form, acted as a catalyst that brought together different political interests that otherwise had very little in common. As a well-developed, powerful political tool in the hands of unscrupulous demagogues and hate mongers supported by the Catholic and Protestant churches, it reached the threshold of the twentieth century. Used to derail honest political public discussion and campaigning from its track, Jews were systematically made responsible for every political problem at the time. Germany, Austria, and France are the most conspicuous examples of countries using unscrupulous and immoral anti-Semitic hate propaganda in politics to gain votes.

Acting in the spirit of the medieval Church, the Church in modern times blamed the Jews of being the source of every novel political development it feared or disliked.[7] Not unlike Pope Benedict VIII (1012-1024) who put on trial and executed Jews under the charge of being responsible for hurricanes and earthquakes as documented by historian Hans Kühner in his *Der Anti-Semitismus der Kirche*, the Church in modern times systematically accused the Jews of being responsible for freemasonry, secularism, liberalism, industrialism, capitalism, urbanization, and parliamentary democracy. To stir up popular opposition to the emerging tendencies of modernity perceived as menacing to the Church, its spokesmen would simply label them a Jewish plot.

World War I changed the borders and regimes of Europe but not its deep-seated rivalries, which turned virulent. A message of hate was being spread not only by the Nazis in Germany and Austria but also by extreme nationalists in every European country. Pitted against each other they found a common language in anti-Semitism. The Church was not a stranger in these developments. The old forgery of the Czar's Secret Service, *The Protocols of the Elders of Zion*, that claimed that the Jews had a secret plan for controlling the world was rediscovered and disseminated by influential Church circles in every country of Europe. In Italy, Monsignor Umberto Benigni, a highly placed official in the Vatican Secretariat of State during the pontificate of Benedict XV published the *Protocols* in Italian to propel his unrelenting anti-Semitic campaign, even accusing Jews of ritual murder. Fr. Ernest Jouin, the leader of the French-Catholic League and champion of the *Protocols*, conducted in France a vicious anti-Semitic campaign in his *Revue Internationale* harping on the alleged Jewish-Masonic world conspiracy. Honored by Benedict XV with the title *Prelate of his Holiness*, Pius XI raised him to *Apostolic Prothonorary* for his activities. In a private audience Pius XI encouraged him in 1923:

> Continue your Review, despite your financial difficulties, for you are combating our mortal enemy. [8]

In 1928 the Supreme Tribunal of the Catholic Church, known through history as the Inquisition or the Holy Office, banned on March 28, 1928, a missionary Catholic movement called the *Friends of Israel* that petitioned the Vatican to remove from the Good Friday liturgy the insulting expressions "the perfidious Jews" and the "perfidy of the Jews." The Friends of Israel, which was backed by nineteen Cardinals, 278 bishops, and 3,000 priests, did not lack ulterior motives for their request—they were interested in the conversion of Jews. The central committee of the movement argued that missionary activity was hindered by the ignoble way the Church related and treated the Jewish people. In a publication under the title *Peace upon Israel* (*Pax super Israel*) they criticized the Church for allowing the libelous ritual-murder accusations against the Jews, which were nothing but "old wives tales," and for its support of anti-Semitic movements and the stigmatization of the Jews as the "deicide" people.

With the exception of Cardinal Ildefonso Schuster, a member of the Supreme Tribunal, who expressed sympathy for the petition of the missionary Friends of Israel and voiced his opinion that such expressions as "perfidious Jews" represented a practice that was "late and superstitious," all the other members of the Holy Office zealously rejected the petition. The wrath of Pius XI fell on Cardinal Schuster for calling the liturgical expressions "late and superstitious." Pius XI ordered Cardinal-Secretary of the Holy Office Rafael Merry Del Val to question Schuster of why he articulated opinions "so grave and offensive to the Church."

The Holy Office reached a decision to issue a ban against the Friends of Israel and to order its dissolution, adding a warning that "no one in the future write or publish books that in any way favor such erroneous initiatives." To cover itself against charges of blatant anti-Semitism, the Holy Office added a caveat, which became a standard formula in all Church pronouncements concerning Jews in the sense that "hatred against the people whom God once chose, that hatred that it is today known as anti-Semitism is unacceptable." Notwithstanding its duplicitous caveat, ancient and modern anti-Semitism found in Merry Del Val a powerful sounding board. He went as far as to launch the accusation that beyond the missionary Friends of Israel stood "the hand and the inspiration of the Jews."

> Today after the war the Jews were attempting more than ever to reconstruct the kingdom of Israel. They penetrated modern society, seeking to hide their history and win the confidence of Christians while forming alliances with Masonry and practicing usury. [9]

In 1928, Father Enrico Rosa, longtime director of *Civiltá cattolica,* explained the ban in an article that carried the title "The Jewish Danger and the Friends of Israel":

> The Church has always sought to protect even its most bitter enemies and persecutors, which is what the Jews are . . . We have tried in these pages to demonstrate how much the Jews are to blame for the Soviet Revolution . . . as they were previously in the French Revolution and as they have been in the more recent one in Hungary . . . In the short time Jews had been given equal rights they have established their hegemony in many sectors of public life, especially in the economy and industry, as well in high finance, where they are indeed said to have dictatorial power. They can dictate laws to states and governments, in political as well as in financial matters, without fear of having any rivals . . . They are first in the large businesses, occupying the highest posts, especially in industry, in the large banks, in diplomacy, and even more predominant in the occult sects, scheming to achieve their world hegemony. [10]

The differences on the racial or religious definition of Jews wouldn't have made much difference to anti-Semites whether Nazi or clerical. However, when the Nazis turned their attention to the historical roots of Christianity to redefine Christianity in terms of their racial premises, contention set in. In 1930, Alfred Rosenberg (1893-1946), the ideologue of the Nazi movement, published *Der Mythus des Zwanzigsten Jahrhunderts*, demanding that Christianity should break its links with the Old Testament and Aryanize the New Testament and its main figures. "The time had come," said Rosenberg, "to establish a Germanic Aryan Church based on the principles of soil, blood, and race" in accordance with the idea of *Positive Christianity* announced in the 1920 Nazi program. The connections of the Church to its ancient Judaic roots had to be severed.

In view of the potential far-reaching consequences that Rosenberg's demand entailed for its future existence as a universal religion, the Church felt threatened and reacted swiftly. For reason of its own survival as a world religion, the Church was not ready to alienate and surrender all the non-Aryan races in its fold to please the Nazis. Its claim of representing a supranational religion that embraces all races and nations would become meaningless. The Church realized that Christianity, as a whole, whose main founding figures were Jews (of all people!) and not Aryans, would be turned into a mockery in terms of Aryan racism. A break with the Old Testament to which the Church appealed throughout the ages to sanction its religious claims, as demanded by Alfred Rosenberg, was seen as demolishing the foundation of Christianity itself.

Afraid that German Catholics might follow in the footsteps of the Protestant German Christians who, in response to Rosenberg's call to Aryanise their religion, founded "a Reich Evangelical Church to which the greatness of the National Socialist state is an article of faith," Rosenberg's demands were declared by the Catholic Church to constitute a "subversion of the very foundations of the Christian Religion and the Christian State." [11] The two leading German cardinals, Bertram and Faulhaber, who otherwise maintained cordial relations with Hitler and the Nazis, expressed from the pulpit their rejection of Rosenberg's *Positive Christianity*. Cardinal Faulhaber formulated the Catholic position in 1931 and again in his Advent sermons in St. Michael's Church at the eve of 1933. He pointed out that baptism and not ties of blood define a Christian and rejected Rosenberg's demands to sever the ties of Christianity to the Old Testament. He called upon the Protestants to join with the Catholics in defending the "Holy Books of the Old Testament." On February 7, 1934, Rosenberg's *Der Mythus des Zwanzigsten Jahrhunderts* and Ernst Bergman's *Die deutsche Nationalkirche* were included in the Church Index of Forbidden Books. [12]

However, when some foreign anti-Nazi circles abroad interpreted Faulhaber's sermons against Rosenberg's demands as an attack on anti-Semitism and a gallant defense of persecuted German Jewry, Faulhaber swiftly rejected any such suggestion with indignation. In a historic letter to the Jewish World Congress in 1934, Faulhaber took good care to point out that his defense of the Hebrew Bible had nothing to do with the "antagonism to the Jews of today." To avoid being suspect of defending Jews or Judaism he stated in a sermon, in line with the ancient anti-Semitic tradition of the Church, that after the appearance of Christianity, God's covenant with the Jewish people had been revoked and the

Jews had become "restless wanderers over the earth." He even negated the contribution of the ancient Jewish nation to the lofty ideals of the Old Testament using defamatory language:

> People of Israel, this did not grow in your own garden of your own planting. This condemnation of usurious land grabbing, this war against the oppression of the farmer by debt, this prohibition of usury, is not the product of your spirit.[13]

Faulhaber's defenders, whose historical memory works selectively, tried again after World War II to revive the myth of his alleged defense of the Jews against the Nazi attacks. The Church declaration *We Remember* found it easy to pin on Faulhaber the label of spirited defender of the Jews on the basis of these sermons. Guenter Levy reacted to this travesty of historical truth:

> It therefore is little sort of falsification of history when Faulhaber's sermons in 1933 are hailed by one recent Catholic writer as a "condemnation of the persecution of the Jews." [14]

The differences between the Church and Rosenberg did not lead to a break between the Catholics and the Nazis. Hitler himself provided them with a formula of accommodation, which they gladly embraced. When an official delegation of the Conference of Bishops visited Hitler for the first time on April 26, 1933, to congratulate him in the name of the episcopate to his becoming chancellor, Hitler used the occasion to exhort the Church to reinvigorate its war against the Jews and join him in a common struggle against them. The master-deceiver tried to put a distance between him and Rosenberg's plans to Aryanize the churches. He told them that being a Catholic, he would not permit the founding of another religion, nor tolerate another *Kulturkampf*. To calm their apprehensions, he assured them that he did not set race over religion and gave the bishops a formula to harmonize Aryan racism with Christianity. Race and race purity could be integrated and harmonized with religion as subordinate values:

> I do not set race over religion, but I recognize the representatives of this race as pestilent for the state and for the Church, and perhaps I am thereby doing Christianity a great service by pushing them out of schools and public functions.

Guenter Lewy points out:

> Soon the German Bishops and theologians expressed their support for the ideas of race and racial purity after Hitler's rise to power. The list includes some of the most prominent theologians such as Karl Adam, Theodor Brauer, and Archbishop Gröber. [15]

Michael Schmaus, a theology professor at Münster wrote:

Catholics had always regarded the fate of the people, anchored in blood and
soil, as a manifestation of divine providence and for that reason they would also
have to share the just concern for maintaining the purity of blood, the basis for
the spiritual structure of the people.

As Catholics and Nazis converged on the "earthly values" of race and race
purity, the Nuremberg Racial Laws adopted by Nazi Germany in September
1935 posed no problem for the Catholic Church. The Fulda Bishops conference
did not express any objection to the Nuremberg Racial Laws and the official
Catholic organ in Germany, the *Klerusblatt*, welcomed them as "indispensable
safeguards for the qualitative make-up of the German people." In the *Handbook
of Contemporary Religious Questions*, published in 1937, Archbishop Gröber of
Freiburg (1872-1948) defended the right to protect the purity of the German race
in the following terms:

Every people bears responsibility for the success of its existence, and the absorption of entirely alien blood will always constitute a risk for a nation that has
proven its historic worth. Consequently, the right to safeguard the purity of the
race, and to devise measures necessary to that end, can be denied to no one.

Cardinal Faulhaber himself, the alleged champion against racism, wrote in
1937 in his draft proposal for *Mit Brennende Sorge*:

Race and state deserve a place of honor among earthly values, but they should
not be overvalued or deified. [16]

Dr. Hans Globke, the trusted confidant of Cardinal Faulhaber became the
main commentator of the Nuremberg Racial Laws. After their approval in 1935,
the Church in Germany fully cooperated in the implementation of the Nuremberg Racial Laws, providing the information kept in its birth, baptism, and marriage archives on the blood purity of the population. Their enthusiasm did not
wane even during the war years when the identification meant deportation and
death, as pointed out by Guenter Lewy. [17]

It is most unfortunate that the polemic between the German Church and the
Nazis was misunderstood for so long, particularly by the Jewish world. It was
nothing but a discussion between "classical" Catholic anti-Semitism and Nazi
racist anti-Semitism. Both varieties shared enough common ground to establish
a working alliance that held them together during the whole Hitler period to almost become indistinguishable one from the other. The primacy of baptism over
race postulated by the Church never went beyond the lukewarm defense of the
non-Aryan Christians, the name used by the Church to refer to the baptized converts whom in theory they were inclined to treat less harshly, although not better
than in medieval times. However, as far as the Jews were concerned they agreed
to their elimination from German life and cooperated during the Hitler era with
the Nazis in every walk of life. Thus they silently stood by as the Jews from

Germany and of conquered Europe were being deported and annihilated to the last man.

## Church Opposition to a Jewish Return to Palestine

In profiling modern Church anti-Semitism one cannot ignore the Church's fierce opposition to the hopes and efforts of the Jewish people to return in any form to their ancient homeland from which they were exiled by force and which they included in their every prayer during two thousand years. While the Church considered legitimate for every other nation in the globe to have a homeland, Church anti-Semitism made an exception in the case of the Jews and denied them that right. That hostility acquired its ultimate tragic significance during the Holocaust as country after country closed tightly their doors to Jewish refugees and every avenue of rescue was shut. Strong opposition to rescue Jews to Mandate Palestine, even children, came forth from the Catholic Church at the most tragic moment of the Jews need and abandonment.

On March 13, 1943, at a time that most of Slovakian Jewry had already been deported to Auschwitz, Msgr. Angelo Roncalli, the future Pope John XXXIII, then apostolic delegate in Turkey, was approached by the representative of the Jewish Agency in Istanbul, Chaim Barlas, asking for the Vatican's intervention before the Catholic government of Slovakia to allow the exit of one thousand Jewish children whom the British government, in an exceptional gesture, agreed to grant visas to Palestine. Msgr. Federico Tardini, the Vatican undersecretary of state became alarmed that the request to rescue the children might help Jews to convert Palestine into a Jewish national home. He wrote in his notes:

> The Holy See has never approved the project of making Palestine a Jewish home. . . But unfortunately England does not yield. . . And the question of the Holy places? Palestine is by this time more sacred for Catholics than for Jews.[18]

Vatican Secretary of State Luigi Maglione (1877-1944) responded on May 4, 1943, to a parallel appeal transferred through Msgr. Godfrey from England concerning the rescue of Jewish children from Europe to Palestine:

> The Vatican had long opposed the notion of a Jewish homeland in Palestine. The land of Palestine was sacred to Catholics because it was the land of Christ, and Catholics would justifiably fear for their rights if that land were occupied by a majority of Jews.

On September 4, 1943, Msgr. Roncalli himself, who otherwise showed his sympathy for the dying Jews of Europe, expressed his own apprehension in a dispatch to Cardinal Maglion concerning the Jewish efforts to rescue Jews to Palestine:

He (Roncalli) confessed to his superior he felt uneasy about the attempts of Jews to reach Palestine, as if they were trying to reconstruct a Jewish kingdom. Moreover he did not think it proper that the charitable activity of the Holy See should be used in this way to help the realization of any messianic dream that the Jews might have. The delegate concluded that any notions of reestablishing a Jewish reign in Palestine were visionary and utopian.

For Catholics and Christian governments loyal to Rome all over the world that policy carried great weight and influenced deeply their decisions. The Vatican Secretariat of State instructed its apostolic delegate in Washington, Msgr. Amleto Cicognani, to actively advocate that policy in Washington with President Roosevelt's representative to the Vatican, Myron Taylor, and to advise the American bishops to be on alert with regard to any change in public policy with regard to Palestine. In a letter to Myron Taylor dated June 22, 1943 he stated:

It is true that at one time Palestine was inhabited by Jews; but how can the principle of bringing back people to this land where they were until nineteen centuries ago, be historically accepted?

In another contemporary document the Vatican state secretary wrote:

Palestine, under a Jewish majority, would give rise to new and grave international problems, would displease Catholics throughout the entire world, would provoke the justifiable protest of the Holy See, and would badly correspond to the charitable concern that the same Holy See has had and continues to have for the Jews.

That a desperate SOS request to save one-thousand Jewish children from being sent to the gas chambers of Auschwitz should have elicited such a harsh reception from the highest authorities of the Church is in itself a most powerful indicator of the deeper roots of the Holocaust.

## Notes

1. Gustav Gundlach, *S.J.Antsemitismus, Lexicon fur Theologie und KircheFreiburg*, Br., 1930. 504. Martin Rhonheimer. *The Holocaust. What Was Not Said*. First Things. November 2003. Lewy Güenther. *The Catholic Church and Nazi Germany*.

2. Beth A. Griech-Pollele, *Bishop von Galen:German Catholicism and National Socialism* (New Haven, CT: Yale University Press, 2002).

3. Griech-Pollele, *Bishop von Galen*, 461.

4. Msgr. Johannes Maria Gföllner, Bishop of Linz. Pastoral letter published in 1935.

5. David I. Kertzer, *The Popes against the Jews: The Vatican's Role in the Rise of Modern Anti-Semitism* (New York: Alfred A. Knopf, 2001).

6. Eleven of the thirty-eight Nobel Prize winners in Germany before 1933 were Jews.

7. Hans Kühner, *Der Anti-Semitismus der Kirche* (Zurich: Verlag Die Waage, 1976), 108.

8. Kertzer, *The Popes against the Jews,* 264–269

9. Kertzer, *The Popes against the Jews*, 269–273. Godman, 26–28.

10. Rhonheimer, *The Holocaust.*

11. Review of the book by M. Barbera SJ in *La Civilta Catholica*, February 3, 1934.

12. Ronald Modras, *The Catholic Church and Anti-Semitism* (Poland: 1933–1939. Harwood Academic Publishers, 1994) 127. Bergmann was a philosophy professor at the University of Leipzig who published his book in 1933

13. Lewy Güenther, *The Catholic Church and Nazi Germany* (New York: Mc Graw Hill Book Co., 1964), 274.

14. Güenther, *The Catholic Church and Nazi Germany.*

15. Güenther, *The Catholic Church and Nazi Germany*, 7.

16. Godman, 143.

17. Güenther, *The Catholic Church and Nazi Germany,* 282. Daniel J. Goldhagen, *Hitler's Willing Executioners* (NewYork: Alfred A. Knopf, 1996), 110.

18. John F. Morley, *Vatican Diplomacy and the Jews During the Holocaust 1939-1943* (New York: Ktav Publishing, 1980).

## Chapter 2
## Hitler's Background

### Anti-Semitism at the Beginnings of the Nazi Movement

In his study on the more recent historical origins of Nazi anti-Semitism, the British historian Gerald Fleming pointed out the direct historical connection between the clerical anti-Semitism of the Austro-Hungarian Empire and Nazi biological anti-Semitism:[1]

> Clerical anti-Semitism, which prevailed mainly in the Austro-Hungarian Empire, must be regarded as a forerunner of the biological-racialist anti-Semitism that the Nazis were to perfect. It represents a long-standing, sinister tradition from which Adolph Hitler demonstrably was unable, and indeed unwilling, to escape . . . With the slogan "By keeping the Jews at Bay, I fight for the good Lord's way", Hitler, the anti-Semitic nationalist, sought to present himself as a new Christus militants . . . Its overtones of traditional Christian anti-Semitism were easy enough to link up with the Nazi brand of biological anti-Semitism. The move from one form to the other constituted a big step, but nonetheless, no more than a step.[2]

Adolf Hitler (1889-1945) was a direct product of Austria's anti-Semitic culture in which clerical and *Volkish* anti-Semitism coexisted side by side at all levels of society. Millions of Germans and Austrians could easily identify with Hitler because they drank from the same poisoned sources without any real sense of contradiction between them. The main perpetrators of the Final Solution—Hitler, Himmler, Heydrich, and Hoess—were born into Catholic families, received a strict Catholic education, and never severed their connection to the Catholic Church.

Baptized and raised as a Catholic, Hitler never renounced his Catholicism. Shortly after his birth, Hitler's father retired and moved the family to Lambach in upper Austria, where Hitler went to Catholic school with the Benedictines at the Abbey of Lambach-am-Traum. He lived for two years in the monastery and participated in its boys' choir. At the Abbey of Lambach-am-Traum, Hitler saw for the first the swastika engraved on the four corners of the monastery, where it had been sculpted several years before by orders of the abbot Theodorich Hagen. Hitler described himself in *Mein Kampf* as an enthusiastic admirer of the clergy during his youth and considered a priest to be the "embodiment of all humanly attainable heights."[3] For two years he seriously considered becoming a priest himself. Until he became chancellor, Hitler dutifully paid his annual Church tax. Konrad Heiden points out that "Hitler in 1918 certainly still went to confession and communion, and is even said later, after 1922, to have received the sacraments from the hands of the National Socialist Abbot Albanus Schachleitner, the former head of the Benedictine monastery of Prague."[4] On July 1, 1933, months after he became the chancellor of the Third Reich he let it be officially announced:

> Reich Chancellor Hitler still belongs to the Catholic Church and has no intention of leaving it.[5]

As late as October 1941, Hitler told his army adjutant, Major-General Gerhard Engel (1906-1976):

> I am now as before a Catholic and will always remain so.[6]

At no moment during the existence of the Third Reich did the Church excommunicate Hitler or place his book *Mein Kampf* in the Index of Forbidden Books. To the contrary, at the very end when Hitler committed suicide in the Reich's chancellery in Berlin and the news reached Pius XII in Rome, the Pope prayed for the "repose of Hitler's soul" in the papal chapel according to the testimony of his housekeeper Pasqualina Lehnert, who joined him there in silent prayer.

The senior cardinal of Germany, Adolf Bertram, gave written instructions to all the parish priests of the archdiocese to hold "a solemn requiem in memory of the Führer" when he received the news of Hitler's suicide late in the evening of May 1, 1945, at Schloss Johannesberg near Lauering. Klaus Scholder points out that such a religious ceremony can only be held for a believing member of the Church and if it is in the public interest of the Church. It meant, says Scholder, that until the very end the Church "continued to see and respect Hitler as the Catholic state head of the Reich."[7]

Hitler spent the formative years of his youth from 1907 to 1914 in Vienna, the capital of the Hapsburg Empire, as an unemployed vagabond. In Vienna's streets and soup kitchens, he acquired his political education before World War I. Vienna's two rival politicians, Karl Lueger (1844-1910) and George Schoennerer (1842-1921), who dominated the Viennese parliamentary and municipal politics during the closing era of the Hapsburg Empire, exerted a profound long-term influence in the formation of his fundamental political ideas. The two rivals are the last visible link in the chain that connects nineteenth-century political anti-Semitism to Hitler and the Nazis. Historian E. B. Bukey characterizes in short words the anti-Semitic environment of Vienna at the time:

> The new anti-Semitic rage that began in Vienna, and spread rapidly through German-speaking Austria was exploited by well-known Jew-baiters such as Schoenerer and the Viennese political boss Karl Lueger. It was also blessed by the Roman Catholic hierarchy and given dangerous intellectual prestige by Social Darwinian apostles of "scientific racism." [8]

Regardless of their differences, both rivals Lueger and Schoenerer gave anti-Semitism a pivotal role in their movements and made systematic use of anti-Semitic propaganda. Schoenerer, as a *Volkish* racial anti-Semite, attacked both Jews and baptized converts alike, while Lueger, a clerical anti-Semite, exempted the apostates from his anti-Semitic rage, extending his "generous benevolence" to them. "I decide who is a Jew," he said, although his most trusted lieutenant, Ernst Schneider, was far less forgiving to them:

> The Austrian government should offer a cash price to any good Christian who killed a Jew. . . If I had to baptize Jews, then I should follow the method of St. John, though in somewhat improved fashion. He held them under water for baptism, but I should immerse them for the duration of five minutes. [9]

Hitler drew lessons indiscriminately from both rivals during the formative years of his youth in Vienna. Their ideas gave dangerous impetus to the two strains of anti-Semitism in the Nazi movement. Many of their contradictory ideas and methods were reintroduced by Hitler in the Nazi movement after World War I. Above all, he learned from them that anti-Semitism paid off well in politics, transcending the secular and religious divisions of the Germans.

Lueger, a master populist politician, won the support of the Vatican and the lower clergy in Austria for his *Christian Social* movement by declaring himself loyal to the Church in Rome and to the Catholic Hapsburg monarchy. The inordinate rise of modern anti-Semitism among the masses in Austria is credited to the support the lower clergy in Vienna lent to Lueger's movement.

Schoenerer, in contrast, was opposed to the Hapsburg monarchy and to the Catholic Church that supported it. He demanded the *Anchluss* of German-speaking Austria in a greater German Reich under the German kaiser and expressed his veneration for Bismarck who unified the German-speaking principalities under the leadership of the German kaiser, although he considered his achievement truncated by the *Ausschluss*—the exclusion of Austria from the Second Reich. He loathed the multiethnic character of the Austro-Hungarian Empire composed of many different nationalities such as Hungarians, Italians, Czechs, Serbs, Croats, Poles, and others, berating what he called the *Slavization* of the Austrian Empire. An exponent of fierce German nationalism and *Volkish* ideology, he was one of the founders of the reactionary nationalist Pan German movement, which proclaimed the union of all German-speaking people and the "right" of German territorial expansion to create a Greater Germany (*Grossdeut-*

*schland*). Schoenerer linked the goal of *Grossdeutschland* to the idea of the superiority of the Nordic race, which he declared to be the *Herrenvolk* or master race of Europe.

While Hitler generally identified with Schoenerer's ideas, he found fault with his tactics, which led him to fight many enemies at the same time, such as the Catholic Church, the Austro-Hungarian monarchy, and the Jews. In contrast, Hitler praised Lueger in *Mein Kampf* for his tactical decision to concentrate all his attacks on one enemy, the Jews, in order to secure the support of the Catholic Church. "Lueger," he wrote in *Mein Kampf*, "became a Christian Social because he viewed anti-Semitism as the way toward the salvation of the state and because in Vienna anti-Semitism could be established only on a religious basis." As for himself he was ready to use racial or religious anti-Semitism, as needed, in an all-encompassing strategy of unmitigated hate that would leave no escape route for the Jews, whether Mosaic or baptized:

> In general the art of all truly great national leaders at all times consists among other things primarily in not dividing the attention of a people, but in concentrating it upon a single foe (the Jews). He (Lueger) avoided any struggle against a religious institution and thus secured the support of that mighty organization which the Church represents . . . He recognized the value of large-scale propaganda and was a virtuoso in influencing the psychological instincts of the broad masses of his adherents. [10]

Unwilling to serve in the multiethnic Austrian army, Hitler left Vienna and arrived in Munich, the capital of Catholic Bavaria in May 1913. When World War I broke out on August 1, 1914, he enlisted, at the age of twenty-five, in the German army. The war turned out very different than what the German expansionist nationalists expected. The war left behind many millions dead and wounded and enormous political upheaval. It led to the abolition of the monarchies of Russia, Germany, Austro-Hungary, and Bavaria and the abdications of Czar Nicholas II of Russia (1917), Wilhelm II of Germany (1918), Charles IV of Austro-Hungary (1918), and King Ludwig III of Bavaria (1918).

Russia was the first country to surrender after the abdication of the Czar in February 1917. On November 8, 1917, Lenin (1870-1924) seized power in Russia and established a Bolshevik dictatorship. Vladimir I.Lenin, leader of the Bolshevik fraction of the Russian Socialists, who lived exiled in Switzerland, was sent in April 1917 by the Kaiser's government in a sealed train to Russia in hope that his anti-war propaganda would undermine the Russian war effort. On March 3, 1918, Russia surrendered to Germany, and signed the treaty of Brest-Litovsk.

On November 11, 1918 Germany surrendered to the Allies after the Kaiser abdicated two days earlier. The Weimar Republic came to power in Germany. On June 28, 1919, the German government ratified the Treaty of Versailles that formally ended the war. Germany lost portions of its territory and all its overseas colonies. It was subjected to rearmament limitations and to the payment of war reparations. The geopolitical map of Europe changed radically with the appearance of Poland, Czechoslovakia, Yugoslavia, and the Baltic countries as new, independent national states.

Lord Keynes figured out that the war reparations that Germany accepted to pay exceeded by three times Germany's ability to pay, but the sums were, nonetheless, benign compared to the reparations that the kaiser imposed in the earlier Brest-Litovsk Treaty on Russia, which were four times greater than the ones later imposed on Germany in Versailles. Aware that the Germans were eager to lay the blame on others but themselves for their defeat, Hindenburg (1847-1934), the German supreme military commander, accused the civilian politicians in Germany's surrender to absolve the army and the officer corps from any responsibility.[11]

After the German defeat, chaos reigned in Germany. A dangerous polarization in the political arena took place. To the right, embittered war veterans, unemployed youth, and other discontents joined the Freikorps, paramilitary organizations led by army ex-officers and other former military personnel. The Freikorps eventually served as the nucleus of the Nazi storm troops, the SA. To the left, Communist-inspired attempts to seize power took place in various parts of Germany, such as the short-lived Spartacist uprising in Berlin (January 5 to 15, 1919) and the abortive Bavarian Soviet Republic in Munich led by Max Levien, Eugen Levine, and Tonja Axelrod (April 7 to May 1, 1919). The government of the Social Democrat Friedrich Ebert used the Freikorps to rapidly crush the Communist insurrections and murder its leaders.

Hitler returned in 1919 to the Lechfeld barracks in Munich with the rank of lance corporal. There he acquired the skills of a political agitator participating in the political indoctrination courses that the Education and Propaganda Department of the Bavarian *Reichswehr* organized under Captain Mayr to safeguard the soldiers from leftist ideologies. From the very beginning Hitler decided to play the anti-Semitic card and defined himself on September 16, 1919, as a rational anti-Semite whose ultimate goal was the "removal of the Jews altogether." In a report on anti-Semitism that Captain Mayr assigned him to write for Adolf Gemlich, a participant in the courses, he wrote:

> Anti-Semitism of the emotional sort finds its expression in the forms of pogroms. Rational Anti-Semitism on the other hand, must lead to a systematic legal opposition and elimination of those special privileges that the Jews hold, in contrast to the other aliens living among us. Its final objective must unswervingly be the removal of the Jews altogether.

Hitler was sent in by the Bavarian Reichswehr as an agent to infiltrate a minuscule political group, the *Deutsche Arbeterpartei* (German Workers' Party), that was reestablished on January 5, 1919. The party was created originally during World War I by Anton Drexler with the support of the army and industrialists to win over the working class to the aspirations of the Pan-German nationalist Fatherland Party, which then sought international recognition for the conquests and annexations of the kaiser. Hitler joined the group on September 12, 1919, in Munich and delivered his first political speech for the party in a

Munich beer cellar on November 13, 1919. He redirected against the Jews Hindenburg's "treason and stab in the back" accusation and blamed the Jews for Germany's collapse in the Great War and the conditions imposed by the Versailles Treaty.

Hitler hurled with impunity every conceivable accusation of disloyalty and treason against the Jews. It did not matter to him that his fabrications went against the true facts of the loyal and patriotic participation of German Jewry in the war effort in which they stood out far beyond their proportion in the population. Although the approximately 500,000 Jews in Germany were less than 1 percent of the population, more than 100,000 Jews, 20 percent of the total, freely joined the Kaiser's army! Eighty thousand of them served in combat and as many as 35,000 were decorated for bravery, while 12,000 lost their lives in the trenches.[12] The names of the fallen soldiers were memorialized in a *Geffallensbuch* published after the war with a foreword by field Marshal Paul von Hindenburg, the chief commander himself.[13] Winston Churchill referred in a memorable speech in 1935 to the patriotic participation of German Jewry in the German war effort during World War I and the "gratitude" they received in payment:

> No past services, no proved patriotism, even wounds sustained in war, could procure immunity for persons whose only crime was that their parents had brought them into the world.

Hitler found responsive listeners among the Germans who needed a scapegoat for their own failings. It made no difference to them that it was a Catholic, the leader of the Center Party Matthias Erzberger who was murdered by the Free Corps in 1921, which negotiated and signed the armistice on November 11, 1918, as head of the German delegation.[14] To them it mattered little that Germany's defeat and its postwar problems had nothing to do with the Jews, as the German historian Klaus Scholder points out:

> Ideologies take little account of reality, and totalitarian ideologies take no account of it at all. In fact the Jewish question had nothing to do at all with the German problems of the postwar period. But that did not disturb either Hitler or Streicher. And there are moments in history when anything seem credible, even what is most absurd.[15]

Munich was at the time the residence of the apostolic nuncio, Msgr. Eugenio Pacelli, the future Pope Pius XII (1876-1958). He arrived in 1917 to the court of King Ludwig III of Bavaria and experienced during his stay the difficult days that followed the king's abdication, including the short-lived Communist revolution. During the short period of the aborted Communist seizure of power in early 1919, the nunciature was invaded by a mob on one occasion demanding food and money; an unsuccessful attempt was made by the revolutionary government to confiscate the limousine of the nuncio. The reports to Rome of the nuncio and his assistant, Msgr. Lorenzo Schiappa, spoke of a "harsh Jewish-Russian revolutionary tyranny."[16] Based on the anti-Semitic undertones of these reports, author John Cornwell, and others who followed in his footsteps, linked Pius XII's later policies to that early experience in Bavaria.[17]

In the biography of Sister Pasqualina Lehnert (1894-1983), the lifetime house-keeper of nuncio Paccelli, a very significant episode that occurred at the end of 1919, which she vividly described to authors Paul Murphy and Rene Arlington, comes to light. She remembered well when a young corporal (Hitler) came knocking at the door of the nunciature in Munich one late night during the winter of 1919 holding a letter of introduction from General Ludendorff (1865-1937) in which he extolled Hitler's bravery while serving as a corporal under his command. Sister Pasqualina recalled Hitler's meeting with the nuncio:

> Hitler told Pacelli that he was out to check the spread of atheistic communism in Munich and elsewhere. Through the door which had been left ajar, Pascalina overheard the prelate say, "Munich has been good to me, so has Germany. I pray Almighty God that this land remain a holy land, in the hands of Our Lord, and free of communism."
>
> Pascalina knew that Pacelli lived in fear of atheistic communism because of its professed aim to annihilate Catholicism. For that reason and despite the Church's claim of strict neutrality, the prelate had made his goal the complete destruction of this insidious new threat to world freedom and brotherly love.
>
> It did not come as a surprise to her, therefore, in light of Pacelli's hatred of the Reds, to see the prelate present Hitler with a large cache of Church money to aid the rising revolutionary and his small, struggling band of anticommunists.
>
> "Go, quell the devil's works," Pacelli told Hitler. "Help spread the love of Almighty God!" "For the love of Almighty God!" she heard the young man reply.[18]

The Germans Workers' Party achieved very little success among the working class and was at the brink of total extinction at the time Hitler visited the nuncio. While at present it is not known if Hitler continued to maintain his contact with the nuncio, who remained in Munich until 1926, that question might someday receive an adequate answer.[19]

On March 31, 1920, Hitler received his discharge from the army with the rank of lance corporal. Hitler and a gang of professional provocateurs, which included Anton Drexler, Dietrich Eckart, and Gottfried Feder, decided to recast the failing group on February 24, 1920, into the *National Socialist Party* (NSPD), Nazi Party in short. In a little beer hall in Munich they came forward with the idea to juxtapose the words, "Nationalism" and "Socialism" to capitalize on the appeal of these ideologies among many Germans. They adopted the swastika symbol of the occultist *Thule Gesellschaft* of Baron Rudolf von Sebottendorf as the emblem of the new party.[20] They also acquired from von Sebottendorf his newspaper *Die Volkischer Beobachter*, which became the official voice of the Nazi Party.

The founding political platform of the *National Socialist Party* was formulated in twenty-five points. The program expressed its support for *Positive Christianity*, without specifying what that meant. The program demanded the union of all Germans in one *Grossdeutschland*, and the Anschluss of Austria to Germany. Racial anti-Semitism figured prominently in the program: Only a person of German blood could belong to the party and consequently, Jews, even if converted, were excluded. In point 4, the program demanded an end to Jewish civil rights; point 5 demanded that citizenship should be taken away from Jews; point 6 postulated that Jews should be inhabilitated to hold public office, and point 7 demanded that where their presence threatened the lives of German citizens they should be deported as aliens.

Several weeks after the founding of the National Socialist Party, Hitler declared in a political meeting on April 6, 1920, according to a report of the Munich police, that he could not rest satisfied with instigating pogroms, but his aim went much farther "to extirpate the Jews root and branch" even if that meant "making a pact with the devil":

> We have no intention of being emotional anti-Semites who want to create the atmosphere of a pogrom; instead our hearths are filled with an inexorable determination to attack the evil at its roots and to extirpate it root and branch. In order to reach our goal every means will be justified, even if we have to make a pact with the devil.

In a party meeting in Salzburg on August 7, 1920, Hitler again formulated explicitly his ultimate aim of eliminating the Jews from Germany:

> The effect of Judaism will never disappear and the poisoning of the people will not end unless the cause—the Jews—are removed from our presence.

Hitler's anti-Semitism acquired more dangerous characteristics under the influence of his mentor and friend Dietrich Eckart (1868-1923), a Volkish unsuccessful playwright, addicted to drugs and alcohol. Eckart was the editor of the official Nazi paper Volkisher Beobachter from December 1920 until his death in December 1923. Eckart, who was waiting for the coming of a German savior that would bring together politics and religion in a new crusade, introduced Hitler to his friends as the long-anticipated savior. A pathological anti-Semite, Eckart raised the *Judenfrage*, the Jewish problem, to cosmic proportions:

> The Jewish question is the chief problem of humanity, in which, indeed, every one of its other problems is contained. Nothing on earth could remain darkened if one could throw light on the secret of the Jews. [21]

In a Germany divided religiously and politically for centuries, these two professional Jew haters saw anti-Semitism as a common denominator that could transcend the religious and secular divisions among the Germans and unite them around a common cause. They conceived its role as a *sammelpunkt*, a point of confluence that could attract Volkish as well as Christian anti-Semites, whether Catholic, Protestant, or secular, under one flag. Aware that a common enemy, even if illusory, has the capacity to unite those allegedly being threatened, Hitler was confident that the Judeophobia of the Germans, whether in its clerical form or in its racist variety, would bridge their internal differences and eventually propel him to power. On the basis of his conversations with Hitler, Eckart published a pamphlet under the title *From Moses to Lenin: A Conversation between Adolph Hitler and Me,* 1924. [22]

In the pamphlet they gathered up all the anti-Semitic traditions they found in Christian history to prove that Christianity always stood in the forefront of the war against the Jews. They developed the thesis that the Church and the Christian state drew their strength from anti-Semitism and only became weakened in modern times when they softened their militant attack against the Jews as a result of liberalism. In consequence, if the modern state and Christian churches were to regain their lost power, they had to renew their old alliance against the Jews and once again isolate and persecute them.

In the early years of his political career Hitler presented himself before his audiences as a zealous Christian knight who rose to avenge the cross, like a modern day Ferrand Martinez—the Spanish rabble-rouser and instigator of medieval Spain who carrying the crucifix moved his thugs from town to town in 1391 to murder and destroy the flourishing Jewish communities of Spain. Hitler tried to revive his own version of a modern Christian avenger. After rhetorically asking in a famous harangue in Munich in 1922, cited by Klaus Scholder, whether a Christian *can* be an anti-Semite, he responded that he *must* be one:

> I tell you that my Christian feelings point me to the man who once in solitude, surrounded by only a few supporters, recognized these Jews and summoned people to fight against them . . . But today after two thousand years, I can recognize his tremendous battle for this world against the Jewish poison, and be most powerfully moved by the fact that he had to shed his blood for it on the cross. [23]

An interview Hitler granted in 1922 to the journalist Josef Hell, a retired army major and editor of the Catholic Munich weekly magazine *Der Gerade Weg,* documents in Hitler's own words his diabolic early decision to choose the Jews as his main enemy, as Lueger had done before him, and to center his movement on Jew hatred. With the cunning premeditation of a predator zeroing in on his prey, he chose the Jews as his victim. The interview, more than any other later statement made by Hitler, represents an early historical source on the genesis of Hitler's evil decision to make anti-Semitism the rallying cry of his movement. Editor Josef Hell asked Hitler, referring to the Jews, why he wanted to destroy this "so undeniably intelligent race—a race to which the Germans and all the Aryans, if not the entire world, owed an incalculable debt in virtually all fields of art and knowledge, research, and economics." Hitler who had previously threatened in a violent tone to "hang all the Jews of Germany in every plaza and public place, until Germany is cleansed of the last Jew," suddenly calmed down and offered an answer that his interviewer characterized as "unexpectedly sober and dispassionate." Major Hell transcribed his statement word by word:

It is manifestly clear and has been proven in practice and by the facts of all revolutions that a struggle for ideals, for improvements of any kind whatsoever must
be supplemented with a struggle against some social class or caste. . . Earlier
revolutions were directed either against the peasants, or the nobility and the clergy, or against dynasties. . . But in no case has revolution succeeded without the
presence of a lightning rod that could conduct and channel the odium of the general masses.

With this very thing in mind I scanned the events in history and put the
question to myself: against which racial element in Germany can I unleash my
propaganda of hate with the greatest prospects of success? I had to find the
right kind of victim, and especially one, against whom the struggle would make
sense, materially speaking. I can assure you I imagined every possible and
thinkable solution to this problem, and weighing every imaginable factor, I
came to the conclusion that a campaign against the Jews would be as popular as
it would be successful. There are few Germans who have not been vexed with
the behavior of Jews or else have not suffered losses through them in some way
or other. Disproportionately to their small number they account for an immense
share of the German national wealth, which can be easily put to profitable use
for the state, as could the holdings of the monasteries, bishops, and nobility.

Once the hatred and the battle against the Jews have been really stirred up,
their resistance will necessarily crumble in the shortest possible time. They are
totally defenseless, and no one will stand up to protect them. [24]

In the interview, Hitler articulated the material benefits that would accrue
to the Germans from depriving the Jews of their wealth. Here was an easy formula to eliminate the Jews as competitors, enrich the German coffers, and provide Germany with the means to rearm itself. This was his blueprint to finance a
new round of territorial conquest in order to undo the injustices of the Versailles
Treaty. Assured that no one would stand up for the Jews, Hitler figured out that
the risks in attacking them were minimal. An evil "cost-benefit" analysis led
him to the conclusion that his demand that the Jews be deprived of their economic positions and capital, as the Christian kings and princes had done in olden
days when they were short of money, would be enormously popular with the
Germans. When Hitler came to power eleven years later, every step in his attack
on the Jews was actually accompanied by pillage and robbery of Jewish property
of unprecedented proportions as he already announced in 1922. Expropriation of
Jewish property made Nazism attractive to the many non-Jews over Europe,
which in one way or another benefited personally from the looting.

It is relevant in this context to cite here Michael A. Musmanno (1897-
1968), one of the American Nuremberg judges, on the systematic robbery of the
wealth of the Jews when Hitler actually came to power:

The story of the robbery of the Jews under the Nazi rulers is something that
staggers the imagination . . . If I had not seen those documents, if I had not
heard the witnesses who described how every item of possession was taken—
from factories, railroads, automobiles, household furniture, and every piece of
wearing apparel down to little, tiny baby shoes all listed, businesslike . . . I

could never believe that so gigantic a program of thievery could be worked out and carried into fulfillment. [25]

Franz Stangl, the commander of Sobibor and Treblinka who was deeply aware of the astronomical value of the wealth plundered from the Jews all over Europe, responded in prison to Gitta Sereny's question on the reason for the extermination of the Jews in the following words:

Stangl: They wanted the Jews' money.
Sereny: You can't be serious? He was bewildered by my reaction of disbelief.
Stangl: But of course, have you any idea of the fantastic sums that were involved? That's how the steel in Sweden was bought.
Sereny: If the racial business was so secondary, then why all that hate propaganda?
Stangl: To condition those who actually had to carry out these policies, to make it possible for them to do what they did. [26]

Imitating Mussolini's March on Rome, Hitler attempted a putsch on November 8 and 9, 1923, to seize the Bavarian government. With the complicity of Generals, Ludendorff and Haushofer, and the help of Ernst Röhm (1887-1934) and his Freikorps members, he tried to seize power. The Munich Beer Hall Putsch failed and Hitler was found guilty of high treason and sentenced to five years imprisonment at the state prison at Landsberg am Lech. The Nazi Party was banned. Hitler, however, was released after only thirteen months from the Landsberg Fortress where he was held in very benign conditions from November 11, 1923, to December 20, 1924.

During his stay in prison, Hitler received the daily visit of Haushofer who indoctrinated him in his rapacious geopolitical theories on race and Lebenstraum. General Karl von Haushofer, a retired Reichswehr general and professor of political geography at the University of Munich, which he named geopolitics, argued that the struggle of races was the determining force in human history, not the struggle of classes, as claimed by Karl Marx. The races were involved in a perennial struggle for living space, *Lebenstraum*, to feed and sustain their kinfolk, and war was the inevitable result. For Haushofer, the state was only an instrument of the race. Race was the content and the state the vessel that lent it form.

Dressing up German territorial expansionist dreams in academic garb in terms of his theory, Haushofer postulated that the vital Lebenstraum of the Germanic Aryan race lay in Europe itself to the east of its borders and not in colonies overseas, as claimed by the prewar nationalists. The phrase *drang nach dem Osten* (drive to the East) acquired ominous significance in his rhetoric. In these four words he expressed the predatory notion that much of the land belonging to Poland, the Baltic countries, Russia, and the Ukraine was vital to the future development of Germany. The east of Europe populated by the "inferior" Slavic race held the vast spaces "needed" for the development of the Germanic race.

The "inferior" races in the expanded German Lebenstraum could only be eliminated or enslaved—never assimilated in the *Volk*.[27]

Under the influence of Haushofer's ideas, Hitler began to dictate a book, part autobiography and part political treatise, to his friend Rudolph Hess. Fr. Bernhard Stempfle, a Catholic priest and member of the Catholic order of Saint Jerome, assisted in editing and proofreading Hitler's *Mein Kampf*. Stempfle like Röhm and many other Nazis, were liquidated by order of Hitler during the Night of the Long Knives in 1934. After Hitler came out from the Landsberg fortress he published *Mein Kampf* in two volumes during 1925 and 1926. He reestablished anew the Nazi Party that had been banned by the government. Imitating Mussolini, he adopted the Roman salute for the Nazi Party.

Haushofer's ideas became an important part of Hitler's political rhetoric. He claimed that protecting the purity of the Aryan race ranked first above any other national concern. The Germans had to protect their blood from being racially contaminated by alien blood, which of course meant, among other things, not only the separation of the Jewish race but also the elimination of the Jews from the Aryan Lebenstraum altogether. In the first mass meeting in 1925 of the reorganized Nazi Party he thundered:

> The greatest danger is and remains for us the poison of foreign peoples in our body. All other dangers are limited in time. Only this alone is eternally present in its consequences for us . . . The peace treaty can be abrogated, reparation obligations can be declared invalid and rejected, political parties can be disposed of, but blood that is once poisoned can never be altered.[28]

The Nazi ideology was reduced to three basic premises:

1. The superiority of the Aryan race and the need to maintain its "purity."

2. The expansion of the German Lebensraum to unite all the German-speaking Aryans in one *Grossdeutschland*.

3. The isolation of the Jews and their elimination from the German Lebensraum.

These three aims soon proved themselves effective in turning the Germans away from Socialism and other messianic movements attracting Germans of different social strata and backgrounds to slavishly follow Hitler.

A debate has been going on in historical literature whether Hitler and the Nazis actually believed their racial myths. What finally matters is that they acted in accordance with these myths to justify mass murder and plunder. The functional role of the race theory as a means to justify organized large-scale murder and robbery was recognized by the Nazis from the very beginning. The Nazi race theory, which postulated the alleged superiority of the Aryan race and the "rights" that it conferred on its privileged members provided the rational to justify the predatory immoral policies that Nazism stood for. It served to justify the displacement of the "inferior" non-Aryan races to provide the alleged Lebenstraum for the Herrenvolk as well as their enslavement and dispossession of their wealth. By declaring that the Jewish race represented the antithesis of the master race, they justified the total elimination of the Jews from German lands and, later on, their physical annihilation in Europe. The German population was conditioned to accept such unprecedented criminal notions as fully justified in terms of the higher racial aims of the Herrenvolk. The Nazi race theory in particular was given supreme importance by Himmler in the ideological indoctrination of the SS to condition them psychologically to actually carry out their unspeakable crimes.

## Hitler Seeks the Support of the Army and the Economic Elite

In his highly popular book *The Rise and Fall of the Third Reich*, William L. Shirer focuses on a fundamental tactical principle that Hitler learned during his vagabond years in Vienna from his political role model, the anti-Semitic mayor of Vienna, Karl Lueger. According to this principle any revolutionary movement, if it wishes to reach and maintain government power, has to establish alliances with key forces in the state. In applying Lueger's tactical principle, Hitler chose at a certain moment in his career to ally himself with the army, the big financiers, and industrialists.[29]

The reasons seem obvious, says Shirer: Hitler needed their combined support to achieve his short and long-term goals. In the long term, Hitler needed them to build up the war machine to launch the army to conquer Europe and "win for Germany a place under the sun," as the kaiser claimed when he plunged Germany into World War I. In the short term he could not hope to finance the campaign that would lead him to power without funds from industrial and financial concerns.

To attract the economic elite, Hitler was shrewd enough to proclaim that the revolution he advocated did not envision a change of the economic system, as would have been the case with a Socialist revolution, but the supremacy of the Aryan master race, which among other things implied that the Jews had to be eliminated from the German economy. In 1920 and 1926 he declared:

> We stand for the maintenance of private property . . . We shall protect free enterprise as the most expedient, or rather the sole possible, economic order.[30]

In his conversations with the president of the Danzig Senate, Rauschning (1932-1934), Hitler very precisely articulated the notion that the Nazi revolution did not reside in conventional socioeconomic changes but in the application of the "scientific" racial principles to society. The struggle to preserve the purity of the Aryan race was the antidote to Marxism, which in the ears of German industrialists and financiers sounded reassuring. Hitler managed at the same time to build his popular power base among the proletariat, exploiting artfully the radical antibourgeoisie voices within National Socialism to promote his revolution, but he never lost sight that the army, industrialists, and financiers were the pillars of his regime, to which all the other sectors, including the workers, had to become subservient.

German industrialists and financiers such as Gustav Krupp, Fritz Thyssen, Alfred Hugenberg, Emil Kirdorf, and the fierce anti-Semite Heinrich Class had a long history that went far back before World War I of patronage of Pan German militaristic organizations that advocated expansionist nationalism and vicious anti-Semitism. Hitler was able to convert them into generous financial supporters of the Nazi movement as well. Encouraged by the prospect of getting rid of their Jewish competitors and coming into possession of the Jewish commercial and industrial establishments, Hitler's campaign to protect the purity of the Aryan race made sense to German industrial and financial elites. In 1929, invited by Hitler, the Ruhr coal magnate Emil Kirdorf and his wife attended the yearly August Nuremberg rally. The eighty-two-year-old magnate wrote a letter of thanks to Hitler:

> You may be proud of the honors and homages done you; there is hardly a crowned head who receives their equal. My wife and I are happy to have been able to witness them . . . I have taken with me from the Nuremberg Congress the consoling certainty that numerous circles will sacrifice themselves to prevent the doom of Germanism from being accomplished in the dishonorable, undignified way I previously feared. With true German greetings from my wife and myself; in friendship, Your Kirdorf. [31]

In 1929 Hitler led a political campaign against the Young Plan of reparations payments. The army found in Hitler a spokesman for its revanchist aims. Many of its high-ranking figures, such as Werner von Blomberg and his chief of staff Colonel Walter von Reichenau, turned into enthusiastic backers of the Nazis during the late 1920s. Even the senior general Hans von Seeckt (1886-1936), the "sorcerer" of German secret rearmament and once a rival of the Nazis, became in the *Reichstag* their close ally attracted by Hitler's revanchism. "Not only do I deem Hitler's inclusion in the government desirable, I think it is a necessity," declared von Seeckt in 1931.[32] Hitler's rhetoric on Lebensraum and Drang nach dem Osten echoed their own ideas, which General Karl von Haushofer, one of their own, had implanted in Hitler.[33] The vast alliances between the industrialists and the Reichswher inclined the two sectors in favor of Hitler.[34]

## Hitler Seeks the Support of the Catholic Church

While Shirer's thesis on Hitler's tactical alliances with the army, industrialists, and financiers has wide explanatory power and throws light on major decisions of his political career, it leaves out a key component of the political equation in Germany—the religious establishment. Shirer, in his scant reference to the religious establishment, presents the Church as a victim of the Nazi regime and ignores completely its key role in Hitler's rise to power, in the consolidation of his regime, and his later Lebenstraum claims and conquest of Europe. This omission leaves a major gap in his otherwise elaborate history of the Third Reich. If one is to understand Hitler's tactics in gaining the backing of key power-er holders in Germany, one cannot ignore his courtship of the fourth pillar of the

German power-constellation, the religious establishment, and his final success in winning it over to his side.

At the very beginning of his political career after World War I, Hitler already realized that the goodwill of the churches, both Catholic and Protestant, was essential to his success. The churches, no less than the industrial-financial establishment and the army, were essential to the achievement of his aims. Vital as the army and the financial-industrial establishments were to Hitler's plans, these institutions could not deliver to him the allegiance of the masses. To win over the masses, Hitler needed the religious establishment, which held sway over the souls of eighty million Germans. Beyond wining over German Catholics and Protestants as individuals, Hitler intended to secure the institutional backing of their churches. This was part of the lesson in political strategy he learned from Lueger. In *Mein Kampf*, Hitler expresses admiration for Lueger for recognizing the decisive role of the Church and for "having avoided any struggle against a religious institution and thus secured the support of that mighty organization which the Church represents." Thus, to win the goodwill of the religious establishment, they declared themselves in their founding program in 1920 in favor of Positive Christianity, and promised in article 24, "liberty for all religious denominations in the State, so far as they are not a danger to the moral feelings of the Germanic race."

Before the Nazis became numerically significant at the end of the 1920s, Hitler was rather unsuccessful in being taken seriously by the power holders in Germany—including the leaders of the religious establishment. The Putsch Hitler attempted in 1923 failed miserably. As a body, the bishops were ambivalent in their position toward the Nazi movement. Some bishops tried to put distance between themselves and the Nazis during the twenties and also applied to them the ecclesiastic prohibition to belong to the Socialists, Communists and Free Masons, and even denied the sacraments to them. Others, in contrast, such as Bishop Schreiber of Berlin or Dr. Haeuser of Augsburg, showed their sympathies very early on by demonstratively participating as clergymen in Nazi celebrations.

For all their early opposition to the Nazis, the bishops limited their censure to what they considered irreconcilable with Catholic doctrine and abstained from passing judgment on their political aims. They had flattering words for what they called the "healthy core of National Socialism," praising the "patriotic nature of the movement, which reasserted the values of religion, love of fatherland, and staunch opposition to Bolshevism" to use their exact words. In their conference-resolutions, the bishops expressed their hope that the Nazi movement might succeed in eliminating from its program the elements conflicting with Catholicism and invitingly left open the door for the recall of their censures as soon as the Nazis would rectify these errors:

> If that were to occur, the Nazi movement could then be considered a patriotic movement, which every friend of the fatherland in principle could support.

Cardinal Faulhaber of Munich had even some warm words of praise in 1924 for his neighbor Hitler, while expressing regret that the "pure spring" of National Socialism had become contaminated by *Kulturkampf*:

> The originally pure spring (of National Socialism) had been poisoned by later tributaries and by Kulturkampf, but Hitler knew better than his underlings that the resurrection of the German nation required the support of Christianity.

As a totalitarian whose ultimate goal was to establish a Nazi monopoly of power, Hitler's aim was to eliminate all political parties other than the Nazis. Hitler could not tolerate political competitors—only submissive subordinates. He consequently made a distinction between religious Catholicism, which he allegedly supported, and political Catholicism, which he rejected. Thus he wished to win over the Church while at the same time undo its political parties and social organizations. He therefore aimed at the eventual disappearance of the two Catholic parties, the Center and the Bavarian People's Party, which represented Catholic interests in the Reichstag and end the participation of priests in politics. In conversations with his friend Artur Dinter in 1925, Hitler made it clear how critical Church support was to his plans to reach power:

> To achieve power, it is important not to fall out with the Catholic Church, which has great influence in Germany . . . What I propose to do is to oppose the Center Party, who by its frequent alliances with the Social Democrats in order to retain its power is acting against the true interests of the Church. We must show the Catholics of Germany that they are in safer hands among the National Socialists than with the Center party. [35]

In his strategy to use the Catholic Church as the stirrup-holder to mount the horse, Hitler shrewdly pointed out to Dinter the particular significance of his being a Catholic.

> Do not imagine that I shall commit Bismarck's mistake. He was a Protestant and did not know how to handle the Catholic Church. Providence has made me born Catholic; I know how to. [36]

The Center Party was founded at the heat of the Kulturkampf in 1870 to defend the political interests of the Catholic Church in Germany. Although a minority party, the Center wielded much political power in the Weimar Republic after World War I. In a parliamentary regime such as the Weimar Republic, a government required a majority in the Reichstag to stay in power. None, however, of the existing political parties in the Reichstag, including the Social Democrats, commanded such an absolute majority, and therefore had to join parliamentary coalitions. [37] By skillfully negotiating its parliamentary votes with the Social Democrats, the Center Party managed to become a partner with them in the fourteen coalition governments that ruled Germany between 1918 and 1930, even holding the chancellorship in eight of them.

Hitler's hopes of convincing the German Catholics that "they are in safer hands among the National Socialists than with the Center party" began to materialize by the end of 1928 when Msgr. Ludwig Kaas (1881-1952) became, with the decisive support of Nuncio Pacelli, the leader of the Catholic Center Party over the lay Catholic trade-union candidate Dr. Adam Stegerwald. Kaas had been a Reichstag member since 1920. On the recommendation of Cardinal Bertram of Breslau he became in 1925 an advisor to Nuncio Pacelli (1876-1958). Whether in his role as nuncio, Vatican secretary of state, or pontiff, Pacelli's influence on German affairs was second to none. He was the ultimate voice in all main decisions pertaining to Catholic interests in Germany during forty-one years, from 1917 when he became nuncio to Germany until his death in 1958. Kaas adhered to Pacelli's policies and as a subordinate kept close to him to the very last day of his life in 1952 as administrator of St. Peter's Cathedral in Rome.[38]

With the designation of Ludwig Kaas as leader of the Center Party, in December 1928 the partnership of the two Catholic parties with the Social Democrats came to an end, and the way to cooperation with the Nazis that Hitler had dreamt for was opened. Although the Center Party had prospered during the Weimar Republic as never before in its history and drawn great benefits from its political partnership with the Social Democrats, it decided to follow Vatican policy and distance itself from the Social Democrats with whom it had shared power since the founding of the Weimar Republic and instead it joined the side of its mortal enemies.

Hitler's historic opportunity came with the Great Depression. The Wall Street crash during the second half of 1929 had serious repercussions in Germany. When the American financiers called back their short-term loans to Germany, the collapse of banks followed in domino fashion. The disappearance of international export markets brought a sharp decline in internal domestic demand causing mass unemployment—the breeding ground of political and social unrest and strife. Five million Germans were left without jobs in 1930. Fear that the Germans would turn to Communism took hold among economic elites and the Church and they began to look to Hitler for a way out.

The reorientation of the Catholic political parties to the right rapidly became a reality. The decade-old Great Coalition, as the parliamentary block of the Social Democrats and Catholics was known, fell apart over the issue of unemployment insurance in 1930. The last coalition government headed by the Socialist Chancellor Hermann Müller-Franken ended on March 27, 1930 when Hindenburg called for new elections to be held on September 14, 1930. The Center Party's fateful decision to terminate their partnership with the Social Democrats and to seek new partners to the right opened the road to power for Hitler.[39]

At the elections of September 1930, the Nazis came out the real beneficiaries of the economic and parliamentary crisis. The Nazi Party's electoral luck underwent a spectacular turnaround that changed the political equation in Germany. By blowing up the communist threat out of all proportion, the Nazis leaped overnight from the 800,000 votes they obtained in 1928, to 6.4 million votes in 1930—an increase from 2.6 percent to 18.3 percent. Instead of twelve seats in the Reichstag they obtained 107 out of a total of 491, a ninefold increase, while the Communist Party only had a modest gain from 10.6 percent to 13.1 percent of the votes [40]

According to the Weimar Constitution, the president had the obligation to call for new elections to the Reichstag within sixty days after the fall of the government. In anticipation of situations where the parties were unable or unwilling to put together a coalition, the Weimar Constitution granted the president emergency powers in its Article 48 to appoint a chancellor by decree. He could remain in power as long as a nonconfidence majority vote against his government was not cast. All the governments following the Müller government were established by a presidential emergency decree without an actual Reichstag majority. Heinrich Brünning (1885-1970), a lay leader of the Center Party, was the first interim chancellor appointed by Hindenburg on the basis of his emergency powers. He held the post for eighteen months, until May 30, 1932, when Hindenburg dismissed him for his unpopular economic policy. Then Franz von Papen and finally General Kurt von Schleicher headed emergency governments with the support of the Catholic and Nationalist parties and the blessing of industrialists and financiers. On January 30, 1933, Hitler was called in by Hindenburg and handed the government on a silver plate.

As a result of the electoral rise of the Nazis in 1930, German industrialists, financiers, army generals, and Catholic political leaders reassessed their previous skepticism and seriously began to toy with the idea to cast their lot with the Nazis. Hitler used the modest gain of the Communist Party, as a sign of imminent Communist takeover and presented himself and his party in his propaganda as the wall holding back the Bolshevik flood. The red scare was part and parcel of the Nazi bag of tricks to capture votes and frighten the rich to open their purses generously to the Nazi Party. A contemporary diary entry by Bella Fromm describes the scare induced by the Nazi propaganda machinery:

> At that time, the National Socialists were scaring the rich out of such wits, as they happened to have by warning them constantly of the coming "Red Tide." It frightened financial contributions out of pockets that, up to this point, had been open only to receive.[41]

Hitler's claim of being the defender of what he called "Christian civilization" against the "red menace" sounded reassuring to the army and industrialists. On the assumption they could use and control Hitler, they began thinking seriously in taking cover behind him. Although they were afraid of the SA, the Nazi Sturm Abteilung, being turned against them at a moment's notice by Nazi radicals, they decided to throw the full weight of their resources and power behind Hitler and pronounced themselves in favor of the Nazis joining the government. The SA, the Nazi paramilitary force created originally to protect Nazi meetings and to disrupt those of their opponents, grew beyond leaps and bounds.

Hundreds of thousands of unemployed and subemployed lumpen proletarians joined the SA ranks.

Under the delusion that Hitler was the best bet against Communism, Kaas pushed vigorously for a coalition with the Nationalists (*Deutschnationale Volkspartei*) and the Nazis. Acting in accord with Church hierarchy, the Party leadership issued calls after the 1930 elections to include the Nazis and Nationalists in what they called a National Concentration Government. Kaas and Brünning both declared themselves in favor of a National Concentration Government that would include the Nazi Party. The proposition to share power in the government with the the Nazis, became the Center Party panacea for solving the problems of Germany. Hitler's goal of winning over the Catholic Church for the Nazi cause was well in its way to be fulfilled.

Brünning, the interim Catholic chancellor, initiated personal talks with Hitler in 1930 on the participation of the Nazis in the government, which he continued during 1931. With the Nazi electoral successes, the resistance of the bishops began rapidly to wane when they saw millions of Catholics voting for the Nazis. What seemed previously unlikely—cooperation with Hitler and the Nazis—became a fact. When Chancellor Brünning visited Rome during the summer of 1931, Vatican secretary of state Pacelli strongly suggested that he form a coalition government with the Nationalists and Nazis, under the condition that they agree to approve a concordat for Germany.

The growing rapprochement between the Church and the Nazis was momentarily jeopardized by the publication of Rosenberg's *Der Mythus des Zwanzigsten Jahrhunderts* in 1930. The Vatican was seriously troubled by Rosenberg's demands of a German Church based on principles of blood and soil. To protect his prospects with the Church and German Catholics, Hitler dispatched in 1931 his second in command, Hermann Göring, as his emissary to the Vatican to clear "misunderstandings." Göring received a friendly reception. *Osservatore Romano* had words of praise for him as a valiant fighter against Bolshevism and able chief of police who had fought against corruption and immorality in Prussia.

Göring's assured Msgr. Giuseppe Pizzardo, the Vatican undersecretary of state and ecclesiastical head of *Catholic Action*, on May 9, 1931, that Rosenberg's book was not to be taken as the official creed of the party but rather as a private opinion of one of its members. As a result of Göring's trip to Rome, a motion by some bishops at the annual August 1931 Fulda Conference to include the Nazi Party together with the Communists, Socialists, and Freethinkers in the list of the forbidden movements whose members were to be denied the Catholic sacraments was defeated.

Hitler's duplicity worked well. While actually promoting militantly through the party the Aryan racial ideology, Hitler was able to convince the Church that he could be trusted as a loyal defender of Christianity against its detractors in the Nazi Party. To reinforce that impression, Hitler studiously sought out opportunities to make known his tactical "differences" with Rosenberg, such as when he told Schacht: "I have always told Rosenberg one doesn't attack petticoats or cassocks." His assurances were well received because the Vatican wanted to believe that were it not for Rosenberg, everything could go well between the Church and the Nazis.

When the time for new presidential elections arrived in 1932, the first since 1925, the Nazis put up Hitler as their candidate for president. President Paul von Hindenburg (1847-1934) decided to run again against Thälmann, Duesterberg and Hitler. On the day of the kaiser's birthday, January 27, 1932, the devout Catholic steel magnate and banker Fritz Thyssen, an admirer of Hitler, brought together the German industrial leaders to a meeting with Hitler in Dusseldorf to request their financial support for the Nazi Party.[42] Fritz Thyssen declared:

> I am voting for Adolf Hitler because I know him well and am firmly convinced that he is the only man who can and will rescue Germany from ruin and disintegration. [43]

The donations of industrialists and bankers came forward generously on the spot: Gustav Krupp and the other directors of I. G. Farben showed their generosity for the Nazi cause as did Florian Kloeckner, a steel and railroads magnate of the Center Party. Alfred Hugenberg, the leader of the Nationalists and director of the Krupp Works, was likewise active in raising millions for the Nazis. Hitler's candidacy received the support of one of the leading figures of Protestantism in Germany, the Lutheran Bishop of Kurmark Otto Dibelius, who called the German Protestants to vote for Hitler regardless of his being a Catholic:

> Seven years ago we expressed our incomprehension of the readiness of certain Protestants to vote for the Catholic candidate of the Center Party. This time we have done nothing of that sort, although among the candidates there is once again a Catholic, namely Hitler. But he is not a candidate of the Roman Catholic Church, rather the leader of a great national movement, to which millions of Protestants belong.

Although Hitler lost against Hindenburg in the presidential elections of March 13, 1932, the results revealed Hitler's great gain in popularity among the German population. Hitler's ominous shadow was already looming large on the German horizon. While Hindenburg drew 49.7 percent of the vote with the support of Social Democrats, Hitler followed second with an impressive 30.1 percent. The Weimar Constitution required an absolute majority to be elected president and a second run took place on April 10, 1932. Hindenburg was elected with 19.4 million votes (53 percent), while Hitler obtained 13.4 million votes, 36.8 percent of the total. Communist candidate Ernst Thälmann was well behind with only 3.7 million votes, no more than 10.2 percent of the total.

As they decided to put their resources and prestige behind Hitler, industrialists and financiers nonetheless remained distrustful and vigilant of Hitler's radical followers, such as Gregor Strasser and Gottfried Fedder, and their quasi-Socialist proposals and anticapitalist rhetoric. They were seriously concerned that the 800,000 lumpen proletarians and thugs organized in the SA under the leadership of Ernest Röhm could be easily turned against them in a flash notice. The SA thugs meanwhile tried out their skills against defenseless Jews all over Germany. General Schleicher, leader of the Nationalist Party, warned at the time against "Brown Bolshevism" in his election speeches, an obvious allusion to the SA. It is ironic that Hitler liquidated all of them, Schleicher, Strasser, and Röhm in the Blood Purge of June 30, 1934.

As the Nazis were escalating their physical and verbal terror attacks against Jews, the helpless representatives of the Central Association of German Jews met privately with Chancellor Brünning—but to no avail. He did nothing to stop the Nazi attacks.[44] George L. Moose was among the earliest authors to point out what today is conventional wisdom that Hitler's anti-Semitic campaign was not peripheral but central to the decision of the industrial-financial elites to support Hitler. They realized that Nazi radical anti-Semitism was serving their survival diverting toward the Jews the revolutionary forces menacing political and economic stability in Germany. Hitler's anti-Semitism served as a lightning rod that channeled all the grievances, real and imagined, against the defenseless Jews— presented cleverly as a mighty world power in Nazi propaganda. Hitler's ability to transform the revolutionary longings and grievances of a large sector of the populace into an anti-Jewish revolution was the source of his success. Not the big capitalist or the economic middleman, but the Jew and his race were the incarnation of the enemy. Once eliminated, the Jews would leave behind their investments, inventories, and wealth. In the words of George L. Mosse:

> The German revolution became the anti-Jewish revolution. The mass enthusiasm which over half a century of Volkish agitation had become explosive, and which, if not resolved, could become dangerous to its own creators was shifted away from the real social and economic grievances and channeled into anti-Semitism. The Jew was made to bear the brunt and, although this too had been standard in the Volkish movement, Hitler made it stick.[45]

Hindenburg dismissed Brünning on May 30, 1932, for his unpopular and ineffective economic policy very soon after his reelection. He announced new elections to the Reichstag to take place on July 31, 1932, and using his emergency powers, appointed his advisor Franz von Papen (1879-1969), known at the time as "Hindenburg's lapdog," as chancellor. As an avowed Catholic, von Papen was officially a member of the Center Party, but his true loyalties lay with the Nationalists. Accused by his party colleagues of disloyalty for having misled them concerning Hindenburg's intentions to dismiss Brünning, he resigned from the Center Party. As chancellor he could only count on the fifty-two votes of the Nationalists to support him in the Reichstag in case of a non-confidence vote. The Catholic Center Party criticized his appointment and published the following official statement requesting that the Nazis be entrusted with the responsibility of forming a new government:

The party therefore rejects the temporary solutions provided by the present cabinet, and demands that the situation should be clarified by placing the responsibility for forming a Government in the hands of the National Socialist Party.

At the parliamentary elections of July 31, 1932, the Nazis came out the largest party in Germany with 12.9 million votes, 36.8 percent of the total. The number of Nazi seats more than doubled from 107 to 230, out of a total of 584 delegates. They were still short of an absolute majority to run a government. The Communists were far behind with 100 deputies, 14.3 percent of the total. Among them there was not a single Jew. According to Goebbels' diary, Hitler was looking at the time to co-opt the votes of the Center Party in the Reichstag to form a parliamentary majority:

Hitler cast his eyes on the Center party to achieve a parliamentary majority, for the Center alone could give him the majority he lacked.[46]

Negotiations with the Center Party began on Hitler's initiative on August 13, 1932. Hitler found Brünning "very compliant," according to Hitler's own account of the meeting. A deal was struck between the Center Party and the Nazis to support the election of Herman Göring, the Nazi number two as president of the Reichstag. Msgr. Kaas mobilized the vote of the two Catholic sister parties, the Center and the Bavarian People's Party, to vote for Göring. With the votes of the Catholic parties the Nazis acquired the highly strategic political position of Reichstag president that they used immediately to begin their Trojan assault on the Weimar Republic.[47]

At the inaugural session of the newly elected Reichstag on August 30, 1932, Göring as Reichstag president seized the opportunity offered to him by his mortal enemies, the Communists, to bring down the von Papen government. When the Communists introduced a nonconfidence motion against the von Papen government, the Nazis and Catholics joined with them and brought down the three-month-old von Papen government by 513 votes against forty-two votes of the Nationalists and five abstentions. The new Reichstag was dissolved right there and then at the first session. Msgr. Kaas issued a statement on October 17, 1932, in favor of the inclusion of the Nazis in a new government:

We call for a strong national government in tune with the interests of the people, which would include the National Socialists.

Hindenburg called for new parliamentary elections on November 6, 1932, in which the Nazis lost thirty-three seats but still emerged as the single largest political party controlling one-third of the seats. Von Papen carried on as chancellor during the crisis until December 2, 1932, when Hindenburg appointed the leader of the Nationalist Party, General Kurt von Schleicher (1882-1934) as chancellor. After barely staying in power for two months, von Schleicher offered his resignation on January 28, 1933, to Hindenburg when he refused his request to dissolve the Reichstag.

Both Catholics and Nationalists were vying for Hitler's favors. The industrialists, the army, the Nationalists, and the Catholic parties all looked to the Nazis as their future partners and expressed to Hindenburg their support to entrust Hitler with forming a government. They had no reservations to entrusting the future of Germany in Hitler's hands, although Nazism was already then the embodiment of evil with its terror, Aryan racism, venomous hatred of the Jews, and glorification of war and foreign conquest.

The Catholic Center Party proposed that Hitler should become chancellor, heading a National Concentration government with the participation of Nationalists and the Catholic Center Party as partners. The Nationalists, on their part, refused to join with the Center in any government and suggested a coalition with the Nazis headed by one of their own, the financier Hjalmar Schacht (1877-1970) as chancellor. Schacht, however, refused the Nationalists offer, and backed Hitler's candidacy. Schacht had been impressed with Hitler's nationalist ideas since January 1931 when Göhring introduced Hitler to him, and he opened the doors for Hitler to many German bankers and industrialists who financially gave him support. In a letter made public by Hitler, Schacht backed Hitler's candidacy in the strongest terms and contacted many politicians urging them to bring in the Nazis as coalition partners:

> Only one man can become chancellor today, and that is Hitler. If he does not become chancellor today, he will in four months.[48]

In a joint statement Hitler and Msgr. Kaas blamed the Nationalists and their spokesman Hugenberg for obstructing a stable coalition government and threatened to bring down any presidentially appointed Nationalist government, even using Communist votes if necessary. Next day, after a friendly conference with Hitler, Msgr. Kaas again declared the readiness of the Catholic party to join in any government with Hitler as chancellor. In his self-serving memoirs, Franz von Papen, whose responsibility for Hitler's rise to power is second only to that of Hindenburg, had these words for his ex-comrades of the Center Party:

> Historians may care to note that the Center Party at this juncture regarded a Cabinet led by Hitler as the only way out of the impasse. I fail to see how this can be equated with the accusation that I was the person responsible for bringing Hitler to power.[49]

In a personal vendetta against his ex-colleagues of the Center Party, von Papen was plotting at the time his intrigues for a Hitler government with the exclusion of the Center Party and only the Nationalists as partners. At a secret meeting with Hitler at the home of Baron Kurt von Schroeder in Cologne on January 4, 1933, von Papen reached an agreement with Hitler to form a Nazi-Nationalist coalition with Hitler as chancellor, himself as vice chancellor, and General Schleicher as defense minister.[50] An influential group of leading industrialists and financiers authorized Ruhr magnate Gustav Krupp to approach

Hindenburg to support Hitler as chancellor. The presence at Hitler's side of Hjalmar Schacht—one of their own—was greatly reassuring to them.

On January 30, 1933, a dark day in world history to remember, Hindenburg called in Hitler to offer him the post of chancellor and to form a new government in a coalition with the Nationalists. The SA celebrated the event that night with a torchlight procession in Berlin. The papal nuncio in Berlin, Cesare Orsenigo, was jubilant with Hitler's accession to power and full of hope that Hitler would now grant the Church in Germany the same rights that Mussolini had given them in Italy through a concordat.[51] Decisions bereft of political vision and moral principles changed the course of history in Germany and the world at large.

# Notes

1. Historian Richard Grunberger expressed it succinctly: Anti-Semitism provided a tempting point of convergence for Nazi dogma and deep–seated Catholic animosity, 1.

2. Gerald Fleming, *Hitler and the Final Solution* (Los Angeles, CA: University of California Press, 1984), 10-11.

3. Stempfle was killed in the night of terror of July 30, 1934, by order of Hitler, seemingly to bury with him the dark secrets of Hitler's niece's suicide. William I. Shirer, *The Rise and Fall of the Third Reich* (New York: Simon and Schuster, 1959), 133, 223.

4. Lewy Güenther, *The Catholic Church and Nazi Germany* (New York: Mc Graw Hill Book Co., 1964), 282. Daniel J. Goldhagen, *Hitler's Willing Executioners* (New York: Alfred A. Knopf, 1996), 6. Schachleitner met Hitler in 1922 for the first time and gave many public lectures in behalf of the Nazis in later years.

5. Konrad Heiden, *The Führer* (New York: Carroll & Graf Publishers, Inc. 1944), 494.

6. Paul I. Murphy and Rene R. Arlington, *La Popessa: The Controversial Biography of Sister Pascalina, the Most Powerful Woman in Vatican History,* (New York: Warner Books, 1983), 228.

7. Klaus Scholder, *A Requiem for Hitler* (Philadelphia, PA: Trinity Press International, 1989).

8. E.B. Bukey, *Hitlers Austria: Popular Sentiment in the Nazi Era, 1938-1945* (Chapel Hill, NC: University of North Carolina Press, 2000).

9. David I. Kertzer, *The Popes against the Jews: The Vatican's Role in the Rise of Modern Anti-Semitism* (New York: Alfred A. Knopf, 2001), 202, 211.

10. Hamman from Jackel/Kuhn.

11. Professor Gerhard Rempel, Political Parties in the Weimar Republic.Western New England College.

12. Klaus P. Fischer, *The History of an Obsession: German Judeophobia and the Holocaust* (New York: Continuum Press, 1998), 120. Jakob Segall, *Die Deutsche Juden als soldaten im Kriege 1914-1918* (Munich: Huber, 1922). The 1925 Census indicates 564,397 Jews in Germany, 0.90 percent of the population.

13. Bella Fromm, *Blood and Banquets: A Berlin Social Diary* (New York: Kensington Publishing Corp, 2002).

14 Fromm, *Blood and Banquets*, 308.

15. Klaus, *A Requiem for Hitler*.

16. John Cornwell, *Hitler's Pope: The Secret History of Pius XII* (New York: Penguin, 2008), 78.

17. Cornwell, *Hitler's Pope,* 74-75. On the basis of Schioppa's visit to Max Levien, head of the Munich Soviet, Pacelli informed Msgr. Gasparri in Rome: "An army of employees were dashing to and fro, giving out orders, waving bits of paper, and in the midst of all this, a gang of young women, of dubious appearance, Jews like all the rest of them, hanging around in all the offices with lecherous demeanor and suggestive smiles. The boss of this female rabble was Levien's mistress, a young Russian woman, a Jew and a divorcée, who was in charge. And it was to her that the nunciature was obliged to pay homage in order to proceed . . . This Levien is a young man, of about thirty or thirty-five, also Russian and a Jew. Pale, dirty, with drugged eyes, hoarse voice, vulgar, repulsive, with a face that is both intelligent and sly."

18. Murphy and Arlington, *La Popessa,* 52. The book was published in May 1983, months before her death in November that year.

19. Pascalina's's vivid recollection of an event that happened thirteen years before Hitler became chancellor may well not contradict Vatican Secretary of State Tarcisio Bertone which refers to Hitler as chancellor. He said in a recent allocution on Pius XII on June 5, 2007: "When did Cardinal Pacelli meet Chancellor Hitler? Never!"

20. Thule Gesellschaft was founded in August 1919.

21. George L. Mosse, *The Crisis of German Ideology: Intellectual Origins of the Third Reich* (New York : Grosset and Dunlap, 1964).

22. Dietrich Eckhart, "Der Bolschewismus von Moses bis Lenin Zwiegesprach zwischen Adolf Hitler und mir, 1924.

23. Klaus Scholder, *A Requiem for Hitler.*

24. Josef Hell, Aufzeichnung, 1922, ZS 640, 5 Institut for Zeitgeschichte. Gerald Fleming, *Hitler and the Final Solution,* 28.

25. Interview of Judge M. M. Musmanno by Rabbi W. Berkowitz. *Heritage and Hope: Dialogues in Judaism.* Thomas Yoseloff, 1965. Algemeiner Journal, May 25, 2001.

26. Gitta Sereny, *Into That Darkness* (New York: McGraw Hill Book Co., 1974), 232.

27. Claus P. Fischer, 92. Fromm, *Blood and Banquets,* 22, 63, 314.

28. Irving vs. Lipstadt. Defense Documents. Hitler's Role in the Persecution of the Jews by the Nazi Regime: Electronic Version, by Heinz Peter Longerich.

29. Shirer, *The Rise and Fall of the Third Reich.*

30. Heiden, *The Führer,* 229.

31. Heiden, *The Führer,* 271-272.

32. Fromm, *Blood and Banquets,* 29

33. Fromm, *Blood and Banquets* 22, 63, 314.

34. Shirer, *The Rise and Fall of the Third Reich,* 265-266. James Pool, *Who Financed Hitler: The Secret Funding of Hitler's Rise to Power, 1919-1933* (New York: Dial Press, 1978), 354-355.

35. Robert d'Harcourt. *Les Catholiques d'Allemagne.* Rhodes, 167.

36. Robert d'Harcourt. *Les Catholiques d'Allemagne.* Rhodes, 167.

37. The governing parties to the left included the Social Democratic Party, the Democratic Party, and the German's People's Party.

38. Member of the Reichstag since 1920, he became the Nuncio's advisor in 1925 on the recommendation of Cardinal Bertram.

39. Cornwell. *Hitler's Pope.*

40. Dorothea Dieckman and Bruno Gebhardt, *Handbuch der deutschen Geschichte.* (Stuttgart: Klett Cotta, 1973). See Erdman K.D.

41. Fromm, *Blood and Banquets.*

42. Fromm, *Blood and Banquets*, 42.

43. Heiden, *The Führer,* 352-353.

44. Donald M. McKale, *Hitler's Shadow War: The Holocaust and World War II* (Lanham, MD: Taylor Trade Publishing, 2006), 35.

45. George L. Mosee, *The Crisis of German Ideology.*

46. Louis Lochner Ed., trans., *The Goebbels Diaries* (New York: Doubleday & Company, 1948).

47. Lewy, *The Catholic Church,* 7.

48. Heiden, T*he Führer*, 392.

49. Brian Connell, Trans., *Franz von Papen. Der Warheit eine Gasse, 1952. Franz von Papen Memoirs* (London, UK: Andre Deutsch, 1952).

50. The meeting was arranged by the industrialist Wilhelm Keppler, Hitler's economic advisor

51. Lewy, *The Catholic Church*, 27.

# Chapter 3
# Hitler in Power: 1933

## The Enabling Act

General Ludendorff (1865-1937), Hindenburg's second in command during World War I, an extreme Nationalist and conservative who had supported Hitler in the 1923 Putsch, had already come to know Hitler better and he had some ominous words for Hindenburg:

> By appointing Hitler as Chancellor of the Reich, you have delivered our holy German fatherland into the hands of one of the greatest demagogues of all time. I solemnly prophesy to you that this unholy man will cast our nation into the abyss . . . Future generations will curse you in your grave for what you have done. [1]

Hitler presented himself in his first public address over the radio on February 1, 1933, as the defender of the moral values of Christianity and family against the specter of Communism:

> Communism with its method of madness is making a powerful and insidious attack upon our dismayed and shattered nation . . . Fourteen years of Marxism have ruined Germany; one year of Bolshevism would destroy her . . . one decisive step is absolutely necessary first: the overcoming of the destroying menace of Communism in Germany . . . The members of the new government . . . regard Christianity as the foundation of our national morality and the family as the basis of our national life. [2]

Carrying on one of his characteristics charades, Hitler called in Msgr. Kaas for talks on his joining a majority coalition government the same day he came to power. Kaas was eager and ready to join Hitler's cabinet, but Hitler had no intention to create a wider coalition with the Center Party whom he wanted out of politics altogether. He formed his government with the Nationalists as sole partners as he made up with von Papen. The Nazis Göring and Frick became members of the first cabinet while the other ministries went to the Nationalists with von Pa-

pen as vice chancellor. Hitler also took care to meet privately with leading army
generals on February 3, 1933 and presented them with his plans for rearmament
and conquest of Lebensraum in the east, which obviously were music to their
ears.[3]

As the door to power was opened to him for the first time, Hitler was resolved not to allow that door ever to close. His plan was to liquidate parliamentary democracy and establish a Nazi monopoly of power using the laws of the
Weimar Republic. As in so many other things, Hitler took the initial clue from
Benito Mussolini who suspended parliamentary democracy in Italy in 1928 to
become absolute dictator of a Fascist corporate state. At that time, with no more
than twelve delegates in the Reichstag, Hitler addressed the Nazi Party on October 29, 1928, with the following words:

> I have not sent my twelve deputies into the Reichstag so they could be function-
> ing members, but only to accelerate the end of parliamentarianism.[4]

Wilhelm Frick, one of the two Nazis who later became cabinet members in
Hitler's first government, spelled out the Nazi aim in the National Socialist Yearbook very clearly:

> Our anti participation in the parliament does not indicate support, but rather an
> undermining of the parliamentary system. It does not indicate that we renounce
> our -parliamentarian attitude but that we are fighting the enemy with his own
> weapons and that we are fighting for our National Socialist goal from the par-
> liamentary platform. (2724-PS).[5]

Hitler's plan contemplated the approval of an Enabling Act or *Ermächtigunggesetz* that would transfer the main legislative powers of the Reichstag to the
chancellor and his cabinet for four years. The Enabling Act would grant the chancellor the authority to govern by decree and even approve laws contrary to the
constitution that previously required a two-thirds Reichstag majority. The approval of the budget, loans, and foreign treaties would be turned over from the
parliament to the cabinet. A decree to dissolve and ban all political parties with
exception of the Nazi Party could then be approved by the cabinet.

Hitler was careful this time to maintain the appearance of constitutional legality and not to repeat the errors of the 1923 Putsch. He made sure that Hindenburg, an old-school monarchist, would not stand in the way to give the Republic
its coup de grace. To pass the Enabling Act in the Reichstag, Hitler needed a two-
thirds majority and a minimal quorum of two-thirds of the delegates, which he
was far from commanding. The Nazis did not despair. They were ready with their
dirty bag of tricks to overcome the hurdle eliminating their parliamentary opponents. Hitler began negotiations with the parties, which he used as a screen to
bring about new Reichstag elections. On February 5, 1933, Hitler sought Hindenburg's approval for new parliamentary elections to change the balance of power
in the Reichstag. Hindenburg agreed and new elections were set for a month later
on March 5, 1933.

The Nazi Party was on the verge of financial bankruptcy at the time and not in a condition to carry out a successful campaign for the upcoming elections. When the industrialists learned that the Nazi Party coffers were empty, they came promptly to their rescue. On Hitler's call, a consortium of around twenty-five of the most powerful German industrialists, with Gustav Krupp and Hjalmar Schacht at the helm, gathered in the home of Herman Göring for a fundraiser on February 20, 1933. The most important representatives of the industrial-financial elite were present, such as Albert Voegler of United Steel, Georg von Schnitzler of I. G. Farben, Edward Schulte, Friedrich Flick, Hugo Stinnes, Fritz Springorum, and many others. While asking for their money, Göring had some encouraging words for them:

> The sacrifices asked for will be easier for industry to bear if it is realized that the election of March 5 will surely be the last one for the next ten years, probably even for the next hundred years. [6]

General Schleicher, the leader of the Nationalist Party who traditionally represented the interests of industrialists, came out in favor of helping the Nazis. He declared that if the Nazi Party were allowed to disintegrate, Germany would have ten million Communists the next day. It is ironic that only one year later, von Schleicher was one of the victims murdered by the Nazis. The industrialists responded generously in anticipation of the upcoming elections, and pledged three million Reich marks to save the Nazi Party from bankruptcy. Their investment paid off handsomely when Hitler's rearmament program soon opened before them unprecedented profit opportunities. With the money in his purse, Goebbels exulted:

> Now it is easy to carry on the fight for we can call on all the state's means. The radio and the press are at our disposal. We shall furnish a masterpiece of agitation. And this time (of course!) there is no lack of money. [7]

The Nazis thought not merely of co-opting initially the votes of Catholics and Nationalists to pass the Enabling Act, but also of physically eliminating from the Reichstag as many of their Communist and Social Democratic opponents as possible without destroying the minimum quorum required. They relied on Göring's cunning to eliminate and silence as many of them as necessary. Göring did not disappoint them. He hatched a diabolic plot to justify the suspension of civil liberties and the arrest of opposition Reichstag members by creating a false alarm of an imminent Communist takeover. The first act of Hitler's so-called prophecy was going to be fulfilled:

> The fight to the finish between Swastika and Soviet Star must appear to the people in the garish light of an attempted Bolshevist revolution. Then you will see that the Lord sent me to do these works. [8]

On February 27, 1933, the Reichstag building was set on fire and the Communists acussed of the crime. Marinus van der Lubbe a deranged ex-Communist was accused of the act.[9] The fire gave credibility to the claim that the Communists were preparing a revolution in Germany and provided the necessary excuse to suspend civil liberties. A campaign of terror and intimidation against the opposition to the left began. The next day, February 28, 1933, at Hitler's request, Hindenburg signed the Decree for the Protection of the People and the State that suspended free speech, free press, freedom of assembly and organization, sanctity of the home, and security of mail and telephone, and granted the government the right of unrestricted imprisonment of suspects. The death penalty was instated for treason, arson, and railroad sabotage.

The first concentration camps were established and the SA dragged political enemies away and beat them to death or tortured them. About 4,000 Communist Party officials were arrested. The hunt was also extended against many Social Democrat Reichstag members. Their newspaper, the *Reichsbanner*, was forbidden in most German states. The Center Party convened its deputies the morning after the Reichstag fire to define its position in face of the crisis. Although no one of them believed the Nazi fabrications about the fire, Kaas passed an internal party resolution, which bid its members to refrain from accusing the Hitler government of incendiarism and falsehood. Cardinal Faulhaber of Munich congratulated in a pastoral letter the Nazi government's campaign against atheism and Communism.[10] On March 13, 1933, Cardinal Faulhaber returned from his trip to Rome with a message from Pope Pius XI to the Conference of Bavarian bishops with words of praise for Hitler for combating Communism:

> The Holy Father Pius XI publicly praised the chancellor Adolf Hitler for the stand that the later had taken against Communism.[11]

The official daily international bulletin of the Vatican, *La Corrispondenza*, came out on March 13, 1933 with a statement that there was a need to reassess the previous negative attitude towards Hitler's movement because "no one could fail to recognize certain nobility in the National Socialist movement."[12]

The words that Karl Bachem, the historian of the Center Party wrote shortly after are characteristic of the Catholic mindset at the time:

> It is enough if cooperation with the National Socialists can protect us against Communists, Bolshevism and anarchy! First remove the danger of Communism then everything will sort itself out.[13]

The parliamentary elections were held as scheduled on March 5, 1933, in an environment of terror and intimidation with the civil liberties suspended. The SA thugs were vandalizing the Weimar flag and hoisting Nazi banners everywhere. The elections increased the number of Nazi seats but still left them dependent on Catholic and Nationalist votes to approve the Enabling Act:

| Party | Votes | Deputies | % |
|-------|-------|----------|---|
| Nazis: | 17.2 million | 288 | 43.9% |

| Social Democrats: | 7.1 million | 119 | 18.7% |
| Communists: | 4.8 million | 81 | 12.7% |
| Catholics: | 5.4 million | 92 | 15.1% |
| Nationalists: | 3.1 million | 52 | 8.6% |

The Nazi-Nationalist coalition had now a majority in the Reichstag with 52.5 percent of the votes, but it was still short of the two-thirds majority required to approve the Enabling Act in parliament. The votes of the Center Party and the elimination of as many opposition votes as possible were their best bet. The Nazis feverishly began preparing for the next decisive battle: the approval of the Enabling Act that would give them the dictatorial powers they were after.

The vote for the Enabling Act was set for March 23, 1933. The Catholic parties held the key to the two-thirds majority required to approve the Enabling Act. Two days after the elections, on March 7, 1933, Hitler passed a resolution in the cabinet meeting to put all their efforts into winning over the Catholic parties to vote in favor of the Enabling Act. The ability of the Catholic parties to tip the scale either way gave their votes a value far beyond their actual numbers.

In his pursuit of a Nazi monopoly of power, Hitler looked forward to the day when Catholic activism would be forced out from the political arena. Hitler wished to capture the Catholics into the Nazi movement and end any independent Catholic political activity. He spoke at the cabinet meeting of the importance of getting the Curia in Rome to agree to dissolve the confessional parties and to remove the clergy from the political scene. Von Papen, the vice chancellor, readily agreed with him:

> The priest in politics we shall eliminate . . . We shall give him back to the pulpit and the altar.[14]

Meanwhile, however, it was necessary to deal with the Center Party and its political leaders. He and the Nazi Interior Minister Frick personally negotiated from March 20 to March 22 with Catholic leaders Kaas, Stegerwald, and Hackelsburger to win their vote for the Enabling Act. Hitler accepted their conditions that he should issue a public declaration in the Reichstag before the vote, guaranteeing the Christian character of the state, the existence of confessional schools, the continuation of the Catholic civil service employees in the government, and the permanence of the states of Bavaria, Prussia, and Baden and of their concordats.The main prize, however, was the understanding that the Nazi government would sign a concordat as soon as possible with the Church. Goebbels expressly made reference to that accord in 1937 in his newspaper *Der Angriff* stating that the main incentive at that moment was Hitler's verbal promise to Kaas to sign a national concordat with the Church in Rome. At the request of the Vatican, the Catholic parties voted for the Enabling Act on the basis of that promise:

> Kaas agreed to the Enabling Act in exchange for the government's agreement to negotiate a Reich concordat with the Holy See.[15]

On March 22, 1933, two days before the vote on the Enabling Act, Himmler, the SS leader and newly appointed police chief of Munich, put in service the Dachau concentration camp in a former powder-milk plant. It was the first of many other camps for the internment of political opponents. The Malicious Practices Act of March 21, 1933, approved a day earlier, allowed the Nazis to carry out mass arrests of political opponents. All the elected Communist Reichstag members were rounded up and sent to concentration camps to prevent them from voting. Frightened to death, twenty Social Democrat deputies went into hiding. Göring proved once again that he was a master of trickery. By eliminating one hundread opposition votes from the Reichstag before the vote even began, he reduced the quorum from 635 to 535 members.[16] Overjoyed, Göring appeared at Hitler's cabinet meeting informing its members that more than a two-thirds majority vote was now guaranteed!

With the burned-down Reichstag building lying in ruins, Hitler convened its members for the crucial vote in the Kroll Opera, across from the Reichstag building, on March 23, 1933. Addressing the Reichstag before the vote, Hitler had no problem with making all the promises that the Center Party leadership requested in order to get their vote. He referred to the Christian denominations as "the most important factor for the maintenance of our society" and "an essential element for safeguarding the soul of the German people" and expressed his desire for "sincere cooperation between Church and State," seemingly in allusion to the negotiations of a treaty with the Vatican. He pledged "to attach the greatest value to friendly relations with the Holy See," adding that he was "endeavoring to develop them":

> The National Government sees in both Christian denominations the most important factor for the maintenance of our society . . . It will respect the agreements concluded between them and the states; their rights will not be touched. It expects, however, that its task of the national and moral renewal of our people will meet with similar appreciation from their side . . . The National Government will permit and guarantee to the Christian denominations the enjoyment of its due influence in schools and education. Its concern will be for the sincere cooperation of Church and State. The struggle against the materialist ideology and for the establishment of a real national community is in the interests of our German nation as much as of our Christian faith . . . The government of the Reich, who regard Christianity as the unshakable foundation of the morals and the moral code of the nation, attach the greatest value to friendly relations with the Holy See and are endeavoring to develop them.[17]

In the evening session, Msgr. Ludwig Kaas and Ritter von Lex, the leaders of the Center and the Catholic Bavarian People's Party respectively, stood up and ceremoniously declared in the name of their parties that on the basis of Hitler's promises they were ready to cast their vote in favor of the Ermächtigunggesetz. The Nazi delegates responded to their newly found soul mates with generous applause. The next day, on March 24, 1933, Göring brought the Enabling Act to a vote. The 535 members assembled there amply exceeded the minimum quorum of 420 members required. No more than 357 favorable votes were necessary to reach a two-thirds majority.

All ninety-two Catholic Center Party members to one man were present and they voted unanimously in favor of the Enabling Act, together with the Nationalists. The only votes cast against were those of the ninety-four Social Democrat delegates who held on bravely. The Enabling Act was passed on the third reading by 441 votes in favor to 94 votes against, surpassing the minimal two-thirds majority of 357 votes. Had the Catholics voted against the act there would only have been 349 votes in favor, eight less than the necessary minimum. The parliamentary Weimar Republic came to an end. The senile Hindenburg had already agreed, even before the vote was taken, to transfer his own constitutional powers to issue decrees to Hitler. From that moment on, Hitler's Third Reich was born; his word became the law in Germany, and legislation fundamentally took the form of Führer edicts. [18]

The highest body of the Church in Germany, the Fulda Conference of Bishops, gathered five days after the vote, on March 29, 1933, and issued a public declaration expressing their trust in the promises Hitler made before the Reichstag. The bishops withdrew the ban against membership in the Nazi Party that they had issued on their last annual conference:

It must be recognized that public and solemn declarations have been issued by the highest representative of the Reich Government, who is simultaneously the authoritarian leader of that movement, which acknowledge the inviolability of the teachings of the Catholic faith and the immutable tasks and rights of the Church. Similarly, the full validity of the treaties concluded between the various German states and the Church is guaranteed.

Without revoking the condemnation contained in our previous statements of certain religious and ethical errors, the Episcopate nevertheless believes it can cherish the hope that those general warnings and prohibitions need no longer be regarded as necessary . . . Members in uniform may now be admitted to the divine services and to the sacraments even if they appear in large numbers. [19]

The Catholic vote for Hitler's Enabling Act and the bishop's declaration were perceived by German Catholics as a go-ahead signal to join the Nazis and rally behind Hitler. Most German Catholic newspapers were now calling for support of the new Reich. The Catholic Teachers Association, the caretakers of Catholic education in Germany, considered its independent existence superfluous and voluntarily dissolved itself and joined the Nazi Teachers League.[20] It published an enthusiastic manifest in favor of the Nazis on April 1, 1933, that is characteristic of the mood that now prevailed in the Catholic camp. The historian of the Center Party, Karl Bachem, defended the Catholic vote and highlighted the new unity of purpose that was forged between the Nazis and the Catholics:

As in the August days of 1914, a feeling of national and German emotion has seized our people . . . Thanks to the warning summons of Adolf Hitler and his movement, and to his work, we have succeeded in breaking through the un-

German spirit that prevailed in the revolution of 1918 . . . At this critical moment, Catholicism must not once again stand aside, adopting a wait and see attitude. We will lend a hand of help with the construction of a new Reich and a
new nation, putting our trust in the leader of the German and Volkisch movement . . . We must—and here we agree completely with the leader of the national
movement—we must first become an internally unified nation of German men
and women . . . Shake hands across the barriers that have hitherto been overem-
phasized, in order once more to become a nation that believes in honor, cleanli-
ness, and loyalty.[21]

Showing a total lack of moral sensitivity in more than one sense, Bachem
compared the alliance with the Nazis to the cooperation accord that the Center
Party established in 1919 with the Social Democrats that saved Germany from
Bolshevism:

The bishops have voted unanimously for the recognition of the new government,
such resistance, no longer morally defensible, would have been impossible for us
. . . It is true that parliamentarism and with it the democratic idea have come to a
dead end . . . So was it justified to try a new way? Certainly, Hitler had inserted
several points in his speech that meet our wishes to a far greater extent than
would have been thought possible, and give us a certain security . . . Just as after
1919, when the association with the Social Democrats saved us from Bolshevism, it is enough if cooperation with the National Socialists can protect us
against Communists, Bolshevism and anarchy! First remove the danger of
Communism then everything will sort itself out . . . It is certain that even Catholics loyal to the Church will now join the National Socialists formations in great
numbers just as in Italy. [22]

A rush to join the Nazi Party ensued. Catholics were joining in masse the
Nazi Party and its organizations. The Catholics did not want to be left out of Hitler's new Germany as Noakes and Pridham point out:

Even before the Center Party was voluntarily dissolved, many of its members
had already been swept away by the spirit of the national uprising and without
reservations joined the Nazi Party. [23]

Civil servants afraid of loosing their jobs or seeking rapid promotion in the
Nazi government rushed to become members in the Nazi Party. Teachers, doctors, lawyers, and other opportunists eager to board the bandwagon stood next in
line. Catholic Heinrich Lammers, a prominent member of the Center Party, timed
so well his Nazi conversion that Hitler appointed him head of the chancellor's
office. New 1.5 million members joined the party which had only counted
850,000 members in January, 1933. Unable to handle the avalanche the Nazi Party offices had to be closed temporarily to the public.

The Enabling Act vote of March 24, 1933, literally changed the course of
history in Germany and the world. Its tragic effects lasted until the Third Reich
went up in flames. In January 1934 the Nazified rubberstamp Reichstag took another step to increase Hitler's power, granting him the authority to change the

constitution at will without the consent of a two-thirds formal majority. At the end of its first four-year-period on April 1, 1937, Hitler's puppet Reichstag rubberstamped the Enabling Act again. In 1943 Hitler made the Enabling Act permanent. It took a world war and tens of millions of deaths to undo the immoral decision of the Church leadership to join Hitler in destroying the democratic political system in Germany. Even if Hitler would conceivably have found other means to carry through his evil designs without the help of the Catholic Church and its political arm, the fact remains that the Church provided him with the crucial support to do it at the crossroads of history.

## The Jewish Situation Deteriorates

A campaign of terror and intimidation against German Jewry was let loose as soon as Hitler came to power. Signs cropped up announcing that Jews were not wanted: "Juden sind hier unerwünscht!" Nazi slogans and posters threatening reprisals against buyers were smeared on Jewish storefronts. SA storm troopers in their brown shirts stood guard outside and prevented anyone from entering them. Streicher's highly visible placards were indoctrinating the Germans everywhere:

Ohne Lösung der Judenfrage keine Erlösung des deutschen Volkes! (Without a solution of the Jewish question there is no salvation for the German people.)

On March 9, 1933, the SA began all over Germany the first physical attacks and killings of Jews. Jewish shops and homes were looted. Storm troopers seized in broad daylight many East European Jews in Berlin to send them to concentration camps. Jewish lawyers were expelled from courtrooms and professors from classrooms. Synagogues and Jewish cemeteries were vandalized.[24] Jewish firms began to be expropriated by the SA and the large Jewish department stores and one-price shops came under heavy pressure to close down. Brutal Nazi commissars were sent in to take over control over the large Jewish-owned newspapers, companies, and organizations. Every Jewish event and gathering began to be supervised by Gestapo agents.

When the Catholic parties voted on March 24, 1933, in favor of the Enabling Act that concentrated all government power in Hitler's hands, they knew perfectly well what kind of "new" Germany they were helping to create. After the approval, the persecution of the Jews took on new momentum. On March 26, 1933, Hitler instructed in Berchtesgaden his newly appointed minister of propaganda Josef Goebbels (1897-1945) to announce a nationwide boycott against all Jewish businesses and professionals.[25] On March 28, Goebbels and Streicher announced that a boycott against Jewish businesses and professionals was to begin on April 1, 1933, allegedly in response to the "atrocity propaganda" Jews were spreading abroad. Goebbels threatened to hold German Jewry hostage:

Perhaps the foreign Jews will think better of the matter when their racial comrades in Germany begin to get it in the neck.[26]

Oskar Wassermann, the president of the Committee for Inter-confessional Peace approached the Catholic bishop's conference with a plea to intervene with the Nazi government to stop the Nazi boycott against the Jews. At a time that the prospects of signing a concordat were already running high, the bishops firmly turned down the request. Cardinal Michael Faulhaber of Munich explained to clergyman Alois Wurm, the editor of the periodical *Seele*, that more important concerns stood in the agenda of the bishops than the fate of the Jews. The Jews, he said, can take care of themselves.

> For the higher ecclesiastical authorities there are immediate issues of much greater importance: Schools, the maintaining of Catholic associations, steriliza-
> tion, are more important for Christianity in our homeland. One must assume that the Jews are capable of helping themselves. [27]

The answer of the Church hierarchy clearly indicates that they considered their relations with Hitler too important to allow the Jewish question to stand in the way. The policy of *nichteinmischung*—not interfering with the Nazis in their persecution of the Jews—was beginning to take shape. In stark contrast to the refusal of the German bishops to intervene, Arturo Toscanini, Fritz Reiner, and eleven of the world's most prominent musicians responded to the persecution of the Jews by cabling a protest to Hitler and announcing they would boycott Germany's cultural enterprises, including the Wagner Festival in Bayreuth. Toscanini demanded that his name be put on top of the names signing the protest cable to Hitler.[28]

As news of the persecutions were spread worldwide by the media, Jews abroad, alarmed by the situation, called for a response that would deter Hitler of further attacks on the defenseless German Jews. The idea of a Jewish counter boycott was proposed in many Jewish circles abroad. The proposal terrified the helpless Jewish leaders in Germany who were pleading with Jewish leaders outside Germany not to endanger German Jewry. When the German American Nazi Ernst Hanfstangl commented to Hitler that the Jews intended to respond with an international boycott against German products, Hitler ran into frenzy and beat his fists:

> Now we shall show them that we are not afraid of international Jewry. The Jews must be crushed. [29]

Already in 1922 Hitler believed that a call to all anti-Semites to unite would be a sure way to gain allies. From the small Bavarian country town of Tölz, Hitler paraphrased Marx's call to the workers of the world to unite against their exploiters and called all anti-Semites and Aryans from all nations to unite against the Jewish race. He thundered there before a gathering of peasants and lumbermen:

> Aryans and anti-Semites of all nations, unite in the struggle against the Jewish race of exploiters and oppresors of all nations! [30]

In his conversations with the president of the Danzig Senate, Hermann Rauschning (1932-1934), Hitler made clear his intended use of anti-Semitism not only internally but also as an instrument of Nazi foreign policy. Hitler, who called anti-Semitism "the most important weapon in my arsenal," saw the Jews as hostages in his international political adventures and as a catalyst to attract all their enemies to the Nazi cause all over the world. He told Rauschning:

> "My" Jews are a valuable hostage that the democracies have provided me with. Anti-Semitic propaganda in every country is an almost indispensable means for the expansion of a political campaign. You will see how little time we will need to change the ideas and norms of the whole world by the simple device of attacking Judaism. It is without a doubt the most important weapon in my arsenal. [31]

On April 8, 1933, at a meeting with Adolf Hitler at the new chancellor's office, Hitler told James G. Mc Donald:

> I will do the thing that the rest of the world would like to do. It doesn't know how to get rid of the Jews. I will show them. [32]

On April 26, 1933, Hitler received for the first time an official delegation representing the Fulda Bishops conference. Bishop Wilhelm Bernning of Osnabrück and Vicar General of Berlin Johannes Steinman came to convey to him the congratulations of the bishops conference to his becoming chancellor. The bishop's secretary registered their conversation in a protocol.

> Hitler welcomed the opportunity to explain himself to a Catholic bishop for he had been accused of being an enemy of Christianity and this charge hurt him deeply. He was convinced that without Christianity one could neither run a personal life nor a state, and Germany in particular needed the kind of religious and moral foundation only Christianity could provide. [33]

Hitler assured the delegation that he rejected Rosenberg's book and that as a Catholic he would not permit the founding of another religion nor tolerate another Kulturkampf:

> For this reason I have turned against Ludendorff and broken company with him and for the same reason I reject the book of Rosenberg. It is not a Party book . . . that book is written by a Protestant. The Protestants can settle matters with him. [34]

Hitler immediately brought up the Jewish question to make the bishops aware at his first official meeting with them what he expected from the Church in this respect. He told them that the struggle against the Jews had the highest priority in his agenda. He exhorted the Church leaders to reinvigorate the war against the Jews and join him in a common struggle against them:

Christianity had in recent centuries failed to exert its strength and its will to overcome the powers, which are hostile to the state and Christianity. I have been attacked because of my handling of the Jewish question. The Catholic Church considered the Jews pestilent for fifteen hundred years, put them in ghettos etc., because it recognized the Jews for what they were. In the epoch of liberalism the danger was no longer recognized. I am moving back toward the time in which a fifteen-hundred-year-long tradition was implemented. I do not set race over religion, but I recognize the representatives of this race as pestilent for the state and for the Church, and perhaps I am thereby doing Christianity a great service by pushing them out of schools and public functions. [35]

Warm handshakes and congratulations sealed the end of the encounter with the Führer, not words of recrimination or reserve. The conversation in its entirety was subsequently transmitted through Nuncio Cesare Orsenigo to the Vatican and received by Vatican Secretary of State Pacelli on May 8, 1933. This first encounter of the bishops with Hitler provides the early background of the policy the Church adopted during the Hitler period with regard to the persecution of the Jews.

When Hitler spoke with the bishops of reinvigorating the persecution of Jews, he was already well on his way to make anti-Semitism the centerpiece of his internal policy. The boycott announced by Goebbels, which allowed the brutal SA thugs to terrorize Jewish businesses and professionals, was called off after three days, on April 3, 1933. In its place, a pernicious legislative program to eliminate the Jews from the German economy and from every field of the arts and culture in which they were so prominent followed. More than 400 anti-Semitic decrees were issued in three weeks during April 1933, making normal Jewish existence in Germany practically impossible. Decrees were issued forbidding Jews to teach in the universities, practice law, practice medicine for insurance companies, write for newspapers, and publish books. They could not work in the theater, film, literature, journalism, and the arts. All Jewish judges in Prussia and Bavaria were dismissed. Gustav Krupp agreed in April 1933 to remove Jewish workers from his factories.

On April 7, 1933, the Law for the Restoration of the Professional Civil Service mandated that government officials of non-Aryan origin were to be retired. An Aryan clause prohibited non-Aryans from taking state examinations in many occupations. The Aryan requirement was made mandatory for membership in professional organizations, societies, and clubs. On April 12, 1933, Wilhelm Frick, the minister of the interior, declared that any mixed descendents with even one Jewish grandparent, regardless of the conversion of these ancestors to Christianity were considered Jews. On April 21, 1933, kosher slaughtering was outlawed in Germany. A law was approved dismissing all Jewish medical doctors, pharmacists, and dentists from hospitals, clinics, and public health centers. On April 25, the Reich sports office ordered all German sports organizations to exclude Jews from competitions and to implement an Aryans-only policy. On April 26, 1933, the fearsome Gestapo was established under Göhring's leadership.

Those Germans seeking professional employment or promotion became obviously enthusiastic supporters and beneficiaries of the elimination of the Jews. To get rid of Jewish competitors and take over their positions and wealth was very appealing to them. German Jews understood that the future of Jews in Germany was bleak indeed, and many began to flee the country in panic, using every transport available, including on foot. Prominent Jewish professors, scientists, and artists were among the refugees. Some were Nobel Prize winners; others would receive the Nobel Prize years later. Walter Benjamin went to France, Lion Feuchtwanger to Switzerland, and Albert Einstein, during an overseas tour in California, vowed never to return to Germany. The refugees began to alert the world to what was occurring in Germany. World newspapers were filled with reports of the atrocities being committed and Jews all over the world reacted with pain and anguish.

During the first two weeks of April more than 10,000 Jews with nothing more than a few belongings in their hands fled from Germany to almost every country in Europe. The refugees went to Denmark, Holland, Belgium, France, Czechoslovakia, Switzerland, and even to Poland. Jewish charities were overwhelmed. Some refugees reached Spain, Portugal, and Great Britain. Although the German immigration quota to the United States was largely unused at the time, it kept to its strict closed-doors policy and did not make an exception for persecuted German Jewry.[36]

The British Colonial Office, which administered the mandate over Palestine, formulated a strict immigration policy to stem Jewish immigration to Palestine. Visa applicants were divided into two major categories: capitalists and noncapitalists. Capitalists who could pay £1000 sterling could obtain a certificate, while non capitalists were subject to a quota system that fluctuated according to a periodic assessment of the local job market. The Jewish Agency would negotiate twice a year with the Colonial Office the number of certificates for non capitalists. The Jewish Agency was responsible for allocating these certificates. Varying between 500 and 1,500, these certificates were a drop in the bucket given the magnitude of the Jewish tragedy in Germany and Europe.

The exodus of persecuted Jews from Germany was held back by the strict monetary restrictions that were originally instituted by the Brünning government in August 1931, which prohibited taking currency out of Germany. They became a formidable barrier when the Hitler government turned these restrictions into a powerful instrument to rob German Jewry. To obtain an immigration permit, a Jew had to pay an exorbitant exit tax, a *Reichsfluchtsteuer* equivalent to 25 percent of his assets, while the rest of his capital remained behind in blocked accounts.

Negotiations with the Nazi government initiated by private Jewish entrepreneur Sam Cohen and the Zionist leader Chaim Arlosoroff culminated in a transfer agreement, the Ha'avarah Agreement, signed with the German Ministry of Economics on August 7, 1933. It allowed the Anglo Palestine Bank to use part of the blocked accounts of German Jews wishing to immigrate to Palestine to buy German products to be sold in Palestine and the Near East.[37] The proceeds of the sales were to be used in the first instance to pay the £1000 required by the mandate government for a capitalist visa to Palestine.

Nazi leaders signed the accord to break the anti-Nazi boycott, hasten the elimination of Jews from Germany, and provide badly needed employment for German industry. The initial accord that forced Jewish Palestine to become a consumer and sales agent of German goods allowed for the exit of a significant number of German Jews to mandate Palestine and to the transfer of 3 million RM of goods, the equivalent of $1 million. The accord deeply divided at the time the Jewish world and the Zionist movement itself, sowing bitter discord and dissension as it ran counter to the anti-Nazi boycott.

George S. Messersmith, the American consul general in Berlin, one of the most perceptive observers of Nazism, assessed the Jewish situation in Germany on May 4, 1933:

> A moral suffering such as I have not seen anywhere and under any conditions heretofore. [38]

On May 10, 1933, Germany made a return to the darkest days of the Middle Ages when students in the universities organized great bonfires in which they burned books by authors they classified as Jewish. Goebbels, the organizer of the book burnings, addressed a roaring crowd of tens of thousands of students gathered in Berlin's *Opernplatz* and turned into ashes the products of the Jewish genius:

> The era of extreme Jewish intellectualism is now at an end. The breakthrough of the German revolution has again cleared the way on the German path . . . The future German man will not just be a man of books, but a man of chara-cter. [39]

When he finished, Nazi-saluting vandals broke out in a frenzied dance of triumph over the spirit of Judaism, singing Nazi songs and anthems. With unusual premonition, the German-Jewish bard Heinrich Heine had written one century earlier, in 1821, in his play *Almansor* the following words referring to the book burnings of the Inquisition:

> Dort, wo man Bücher verbrennt, verbrennt man am Ende auch Menschen. (Where they burn books, they will end burning human beings.) [40]

## Liquidation of the Political Parties: The Concordat

After the approval of the Enabling Act on March 24, 1933, Hitler's next objective was the dissolution of all political parties with the exception of the Nazis. As long as legislative power lay in the hands of the Reichstag such a ban was unthinkable—they would not have approved their own suicide. But once the powers of the Reichstag lay in the hands of Hitler and his cabinet, he could issue a dissolution decree. He was fully prepared to use force against the Communist and Social Democrat parties if they refused to disband. As to the Catholic parties he preferred the carrot instead of the stick to obtain the voluntary agreement of the Church to their dissolution. The sweet carrot was his offer to the Vatican to negotiate a concordat.

Diplomatic treaties between the Vatican and the different governments, known as concordats, became the favorite formula of Pius XI to guarantee Church rights. Seeking accommodation with the one-party Fascist dictatorships of Europe, Pius XI broke away from the earlier Vatican policy of Pope Leon XIII that depended on local Catholic parties to protect these interests. He assumed that Catholic lay organizations working from within the Fascist corporate states could be at least as effective as Catholic political parties. The Fascist dictators delighted with the new policy that cleared the political playing field for them and they stood in line to sign concordats with the Vatican.

Msgr. Eugenio Pacelli, the Vatican's main diplomatic negotiator of concordats, signed a total of eighteen concordats in record time with such reactionary regimes as Poland, Portugal, and Italy, among others. The Vatican was especially eager to sign concordats with countries where Catholics were in the minority and Catholic political parties could not hope to gain political control such as Germany, Yugoslavia, and Romania. Nuncio Pacelli expressed the Vatican's desire for a concordat with the Weimar Republic in 1920 for the first time when he presented his diplomatic credentials to President Friedrich Eber. During his tenure as nuncio, Pacelli concluded concordats with Bavaria (1924), Prussia (1929), and Baden (1932) but failed in his effort to sign a concordat with the Weimar Republic, despite his repeated attempts from 1920 to 1932.

The issue of the existence of separate confessional schools stood in the way of concluding a treaty with the Weimar Republic due to the opposition of the Social Democrats. Even when Catholic chancellors from the Center party, such as Fehrenbuch, Wirth, Marx, Brüning, and von Papen, headed the government coalition, they were unable to overcome the opposition. Just three months before the installation of Hitler as chancellor, during November 1932, von Papen was an actor in Pacelli's latest failed attempt to negotiate a Reich concordat with the Weimar government.[41]

Hitler realized the enormous leverage of a concordat in dealing with the Church. In Italy, the Lateran Treaty signed by the Holy See with Mussolini in 1929 brought to an end the feud that had persisted since 1870. Mussolini recognized Catholicism as the official religion of the country and the Vatican as a sovereign state; he guaranteed the Vatican's freedom of access and the provision of its necessary services and communications. In exchange, the Catholic Church disallowed Catholic political parties and the direct participation of priests in politics, leaving completely the political arena to the Fascists. Pius XI hailed Mussolini as the man of Providence who "restored God to Italy and Italy to God." Hitler, an early apprentice of Mussolini, grasped the political logic of Mussolini's move and envisioned the political trading value of a concordat in Germany at the right moment. [42]

When Hitler rose to power, von Papen brought to his immediate attention the political leverage that a concordat could provide him.[43] A concordat was after all a small price to pay to obtain the agreement of the Church to end parliamentary democracy in Germany and remove the Catholic parties out of the way. Different independent historical sources confirm that it was Hitler who initiated the concordat proposal in 1933. Pius XII himself stated that much in an address to the Sacred College after World War II on June 2, 1945:

> Since it was the German government, which made the proposal, the responsibility for all the regrettable consequences would have fallen on the Holy See if it had refused the proposed concordat. [44]

In his negotiations with Msgr. Kaas to win the Center Party vote for the Enabling Act, Hitler floated the alluring propositions of signing a concordat with the Vatican that would guarantee the inviolability of its rights and a steady annual income to support the Church. The bait worked exactly as Hitler had foreseen and immediately began to produce high political dividends for the Nazis even before formal negotiations began.[45] With the promise of negotiating a concordat, Hitler extracted from the Church concession after concession. Although Hitler's aim of removing the clergy and the Catholic parties from the political scene was not acceptable to many of the German Catholic lay leaders, the Vatican was ready to cut a deal as Pius XII's statement confirms. Msgr. Kaas was instructed to mobilize his deputies to vote in favor of the Enabling Act and to agree to the dissolution of the Catholic parties and the depoliticization of the clergy.

The Enabling Act was approved on March 24, 1933. The same day Msgr. Kaas left in a hurry for Rome without any public explanation for his sudden trip. Six days later, on March 30, 1933, a press report in the *Tägliche Rundschau* announced that negotiations of a concordat that would bring about final reconciliation between the Church and the Nazi regime were underway. On March 31, 1933, Kaas was called back from Rome to Berlin for talks with Hitler. He met twice with him on April 2, 1931, and informed Hitler that the Vatican was willing and ready to negotiate a concordat.

According to Church law, a concordat had the status of a *causa major* that had to be negotiated in Rome. Hitler appointed Franz von Papen, the vice chancellor, as the German chief negotiator and gave him the authority to bypass the Foreign Ministry in his direct communications with him.[46] For the Church the appointed negotiators were Msgrs. Eugenio Pacelli and Ludwig Kaas. On April 6, von Papen announced officially in the name of the German government that he was traveling to Rome to propose the conclusion of a concordat. That day the *Paris Journal* reported that the German government made overtures to the Vatican to sign a concordat that would exclude priests from political office. On April 6, 1933, Ludwig Kaas resigned as leader of the Center Party, leaving to Brünning the unsavory task of pulling the plug on the Center party. Nobody could have characterized better than Kaas himself his service to The Nazi cause as he did when he resigned:

> I did my best to counteract the opposition trying to block the path of the new Germany.[47]

Kaas left in his diary a testimony of his conversations with von Papen on April 7 in Munich on their way to Rome to negotiate the concordat. When von Papen expressed to Kaas Hitler's personal interest in the concordat, Kaas expressed his enthusiasm for National Socialism:

> If that were the case, I would surely not be ungenerous. On the contrary, nothing would personally please me more than the possibility of winning the great National Socialist movement to such a policy; It above all, as well as the state would gain strength; a process which until now, unfortunately, had not fully come to fruition. [48]

In Rome, von Papen was received with full state honors by Mussolini whom he met for the first time. "Mussolini," writes von Papen, "gave it, [the concordat], his enthusiastic support." To show his personal interest and support for the concordat, Hitler, as he had done in the past in the Rosenberg dispute, dispatched Hermann Göring to the Vatican. The audience with Pius XI of von Papen and Göring on April 11, 1933, is described by von Papen:

> The Pope greeted me with paternal affection, expressing his pleasure that at the head of the German government now was a man like [Hitler] who uncompromisingly opposed to Communism and Soviet Nihilism in all its forms. [49]

Göring described his visit to the Pope at the Nuremberg trial:

> Shortly before that agreement was concluded by Herr von Papen, I visited the Pope myself. I had numerous connections with the higher Catholic clergy because of my Catholic mother, and thus—I am myself a Protestant—I had a view of both camps. [50]

On April 15, Msgr. Kaas received in Rome instructions from Secretary of State Pacelli to prepare a draft of the concordat. On Hitler's birthday, April 20, Kaas sent from the Vatican a congratulatory telegram, which was greatly publicized in the German press. For many German Catholics this was a signal to join the Nazi Party:

> For today's birthday sincere good wishes and the assurance of unflinching cooperation in the great enterprise of creating a Germany internally united, enjoying social peace and externally free. [51]

On April 22, 1933, Msgr. Giuseppe Pizzardo, the Vatican undersecretary of state told British Ambassador Sir Robert Clive that the Curia had already given up on the Center Party:

> The Holy See is not interested in the Center Party. We are more concerned with the mass of Catholic voters in Germany than in Catholic deputies who represent them in the Reichstag. [52]

On April 28, 1933, Hitler wrote a personal letter to Cardinal Bertram in which he assured him that his government only had in mind sincere collaboration with the Church, for the benefit of both Church and state. Neither the Catholic youth organizations nor the Catholic civil service employees had anything to fear, provided they did not show any hostility toward the party or the government. [53]

With concordat negotiations underway, Cardinal Pacelli requested that the Fulda Conference of Bishops be called together to discuss the issues linked to signing of the treaty, including the dissolution of the Catholic parties and political organizations. The conference was convened to a plenary session—the first in almost a century since 1848—on May 30 and June 1, 1933. Although the Catholic parties had served well Catholic interests since 1870, the Fulda Bishops conference approved the dissolution of the Center and the Bavarian People's Parties.

The widespread rise of sympathy for the Nazis among Catholics in Germany who massively joined the Nazi Party deeply influenced the decisions taken. The conference chose Konrad Gröber (1872-1948), Archbishop of Freiburg, an early Nazi sympathizer and "promoting member" of the SS, to represent them in Rome at the negotiating table. No one is more authorized than von Papen to confirm the direct connection between the dissolution of the Catholic parties and the concordat. In his address before the Association of Catholic Academicians at the Benedictine monastery at Maria Laach on July 22, 1933, von Papen stated:

> As a matter of fact, there also exists, of course, an undeniable inner connection between the dissolution of the German Center Party that has just taken place and the conclusion of the concordat.[54]

At the conference, the question of baptized converts or non-Aryan Christians that were included in the anti-Semitic decrees also came up for discussion. Passing over in silence the persecutions against the Jews, the bishops put in a short sentence against including baptized converts—those newly reborn through the holy sacrament of baptism:

> The excessive stress on race and blood leads to injustices which burden the Christian conscience, especially when they affect men who through the holy sacrament of baptism have been reborn.

The bishops, however, did not condition the conclusion of the concordat to the acceptance of the suggestion. Instead, in their resolution they expressed support and sympathy for Hitler's objectives:

> We German Bishops are far from underestimating or even preventing this national awakening . . . Our German nation, after years of bondage, disregard for our national right, and shameful interference with them, must again receive that freedom and place of honor in the family of nations which is its due on account of its numerical size and its cultural ability and performance.

After the decisions of the plenary session of the Fulda Conference were made public, Catholic writers and publications told their readers that as Catholics they should now find no difficulty in wholeheartedly embracing the world of National Socialism. There is vast historic documentation that bears witness to the unity of purpose that prevailed on both sides at the time. The Seamless Robe that had not been displayed publicly since 1893 was taken out for the unique festive occasion in the cathedral of Trier.[55] Bishop Bornewasser addressed a Catholic youth gathering in the cathedral of that ancient city:

> With raised heads and firm step we have entered the new Reich and we are prepared to serve it with all the might of our body and soul.

The Association of Catholic Newspapers in Bavaria adopted in a resolution in June 1933 to put the Catholic press at the service of the Nazi state, supporting its policies:

> To support the policy of national liberation by the present government, the strengthening of the authority of the state . . . the struggle against Liberalism, Marxism, and above all Bolshevism and for a peaceful understanding between Church and State.

In a festive mass meeting in Berlin on Catholics Day on June 25, Nuncio Orsenigo was saluted by an SA contingent with their raised swastika flags. The leader of Catholic Action in Berlin, Dr. Erich Klausener, later murdered by the Nazis, announced there that great tasks lay ahead for the Catholics in the new awakening of the German nation. Little did he suspect that the "awakening" he was speaking of would take his life and that of his wife exactly one year after, in the Night of the Long Knives!

As the concordat negotiations were coming to a close, the Nazis were trying to put pressure and weaken the Catholic position in the negotiations. Catholic civil servants were dismissed from their government jobs and catholic lay associations were ordered closed. In June a campaign against immorality in the monasteries took the form of arrests of priests under the accusation of immorality and black market charges. What superficially seemed an incongruous policy of negotiating a concordat while harassing priests and Catholic civil servants was in reality classical Nazi double-faced pressure tactics. Von Papen gave some friendly advice to Hitler:

> I pointed out that the Vatican would refuse to recognize him [Hitler] as a possible partner to an agreement unless he immediately put a stop to this sordid campaign. He told me to assure the Papal Secretary of State that he would clamp down on the offenders at once. [56]

Hitler sent a message to Cardinal Pacelli through von Papen on July 1, 1933, with assurances that after the conclusion of the concordat he would arrange full pacification between the Nazi regime and the Church. Well aware of the powerful impression that a declaration that he was and would remain a loyal Catholic would make on the Church, Hitler ordered that day in Berlin that an official announcement be made in his name:

> Reich chancellor Hitler still belongs to the Catholic Church and has no intention of leaving it. [57]

A final text of the concordat was agreed in Rome on July 2, 1933, after its revision by Pope Pius XI. Article 1 guaranteed the freedom of profession and public practice of the Catholic religion. Article 23 guaranteed the continued existence of Catholic denominational schools and Article 21 the provision of Catholic religious instruction in the public schools. The concordat provided the Church with a vast and stable source of income from the religious tax collected by the government. Fifty percent of the religious tax collected by German regional governments was to be designated to the Catholic Church. Considering that German Catholics were not used to support monetarily for their priests nor their schools, as pointed out by historian Guenter Lewy, this aspect of the concordat was particularly alluring to the Church.

In article 16 the concordat demanded an oath from every bishop before a Reich representative of the state concerned or the president of the Reich of unreserved loyalty to the Third Reich. That oath was very soon transformed into a personal oath of loyalty to the Führer:

> Before God and on the Holy Gospels I swear and promise as becomes a bishop, loyalty to the German Reich and to the [regional-EC] State of . . . I swear and promise to honor the legally constituted Government and to cause the clergy of my diocese to honor it. In the performance of my spiritual office and in my solicitude for the welfare and the interests of the German Reich, I will endeavor to avoid all detrimental acts which might endanger it. [58]

Article 32 forbade priests and members of religious orders to become members of political parties. The prohibition was very soon exposed as a subterfuge to nazifiy the clergy when the Nazi legislation made an explicit exception for Catholic priests joining the Nazi Party, on grounds that the general ban on party membership could not possibly apply to the "movement sustaining the state.

In the short term, the concordat was an expedient way to obtain the Church's agreement to the dissolution of the Catholic parties. In the long run it was intended to make the Church economically dependent on the state. A Church whose salaries and budget are covered by the state would necessarily become its obedient servant. The subsidy to the Church increased from 150 million marks a year in 1933 to 500 million marks in 1938 and to 450 million marks in 1943. After the defeat of the Third Reich, the concordat remained in force in West Germany, surpassing the yearly amount of 5 billion marks, the equivalent of $2 billion. In his conversations with Rauschning, Hitler laid out to him the rational of his Church policy:

They (the Church) will swallow anything in order to keep their material advantages . . . They will recognize a firm will, and we need only to show them once or twice who is master. They will know which way the wind blows. [59]

The two Catholic parties were voluntarily dissolved a few days before the concordat was initialed in Rome in compliance with the decision of the Fulda Conference. The Catholic Bavarian People's Party was dissolved voluntarily on July 4, 1933, and the Center Party followed suit the next day on July 5, 1933. All the Catholic organizations with any political function, including Catholic labor unions, were also dissolved in the process. Reichstag members of both parties were incorporated into the Nazi block in the parliament.

The concordat was initialed by Pacelli and von Papen on July 8, 1933, and made public the next day.[60] It still required the approval of the Hitler cabinet before its signing could take place in Rome. On July 13, Secretary of State Pacelli told the British Minister to the Vatican Sir Robert Clive (1933-1934):

Against Herr Hitler, His Eminence had nothing to say. He considered that Hitler was becoming more moderate.[61]

Hitler brought the concordat for approval to the cabinet on July 14, 1933, as an urgent matter of state that could not be postponed. The transcripts of Hitler's cabinet deliberations contain facts of unparalleled historical importance of the role that Hitler's war against the Jews played in the signature of the concordat. They were published for the first time in 1957. From the protocol of the cabinet meeting that day it becomes clear that the concordat was much more than a means to get the Church's agreement to the destruction of parliamentary democracy and the dissolution of the political parties in Germany—it was part of Hitler's wider plan to consolidate an alliance with the Church for a crusade against Jewry. Hitler considered the Church to be a natural ally in a global war against Jewry. He stated unambiguously at that cabinet meeting that this was his main reason for the treaty. The signature of the concordat, he said, was essential to create an "area of trust" with the Church that was critical to the struggle against "International Jewry":

He [Hitler] expressed the opinion that one should consider the concordat a great achievement because the concordat gave Germany an opportunity and created an area of trust that was particularly significant in the developing struggle against international Jewry. [62]

According to a slightly different version of Hitler's statement cited by Hochhuth in his historical addendum to his drama, Hitler made little of the intrinsic merits of the concordat while underscoring its main value as the means to establish a basis of cooperation with the Church in the war against the Jews:

This concordat, whose contents do not interest me at all, nevertheless creates an area of trust that will be very useful in our uncompromising struggle against international Jewry. [63]

Hitler's statement in both versions leaves no doubt of the crucial connection between the concordat and his war against the Jews. The concordat appears here as a quid-pro-quo deal between the Church and Nazi Germany to cooperate in the war against the Jews. His urgency in concluding the treaty in order to co-opt the Catholic Church in the "uncompromising struggle against international Jewry" is not surprising at all if one remembers his words to the bishops delegation on April 26, 1933. It goes a long way to explain the Church's policy of silent complicity in face of the annihilation of the Jewish people during the long twelve years of the Third Reich.

The cabinet approved unanimously the concordat right there and then without any further discussion. The protocol of the cabinet meeting also contains Hitler's assessment of the benefits he achieved through the concordat:

1. That the Vatican had negotiated at all,
2. That the Vatican should have been persuaded to bring about good relations with this purely national German State,
3. That the Church should have withdrawn from activity in associations and parties, and, for instance, have abandoned even the Christian labor unions.

Various other laws were also approved in the cabinet meeting of July 14, beginning with the decree that banned all political parties in Germany and declared the Nazi Party the only legal political party. "In Germany the National Socialist Workers Party is the sole existing political party" states the introduction to the decree. The following decrees were also approved that day: 1) a Denaturalization Law authorizing the government to take away citizenship and property from the so-called *Ost-Juden* and to expel them from the country if they had settled in Germany after 1918; 2) a Law for the Prevention of Progeny with Hereditary Disease authorizing the sterilization of the blind, deaf, alcoholic, mentally handicapped, manic-depressive, schizophrenic, and hereditary-epileptic; c) a Law against Dangerous Habitual Criminals that mandated the castration of serious moral offenders, but which was really meant to be used against enemies of the regime.[64] These immoral decrees were the forerunners of the euthanasia program of World War II and of the forced sterilization of as many as 400,000 men and women, including many Gypsies and children born to black soldiers and German women during the French occupation of the Ruhr in 1924.[65]

On June 29, 1933, Hitler dispatched von Papen to Rome to conclude negotiations. In Rome, Mussolini urged von Papen not to delay the signature of the treaty:

Mussolini, whom I saw again, insisted on the importance of arranging things as quickly as possible. "The signing of this agreement with the Vatican will establish the credit of your government abroad for the first time," he said . . . It really seemed as if the regeneration of the Christian way of life in the center of Europe had been placed on a firm basis. [66]

On July 17, 1933, Hitler announced officially that the Nazi revolution had come to a successful close. The parliamentary Weimar Republic ceased to exist and a one-party totalitarian Nazi state, the Third Reich, was now fully established. The Communist Party had been declared illegal two months earlier on May 2 as a threat to the state. The Social Democratic Party was dissolved forcibly on July 22, 1933, and the Nationalists dissolved their party voluntarily on July 28, 1933, leaving the Nazis the sole masters of the political arena.

On July 20, 1933, Vatican Secretary of State Pacelli and the German vice chancellor von Papen signed the concordat in Rome in a solemn ceremony that included a symbolic exchange of gifts. The Church's readiness to sign a concordat with a regime adopting laws that mandated sterilization and castration of the disabled and mentally sick, violating hallowed moral and religion imperatives, is tangible proof of how little the Church cared about moral principles when it concerned its interests. That same day in Nuremberg the SA arrested 300 Jewish store owners and paraded them through the streets for many long hours.

Cardinal Faulhaber of Munich sent congratulations to the Führer in which he underlined with special pride Hitler's feat of obtaining the Vatican's recognition:

> What the old parliaments and parties did not accomplish in sixty years, your statesmanlike foresight has achieved in six months. For Germany's prestige in East and West and before the entire world this handshake with the Papacy, the greatest moral power in the history of the world, is a feat of immeasurable blessings . . . Coming from the bottom of our heart: May God preserve the Reich Chancellor for our people. [67]

Four years later, Cardinal Faulhaber's pride on the role played by the Church in making Hitler internationally respectable did not wane and he again expressed in a sermon delivered in the cathedral of Munich on February 14, 1937, his feelings:

> At a time when the heads of the of the major nations in the world faced the new Germany with cool reserve and considerable suspicion, the Catholic Church, the greatest moral power on earth, through the concordat expressed its confidence in the new German government. This was a deed of immeasurable significance for the reputation of the government abroad.[68]

The *Volkischer Beobachter*, the official Nazi organ, expressed the same thoughts on the significance of the signing of the concordat in its edition of July 24, 1933:

> This fact signifies a tremendous moral strengthening of the National Socialist government of the Reich and its reputation. [69]

Upon his return from Rome after signing the concordat, von Papen spoke on July 22, 1933, before the Catholic academicians at the Benedictine Monastery of Maria Laach and told his audience that the fight against Bolshevism that Hitler was leading had convinced the Pope to conclude the concordat with Germany. The imprisonment of approximately 100,000 opponents of the Nazis as Communists after the Reichstag fire in newly created concentration camps was sure proof that Hitler was fighting Bolshevism:

> Although the Pope was warned against concluding a treaty with so unworthy a partner as the Reich led by Hitler, he nevertheless decided in favor, in the recognition that the new Germany had fought a decisive battle against Bolshevism and the atheist movement. The Pope told me he had full confidence in the assurances of the Reich chancellor that the national renaissance would be carried out upon the sole foundation of Christianity. [70]

On August 14, 1933, James G. McDonald, League of Nations high commissioner for refugees, visited Vatican Secretary of State Cardinal Pacelli and discussed with him the situation of the Jews in Germany. He left with the sad impression that the Jews could expect no help from the Vatican. Describing himself as "deeply disappointed" he wrote to his friend, the financier Felix Warburg:

> Deeply disappointed by the Cardinal . . . Cardinal Pacelli was noncommittal but left me with definite impression that no vigorous cooperation could be expected from that direction.

To become official, the concordat required final ratification. It was put on hold by the Vatican when the Nazis, in a test of wills, closed down various Catholic lay organizations under the claim that they were political, not religious, and began to impose severe restrictions on the Catholic press. At the request of Cardinal Pacelli the Fulda Conference gathered again from August 29 to August 31, 1933, to decide whether the ratification of the concordat should proceed. The conference urged the Vatican not to delay the ratification in order not to weaken the episcopate's position vis-à-vis the government. Cardinal Bertram of Breslau, the president of the bishop's conference, added a note in his positive response of September 2 to Cardinal Pacelli, whether it was possible to "put in a word at the last moment for the non-Aryan Catholics."

The final ratification of the concordat took place on September 10, 1933, in Rome. Cardinal Pacelli, the Vatican secretary of state, and Msgr. Giuseppe Pizzardo, the Vatican secretary for extraordinary ecclesiastical affairs, represented the Vatican. German ambassador Baron Diego von Bergen and the embassy councilor Eugen Klee represented the Third Reich. Cardinal Pacelli brought up the question of the status of baptized non-Aryans, which were being persecuted as Jews. He made the request that a secret clause be included recognizing that they were Catholics not Jews:

> Baptized Jews were Catholics with all the safeguards that this would imply. [71]

Convinced that the Vatican would not risk the treaty for baptized Jews, Eugen Klee opposed the demand, arguing that the issue was not religious but racial in nature. Catholic converts, he argued, were included in the anti-Jewish measures not because they were Catholics but because they belonged to the Jewish race; the question therefore was unrelated to religion.

Councilor Klee reminded Msgr. Pizzardo that racial purity had been pursued by the Church itself even to a greater degree than by Nazi Germany and was applied by the Church to baptized converts and their descendents over the centuries. He took as a model the *Statute of Blood Purity* adopted by the Jesuit Order since its foundation in the sixteenth century that required anyone entering its ranks to prove that he had no Jewish blood as far back as five generations (the restriction was "relaxed" by the Order to four generations in 1923). Jesuit racial rules were far more demanding than the Nazi racial limitations, said Klee:

> I explained to undersecretary Pizzardo also orally that these laws of one of the most eminent orders of the Catholic Church, which has been upheld throughout centuries and which must have therefore well proven to be necessary, go still beyond the measures that were adopted in Germany. They therefore show clearly how justified the concerns of the German government are for the racial preservation of the German people. [72]

Klee would only consent to forward Pacelli's diplomatic note to Berlin if it included a preamble accepting the principle of noninterference, nichteinmischung, with regard to the Jewish question. Cardinal Pacelli agreed to introduce such a clause: "The Holy See has no intention of interfering in Germany's internal affairs." It meant that as far as the Jews were concerned, the Church would not interfere with the Nazi government, provided baptized non-Aryans were excluded. The tragic fate of German and European Jewry was sealed. E. C. Helmreich comments on the meaning of that sentence:

> There also was at least an indirect recognition that the broader Jewish question was an internal German problem, which was not a matter for discussion on the level of foreign policy. [73]

Klee finally forwarded by telegraph the Vatican note to Berlin on September 9, 1933:

> The Holy See has no intention of interfering in Germany's internal affairs but would like to add a word in behalf of those German Catholics who themselves have gone over from Judaism to the Christian religion, or who are descended in the first generation, or more remotely from Jews who adopted the Catholic faith, and who, for reasons known to the Reich government, are likewise suffering from social and economic difficulties. [74]

Berlin rejected the request of a written secret clause but agreed to give a verbal promise that baptized non-Aryans would be protected from the actions undertaken against the Jews. Pacelli relayed to Bertram the news of the ratification, adding: "The determining factor had been the highly esteemed views of the Fulda Bishops conference." Anthony Rhodes describes the agreement on the basis of von Bergen's memoirs:[75]

> According to von Bergen . . . it was only after the German government had given a verbal promise to Cardinal Pacelli that baptized Jews would not be victimized and would be regarded as Christians that the Vatican yielded.

The secret verbal agreement served as the basis of the Church's policy during the tragic years of the Third Reich not to interfere with the actions against the Jews undertaken by the Third Reich. Michael Phayer's assessment of the consequences of the concordat, are relevant here:

> The concordat had conditioned the Bishops to refrain from speaking about issues not directly related to Church matters. In their minds this stricture blocked them from commenting on what was happening to Mosaic Jews. [76]

The systematic silence of the Church that prevailed during the Holocaust can thus be understood by the light of the secret verbal agreement as an expression of the Vatican's strict adherence to the accords that accompanied the concordat.[77] German bishops and the Vatican kept quiet about the persecutions against the Jews and abstained from expressing any sympathy with their plight in compliance of the treaty. In the encyclical *Mit Brennender Sorge* that was issued in 1937 to protest Nazi violations of the concordat, Pius XI gives particular emphasis to the fact that in contrast to the Reich government the Vatican adhered scrupulously in all its actions without exception, to the terms of the concordat, which obviously includes the Church's strict refusal to oppose the Nazis in their solution of the Jewish question:

> Whoever had left in his soul an atom of love for truth . . . must admit that, in the course of these trying years following upon the conclusion of the concordat, every one of Our words, every one of Our acts, has been inspired by the binding law of treaties. [78]

The ratification of the concordat was celebrated as a unique historical event by special services in all the Catholic churches of Germany. A most solemn High Mass was held in St. Hedwig's cathedral in Berlin with the participation of papal Nuncio Cesare Orsenigo and high Nazi officials. Formations of all Catholic SS and SA in their uniforms and flags saluted. Thousands, unable to enter the cathedral, surrounded the adjoining square. The preacher celebrating the event praised the Führer in the most glowing terms possible from the pulpit:

> A man of marked devotion to God and sincerely concerned for the well-being of the German people that will be governed in accordance with the will of the Divine Creator.[79]

The first German bishop to take the oath of allegiance prescribed by the concordat was the newly appointed Bishop of Münster, Clement August von Galen, who swore before Göring on October 23, 1933, in Berlin. For him, as for the other German bishops, Hitler remained until the very end the legitimate authority of Germany to whom they had sworn loyalty.[80] Enthusiasm for the Nazis ran high among the hierarchy. Catholic prelates publicly praised Hitler's "achievements." Many of the highest members of the German Catholic hierarchy, such as Berning, Gröber, and Wolker, sang publicly their praises of the new regime in hyperbolic terms. The most prominent Catholic theologians and historians, such as Karl Adam of Tubingen, Joseph Lortz, Michael Schmaus of Munster, and Theodor Brauer of Cologne, "discovered" in their books printed with official Catholic imprimatur basic similarities between Catholicism and the Nazi Weltanschauung. Bishop Burger declared:

> The aims of the Reich government have long been those of the Catholic Church.[81]

Karl Adam, a prominent theologian wrote:

> Now he stands before us, he whom the voices of our poets and sages have summoned, the liberator of the German genius. He has removed the blindfolds from our eyes and, through all political, economic, social and confessional covers, has enabled us to see and love again the one essential thing: our unity of blood, our German self, the homo Germanus.[82]

Bishop Berning exhorted his listeners in a mass meeting in Bremen in November 1933 to serve the new Germany with love. Cardinal Bertram of Breslau, the senior cardinal of Germany, expressed publicly his appreciation of the new regime in the name of the Fulda Conference of Bishops. His letter to Catholic students of theology after the concordat was signed is highly suggestive of the degree of identification of the Catholic clergy with the Hitler Reich:

> No one should any longer doubt the sincerity of the Church in accepting and standing up for the new order. [83]

No one doubted then and no one doubts today that the enthusiasm shown by the Catholic clergy and millions of Catholics for Hitler was sincere. The euphoria that enveloped the German Catholics after the approval of the concordat was more than an outpouring of joy for the concordat—it was an expression of internal identification with Nazism and its aims. Hitler's Third Reich was perceived by German Catholics as the fulfillment of the ages says Kurt Scholder. The euphoria reached a climax at all levels among laymen as among the bishops:

> In summer and autumn 1933 the enthusiasm for National Socialism and the new Reich reached a climax in both churches . . . The "Third Reich" was in part un-

derstood as the fulfillment of the ages and seen as in enthusiastic terms as a new combination of politics and faith. [84]

The Jesuits in their monthly *Stimmen der Zeit* expressed in their summary of 1933 the unity of purpose between the *kreuz* and the *hakenkreuz*, between the cross and the swastika:

> The speedy conclusion of the concordat has demonstrated that hostility need not prevail between the swastika and the Christian cross. On the contrary: the symbol of nature only finds its fulfillment and consummation in the symbol of grace.[85]

The identification with Nazi values that ensued after the approval of the concordat did not pass unnoticed in the Vatican even early on; Fr. Robert Leiber, secretary to Cardinal Pacelli, expressed his apprehension in a private letter to him on August 17, 1933:

> I am particularly anxious over the ideological confusion that had been brought into the minds of German Catholics. The National Socialists are doing everything they can to convince the Catholic population that an ideological agreement has also been reached between the Nazis and the Church. Already for six months now, the Catholic authorities no longer dare nor are given the opportunity to expose and emphasize the ideological differences between the party and the Church. A number of professors at Catholic theological faculties have already come around to that point of view and are teaching that it is not the function of the State to serve the people, but the people to serve the State. [86]

Signature of the concordat in Rome in 1933. From left to right: Fr. Ludwig Kass, Franz von Papen, Vatican Undersecretary Msgr Giuseppe Pizzardo (standing), Vatican Secretary of State Eugenio Pacelli, Cardinal Alfredo Ottaviani (standing), German ambassador Rudolf Buttman, Msgr Giovanni B. Montini (standing far right, future Pope Paul VI). USHMM.

The defeat of the Third Reich in 1945 did not bring about a change of heart with respect to the concordat. Pope Pius XII considered it of such fundamental importance that he gave instructions to his postwar envoy to Germany, Bishop Muench, to preserve the treaty to the last detail. Pius XII went to great lengths to overcome the objections of occupying powers and the doubts of the German bishops themselves. When the postwar negotiations did not go well at the beginning, Pius XII reminded the German people in a public telegram to Cardinal Frings the kindness and generosity he had shown to the German people immediately after the war. [87]

The general conclusions on the consequences of the concordat can hardly be contested. By signing the concordat the Church entered into a Faustian pact with the Nazis and became a pawn in Hitler's war against Jewry. Millennial Church anti-Semitism and alluring benefits reinforced each other in a deal for which the Jews of Europe paid the ultimate price.

# Notes

1. Jean Medawar and David Pyke, *Hitler's Gift* ( New York: Arcade Publishing, 2001), 15.

2 . Max Domarus, *The Speeches of Adolf Hitler Volume 4* (Mundelein, Il.: Bolchazy-Carducci Publishers), 369-370.

3. Jeremy Noakes and Geoffrey Pridham, *Nazism 1919-1945* (Exter, UK: The University of Exeter Press, 1998), 628-629.

4. Domarus, *The Speeches of Adolf Hitler.*

5. *Nationalsozialistisches Jahrbuch* (National Socialist Yearbook). Franz Eher Nachfolger of München (Munich), Germany 1927-1944. 2724-PS

6. Taylor Telford, *Sword and Swastika* (Mount Pleasant, SC: Nautical & Aviation Pub Co of America), 73-75.

7. Angela Hermann, ed., *Die Tagebücher von Joseph Goebbels*, (München 2006), Band 2/III.

8. Konrad Heiden, *The Führer* (New York: Carroll & Graf Publishers, Inc. 1944), 434.

9. Van der Lubbe was guillotined a year later in Leipzig on January 10, 1934 by the Nazis.

10. A.A. Bezihungen, *Des Heiligen Stuhl zu Deutschland, Vol.4.* Rhodes Anthony, *The Vatican in the Age of Dictators, 1922-1945* (London: Hodder & Stoughton, 1973).

11. Niederschrift der Konferenz der bayerischen Bischofe in Regensburg am 20, April 1933, 1 (DA Eichstatt). Guenter Lewy, *The Catholic Church and Nazi Germany* (Cambridge, MA: Da Capo Press, 1964), 30.

12. In its daily international bulletin, *La Corrispondenza*, a Vatican spokesman stated on March 13, 1933 that one could not fail to recognize a "certain nobility" in the National Socialist movement.

13. Noakes and Pridham, *Nazism, 628-629*

14. Heiden, *The Führer*, Domarus, *Hitler, 4 vol.*

15. Klaus Scholder, *The Churches and the Third Reich* (Minneapolis, MN: Fortress Press, 1988), 246. John Cornwell, *Hitler's Pope: The Secret History of Pius XII* (New York: Viking, 2008), 135.

16. Brian Connell, Trans., *Franz von Papen. Der Warheit eine Gasse, 1952. Franz von Papen Memoirs* (London, UK: Andre Deutsch, 1952), 270.

17. Lewy, *The Catholic Church*, 34.

18. Von Papen, *Der Warheit eine Gasse*, 262.

19. Lewy, *The Catholic Church,* 40.

20. Lewy, *The Catholic Church,* 40.

21. Noakes and Pridham, *Documents on Nazism,* 196-197.

22. Noakes and Pridham, *Documents on Nazism.*

23. Noakes and Pridham, *Documents on Nazism.*

24. Saul Friedlander, *Nazi Germany and the Jews, Vol.1.* (New York: Harper Collins Publishers, 1997).

25. Donald M. McKale, *Hitler's Shadow War* (Lanham, Md.: Taylor Trade Publishing, 2006), 42.

26. Angela Hermann, ed., *Die Tagebücher von Joseph Goebbels, Teil I Aufzeichnungen 1923-1941* (München: 2006), Band 2/III.

27. Friedlander, *Nazi Germany and the Jews.*

28. Edwin Black, *The Transfer Agreement* (New York: Scribner, 1984), 61.

29. When the late James G. McDonald visited Germany, Hanfstangl told him of this incident on April 3, 1933.

30. Heiden, *The Führer*, 105.

31. Herman Rauschning, *Hitler Speaks* (London, UK: Thornton Butterworth 1939).

32 . James G. McDonald, *Advocate for the Doomed: The Diaries and Papers of James G. McDonald, 1932-1935* (Indiana University Press, 2007), 91.

33. *Akten deutscher Bischofe*, vol. 1, 100-102. Müller, *Kirche und NS*, 109-117. Lewy, *The Catholic Church*, 50-51. S. Friedlander, 47. E. C. Helmreich, *The German Churches under Hitler* (Detroit, MI: Wayne University Press, 1979), 253-256.

34. *Akten deutscher Bischofe*, vol. 1, 100-102. Müller, *Kirche und NS*, 109-117. Guenter Lewy, 50-51. S. Friedlander, 47. Helmreich, *The German Churches under Hitler*, 253-256.

35. Peter Godman, *Hitler and the Vatican* (New York: Free Press, 2004), 32.

36. Black, *The Transfer Agreement*, 71.

37. Black, *The Transfer Agreement.*

38. David Bankier, ed., *Probing the Depths of German Antisemitism: German Society and the Persecution of the Jews, 1933-1941* (Oxford, UK: Berghahn Books, 2000), 503-513. Koonz, 43.

39. Christian Graf von Krockow, *Scheiterhaufen. Größe und Elend des deutschen Geistes. rororo-Sachbuch* (Reinbek: Rowohlt Verlag, 1993), 13-14. USHMM, Holocaust Encyclopedia.

40. Von Krockow, *Scheiterhaufen.*

41. Scholder, *A Requiem,* 67.

42. Godman, *Hitler and the Vatican.*

43. Von Papen, *Der Warheit eine Gasse,* 261

44. Anthony Rhodes, *The Vatican in the Age of Dictators*. In his hand-written draft corrections to the Italian version of Mit Brennende Sorge, Pacelli makes the same claim. Goodman, *Hitler and the Vatican*, 145.

45. Scholder, *A Requiem for Hitler*.

46. Von Papen, *Der Warheit eine Gasse*, 280.

47. Von Papen, *Der Warheit eine Gasse*, 280. Rudolf Morsey, *Stimmen der Zeit*, 427.

48. Rudolf Morsey, *Stimmen der Zeit*, 427. Lewy, *The Catholic Church*, 68.

49. Von Papen. *Der Warheit eine Gasse*, 1952.

50. *Trial of The Major War Criminals Before the International Military Tribunal*, Nuremberg, Vol.9, 1945.

51. Guenter Lewy, *The Catholic Church*.

52. Anthony Rhodes, *The Vatican in the Age of Dictators*.

53. Anthony Rhodes, *The Vatican in the Age of Dictators*, 170

54. Rudolf Morsey, *Stimmen der Zeit*, 86.

55. James Carroll, *Constantine's Sword: The Church and the Jews* (Boston, Ma.: Houghton Mifflin Company, 2001).

56. Von Papen. *Der Warheit eine Gasse*.

57. Heiden, *The Führer*, 494.

58. Alfred Metzner, *Konkordate seit 1800* (Verlag, 1964), 35.

59. Lewy, *The Catholic Church and Nazi Germany*, 86.

60. The *Four Power Act* negotiations promoted by Mussolini between Great Britain, France, Italy and Germany was also being negotiated in Rome at the time. German diplomats initialed in Rome on July 7 the treaty. The later rejection by the French Parliament prevented *Four Power Act* from coming into force.

61. Anthony Rhodes, *The Vatican in the Age of Dictators*. FO dispatch from Sir Robert Clive July 13, 1933.

62. Der Nationalsozialismus: Dokumente 1933-1945, Frankfurt am Main, 1957, 130.

63. Rolf Hochhuth, *The Deputy. Sidelights on History* (New York: Grove Press: 1964).

64. Deborah Dwork. & Robert Jan Van Pelt, *Holocaust: A History* (New York: W. W. Norton and Company, 2002), 73.

65. McKale, *Hitler's Shadow War*, 51.

66. Brian Connell, *Franz von Papen Memoirs*.

67. Ian Kershaw, *Hitler, 1889-1936*.

68. Munchener Kardinalspredigten Third Series, Munich, 1937, 4-5. Lewy, *The Catholic Church*, 90.

69. Lewy, *The Catholic Church*, 86.

70. Lewy, *The Catholic Church*, 86

71. Anthony Rhodes, *The Vatican in the Age of Dictators* 180.

72. Repgen Konrad, Ed. *Staatliche Akten uber die Reichskonkordatsverhandlungen, 1933*. (Mainz: Matthias Gruenwald Verlag, 1969), 419. Goldhagen, *Hitler's Willing Executioners*, 155.

73. Helmreich, *The German Churches*, 253-256.

74. Helmreich, *The German Churches*, 253-256.

75. Rhodes, *The Vatican*, 180. *A.A. Abschluss von Konkordaten mit Deutschland*. Helmreich, *The German Churches*, 254-256.

76. Phayer, *The Catholic Church and the Holocaust*, 74.

77. Helmreich, *The German Churches*, 253-255. Anthony Rhodes, *The Vatican in the Age of Dictators*. A. A. Pol II, *Betzihungen des Vatican zu Deutschland*.

78. John Peter Pham, *Heirs of the Fisherman: Behind the Scenes of Papal Death and Succession* (UK: Oxford University Press, 2006).

79. Lewy, *The Catholic Church*, 106

80. Gordon Zahn, *German Catholics and Hitler's Wars: A Study in Social Control* (New York: Sheed and Ward, 1962), 90.

81. Lewy, *The Catholic Church*, 105-110.

82. Lewy, *The Catholic Church*, 105-110.

83. Lewy, *The Catholic Church*, 107.

84. Scholder, *A Requiem.*

85. Lewy, *The Catholic Church*, 111-112.

86. Gitta Sereny, *Into That Darkness* (New York: McGraw Hill Book Company, 1974), 61.

87. Phayer, *The Catholic Church and the Holocaust*, 218. Muench Diary, Ludwig Volk.

# Chapter 4
# German Rearmament

## German Bishops Support Rearmament

For more than twelve years before coming to power, Hitler vented his rage against the Versailles Treaty to gain popularity among the German people. He denounced a long list of grievances against the treaty, which he vowed to undo once in power. First in his list stood the recall of the rearmament restrictions imposed on Germany, followed by the return of the Saargebiet, the rearmament of the Rhinelanland, the anchluss of Austria and the Sudetenland, the return of the Ports of Memel and Danzig, the Polish Corridor and Upper Silesia.

Hitler's declared objective to redress the injustices of Versailles was not by any means his ultimate aim, but only a stepping stone to a far more ambitious goal—the acquisition of new Lebensraum (living space) in the east through war. Already in 1925, Hitler rejected in *Mein Kampf* the notion that the restoration of the German boundaries of 1914 would be enough to satisfy his ambitions:

> To demand that the 1914 frontiers should be restored is a glaring political absurdity that is fraught with such consequences as to make the claim itself appear criminal. The confines of the Reich as they existed in 1914 were thoroughly illogical because they were not really complete, in the sense of including all the members of the German nation. Nor were they reasonable, in view of the geographical exigencies of military defense. They were not the consequences of a political plan which had been well considered and carried out, but they were temporary frontiers established in virtue of a political struggle that had not been brought to a finish; and indeed, they were partly the chance result of circumstances. [1]

Hitler and the Nazis understood well the power of propaganda to pave the way to their objectives. Goebbels' powerful propaganda apparatus received the greatest measure of support. It not only mobilized the newspapers and periodicals but the radio and movies as well. Documentary films and newsreels were used to prepare the Germans for the aggressive role that Hitler envisioned for them. Germany reached the highest number of radios per capita in the world by 1934. Sirens would sound all over Germany interrupting current activities to announce that Hitler was going to speak. Germans sat in offices, factories and homes glued to their apparatus to listen to the Führer.[2] The Versailles grievances and the threat of Bolshevism were useful as a veneer to cover up his vast plans for rearmament. In his private conversation with Kurt G. W. Ludecke, Hitler explained his tactics:

> I have got to keep the Versailles Powers in line by holding aloft the bogy of Bolshevism—make them believe that a Nazi Germany is the last bulwark against the Red flood. That's the only way to come through the danger period, to get rid of Versailles and rearm. I can talk peace and mean war. [3]

As a first step in his plan, Hitler denounced, on October 14, 1933, the disarmament limitations imposed by the Versailles Treaty. He withdrew unilaterally from the disarmament conference and the League of Nations to allegedly "save" Germany and Christian civilization from Bolshevism. As Hitler broke one international agreement after another, he was careful not to risk an early war for which Germany was not yet prepared. While carrying out the greatest rearmament program and military preparation for war ever undertaken by any nation, he accused the Jews of pushing the world to war and cynically spoke of peace and peaceful methods to redress the alleged grievances of Versailles.

With a difference of only five weeks, the Depression brought Adolph Hitler and Franklin D. Roosevelt to power. While Roosevelt led America out of the Depression by building dams and federal highways, Hitler did it in Germany by rearming and preparing for war. Rearmament played a key role in the reactivation of the German economy and the elimination of unemployment. The masses of unemployed laborers found work in the armament industry and its subsidiaries, while the industrialists reaped enormous profits. Even the autobahnen he built were meant to facilitate the movement of troops.

Hitler's withdrawal from the disarmament conference and the League of Nations was greeted enthusiastically by the Catholic Church and its lay leaders in Germany. Msgr. Steinman and Dr. Klausener (murdered by Hitler only a few months later) sent a message of solidarity in the name of Catholic action to Hitler on October 15, 1933:

> In this hour of decision for the nation, the Catholics of the diocese of Berlin, possessed of unshakable love to people and fatherland, unanimously support the Führer and Chancellor in his struggle for equal rights, the honor of the nation and the restoration of a just peace between all people. [4]

Hitler called for a referendum for November 12, 1933, and also announced "elections" to the Reichstag to demonstrate to Western powers that the German people stood solidly behind him. Calling referendums and Reichstag elections with handpicked Nazi candidates became Hitler's standard prop to rally Germans behind his risky adventures. German bishops called Catholics to vote in the referendum and support the withdrawal from the disarmament conference and the League of Nations. Cardinal Faulhaber issued a call in the name of the Bavarian bishops asking for a favorable vote to support the Führer. Faulhaber emphasized in his call that rearmament was needed to protect the German people against Bolshevism and as a means to create jobs for the unemployed:

> In this way the Catholics will profess anew their loyalty to people and fatherland and their agreement with the farsighted and forceful efforts of the Führer to spare the German people the terror of war and the horrors of Bolshevism, to secure public order and create work for the unemployed. [5]

Archbishop Gröber, in his exhortation, called Catholics to fulfill their patriotic duty on November 12, 1933, and support Hitler with their votes. He assured the Germans that the Führer's actions were "in consonance with national honor as well as with the Christian law of morality and international law." [6] The referendum of November 12, 1933 gave Hitler a resounding victory with 95 percent of the votes in favor of withdrawal from the disarmament conference and the League of Nations.

During the Weimar years, the Reichswehr generals were covertly violating the disarmament restrictions of the Versailles Treaty, conducting with the Soviet Red Army clandestine military activities. After leaving the disarmament conference, the Reichswehr began to rearm openly and defiantly on a much larger scale. With Hitler at the helm, Reichswehr generals now saw themselves in the frontline again, leading armed forces that grew in might day by day. Industrialists and generals closed ranks behind Hitler. Under the leadership of Schacht and Göhring and the support of industrialists such as Alfred Hugenberg and Gustav Krupp, German industry was mobilized for rearmament. New enormous armament factories were being built to equip the army, navy, and the newly created Luftwaffe, while synthetic substitutes for scarce raw materials such as oil and rubber were being developed.

As German military strength grew in magnitude, Hitler's claims against Versailles matured rapidly one after another, with no one willing to stop him. Vacillating Western powers, unwilling to face their historic responsibilities, allowed him to win one easy victory after another with the help of subversion, intimidation, and a mighty propaganda apparatus.

With the capture of the German diplomatic documents after the war, a secret annex to the concordat, signed on November 2, 1933, came to light. The annex was negotiated in early August 1933 before Hitler denounced the Versailles Treaty by Cardinal Pacelli and German Ambassador Count Diego von Bergen (he had been in charge of political subversion within Russia during World War I) and embassy councelor Eugen Klee. In the addendum, the two sides agreed to establish a common front against Soviet Russia. They agreed that the Church would get full rights to provide field chaplains in the event of a German invasion of the Soviet Union. Their duties in the German army were defined. Anthony Rhodes and E. C. Helmreich both point out that the Vatican was the first power to give official recognition to army conscription in Nazi Germany in violation of the Versailles Treaty. To shield the Vatican from the negative reaction that such a breach of Versailles was bound to produce, Cardinal Pacelli, the Vatican secretary of state, was anxious that the annex be kept secret. In compliance with his wishes, German Ambassador von Bergen requested that "a special courier should bring the documents from Berlin in order to maintain secrecy about the additions."[7]

The annex produced its bitter fruits during World War II when German armies invaded the Soviet Union accompanied by approximately one thousand priests, Protestant and Catholic. The military chaplains became part of the operation that mass murdered 1.5 million Jews in the outskirts of the towns of the Ukraine, the Baltics, and Bielorussssia.

## The Night of the Long Knives

Hitler's alliance with army generals, industrialists, and the Church became strained when Ernest Röhm, commander of the SA (*Sturm Abteilung*), demanded in June 1933 in a Nazi Party publication a purge of the army's officer corps and the replacement of the professional army by a revolutionary or national militia formed by the SA. The SA, the paramilitary force of lumpen proletarians led by Röhm, which was originally created to protect Nazi meetings and terrorize opponents, swelled to a menacing force of 3 million armed members. The professional German army counted no more than 100,000 soldiers as restricted by the Versailles Treaty. Army officers and industrialists feared that Röhm's thugs could easily get out of control and turn against them in a radical revolution under the banner of the Nazi movement. Hindenburg and the army generals were suspicious with Hitler's failure to control Röhm and they showed their displeasure to him.[8]

In an attempt to mollify them, Hitler oversaw in the Defense Ministry on February 28, 1934, the signature of an agreement between General Blomberg and Röhm defining the respective responsibilities of the Reichswehr and the SA. Soon the SS, the elite Nazi corps, accused Röhm of calling Hitler a traitor and of having vowed to overthrow him. On June 3 and June 7, 1934, Hitler again met with Röhm who agreed to furlough the SA for one month beginning July 1. On June 21, 1934, Hindenburg, on his death bed in Neudeck, called in Hitler and told him that unless he restored order he would declare martial law and would turn over power to the army.

Unwilling to risk the loss of the support of the army and industrialists, Hitler chose to eliminate his comrade Ernest Röhm. With the help of Göring and Himmler and using army equipment and vehicles, Hitler ordered, on June 30, 1934, that Röhm and three hundred of his lieutenants be liquidated in the "Night of the Long Knives" on charges of planning a Putsch. Hindenburg and the Reichswehr were appeased with Hitler's action and showered praise on him for his decision to defend the army's independence. On July 1, 1934, General Blomberg congratulated Hitler in the name of Reichswehr for curbing Röhm. On July 2, 1934, Hindenburg thanked Hitler in a telegram for saving the German people from a catastrophe.

The purge gave Hitler and his team the opportunity to settle accounts with other potentially dangerous rivals or holders of embarrassing secrets. Hitler was affraid that these secrets would come to the open. His payments to blackmailers at the time confirm these hypotheses. Among the victims liquidated were General Schleicher and his wife, Nazi radical Gregor Strasser, and Hyeronomite priest Bernhard Sempfle. Sempfle, who edited *Mein Kampf* for Hitler, knew the truth of Hitler's niece's suicide when she was living at his side.

A number of prominent Catholic lay leaders were murdered during the Night of the Long Knives, such as Erich Klausener, the leader of Catholic Action, who only a year before had welcomed the Nazi rise to power with great enthusiasm, Adalbert Probst, the leader of the Catholic sports organizations, Dr. Fritz Gerlich, former editor of *Die Gerade Weg*, and Dr. Fritz Beck, a leader of Catholic students. Notwithstanding the crimes committed against their own, Church authorities chose to close their eyes and ordered the clergy to "observe due restraint and not to lose sight of the general good of the Church."[9]

In expectation of Hindenburg's imminent death, the Reichstag approved a law on August 1, 1934, that merged the offices of president and chancellor and vested them in one person after his death. When Hindenburg died the next day, on August 2, 1934, Hitler became the absolute master of Germany. In a referendum on August 19, 1934, 88 percent of German voters approved Hitler's dual function as chancellor and Führer of Germany. A new oath of personal allegiance was approved on August 20, 1934, swearing loyalty to the "Führer of the German Reich," the commander in chief of the armed forces. Hitler, not the constitution, was recognized as the embodiment of the German state to whom the Germans owed and swore personal allegiance.

Hitler had now in his hands unrestricted powers to mobilize Germany's full potential for rearmament and the expansion of the German Lebensraum. Von Papen resigned as vice chancellor and his place was left vacant. On December, 1934, a new law forbidding malicious slander against the state and the party gave the Nazis additional legal power to carry out mass arrests of opponents and silence any dissident voices.

## The Church Bells Toll for Hitler's Marching Troops

After having broken loose from the disarmament limitations, Hitler's next item in his list was to reunite the Saargebiet with the Third Reich. The Saar territory, in the west of Germany, had been separated from Germany and occupied by

France in 1919 and placed under the administration of the League of Nations by the Versailles Conference in 1922. According to the treaty, the League of Nations was to hold a plebiscite on January 13, 1935, at which the Saar population was to decide between the status quo, or whether to join Germany or France.

In anticipation of the plebiscite, the Nazis created in the Saar in 1933 a Nazi organization, the Deutsche Front, in favor of reunification with the Third Reich. The population in the Saar was overwhelmingly Catholic (72.6 percent in 1927), and the position of the Catholic Church on the issue was to play a decisive role in deciding the outcome. The Catholic Center Party of the Saar dissolved itself voluntarily in October 1933 following its mother party in Germany and joined the Deutsche Front. However, after the Night of the Long Knives in which Catholic lay leaders were murdered by the Nazis, some Saar Catholics, including seventy priests, organized on November 30, 1934, a new Catholic party, the *Volksbund*, to prevent the return of the Saargebiet to the Third Reich. The voices of the dissident priests were silenced when the bishops of Germany and particularly their superiors, the Bishops of Trier and Speyer, unhesitatingly supported the return of the territory to Germany even after the bloodbath of June 30, 1934. The bishops of Bavaria and Cologne issued proclamations to Saar Catholics on January 6, 1935, in which they appealed to their German patriotism and called them to pray for reunification:

> This decision . . . is fraught with fateful consequences for the future of our fatherland no true German can face with indifference. As German Catholics we are duty bound to stand up for the greatness, welfare, and peace of our fatherland. [10]

A last minute proclamation was also issued before the plebiscite by the spiritual leaders of the Catholic youth in Germany, Wolker and Esch, calling the Saar Catholics "to rejoin their brothers as the unity of blood and language, law and history demanded." Nazi evil reached new summits when the Nazis threatend to annihilate the Jews, if the Saar question was not solved their way:

> If the Saar struggle gives rise to a fight or even a war, we shall not hesitate to annihilate the whole Jewish society, root and branch. [11]

The plebiscite that took place on January 13, 1935, resulted in a great victory for Hitler. More than 90 percent of the population of the Saargebiet voted in favor of union with the Third Reich. Flags were displayed on the churches and religious thanksgiving services were held after the plebiscite. The bells of all the churches were tolled in jubilation on the day of the transfer on March 1, 1935. The Church had once again rendered its loyal services to the Third Reich.

Greatly emboldened by the Saar victory, Hitler took his next step. He repudiated on March 5, 1935, the clauses of the Versailles Treaty that intended to prevent Germany again turn into a military threat to Europe. On March 16, he reintroduced compulsory military service, requiring all young men to serve one year in the armed forces. The enlargement of the army to thirty-six divisions, the approximate equivalent of 500,000 soldiers—five times larger than the size allowed by the treaty—was publicly announced. The Reichswehr changed its name to *Wehrmacht*. The Luftwaffe was established and the German navy underwent an enormous program of modernization and expansion. Great Britain and France protested but otherwise did nothing against the unilateral defiant action. After denouncing the Versailles Treaty in early 1935, Hitler issued secret orders to Minister of Defense General Blomberg to prepare plans for the military occupation of the Rhineland, the thirty-mile-wide demilitarized buffer zone in western Germany.

The episcopate was overjoyed with the denunciation of the Versailles Treaty and the rearmament program. In his 1936 New Year's sermon, Archbishop Gröber of Freiburg addressed Catholics in support of Hitler's military actions:

> The strength of the German people has blossomed forth manifold and unemployment has decreased to a surprising degree. Newly rearmed, the Reich again now takes its place in the family of nations and in place of the dishonor that since the Versailles Treaty has besmirched the German name the world is faced by a united, upward-striving and power-conscious state. [12]

Taking a new gamble, Hitler, in open violation of Germany's international accords, ordered the Wehrmacht units on March 7, 1936, to cross the Hohenzollern Bridge in Cologne and reocuppy the Rhineland under the pretext that the Franco-Soviet alliance talks had rendered obsolete the demilitarization of the Rhineland agreement of the Versailles Treaty and the Locarno Pact of 1925.[13] Once again Western powers dodged their responsibilities and remained passive, exactly as Hitler had hoped. Former Lance Corporal Hitler, now supreme military strategist of the Wehrmacht, described his gamble:

> The two days after the move into the Rhineland were the most nerve-racking in my life. If the French had marched into the Rhineland, we would have had to withdraw with our tail between our legs, for the military resources at our disposal would have been wholly inadequate for even a moderate resistance. [14]

Schacht explained why the Führer had taken such a serious gamble considering that Germany was not yet prepared militarily for a confrontation:

> In order to make his hold on the government secure, the Führer felt he must present the German people with a military victory.[15]

The bishops in the Rhineland were overjoyed and welcomed the incoming Wehrmacht military units with patriotic messages congratulating them for "protecting German honor and justice." To celebrate the occasion, Nazi banners were flown high on Church buildings and bells tolled in jubilation when the German military units marched in the Rhineland.[16] Hitler again announced a plebiscite and new "elections" to the Reichstag. Catholic bishops all over Germany joined in recommending a support vote. Despite their misgivings due to the many violations of the concordat by Hitler, the bishops published ardent patriotic proclamations that were read from the pulpits before the plebiscite was held. On March 29, 1936, 98.8 percent of the 45 million Germans who went to the polls approved the reoccupation and remilitarization of the Rhineland.

## Nuremberg Racial Laws

When Hitler came to power in 1933 there were in Germany 503,000 Jews, 0.76 percent of the total German population. During the first year of his rise to power, around 40,000 Jews, among them 2,600 Jewish scientists and scholars, left, notwithstanding the severe property losses involved. Another 22,000 Jews managed to get out in 1934. The growing difficulty of obtaining visas in addition to the losses involved in migrating were major obstacles to the flight. Those staying behind harbored the false hope that Hitler would not last for long in power and the situation for Jews would improve. An internal exodus from the smaller towns and villages took place to the larger cities of Germany, such as Berlin, Hamburg, Frankfurt, and Munich, where Jews could at least count on some support from Jewish help organizations.

New anti-Semitic measures were raining day after day on Jewish heads. To eliminate Jews from every branch of cultural activity, Goebbels established the Chamber of Culture on September 22, 1933. On October 4, 1933, Jews were prohibited from serving as newspaper editors. Jews were excluded from health insurance on May 14, 1934; on May 31, 1934, all Jews were dismissed from the army. The tax-free status of Jewish religious organizations was terminated on October 16, 1934; Jewish children were banned from using the same playgrounds and locker rooms with Aryans in November 1934.

In the summer of 1935 Nazi propaganda gave new impetus to the race question and concentrated with uncommon intensity on the danger to which the Aryan race was being exposed by the presence of Jewish racial defilers. Their presence represented a threat to the purity of the Aryan race. Demonstrations against the so-called race defilers were organized by the Nazi Party, demanding that legislation be introduced establishing heavy penalties for mixed marriages and sexual relations between Aryan and Jews.

Violent anti-Semitic riots were organized by SA thugs and the *Hitler-Jugend*. On August 1, 1935, *Juden Verboten* signs began to appear all over Germany, forbidding the entrance of Jews to public facilities, restaurants, shops, and villages. Jewish property was vandalized and destroyed. On August 6, 1935, large Jewish commercial business including the popular Globus Department store in Lübeck was destroyed. A massive Nazi demonstration against Jews was organized on August 11, 1935, in Berlin, followed on August 15 by a mass rally organized by Streicher in the Berlin Sportspalast, demanding stricter measures against the Jews.

Hjalmar Schacht, the czar of German rearmament, although very much in agreement with the elimination of the Jews, was concerned that the SA riots would produce negative repercussions on the rearmament program. As president of the Reichsbank in 1933, economics minister in 1934, and plenipotentiary-general for the war economy in 1935, Schacht played a pivotal role in implementing iron controls that led to the elimination of Jews from the economy and the Aryanization of their properties. Schacht wanted the Jews out, while keeping their property intact for Aryans. He personally presided over the Aryanization of the banks owned by Jews. He felt that his anti-Semitic economic decrees and administrative procedures were more effective than riots. Speaking in Koenisberg on August 18, 1935, at the German Eastern Fair he formulated his position:

> The Jew must realize that his influence is gone for all time. We desire to keep our people and our culture distinctive, just as the Jews have always demanded this of themselves since the time of the prophet Ezra. But the solution of these problems must be brought about under state leadership, and cannot be left to unregulated individual actions, which mean a disturbing influence on the national economy.[17]

On August 20, 1935, a ministerial meeting was called on Schacht's request. Schacht stated that he shared Hitler's goals on the Jewish question but complained that the "drift into lawlessness among other things is putting the economic basis of rearmament at risk."[18] He favored orderly Aryanization without outward violence that could trigger international protests, threaten Germany's international commerce, and endanger the economic process of rearmament.

Soon after, on September 10, 1935, to the occasion of the annual Nazi Party rally in Nuremberg, the adoption of comprehensive legislation on the race question was announced. Hitler ordered the minister of the interior to prepare legislation to "protect" the Aryan *Herrenvolk* (master race) from the Jewish racial threat. The *Judenreferent* (division head on the Jewish question) in the Interior Ministry, Dr. Bernard Lösener and Dr. Wilhelm Stuckart (1902-1953), later one of the main figures at the Wahnsee Conference, drafted the legislation known as the Nuremberg Laws. At a special Reichstag session in Nuremberg, two new constitutional laws, the Reich Citizenship Law (Reichsbürgergesetz), and the Law for the Protection of German Blood and German Honor (Blutschutzgesetz) were approved.

The Reich Citizenship Law deprived the Jews of citizenship and civil rights and placed them in the category of *Staatsangehorige* (subjects). Only Aryans could be *Reichsbuerger* (citizens of the German Reich). Jews could not vote or hold public office. They were prohibited from raising the German flag. The exemptions that Hindenburg had procured in 1933 for Jewish World War I veterans and senior state officials were terminated. The last remaining Jewish officers in the armed forces were to be discharged on December 31, 1935. The Law for the Protection of German Blood and German Honor prohibited marriages and sexual relationships between Jews and Aryans to "protect" the racial purity of the Aryan race from defilement and bastardization (*rassenschande*). It banned the employment of German maids under the age of forty-five in Jewish households, and prescribed incarceration and hard labor for violating the laws.

After the approval of the Nuremberg Laws, Hitler issued a warning that harsher means were in store if the Nuremberg Laws did not achieve their goal. The problem would then be handed over, he said, to the National Socialist Party for Final Solution, but he stoped short of clearly specifying what he meant by the term:

> If these arrangements for a separate, secular solution broke down, it might become necessary to pass a law handling over the problem to the National Socialist Party for final solution.[19]

Three months after the adoption of the Nuremberg Laws, Schacht spoke before the Chamber of Commerce of Saxony expressing his satisfaction with the newly approved Nuremberg Laws:

> We have to agree to the Jewish policy of the Führer and, you may be surprised to hear, that of Julius Streicher as well. The race problem will be solved by the Nuremberg Laws and by throwing the Jews out of the administration, the theaters and so on.[20]

German so-called race scientists and legal scholars who claimed that Jews were a race were unable to provide any particular physical or biological trait specific to Jews despite all their efforts. The taskforce led by the official leader of Reich physicians, Dr. Gerhard Wagner, who tried since 1933 to find a specific blood type that would identify Jews, admitted that they failed to find any biological marker of Jewishness.[21] For lack of nothing better, the Nuremberg legal "experts" had to go back to medieval anti-Semitic laws and statutes of blood purity legislated by the Church that relied on religious affiliation of the ancestors of a person to determine his so-called racial identity.

Two months after the approval of the Nuremberg Laws, special courts to try cases related to the laws were set up on October 13, 1936, by the German Ministry of Justice. Thirteen supplementary ordinances specifying the bylaws required for their implementation were issued on November 14, 1935. Only a person with four Christian grandparents qualified as a pure Aryan. In article 5-1 the decree defined as a Jew anyone descending from three Jewish grandparents. Those with two Jewish grandparents were classified as first-degree *mischlinge* and designated as Jews if they belonged to the Jewish religion or were married to a Jewish spouse. Those with only one Jewish grandparent were considered second-degree mischlinge. People married to Jews were declared to be Jews in article 5-2.

Dr. Hans Globke (1898-1973), the legal advisor of the minister of the interior who drafted the Enabling Act in 1933, wrote the commentary to the Reich

Citizenship Law that became the standard reference of the Nuremberg Laws that turned German Jews into pariahs. A practicing Catholic, former prominent member of the Catholic Center Party, and close friend and confidant of Cardinal Faulhaber of Munich, Globke was later responsible for the addition in 1938 of the names Israel and Sara in the documents of every German Jew and Jewess. He assisted Himmler in promoting the adoption of anti-Semitic legislation similar to the Nuremberg Laws in the different countries allied with Germany. After the war, Globke joined the Christian Democratic Party and became a leading member of Adenauer's government until 1963. He testified in favor of his colleague Stuckart at the postwar trial helping him to get away with a four-year prison sentence.

Not only did the Catholic Church not object to the Nuremberg Laws, but also the official Catholic organ in Germany, the *Klerusblatt*, welcomed the laws in January 1936 and justified them with the argument that they were "indispensable safeguards for the qualitative make-up of the German people." While rejecting Rosenberg's demand to redefine the Christian religion in racial terms and placed his works in the *Index* on February 9, 1934, the Catholic Church found no problem with the notion that the German people as Aryans had the right to "protect" their race against the Jewish "threat." Archbishop Gröber (1872-1948) commented on the Nuremberg Laws:

> Every people bears responsibility for the success of its existence, and the absorption of entirely alien blood will always constitute a risk for a nation that has proven its historic worth. Consequently, the right to safeguard the purity of the race, and to devise measures necessary to that end, can be denied to no one. [22]

The implementation of the Nuremberg Laws depended on the birth and marriage certificates kept by the churches in their archives. These archives were the only source of birth records before 1875. Catholic and Protestant churches more than willingly cooperated with the Nazi regime and provided them with the baptismal and marriage information necessary to identify Jews. Guenther Lewy points out that their enthusiasm did not wane even during the war years when the identification meant deportation and death:

> The very question whether the Church should lend its help to the Nazi state in sorting out people of Jewish descent was never debated. On the contrary, a priest wrote in the Klerusblatt in September 1935: "We have always unselfishly worked for the people without regard to gratitude or ingratitude. We shall also do our best to help in this service to the people." And the cooperation continued right through the war years, when the price of being Jewish was no longer dismissal from a government job and loss of livelihood, but deportation and outright physical destruction. [23]

If initially the Nurenberg Laws served to identify and expel Jews from different sectors of German economic, cultural, and social life, they eventually led during World War II to their deportation and destruction. Seen from a wider perspective, the Nuremberg Laws laid the groundwork of Hitler's plans to physically eliminate them completely from the totality of the expanding German Lebensraum under the "rationale" that the biologic presence of the Jew "endangered" the purity of the Germanic race. The means to achieve that goal became for Germans a tactical question to be resolved according to the circumstances. Professor Hilberg's assessment of the significance of German race legislation from its early beginning in 1933 is certainly applicable to the Nuremberg Laws:

> When in the early days of 1933 the first civil servant wrote the definition of "non-Aryan" into a civil service ordinance, the fate of European Jewry was sealed.[24]

## The Berlin Olympics

The XI International Olympic Games celebrated in Berlin from August 1 to August 16, 1936, contributed in a major way to internationally strengthen the Nazi regime. The mere participation of forty-nine countries represented a tangible display of international support for the Hitler regime. Long before the games, the American ambassadors to Berlin and Vienna, William Dodd and George Messersmith, warned the U.S. State Department that the Nazi government had taken over the Olympics for their own purposes and that the alleged "Olympic training courses for Jewish athletes" was another Nazi ruse to deceive the world.

The Nazis were obviously deeply aware of the propaganda effect of the event and staged the Olympic Games as a colossal show. The pagan pageantry of the games and the Führer worship that accompanied them outdid ancient Rome. Like a deified Roman emperor, Hitler inaugurated the Olympics in Berlin before a crowd of 110,000 spectators on August 1, 1936. The Wagnerian rallies and parades that accompanied the games served to convince the Herrenvolk that the day they would rule Europe was near.[25] A sea of swastikas drowned the Olympic symbols. The Aryan sport placards proclaimed that modern Germany was heir to the culture of ancient Greece.

Anti-Semitic activity was put under cover during the two weeks of the games to convince the world that the atrocity stories were merely Jewish propaganda inventions. The faint voice of oppressed and frightened German Jewry was silenced. American ambassador Dodd reported back to Washington that Jews in Germany "awaited with fear and trembling the end of the short Olympic truce." When the Olympics were over, Avery Brundage (1887-1975), president of the American Olympic Committee, went overboard with his euphoric report of the games to the American Olympic Committee:

> The Games of the XIth Olympiad of Berlin, Germany, was the greatest and most glorious athletic festival ever conducted—the most spectacular and colossal of all time . . . The 1936 Olympic Games were removed from their normal

plane and lifted to a dazzling precedent which probably no country can hope to follow.[26]

When Hitler rose to power in 1933 and began to persecute German Jewry, demands were raised by the American Amateur Athletic Union and by Western countries in favor of transferring the XI Summer Olympic Games from Berlin to Rome or Tokyo, or to cancel them altogether and were printed in the *New York Times* on April 18, 1933. On November 20, 1933, the Athletic Union called for a boycott of the Games in view of Germany's violation of the principle of equality of all races that the Olympic Games were supposed to respect. Brundage, who originally declared his support for the position of the American Amateur Athletic Union, soon made a turnabout after an inspection visit to the Berlin Olympic facilities in September 1934. Under the influence of the Nazi representative in the International Olympic Committee, SA Major General Karl Ritter von Halt (1891-1964), and of other Nazis, he became a champion of holding the Olympics in Berlin.[27] Upon his return to the United States on September 25, 1934, Brundage recommended in the strongest terms that the preparations for the Games in Berlin should continue undisturbed. Following his report, the American Olympic Committee voted unanimously on September 26, 1934, to participate in the Berlin Games.

When a new wave of brutal physical attacks against Jews began in 1935 followed by the approval of the Nuremberg Laws, Judge Jeremiah Mahoney, an American Catholic, president of the American Amateur Athletic Union, led a strong movement to boycott the upcoming Games. Jewish organizations together with the American Federation of Labor, the National Association for the Advancement of Colored People, and forty-one American college presidents supported the demand for a boycott. The Catholic governors of New York and Massachusetts, Al Smith and James Curley, supported the boycott. Mahoney issued a call in July 1935:

> I believe that for America to participate in the Olympics in Germany means giving American and moral support to the Nazi regime, which is opposed to all that Americans, hold dearest.[28]

Horrified by what was happening in Germany, Ernest Lee Jahncke (1870-1960), one of three American members of the International Olympic Committee and previously assistant secretary of the navy under President Herbert Hoover, perceived the deeper moral and political implications of participating in the games. In a letter to Count Henri Baillet-Latour, president of the International Olympic Committee, on November 25, 1935, he wrote:

> Neither Americans nor representatives of other countries can take part in the Games in Nazi Germany without at least acquiescing in the contempt of the Nazis for fair play and their sordid exploitation of the Games.[29]

Jahncke's courageous opposition earned him the rare honor of being the only member of the IOC ever to be expelled from that body. Two days before the inauguration of the games, on July 30, 1936, Jahncke was ousted from the International Olympic Committee and replaced by Brundage, the president of the American Olympic Committee.

Influenced by Nazi allegations of a Jewish-Communist plot, Brundage managed to vote down the proposal of a boycott in the Amateur Athletic Union by a majority of only two and a half votes on December 8, 1935, arguing that American athletes should not become involved in a "Jew-Nazi" fight. He countered Mahoney's call for a boycott declaring before the press with well-feigned candor that he knew of no reason to boycott Germany:

> Brundage asserted here today that he knew of no racial or religious reasons why the United States should consider withdrawal of its athletes from the Games.[30]

The failure to stand up to Hitler by moving the Games from Berlin or to boycott the games had the same effect as the unwillingness of the Western powers and the League of Nations to stand up to Hitler's breaches of international agreements. Hitler, who drew enormous political capital from the event, was strengthened in his conviction that he could go ahead with his plans of aggression and with his war against the Jews and no one would stop him. He also tried to draw support for his claim of Aryan superiority from the Olympics. Although the medals won by black and Jewish sportsmen were a clear denial of the Nazi racial myths, the Nazis were counting their harvest of gold medals to "prove" Aryan superiority. Even Max Schmeling's victory over Joe Louis in a boxing match prior to the Olympics was used by Goebbel's press as proof of the alleged superiority of the Aryan race. In more than one sense, the Berlin Olympics were part of the chain of events that led to the Holocaust as properly recognized by the U.S. Holocaust Memorial Museum in its 1996 exhibition on the 1936 Berlin Olympic Games.

The success of the Olympics wetted the Führer's appetite. He made plans for inheriting Olympic Games for all future. When Albert Speer presented Hitler after the Games with a model of a gigantic stadium for Nuremberg of 400,000 seats and commented that it did not conform to Olympic standards, Hitler dismissed his concerns:

> Do not worry. In 1940 the Olympic Games will take place in Tokyo. But thereafter they will take place in Germany for all times to come.

# The Church Supports Mussolini in Ethiopia and Franco in Spain

Like Hitler, Mussolini tried to justify his policy of heavy spending on rearmament, arguing that Italy was overcrowded and needed new territorial space. Abyssinia in East Africa was singled out as prey. He amassed troops in Somaliland and Eritrea and stockpiled large quantities of ammunition and supplies to attack. Acting with treachery, he signed a friendship treaty with Emperor Haile Selasie in December 1934 while preparing for the attack. When he felt he was ready, Mussolini accused the Abyssinians of aggression at the Wal Wal oasis.

Instead of censuring Mussolini's expansion plans, Pope Pius XI provided moral support. On August 27, 1935, the Pope stated that while it was true that war horrified him, a defensive war necessary for the expansion of an increasing population could be just and right. Some days later, while the discussion on the Italo-Ethiopian problem reached its most critical point, Pius XI declared that, although he was praying for peace, he wished that "the hopes, the rights, and the needs of the Italian people should be satisfied, recognized, and guaranteed with justice and peace."

The Ethiopian Orthodox Union Church was the official religion in Abyssinia. Closely related to the Coptic Church of Egypt, it was one of the oldest Christian denominations in the world and dated its beginnings to the fourth century, long before Europe accepted Christianity. Moslems were also an important sector of the population. The Jewish community there, the Beta Israel or Falashas, was one of the oldest Jewish tribes in the world whose origins went back to the times of the First Temple.

On October 3, 1935, Mussolini ordered the Italian troops in Somaliland and Eritrea to attack Abyssinia. Equipped with pre-World War I rifles the Abyssinian army could not withstand Mussolini's armored vehicles and mustard gas. Abyssinia, a member of the League of Nations, appealed to that world organization for help. The situation was clear; a predatory aggression against a weak nation had taken place. The League, which was created to maintain peace by resolving international disputes without resorting to war, condemned the attack and recommended to impose economic sanctions on Italy. But the sanctions were doomed to failure when vital materials such as oil were left out of the embargo.

Unwilling to stand up for international law and justice, Great Britain and France chose the route of appeasement. The French Foreign Minister, the future collaborationist Pierre Laval, refused to go along with the League of Nations resolution. British Foreign Secretary Samuel Hoare and Laval came up in December 1935 with the Hoare-Laval Plan, which proposed that two large areas of Abyssinia should go to Italy and a gap in the middle—the so-called corridor of camels to the Abyssinians. A national outcry in Britain against the betrayal of Abyssinia forced Hoare to resign, and the plan was dropped while Mussolini's troops continued to advance. The capital, Addis Ababa, fell on May 3, 1936. To fulfill his promise of creating an Italian East African Empire, Mussolini exiled Haile Selassie and united Somaliland, Eritrea, and Abyssinia under Victor Emmanuel III as its emperor. A week later, the Pius XI in his address of May 12, 1936, joined in the joy of the triumph:

> I partake in the triumphant joy of an entire, great, and good people over a peace which, it is hoped and intended, will be an effective contribution and prelude to the true peace in Europe and the world.

The Italian episcopate enthusiastically supported Mussolini and the Abyssinian campaign at a time when, according to the concordat of 1929, bishops were strictly forbidden to take part in any political activity. Seven Italian cardinals, twenty-nine archbishops, and sixty-one bishops expressed direct support for the Abyssinia campaign according to Harvard historian Gaetano Salvemini. When Mussolini asked the Italian women to give up their gold and silver rings for the war, many bishops and priests led the way by giving the jewels and gold belonging to their churches, even offering the church bells so that they might be made into guns.

Although Abyssinia was home to one of the oldest Christian denominations in the world, the Italian bishops hailed Mussolini's campaign as a missionary crusade to spread Catholicism. Priests, missionaries, nuns, and Catholic organizations followed in the footsteps of the Italian army in Abyssinia. The archbishop of Taranto, symbolically celebrating Mass on a submarine, declared:

> The war against Ethiopia should be considered as a holy war, a crusade, because the Italian victory would open Ethiopia, a country of infidels and schismatics, to the expansion of the Catholic Faith.[31]

The Cardinal Archbishop of Milan Schuster declared:

> The Italian (Fascist) flag, is at the moment bringing in triumph the Cross of Christ in Ethiopia, to free the road for the emancipation of the slaves, opening it at the same time to our missionary propaganda.[32]

The failure of the sanctions and the readiness of Western powers to reward a nation that had used blatant aggression delivered a fatal blow to the League of Nations and to international law. The crisis of Abyssinia brought Nazi Germany and Fascist Italy close together for the first time and laid bare the weakness of the organization. The slide toward the Second World War became unstoppable.

Barely two months after Mussolini's conquest of Abyssinia the rehearsal of World War II in the form of a bloody civil war began in Spain when the Popular Front of moderate Republicans and leftists won the national elections on February 16, 1936, and drove the conservatives from office. A number of discontented generals led by General Francisco Franco led the rebellion. A coalition of the nobility, the military, and the Fascist Falange, supported by the Catholic Church, declared a rebelion against the legally elected Republican governments of Spain and Spanish Morocco on July 17, 1936. The military help of Hitler and Mussolini made possible the victory of the rebels, while the Allied powers refused to help the legally elected Spanish Republic and declared an arms embargo against it.

On July 25, 1936, a date considered by many historians as the virtual beginning of World War II, Hitler took the crucial decision to actively support the rebels when two emissaries of Franco reached him in Bayreuth with an urgent appeal for military help to save the rebels from imminent defeat. He made the decision late that night and issued orders to Blomberg and Göring to send twenty Junker fifty-two transport planes with military supplies. The planes took off to Spain four days later, tipping the military balance in favor of Franco's rebels. Mussolini followed Hitler's example some months later, sending military planes to assist Franco on December 28, 1936.

Hitler's decision to back militarily the Franco rebels found enormous favor in the eyes of the Vatican, which considered the Falangist rebellion to be a crusade against Bolshevism. Nothing could have been more effective to bring the Church together with the Nazis then the red scare. The Vatican made an offer to the Third Reich during the summer of 1936 to form a common front against Communism.[33] The Vatican saw Hitler's Reich as the bulwark against Bolshevism in Europe and as its global ally in the struggle against Communism, in spite of the serious difficulties that Catholic lay organizations faced in Nazi Germany at the time. A propaganda campaign of enormous proportions exploited the alleged threat of Bolshevism in Spain to inflame world opinion against the Spanish Republic. When the majority of Spanish bishops called for a crusade against Communism, Pope Pius XI addressed his blessings on September 14, 1936, to "those who have assumed the difficult and dangerous task of defending and restoring the rights and honor of Church and religion."

The German bishops that gathered at the Fulda Conference from August 18 to August 20, 1936, issued a pastoral letter putting German Catholicism at Hitler's command in the fight against Bolshevism:

> As always when the call of the Fatherland is sounded, we German Catholics are prepared to place ourselves at the disposition of the Führer in his campaign against a creed that threatens the entire universe . . . With diabolical purpose and tenacity Bolshevism is advancing from east and west against Germany as the heart of Europe, to take it as it were in a fateful pincer movement.[34]

Cardinal Michael Faulhaber of Munich was invited to meet with Hitler on November 4, 1936, in his private residence at the Oberzalsberg at the height of the Spanish civil war. The cardinal left a record of the conversation full of admiration for the Führer, including his own approving reaction to the "Bolshevik-Jewish" calumny, which now took the place of the nineteenth-century Church canard about the Masonic-Jewish conspiracy:

Hitler spoke openly, confidentially, emotionally, at times in a spirited way; He lashed out at Bolshevism and at the Jews: How the subhumans, incited by the Jews, created havoc in Spain like beasts, on this he was well informed . . . He would not miss the historical moment . . . Unless National Socialism gets the better of Bolshevism, all is up in Europe for Christianity and the Church. Either National Socialism and the Church will win together or they will both go under . . . All of this was expressed in a moving way in his great speech at the Nuremberg Party rally.[35]

Faulhaber reminded Hitler that he was personally present when Pope Pius XI called the chancellor the first statesman who, together with the Pope, had clearly recognized the Bolshevik threat. With extreme servility he told the modern Attila:

As head of the German Reich you are, for us, the authority willed by God, the legal superior, to whom we owe reverence and obedience.

At the November bishops conference in Regensburg, Cardinal Faulhaber informed the bishops about his conversation with the Führer. On December 13, 1936, the Bavarian bishops issued a pastoral letter that reveals the degree of identification with the Nazi regime they reached despite the difficulties that the Catholic press and organizations were experiencing at the time:

Nothing could be further from our intentions than to adopt a hostile attitude toward, or a renunciation of, the present form taken by our government. For us, respect of authority, love of Fatherland, and the fulfillment of our duty to the State are matters not only of conscience but of divine ordinance . . . The Führer can be certain that we bishops are prepared to give all moral support to his historic struggle against Bolshevism. We will not criticize things that are purely political, what we do ask is that our holy Church be permitted to enjoy her God-given rights and her freedom . . . We pray to the Almighty that he take under his protection the life of our Führer and Reich Chancellor, and that he grant his blessing to your statesmanly goals.[36]

A few days later, the Fulda Bishops conference published a "Christmas Pastoral Message from the German Bishops on Defense against Bolshevism," expressing their unconditional support for Hitler: [37]

The German Bishops consider it their duty to support the head of the German Reich by all the means the Church has at its disposal. [38]

In a personal letter of support to the Führer written by Cardinal Faulhaber after the conference, he highlighted the major international significance of the bishop's declaration:

Abroad, too, this unanimous commitment of the German bishops to the Führer and his role in world history, the repelling of Bolshevism, will not go unheard.[39]

In a sermon on December 1936, Cardinal Faulhaber expressed from the pulpit the unique nature of the alliance between Germany and the Church in the war against Bolshevism:

If ever the German people were to face the task of assuming the leadership in the defense against Bolshevism, then they cannot and may not forgo their strongest ally in this struggle, Christianity.[40]

## Preparing the Conquest of Lebensraum: The 1937 Hossbach Conference

Emboldened by his successes in the Saargebiet, the Rhineland, and Spain, Hitler began to move forward with his plans to conquer new Lebensraum in the east. In the battlefields of Spain, Hitler's generals rehearsed World War II. New weapons, aircraft, and military techniques were tested for the first time. Göhring's Luftwaffe showed its prowess against undefended civilian population. In Guernica, its planes threw bombs on civilians, killing 1,650 people and injuring 900 more. The successes in the Spanish civil war convinced Hitler to move ahead his timetable for war. In a memorandum he wrote in August 1936 in Obersalzberg, Hitler put down on paper his decision to prepare for war in the next four years.

1) The German army must be ready to fight in four years.
2) The German economy must be on a war footing in four years. [41]

At the 1936 annual rally of the Nazi Party in Nuremberg, Hitler announced a four-year plan to have Germany militarily ready for war within the next four years. He appointed Göhring head of the Four-Year Plan Office. On December 9, 1936, Schacht in a speech delivered in Frankfurt formulated in terms very similar to Hitler's, Germany's need of new Lebensraum:

Germany has too little living space for its population. She has made every effort, and certainly greater efforts than any other nation, to extract from her own existing small space, whatever is necessary for the securing of her livelihood. However, in spite of all these efforts the space does not suffice.[42]

Hitler and Mussolini signed the Berlin-Rome Pact and established the Axis on October 25, 1936. One month later, on November 25, Japan signed a parallel pact with Germany, radically changing the balance of power in Europe and the world. Hungary, Romania, and Bulgaria later joined the Axis. On November 5, 1937, three months before he carried out the Anschluss of Austria, Hitler called together a secret conference that is known in literature as the Hossbach conference after his military adjutant, Oberst Friedrich Hossbach (1894-1980). His protocol of the conference is the main historical source of the deliberations. Hitler summoned to the meeting Foreign Minister Konstantin von Neurath (1873-1956), Minister of War Werner von Blomberg (1878-1946), and the three highest commanders of the armed forces: Werner von Fritsch (1880-1939) of the army, Erich Raeder (1876-1960) of the navy, and Hermann Göhring (1893-1946) of the Luftwaffe.

At the Hosbach conference, Hitler first presented his ministers with an overview of Nazi geopolitics. He put forward the proposition that the ultimate aim of German policy was the preservation of the purity of the German racial community. However, the continuation of a tightly packed racial core in the limited territorial boundaries of Germany posed the greatest danger to the preservation of the German race. The possibility of an autarchic German economy was unrealistic in view of Germany's limited natural resources and minimal agricultural potential to cover its food needs. The expansion of foreign trade was not a viable option either, considering the instability of export markets and the British domination of the seas. He then offered his own predatory solution: Germany's future was wholly dependent on obtaining new breathing space in Europe itself and not in faraway colonies as was held in the kaiser's days. German military might should be used to conquer agricultural lands in Eastern Europe, wherever it could be gotten at the lowest cost:

> There had never been spaces without a master and there were none today. The attacker must always come up against a possessor. [43]

After venturing some possible timetables for war, he stated that the Anschluss of Austria and the annexation of Czechoslovakia stood first in line in preparation of war "to remove any threats from the flanks."[44] Blomberg, Fritsch, and Neurath, who voiced their reservations on the premature timing of the plan, were out of office in less than three months.

To set the scene for World War II, Hitler instigated riots and disturbances in Austria and Czechoslovakia through his local Nazi agents and allies to "prove" before the world that the rights of German minorities were being violated and that German military intervention was justified. Less than a month after the conference, on November 30, 1937, Hitler met with Goebbels and spent a long time with him commenting on the Jewish question. Goebbels recorded their conversation in his diary:

> The Führer talked about the Jewish question for a long time . . . The Jews must disappear from Germany, yes out of all Europe. That will take some time still, but it will happen and must happen. The Führer is firmly committed to this. [45]

Although the Nazi government was trying to systematically diminish the power of the Catholic Church in Germany, the enthusiasm and patriotic zeal for the new Reich did not wane among the bishops and lay Catholic in Germany.

Just as they helped Hitler to come to power and consolidate his regime they played a crucial role in preparing the Reich for its future war to conquer Lebensraum. Hitler's Lebensraum ideas found their way to the writings of Catholic theologians and bishops such as Otto Schilling, Bishop Conrad Gröber, and Bishop Berning. The bishops became committed to the call of a Grossdeutschland and the expansion of the German Lebensraum. Without any regard whatsoever for the terrible implications that the plans of the Führer to widen the Lebensraum entailed for other nations, the Catholic press and publications praised these plans in increasingly enthusiastic terms even during the war years when its ominous meaning became clear in occupied Poland and the Soviet Union.[46]

As the financial debt for rearmament began to grow rapidly and became highly problematic for the German economy, the plunder of Jewish assets provided much of the funds needed. What Hitler laid out before Major Hell in 1922 was now put into practice. Under the expert hands of the two master-looters, Schacht and Göhring, decrees were issued to deprive Jews of their properties to finance German rearmament. By the end of 1937 state-ordered confiscation became mandatory. Any Jewish firms that had not Aryanized voluntarily had to be taken over by Germans. Aryan firms acquired Jewish enterprises and stocks for a minimal fraction of their true value. The government then took away as a tax 60 to 80 percent of the reduced price the German firms paid the Jewish owners.

The Aryanization of the highly valuable mining companies of Julius and Ignaz Petschek is only one of the countless examples of the gigantic looting operation. The great German banks found in these transactions a veritable gold mine. Banks such as the Deutsche Bank, the Dresdener Bank, and the Commerz Bank were major players and beneficiaries of the robbery. The so-called wizard of the German economy, Dr. Schacht, found in these activities a fertile field for his financial skills. To also put their hands on the assets of converted Jews and their descendents, the German legal masterminds tried to widen the Jew definition as much as possible. The Nuremberg Laws adopted in 1935 facilitated the task. The Nazi race theory and venomous propaganda served them well to carry out the task.

## The Encyclical *Mit Brennender Sorge*

Treaties were for Hitler disposable devices to deceive and outwit his momentary partners. When a treaty had outlived its deceptive purpose, the master-deceiver would break shamelessly his commitments and promises and leap treacherously upon his prey.[47] Thus he signed a nonaggression treaty with Poland in 1934, the Munich accord in 1938, and the Ribbentrop-Molotov pact in 1939, all of which he broke when it suited him. The concordat somehow survived because he still needed it. According to Chancellor Brünning, Hitler boasted before the signature of the concordat that he would be among the very few who were able to outwit the Vatican:

I shall be one of the few men in history to have deceived the Vatican.[48]

Hitler never really intended to keep the promises he gave the Church in the concordat, but instead planned to turn it into a pliable instrument serving the interests of the Nazi state. As a totalitarian going after the body and soul of every German, and particularly the young, he had no room for more than one master in Germany. He could not tolerate rivals, whether secular or religious, competing for the soul of the people. All the sectors of public life had to be re-gimented and controlled in accordance with the interests of the Nazi state, whether political parties, churches, trade unions, private organizations, and par-ticularly the media.

In 1936 the Nazis, for the first time, voiced the claim that the concordat was outdated. Cardinal Bertram informed Cardinal Pacelli on April 21, 1936, of the threat.[49] As both sides had their own reasons for the concordat to continue, it survived over the years intact. Hitler's claim to be Christianity's defender against Bolshevism required that he maintain it in force. As long as the concor-dat was still useful to him, Hitler created conflicts to scare the Church into meek obedience. The ruthless dictator and power manipulator wanted to subdue and control the Church as much as he could, without reaching the breaking point. "In fact" says Scholder "right up to the end of the war no German bishop on either the Catholic side or the Protestant side was arrested for political reasons."

Without the willingness of the Church to be deceived, Hitler could never have been successful in his boast. Before the ink on the concordat dried, Hitler was violating the promises he signed. The violations of the concordat obviously angered the Church, and the bishops complained, but the thought of cancelling the treaty was unthinkable to them. Hitler was well aware of that and he streched his actions to the limit. He told Rauschning "the Church will swallow anything in order to keep its material advantages."

By means of the concordat and its monetary subsidies, the Church was co-opted and transformed into a docile instrument of the Nazi state exactly as Hitler intended. In this, Hitler was successful beyond imagination. The concordat se-cured the loyalty of the Church to the Third Reich, excluding the possibility of any political resistance on its part. The Church lost the initiative vis-à-vis Hitler and became subservient to his will. The concordat was a one-way street with no return, instead of independence, it bought servility.

While the Vatican adhered scrupulously to the concordat until the very end, the Nazis violated the treaty from the very beginning. The Church lost posi-tion after position and was unable to do much about it. Catholic organizations were taken over from within with minimal resistance under the argument that they were political organizations barred by the concordat. The first to go were the Catholic trade unions and associations.

On January 24, 1934, Rosenberg was appointed deputy of the Führer for the spiritual and ideological training of the Nazi Party. A new version of the book of Psalms in which every reference to the Jews was erased was published on February 2, 1934. Six days later the Gestapo ordered all Bible-study groups to disband. On February 9, 1934, the Vatican placed Rosenberg's book *The Myth of the XX Century* in the Index of Forbidden Books. *Civilta Cattolica* expressed its criticism of Rosenberg's brand of anti-Semitism, recommending instead its own more genuine variety:

> The anti-Semitism of the Nazis does not stem from the religious convictions or the Christian conscience . . . but from the desire to upset the order of religion and society . . . We could understand them and even praise them, if their policy were restricted within acceptable bounds of defense against the Jewish organizations and institutions. [50]

The Nazi aim of controlling the Church was pursued with even greater zeal during 1935 and 1936. The Gestapo issued court warrants against lower-level priests. Great numbers of monks and nuns were arraigned in German courts in 1936 and 1937 under charges ranging from sexual misconduct to illegal currency transactions. As many as 700 priests were indicted under accusations of sexual misconduct and black-market operations.

Although the Catholic press became—in the words of Gordon Zahn— "captive auxiliaries of Goebbels' propaganda ministry" that was not good enough for Goebbels. He preferred direct control of public opinion. Pressure was exerted on subscribers of Catholic newspapers to switch to Nazi newspapers. To drive as many Catholic newspapers out of business and control the rest, he used such means as withdrawal of paper allocations, censorship by government and party officials, selective licensing of journalists as a function of Nazi loyalty, and outright suspensions. The Church witnessed the disappearance of the majority of Catholic newspapers and the loss of the independence of those few left.

The indoctrination of German youth was crucial to the fulfillment of the Nazi program. As early as 1934 the Church totally surrendered to the Nazis its sport and youth organizations and finally in 1935 the Catholic youth organizations were dissolved. In 1936 the *Hitler Jugend* became the official youth organization of the state, and in 1939 membership in the Hitler Jugend became mandatory; it reached 8.9 million members at the threshold of the war. The churches emptied of young people as the activities of the Nazi youth organizations were intentionally scheduled for Sundays during services. The Nazi leadership boasted that the influence of the Church on the youth in Germany was practically null. [51]

The takeover of the Catholic school system took place at an incredible pace. Confessional schools were subjected to a well-planed campaign of attrition. The government withdrew its subsidies and tax concessions and prohibited civil servants and the military from sending their children to them. Pressure was applied on Catholic parents to take out their children. In Munich, the capital of Catholic Bavaria, the percentage of families sending their children to Catholic schools decreased from 65 percent in 1933 to 3 percent in 1937. [52] Confessional schools suffered, in consequence, a great decline in their matriculation and many closed.

Catholic teachers colleges were suppressed. At the audience of the Pope-with German cardinals on January 17, 1937, Cardinal Bertram informed that he had just received a document from the German Minister of Education to the effect that "there shall be no more Catholic kindergartens."[53] For the sake of appearance of formal compliance with the concordat, spurious religious instruction was provided in the public schools.

But there certainly was much more than the wish to maintain the concordat under all circumstances that underlay Church policy. The great sympathy felt by millions of the German Catholics and their bishops for Hitler developed into full identification, pushing to the background the differences of the Church with the Nazi regime. Nazi Catholic youth groups under the leadership of clergymen were formed in Church institutions and in seminaries all over Germany, while millions of Catholics joined the Nazi ranks. German patriotism came to have incomparably greater weight and significance for German Catholics than their religion. George L. Mosse describes well the identification process:

> Many ecclesiastics, both Protestant and Catholic, felt a personal allegiance to the party, the state, and the Germanic ideology and openly voiced their convictions from the pulpit. Others believed that the German task, like that of the Holy Crusade, could be accommodated within the Christian dogma. Still others saw in the Nazi victory a revitalization of the German spirit and were grateful to the party, its ideology, and its leaders . . . Throughout the country many congregations, joined the festivities, marched alongside the proudly victorious Nazi troops, and saw no conflict between their faiths and Nazi-ideology. [54]

Even when provoked by the Nazis, the bishops kept their allegiance to Hitler intact. "On the whole," says Scholder, "there was hardly any doubt about the reliability of the churches within the nation and their loyalty to the State." When the German press reported in June 1936 that a Swiss Catholic asked children to pray for the death of Hitler and accused all Catholics of sympathizing with sedition, Cardinal Faulhaber was swift to respond on June 7, 1936, with a patriotic sermon:

> A lunatic abroad has had an attack of madness—does this justify wholesale suspicion of German Catholics? . . . We will today give an answer, a Christian answer: Catholic men we will now pray together a paternoster for the life of the Führer. This is our answer. [55]

In his assessment of the attitude maintained by the bishops over the years of the Nazi regime, Guenter Lewy concludes:

> It is hard to resist the conclusion that it was the attraction felt for certain elements in the Nazi ideology more than anything else that prevented the German episcopate from apprehending the true inhumanity of National Socialism in

1933 as well as in later years . . . No matter what the regime did, the Nazi state remained the lawful authority that had to be obeyed in accordance with the divine command. [56]

Hitler greeting a German cardinal in an official Nazi ceremony. USHMM.

Many bishops and theologians continued to stress the coincidences of Catholicism and National Socialism well after their newspapers, youth organizations, and schools were emptying and disappearing. Cardinal Bertram told the clergy in a synod in Breslau in 1935 that many National Socialist ideas were already contained in Catholicism and that the Church had always admitted the significance of race, soil, and blood, which it consecrated through Christianity.[57] The Fulda Conference of Bishops continued taking pride in the fact that the concordat was the first international treaty signed by Hitler that opened for him the doors of international recognition and trust. In their congratulations to the Führer in 1935 they reminded him of this fact:

> Pope Pius XI exchanged the handshake of trust with you through the oncordat—the first foreign sovereign to do so . . . Pope Pius XI spoke high praise of you . . . Millions in foreign countries, Catholics and non-Catholics alike, have overcome their original mistrust because of this expression of papal trust, and have placed their trust in your regime.[58]

Klaus Scholder rightly rejects the allegation that the concordat was nothing more than a formal regulatory instrument. He contends that the unshakeable loyalty of the German bishops to Hitler until the very end originated and was

upheld by the concordat. Referring to Cardinal Bertram's order to hold a solemn
requiem for Hitler after his death in 1945, he states:

> Although today the concordat may be described as "the form of a legal treaty
> preventing the assimilation of the Catholic Church in the Third Reich," for the
> President of the German Conference of Bishops at that time it was on the con-
> trary one of the decisive reasons for his unshakeable loyalty to Hitler. [59]

According to Church historian Peter Godman, the Vatican already pon-
dered in 1934 the possibility of an ideological confrontation with the Nazis and,
not just with Rosenberg, in view of the difficulties that Catholic schools, youth
organizations, and newspapers were experiencing and commissioned three
priests to produce a report. At the end, Pius XI decided to shelve indefinitely the
secret report and sent it for safe keeping to America.

During the spring of 1936 the Vatican again raised the possibility of publishing a White Book on the violations of the concordat, as could be learned
from a memorandum of the British minister to the Vatican, Francis Osborne.
However, the general of the Jesuit Order in Rome, Ledochovsky, who had the
ear of the Pope more than any other Vatican dignitary, persuaded him not to do
so because "the Nazis, with all their faults were still the principal bulwark
against Communism."[60]

As the Nazis were progressively taking control of every Catholic position
in Germany, Pius XI finally decided in 1937 to react publicly against the violations of the concordat. With the assistance of German cardinals visiting Rome in
early 1937 and of his secretary of state Pacelli, Pius XI sought to produce a document that would condemn the violations of the concordat without endangering
the treaty. The result was the encyclical *Mit Brennender Sorge* (*With Burning
Concern*) issued on March 14, 1937, in Rome. The encyclical contrasts the strict
conscientious observance of the concordat on the part of the Vatican with the
wholesale violations of its terms by the other side:

> In the course of these anxious and trying years following upon the conclusion
> of the concordat, every one of Our words, every one of Our acts, has been in-
> spired by the binding law of treaties . . . the other part emasculated the terms of
> the treaty, distorted their meaning, and eventually considered its more or less
> official violation as a normal policy.

The encyclical denounced the Nazi government's coercion against the
Catholic schools in violation of the concordat:

> Even now that a campaign against the confessional schools, which are guaran-
> teed by the concordat, and the destruction of free election, where Catholics
> have a right to their children's Catholic education, afford evidence, in a matter
> so essential to the life of the Church, of the extreme gravity of the situation and
> the anxiety of every Christian conscience.

It refers to the intimidation suffered by members of religious orders, priests, and Catholic functionaries to induce them to leave the Church:

> Voices are swelling into a chorus urging people to leave the Church . . . Secret and open measures of intimidation, the threat of economic and civic disabilities, bear on the loyalty of certain classes of Catholic functionaries, a pressure which violates every human right and dignity . . . Our paternal gratitude goes out to Religious and nuns, as well as our sympathy for so many who, as a result of administrative measures hostile to Religious Orders, have been wrenched from the work of their vocation.

The encyclical also reiterated its opposition to Rosenberg's ideas that were becoming the official ideology of the Nazi movement. It rejected once again, Rosenberg's claims to create a Germanic National Church based on the myths of race, blood, and soil, and his demands to rewrite the Gospel according to the interests of the state and to repudiate the Old Testament:

> None but superficial minds could stumble into concepts of a national God, of a national religion . . . Should men . . . come and offer you the seduction of a National German Church, be convinced that it is nothing but a denial of the one Church . . . Whoever exalts race, or the people, or the State, or a particular form of State, or the depositaries of power, or any other fundamental value of the human community—however necessary and honorable be their function in worldly things—whoever raises these notions above their standard value and divinizes them to the idolatrous level, distorts and perverts an order of the world planned and created by God . . . The Gospel is final and permanent. It knows no retouches of human hands; it admits no substitutes or arbitrary alternatives such as certain leaders pretend to draw from the so-called myth of race and blood . . . Nothing but ignorance can blind one to the treasures hoarded in the Old testament . . . Whoever wishes to see banished from church and school the Biblical history and the wise doctrines of the Old testament blasphemes the name of God. [61]

After the encyclical was read from the pulpits in Germany on March 14, 1937, the Nazis protested. Cardinal Pacelli responded that the encyclical was not an attack on the Nazi regime at all but against the measures taken against the Church, because it very carefully "allowed a distinction between the Reich government and the measures hostile to the Church . . . the Holy See did not intend to interfere with what kind of government a people choose."[62] The main Catholic publication in Poland, *Maly Dziennik,* explained the encyclical to the Polish Catholics in very similar terms:

> The Holy Father does not condemn the National-Socialist system but only those aspects of the Nazi ideology that are incompatible with Catholic dogma or whatever in practice Hitler's subordinates do against the commandments of the faith.[63]

The Nazis responded awarding Rosenberg the National Prize at the 1937 Nuremberg Nazi Party Conference. They disseminated a spurious report published in the Nazi magazine *Die Sonne* in 1936 that the Pope's grandmother was a Dutch Jewish woman called Lipmann and that he employed in the Vatican library a Jewish rabbi named Levy. This typical ruse was intended to discredit the Pope and his encyclical by his alleged Jewish ancestry.[64] When Hans Frank, the Nazi minister of Justice (later the brutal governor of occupied Poland), visited Rome, Pius XI refused to grant him a private audience despite Cardinal Pacelli's insistence. Von Bergen, the German ambassador reported to Berlin:

> Pacelli told me His Holiness is filled with personal ill-humor over Germany. He refused the audience . . . The Pope also feels particularly wounded by the repeated assertion that he is of Jewish origin. He has nothing against the Jews, but a great deal against false statements of facts.[65]

The relations of Pope Pius XI and the Hitler government reached their nadir in 1938, the last year of his life, after the publication of *Mit Brennender Sorge*. When Hitler made a state visit to Rome May 3-9, 1938, to reciprocate Mussolini's visit to Germany, he refrained from requesting a papal audience, although protocol required that as a head of state visiting the Quirinal he should do so. In response to Hitler's slighting, Pius XI withdrew to Castelgandolfo and ordered that the Vatican museums be closed during the visit.[66]

While *Mit Brennender Sorge* did not deal at all with the terrible persecution of Jews in Germany, the Church apologists use it to "prove" the Church's concern for them. The declaration was not, nor intended to be in any sense, a protest against the persecution of German Jewry, as they have tried to misrepresent the document after the war. Whatever its merits as a protest against the violations of the concordat, it did not address the question of the fierce persecution of German Jewry by the Nazis. It was only in 1938 that Pius XI commisioned an encyclical to formulate the position of the Church on racism and on the Jews. That encyclical, *Humani Generis Unitas*, to be discussed in a later chapter, was never published but has come to light in recent years. Full of undisguised hostility towards the Jewish people, it led Fr. Johannes Nota to declare, when he discovered the original text in 1976: "God be praised that this draft remained only a draft."

# Notes

1 . Adolf Hitler, *Mein Kampf* (Boston, MA: Mariner Book, 1998).

2. Claudia Koonz, *The Nazi Conscience* (Cambridge, MA: Belknapp Press of Harvard University, 2005), 93-94.

3. Kurt G. W. Ludecke, *I Knew Hitler: The Story of a Nazi who escaped the Blood Surge* (London, 1938), 422. Jarman, Lewy, *The Catholic Church.*

4. Güenther Lewy, *The Catholic Church and Nazi Germany* (New York: Mc Graw Hill Book Co., 1964), 177.

5. Lewy, *The Catholic Church*, 179-180.

6. Lewy, *The Catholic Church*, 179-180.

7. Anthony Rhodes, *The Vatican in the Age of Dictators 1922-1945* (London, UK: Hodder and Stoughton, 1973), 180. Helmreich, 254. A.A. Abschluss von Konkordaten mit Deutschland, Vol. 10. Pacelli–Klee conversation. August 11, 1933.

8. Gordon A. Craig. *Germany 1866–1945* (New York: Oxford University Press, 1978), 587. Donald M. McKale, *Hitler's Shadow War: The Holocaust and World War II* (Lanham, MD: Taylor Trade Publishing, 2006), 61. Koonz, *The Nazi conscience*, 96

9. Klaus Scholder, *A Requiem for Hitler* (Philadelphia, PA: Trinity Press Int., 1989), 132.

10. Lewy, *The Catholic Church*, 192.

11. David Bankier, *The Germans and the Final Solution: Public Opinion Under Nazism* (Malden, MA: Blackwell Publishing 1992), 34.

12. Lewy, *The Catholic Church*, 201.

13. On May 2, 1935, a Franco–Soviet alliance was signed to counter Germany's military resurgence.

14. Alan Bullock, *Hitler: A Study in Tyranny* (London, UK: Odhams, 1952).

15. Jewish Virtual Library, Schacht (EC-458). *"The Avalon Project"*. Nuremberg Trial Proceedings Vol. 5. January 11, 1946.

16. William I. Shirer, *The Rise and Fall of the Third Reich* (New York: Simon and Schuster, 1959).

17. Jewish Virtual Library. (EC–433).

18. Donald M. McKale, *Hitler's Shadow War*, 72. Jeremy Noakes and Geoffrey Pridham, *Nazism 1919-1945* (Exter, UK: The University of Exeter Press, 1998), 531.

19. Max Domarus, *Hitler: Reden und Proklamationen 1932–1945* (Wurzburg, 1962), 537.

20. Donald M. McKale, *Hitler's Shadow War: The Holocaust and World War II* (Lanham, MD: Taylor Trade Publishing, 2006), 73. Albert Fischer. Yad Vashem. David Bankier, ed., *Probing the Depths of German Antisemitism: German Society and the Persecution of the Jews, 1933-1941* (Oxford, UK: Berghahn Books, 2000), 216.

21. McKale, *Hitler's Shadow War*, 77. On September 12, 1935, Wagner announced the intention of promulgating a law for the protection of German blood.

22. Lewy, *The Catholic Church,* 275.

23. Lewy, *The Catholic Church*, 282. Goldhagen Daniel J. *Hitler's Willing Executioners*. (New York: Alfred A. Knopf, 1996), 110

24. Raul Hilberg, *The Destruction of the European Jews* (Teaneck, NJ: Holmes & Meier, 1985), 305.

25. Susan. D. Bachrach, *United States Holocaust Museum. The Nazi Olympics Berlin 1936*. (New York: Little Brown and Company, 2000).

26. Bachrach, *The Nazi Olympics*.

27. Brundage did not forget his Nazi friends. He brought back his Nazi mentor SA General Karl Ritter von Halt to a leading position in the IOC in 1952.

28. Bachrach, *The Nazi Olympics*.

29. Bachrach, *The Nazi Olympics*.

30. *The New York Times*.

31. Avro Manhattan. *The Vatican in World Politics*. *Chap. 9.* (Gaer Associations, Inc, 1949).

32. T. L Gardini, *Towards the new Italy* (Surrey, UK: L. Drummond, 1943)

33. Rhodes, *The Vatican.*

34. Lewy, *The Catholic Church,* 206.

35. Lewy, *The Catholic Church,* 207-209.

36. Lewy, *The Catholic Church,* 208.

37. Lewy, *The Catholic Church,* 207-209.

38. Lewy, *The Catholic Church,* 207-210.

39. Lewy, *The Catholic Church,* 207-210.

40. Lewy, *The Catholic Church,* 207-210.

41. Scholder, *A Requiem for Hitler,* 143.

42. Jewish Virtual Library (EC–433).

43. Documents on German Foreign Policy. U.S. Printing Office, 1957-1964, Series D, Vol.1 Document 19, pages 29-39.

44. Taylor Telford, *Sword and Swastika* (Mount Pleasant, SC: Nautical & Aviation Pub Co of America), 140.

45. *Die Tagebücher von Joseph Goebbels*, Teil I Aufzeichnungen 1923-1941: ed. Angela Hermann, München 2006 Band 2/III.

46. Lewy, *The Catholic Church,* 165, 220. Phayer, *The Catholic Church and the Holocaust,* 92.

47. G. Messersmith declared in an affidavit at Nuremberg how the highest ranking Nazis Gohring, Goebbels, Frank, etc. scoffed at the idea of to the binding character of treaties.

48. Rhodes Anthony, 178. F.O. 371/30898. Statement to E. Munster at the Francois Xavier University of Nova Scotia on January 3, 1942.

49. Godman Peter, *Hitler and the Vatican.* (New York: Free Press, 2004), 110.

50. Lewy, *The Catholic Church.*

51. Rhodes, *The Vatican,* 225.

52. Rhodes, *The Vatican,* 187.

53. Godman Peter. *Hitler and the Vatican* (New York: Free Press, 2004), 136.

54 .George L Mosse, *The Crisis of German ideology, Intellectual Origins of the Third Reich,* (New York: Grosset and Dunlap, 1964).

55. Lewy, *The Catholic Church,* AB Munich.

56. Lewy, *The Catholic Church,* 101

57. Lewy, *The Catholic Church,* 162.

58. Katholische Kirche und Nationalsozialismus: Dokumente 1930–1935. Nymphenburger Verlagshandlung, Munich 1963. James Carroll, *Constantine's Sword: The Church and the Jews* (Boston, Ma.: Houghton Mifflin Company, 2001), 505.

59. Scholder, *A Requiem for Hitler,* 167.

60. Rhodes, *The Vatican,* 202.

61. Anne Fremantle, *The Papal Encyclicalsin their Historical Context* (New York: Mentor, 1956). Mit Brennender Sorge. Encyclical on the Church and the German Reich His Holiness Pope Pius XI. March 14, 1937.

62. Rhodes, *The Vatican.*

63. Ronald Modras, *The Catholic Church and Anti-Semitism. Poland, 1933–1939* (Newark, NJ: Harwood Academic Publishers, 1994).

64. Georges Passelecq and Bernard Suchecky, *The Hidden Encyclical of Pius XI* (Orlando, FL: Harcourt Press, 1997), 192, 200.

65. *A.A. Pol II Bezihungen des Vatikans zu Deutschland, Vol 5, von Bergen to Berlin, April 6, 1936.* Rhodes, *The Vatican,* 200.

66. Rhodes, *The Vatican,* 207.

## Chapter 5
## Hitler's Grossdeutschland

### The Anschluss of Austria

With the defeat of the Austro-Hungarian Empire in World War I, Austria emerged as a small Republic of 6.5 million German-speaking people. The Treaty of St. Germain that the victorious Allies signed with the Austrian government on September 10, 1919, broke up the empire along its ethnic fault lines: Hungary, Czechoslovakia, Poland, and the State of Slovenes, Croats and Serbs became independent. The treaty required Austria to refrain from directly or indirectly compromising its independence by merging with Germany. As a result, the Anschluss resolution approved by the Provisional National Assembly on November 12, 1918, that declared Austria part of Germany was renounced. In the new Austrian Republic (1919-1938), the Catholic Church remained the official state religion. Its subsidies and its monopoly on education were left intact.

In an overwhelming Catholic country such as Austria where more than 90 percent of its population identified itself as Roman Catholics, the decisions taken by the Church played a decisive role. The Christian Social Party (CSP) represented Catholic political interests in the interwar years. The Christian Socials used anti-Semitism, as did their predecessors, to maintain their popularity. They championed a radical form of anti-Semitism that they inherited from Karl Lueger and his supporters. By the time of the Anschluss "many priests were outspoken anti-Semites while; others only moderately so" indicates Michael Phayer.[1] Even the so-called alleged opponents of the Nazis in the episcopate such as the Metropolitan, Johannes Maria Gföllner of Hitler's hometown Linz, were outspoken anti-Semites who considered it a Christian duty to fight Judaism. In a pastoral letter published in 1935 Gföllner called Christians to unite with the Aryans against the Jews and Judaism.[2]

Another prominent Austrian bishop, Alois Hudal, the rector of the Collegio Santa Maria del'Anima in Rome, was calling in his booklet *The Foundations of National Socialism* (1936) for a Catholic-Nazi covenant to fight Jewry and

Marxism. He argued that there was no basis for an equal treatment of the Jews in the law according to Church doctrine. He blamed liberalism and the French revolution for having granted equal rights to the Jews. The copy of his booklet that he sent to the Führer bears his handwritten dedication "To the architect of German greatness." [3]

The new Austrian Republic was led in the beginning, like the Weimar Republic, by a coalition government of Social Democrats and Catholics, with Social Democrat Karl Renner (1870-1950), as chancellor.[4] The coalition with the Social Democrats was short lived and broken up for good on June 1920, eight years earlier than in Germany, due to the resolute opposition of the Catholic Church obsessed by its fear of Marxism and Socialism. From 1920 until the Anschluss in 1938, all the ensuing Austrian governments were dominated by the Christian Social Party. The party had the full backing of the Vatican, although it was suspect in the eyes of the Austrian higher clergy.

The Christian Socials followed Italian Fascism and aligned themselves behind Mussolini, who supported them politically. A Roman Catholic priest, Ignaz Seipel (1876-1932), was the chancellor of the Christian Social government between 1922 and 1929. Seipel had the support of the *Heimwehr*, a Nationalist paramilitary organization similar to Germany's Freikorps, which was backed by Mussolini and various Austrian bishops as a counterforce to the alleged threat of a Marxist takeover. Before the signature of the Berlin-Rome Pact of October 25, Fascist Italy was interested in the existence of an independent Austria and served as an effective shield against Hitler's Anschluss plans. However, when Mussolini joined the Axis in 1936 and sought Hitler's consent to the invasion of Abyssinia, he soon withdrew his support for Austrian independence and independent Austria was doomed.

Seipel's criticism of parliamentary democracy set the stage for the dictatorial government of his successor and protégé Engelbert Dollfuss (1932-1934). Dollfuss, a militant Catholic abolished parliamentarism, liquidated the Constitutional Court, and savagely repressed Social Democrats and parties of the left. He dissolved all political parties in 1933 and created the so-called Fatherland Front (*Vaterländische Front*), a Fascist Christian Party, declaring before the Catholic-dominated assembly that his aim was to establish a corporatist system in accordance with the papal social encyclicals. In 1934 he signed a concordat with the Vatican.

National Socialism found fertile ground in Austria, Hitler's birth land, even before he came to power in Germany. Many Catholics who during the Hapsburg Empire favored the existence of a separate Austro-Hungarian Empire under the rule of the Catholic Hapsburg dynasty were now in favor of the union of Austria and Germany as the Pan-Germans of old had demanded. When Hitler proclaimed in 1926 in the first page of *Mein Kampf*, "German Austria must return to the Great German Motherland," many Austrians agreed with him. The first of the twenty-five points of the Nazi Program of 1920 demanded the union of all German-speaking people in a Greater Germany. Pan-Germans flocked to the Austrian Nazi Party.

There were also in the Nazi Party vast numbers of *Nazikatholiken*, Nazi Catholics whom anti-Semitism, more than anything else, attracted them to the party. Arthur Seyss-Inquart (1892-1946), was one of them. A founding member of the *Deutsche Gemeinschaft* or German Brotherhood—a secret society created by Catholics and Pan-German Nationalists in Austria on December 28, 1918, to combat Free Masons, Marxists, and above all Jews. Its members were required to take an oath that no Jewish blood ran in their veins. The preamble to their constitution stated:[5]

> The purpose of this organization is the liberation of the German people from Jewish influences, and combat against Jewry with all available means. The organization is secret. Since a contact of the organization with the public can't be avoided it has to be done under pretense of unsuspicious purposes and without showing the actual setup.[6]

The *Deutsche Gemeinschaft*, which laid the foundation of the future Austrian Nazi Party, was dissolved when the Austrian Nazi Party came into being. Seyss-Inquart declared in Nuremberg that Dollfuss and Schuschnigg had also been members of the Deutsche Gemeinschaft. Seyss-Inquart who eventually became the first Nazi Reich commissar of Austria shared with them the idea of unification with Germany, although they, unlike Seys-Inquart, refused to cede their power to the Nazis.[7] In a letter to Himmler dated August 19, 1939, presented at the Nuremberg Trial, Seyss-Inquart referred to his early membership after World War I in the German Brotherhood together with Engelbert Dollfuss, the future Austrian chancellor.

> It must be known to you that at the time of the Black-Red coalition (the Catholic-Social Democrats Renner government), there existed an extremely secret organization under the name of "German Community." Here met all sorts of Nationalists and Catholic elements who, at least at that time, were anti-Semitic and anti-Marxists . . . Dollfuss was also active there. He was of my age, and was a very active anti-Semite. It is through success of the activities of this organization that the Black-Red Coalition was broken and the Marxists never came back in the government. After the establishment of National Socialism, this organization was dissolved.[8]

Hitler set up in Austria a powerful Nazi apparatus of propaganda and subversion that aimed at taking over the country from within without a war. Through German Ambassador Reith and the German Legation, the Austrian Nazis and their front organizations secretly received funds for their activities. The Nazis promoted social unrest to create a crisis that would bring them nearer to their goal. Inflamed by Hitler's demagogic broadcasts, the Austrian Nazis organized riots and street fights, burned down buildings, attacked railroads, and blew up bridges and telecommunications in preparation of a coup.[9]

On July 25, 1934, less than a month after the Night of the Long Knives, the Austrian Nazis, with assistance of German SS, attempted a coup and assassinated Chancellor Engelbert Dollfuss. The coup was put down by Justice Minister Kurt von Schuschnigg (1897-1977), who like his predecessor resisted giving up his power to the Nazis. The Nazi Party was banned and the leaders of the Putsch were tried and thirteen of them received the death penalty. Some members fled with the help of the German ambassador. Outside of legality, the Nazis were growing stronger day by day in Austria.

The power struggle that developed between the Christian Socials in control of the government and the Austrian Nazis mirrored Italian-German changing relations. When Dolfuss was assassinated by the Nazis in 1934, Mussolini's swift movement of troops to the Brenner Pass convinced Hitler to postpone his Anschluss plans for a while. Cardinal Theodor Innitzer of Vienna and the Austrian higher clergy backed the government. They declared themselves in favor of maintaining Austria's independence, notwithstanding their Pan-German nationalism. At the same time, like their colleagues in Germany during the 1920s they had warm words for what they considered the positive elements of Nazi ideology in which individualism and liberalism were repudiated giving way to authority and bonds of blood to create a homogeneous community.

After Göhring almost had him killed in the Night of the Long Knives, Hitler summoned Franz von Papen to Berlin on July 3, 1934, a short time after he resigned as vice chancellor. Hitler dispatched von Papen as his Trojan horse to Vienna to reestablish friendly relations with the Schuschnigg government after the failed coup and create a cover for illegal Nazis activities. As a devout Catholic who was held in high esteem by the Vatican, few could match von Papen's capacity for the job. Just as he helped Hitler arrive to power in Germany and to gain the support of the Catholic Church for the Führer, he asked him to win over Austria and the support of the Vatican and the Austrian bishops. At his trial in Nuremberg, he described his mission:

> It was my first purpose in the diplomatic field to deprive the Austrian problem of its European character, and to develop it gradually into an exclusively internal problem between the Reich and Austria. It therefore had to be my primary aim to convince the Vatican that a union could not endanger the Vatican's interests. [10]

Von Papen arrived in August 1934 in Vienna to carry out his infiltration plan. Upon his arrival, von Papen called for a rapprochement between Austria and Germany. The perceptive American ambassador to Vienna, George S. Messersmith, warned the State Department in an official dispatch of October 10, 1935, on the dangerous nature of men like von Papen:

> Europe will not get away from the myth that Neurath, Papen, and Mackensen are not dangerous people and that they are "diplomats of the old school." They are in fact servile instruments of the regime and just because the outside world looks upon them as harmless, they are able to work more effectively. They are able to sow discord just because they propagate the myth that they are not in sympathy with the regime. [11]

Messersmith summarized the conversation he had with von Papen after his arrival to Vienna in an affidavit at the Nuremberg trial:

> In the baldest and most cynical manner he then proceeded to tell me that all of Southeastern Europe, to the borders of Turkey, was Germany's natural hinterland, and that he had been charged with the mission of facilitating German economic and political control over this region for Germany. He blandly and directly said that getting control of Austria was the first step . . . He said he intended to use his reputation as a good Catholic to gain influence with certain Austrians, such as Cardinal Innitzer, towards that end. He said that he was telling me this because the German government was bound on this objective of getting this control of SE Europe and there was nothing which could stop it and that our policy and that of England and France was not realistic. [12]

Hitler, the master deceiver, denied at the time in his public appearances any intention to annex Austria or to meddle in its inner affairs. On May 21, 1935, he solemnly declared in the Reichstag:

> Germany neither intends nor wishes to interfere in the internal affairs of Austria, to annex Austria or to conclude an Anschluss. [13]

To create the impression before the inauguration of the Berlin Olympics that Germany was ruled by a reasonable government seeking peace and understanding, von Papen signed, on July 11, 1936, a gentlemen's agreement with Austria. Cardinal Theodor Innitzer of Vienna (1875-1955) hailed the July agreement as an end to civil war. In the agreement, Germany pledged to respect Austria's independence and sovereignty. These promises were given in exchange of the inclusion of Nazi stooges in the Austrian cabinet. Messersmith explained in his affidavit at Nuremberg the essence of the Hitler-von Papen strategy:

> At the beginning of the Nazi regime, Germany was of course, far too weak to permit any open threats of force . . . Instead it was the avowed and declared policy of the Nazi government to accomplish the same results which they later accomplished through force, by the methods which had proved so successful for them in Germany: Obtain a foothold in the Cabinet, particularly in the Ministry of the Interior, which controlled the police, and then quickly eliminate opposition elements. [14]

Arthur Seyss-Inquart, the top *Nazikatholik* in Austria, an insider among the Austrian Catholic leading-circles as well as among the Nazis, was appointed state councilor. A devout Catholic who attended mass almost daily with his family, even as Reich commissar, Seyss-Inquart became later famous as the executioner of Dutch Jewry. He is described as "an ardent Catholic propagandist who was often heard in Vienna as lecturer propounding Catholic principles and supporter of many Catholic organizations of all kinds." Although the Austrian Nazi Party did not achieve legal recognition through the July agreement, the Nazis regained their political maneuvering space inside and outside of the patriotic front. The July agreement led other European nations to view the Anschluss issue as a purely internal German affair in which outside interference was not called for, as Hitler and von Papen had intended. But Hitler needed the truce only to gain military strength and it did not last more than eighteen months. The agreement, like all of Hitler's treaties, proved to be a worthless piece of paper. Göhring, in charge of the German rearmament program, laid his covetous eyes on Austrian human and financial resources and he pushed for immediate action to take over Austria. After the Hosbach Conference in 1937, the Nazis began again to stir unrest in Austria.

Von Papen's final assignment in Austria was to convince Schuschnigg that the most effective means to discipline Austrian Nazis was to go to Obersalzberg to meet the Führer. Hitler, who had already decided that the time had come for the Anchluss of Austria, demanded from him to sign an accord lifting the ban against the Nazi Party, appoint Austrian Nazi sympathizers to key positions in the Austrian government, and amnesty all Nazi terrorists in prison, including those involved in the Dollfuss assassination. Schuschnigg signed. Schuschnigg's attempts to hold on to power were from that moment on doomed to failure. One month after the signature, the Anschluss of Austria to Germany took place. Overjoyed the Führer turned around to von Papen after the signature to thank him for a job well done:

> Herr von Papen, through your assistance I was appointed Chancellor of Germany and thus the Reich was saved from the abyss of communism. I will never forget that. Ja wohl, Mein Führer, replied von Papen. [15]

Fourteen years after the end of World War II in 1959, von Papen also received the gratitude of the Vatican, which honored him by renaming him privy chamberlain to the Pope.

On February 16, 1938, Schuschnigg reorganized his cabinet and appointed Seyss-Inquart minister of the interior with control over the police. Other Nazis were appointed to the key cabinet posts of the army and the economy. In an attempt to maintain his power through the Fatherland Front, Schuschnigg stopped short from legalizing the Nazi Party. Right after Seyss-Inquart took possession as minister of the interior, the Nazis stormed the streets in Vienna and other cities and began riots, Schuschnigg sought assistance from the Social Democrats whom his regime had savagely repressed, promising them he would make concessions to the workers. The Social Democrats and Monarchists came out to demonstrate in the streets against the Nazis and the Anschluss. Their awakening alarmed the Church and cleaved a wedge between the Church and the Schuschnigg government.

Schuschnigg's announcement in Innsbruck on March 9, 1938, to hold a plebiscite four days later on March 13, incensed Hitler. He demanded from President Wilhelm Miklas (1872-1956) to replace Schuschnigg immediately by Seyss-Inquart and delay the plebiscite. On March 11, Schuschnigg resigned.

Later that night, Seyss-Inquart was appointed chancellor.[16] The German embassy informed Berlin that Seyss-Inquart agreed to the entrance of German troops to Austria to "establish peace and order." The road was now clear for the Anschluss. Cardinal Theodor Innitzer, the primate of Austria, published a call in the *Reichpost* immediately after Schuschnigg's resignation calling for Austrian Catholics to support the Anschluss.[17] Innitzer's about-face came as a surprise because of the declarations in favor of the independence of Austria he had made as late as February 1938.

On March 12, 1938, three months after the Hosbach Conference, Hitler carried out the Anschluss of Austria in defiant violation of the St. Germain Treaty. The Wehrmacht marched into Austria on March 12, at daybreak without one shot being fired by the Austrian Army to stop them. Within an hour, the Austrian police all over Austria were wearing swastikas. Arthur Seyss-Inquart was sworn in as chancellor by President Wilhelm Miklas. The new Austrian cabinet convened on March 13 and unanimously approved the Anschluss. After the resignation of the president, Seyss-Inquart signed the Anschluss decree in the name of Austria. A homologous decree was approved by the Reich cabinet and signed by Hitler. Renamed Ostmark, Austria became a province of the Third Reich with Seyss-Inquart as *Statthalter*, its first governor—a post he held until April 30, 1939.

Cardinal Innitzer found the new cabinet of Nazikatholiken appointed by Seyss-Inquart very reassuring.[18] The next day, March 13, 1938, Hitler entered to Vienna triumphantly and received an apotheotic welcome from his fellow countrymen. Cardinal Innitzer and the other bishops ordered the ringing of bells and the display of swastika banners on the churches to welcome the Führer's entry into the capital. Arranged by von Papen, Innitzer paid a personal visit to the Führer in the Hotel Imperial to congratulate him and welcome him to Austria. According to Baldur van Shirach, Cardinal Innitzer gave the Nazi salute at that meeting. The resistance of the Catholics of Austria to become part of the German Reich ended in a submissive acceptance and identification with the Nazis. In this case again, the Catholic Church rendered invaluable help to Hitler at the crossroads of history. At the Nuremberg Trial, von Papen, the architect of the Nazi-Catholic partnership, gave the following explanation for arranging the meeting:

> With our march into Austria and the Anschliss of Austria to the Reich, Hitler had joined a Catholic country to Germany; and the problem, which was to be solved, was winning this country from the interior as well. That was possible only if Hitler recognized the religious basis, recognized what rights Catholicism had in this country; for this reason I arranged a talk between Cardinal Innitzer and Hitler in order to make sure that Hitler in the future would follow a policy which stood on a Christian basis in Austria. By arranging this interview, I thought I would be able to do one last service for Austria.[19]

Cardinal Innitzer explained after the war that von Papen persuaded him that "under the Nazis the Church would be able to carry on its activities better than before."[20] The same day of his visit to Hitler, Cardinal Innitzer addressed an enthusiastic letter "To the Catholic clergy and to faithful Catholics in the archdiocese of Vienna and Burgenland." He called them to support "the great German State and the Führer" and even urged them to encourage the youth to join the Nazi youth organizations. Innitzer published his proclamation long after the encyclical *Mit Brennender Sorge* was issued protesting the injuries suffered by the Church in the Third Reich. He wrote:

> Those who are entrusted with souls and the faithful will unconditionally support the great German State and the Führer, because the historical struggle against the criminal illusion of Bolshevism and for the security of German life, for work and bread, for the power and honor of the Reich and for the unity of the German nation, is obviously accompanied by the blessing of divine Providence . . . I urge the heads of youth organizations to promote membership in the German Reich's youth organizations.
>     "The Church will not regret its fidelity to the great German state." This statement by the Führer is a guarantee that the true mission of the Church can be fulfilled. And so Catholics in their totality serve in the best way the good of the Reich, the nation, and the fatherland. [21]

On March 15, 1938, Innitzer again paid a personal visit to the Führer. To make sure that the Anschluss plebiscite would not produce any unwanted surprises, Hitler announced on March 18, 1938, that a plebiscite on the Anschluss and new elections for deputies to the Reichstag would also be held in Germany on April 10, 1938. All the Austrian bishops signed a proclamation on March 18 with the Heil Hitler salute to be read in all the churches in Austria on March 27 urging the faithful to vote yes, in favor of the annexation of Austria to the German Reich. Cardinal Innitzer sent a message to Cardinal Adolph Bertram, on April 1, 1938, expressing his wish that the German bishops would similarly urge the Germans to vote yes to the Anschluss. Preceding his signature Innitzer added in his own handwriting "Und Heil Hitler!" The proclamation of the Austrian Bishops is one of the most eloquent expressions of the identification of the Austrian Church with the Third Reich:

> We joyfully acknowledge the eminent work that the National Socialist movement has done and is still doing in the domain of national construction and economy as well as in the domain of social welfare, for the benefit of the Reich and the German nation, and notably for the poorest strata of the population. We are also convinced that the activity of the National Socialist movement has averted the danger of an all-destroying atheistic Bolshevism. For the future, the bishops confer their heartiest blessings on this activity, and they will instruct the faithful to this effect.
>     On the day of the plebiscite, it goes without saying that it is for us a national duty, as Germans, to vote for the German Reich, and we also expect all believing Christians to demonstrate that they know what they owe to their nation. [22]

Recalling the experience with the Nazis in Germany, the Vatican considered that Cardinal Innitzer and the Austrian bishops had moved too fast before securing solid guarantees on the rights of the Catholic Church in Austria in exchange of their support.[23] *L'Osservatore Romano* published a statement that the declaration of the Austrian Episcopate had not been consulted with the Vatican and summoned Cardinal Innitzer to Rome for consultations. The whole episode has been seized to misrepresent the Vatican's position as a protest against the Anschluss. The truth is very different: Pius XI was concerned that Cardinal Innitzer had missed an opportunity to include a clear reference to the protection of the rights of the Catholic Church and he told Innitzer at the audience: "It was very simple-minded of you to believe in any promise made by Hitler." An addition to the bishop's proclamation was agreed to in Rome on April 6, 1938, which content is known from a copy forwarded to the American Ambassador in London, Joseph P. Kennedy:

a) That in all matters pertaining the Austrian concordat no change be made without previous understanding with the Holy See.
b) That in a particular way all rules in connection with the schools and the educational activities as well as the training of the youth be made according to the doctrine of the Catholic religion.
c) That the propaganda against religion and the Church be forbidden.
d) That the rights of Catholics to proclaim, defend, and practice Catholic Faith .
. . be respected. Rome, April 6, 1938. Signed: Th. Cardinal Innitzer [24]

A day before the April 10 plebiscite, all the churches in Austria and Germany complied with the request of the Nazi government to toll their bells as a sign of "overwhelming expression of confidence of the entire nation in the Führer and his work." Historian Evan Burr Bukey comments: "In a Catholic nation as Austria, the recommendation of the Bishops carried great weight. Nearly everyone obeyed the Bishop's call to endorse the Anschluss." Austrians and Germans voted in favor of the Anschluss, which was ratified by an unprecedented 99.73 percent vote in Austria and a 99.08 percent vote in Germany. The Austrian Army was integrated into the Wehrmacht without the formation of separate Austrian units. Around 800,000 Austrians served in the Wehrmacht and another 150,000 in the Waffen SS during World War II.

The Church in Austria did not escape Nazi pressure in order to minimize its influence and power. The bishops who had welcomed the Anschluss soon witnessed the dissolution of many Catholic organizations and the obstruction of their educational activities. Nonetheless, as good patriots supporting in the home front the victorious armies of the Führer they remained silent during the war. After the war, however, they had no problem with presenting themselves as victims of the Nazis involved in a battle against them.[25] Cardinal Innitzer remained archbishop of Vienna and primate of Austria until 1955, long after the war. It is more than ironic that he was eulogized as an alleged anti-Nazi and saver of Jews, although his activities never crossed the line beyond the non-Aryan Christians whom the Nazis classified in racial terms as Jews.[26]

## The Jews, First Victims of the Anschluss

There were around 185,000 Jews in Austria, 2.8 percent of the population. Most of them were concentrated in Vienna, a city that acquired its unique place in European culture through its Jewish scientists, writers, and artists, such as Sigmund Freud, Alfred Adler, Gustav Mahler, Arnold Schoenberg, Alfred Loos, Arthur Schnitzler, Hugo von Hofmanstahl, Franz Kafka, and Franz Lehar to mention some of the more famous among them. Although Vienna was a pulsating center of genuine Jewish religious and cultural life, it also counted a substantial number of apostates, around 8,000, who converted to Christianity. Hitler intended to eliminate them together with the Jews.

The Austrians gave full vent to their inveterate anti-Semitism after the Anschluss with a zest that outdid the Germans. After all, Austria had written the book on anti-Semitism. The country that nurtured Hitler and produced Eichmann, Globocnik, and Kaltenbrunner, as well as the majority of the bureaucrats that implemented the Final Solution, celebrated the Anschluss with an unprecedented orgy of brutality. A British correspondent estimated that as many as 100,000 Viennese were rampaging through the Jewish quarter on the evening of March 11 chanting: "Death to the Jews! One Reich, One People, One Leader!" Yesterday's neighbors and friends turned their backs on the Jews. All Jewish organizations, 444 in Vienna and 181 in the rest of the country, were closed down. More than 110 Jewish personalities of all walks of life were deported to Dachau, followed not long after by 1,700 Jewish intellectuals and professionals.

Jews of all ages, including women and children, were ordered to dress in their best and taken to wash streets and buildings in Vienna. Kneeling before cheering crowds, venerable rabbis and figures of that great Jewish community were forced to scrub the center streets of Vienna with toothbrushes, while unspeakable abuse was heaped on them.[27] In Währing, a wealthy section of Vienna, Nazi brutishness reached its peak when Jewish women were ordered to dress in their fur coats to scrub the streets while the Nazi officials urinated on their lowered heads.[28] The photographs of ordinary Germans and Austrians enjoying the sight remain as a testimony to their complicity and moral decay.

March 13 and 14, the Gestapo carried out large-scale looting in wealthy Jewish homes, plundering rugs, furniture, and artworks that they shipped to Berlin. Germans and Austrians needed no explanations of the *Volkisher Beobachter*'s recommendation: "The Jew must go—but his cash stays here." The wealth of Austrian Jewry was systematically plundered under Göring's covetous eyes: Priceless works of art were confiscated and shipped to Berlin. Baron Louis de Rothschild was arrested and his priceless famous art collection confiscated. SS General Wulff participated together with Heydrich in the seizure of Baron Rothschild's invaluable art collection in exchange for his life.[29]

Gangs of local Nazis raided the city for weeks, cleaning out Jewish department stores and private homes. Jewish businesses and dwellings were taken over and those who refused to surrender their properties were arrested. Aryan supervisors were systematically taking over every business owned by Jews. By September 1938 Nazi supervisors already controlled 5,210 firms.[30]

The Reich commissioner issued a decree requiring Jews to register property valued more than 5,000 Reich marks.[31] A specific law prohibiting Jews from holding directorial and managerial positions was approved. Other decrees banned Jews from most occupations to destroy the very basis of Jewish economic existence. The Nuremberg laws were declared in force in Austria on May 23, 193,8 long before Reich legislation in general became the law in Austria. On June 29, 1938, a total of 40,000 Jews, including spouses in mixed marriages, were dismissed from their jobs in the private sector.

In London, American Ambassador Joseph P. Kennedy expressed full understanding of the German policy to the German ambassador on June 15, 1938. Kennedy only objected to the excessive noise that accompanied its implementation. In his telegraphic communication to Berlin the German ambassador summarized Kennedy's position in the following words:

> He said Germany was hurting her own cause, not so much because we want to get rid of the Jews but rather by the way we set out to accomplish this purpose with such a lot of noise. At home in Boston, for instance, Kennedy said there were clubs to which no Jews have been admitted in fifty years . . . people simply avoided making a fuss about it. He himself understood our policy on Jews completely. [32]

The physical elimination of the Jews became a high priority objective for the Nazis immediately after the Anschluss as a precondition of Grossdeutschland. A memorandum of the German Foreign Ministry of January 25, 1939, highlights the connection between the aim of a Greater Germany and the elimination of the Jews:

> It is probably no coincidence that the fateful year of 1938 brought not only the realization of the concept of a Greater Germany, but at the same time has brought the Jewish Question close to solution. For the Jewish policy was both precondition and consequence of the events of 1938. [33]

Adolph Eichmann (1906-1962), a fellow Austrian, was sent by Himmler and Heydrich to Vienna to expedite the process of expelling the Jews. There he honed his skills as a large-scale deportation specialist. On August 1, 1938, Eichmann in representation of the SS opened in the confiscated palatial residence of Baron Rothschild the offices of the *Zentralstelle Fuer Juedische Auswanderung* (Center for Jewish Emigration), the only agency authorized to issue exit permits for Jews from Austria. In a record time of six months, Eichmann expelled 50,000 Austrian Jews. Jews not born in Austria itself were taken by force to the borders and unceremoniously pushed over to the neighboring countries. Eichmann's superiors, Himmler, Heydrich, and Mueller, were full of admiration for his feat.

The ferocity of Austrian anti-Semitism left no doubt in Jewish minds on the need to flee as quickly as possible. Endless lines of Jews stood outside every consulate in Vienna day and night to obtain exit visas, while Jews were being terrorized in the streets. The many not lucky enough to obtain a visa were left behind to face a tragic destiny. Before the outbreak of World War II, a total of 126,445 Austrian Jews managed to exit and migrate to every corner of the world. Unfortunately, the Nazis caught up with some of them in neighboring countries when they occupied Europe. The 67,000 Jews left behind in Austria were deported to ghettos and death camps after November 10, 1941. Only 2,000 of them survived while the rest was murdered in the ghettos and death camps.[34]

Some Western European countries agreed to accept a maximum of 10,000 Austrian Jewish children after Kristalnacht. Families who were unable to obtain visas stood before the heart-breaking decision to separate themselves from their children and send them alone to unknown charitable families abroad. Actually, only 2,844 children were rescued from Austria, a token remnant of that great community. Beginning with a group of 200 children in December 1938, forty-three kindertransportn left Austria. Most of them went to Britain, which received 2,262 of them.[35]

The Austrian episcopate and the Vatican in Rome refused to hear or see what was being done to the Jewish community in Austria and Germany. Neither then nor at Kristallnacht on November 10, 1938, did the Austrian episcopate react in any way to the outrage. Many in the clergy and among Catholic laymen saw this as the long hoped for opportunity to reverse Jewish emancipation.[36] Historian Bukey comments:

> At no time during the Anschluss era, did the Austrian Church speak out against the Nazi persecution of the Jews, not even after the devastation of Crystal Night . . . Their silence and that of other Austrian and German bishops in the face of the monstrous brutalities of Crystal Night was particularly deafening.[37]

## The Evian Conference

Until *Kristalnacht* (Crystal Night) in 1938, only 130,000 Jews, one-quarter of German Jewry, managed to get out from the Third Reich. Some stayed because they still harbored a glimmer of hope that the situation would improve, but most were unable to leave as a result of the closed door policy that the Great Depression and anti-Semitism brought about. The systematic robbery of Jewish wealth by the Nazis made the pursuit of visas far more difficult, as nobody wanted penniless Jews as immigrants.

The U.S. immigration quota system adopted since 1924 by Congress stood as a major barrier to the rescue of Jews from Germany and Austria. Most Jews were unable to comply with the LPC clause (Likely to become a Public Charge), which required that the applicant prove that he had enough money to support himself, or that he produce an affidavit guaranteeing his support by relatives. The efforts to influence Congress to draw a distinction between regular immigrants and persecuted refugees in order to relax for them the harsh restrictions were unsuccessful. As a result of this law and the bureaucratic obstruction of the State Department, the German immigration quota to the United States went underused almost until the war in spite of the enormous line of applicants trying to get out from the Third Reich.

With the onset of the Great Depression, the situation worsened radically. Under anti-Semitic influence, Latin American countries began to circulate orders to their consulates to stop issuing visas to Jews, although they certainly were in dire need of entrepreneurial talent for their development and could have benefited greatly from the skills and energy of European Jews. Mexico had circulated repeatedly such memoranda to its consulates since 1933.[38] On June 7, 1937, the Brazilian Ministry of Foreign Affairs issued a secret memorandum to its consulates not to grant visas to Jews.[39] On July 12, 1938, the Argentinean Foreign Minister Jose Maria Cantilo issued a secret order known as Directive 11, banning Jewish immigration to Argentina.[40] Even tourist and transit visas to Jews were included in the ban.

The Nazis were keenly aware that a mass flight of homeless Jewish refugees would increase anti-Semitism in host countries. They considered this effect to be highly favorable to their aim of promoting anti-Semitism worldwide. In a memorandum, the German Foreign Ministry gloated over the fact that Jewish immigration faced growing resistance everywhere, not the least as a result of the policies sponsored by the Nazis themselves, including the anti-Semitic propaganda against Jewish immigrants fanned by them and their local allies. The Foreign Ministry memorandum suggested the use of the anti-immigrant bias to strengthen anti-Semitism all over the world and gain support for Nazi policies worldwide:

> By now almost all countries in the world have sealed their borders hermetically against the burdensome Jewish intruders . . . The influx of Jews arouses the resistance of the native population in all parts of the world and thus provides the best propaganda for Germany's policy towards the Jews . . . It must be the aim of German foreign policy to strengthen this wave of anti-Semitism. The poorer the Jewish immigrant is, the greater the burden he constitutes for the country into which he has immigrated, the stronger the reaction will be in the host country, and the more desirable the effect in support of German propaganda.[41]

The Arabs also began to look for German support through various channels. An Arab delegation was invited to attend as honorary guests at the Nuremberg Nazi Party Congress on September 16, 1937[42] Under the Ha'avarah Agreement established in 1933 between the Jewish Agency and the Nazi government, almost 60,000 Jews had been able to leave from Nazi Germany to Palestine. When the Nazis saw that the Ha'avarah Agreement was helping the development of the *Yishuv*, they practically ceased its operation by the end of 1937. A German Foreign Ministry memorandum dated January 25, 1939, explained the Nazi policy:

The transfer of Jewish property from Germany contributes in no small measure to the development of a Jewish State, which even in miniature form could provide world Jewry with a basis of action similar to that of the Vatican State for political Catholicism. The realization that Jewry will always be the implacable enemy of the Third Reich forces us to the decision to prevent any strengthening of the Jewish position.[43]

Obtaining a visa became even more difficult when Nazi Germany issued a decree in 1938 adding the names Israel and Sara to every passport of a Jew or Jewess. A *J* for Jude was stamped on their passports on the request of the Swiss government so their border guards would know whom to turn away. The sign became a death sentence for tens of thousands of Jewish refuges trying unsuccessfully to flee the borders of the Third Reich.[44]

The increasingly restrictive immigration policy of the British Mandate Government in Palestine and the end of the Ha'avarah Agreement were most inmical to collective rescue efforts. In April 1936 Arab riots began again under the instigation of the Mufti of Jerusalem Haj Amin el Husseini and the Arab Higher Command. The Arabs demanded from the Mandate government to stop Jewish immigration and land acquisition in Palestine altogether. A Royal Commission presided by Lord Earl Peel recommended on July 1937, to give Arab opposition to Jewish immigration a decisive voice. The British Colonial Office reduced the yearly immigration quota drastically from a record high of 66,000 certificates in 1936 to only 14,000 in 1938. When Hitler annexed Austria in March 1938, the British Colonial Office further restricted the number—at the moment of greatest need—to three thousand certificates for the next six months.

Although the League of Nations took note very early of the plight of German Jewry and created a Commission for Refugees with James G. McDonald as high commissioner in 1933, the organization did not support his work. McDonald resigned his post in 1935 accusing the organization of ignoring the plight of German Jewry. Polish anti-Semitism added another tragic dimension to the plight of European Jewry. The more difficult it became for Jews to emigrate, the more vocal became the campaign against their presence in Poland and stronger the demand to get rid of them.

The Polish eliminationist policy eventually acquired a deadly significance for Polish Jewry. At every international forum, including the League of Nations, the Polish anti-Semitic representatives demanded that the 3.5 million Polish Jews be massively transferred to the colonies of the Western powers. The Polish delegates expressed without any inhibitions in the League of Nations their "surprise" of why anyone would get indignant at the Poles when they only followed in the footsteps of a "great and cultured nation", referring to the Germans.[45]

The tragic situation of the Jews in Nazi Germany turned into a political conundrum for American President F. D. Roosevelt when the American Jews demanded from his government a humane response to the plight of persecuted German Jewry. Facing a congress fiercely opposed to immigration, and surrounded by advisors and officials hostile to Jews, FDR had to maneuver his way within the turbulent waters of American politics. On March 25, 1938, Roosevelt announced he was calling an international conference at Evian-les-Bains, in France to help the emigration of political refugees from Germany. A report by the U.S. State Department, brought to light by William Perl, written shortly after the Evian conference on November 15, 1938, states explicitly that the American initiative intended to use the forum as an escape valve to divert the pressure exerted on the American government to liberalize its immigration policy to save the Jews of Germany and Austria:

> After the absorption of Austria by Germany on March 12, with the resultant immediate and ruthless application of the Nuremberg laws to Austria, pressure on the Department "to do something" increased. It was obvious that this pressure was going to be both exceedingly strong and prolonged. The Secretary Mr. Welles, Mr. Messersmith and Mr. Moffet decided that it would be inadvisable for the Department merely to resist the pressure, and that it would be far preferable to get out in front and attempt to guide their pressure, primarily with a view towards forestalling attempts to have the immigration laws liberalized. The idea of the Evian intergovernmental meeting was suggested by Mr. Welles and approved by the President on March 22.[46]

The invited governments were given previous written assurances that the conference would recommend or even consider the need of changing their restrictive quotas and immigration policies. Roosevelt also agreed beforehand to the British demand to exclude Palestine altogether from the agenda of the conference. At a time when the United States itself, the caller of the conference, had closed its gates to persecuted Jews of Europe through its highly restrictive quota system, much less could be expected from the other countries. The isolationist, anti-Semitic, and xenophobic sentiments in Congress and among higher government officials—far more than the economic depression—blocked the way to relax the rules for persecuted Jews of Germany. The Evian Conference was not called together to save Jews but to save face, and even that was not achieved when it turned into a charade that provided Hitler's propaganda machine with proof that no one wanted the Jews.[47]

Hitler reacted with mockery to the announcement of the conference in an electoral speech in Konigsberg, saying that as far he was concerned "he would be happy to see the Jews go even on luxury ships."[48] The Evian conference began on July 6, 1938, in Hotel Royal at Evian-les-Baines with official representatives of twenty-nine nations and observers from Poland and Romania. Some countries, like Italy and South Africa, declined the invitation. President Roosevelt appointed Myron C. Taylor (1874-1959), who later was his envoy to the Vatican (1939-1950) as head of the American delegation, and James G. McDonald (1907-1991) as a delegate.[49]

Eichmann, in charge of the Blietz clearing of Austria of its Jews, found a way to make his presence felt at the conference. He dispatched a Jew from Vienna, Dr. Heinrich Neumann, to the conference with a ransom proposal for the mass transfer of 40,000 Jews from recently occupied Vienna. The conference, however, refused to discuss the offer under the technical argument that

Austria no longer existed. The delegates of Poland and Romania demanded at the conference that the emigration of Jews from their countries be given equal priority to that of Germany, even threatening with pogroms if that did not happen. In the words of Historian H. L. Feingold:

> Observers from Poland and Romania were present at Evian and their governments had already made it clear that they expected equal opportunity with Germany to rid themselves of their Jews. Poland went so far as to hint to the State Department that suitable pogroms could occur to impress the powers with the urgency of its situations.[50]

T. W. White, representing Australia, an almost empty continent with an enormous potential for population absorption, justified at the conference the Australian refusal to accept Jewish refugees by stating: "As we have no racial problem, we are not desirous to import one."[51] A very similar response came forward from Canada, which was at the time under Mackenzie King, fiercely against Jewish immigration. King recorded in his diary that any action permitting an appreciable number of Jews to settle in Canada would undermine the unity of the Nation:

> This is no time for Canada to act on humanitarian grounds, but that Canada must be guided by realities and political considerations.[52]

The hope that Latin American countries would provide a haven for the refugees came to naught when delegate after delegate used flowering Latin rhetoric to turn down the request. The Peruvian delegate, Francisco Garcia Calderón (1881-1953), could not miss the opportunity to jest on the hurting back of persecuted Jewry. Trying to impress his colleagues that he too was conversant with philosophy, he quoted Nietzsche's saying that "Jewish influence, like leaven or ferment, is of value to all nations," than added with mockery that Peru had already enough ferment, referring to the tiny Jewish community in Lima of a few hundred souls. Calderón pointed to the United States as Peru's role model for its closed-door policy and explained that the Peruvian immigration policy, like the American, was designed to protect Peru's racial composition, whatever that meant.[53]

The Conference doomed the last glimmers of hope to rescue German Jewry. After deliberating for nine days, the twenty-nine participants, with the sole exception of the Dominican representative, refused to accept any Jewish refugees to their shores.[54] The Mexican delegate offered one hundred visas per year for the Jewish refugees; the rest, none. Any illusions that existed about rescuing the Jews of Germany and the rest of Europe from the claws of the Nazis through migration were shattered by the conference. Western democracies proved they cared very little about the tragic destiny that awaited the Jews under the Germans and refused them safe haven anywhere in their dominions. With little else to show for their presence, the delegates filled their time with pleasure cruises on Lake Geneva, casino gambling, water skiing, mineral baths, and golf.

In his report of the conference to Cordell Hull, Myron Taylor expresses his frustration with the Latin American delegates, "who are extremely troublesome, raising objection after objection simply for the sake of self-advertisement, without having anything constructive to offer." Taylor expressed his serious doubts on the usefulness of involving them in the future in the work of the Intergovernmental Committee to be created in London.[55]

Although the record is very clear in this respect, the immigration initiatives undertaken by the Church for small groups of baptized non-Aryan Christian refugees to go to Latin America are misrepresented as efforts to rescue Jews. The most highly publicized initiative is the Brazilian intervention that was undertaken by the Vatican in 1939 exclusively for baptized converts with the explicit stipulation that *Mosaic* Jews should *not* be included. It originated in a letter of Cardinal Faulhaber and Bishop Berning on March 31, 1939, to Vatican Secretary of State Cardinal Luigi Maglione in which they suggested that the Vatican intervene with Brazilian dictator Getulio Vargas to request visas for baptized converts who were being persecuted by the Nazi government.

The Brazilian government responded to Cardinal Maglione's request (April 5, 1939) and promised 3,000 visas for the baptized converts; one thousand of these visas were to be distributed directly by the Brazilian consulates and two thousand through the Vatican San Raffaelo Society. Mirroring the exact terms of the original request, the Brazilian government clearly specified that the visas would only be extended to "sincere Catholics who deserve to be helped." Father Anthon Weber, a Palatine priest in charge of the San Raffaelo Society in Rome explained to Gitta Sereny how he made sure that no real Jew would come through the cracks in obtaining such a visa:

> I was responsible for baptized Jews only. Of course they were all claiming to be Catholics . . . I made them recite the Lord's Prayer and the Ave Maria; that proved in a hurry who was genuine and who wasn't. [56]

The Brazilian government soon reneged on its offer and withheld 2,000 of the visas under the claim that the arriving refugees were "showing inadequate adaptation to the customs of the country, behaved improperly, and were unwilling to work." There are good reasons to believe, as suggested by Daniel Goldhagen and Shira Schoenberg, that these accusations against the refugees originated in the return to Judaism of some of them after their arrival to Brazil.

Very similar was the hostility shown to refugees of Jewish descent who managed to reach Chile and Bolivia. The apostolic delegates of Bolivia and Chile maligned the arriving refugees in their reports to the Vatican as "invasive" and "cynically exploitative" and accused them of being engaged in "dishonest dealings, violence, immorality, and even disrespect for religion." The animosity in the reports of the apostolic delegates against the persecuted refugees uprooted from their families, homes, and possessions is evident. The impact of these reports on subsequent immigration can only be guessed in view of the scarce information available. Future access to Vatican and Latin American government archives may, in the future, allow a better understanding of the dismal record of the Latin American countries in responding to the Jewish tragedy in Europe.

# Kristallnacht

As soon as Germany annexed Austria in March 1938, foreign-born Jews were rounded up and dumped by the Gestapo at the borders without allowing them to take along any monetary means whatsoever. They were ordered to run across no-man's land to the other side of the borders of the neighboring countries. The anti-Semitic Fascist Polish government foresaw the expulsion of Polish Jews from Austria when the Anschluss took place and took preventive measures to block their return to Poland. The Polish issued a denaturalization decree on March 25, 1938, taking away Polish citizenship from those living abroad for more than five years. As a consequence of the decree, Polish Jews in Austria and Germany became stateless pariahs overnight. In June 1938, the Polish government again announced that those Polish Jews who would return in contravention of the new denaturalization law would be interned in the infamous Bereza Kartuska concentration camp where political prisoners were held.

Ten weeks after the Evian Conference, forced deportations of so-called foreign Jews began on October 26, 1938, from Germany to the Polish border at Zbaszyn. From a total of 56,430 Polish Jews living in Germany, 18,000 helpless unsuspecting Polish Jews, some living there as much as fifty years or more, were rounded up overnight by the Gestapo and taken by force to the Polish border. Twelve thousand of them ended up, on October 28, 1938 at the no-man's land across the village of Zbaszyn near Pozen. Before forcing them to run in heavy rain to the Polish side, the Germans confiscated their suitcases and any money over ten marks and told them with mocking sadism: "You didn't bring in any more into Germany and you can't take any more out." When the Jews reached the Polish side, the Poles refused entry to most of them on the basis of the new Polish denaturalization law.

Wandering back and forth between the two lines, without food for days, most expelled Jews were taken into custody in a Polish concentration camp and housed in unheated stables. The others reentered Germany to find their final tragic destiny at a later date. As the Polish government held the expelled Jews in Zbaszyn, Hitler was successful in proving to the whole world that as far as the Jews were concerned both Germany and Poland shared the same goal—the elimination of Jews from their midst. What looked to some as a conflict between Germany and Poland was in truth a display of shared policies and intentions: a game in which both used the hapless Jews as their punching bag. Poland played well its part as the anvil on which Jewry would be crushed by the German hammer.

The Zbaszyn outrage unchained the tragic sequence of events that led to Kristallnacht. Among the expelled Polish Jews at Zbaszyn was a Jew from Radomsk living in Hanover since 1911, Zindel Grynspan, the father of Herschel Grynspan. He lived to testify at the Eichmann trial in Jerusalem in 1961 on the events that he was involved. A postal card he wrote from no-man's land to his seventeen-year-old son Herschel in Paris, describing the tragedy that befell the family, moved Herschel to a desperate lonely act of revenge. Unemployed and barely subsisting illegally in Paris, Herschel went to the German Embassy in Paris and shot, on November 6, 1938, Ernest Von Rath, the first German officer he met there. The Germans, who long before had been waiting for an opportunity to carry a spectacular major pogrom on the Jews in Germany, seized the opportunity of von Rath's death to prove to Western powers that they were deadly serious about their intentions to make the Third Reich Judenrein.

On November 9 and 10, 1938, Goebbels and Streicher staged the Kristallnacht pogrom all over Germany and provided the world with a bloody sample of what lay in store for the Jews. They orchestrated a wave of terror that enveloped the Jews all over Germany. Hundreds of synagogues were put on fire and destroyed; the glass of many thousands of shattered Jewish storefronts shimmered in the night, while the fire of the synagogues illuminated the sky. In Vienna and other Austrian cities the pogrom was carried out with even greater brutality than in Berlin and Frankfurt. Thirty thousand Jews were arrested in their homes all over Germany and Austria and sent to Dachau, most of them never to return. Others were abducted in the streets and tortured to death at Gestapo headquarters. Their families received a notification demanding a payment of twelve marks to have delivered to them a small box with the ashes of their dear ones. Whatever illusions the Jews in Germany still harbored were shattered with Kristallnacht. The pogrom was a violent message that the Third Reich would not stop at any means to eliminate the Jews.

Austrian brutality against the Jews reached its peak at Kristallnacht. Great crowds of spectators, including housewives and children, were attracted to the spectacle. "It should come as no surprise," points out historian Evan Burr Bukey, "that aside from Middle Franconia, the level of violence and bloodshed in Vienna exceeded that of any other locality in Greater Germany." All the synagogues in Vienna, around fifty in number, were destroyed, with the exception of the small *Bet-Hamidrash* of the Schiff Shul. More than 4,000 Jewish businesses were plundered. More than 6,000 Jews were arrested, of which 3,000 were dispatched to Dachau from where they never returned. The Gestapo took Jews from their homes and herded them in cellars, while hundreds of Jewish women were arrested, stripped naked, and subjected to humiliating actions. Many Jews were murdered and many hundreds committed suicide.

A collective atonement fine of one billion reichsmark was levied on German Jewry on November 12, 1938, by order of Hermann Göring. Each Jew in possession of property valued above 50,000 reichsmark was required to pay 20 percent of its value to cover the fine. The quota was soon raised to 25 percent. All the Jewish retail stores were ordered out of business. On December 3, 1938, real estate, industries, and securities owned by Jews were Aryanized. Combined with the loss of employment opportunities, these confiscatory taxes brought about the total pauperization of German and Austrian Jewry. On November 15, all Jewish children were expelled from German public schools. For Jews wishing to leave, the Nazis required the payment of a security tax and a 25 percent flight tax on property worth over 200,000 reichsmark and on a yearly income above 20,000 reichsmark. During the winter months that followed another 118,000 Jews fled from Germany in haste in every direction.

Foreign diplomats and visitors witnessed in the streets of Germany and Austria the outpouring of unrestricted brutality against the defenseless Jews. The Austrian Church hierarchy whose Nazi sympathies were so enthusiastically displayed at the time of the Anschluss showed their patriotic solidarity with quiet approval. No condemnation of this act of organized savagery came forth from Pius XI or Secretary of State Pacelli. Neither did the German episcopate as a whole, through its spokesmen, nor the thousands of Catholic clergymen individually—with the sole exception of Msgr. Bernard Lichtemberg, provost of St. Hedwig Cathedral in Berlin—utter a word of condemnation in any form. None of them followed his courageous example when he raised his lonely voice in his parish in November, 1938 against the burning of synagogues:

> What happened here yesterday, we know; what will happen we do not know; but we are witnesses of what is happening today. Outside, a synagogue is burning—and a synagogue too, is a house of God.[57]

The Evian Conference actually served to promote the Nazi agenda. Hitler himself could not have devised a better way to justify the German policy toward Jews than by proving that no one wanted them. The Nazis saw the conference as the green light to proceed with their plans of the Final Solution, which allowed them to get rid of the Jews not in reservations but via the smoking chimneys of the death camp crematoriums. Two days after the Kristallnacht pogrom Göring informed at a joint conference of representatives of the Nazi Party and government ministers that Hitler was considering Madagascar for the internment of German Jewry, and was on the way of putting forward a foreign policy initiative with that idea in mind:

> Hitler would now finally make a foreign policy thrust, beginning with the powers who had raised the Jewish question, in order really to arrive at a solution to the Madagascar question. This is what he explained to me on November 9. It doesn't work otherwise. He also wants to tell the other states: Why do you constantly talk about the Jews? Take them![58]

## Territorial Reservations for the Jews

To cover up the fiasco of the Evian conference the gathering ended with setting up an Intergovernmental Committee on Political Refugees (IGC) in London to search for a territory somewhere on the planet for the resettlement of Jews. George Rublee (1868-1957), a friend of President Roosevelt, was named chairman of the IGC. While the IGC actually did little or nothing for the refugees, it served well the U.S. State Department and the British Foreign Office to juggle illusionary plans of Jewish resettlement before world opinion. These plans that

were never meant to materialize, were located in far away undeveloped territories such as Kenya, Northern Rhodesia, Alaska, Angola, Mindanao, British
Guiana, Madagascar, and Ethiopia. A cruel game of deception was played on the
backs of a people threatened with extinction. The history of the IGC and the trail
of paper proposals it left behind is one of the saddest chapters of the Holocaust.

The Nazis joined the international charade of territorial reservations for the
Jews as an excellent means of diversion from their real intentions. They issued a
memorandum in favor of an international solution to the Jewish problem that
would eliminate the "danger" the Jews posed to the "national character" of the
nations by isolating them in large territorial ghettos or reservations:

> The aim of this German policy is a future international solution of the Jewish
> question, dictated not by false pity for "a Jewish religious minority that has
> been driven out" but by the mature realization by all nations of the nature of the
> danger that Jewry spells for the national character of the nations. [59]

Alfred Rosenberg reacted to the Evian Conference with an article in the
*Volkischer Beobachter* on July 8, 1938, under the title "Wohin mit den Juden?"
Referring to a French plan to resettle 10,000 of the German Jewish refugees in
France to Madagascar, Rosenberg challenged France to make available the isl-
and for the transfer of all the Jews of Europe and expressed satisfaction that the
"resettlement" of the Jews to far away isolated reservations in the African colonies dovetailed with the idea of clearing the German Lebensraum in Europe.[60]

The Madagascar plan was not new. It was born in Germany in 1866 when
the notorious German anti-Semite Paul de Lagarde proposed in his *Deutsche
Schrifften* to get rid of the Jews by sending them off to the remote island of Ma-
dagscar. The Madagascar idea was resuscitated in 1927 by the Polish anti-
Semitic government and dressed up as a "solution" to the Jewish problem in
1936. A fact-finding committee of four members under the chairmanship of
Captain Mieczyslaw Lepecki was established in 1937 by the Polish government
to study its feasibility. They obtained permission from the French colonial minister to visit the colony. Given the harrowing situation faced by the Jews in
Poland, the idea initially even awakened interest in some Jewish circles and led
to the participation of two Jewish activists, Leon Alter of the Jewish Emigrant
Association (JEAS) and Shlomo Dick, an agricultural engineer from Tel Aviv. [61]

The arrival of the delegation to Madagascar in 1937 sparked a local riot.
The Jewish members withdrew from the committee when they came to the conclusion that no more than a few hundred Jewish families could at best be settled
there. Captain Lepecki was more optimistic and reached a figure of between
40,000 to 60,000 Jews. The minimal absorption capacity of the island at the
time, its backward condition, the strong opposition that a mass movement of
population was bound to arise in the existing population of 4 million people, and
last but not least, the refusal of the Jews themselves to be exiled, convinced its
Jewish members that the plan was nothing but a diversion. The Nazi press made
its own mocking comments at the time on the Polish proposal:

Madagascar could become a promised land for the Jews Poland wants to get rid of, only if they could lead a life of masters there, without effort of their own, and at the expense of others. It is therefore questionable whether the invitation for an exodus of the Children of Israel to Madagascar will soon free Poland of any great part of these parasites. [62]

On September 20, 1938, Hitler met with Polish Ambassador Joszef Lipski in Obersalzberg to invite the Poles to participate in the attack on Czechoslovakia and share in the spoils. On the occasion Hitler made reference to his interest in creating reservations for Jews in the overseas colonies of Western powers to clear not only the Third Reich from Jews but also Poland, Hungary, and Romania. The ambassador transcribed verbatim his conversation with Hitler to Polish Foreign Minister Joseph Beck:

Hitler told me he had in mind an idea for settling the Jewish problem by way of emigration to the colonies with an understanding with Poland, Hungary, and possibly also Romania. [63]

Lipski was so impressed with Hitler's proposal of helping Poland get rid of its Jewish population by sending them off to colonial reservations that he responded enthusiastically to Hitler, as described in the ambassador's own words in a memo to his superior:

I told him that if he finds such a solution, we will erect him a beautiful monument in Warsaw. [64]

In October 1938 Hitler personally raised the question of using Madagascar for the resettlement of German Jews with the French ambassador, Andre Francois-Poncet, as noted by historian Philipp Friedman. [65] On December 8, 1938, French Foreign Minister Georges Bonnet met with his German counterpart von Ribbentrop. When Bonnet complained that the stream of refugees from Germany burdened the French economy, Ribbentrop responded that for Germany ridding itself of its Jews was a question of national survival and added that "the difficulty of the Jewish problem lay in the fact that no country wished to receive them." Bonnet mentioned at the meeting that France intended to resettle 10,000 German-Jewish refugees from Germany to Madagascar and suggested that allowing the Jews to leave from Third Reich with more of their capital might facilitate their resettlement. Ribbentrop responded in typical Nazi fashion:

All Jewish property should be considered stolen since all Jews were criminals and they should leave Germany as they entered — penniless. [66]

On December 14, 1938, Hjalmar Schacht (1877-1970), director of the Reich's bank, appeared in London at a meeting of the IGC with a giant extortion scheme intended to shore up the deteriorating foreign balance situation of Germany that was jeopardizing its rearmament program. He proposed a plan to re-

settle 400,000 Jews in a territorial destination to be provided by Western colonial powers. A Jewish corporation would release a thirty-year-bond issue to raise
the necessary means. The German government would provide collateral after
impounding one-quarter of the wealth of German Jewry, already greatly diminished by Nazi plunder, but still the equivalent of 1.5 billion reichsmark. The
bond debt raised by international Jewry would only be serviced when and if the
foreign exchange balance of the Reich would show a surplus, thus holding world
Jewry hostage to the state of the German economy. On January 20, 1939,
Schacht resigned as director of the Reich's bank. On February 11, 1939, the
German Foreign Office sent out a circular to its embassies announcing that
Germany was searching for resettlement areas for the Jews on its own:

> Germany would take the search of resettlement areas into its own hands be-
> cause it has a major interest in seeing that Jews continue to be dispersed. [67]

The Nazis were widening the horizons of their anti-Jewish policy in 1939.
It was not only a matter of clearing the Jews from the Third Reich but also of
making all of Europe Judenfrei. Rosenberg raised the issue of a Jewish reservation in the *Volkischer Beobachter* on January 16, and again on February 8, 1939
after holding a news conference on February 7. The reservation he had in mind
had to allow the concentration of the 15 million of Jews from all over the world.
The Western powers would have to provide a territory with no Europeans living
there, such as Madagascar or Guiana. Germany would administer the reservation, which meant, as pointed out by Jonny Moser, that Jews would be removed
from Germany but not from German control and would remain hostages in
German hands. The territory would be "placed under an administration well-
versed in the use of police control." By its very nature the reservation would be
excluded from the present or future possibility of developing into a state.

Eichmann was instructed by his superiors to look into a "foreign policy solution" such as the Madagascar project. A plan was drawn up that proposed the
establishment of a Judenreservat for 4 million Jews offshore the African continent in the French colony of Madagascar under German administration. German
naval bases would be established under the command of a German police governor directly responsible to Himmler.

Considering that 4 million people were to be sent to a place that could only
absorb a few thousand people led German historian Peter Longerich to draw the
conclusion that the reservation was not meant to be different in any significant
way from the ghettos and concentration camps that the Nazis created a little later
in Europe as provisional gathering places to starve the Jews before their slaughter.

> The territorial solution was ultimately intended to lead to the death of the vast
> majority of Jews . . . What happened from 1941 onwards was the accomplish-
> ment of the annihilation that had been envisaged as early as 1939. However, it
> had been made dependent on certain conditions, and was seen as a long-term
> process. What had begun as general, long-term considerations about ensuring

that the Jews die out within the area under German rule was developed into a comprehensive program of mass murder that, in the opinion of the planners, should in essence be completed before the end of the war . . . The mere fact that Madagascar lacked the basic conditions necessary for the existence of four million European Jews makes it clear that the plan itself was a threat to the further existence of Jews in the area of German dominance.[68]

A far-away location totally out of sight such as Madagascar was ideally suited to disguise and hide the machinery of death to exterminate the Jews. After starvation and disease would do their part, Himmler's killers would do the rest. Phillip Bouhler (1899-1945), the head of the German euthanasia program in Hitler's chancellery, was to become the governor of the island. The designation of this master killer is one more indication that the Nazis intended to use Madagascar as a well-guarded slaughterhouse to annihilate Jewry. In a memorandum to the Führer from Himmler dated May 25, 1940, he clearly spells out the objective of the plan as a sure way to extinguish the "concept of Jew":

> I hope to see that by means of the possibility of a large emigration of all Jews to Africa or to some other colony that the concept of Jew will be fully extinguished.[69]

The Nazis planned to teach the new generations in a Nazi-dominated world that there once was a Jewish race that mysteriously vanished from Europe for unknown reasons. A special museum in Prague was being organized where the highly cultured Aryans and their children could come to learn after the war about the vanished Jewish race.

## Adrift on the Seven Seas

On May 17, 1939, the British Colonial Office under Sir Malcolm MacDonald dealt a terrible blow to the hopes of rescuing part of European Jewry from doom, when it issued a new British White Paper on Palestine to win over the Arabs to their side in case of war. The new British White Paper legitimized the Arab opposition to Jewish immigration and reduced the immigration quota to minimal numbers:

> The fear of indefinite Jewish immigration is widespread among the Arab population and this fear has made possible disturbances.[70]

The MacDonald White Paper recommended a final yearly quota of 10,000 immigrant visas and 5,000 refugee emergency permits for the next five years beginning April 1939, with no subsequent immigration without Arab approval. When Britain entered the war on September 1, 1939, MacDonald announced that Jewish refugees from the Third Reich were considered enemy aliens ineligible for a visa to Palestine or anywhere in the British Empire.

Small numbers of Jews had been reaching the shores of Palestine illegally, circumventing the British blockade, since 1934. The first ship with illegal immigrants, the *Vellos*, broke through the British blockade and arrived on February 10, 1934, with 350 people.[71] The movement of illegal Jewish immigration to Palestine in old and worn ships moving through the Danube and the Black Sea increased against all odds. Despite the enormous difficulties involved, illegal ships kept coming until the establishment of the State of Israel in 1948, although some were sunk and never made it to the land of their dreams.

A Children's Rescue Bill was introduced in the U.S. Congress on February 9, 1939, by New York Senator Robert Wagner and Massachusetts Representative Edith Nourse Rogers to admit by special action 20,000 refugee children in two years. To counter the bill, North Carolina Senator Robert Reynolds introduced a bill to abolish all immigration for the next ten years. When called to intervene in favor of the Children's Rescue Bill, President Roosevelt refused to become involved. With his own handwriting he noted on the request "file-no action," knowing well that he was signing the death sentence of the Children's Rescue bill. The Wagner-Rogers bill never left the Committee and 20,000 children were denied an opportunity to save their lives. The demise of the Wagner-Rogers bill dealt a terrible blow to the rescue efforts of Jewish organizations.[72]

On January 24, 1939, Heydrich was charged with the reorganization of the emigration apparatus in Germany, and instructed to solve the Jewish problem by "emigration or evacuation."[73] Heydrich ordered, in March 1939, a frightened group of German Jewish leaders in Berlin to carry a message to the IGC in London that dire consequences would follow for German Jews if the commission failed to come up with evacuation sites. When the heartbroken group returned empty-handed, Heydrich kept his word and ordered the Gestapo to begin a new series of roundups of Jews. Jews were hunted in the streets and pushed over the borders and dumped at the Polish borders as in the past.

Heydrich allowed the sailings of boats with Jewish refugees from German ports to the American continent and the Far East to prove that nobody wanted them. The sale of landing permits and visas to Latin American countries flourished protected by the Gestapo. Their prices fluctuated between $500 and $600 per capita. The first ship to sale to the ocean with hapless Jews was the *St. Louis* followed by the *SS Ordina*, the *SS Quanza*, and the *SS Flanders*.[74] At least other thirteen ships followed with their cargo of Jewish refugees such as the *Struma*, the *Caribia*, the *Salvador*, the *Konigstein*, the *Colorado*, the *Navemar*, the *Hilda*, the *Atrato*, the *Libertad*, the *Monte Rosa*, the *Pentcho*, and the *Donau the Bredveit*, without finding a port to unload their human cargo.[75] In addition many refugees who boarded the regular transatlantic ships were denied landing. Some of the voyages ended in tragedy, as in the case of the *Struma* that was sunk in Turkish waters; the others returned to Europe to their doom.

The *St. Louis* sailed from Hamburg on May 13, 1939, carrying 936 German Jewish refugees with landing permits to Havana for which each paid the legal fee of $150. The visas were signed by the Cuban director general of immigration, Manuel Benitez Gonzalez, a protégé of Fulgencio Batista. The news of the coming ship was used by the Cuban ex-president Ramon Grau San Martin (1887-1969) to instigate a massive anti-Semitic rally in which the speakers incited the people to fight the Jews until the last one was driven out from Cuba. The Cuban Jewish community at the time had hardly reached the number of 4,000 souls. A week before the arrival of the ship, the Cuban government invalidated the permits. When the ship arrived in Havana on May 27, 1939, President Federico Laredo Brun (1875-1950) refused to honor the visas and did not allow them to disembark. The negotiations between the representative of the Joint Distribution Committee (JDC) and the government fell through when the JDC was slow in meeting the bribery demands of the Cubans.[76] On June 2, 1939, Laredo Brun ordered the ship to leave Havana harbor.

The ship sailed to Miami where it arrived on June 3, 1939. U.S. authorities denied them asylum, including to those refugees in possession of valid quota numbers for future entrance to the United States. The ship returned to Europe. The JDC found asylum for them in England, the Netherlands, and France, but very soon the Germans caught up with them. Many of them found their end in death camps. The tragic story repeated itself when regular transatlantic ships reached their South American disembarkation points. The SS Conte Grand and the SS General San Martin docked in Buenos Aires on February 25, 1939, with sixty-eight and twenty-seven respectively Jews among their passengers. With the sole exception of two, all the rest were sent back to Europe. It is known that more than 200 Jews that arrived in twenty-three regular ships to Argentina during 1939 were denied entrance.[77]

The ordeal of these ships, like the Zbaszyn outrage, epitomizes the tragedy of the Jewish refugees driven out of their homes to sail the seven seas to face callous rejection. The judgment expressed by U.S. Senator Clairborne Pell, in his introduction to William Perl's The Holocaust Conspiracy, is far from being a hollow claim:

> In my view, just about every Jew who was killed could have been saved if the governments of the Allied powers had provided timely refuge to European Jews who lived in countries coming under the control of Hitler's forces. Increasingly their failure to do so is being recognized as a "conspiracy of silence." [78]

## The Dismemberment of Czechoslovakia

After the Anschluss of Austria, Hitler lost no time in going after his next prey in his campaign to undo the alleged injustices of the Versailles Treaty. Czechoslovakia was marked as his next prey not only because it stood in the way of Hitler's territorial Lebensraum ambitions, but also it was a model of democracy and freedom that stood out in a continent dominated by Fascist dictatorships. The liberal parliamentary democracy founded by Tomas Masaryk was a successful social experiment of a multiethnic society in a region divided by fierce nationalism. It was the embodiment of Masaryk's lofty vision of an open society where minority rights and institutions were guaranteed in its constitution. Karl Popper looked back with admiration to Masaryk's founding vision of an open society in a lecture he gave in Prague in 1994:

> He was one of the most important pioneers of what I have called one or two years after Masaryk's death, the Open Society. He was a pioneer of an open society, both in theory and in practice; indeed, the greatest of its pioneers between Abraham Lincoln and Winston Churchill.
>
> Czechoslovakia was a financial, an industrial, a political, an educational, and a cultural success; and it was well defended. Never was a new state—after all, the result of a revolution—so peaceful and so successful, and so much the creative achievement of one man. And all this was not due to the absence of great difficulties; it was the result of Masaryk's philosophy, his wisdom, and his personality in which personal courage, and truthfulness, and openness, played so conspicuous a role. He described his own philosophy as a critical realism. This is indeed what it was. But humanism, or humanitarianism, also played a dominant role. [79]

The Czechoslovak Republic of 14.5 million people was a mosaic of ethnic groups: Czechs, Germans, Slovaks, Ukrainians, Magyars, Poles, and Jews. The 7 million Czechs were the dominating majority ethnic group, followed by 3 million Germans and 2 million Slovaks. The Jews were the smallest minority, with around 350,000 people. Czech and Slovak were recognized as the official languages of the country, while the other minority languages and their cultures were allowed full freedom. Germans and Slovaks were overwhelmingly Catholics while the Czechs were Hussite Christians. The educational and cultural institutions of the minorities were preserved and provided with monetary support by the state in proportion to their respective populations.

Hitler's eyes were set on the Sudetenland, a part of Chechoslovakia on the border with Germany that had been awarded to Czechoslovakia by the Versailles Treaty in 1919. With its impregnable installations and strategic situation the Sudetenland was the most crucial element in the military defense of Czechoslovakia. Under the mantle of protector of the Sudeten Germans, Hitler demanded what he called self-determination for the Sudetenland. Hitler claimed that the ethnic Germans in Czechoslovakia were being oppressed by the Czechs. Goebbel's propaganda took good care to spread stories of atrocities allegedly committed by the Czech government against ethnic Germans while it accused falsely democratic Czechoslovakia of being a nest of Bolshevism and a base for Soviet military forces.

As he had done elsewhere, Hitler used his Fifth Column to undermine the Czechoslovak Republic. As in Austria, he relied on local Nazis and Nazikatholicn to fan the flames of ethnic strife and hatred. Financial support flowed from Berlin to them. Among the German-speaking minority he had the help of Konrad Henlein (1898-1945)—the Seyss-Inquart of Czechoslovakia—and his *Sudetendeutsche Partei*. Among the Slovak minority he relied on the support of Fr. Andrej Hlinka (1864-1938) and his Hlinka Slovak People Party (HSLS). These two separatist groups, which originally demanded national autonomy, soon became under the direct influence and support of Hitler virulent champions of complete secession and independence.

Ninety percent of the Sudeten Germans were Catholic. Their leader Konrad Henlein, a Nazikatholic, maintained secret contacts with the Hitler government. Founder of the Sudeten German Homefront in 1934 and the Sudetendeutsche Partei SDP in 1935, he originally did not go beyond demanding Sudeten autonomy, but by 1937, most of the leaders of his party were already openly supporting Hitler's Pan-German claims of annexation of the Sudeten to the Third Reich. Henlein's storm troops, the *Freiwilliger Selbtschutz*, were patterned after the Nazi SS. They organized terrorist acts, military espionage, abductions of opponents, and infiltration of organizations and businesses. The Henlein press scared its readers with the Bolshevik threat, spread anti-Semitic propaganda and organized a boycott against Jewish lawyers, doctors, and businesses.

In Catholic Slovakia, Hitler found allies among the Slovak clero-Fascist separatists and their leader, a Catholic priest Fr. Andrej Hlinka (1864-1938), founder of the Hlinka Slovak People Party. The Vatican was an important player in the Chechoslovak political game. It supported Hlinka and his clerical Slovak separatist movement. When the nuncio published a letter in 1934 in favor of the claims of Slovak separatists, he was expelled from the country. From that moment on, the Vatican began to work for the disintegration of the Czechoslovak Republic, in parallel to the Nazis.

After Hlinka's death in 1938, his deputy Fr. Josef Tiso (1887-1947), the parish priest of Banovce, became the leader of the party. On direct instructions of Hlinka, Tiso had established close cooperation with Henlein. The party's Hlinka Guard and Hlinka Youth were a copy of the Nazi SS and Hitlerjugend. Under such slogans as, "First to go are the Czech bosses, to be followed by Jews and Protestants," they organized pogroms, and plundered Jewish property long before the war. Karol Sidor, one of the top leaders of the Hlinka Party, later Slovakia's ambassador to the Vatican, called in the Czechoslovakian parliament for the expulsion of Jews from Slovakia and Carpatho-Russia to Soviet Birobidjan.[80] Under Hitler's directives, the Hlinkas turned their autonomy claims into a demand for secession and complete independence of Slovakia.

On March 28, 1938, Hitler met with Konrad Henlein and instructed him to bring the internal political situation to a crisis by raising impossible political demands on the Czechoslovak government. On May 30, 1938, Hitler ordered his generals to prepare the armed forces for the invasion of Czechoslovakia. To prevent Czechoslovakia's neighbors in Central Europe providing support to Chechoslovakia, Hitler offered them a share of the spoils. To Hungary he offered the northeastern territorial region of Czechoslovakia; to Poland the Teschen province (Cieszyn). In a meeting with Polish Ambassador Joszef Lipski in Obersalzberg on September 20, 1938, Hitler invited the Poles to join in the attack of Czechoslovakia and seize from them Teschen. To lull the Western powers into inaction, Mussolini stated in an open letter to Lord Runciman that from his private conversations with the Führer he was convinced that he only wanted to reunite the German fringe of Czechoslovakia, without any further territorial demands.

In his meeting with the Führer on September 15, 1938, Henlein expressed the concerns of the Sudeten Catholics that annexation to Germany would bring about the Nazi suppression of Catholic organizations as it had happened in Germany and was already occurring in Austria. Hitler gave solemn promises that he would fully respect all the rights and privileges of the Catholic Church in the Sudetenland after the annexation. The Henlein thugs were ordered in September 1938 to raise the level of violence to new heights, attacking Czech and Jewish targets.

On September 26, 1938, Hitler issued an ultimatum threatening to go to war by October 1, if the Sudetenland was not handed over to Germany pacifically. Unwilling to risk war or take any military action to stop Hitler, Neville Chamberlain (1869-1940), the prime minister of Great Britain, and Édouard Daladier (1884-1970) of France, anxious to appease Hitler, rushed to a conference in Munich with Hitler and Mussolini on September 29. Czechoslovakia itself was excluded from that conclave. Britain and France betrayed Czechoslovakia and signed that day an accord with Hitler, ceding the Sudeten, around 38 percent of the territory of Bohemia and Moravia, to the Third Reich. Chamberlain flew home waving the worthless sheet of paper of the Munich Accord, claiming he had saved world peace. As it turned out, the agreement paved the way to the final dismemberment of the unfortunate nation and led to World War II. In the House of Commons Winston Churchill pronounced with unsurpassed eloquence his prophetic words:

> England has been offered a choice between war and shame. She has chosen shame and will get war.[81]

German troops took over the Sudeten without a single shot on October 1, 1938. Eduard Benes (1884-1948), the prime minister of Czechoslovakia, resigned on October 5, leaving behind Emil Hácha (1872-1945) to write the final chapter of the liquidation of the Republic. Almost all the 20,000 Jews living in the Sudetenland fled in fear to the still free parts of Bohemia and Moravia. On Hitler's invitation, Hungary seized 12,000 square kilometers in the Danube Valley with a population of 1 million people. Poland took over 650 square miles in Cieszyn on October 2, with 240,000 people. In the words of William L. Shirer:

> The Poles and the Hungarians, after threatening military action against the helpless nation, now swept down, like vultures, to get a slice of Czechoslovak territory. Poland at the insistence of Foreign Minister Józef Beck, took some 650 square miles of territory around Teschen, comprising a population of 228,000 inhabitants, of whom 133,000 were Czechs.[82]

Following Hitler's dictat, Slovak clerical leaders gathered at Zilina on October 6, and declared Slovakia an autonomous state within Czechoslovakia, with Tiso as prime minister. The Russian-Ukranian separatists under the leadership of

Avhustyn Voloshyn also established an autonomous state in Subcarpathian Ruthenia on October 8, 1938 which they renamed Carpatho Ukraine. Its existence,
however, was very short when Hungary seized Carpatho Ukraine with Hitler's
permission.

The German bishops were overjoyed with the annexation of the Sudetenland to the Third Reich. The Third Reich, which in 1937 had a population of 65
million, now grew to 78 million people in its expanded Grossdeutchland. Not
only were they overjoyed with the expansion of the German Lebensraum, but no
less with the increase of the proportion of Catholics in the Reich by 10 percent
as a result of the annexation. In a special pastoral letter, Cardinal Bertram expressed his joy over the annexation and welcomed the Sudeten Germans to their
return to the *Heimat*. He called upon the Sudeten population to render "willing
obedience and respect to the new authorities." The Fulda Conference of Bishops
acted on the proposal of Cardinal Faulhaber to congratulate the Führer. Hitler
was informed that the bells would be tolled in all the Churches of the Third
Reich as a sign of celebration:

> The great deed of safeguarding international peace moves the German episco-
> pate, acting in the name of the Catholics of all the German dioceses, respectful-
> ly to tender congratulations and thanks and to order a festive peal of bells on
> Sunday. In the name of the Cardinals of Germany: Archbishop Cardinal Ber-
> tram.[83]

Special Thanksgiving services were held the following Sunday in all the
churches over Germany while the Church bells were tolled in jubilation. The
Munich diocesan Sunday newspaper reminded the faithful to remember in gratitude their Führer who had made possible the achievement:

> We did not forget to thank the man who has preserved the peace for us and yet
> at the same time has achieved the freedom of our German brothers in Bohemia.
> Together with the German Cardinals the entire Catholic community in the
> Greater German Reich thanks the Führer for the act of peace.[84]

In his New Year's Eve sermon of 1939, Cardinal Faulhaber of Munich
found great reassurance in the fact that the destiny of Germany was in the "secure hands of a leader who did not smoke nor drink":

> That is one advantage of our time; in the highest office of the Reich we have
> the example of a simple and modest alcohol—and nicotine—free way of life.[85]

After World War II, the West German Federal Republic remembered and
honored Cardinal Faulhaber with its highest award, the Grand Cross of the Order of Merit.

On March 14, 1939, Slovakia separated completely from Czechoslovakia,
declaring itself an independent state under German protection. Catholicism was
declared the official religion of the country. Slovakia became what was probably

at the time the most clerically oriented state in the world. It chose a Catholic priest, Josef Tiso (1887-1947), as its first president. He was joined by other Catholic priests and pro-clerical laymen in the government such as Prime Minister Vojtech Tuka who prided himself of attending daily mass and of periodically going to confession. When Tiso became Slovakia's first president on October 26, 1939, Pope Pius XII sent him his blessings to his appointment and addressed him as "My dear son." Tiso solemnly pledged to turn Slovakia into a "model Catholic State."

Although it was contrary to Vatican policy to recognize territorial changes during a war, the Vatican granted Slovakia immediate de jure recognition in a gesture of appreciation for its Catholic loyalty, and appointed Msgr. Giussepe Burzio as the Vatican's charge d'affaires in Bratislava. In stark contrast, the Vatican denied diplomatic recognition to the Czechoslovak government in exile that Edward Benes established in London in 1940.[86]

Around five months after taking the reins of what was left of Czecoslovakia, President Emil Hácha was summoned to Berlin on March 15, 1939. He was offered the choice of signing away his country or facing 700 Nazi bombers over Prague within four hours. Without the impregnable defenses of the Sudetenland, the country was indefensible. President Hacha signed. Bohemia and Moravia were easily occupied by the Wehrmacht. Czechoslovakia's most valuable armament industry was now in Hitler's hands to support his future military adventures.

Next day Hitler marched into Prague. The Czech Republic ceased to exist. From Hradcany Castle, the ancient seat of government, Hitler declared Bohemia and Moravia a German protectorate and appointed Konstantin von Neurath (1873-1956) as protector. After Hitler's entrance to Prague, Western powers petitioned Pius XII to protest the invasion. Pius XII firmly rejected the request. German Ambassador von Bergen's report to Berlin on March 22, 1939 describes his response:

> The Pope has declined these requests very firmly. He has given those around him to understand that he sees no reason to interfere in historic processes in which from the political point of view, the Church is not interested. [87]

The German bishops supported Hitler's foreign policy and celebrated his international successes. They committed themselves without reservations to his ideal of a Grossdeutschland and the expansion of the German Lebensraum. The main Catholic official publication in Germany, the *Klerusblatt*, exulted on April 12, 1939:

> The frontiers imposed upon us by the "hate-peace" of Versailles are broken; the Lebensraum of the German people has been widened. Multitudes of unemployed again have work. God's holy providence has provided that in a decisive hour, Hitler is entrusted with the leadership of the German people.[88]

The ominous shadow of Nazi domination fell upon the Jewish community of Czechoslovakia, one of the oldest in Europe. The 120,000 Jews in the Protectorate of Bohemia and Moravia and the 56,000 Jewish refugees from Nazi Germany and Austria that President Masaryk had accepted were now once more in German clutches. Even the 15,000 apostates in the protectorate that had converted to Christianity were now in mortal danger. To make the newly acquired addition to the German Lebensraum Judenfrei, protector Von Neurath approved on June 21, 1939, a long list of anti-Semitic decrees that replicated the anti-Semitic legislation in force in Germany. The legislation wiped out the economic base of Jewish existence and made possible the confiscation of Jewish property and eventually the deportation of the Jews.

Aryanization of Jewish property began in the summer of 1939. On July 26, Eichmann set up an office for Jewish emigration in Prague as he had done in Vienna. The first deportations of Czech Jews from the protectorate to occupied Poland began in October 1939. By October 1942, 78,150 Jews of Bohemia and Moravia had been deported to the death camps of Sobibor, Belzec, and Auschwitz. Only 13,000 Jews survived the Holocaust in former Czechoslovakia, 8,000 of them in Theresienstadt.[89]

# Notes

1. Michael Phayer, *The Catholic Church and the Holocaust, 1930–1965* (Indiana University Press, 2000), 10. Karl Thieme.
2. See chapter 1 for the full text of his declaration.
3. Bishop Alois Hudal, *Die Grundlagen des Nationalsozialismus: Eine ideengeschichtliche Untersuchung von katholischer Warte* (Leipzig, 1936), 13, 88.
4. In the first elections to the Austrian Constitutional Assembly in February 16, 1919, the Social Democrats came out first with forty-one percent of the votes, followed by the Catholics (Christian Socials) with 36 percent of the votes and the Pan–Germans with 13 percent of the votes.
5. Seyss–Inquart presented at Nuremberg a copy of the minutes of the founding meeting.
6. *Nazi Conspiracy and Aggression. Vol. USGPD* (Washington DC, 1946). Seyss–Inquart Nuremberg Charges, Part 1, 956–1004 (3400–PS).
7. *Nazi Conspiracy and Aggression. Vol. USGPD* (3425–PS). The Catholic Trade Unions and the Freeheitsbund were working for the Anschluss.
8. *Nazi Conspiracy and Aggression, Vol. USGPD*, Seyss–Inquart Nuremberg Charges, Part 1, 956–1004. (3271–PS).
9. Nazi Conspiracy and Aggression. *Vol. II. USGPD*, 956–1004. Nuremberg Charges.
10. *Nazi Conspiracy and Aggression. Vol. USGPD.*
11. *"The Avalon Project." Nuremberg Trial Proceedings Volume II*, 7th day.
12. *"The Avalon Project." Nazi Conspiracy and Aggression Volume IV* Document No. 1760-PS.

13. William L Shirer, *20th Century Journey: A Memoir of a Life and the Times, Volume II, The Nightmare Years* (New York: Little, Brown & Company, 1984). *"The Avalon Project."*

14. *"The Avalon Project."* (TC–22).

15. *"The Avalon Project."* (2995–PS).

16. Shirer, *20th Century Journey.*

17. Evan Burr Bukey, *Hitler's Austria: Popular Sentiment in the Nazi Era, 1938-1945* (Chapel Hill, NC: The University of North Carolina Press, 2001).

18. Bukey, *Hitler's Austria,* 97.

19. Baldur van Schirach, *Nurenberg Trial Proceedings Vol. 16: Ich Glaubte in Hitler.*

20. *Agenzia Romana Informazione* (F.O. 371/46674), Anthony Rhodes, *The Vatican in the Age of Dictators 1922-1945* (London, UK: Hodder and Stoughton, 1973), 151.

21. Georges Passelecq and Bernard Suchecky, *The Hidden Encyclical of Pius XI* (Orlando, FL: Harcourt Press, 1997), 50.

22. Güenther Lewy, *The Catholic Church and Nazi Germany* (New York: McGraw Hill Book Co., 1964), 212-216. Bukey, *Hitler's Austria,* 35-36.

23. Evan Burr Bukey: *Hitler's Austria,* 98.

24. Joseph P. Kennedy Collection at the John F. Kennedy Library.

25. *Nuremberg Trial Proceedings, Vol. 4. "The Avalon Project."*

26. Through the *Hilfstelle der Caritas fur nichtarische Christen* to leave Austria and acted in their behalf to thwart the Nazi attempt to void the marriages between Non–Aryan Christians and Christians in 1942.

27. The eminent Hasidic Rabbis of Sadigura and Kopischnitz were among them. The Rebbi of Sadigura would later sweep the sidewalk of his Bet Hamidrash in Tel Aviv before day–break in a symbolic act of humility and gratitude to G–d.

28. George E. Berkley, *Vienna and Its Jews: The Tragedy of Success, 1880S-1980s* (Lanham, MD: Madison Books, 1988), 259. Herbert Rosenkranz. Verfolgung and Selbstbehauptung, 22-23. Daniel J. Goldhagen, *Hitler's Willing Executioners* (New York: Alfred A. Knopf, 1996), 286-287.

29. Donald M. McKale, *Hitler's Shadow War: The Holocaust and World War II* (Lanham, MD: Taylor Trade Publishing, 2006), 102.

30. Lewy, *The Catholic Church*, 213.

31. Decree on the Declaration of Jewish Assets

32 . William Stevenson, *A Man Called Intrepid* (Orlando, FL: Harcourt Press, 1976).

33. Akten zur deutschen auswaertigen Politik 1918–1945, series D (1937–1945), Vol. V, Baden–Baden, 1953, pp. 780–785.

34. *Encyclopedia of the Holocaust* (New York: Macmillan Publishing Company, 1990).

35. *Encyclopedia of the Holocaust.*

36. Bukey, *Hitler's Austria,* 110.

37. Bukey, *Hitler's Austria,* 106.

38. Alicia Gojman de Bacal, *Comunidad Ashkenazi de Mexico Vol. 7.* (Mexico: 1993).

39. Jeffrey Lesser, *Welcoming the Undesirables: Brazil and the Jewish Question* (University of California Press, 1994).

40. Uki Goni, *The Real Odessa: How Peron Brought the Nazi War Criminals to Argentina* (London, UK: Granta Books, 2003).

41. Akten zur deutschen auswaertigen Politik 1918–1945, series D (1937–1945), Vol. V, Baden–Baden, 1953, pp. 780–785.

42. Bella Fromm, *Blood and Banquets: A Berlin Social Diary* (New York: Kensington Publishing Corp, 2002), 255.

43. Akten zur deutschen auswaertigen Politik 1918–1945, series D (1937–1945), Vol. V, Baden–Baden, 1953, pp. 780–785.

44. Dr. Heinrich Rothmund, Chief of the Swiss Federal Police, was the originator of the idea.

45. Hannah Arendt, *Eichmann in Jerusalem: A Report on the Banality of Evil* (New York: Viking Press, 1963), 66.

46. National Archives 840.48, Division of European Affairs, Memo on Refugee Problems, attached to Division of American Republics, November 18, 1938. William Perl. *The Holocaust Conspiracy*. (New York: Shapolsky Publishers, 1989), 122, 43. Perl was one of the US prosecutors at the War Crimes trial in Dachau.

47. Robert Michael, *A Concise History of American Anti-Semitism* (Lanham, MD: Rowman & Litlefield Publishers, 2005), 185. "Between the attack on Pearl Harbor and the end of World War II (1941–1945) when millions of Jews were being sent to their death, the US only admitted a total of 21,000 refugees most of them Jews, the equivalent of less than one tenth of the US quota available for all the Axis–controlled countries."

48. Henry L. Feingold, *The Politics of Rescue: The Roosevelt Administration and the Holocaust, 1938-1945* (Newark, NJ: Rutgers University Press, 1970), 27.

49. D. Wyman (*Abandonment of the Jews*, 313). FDR's vision of Jewish issues was prejudiced and without a factual base. At the Casablanca Conference he referred to the "*understandable* complaints which the Germans bore towards the Jews, who although only 2 percent approximately of the population, represented over fifty percent of the lawyers, doctors, school teachers, college professors etc." Actually, they only held 2.3 percent of the professional positions as a whole: 0.5 percent of the teacher positions and 2.3 percent of the professorships. In the liberal medical and legal professions Jews represented 10.9 percent and 16.3 percent.

50. Feingold, The Politics of Rescue (Foreign Relations of the US papers FRUS, I), 778–780, August 30, 1938; 835–836, Nov. 19, 1938.

51. Martin Gilbert, *The Holocaust* (New York: Henry Holt and Company, 1987).

52. J. W. Pickersgill and D. F. Forster, *The Mackenzie King Record* (Toronto ON: University of Toronto Press, 1960).

53. Gilbert, *The Holocaust*. Feingold, *The Politics of Rescue,* 32.

54. Although Sto. Domingo offered 100,000 visas, it actually only granted 5,000.

55. John Mendelssohn, Ed. *The Holocaust. Vol V.* (New York: Garland Publishers, 1982), 260.

56. Gitta Sereny, *Into that Darkness* (New York: McGraw Hill Book Co., 1974), 318.

57. Lewy, *The Catholic Church,* 284. Saul Friedlander, *Nazi Germany and the Jews, Vol.1.* (New York: Harper Collins Publishers, 1997).

58. Hitler's Role in the Persecution of the Jews by the Nazi Regime: Electronic Version, by Heinz Peter Longerich.

59. Volkischer Beobachter. Article Wohin mit den Juden? July 8, 1938. Shirer, 20th Century Journey 588. Philip Friedman, *The Lublin Reservation and the Madagascar*

*Plan: Two Aspects of Nazi Jewish Policy during the Second World War* [Appeared in "YIVO Annual of Social Science" and in his "Roads to Extinction" (1980).] , 13 (1955), 167.

60. Friedman, *The Lublin Reservation and the Madagascar Plan*, 167. Shirer, *20th Century Journey,* 588.

61. Bela Vago and George L. Moose, eds. Jews *and Non–Jews in Eastern Europe*, Leni Yahil, *The Holocaust The Fate of European Jewry* (Oxford University Press, 1969). Francis Nicosia, *The Third Reich and the Palestine Question* (Edison, NJ: Transaction Publishers, 1984), 165. Yiddishe Enziklopedie, Yidn D, 242.

62. Westdeutscher Beobachter, 12/9/37. Friedlander, *Nazi Germany and the Jews.* 97.

63. Lipski.Columbia University. Doc. 99.

64. Lipski.Columbia University. Doc. 99.

65. Friedman, *The Lublin Reservation and the Madagascar Plan,* 167.

66. Feingold, *The Politics of Rescue.* Holocaust Library NY, 1970, 47.

67. Leni Yahil, *Madagascar: Phantom of a Solution for the Jewish Question* [Appeared in "Jews and Non-Jews in Eastern Europe, 1918-1945" (1974).] 683-702. Friedman, *The Lublin Reservation and the Madagascar Plan,* 703-729. Jonny Moser, *"Nisko: The First Experiment in Deportation"* [Appeared in the "Simon Wiesenthal Center Annual" 2 (1985).] 730-759.

68. Peter Longerich, *"Policy of Destruction Nazi Anti–Jewish Policy and the Genesis of the Final Solution",* 1999 Meyerhoff Lecture at the Holocaust Memorial Museum, Washington, DC.

69. *Encyclopedia of the Holocaust,* Macmillan Library Reference USA, 1990

70. British White Paper of 1939. *"The Avalon Project."* Yale University. Raul Hilberg. *The Destruction of the European Jews*, (1971) (New York: New Viewpoints, 1973), 716 -729. J. C. Hurewitz, *The Struggle for Palestine* (Schoken Books, 1976).

71. The first illegal immigrant ship the "Vellos," breached the blockade on February 10, 1934.

72. Perl, *The Holocaust Conspiracy*, 19-21.

73. Feingold, *The Politics of Rescue*, 54-56.

74. Feingold, *The Politics of Rescue*, 65-66. Also Dwork & van Pelt.

75. The Kupferberg Holocaust Center held an exhibit "Ships to Nowhere" in 2007 to commemorate the tragic voyages.

76. Morse, *Six Million*, 278–280.

77. Goñi, *The Real Odessa*, 31.

78. Perl, *The Holocaust Conspiracy.* Pell was the former Chairman of the US Senate Committee on Foreign Relations (a name well–known in the US through the Pell Grants he helped establish).

79. Karl Popper Lecture at the University of Prague on May 25, 1944.

80. Fuchs, 141.

81. Shirer, *20th Century Journey,* 402.

82. William L. Shirer, *The Rise and Fall of the Third Reich* (New York: Simon and Schuster, 1960), 421.

83. Lewy, *The Catholic Church,* 218.

84. Lewy, *The Catholic Church,* 219. *Munchener Katholische Kirchenzeitung,* no. 42. October 16, 1938.

85. Friedlander, *Nazi Germany and the Jews.*
86. Livia Ritkirchen, *Churban Yahadut Slovakia,* 28–29.
87. Lewy, *The Catholic Church,* 220.
88. Lewy, *The Catholic Church,* 222. *Kerusblatt no. 15,* April 12, 1939, 221-222.
89. Friedman, *The Lublin Reservation and the Madagascar Plan,* 102.

## Chapter 6
## Catholic Europe "Defends" Itself from the Jews

### *Humani Generis Unitas,*
### the Encyclical that Did Not Come to Be

In 1938, some months before his death, Pius XI thought of publishing an encyclical on racism and anti-Semitism. He commissioned three Jesuit priests, John Lafarge (1880-1963), Gustav Desbuquois (1869-1959), and Gustav Gundlach (1892-1963) to produce a draft. The result was the encyclical *Humani Generis Unitas (The Unity of the Human Race)*. That encyclical never saw light, although it seems to have reached the desk of the ailing Pope who died not long after, in February 1939.

Through the encyclicals *Mit Brennender Sorge* and the unpublished *Humani Generis Unitas*, Pius XI was trying in vain to regain the initiative that he had lost vis-à-vis the Nazis and achieve some measure of control of the Frankenstein he helped to create. But it was too little too late. His successor, Pius XII, gave up on any such ideas and adopted a policy of compliant submission when he rose to the papal throne in early 1939, a few months before World War II.

The draft of *Humani Generis Unitas* remained completely hidden until 1973 when parts of it were brought to light for the first time by the *National Catholic Reporter*. After a difficult search, Fr. Johannes Nota, a Dutch Jesuit priest who was living at the time in Thorold, Ontario, near Niagara Falls, obtained the missing parts of the document dealing with anti-Semitism. He published the draft in 1976 in the *Internationale Katholische Zeitschrift*. In 1995, authors Georges Passelecq and Bernard Suchecky published a book on the encyclical that included the 100-page-draft of the document.[1]

Like much that has to do with Church policy during the Holocaust, the unpublished encyclical has been surrounded with a mythical halo as a courageous attack on Nazi anti-Semitism. Scholars Gordon Zahn and Conor Cruise O'Brien regret that the encyclical was not published, which they consider a lost chance to save Jews.[2] While they are right that a call from Rome to stop the persecution of the Jews could have made a difference, the unpublished encyclical not only failed in this respect but could have made things much worse if it were published, adding Catholic anti-Semitic oil to the Nazi fire. When Fr. Johannes Nota learned first hand its contents, he wrote:

> *If one puts these sentences back into the context of the racist legislation adopted in Germany at that period, one can say today: God be praised that this draft remained only a draft. Amen.*[3]

Fr. Edward H. Flannery (1912-1998) commented on the choice of Gundlach as one of the writers of the draft:

> It is quite clear there that the main author of the unpublished encyclical was Gustav Gundlach . . . hardly the person to prepare the section on anti-Semitism at the crucial moment of history![4]

Written at a time (1938) that the persecution of the Jews took a turn for the worse, the encyclical that was supposed to combat anti-Semitism became in the hands of Gundlach and his two colleagues an accusatory diatribe against the Jewish people to justify their separation from the rest of humanity. It is dominated by the same mean-spirited approach that Gundlach took some years earlier to justify the political governmental form of anti-Semitism. While dissociating the Church from Nazi racism, the text basically considers anti-Semitism a "justified defense against Jewish influence." Although the draft recognizes that "Israel remains the chosen people, for its election has never been revoked" (paragraph 140), it denigrates the Jews in classical anti-Semitic terms as "blinded by a vision of material domination and gain."

When referring to the "ardent hope for the eventual conversion of the Jews" it stresses the need of safeguarding the Christians against spiritual contagion to which contact with Jews can expose them, echoing Nazi rhetoric that referred to the Jews as a dangerous source of contagion. Calling Jewish emancipation "an error," the draft defends the "social separation of the people of Israel" as a divinely willed necessity to "prevent harmful contacts between Christians and Jews":

> Such hopes do not blind the Church to the need of safeguarding her children against spiritual contagion. Nor is this need diminished in our time as long as the unbelief of the Jewish people persists, as long as there is active hostility to the Christian religion, just so long must the church use every effort to see that the effects of this unbelief and hostility are not to redound to the ruin of the faith and morals of her own members. (par.142).[5]

Taking a fatal swerve from the subject of religious rivalry to racial persecution, the draft includes a terrifying paragraph when referring to the Nazi campaign against the Jewish people:

Unjust and pitiless it may be, this campaign against the Jews has at least this advantage that it recalls the true nature, the authentic basis of the social separation of the Jews from the rest of humanity (par. 133). [6]

The equality and justice it denies to the Jews, it offers to the baptized Jews condemning as "unjust and a violation of charity, laws which withhold civil rights from baptized Jews, thus interfering illegitimately with the Church's marriage laws." Fr. Edward H. Flannery summation goes to the esence of the issue: [7]

In those fourteen pages one finds several harsh and insulting references to Jews and Judaism. The Jewish "people" are held guilty of the death of Jesus—which was never true and has been rejected in Nostra Aetate of the II Vatican Council and also by Pope John Paul II. Catholics are then warned of the "spiritual dangers to which contact with Jews can expose souls." Jews, we are told, are "blinded by vision of material domination and gain," and thus are "spiritually blind." And we are told that "The historic enmity of the Jewish people to Christianity" has created "a perpetual tension between Christians and Jews" with no reference to the historic Christian contribution to that enmity. The draft, in short, does not recognize a Christian anti-Semitism in any real sense of the word, but views it more as an ethical and theological conflict—which hardly accounts for the centuries of humiliations, oppression, pogroms and murder of Jews in Christian lands . . . Despite the good parts, the draft would have done more harm than good. The best epitaph for the unfortunate draft is that of Johannes Nota, a Dutch Jesuit: "God be praised that this draft remained only a draft. [8]"

Regardless of the unresolved question whether the encyclical was approved or even read by Pius XI, who was already very sick at the time it was brought to him, the fact remains that he never made, even after Kristalnacht, any official pronouncement condemning the Nazi persecution of the Jews. The conclusions of authors Passelecq and Suchecky can hardly be contested:

But when all is said in favor of Pius XI, we must admit that there was an inherent flaw in whatever efforts he made. He was hobbled by his church's history of dealings with the Jews—a fact that comes out in the very document that he wanted to use in defense of Jewish rights. That document, drafted by LaFarge, repeats the theological nonsense about an historic curse on the Jews for their rejection of Christ. The conditions for transcending that traditional "teaching" had not yet arrived. [9]

## A Comment by Pius XI that Made Rounds around the World

Very much as with the unpublished encyclical, a spontaneous comment on anti-Semitism that Pius XI made during a private audience to a group of pilgrims from the Belgian Catholic radio on July 14, 1938, has been greatly misrepresented. When the pilgrims presented the Pope with a prayer book and his eyes fell upon the name of Abraham, he commented that Christians cannot be anti-semites because they are spiritual descendants of Abraham. The comment was based on the traditional Church position that recognized Christianity's original link to the Old Testament and Abraham's role as father of all believers in God. It was directed against the attempts of Rosenberg and the Nazis to sever Christianity's connection to the Old Testament and its Semitic roots:

> Notice that Abraham is called our patriarch, our forefather. We are the spiritual offspring of Abraham . . . We are spiritually Semites . . . Anti-Semitism is a repugnant movement, a movement in which we Christians can have no share. [10]

Lest anyone misunderstood his words as referring to contemporary Jewry, Pius XI, like Gundlach and Faulhaber before him, immediately clarified the meaning of his words by explicitly adding the old caveat that as far as contemporary Jews were concerned, Christians had a right to "defend" and protect themselves from them:

> We recognize that anyone has the right to defend himself, to take steps to protect himself against anything that threatens his legitimate interests. But anti-Semitism is inadmissible. [11]

Although one might have thought that Pius XI was saying that the persecuted Jews had a right to defend themselves, as might have been expected at such trying times, he was in fact stating the very opposite. He was saying that Christian countries had a right to "defend" themselves from the Jews. These were again the same innocent sounding but most ominous words that Gundlach had formulated in 1930 and that were being repeated by Catholic publications all over Europe to justify persecutions and legislation against the Jews:

> Self-defense was justified to prevent the harmful characteristics and influences of the Jewish race. [12]

The comment being private was not registered in the Vatican's official *Acta*, in *L'Osservatore Romano* or in *Civiltá Cattolica*. It was also not quoted by the Italian Catholic press at the time but it made, nonetheless, the rounds all over the world. It was misinterpreted by well-meaning people at the time as a condemnation of the persecution of contemporary Jewry. It is, of course, comprehensible that Jews and righteous non-Jews were anxious to interpret these words as a condemnation of the terrible persecution to which Jews were being subjected. However, when a Jewish newspaper in Hungary at the time praised Pius XI for his opposition to "racist neo-paganism," *Civiltá Cattolica* through Fr. Mario Barbera, took good care to put things right and rejected the praises coming from the Jewish side. It warned its worldwide audience that the fight against racism must not be misinterpreted as having anything to do with the persecution of the contemporary Jews:

It is clear that the Hungarian Catholics are not eager to have such allies for the Church.[13]

## The Anti-Semitic Campaign in the Catholic Press

At the approval of the concordat on July 14, 1933, Hitler made it clear before his cabinet that the main reason for signing the treaty with the Vatican was to involve the Catholic Church in "the struggle against World Jewry." Hitler's expectations that the Catholic Church would cooperate with him in his anti-Semitic campaign were fully met during the twelve years of his regime. The Church did not disappoint him in this respect. Catholic newspapers and all types of publications and books all over Europe defamed and denigrated Jews in a manner not much different than was being done by the Nazis at the time. For the public at large there was hardly any difference between the hate campaigns against Jews conducted in the Catholic press in Europe from the campaign the Nazis were carrying out in their publications, regardless of the pro-forma caveats concerning racial anti-Semitism. The Church and the Nazis, points out David Kertzer, were vying with each other during the 1930s to keep or gain new followers by trying to prove who was a better anti-Semite.

> Nazi anti-Semitism was a problem for the Church in the thirties not because of its negative portrayal of Jews, much of which was shared by the Church itself; the problem stemmed, on the contrary, from the danger that the Nazis would exploit an appeal that was previously identified with the Church to attract Catholics to a non-Christian cause. Church leaders were eager to show people that they need not have to join the Nazis to be against the Jews.[14]

Researchers studying the collections of periodicals available in world libraries, as Ronald Modras so carefully did in the case of prewar Poland, are astonished and overwhelmed by the virulence and magnitude of the daily anti-Semitic attacks in the Catholic press at the time. Contemporary Catholic periodicals and publications were full of anti-Jewish libels and venom without stop all over Europe. They were engaged in anti-Semitic attacks as a matter of daily routine and needed no particular prodding to reinforce their attacks on Jews. In Poland, Romania, Hungary, France, Austria, Italy, and the rest of continental Europe the Catholic press conducted a merciless campaign to smear the imaginary Jewish enemy menacing Christian Europe. The word Jew was used by them as synonym of Bolshevik, Freemason, liberal, and international Capitalist.

The systematic Catholic campaign conditioned public opinion to accept the Nazi persecution as morally justified and prepared Europe for the Final Solution. In their enthusiasm for the results of the National Socialist revolution in Germany, the clergy in neighboring countries soon let people know from their pulpits and publications that the persecution of the Jews was in essence justified. It was right to eliminate the Jews as a *fremdkörper*—an alien body. Even in America, the Catholic radio priest Fr. Charles E. Coughlin (1891-1979) was spreading hate against Jews to tens of millions of listeners from his radio station in Detroit during the 1930s until 1942. Well protected by his superior, Bishop Michael James Gallagher of Detroit (1866-1937), Coughlin was never disciplined by the hierarchy until America entered the war.

The Catholic press all over the world was following the lead of the bell-wether of Catholic publication *La Civiltá Cattolica*, published in Rome, which stood under the direct surveillance of the Pope and the Curia. Founded in 1850 by direct instructions of Pope Pius IX (1846-1878) it unceasingly attacked, vilified, and defamed the Jewish people for over a century. Susan Zuccotti has highlighted the authoritative position held by this Jesuit publication:

> Of the journal in the 1920s and 1930s, one prominent Church historian has written that it was "extremely authoritative because of its tight ties with the Vatican secretary of state. Another respected scholar has observed, "As always, the views of La Civiltà Cattolica were in accord with those of the Pontiff" . . . As another indication of Vatican involvement, many articles from La Civiltà Cattolica, including those about Jews, were reprinted with attribution or merely summarized in *L'Osservatore Romano*, the Vatican's daily newspaper.[15]

Every conceivable canard, in particular the accusation of a Jewish-Masonic conspiracy to dominate the world, found its expression in the pages of *La Civiltà Cattolica*: Jews allegedly aspired to rule the world through capitalist financial domination and revolutionary Communism; they were in control of international banking, finance, politics, and the press; the Freemasons were mere pawns of the Jews, doing their bidding. The preposterous accusation was made that "Jews use Masonry as a means to rule the world, to prepare the way for their Messiah." According to the journal, none others but the Jews stood behind religious persecutions against Catholics and the clergy; they were the source of "the anti-Christian struggle that is the sorry end product of the entire Liberal and Masonic movement." All the modern political developments that the Church disliked at the time were ascribed to the Jews by *Civiltà Cattolica* whether liberalism, Socialism, communism, constitutionalism, democracy, and even rationalism, and atheism.[16] When the Holy Office banned the missionary "Friends of Israel" in 1928, the editor of *La Civiltà Cattolica*, Enrique Rosa SJ, wrote:

> Jews are a danger to the whole world because of their pernicious infiltration, their hidden influence, and their resulting disproportionate power which violates both reason and the common good . . . This danger is especially acute for people in Christian countries. [17]

An article published in *Civiltà Cattolica* on June 19, 1937, is typical of the style, although not necessarily of the contents, which were often far more incendiary and defamatory:

> Even when the Zionist state becomes a reality, there will still be several million sons of Israel in the world, who will not be very different from what they are today: speculators who soak up gold, Messianic and revolutionaries . . . The tragic aspect of the Jewish question is that Israel everlastingly tries to assimilate

itself but never succeeds. The Jewish question is insoluble and it therefore was useless to try and find a solution . . . There is only one hope left to the Christians, the conversion of Israel. That would be the final solution. [18]

The Fascist official paper *Il Regime Fascista* commented on August 30, 1938:

We confess that in both planning and execution, Fascism is far inferior to the rigor of *La Civiltà Cattolica*. Modern states and societies, including the healthiest and most courageous nations of Europe, Italy and Germany still have much to learn from the Fathers of the Society of Jesus. [19]

The articles published in this authoritative forum of papal opinion in the late 1930s and 1940s, adopted an even more hostile tone in their attacks against the Jewish people. At the height of the Holocaust, in 1941 and 1942, when millions of Jews were being gassed, *La Civiltá Cattolica* published two articles in which the Jews were accused of ritual murder! Sam Waagenaar points out how such pronouncements vanished opportunistically after the war from Catholic publications. Very different claims of having helped and defended the Jews took their place after the defeat of the Axis:

Such sentiments and opinions would, after the war, disappear from the variously repeated texts about how much the Vatican had done for the Jews of Rome conveniently forgetting what some of its highest dignitaries had done against them and against Jews in general. [20]

# From Words to Actions
## Anti-Semitic Legislation in Catholic Europe

All along his political career, Hitler held on to his original political idea of cementing his alliances by means of anti-Semitism. Already in 1922, Hitler, paraphrasing Marx's call to the workers of the world to unite against their exploiters, called all the anti-Semites and Aryans from the world to unite against the Jewish race. Czech Foreign Minister Frantisek Chvalkovsky was greatly impressed to learn directly from Hitler in early January 1939 that anti-Semitism was the glue that held together his international alliances:

What appears to have most impressed him [Chvalkovsky] was the importance that Herr Hitler and Herr von Ribbentrop attached to the Jewish Question— absolutely out of proportion to the importance assigned to other questions dealt with.

Germany will seek to form a bloc of anti-Semitic states, for she could not adopt a friendly attitude towards states in which the Jews either by their economic activity or as result of their high positions could exercise any kind of influence. [21]

But there was a deeper dimension to Hitler's anti-Semitism at least as important: its capacity to internally weaken the immune system of the countries he wished to conquer or control. He used anti-Semitism as the Trojan horse to enter these countries and create a fifth column to undermine their strength by attacking and destroying their Jews. It was an important element in his tactics before attacking or taking control of a country.

Hitler did not have to look far for partners ready to become part of a bloc of anti-Semitic states in Europe. The soil of Christian Europe had been well prepared in modern times by the Catholic press and politicians all over Europe and Hitler saw the opportunity to harvest the hatred they had so diligently sown to create his bloc of anti-Semitic states. The clero-Fascist parties of Europe were quite willing and ready to join him in a coordinated attack on the Jews: The Arrow Cross in Hungary, the Hlinka Party in Slovakia, the Ustashi in Croatia, the Rexists in Belgium, the Laval collaborationists in France, and the Fascists in Italy all combined their clericalism and Fascism with rabid anti-Semitism. In negotiations with the heads of these states, Hitler found common ground in anti-Semitism. They often preempted Hitler and proudly displayed what they had already achieved in this respect on their own in their countries.

The anti-Semitic campaign in the Catholic press of Fascist Christian countries of Europe did not stop at defamation, but was directed at promoting anti-Jewish legislation during the late 1930s. That legislation aimed at stripping the Jews from their civic and political rights as in pre-emancipation days and reduce them to the condition of pariahs. The Catholic clergy and Catholic political parties were among the most vocal and politically active promoters of these infamous laws, which prepared the public for the Final Solution of the Jewish question that the Nazis were preparing to carry out. Their role in the adoption of anti-Semitic laws was not one of passive onlookers but of frontline participants and promoters a la par with the Nazis.

Not only did anti-Jewish laws delegitimize the Jews and deprive them of their basic human rights and possessions but also placed them outside the pale of humanity in the eyes of society. They conditioned the public to view the crimes against Jews as legal, normal, and acceptable. The enclosure of the Jews in ghettos was seen as a natural sequel of them. When finally the Jews were deported from these legal ghettoes to an unknown destiny in the east, a well-conditioned, morally immunized population, expecting short-term and long-term windfalls from the elimination of the Jews, greeted their disappearance with delight.

The clero-Fascist governments consulted both their own Church authorities and the Vatican in Rome concerning these laws. They needed their moral sanction to justify their actions before their own people. The guidelines Church authorities provided carried enormous weight in the eyes of their people. Canonical law specialists in the Vatican responded approvingly. They did not find Nazi persecution of the Jews radically different from historical precedent in canon law and took a tolerant view toward their evil actions. One of the most revealing documents in this respect is the Bérard Report for Vichy France authored by

Msgrs. Giovanni Montini and Domenico Tardini that approved the anti-Semitic Vichy laws.

Professor Raul Hilberg points out the striking parallelism, which is by no means accidental, between historical Christian anti-Semitic legislation rooted in canonical law and Nazi legislation.[22] Throughout the ages beginning with the Synod of Elvira in the year 306 the Church decreed laws against the Jews until modern times. Especially noteworthy are the anti-Jewish legislations of the Fourth Lateran Council under the Pope Innocent III in 1215, and the bull Cum Nimis Absurdum decreed by Pope Paul IV on July 14, 1555. Even the deportation of the Jews to the east which preceded their physical annihilation, had its precedent in the mass expulsions of entire Jewish communities during the Middle Ages. That legislation sanctioned ghettoization, mass expulsions, confiscations, abductions, and massacres.

The Church, as already stated, did differ with the Nazis with regard to baptized Jews who converted to Christianity and their descendents. For the Church, the converts were in principle Christians who had "won the right" to be exempted from anti-Semitic legislation by their baptism. But both, the Church and Nazi Germany, agreed on the fundamental principle of placing Jews outside the pale of society. Despite their formal disagreement with the racial premises of Nazi laws, the Church welcomed the laws themselves as "a defense of Christian society against Jewish influence in the religious, cultural, social and economic spheres."

These laws became part of the process that culminated in the gas chambers and killing fields of Eastern Europe. To begin with, these laws prescribed a census of every Jewish man, woman, and child. The registration lists with the names and addresses became the database that served to round up, concentrate, and deport them for "resettlement to the east"—the Nazi code for the Final Solution. The information was most cooperatively provided and updated by Church and civil authorities. Himmler's emissaries in charge of the Final Solution worked in close cooperation with them. They made it possible to identify Jewish citizens in each country—an undertaking, that would otherwise have been almost impossible to carry out in Western Europe.

It is therefore true in the strictest sense of the word that the anti-Jewish legislation that the Church supported and promoted was the crucial preparatory stage of the Final Solution. Even if it were true that the Vatican and the bishops were unaware of what awaited the Jews at the end of their deportation journeys, the adoption of anti-Jewish legislation by itself without knowledge of the final fate of the deported Jews, stands out as a heinous crime against a defenseless people according to any standard of justice and morality. An overview of the adoption of anti-Semitic legislation in Italy, Hungary, and Slovakia will make evident the central role that Catholic hierarchies and their lay political representatives played in their approval.

# Poland

The inclusionary vision of a *Panstwo Narodowosciowe*, a pan-national state, which inspired the struggle of an independent Poland during the nineteenth century, promising all participants in this struggle, including Jews, a rightful place in a free Poland, was discarded after World War I, particularly under the influence of the Polish National Democratic Party (ND) of Roman Dmovski (1864-1939). Its place was taken by an exclusionary xenophobic vision of a Catholic, monocultural and homogeneous Poland in which Jews had no place. By the short equation *Polak=Katolik*, the Pole is a Catholic, Polish Jewry was delegitimized in one stroke. Catholic Poles proclaimed themselves the hosts, while the Jews, whose presence in Poland dated back to the beginnings of Polish history, were declared invited guests whose presence was not welcome any more. The host-guest paradigm that delegitimized Jews as equal citizens became a center piece in Polish political discourse between the two world wars.

Roman Dmovski, who led the Polish delegation to Versailles, opportunistically signed the Versailles Treaty to obtain international approval for the new state, but trampled upon it even before the ink of their signatures had dried. The minority rights clause became the source of their bitter resentment and fierce political maneuvering. The spokesmen of the new Poland did everything in their power to popularize and hammer in the immoral and deadly notion that there were *too many* Jews in Poland. The slogan "There are too many Jews in Poland" reverberated from one end of Poland to the other in the period between the two world wars, and it was turned into an unquestioned self-evident premise of their political discourse. In the streets, the markets, the schools, the newspapers, the universities, Jewish men, women, and children of all ages would be abused and told to go to Palestine: *Szydzi do Palestyny*! Jews go to Palestine! Economic policies and legislation were designed to undermine the Jewish economic base and induce the emigration of as many Jews as fast as possible.

An economic boycott was activated without interruption from 1918 until World War II and a *numerus clausus* restricting Jewish access to higher education was adopted. Jews, who represented around 10 percent of the population, were forced to pay 40 percent of the taxes. Unwilling to solve the Polish agrarian problem through land reform, the government subscribed to the idea of "solving" the problem by pushing out the Jews from their economic positions in the small towns, the *shtetlach*, where they lived for centuries, so the peasants could take over their businesses and homes.[23] This became the basis of the state economic policy that advocated forced mass emigration of 3.5 million Jews from Poland. Not in vain did the most influential economist of the twentieth century, Lord Keynes, refer to Poland as "an economic impossibility whose only industry is Jew-baiting."[24]

Anti-Semitic activism received new impetus at the end of Marshall Jozef Pilsudski's life (1867-1935) with the growing rapprochement between Poland and the Third Reich after he signed a ten-year non-aggression pact and trade agreement with Hitler in 1934, months before his death. The pact allowed Hitler time for rearmament and diverted Pilsudski's heirs from timely preparing to confront the German menace. It also acted as an incentive to join Hitler's war against the Jews. On September 13, 1934, Pilsudski's foreign minister, Colonel Josef Beck, went before the League of Nations in Geneva to unilaterally revoke the Minority Rights Treaty that protected the rights of minorities, including those of the Jews.

Following the example of the SA thugs and Hitlerjugend in neighboring Germany, Polish students began in the early 1930s a systematic anti-Semitic campaign all over Poland, demanding that the entry of Jews to universities should be restricted. They physically attacked their Jewish fellow students within university grounds. Invited by the University of Warsaw, Goebbels came to Warsaw to lecture. Outside in the streets, the students joined the Endek shifts stationed at Jewish-owned stores to prevent the entrance of Polish customers; they distributed anti-Semitic literature, organized riots, attacked Jewish shopkeepers, and threw Jews down from moving trains.

The Catholic Church stood in the center of Polish anti-Semitism during the entire interwar period. Ronald Modras summarized in short words the role played by the Catholic Church and the Catholic press in Poland in the anti-Semitic offensive in the 1930s:

> The Catholic clergy were not innocent bystanders or passive observers of the wave of anti-Semitism encompassing Poland in the late half of the 1930s.[25]

In an effort to stop the physical attacks and terror against Jews, a delegation of prominent rabbis led by Rabbi Ytzjack M. Kanal, accompanied by Rabbis Perlman, Langleben, and Fajner, went to plead with Cardinal Aleksander Kakowski (1862-1938) in Warsaw on June 7, 1934. The highly influential prelate had ordained as bishop in Warsaw in 1919 the future Pius XI, the first apostolic nuncio to the Polish government at the time. The rabbis pleaded with Kakowski to use his moral authority and issue a pastoral to his flock to stop the attacks:

> In the name of the Rabbis and Jews of this illustrious Republic, we entreat you, Cardinal, to issue a pastoral about this to all Polish Catholics. [26]

Cardinal Kakowski refused; he told them that, although as a Christian he might condemn such attacks, as a Pole he could not. Further rapprochement between Church and the government took place after Pilsudski's death. His political heirs, known as the "Colonels Clique," which included Marshall Edward Smigly Rydz, Colonel Josef Beck, Colonel Adam Koc, and Polish President Ignacy Mozicki, embraced the Nationalists and adopted an official, clear anti-Semitic domestic policy:

> The effect of these separate political aspirations [of Jews] and the effect of their numbers, plus their major influence over many areas of social and national life,

is to make the Jews, in the present state of affairs, an element that weakens the normal development of national and state strength in Poland.

Marshall Smigly Rydz, Pilsudski's successor, instituted in 1936 compulsory separate ghetto benches for Jewish students. They responded by standing in the sides and rear of the lecture halls not to surrender to the degradation. Polish students, who greatly outnumbered the protesters, used physical violence against them to force them to occupy the ghetto benches while the school administrators would expel the standing students altogether.

On June 4, 1936, Felicjan Slawoj-Skladovski, the Polish prime minister, declared his support for an economic war against the Jews, as if one was already not being waged uninterruptedly. Since 1923, anti-Semitic politicians such as Dmowski allied with Catholic priests such as Wiribowski tried to outlaw kosher slaughtering (*Schechita*) in Poland to eliminate Jewish competition in the meatpacking business. Laws restricting and banning kosher slaughtering were introduced in 1923, 1936, and 1939. The last law that pretended a total ban on kosher slaughtering came before the Senate when the war broke out.

A pastoral letter issued in 1936 by the primate of Poland, Cardinal August Hlond (1881-1948), the archbishop of Poznan and Gniezno, called for the elimination and separation of the Jews to shield the Poles from dangerous Jewish influence. His pastoral letter, which was read in all the churches over Poland, defamed and vilified Polish Jewry:

> There will be a Jewish problem as long as the Jews remain . . . It is a fact that the Jews are fighting against the Catholic Church, persisting in free thinking, and are the vanguard of godlessness, Bolshevism and subversion. [27]

He did not hesitate to give his unreserved blessing to the boycott against Jewish business:

> In commercial relations it is right to favor one's own people, to avoid Jewish shops and Jewish stalls on the market. [28]

While Hlond was candid enough to admit that there are Jews who are "also faithful, righteous, honest, charitable and well-meaning" and that "in many Jewish families there is a wholesome and edifying family spirit," he went on to slander and vilify Polish Jewry as a whole:

> It is true that in the schools the influence of Jewish youth upon the Catholic is in general negative from the religious and moral viewpoint . . . It is necessary to find protection from the harmful moral influence of the Jews, to keep away from their anti-Christian culture, and in particular to boycott the Jewish press and demoralizing Jewish publications.

Piously preaching that hatred "even" to Jews was un-Christian, Hlond pronounced himself against physical attacks on them not because it was immoral to do so, but for the reason that "the blood which sometimes flows on such occasions is Polish blood." Such a declaration by the head of the Polish Catholic Church, its most authorized spokesmen, served as a sign to escalate the struggle against the Jews in Poland. The Catholic Conservative Party declared itself in favor of the policy of displacing Jews from the small towns "because assisting the peasants to move to the *shtetlach* and engage in business will force the Jews to emigrate from Poland."

The peasant parties, until then largely neutral, enthusiastically endorsed the idea that the creation of a Polish middle class was a national priority that could only be achieved by displacing Jews from the towns and replacing them with villagers. The Catholic press led by the *Maly Dziennik*, the largest Catholic circulating daily, followed suit and unceasingly disparaged Jews and Judaism. *Spravy Catolicke* wrote on October 11, 1936: "The Jews are ulcers in the Polish body." *Gazetta Swiatechna*, an influential Catholic publication, explained to the Polish public in 1936 the rationale of its intensified anti-Semitic campaign:

> The hatred between Poles and Jews is highly beneficial to our Polish trade and to our country.[29]

In February 1937, Pilsudski's heirs organized the anti-Semitic Camp of National Unity (*Oboz Zjednoczenia Narodowego*, [OZON]), to tighten their control on the government. OZON was open to everyone except Jews. Historian Davies points out:

> After Pilsudski's death, the OZON leadership saw little place for the Jews in their vision of Polish national unity . . . Polish Jews in the 1930s were indeed subjected to a number of ugly threats and denigrations, and to a mounting campaign of economic hardship and emotional insecurity. [30]

OZON ideologue Colonel Adam Koc officially included in the OZON program the demand that Jews should be forced to emigrate from Poland. Speaking in lofty terms of the great cultural traditions and honor of Poland that did not allow such a great nation to use dishonorable means to achieve this goal, this chivalrous gentleman had some "honorable" recommendations to make:

> Until their expulsion will be carried out, it is necessary as a first step to abolish their civic rights and confiscate their properties. All the large industries will have to be nationalized.[31]

Under the guise of pseudoeconomics, figures were provided according to which there were "at least one and a half million Jews too many in Poland." The numbers of the "surplus" Jews began to grow in the 1930s: the Deputy-President of the *Sejm*, Mieszinski, declared before Parliament that in Poland a country of 35 million people, there was no room for more than 50,000 Jews at most![32] On June 16, 1937, General Lucjan Zieligowski went a step further and declared in the Polish Senate:

There is no place in Poland for the Jews.

On December 15, 1937, fifteen Polish Catholic bishops called for the legal segregation of Jewish children in Polish elementary schools. This was the beginning of a growing campaign to segregate Jews in every walk of life, from railways to housing districts. In hundreds of markets, Jewish traders and stall keepers were separated from the Poles, and in some cities Jewish coachmen and taxis were isolated from the rest. Polish lawyers began to demand separate benches in the courts for their Jewish colleagues.[33]

During Kristallnacht the Catholic newspapers in Poland went as far in their anti-Semitic zeal as to condone the atrocity. The newspaper of Cardinal Adam Sapieha of Kraków found words of excuse for the Nazis and their heinous crimes. Little did he know that in less than a year Poland itself would experience on its own flesh the meaning of German "benevolence." On December 9, 1938, deputies of the ruling party began gathering signatures in the *Sejm* to declare Jews temporary citizens, and two weeks later 117 deputies introduced a resolution demanding "a radical and immediate solution of the Jewish question in Poland through emigration."[34]

## Italy

Italy began to introduce anti-Semitic legislation against the ancient and small Jewish community of 57,000 souls, whose presence in Italy antedated that of Christianity, exactly one year before World War II broke out in September 1938. In formulating anti-Jewish laws, points out Waagenaar, Mussolini's legal experts went through "the many Church edicts that had plagued the Jews of Rome since 1555 and even before, and which had persisted till 1870."[35]

To prove that the new anti-Jewish laws to be approved stood on the firm ground of Church tradition, the Fascist daily *Il Regime Fascista* brought up from oblivion on August 30, 1938, a famous series of rabidly anti-Semitic articles on the "Jewish Question" published way back in 1890 in *La Civiltá Cattolica*. These articles argued in favor of repealing Jewish emancipation and stripping the Jews from citizenship and civic equality, because "as long as governments remained faithful to the principles of the French Revolution, they would suffer under the Jewish yoke." The Fascist daily concluded with an exhortation to accept the Jesuit recommendations of 1895:

> Italy has much to learn from the Fathers of the Company of Jesus, Fascism is quite inferior, both in its propositions and in their execution, to the rigor of *La Civiltá Cattolica*.[36]

The editors of *La Civiltá Cattolica* responded to the Fascist provocation in the middle of September 1938 with full agreement. They restated their old canards and libels against the Jewish people and reendorsed the thesis of 1895 that the emancipation of the Jews must be repealed by adopting even more stringent laws against them:

> The Catholic battle against the Jews is to be understood as a struggle inspired solely by the need for the legitimate defense of Christian people against a foreign nation in the nations where they live and against the sworn enemy of their well-being. This suggests measures to render such people harmless. [37]

Not to arouse Jewish suspicion, a census was taken of the entire Jewish population in Italy on August 1938 before the introduction of the first round of anti-Semitic legislation. The first anti-Jewish decree Provisions for the Defense of the Race in the Fascist School was adopted on September 5, 1938. It mandated the immediate dismissal of all Jewish teachers in public schools and the exclusion of Jewish children from elementary and secondary public schools. It also banned matriculation to newly entering Jewish students in universities. An additional decree issued on September 7 terminated the right of residence for foreign-born Jews and Jews who became naturalized citizens after January 1, 1919. They were deprived of their citizenship and given a maximum period of six months to voluntarily leave the country or face forced expulsion.

A more severe and comprehensive set of anti-Semitic laws, known as the November Laws, was adopted on November 17, 1938. The November Laws forbade the employment of Jews in civil service at the national, provincial, and municipal level, as well as in banks and private insurance companies. Jews were excluded from the armed forces and the Fascist Party. They were not allowed to own land, factories, or businesses above a certain ceiling value; properties owned by Jews above that value were to be confiscated. Jews could not employ Aryan domestic servants. The laws outlawed mixed marriages between baptized Jewish converts and Christian Italians. The offspring of such mixed marriages, if baptized after October 1, 1938, were considered Jewish.

The anti-Semitic laws obviously required a definition of who was considered a Jew. In his growing rapprochement to Hitler, Mussolini also accepted race as the primary criterion to define Jewish identity, giving religion a subordinate role. The definition, which largely followed the German model, was formulated in the Declaration on Race presented by Mussolini before the Fascist Grand Council, which approved it on October 6 and 7. As a result of the legislation, baptized converts whose parents were Jewish were considered Jewish and also their children were considered Jewish. Children of mixed marriages in which only one of the partners was of Aryan stock were also considered Jewish if baptized after the promulgation of the law. An exception was made for those who were baptized before that date.

The Church, which objected to the inclusion of baptized converts in anti-Semitic laws, had no other objection to them except the ban on marriages between baptized non-Aryan converts and Aryan Christians. Afraid that Mussolini's intrusion in the area of marriages, so jealously guarded in Italy by the Church, might turn out to be the beginning of more serious violations of the Lateran Treaty, *Osservatore Romano* focused its criticism during the deliberations of the Grand Council exclusively on the marriage provisions of the anti-Semitic laws, implicitly accepting the rest. Secretary of State Maglione instructed the nuncio and Tacchi-Venturi to intervene with the Italian government to exempt the converts. In a very clear statement the Italian ambassador to the Holy See transmitted, on October 10, 1938, the Vatican viewpoint to his superior, the Italian Foreign Minister Galeazzo Ciano, in the following words:

> The proposal to prohibit marriages between non-Jewish Catholics and converts of Judaism is the only point of the racist proclamation of the Grand Council to which the Church would formulate objections.[38]

Pope Pius XI, Achile Ratti, considered the ban on marriages between converts and old Christians an infringement of the Italian concordat, which had given the Church exclusive jurisdiction over the area of marriages. He wrote a letter to Mussolini and to the king, expressing his opposition to the government intrusion into the marriage area. In a private audience with the students of Propaganda Fide, Pius XI expressed his regret that Italy had felt the necessity to imitate Germany in accepting race instead of religion as a criterion of ethnic identity. On Mussolini's instructions, Italian Foreign Minister Galeazzo Ciano called the papal nuncio to Italy, Monsignor Francesco Borgoncini-Duca, to present a formal protest against the Pope's critical expression. To his delight, Ciano found the nuncio very much on his side. Ciano wrote down in his diary:

> He [the nuncio] seems fairly convinced . . . I want to add that he personally revealed himself as very anti-Semitic.[39]

To dissipate any impression that the Pope's statement might be misinterpreted as a defense of the Jews, one of the leading figures of the Italian episcopate, the patriarch of Venice Cardinal Adeodato Piazza, in the best tradition of the Holy Office gave an explanation of the Church's objections in a homily on January 6, 1939, in which he denied that the Church intended to protect the Jews and contrasted the Church's "balance, moderation, and Christian charity with Jewish arrogance":

> To say simply that the Church protects the Jews, is to assert what is not true; for the Church, properly speaking, protects by divine mandate only the freedom of its universal mission, which is to communicate its supernatural good to each and all . . . It is true that it had to defend itself as well as its faithful, and not rarely, with the means it had at its disposition, against dangerous contacts and the Jewish invasion, which seems in truth the hereditary mark of this people. But one must also recognize, if one does not wish to lie, that in the reactions too often provoked by Jewish arrogance, one may find, in the Church, suggestions and examples of balance, moderation, and Christian charity.[40]

Outside of Italy the Pope's criticism was understood in the same sense. The Catholic Polish publication *Przewodnik Katolocki*, cited by R. Modras, wrote in 1938:

The Pope's criticism of the Italian race laws was not the 50,000 Jews of Italy, but the Church's mission to draw all nations into one fold. Racism was condemned because it constituted an obstacle to the missionary activity of the Church. [41]

A homily by Bishop Giovanni Cazzani of Cremona published in *L'Osservatore Romano* on January 15, 1939, is characteristic of the support that the Italian bishops on their part expressed in favor of the legislation against the Jews. The homily cited by David Kertzer and Susan Zuccotti could easily have gained the approval of Streicher and Rosenberg:

> The Church has never denied the state's right to limit or to impede the economic, social, and moral influence of the Jews, when this has been harmful to the nation's tranquility and welfare. The Church has never said or done anything to defend the Jews, the Judaics, or Judaism.
>
> The Church has always regarded living side by side with Jews, as long as they remain Jews, as dangerous to the faith and tranquility of Christian people. It is for this reason that you should find an old and long tradition of ecclesiastical legislation and discipline, intended to brake and limit the action and influence of the Jews in of Christians, and the contact of Christians with them, isolating the Jews and not allowing them the exercise of those offices and professions in which they could dominate or influence the spirit, the education, the customs of Christians.[42]

The Cardinal of Florence Dalla Costa issued a similar declaration in early 1939 in support of the anti-Jewish legislation:

> As for the Jews no one can forget the ruinous work that they have often undertaken not only against the spirit of the Church, but also in detriment of civil coexistence. One needs to recall that, with the outbreak of the First World War, Italian Jewry succeeded in seeing that the Vicar of the Prince of Peace, the Holy Father, was excluded from the future peace conference. Above all, however, the Church has in every epoch judged living together with the Jews to be dangerous to the Faith and to the tranquility of the Christian people. Hence the laws promulgated by the Church for centuries aimed at isolating the Jews. The Church has never changed its policy of forbidding Christians from working in Jewish homes, or forbidding Christian children from being taught by Jews.[43]

When the anti-Semitic author Alfredo Romanini reprinted in 1939[44] his rabid anti-Semitic pamphlet—*Jews, Christianity, Fascism*—in which Jews were depicted as seeking to dominate and enslave the world, it received the enthusiastic endorsement of the most prominent members of the Italian Catholic hierarchy who were very close to the Pope, such as Cardinal Adeodato Piazza of Venice (1884-1957), Cardinal Mario Nasalli Rocca of Bolognia (1903-1988), Cardinal Luigi Lavitrano of Palermo (1874-1950), and Archbishop Giussepe Nogara of Udine (1872-1952). Cardinal Piazza blessed Romanini for his book with "all my heart, for this work is most opportune to make known the grave danger that hangs over the world." The other Cardinals praised Romanini's book as "excellent, and of unquestionable usefullness in the understanding of the Jewish problem." Here is a characteristic paragraph of Romanini's dishonorable book that the high Italian prelates found so illuminating:

> Jews aspired to dominate Europe first, to be followed by the enslavement of the world: Banks, industries, newspapers, film studios, railroads and steamship lines were in the hands of Jews . . . high Jewish finance had been dominating European politics for over half a century . . . Mussolini is the chief who raises himself powerfully and majestically against this malicious Israel, which thirsts after a Christian-Aryan vendetta, and which desires world domination with its gold, corruption, Masonic thirst and international organizations of various names and colors, having as its goal the brutalization of the masses. [45]

Msgr. Agostino Gemelli, president of the Pontifical Academy of Science, rector of the Catholic University of Milan and a frequent visitor of the Vatican, spoke in Bolognia on January 9, 1939, on the Jewish question:

> In politics we have only one Chief, Il Duce—whom a great and august voice [referring to the Pope] has called incomparable! . . . It is tragic to view this situation as we have seen it through the centuries, a situation in which the sentence is carried out on the Christ-killing people, as a result of which they wander through the world, unable to find the peace of a fatherland, while the consequences of their horrible deed persecute them wherever they are for all times. [46]

The anti-Semitic November Laws were still considered not strong enough, and the Fascist Grand Council approved a more pernicious anti-Jewish Code on June 29, 1939. Administrative addendums to the laws prohibited Jews from publishing books, holding public conferences, owning radios, being listed in telephone directories, using popular vacation resorts, and even placing any type of advertisements in the newspapers, including death notices. The code itself forbade Jewish professionals to practice their professions among Christians. Included in the prohibition were doctors, lawyers, engineers, mathematicians, accountants, chemists, pharmacists, veterinarians, agronomists, and architects. Jews could not be judges, notaries, or journalists.

The anti-Jewish laws came as a terrible shock to Italian Jewry. The laws were enforced rigorously producing enormous suffering. All Jewish civil servants were dismissed from their jobs. Distinguished military officers with a lifetime record of service were discharged from the armed forces, including twenty-five Jewish army generals and five navy admirals, among them General Pugliese the head of Naval Construction. One officer, Colonel Segre, committed suicide before his troops. [47] Thousands of Jewish professionals lost their employment while their non-Jewish competitors profited from their elimination. Expropriation of property was carried out with devastating consequences in a material and psychological sense.

Although converts were included in the anti-Semitic laws, the legislation, nonetheless, turned out to be a boon to missionary activity, especially among those in mixed marriages. Hoping to escape the iron grip of the anti-Jewish laws, 4,000 Jews yielded to fear and converted to Catholicism at the time. A limited number of Italian Jews managed to escape to other countries.

The authoritative sources previously mentioned should be enough to demolish the false allegations that the Church opposed Mussolini's anti-Semitic laws. Professor Kertzer's balanced summation of the issue is uncontestable and clear: The anti-Jewish legislation in Italy was received favorably by the Pope and the Italian highest Church dignitaries because it embodied the same principles that the Church championed throughout the ages:

> Anyone should not find it surprising that in response to these measures against the Jews neither the Pope nor the Vatican hierarchy uttered a single word of protest. The explanation for this fact is simple: Mussolini's new laws embodied measures and views long championed by the Church itself.
>
> There was, however, one aspect of the Italian racial laws that did draw papal protest and, indeed, clearly angered the aging Pope. The new law treated a Jew who had converted to Catholicism as a Jew, and hence forbade marriages between Catholics who had been born Jewish and other Catholics.[48]

# Hungary

Hungary under the regency of Admiral Miklos Horthy (1868-1957) was really the first Catholic country in Europe outside of Germany to officially adopt anti-Jewish legislation. Two and a half years before it officially joined the Axis, the Hungarian parliament approved on May 29, 1938, its first anti-Jewish law under the innocently sounding title of Bill for a More Effective Guarantee of a Balanced Social and Economic Life. The law aimed at reducing the political-economic rights of Jews by imposing quotas on Jewish participation in free professions, particularly in the field of journalism, as demanded by the Hungarian anti-Semites.

The highest-ranking Catholic clergy of Hungary stood in the forefront of the campaign in the press and the Parliament to promote anti-Semitic legislation. The two branches of the Catholic Church, the Latin and the Greek, convened in full at the residence of the Primate of Hungary Cardinal Jusztinián Serédi (1884-1945), a member of the Upper House of Parliament, and unanimously adopted a resolution expressing their support for the aforementioned law congratulating the government:

> The synod registers with satisfaction the fact that the Royal Government of Hungary strives to defend the interests of the Christian public in face of Jewish spiritual domination.[49]

Cardinal Serédi saw this law as a mere modest beginning of a much wider body of legislation against the Jews, which he advocated, as he made it clear in his address to Parliament:

> Nevertheless, it is necessary to take additional measures against the Jews. We must uproot decisively all those phenomena that Judaism has introduced into our economic, our social, and our public lives, as well as into our legal system. The reasons for this struggle are the same that led the Church in our homeland to oppose bitterly the liberal outlook ever since the granting of full recognition to the Jewish religion.

On April 15, 1939, Cardinal Jusztinián Serédi spoke officially in the name of the Synod of Catholic Bishops in the Upper House of Parliament to express their support for a new round of discriminatory legislation. In the same exact terms used by the Church all over Europe, he described the infamous legislation as an act of "self-defense" against the Jews who in the press, art, literature, poetry, and music "had cast doubt upon values sacred to Christians":

> I declare that in our treatment of the Jewish question I perceive an act of justifiable self-defense . . . The concept of imposing limitations on the Jews is acceptable to all. Part of the Jewish population—disguised as the press, art, literature, poetry, and music—has cast doubt upon values sacred to Christians. They have done so with the acquiescence of the other Jews and despite the constant protests of Catholics . . . The influence of the Jews must be curtailed, for they have sinned much against Christian-Hungary . . . We must ascribe the responsibility to the liberal regime that facilitated the Jewish tricks, despite the constant protest of Catholic Hungarians. [50]

Both houses of the Hungarian Parliament approved a second, more pernicious, round of anti-Semitic laws on May 4, 1939. Under the title Law to Limit the Expansion of Jews in the Public and Economic Domain the new law abolished the political rights of Jews. The law canceled the Jewish right to vote and barred Jews from the civil service, universities, professional organizations, and newspapers. It excluded the Jews completely from all participation in Hungary's cultural life including journalism, teaching, theater, music, films, radio, and from every kind of cultural activity. Employment of Jews in commerce, industry, banking, and trade was limited to a maximum of 9 percent. Jews were forbidden to acquire land and the government could compel them to sell or lease their lands. The consequences of the second round of anti-Semitic laws were very serious for Hungarian Jewry, as pointed out by the late Moshe Y. Herczl. As many as 70,000 breadwinners and their 200,000 dependents, one-quarter of Hungarian Jewry, lost their livelihood overnight, while many were reduced to near starvation.

For the Arrow-Cross Party, the Hungarian Nazikatholics, the legislation did not go far enough. They criticized the legislation during parliamentary debates and commented editorially that their aim was a Hungary without Jews:

We don't view the anti-Jewish law as a final solution to the Jewish problem . . .
We are interested in a country which will be free of Jews. [51]

Moshe Herczl rightly points out that the connection between the words of 1939 and the terrible deeds that followed in 1941 and 1944 is not a coincidence. There is a direct link between the statements of a "Hungary without Jews" and the mass killings committed by the Hungarians in the Ukraine in 1941 and the deportation of the majority of Hungarian Jews to Auschwitz in 1944.

## Slovakia

One of the first actions undertaken by the new independent Slovak state under the leadership of Fr. Tiso after its secession from Czechoslovakia in 1939 was to adopt anti-Semitic legislation. On April 18, 1939, barely one month after its declaration of independence, Slovakia approved its first anti-Semitic legislation to allegedly "defend itself against the Jews and eliminate Jewish influence from Slovakian life." The soil of Catholic Slovakia had been well prepared for it by the systematic anti-Semitic propaganda of the Catholic Hlinka People's Party, which poisoned the Slovakian people in the interwar period.

Intensive Jewish life pulsated in Slovakia during countless generations. Cities like Bratislava, Nitra, Surany, Galanta, and Tyrnau were important Jewish centers. The preeminent yeshiva of central Europe flourished for many generations in Bratislava. Before the Munich Conference there were about 138,000 Jews living in the Slovak portion of Czechoslovakia. Their number was reduced to about 89,000 when Slovakia became independent and Carpatho-Ruthenia was lost to Hungary.

Three rounds of progressively harsher anti-Jewish legislation were approved between April 18, 1939, and May 15, 1942. In their anti-Semitic zeal, Nazis and Catholics were outdoing each other in their support for such legislation. The first Codex Judaicus banned Jewish children from middle and higher-level general schools. It restricted Jews in their change of residence and required them to obtain a special permit to travel from one city to another. Jews were only allowed to shop at certain hours and were forbidden to employ non-Jewish maids. Jews could not teach in institutions of higher education, hold civil service jobs, serve in the army, or participate in sport clubs. The licenses of Jewish physicians, pharmacists, and lawyers were revoked. In his report to Cardinal Maglione, the new apostolic delegate Burzio, who had only recently arrived, expressed his approval of the infamous legislation in blatant anti-Semitic terms:

Some or all of these measures are justified given the preponderant influence of Jews in business. [52]

Although the criterion adopted by Slovak clerical leaders to define Jewish identity in the Codex Judaicus was religious and not racial, Jews who converted to Christianity after October 30, 1918, were considered Jews for all legal purposes. There were about 20,000 baptized Jews in Slovakia. In his report to the Vatican, Msgr. Burzio was concerned that, as a result of the legislation, children of the post-1918 converts would end up attending Jewish schools and eventually return to Judaism. In his response of October 5, 1940 to Burzio, Cardinal Maglione asks him to keep him informed on his further efforts to guarantee the Christian education of the children of the converts.

## France

When Petain was to adopt his second Statut des Juifs, at the time that the Einsatzgruppen were already murdering Jews in Russia, he turned to the Vatican through his ambassador to the Vatican, Léon Bérard, on August 7, 1941, to obtain from the highest Church authorities in Rome the go-ahead. A note written by Cardinal Maglione identifies the specialists who wrote the response to Bérard as none other than Msgr. Giovanni Battista Montini, the future Pope Paul VI, and Msgr. Domenico Tardini. The reply published in recent years is one of the most explicit and important documents that throws light on Vatican policy on anti-Jewish legislation during World War II.

The text of Bérard's extensive reply informs Petain that the Vatican experts found no objections against the legislation from a doctrinal viewpoint. Referring to historical precedent of Church practice with respect to the Jews, Vatican specialists found it justified that Jews should not hold any position of authority over Christians, and that their access to universities and the professions should be minimized. Even the requirement to wear the yellow star, Bérard was told, was well established in ecclesiastical law:

> St. Thomas nevertheless recommends that appropriate measures be taken to limit their action in society and to restrict their influence. It would be contrary to reason to allow them to exercise the powers of government in a Christian state and, by so doing, subject Catholics to their authority. Consequently, it is legitimate to deny them access to functions in the public arena and equally legitimate to admit them only by fixed quotas to universities (numerus clausus) and to the liberal professions. [53]

The report informs Petain that Vatican experts only objected to the clause that considered Catholic converts with three Jewish grandparents as Jews and to the prohibition of intermarriage, because it gave the state a foothold in the area of marriages, which the Vatican opposed as a matter of principle. Bérard was advised that the rejection of the Nazi race theory by the Church did not necessarily imply objections against the Statut des Juifs as a whole from a Catholic doctrinal viewpoint. He was given the strongest assurances that, unlike the case of Italy, no conflict, censure, or even objections from the Church to the Statut des Juifs would follow:

It cannot, however, be inferred from these teachings regarding racial ideas—far from it—that the Church necessarily condemns every particular measure taken by any state against what is called the Jewish race. Its thought on this matter embraces distinctions and nuances which should be noted . . .

I have indicated the only point on which the law of June 2, 1941 is at odds with a principle professed by the Roman Church (on restrictions based on race not religion). It does not follow at all from this doctrinal divergence that the French State is threatened, I will not say by a conflict like that which has arisen between the Holy See and the Fascist government, but even by censure or dis-approval which the Holy See might come to express in one way or another with regard to the statute on the Jews . . . As I have been told by an authorized person at the Vatican, no quarrel will be started with us because of the statute on the Jews.

The Vatican response reveals the moral duplicity in which perfunctory rejection of some forms of Aryan racism went hand in hand with approval of anti-Semitic persecutory legislation. Encouraged by the positive response of the Vatican, Petain and Laval put aside any doubts they might have entertained on the Statut des Juifs. They had the go-ahead from the Holy See to proceed with the anti-Jewish laws. Fr. Morley comments on the significance of the Bérard report:

The importance of the document rests on the implication that it removed from Petain's mind any doubts he might have had about the Christian reaction to the racial legislation.[54]

## The Death of Pius XI and the Rise of Pius XII

Pope Pius XI, Achille Ratti (1857-1939), died on February 9, 1939 at the most critical moment in modern history, when Hitler was making preparations to march on Poland. Less than a month later, on March 2, 1939, Cardinal Eugenio Pacelli (1876-1958), the Vatican secretary of state, was chosen as his successor, in one of the shortest conclaves in Church history. Only three days after his election, Pius XII announced to the German cardinals present in Rome that he intended to send a "message of peace" to Hitler, following the precedent of Leo XIII who brought an end to the Kulturkampf in the days of Bismarck. It meant that he intended to put behind the differences with the Third Reich that his predecessor seemed to be increasingly emphasizing and to begin a new chapter in the Vatican's relations with the Third Reich.

With a world war in sight, Hitler realized that he had to maintain good relations with the center of Christianity to be able to parade before the world as the defender of "Christian Civilization against the onslaught of the Red menace." Internally, Hitler grasped the key role played by the Church in keeping the domestic front quiet during the war. While millions of German Catholics were fighting under his command with the blessings of their bishops and chaplains he had to postpone his power struggle with the Church for after the war. Hitler ordered a truce on the religious domestic front for the duration of the war.

If filled churches help me to keep the people quiet, then in view of the burden
of war there can be no objection to them.[55]

The Ministry of Ecclesiastical Affairs restored on January 6, 1940, on the
basis of the Führer's amnesty of September 9, 1939, the salaries of a large number of priests who had their state subsidy cut off because of minor infractions of
the law. Hitler prohibited "any action against the Catholic and Protestant
churches for the duration of the war." Klaus Scholder points out that the truce
with the Church held out well all through the war:

> In fact right up to the end of the war, no German Bishop on either the Catholic
> side or the Protestant side was arrested for political reasons.[56]

To demonstrate his special appreciation for Germany and its Führer, Pius
XII sent his first official letter communicating his election as Pope to Hitler on
March 6, 1939, before any other head of state. Msgr. Alberto Giovanetti, one of
the official historians of Pius XII, recognizes that this particular letter, which
was discussed beforehand with German cardinals then in Rome, went far beyond
the diplomatic formalities of all other communications to heads of state: "This
letter differs totally in form and substance from all the other official letters sent
by the Vatican at that time." It remains a most eloquent example of the Pope's
sympathies.[57] In another sign of deference to Germany, Diego von Bergen, the
German ambassador to the Vatican (1920-1943), was the first diplomatic representative to be received by the new Pope on March 5, 1939. He was made aware
of this distinction by the Pope himself. In a memorandum to Berlin, von Bergen
highlights the special meaning of the Pope's inaugural letter to Hitler:

> The Pope has intimidated to me that the Führer was the first Head of State
> whom he notified of his election as Pope; he had also broken with the usual
> protocol when he not only signed, as was customary, the letter drawn in Latin,
> but also the German draft, which was not to be considered as a mere transla-
> tion. He also wished by these means to intimate his sympathetic attitude to
> Germany and his desire for peace.[58]

At the express wish of Pius XII, Nuncio Orsenigo, in an exceptional display of friendship toward the Führer, opened the great congratulatory court at
Hitler's fiftieth birthday on April 20, 1939. That date became a special occasion
for celebration for the Church in Germany.[59] All the Catholic churches in Germany celebrated special masses and tolled their bells "to implore the divine
blessing upon Führer and people," and most of them hoisted the swastika flag.

Hitler with Vatican Nuncio Cesare Orsenigo in Berlin. USHMM

Pius XII's admiration for Germany was reciprocated. A day before the election of the Pope in Rome, Count Galeazzo Ciano, Mussolini's son-in-law and Italian Foreign Minister, was told by Italian Ambassador to the Vatican Pignatti di Custoza that Cardinal Pacelli was the candidate favored by the Germans. It is relevant to cite Hitler's flattering statement about Pius XII made in 1941 to SS General Karl Wulff, Himmler's liaison with Hitler. At Pius XII's beatification trial in 1972, Wulff testified that Hitler expressed personally to him his admiration for Pius XII in 1941:

> If I could nominate a German Pope for German Catholics, I would without any hesitation choose Pacelli.[60]

Biographers and Church historians reflect on the exceptional fondness shown by Pope Pius XII to Germany, which he expressed on every occasion to his German visitors and in congratulation letters to the Führer and his underlings. A message delivered in German before a group of German pilgrims on April 25, 1939, gives expression to his feelings for Germany at a time that the Third Reich had already swallowed up Austria and Czechoslovakia and was preparing for war against Poland:

> We have always loved Germany, where We were privileged to spend years of Our life, and We love it much more now. We rejoice at the greatness of Germany, at her resurgence and her prosperity, and it would be false to maintain that We do not desire a flourishing, great, and strong Germany. We wish too, that the rights of God and the Church may always be recognized, because the

more these rights are guarded and made the basis of constructive effort, the more stable will be the foundation on which greatness is built.[61]

Pius XII had served as nuncio in Germany for twelve years (1917-1929) before he became Vatican secretary of state in 1929. His first acquaintance with Germany took place during World War I when he was delegated by the Vatican as a peace negotiator to the Kaiser to explore the possibility of a compromise-peace. Although his early diplomatic venture was unsuccessful, it stood him well to be appointed nuncio to Bavaria in 1917. Nuncio Pacelli resided until 1926 in Munich and then transferred to Berlin where he stayed until 1929. In Munich, the cradle of the Nazi movement, he witnessed closely its development from the very beginning. It was there that Corporal Hitler came with an introduction letter from Ludendorff in late 1919 to solicit funds from the nuncio for the *Deutsche Arbeterpartei* and received "a large cache of Church money" to fight the red menace. [62]

Elevated to cardinal in 1929, Pacelli returned to Rome where he was promoted to Vatican secretary of state at the death of Cardinal Pietro Gasparri. From Rome he continued his close surveillance of German affairs. Germany was the center piece of Pacelli's global vision of Church's interests. He relied on Nazi Germany, of all people, as the main defense against Communism—the dam that stood between Europe and Communist expansion. His admiration for Germany and things German knew no bounds. Franz von Papen (1879-1969), one of his admirers who helped Hitler climb to power, praised his knowledge of Germany in the following hyperbolic terms:

It must be hundreds of years since a Pope knew Germany and the German people, with all their virtues and faults, as well as he does.[63]

From the day he came to Germany as nuncio in 1917 until his death in 1958, Pius XII identified himself so thoroughly with Germany, as if he was a member of the German episcopate. Their differences with National Socialism did not prevent them from supporting Hitler in all his aggressive adventures, although it meant giving endorsement to a regime of unprecedented evil. Except where it directly affected the interests of the Church, the bishops kept their peace as disciplined soldiers who had taken an oath of loyalty to their Führer. Pius XII was perfectly attuned to them and even as Pope saw world problems their way. With their silence they rendered a service of incalculable value to Hitler, leaving the playing field completely free to him.

In his personal life, Pius XII showed a preference for things German. His two closest assistants Leiber and Kaas were German priests. His housekeeper Pasqualina Lehnert was a German nun. His confessor, Fr. Augustin Bea was German, as was Fr. Hendrich who helped draft his speeches He was surrounded by many other German prelates as advisors such as Gustav Gundlach, Pancrasius Pfeiffer, Msgr. Wüstenberg, and Alois Hudal. He spoke in German with them and showed special predilection for the German newspapers in his daily personal review of the press.[64] Last, but not least, the fact that Italy and Germany were on the same side in the war and that he and the Curia were Italians was another concurring factor that strengthened his pro-German leaning.

Throughout his career as nuncio, secretary of state, [65] and Pope, Pius XII was highly supportive of the German grievances against the Versailles Treaty and approved Hitler's efforts to undo its effects and enlarge the German Lebensraum. All his pronouncements along the years on the question led Michael Phayer to draw the following conclusion:

> From the beginning of the war to its very end, Pius XII sought to undo the consequences of the First World War by enlarging Germany. Even as Germany's fate became clear late in the war, Pius wrote to Cardinal Michael Faulhaber of Munich in 1944 indicating that in a negotiated peace Germany should not have to give up Austria and the Sudeten province of Czechoslovakia. [66]

Heinrich Brünning (1885-1970), the Catholic leader of the Center Party and German ex-Chancellor, knew Pacelli well for many years. At the time of the election of Pius XII, Brünning, then in exile, spoke his mind before Lord Robert Vansittart (1881-1957), the British undersecretary of foreign affairs. In his report Vansittart summarized Brünning's view on what could be expected from Pacelli's election:

> This devout German Catholic [Brünning] considers there is much naivety in Pacelli's make-up, particularly in that he believes in temporizing with the present regimes in Germany and Italy. [67]

Brünning was proven right; Pius XII avoided carefully any explicit criticism of the Third Reich during the war, even in the most critical situations, and always reassured the Nazi government that his words, even when they might sound as a criticism were never meant against them. Until his death in 1958, Pius XII was eager to maintain his image before the Germans as their unconditional friend. To assure Hitler that he was not critical of Germany's political system, Pius XII reminded German ambassador Diego von Bergen, of the statement he made as Vatican secretary of state before the International Eucharistic Congress in Budapest on May 27, 1938, nine months before he became Pope:

> It is not the business of the Church to take sides in purely temporal matters and concerns between the various systems and methods that may be considered for mastering urgent problems of the day.

At that important Catholic forum, Msgr. Pacelli sought to win the goodwill of anti-Semites everywhere when he referred to the Jews of this day and age with contempt. He extolled Christian love as Christianity's wonderful contribution to the world but seemed to forget his "Christian love and charity" when he unexpectedly referred to the contemporary Jewish people:

This neighborly love—this wonderful Christian contribution to the world—which cannot be expressed either in figures or in literature, exists everywhere and makes its sublime contribution to the solution of the raging problems of social distress and we shall be worthy of it only if our encouragement of love is from now on the alpha and omega of our entire existence.

As opposed to the foes who cried out to his face "crucify him," we sing him hymns of our loyalty and our love. We act in this fashion, not out of bitterness, not out of a sense of superiority, not out of arrogance toward the Jews whose lips curse him and whose hearts reject him even today.[68]

Germany was the center and axis of Pius XII's global policy. Historian Klaus Scholder cites a report by his closest collaborator, the German Jesuit Robert Leiber, which states that German affairs occupied the cardinal secretary of state as much as, "if not more than all the rest put together and even ten years later, in 1939, Pacelli rose to become Pope Pius XII, things did not change." He maintained the closest contact with the bishops of Germany. "Probably no one," says Scholder "more persistently shaped the ecclesiastical and political destiny of German Catholicism in the first half of this century than this true Roman."[69]

Every year until the collapse of the Third Reich, Cardinal Bertram would congratulate the Führer in the name of the bishops on his birthday and reaffirm their loyalty to Volk, army, Fatherland, and Führer. At the occasion of Hitler's fifty-first birthday in April 1940, Cardinal Bertram sent an enthusiastic message in the name of the bishops conference, celebrating German victories and expressing their loyalty to the Führer.

A review of the incomparably great successes and events of recent years and the gravity of this war which has come over us gives me, as chairman of the Fulda Bishops' Conference, special reason, in the name of the bishops of all the dioceses in Germany, to convey to you on your birthday the warmest felicitations . . . I beg to be allowed to call to remembrance that our aims do not stand in any contradiction to the programme of the National Socialist party and that they find a clear echo in your own policy statement of 23.03.1933 and commitment of 28.04.1933 . . . With the most reverend obedience, Cardinal Adolf Bertram, Archbishop of Breslau.[70]

When Hitler escaped an assassination attempt on November 11, 1939, Pius XII sent him a congratulatory telegram expressing his "deep satisfaction" that he had come out unscathed. Four years later when Hitler narrowly escaped a much closer call on his life on July 20, 1944, Pius XII again congratulated him on his survival.[71] Cardinal Faulhaber and all the bishops of Bavaria sent a message of congratulations to Hitler after the 1939 attempt and conducted a solemn *Te Deum* service at the Munich Cathedral:

To thank Providence for the Führer's fortunate escape . . . We Catholic Christians are joined with entire German Volk in the burning wish that the God may protect our Führer and Volk. [72]

A wave of patriotic German nationalism enveloped the German clergy when Germany attacked Poland and World War II began. The German bishops declared Hitler's aggression as just and legitimate in a theological sense and called every German Catholic to fulfill his patriotic duty and rally to the defense of Volk, Vaterland, and Heimat. Their Nationalist goals blended easily with Nazi racial goals, offering without reservations their support to the expansion of the German Lebensraum. They issued a patriotic exhortation to the German people demanding "obedience toward the Führer and prayers for Führer and Reich." When Poland surrendered, the church bells were tolled for one full week in jubilation all over Germany by order of the bishops. Refusal by Catholics to serve in the German army during the war was almost nonexistent as support of Hitler was declared a religious duty.[73]

# Notes

1. Georges Passelecq and Bernard Suchecky, *The Hidden Encyclical of Pius XI* (Orlando, Fl.: Harcourt Press, 1997).

2. Conor Cruise O'Brien, *"A Lost Chance to Save the Jews?"* (NY Review of Books. April, 1989), 27.

3. Fr. Edward H. Flannery *"Good thing Papal draft was never signed"* (Providence Journal Bulletin).

4. Fr. Edward H. Flannery (1912-1998). *The Catholic Church and the Holocaust,* (1930-1965). Fr. Edward H. Flannery, *The Anguish of the Jews: Twenty-Three Centuries of Antisemitism* (Mahwah, NJ: Stimulus Books, 2004).

5. Passelecq and Suchecky, *The Hidden Encyclical of Pius XI.*

6. Passelecq and Suchecky, *The Hidden Encyclical of Pius XI.*

7. Fr. Edward H. Flannery, *"Good thing Papal draft was never signed."*

8. Passelecq and Suchecky, *The Hidden Encyclical of Pius XI.* Flannery *"The Catholic Church and the Holocaust."* Flannery, *"The Anguish of the Jews."*

9. Passelecq and Suchecky, *The Hidden Encyclical of Pius XI,* xxi.

10. David I. Kertzer, *The Popes Against the Jews* (New York: Alfred A. Knopf, 2001), 279-280.

11. Kertzer, *The Popes Against the Jews,* 279-280.

12. Kertzer, *The Popes Against the Jews,* 279-280.

13. Kertzer, *The Popes Against the Jews,* 278.

14. Kertzer, *The Popes Against the Jews,* 275.

15. Susan Zucotti, *Under His Very Windows: The Vatican and the Holocaust in Italy* (New Haven, Ct: Yale University Press, 2000), 11.

16. December 41: *"The Great Dilemma".* March 42: *"The Actors of the Trials of J."* Michael Phayer, *The Catholic Church and the Holocaust, 1930-1965* (Indiana University Press, 2001), 8.

17. Martin Rhonheimer. *The Holocaust: What Was Not Said* (New York: First Things, 2003), 18-28, 137.

18. Sam Waagenaar, *The Pope's Jews* (La Salle, IL: Open Court Publishers, 1974), 321. *"Civiltà Cattolica",* June 19, 1937.

19. Waagenaar, *The Pope's Jews.*

20. Waagenaar, *The Pope's Jews.*

21. Deborah Dwork and Robert Jan Van Pelt, *Holocaust: A History* (New York: W. W. Norton and Company, 2002), 140-141. The memorandum describes a meeting between Hitler and Ribbentrop with Frantisek Chvalkovsky, the Czechoslovak Foreign Minister. Source: Le Livre Jaune Francais: Documents Diplomatiques, 1938-1939: Paris 1939.

22. Raul Hilberg, *The Destruction of the European Jews* (Teaneck, NJ: Holmes & Meier, 1985).

23. *Algemeine Enziklopedie in Yiddish* (New York: Yidn D. CYCO, 1950), 238.

24. Norman Davies, *God's Playground, A History of Poland* (New York: Columbia University Press, 1982), 263.

25. Ronald Modras, *Catholic Church and Antisemitism: Poland, 1933-1939* (Florence, KY: Routledge, 1994), 396.

26. Modras, *The Catholic Church and Anti-Semitism.*

27. Modras, *The Catholic Church and Anti-Semitism.* Joseph Marcus, *Social and Political History of the Jews in Poland, 1919-1939* (Berlin, Germany: Mouton de Gruyter, 1983).

28. Abraham L. Peck, *American Jewish Archives vol. 8.,* (Cincinnati, OH: Wayne State University Press, 1990), 21.

29. *Gazetta Swiatechna* (no. 2915, 1936).

30. Davies, *God's Playground.*

31. S. Dubnow, *"Divrei Yimei Olam"* (Tel Aviv: Dvir, 1958), vol. 10, 294. *Algemeine Enziklopedie*, 238–239.

32. *Algemeine Enziklopedie*, 239.

33. William Zuckerman, *"The Nation"* (April 2, 1938. Vol. 146, No. 14), 379–381.

34. *Algemeine Enziklopedie*, 242.

35. Waagenaar, *The Pope's Jews.*

36. *"Il Regime Fascista"*, August 30, 1938.

37. Kertzer, *The Popes Against the Jews,* 287.

38. Renzo De Felice, *Storia degli ebrei italiani sotto il fascismo* (Eunadi, Turin: 1988). Zuccotti, *Under His Very Windows*, 48.

39. De Felice, *Storia degli ebrei italiani.* Zuccotti, *Under His Very Windows*, 48.

40. Waagenaar, *The Pope's Jews.*

41. Modras, *The Catholic Church and Anti-Semitism.*

42. Kertzer. *The Popes Against the Jews.* Susan Zuccoti, *Under His Very Windows.*

43. Kertzer, *The Popes Against the Jews*, 285. Published in the bulletin of the archdiocese.

44. Alfredo Romanini, *Ebrei–Cristianesimo–Fascismo.*

45. Waagenaar, *The Pope's Jews.* Meir Michaelis, *"Fascist Policy toward Italian Jews* (US: Oxford University Press, 1979)

46. Waagenaar, *The Pope's Jews.*

47. John F. Morley, *Vatican Diplomacy and the Jews During the Holocaust 1939-1943* (New York: Ktav Publishing, 1980), 168. Susan Zucotti, *The Italians and the Holocaust* (New York: Basic Books, 1987), 43. Zuccotti, *Under His Very Window.*

48. Kertzer, *The Popes Against the Jews,* 287. Moshe Y. Herczl, *Christianity and the Holocaust of Hungarian Jewry.* (New York: NYU Press, 1993), 99.

49. Herczl, *Christianity and the Holocaust of Hungarian Jewry.*

50. Herczl, *Christianity and the Holocaust of Hungarian Jewry,* 111.

51. Herczl, *Christianity and the Holocaust of Hungarian Jewry.* 128.

52. Morley, *Vatican Diplomacy and the Jews.*

53. Zuccotti, *Under His Very Window*, 55. Michael R. Marus and Robert O. Paxton. *Vichy France and the Jews.* (Stanford, CA: Stanford University Press, 1995), 200-203.

54. Morley, *Vatican Diplomacy and the Jews.*

55. Louis Lochner, Ed. *The Goebbels Diaries* (New York: Doubleday & Company, 1948), 141.

56. Klaus Scholder, *A Requiem for Hitler* (Philadelphia, PA: Trinity Press Int., 1989), 117.

57. B. Schneider, *Acts, Vol. 2 Lettres aux Eveques Allemands*, *The Briefe Pius XII,* (Mainz 1966) 318, 299. Anthony Rhodes, *The Vatican in the Age of Dictators 1922-1945* (London, UK: Hodder and Stoughton, 1973), 226-228.

58. Friedlander, *Nazi Germany and the Jews*, 15.

59. Scholder, *A Requiem for Hitler*, 161. Güenther Lewy, *The Catholic Church and Nazi Germany* (New York: Mc Graw Hill Book Co., 1964), 221.

60. Interview published in Der Stern, April 16, 1972.

61. Saul Friedlander, *Pius XII and the Third Reich* (New York: Alfred A. Knopf, 1966).

62. Paul I. Murphy and Rene R. Arlington, *La Popessa: The Controversial Biography of Sister Pascalina, the Most Powerful Woman in Vatican History* (New York: Warner Books, 1983).

63. Franz Von Papen, *Memoirs* (New York: E. P. Dutton & Co. 1953), 126.

64. Carlo Falconi, *The Silence of Pius XII* (Boston: Little, Brown, 1970).

65. Murphy and Arlington, *La Popessa*, 249-250.

66. Phayer, *The Catholic Church and the Holocaust.*

67. Rhodes, *The Vatican in the Age of Dictators,* 226.

68. Herczl, *Christianity and the Holocaust.*

69. Scholder, *A Requiem for Hitler.*

70. Johann Neumann, *1945: The German Churches Before and Afterwards* (1995).

71. Pierre SJ Blet, *Pius XII and the Second World War According to the Archives of the Vatican.* (New York: Paulist Press, 1999).

72. Lewy, *The Catholic Church and Nazi Germany,* 310-311.

73. Gordon Zahn, *German Catholics and Hitler's Wars: A Study in Social Control* (New York: Sheed and Ward, 1962), 54. Only seven German Catholics refused, six were executed and one was put into a military mental asylum.

## Chapter 7
## World War II

### The Attack on Poland

On September 12, 1938, Hitler spoke in praise of the late Polish Marshal Josef Pilsudski (1867-1935) whom he called a great Polish patriot for having signed in 1934 a nonaggression pact with Germany that guaranteed the inviolability of German-Polish borders:

> When in Poland a great statesman and patriot was ready to conclude a pact with us, we immediately accepted the treaty recognizing our respective frontiers as inviolable. This treaty has done more for peace than all the chattering in Geneva put together. [1]

A week later, Hitler extended an invitation to Poland to join in the rape of Czechoslovakia and promised Poland the Tsechen region in reward. No more than four months later, Hitler swallowed his words about the inviolability of the German-Polish borders and shamelessly demanded from Poland the return of the free city of Danzig and an extraterritorial passage across Poland to link Germany to East Prussia. [2] On January 5, 1939, he expressed his demands in Berchtesgaden to Polish Foreign Minister Joseph Beck. Three weeks later, on January 30, 1939, at the commemoration of the sixth anniversary of his rise to power, Hitler threatened with brazen cynicism in the Reichstag the Allied Powers with the annihilation of the Jewish race if his territorial demands of a corridor in Poland were denied:

> And one thing I wish to say on this day, which perhaps is memorable not only for us Germans. In my life I have often been a prophet and most of the time I have been laughed at . . . Today, I want to be a prophet once more: should international Jewry of finance succeed, both within and beyond Europe, in plunging mankind into yet another world war, then the result will not be a Bolshevization of the earth and the victory of Jewry, but the annihilation of the Jewish race in Europe. [3]

After the invasion of Bohemia and Moravia, another territorial gain came easily in Hitler's way—the Port of Memel in Lithuania. As a result of a threatening ultimatum, Lithuania surrendered three days later to the Reich the Port of Memel without a single shot after signing on March 22, 1939, a so-called non-aggression treaty with Germany. In Spain, Franco announced victory over the Spanish Republic on April 1, 1939, when the last strongholds of resistance in Barcelona and Madrid surrendered. In a radio address "Con Inmenso Gozo" on April 16, 1939, Pius XII congratulated the Spanish rebels for their victory:

> Immense joy and fatherly congratulations for the gift of peace and victory with which God has deigned to crown the Christian heroism of your faith and charity, proved through such great and generous sufferings.[4]

The chain of successes convinced Hitler that it was about time to begin his march *Nach Osten*. On March 25, 1939, Hitler ordered the Wehrmacht to prepare military operation plans for war with Poland. Three days later, on April 28, 1939, Hitler rescinded unilaterally the 1934 Polish-German non aggression pact, in open violation of its terms.

Applying the tactics that worked so well for him in Austria and Chechoslovakia, Goebbeles launched a propaganda campaign claiming that Poland was mistreating the German minority. Germany raised the tone of its denunciations of Polish atrocities, demanding the unconditional transfer of Danzig and the creation of the Polish Corridor. Nazi agents disguised as tourists were sent to inflame the conflict and Nazi armed bands began to infiltrate the city. The Polish-German borders, which Hitler had declared inviolable only months earlier, he now declared intolerable. German troops were strategically gathered at the Polish borders. For five months Poland lived in a state of semi-mobilization, and by the time the crisis reached a critical stage in August, millions of men had been mobilized.

The British and the French finally realized that Hitler's territorial ambitions would not be satisfied with another concession and that Hitler's Lebensraum dreams went far beyond Danzig. They finally grasped that the German generals were trying to win time to better prepare for a major future confrontation with the West at the moment of their choice. Appeasement could only lead to the most dangerous of future consequences. The British government convinced the French government to issue a joint declaration guaranteeing the integrity of Poland. Winston Churchill, then in opposition, pointed out the irony of defending Poland after having betrayed Czechoslovakia, a country that shamefully joined with Hitler in the rape of Czechoslovakia:

> And now . . . Great Britain advances leading France by the hand to guarantee the integrity of Poland, that very Poland which with hyena-appetite had only six months before joined in the pillage and destruction of the Czechoslovak State.[5]

Hitler was not much impressed with Allied guarantees to Poland after having tested for years their lack of resolve. He and his generals were nevertheless apprehensive about a possible Soviet alliance with Western powers and the eventuality of having to fight on two fronts simultaneously as in World War I. To neutralize the Soviets, Hitler again used the bait that proved so successful in attracting Poland and Hungary in the rape of Czechoslovakia. He offered Stalin Eastern Poland if he joined him in attacking their mutual neighbor. Stalin obligingly accepted. Ribbentrop and Molotov signed a nonaggression pact in Moscow on August 23, 1939, to which they attached a secret appendix, in which they agreed to divide Poland between them along the rivers Narew, Vistula, and San. They also defined their spheres of influence in Eastern Europe: Finland, Estonia, Latvia, and Bessarabia were assigned to the Soviet sphere of influence. In a later addendum, Lithuania was also included in the Soviet sphere.

On June 4, 1939, Pius XII announced to the British representative, Francis d'Arcy Osborne, his readiness to act as a mediator between the Third Reich and Poland. Sir Orme Sargent, the principal secretary of the British Foreign Office, was critical of the attitude of the Pope:

> I feel that he would be able to influence events far more effectively as champion of certain moral principles in the world of today than he is likely as a possible but improbable candidate for the post of mediator between the Axis and the Democracies.[6]

The French ambassador to the Vatican, François Charles-Roux, reacted to Pius XII's offer critically indicating that the surest way to prevent war was for the Pope to use his moral authority to condemn Hitler's new attempt of annexation of Polish territory instead of offering to act as a mediator, but Charles-Roux's words made no impression on Pius XII.[7]

> Matters have reached the point when to preserve the peace the Holy Father, whose efforts to preserve it have been so untiring, should now state with the authority which He alone disposes that a country whose huge territorial annexations have only increased its insatiable appetite is entirely responsible for the present dangerous situation.[8]

Instead of condemning Germany for its territorial demands, Pius XII instead urged the Polish government through his nuncio in Warsaw, Msgr. Filippo Cortesi, to give in to the German demands. On August 30, 1939, one day before the German attack on Poland, the Vatican sent a note through its Nuncio urging the government of Poland to recognize officially that "Poland does not oppose the return of Danzig to Germany." Colonel Josef Beck (1894-1944), the Polish Foreign Minister had this much to say in his memoirs on the Pope's advice:[9]

> The initiative of the Holy See was unfortunate. In the last days of August 1939 the Pope approached us suggesting that the cession of Danzig would save the

peace. I replied that the publication of this proposal would offend the most sensitive feelings of the Catholic majority of citizens in this country. [10]

To justify an attack on Poland, Heydrich's SS men, disguised as Polish officers, staged a sham attack on a German radio station in the border town of Gleiwitz during the night of August 31, 1939. Replicating the tactics they used in the Reichstag fire, the Germans blamed the Poles for the attack. Next day, September 1, Hitler declared war on Poland in the Reichstag, claiming that Poland had attacked Germany and German forces were being forced to respond in self-defense. The Fulda Conference issued a pastoral letter from the German bishops expressing their unconditional support to the Führer and the war:

> We encourage and exhort our Catholic soldiers to do their duty in obedience to the Führer, ready for sacrifice and with the commitment of the whole being . . . We pray that God grant us victory . . . inspired by God's love we stand behind our Führer. [11]

Cardinal Faulhaber of Munich demanded in the name of Christian duty from the Catholics to offer their patriotic support to the war. Cardinal von Galen, the opponent of the euthanasia program, was no less passionate in his support of the war effort. The major role played by German bishops in supporting Hitler's war among the German Catholics is highlighted by the late Gordon C. Zahn:

> The German bishops, including Galen, did take a specific and express public stand by placing their followers under a moral obligation to support Hitler's wars. The ordinary Catholic, the man-in-the-pew who went to war, dropped the bombs, and sank the ships, could do so partly because his bishops told him he not only had a right to do so but was actually duty-bound to do so. [12]

Hitler ordered the Luftwaffe to bombard Polish cities and Wermacht panzer divisions to march on Poland. With more than 2,000 tanks and 1,000 planes, the Germans broke through Polish defenses along the border. Although Britain and France formally stood by their guarantee to Poland and declared war on Germany on September 3, 1939, they abstained from launching a military counteroffensive that could have changed the course of the war. The German Blitzkrieg strategy was a total success for the Wehrmacht. Poland's cavalry was no match for the motorized German Panzer divisions that encircled Warsaw. After seventeen days of heavy shelling, the desperate resistance led mainly by civilians broke down. Warsaw capitulated on September 27, 1939. By order of the German bishops, the Church bells were tolled jubilantly throughout Germany for a full week at midday to celebrate the German victory.

It is only a matter of speculation what the Vatican policy might have been with respect to the attack on Poland had Pius XI still been alive in September 1939. An Italian by birth, the previous Pope had strong ties to Poland. Consecrated bishop in Poland by Cardinal Kakovski on October 29, 1919, he often referred to himself as a Polish bishop. After serving as apostolic visitor in Poland in 1918 and nuncio in 1919, he succeeded Benedict XV as Pope in 1922. One thing, however, can be stated with near certainty: the death of Pius XI and the rise of Pius XII made it much easier for Hitler to attack Catholic Poland without fear of repercussion from the center of Catholicism. This was well understood by von Bergen who pointed out to his superiors in Berlin in January 1940 how fortunate they were to have Pius XII and not his predecessor as Pope at the time:

Pius XI would have behaved quite differently over the Polish war.[13]

Pius XII saw the German invasion of Poland, according to Catholic historian Friedrich Heer of Vienna (1916-1983), as an opportunity for the Poles to join with the Germans in an alliance against Soviet Russia:

Let us end this war between brothers and unite our forces against the common enemy of atheism—Russia.[14]

Instead, Pius XII witnessed how Nazi Germany joined with Communist Russia in crushing Poland. Despite the pleas of the Polish government and Western powers to condemn the German attack, Pius XII remained silent. On September 7, 1939, von Bergen reported to the German Foreign Ministry:

The Pope's refusal to take sides against Germany would be entirely in harmony with assurances he has repeatedly conveyed to me through trusted agent in recent weeks.[15]

Poland held out for a full month and surrendered formally to the Germans on October 1, 1939. The last islands of resistance around Gdynia fell on October 2 and organized Polish military resistance ceased completely on October 6. Poland lost 300,000 men. Approximately 450,000 prisoners fell in the hands of the Germans and 200,000 in the hands of the Soviets. The Northern and Western regions of Poland were annexed formally to the Third Reich as part of Grossdeutchland on October 8, under the names Reichsgaue of Danzig-Westpreussen and Wartheland.[16] They were subjected without delay to intense Germanization under Gauleiter Arthur Greiser (1897-1946). The rest of Poland, renamed the Generalgouvernement, was given the status of a colony under the administration of the brutal SA stormtrooper Hans Frank (1900-1946) as governor-general and Seyss-Inquart as his deputy.

Hitler intended to radically change the political geography and demography of Europe in a short period. On October 7, 1939, he created the Reich Commission for the Consolidation of Germandom (RKFDV) to carry out the Germanization of the conquered territories and appointed Himmler head of the commission. The 1940 edition of *Der Menscheneinsatz*, a confidential publication of the commision, clearly spelled out its aim of removing foreign races from the incorporated eastern territories:

> The removal of foreign races from the incorporated Eastern Territories is one of the most essential goals to be accomplished in the German East. This is the chief national political task, which has to be executed in the incorporated Eastern Territories by the Reichsfuehrer SS, Reich Commissioner for the strengthening of the national character of the German people. [17]

In accordance with Himmler's racial plan, nearly 1 million Polish citizens were expelled from Danzig-Westpreussen and Wartheland and driven east to the Generalgouvernement to make room for around 600,000 Volksdeutsche from Eastern Europe and 400,000 from the German Reich. Millions of Polish citizens were rounded up for compulsory labor, both inside Poland and in the Reich. The uprooting was accompanied by an unprecedented program of systematic looting and robbery of property. Göhring's Haupttreuhandelstelle Ost, created on October 19, 1939, coordinated the massive confiscation and looting of Jewish and Polish property and the exploitation of the occupied territories.

In a bloody action under the code name "Operation Tannenberg" (Unternehmen Tannenberg), at least 20,000 of the most prominent Polish citizens were murdered in 760 mass executions by the SS Einsatzkommandos, between September and October 1939. The victims were rounded in the streets during so-called lapankas and often executed on the spot. Others were sent to forced labor in Germany or to the new concentration camp established in Auschwitz. Some were held hostage in the Pawiak Prison in Warsaw and later executed. News of the German massive arrest and displacement of population and killing of Polish intelligentsia did not move the Pope to action. Francis Osborne, the British representative in the Vatican, was appalled by the Pope's silence:

> An ostrich-like policy towards notorious atrocities . . . Through his inaction the great moral authority enjoyed by the Papacy throughout the world under Pius XI has been notably diminished. [18]

After many appeals from Polish Church leaders, Pius XII finally issued, on October 20, 1939, seven weeks after the invasion, a belated encyclical *Summi Pontificatus* expressing compassion for the displaced Poles, but refraining from condemning Germany by name. In December 1939, after Cardinal Hlond fled Poland and arrived in Rome, Vatican Radio broadcasted a report that originated with Cardinal Hlond on the terror in Poland. The report compared the terror in Poland "with that imposed on Spain in 1936 by the Communists." When German Ambassador Diego von Bergen protested against the broadcasts in the name of the German government, the broadcasts were promptly silenced. On January 29, 1940, Ambassador Bergen confirmed the cessation of all broadcasts about atrocities in Poland.

At the 1940 New Year reception in the Vatican, Pius XII personally took care to dissipate any idea that he was opposed to the Hitler regime and assured the German chargé d'affaires of his special feelings for Germany. Msgr. Montini, the future Paul VI, was able to smooth things out by assuring von Bergen that nothing could be further from the truth than to think that the Vatican was anti-

German. After all "the Pope regarded the German claims on Poland with a reasonable eye and had advised Poland to accept the claims on Danzig through its Nuncio in Poland":

> Certainly the Pope did not want Germany to be defeated, because this would open the way to atheistic Communism in Europe.[19]

On Christmas Eve 1939, four months after the bloody invasion and partition of Poland, Pius XII proposed in an address to the College of Cardinals a peace plan.[20] Nazi diplomacy at the time ignored the Pope's peace plan altogether. Three years later, however, when the tide turned against Germany and the Third Reich faced the Allied demand of unconditional surrender, to which Pius XII strongly objected, the Nazis suddenly found the Vatican plan useful in order to mobilize the Vatican as a mediator in a negotiated peace.

To test out if Western powers would agree that Germany could keep conquered lands in a negotiated peace-agreement, leading figures of the German General Staff, which included General Ludwig Beck (1880-1944) delegated secretly in early February 1940, Dr. Josef Müller a Catholic trusted by Pius XII to inform him they were ready for peace if Germany would be left in possession of the lands it held. They claimed that they were even ready to stage a coup and depose the Führer if given assurances that a peace would not be "another Compiegne nor Wilsonian in nature." The Pope informed the English government of the proposal through its representative Sir Francis Osborne, but the English government didn't take the bait and responded that until Hitler and his gang were actually eliminated, their offer lacked credibility and any negotiations and promises were premature.[21]

As the Wehrmacht was preparing to invade neutral Holland, Belgium and Norway in early 1940, Hitler again took the necessary steps to make sure that the Vatican would hold its peace. Hitler timely dispatched his Foreign Minister von Ribbentrop to Rome to meet the Pope on March 11, 1940. To impress the Pope with the inevitability of a Nazi victory Ribbentrop boasted that "German soldiers would be in Paris by June and in London by August."[22] He then pointed out the great benefits the Church was reaping through the concordat and the risks involved in marching out of step with the Third Reich. Like a magic spell, the concordat did not fail to act as a most persuasive means to keep the Vatican in line. It gave Hitler powerful leverage over the Church, and he used it in a carrot and stick strategy. Ribbentrop needed nothing more than to remind Pius XII that the concordat was bringing in the Church in Germany a yearly income of 1 billion Reichsmark, "an achievement" he said "of which no other state could boast."

Ribbentropp did not forget to highlight the benevolence shown by the Führer by squashing more than 7,000 criminal court cases against Catholic priests in Germany. To make sure that the Pope did not take for granted his blessings, he pointed out that although the Führer considered the concordat to be outdated he was willing to wait until the after the war to revise its terms. The report summarizes Ribbentropp's words:

The Führer, he [Ribbentrop] said, was of the opinion that an agreement on fun-
damentals between National Socialism and the Catholic Church was entirely
possible . . . An understanding depended on one cardinal prerequisite, namely,
that the Catholic clergy in Germany renounce political activity in any shape or
form and confine themselves exclusively to the cure of souls, which alone was
their concern . . . We must not repeat an error such as the hasty conclusion of a
concordat . . . which must already be considered out of date. In the Führer's
opinion, therefore, the important thing for the time being was to maintain—and
if possible, extend—the existing truce . . . In this respect very considerable advance concessions had been made on the German side. The Führer had
squashed no fewer than 7,000 cases against Catholic priests. It should also not
be forgotten that the National-Socialist state was spending one billion Reichsmark [$400 million dollars at the then prevailing rate annually], an achieve-
ment of which no other state could boast. [23]

The message hit home; Pius XII responded with a love declaration to Germany and dispelled any doubts concerning his readiness to join to the Führer's
wishes. Both Ribbentrop's and the Vatican's accounts of the meeting fully coin-
cide on the Pope's accommodating response to Hitler's "promises." Monsignor
Giovanetti the Vatican's official historian's comments leave no doubts in this
respect:

During the interview he had been granted, Ribbentrop had been able to observe
with deep satisfaction that the Pope's heart was still in Germany and that he
displayed great goodwill in the matter of reaching an understanding. [24]

The following day, March 12, 1940, Hitler sent a telegram to the Pope,
congratulating him personally on the first anniversary of his election to the papacy. Cardinal Bertram gave new religious sanction to Hitler's war at the time.
He called Germany's war for new Lebensraum a "holy struggle whose purpose
was the highest of earthly goals: life in accordance with God's command."

## The Soviet Occupation of Eastern Poland (1939-1941)

Soviet Russia, Hitler's partner in the assault on Poland, played it safe and waited
until heavy fighting was practically over to enter the war and occupy eastern
Poland on September 17, 1939. On September 28, 1939, the Soviets transferred
the Vilna region of Poland to Lithuania. Next day Germany and the USSR
signed a new treaty modifying territorial arrangements in Poland and consigning
Lithuania to the Soviet sphere. The Bug River became the new demarcation line
between German- and Soviet-occupied Poland. Eastern Poland was incorporated
by the Soviets into the Ukraine and Byelorussia.

The Soviet Union also sided with Germany on the diplomatic front and accused Great Britain and France of engaging in a purely imperialist war. Communist parties all over the world followed Moscow's instructions and in a
shameless turnabout supported the conclusion of a peace treaty with Hitler on a

status quo basis that would recognize Hitler's conquests in Czechoslovakia and Poland.

The secret accords of the Molotov-Ribbentrop nonaggression pact gave the Soviets free hands in the east from which they tried to draw maximum benefit. Stalin began a chain of aggressions against his small neighbors. He ordered an attack on Finland on November 30, 1939. Finland held out until March 1940 and was forced to give up around 10 percent of its territory and 20 percent of its industrial capacity to the Soviet Union at the signing of a "peace" treaty. Lithuania, Latvia, and Estonia were next on the list to be swallowed up. In mid-June 1940 when the eyes of the world were fixed on the fall of Paris, the Soviets furtively occupied the three Baltic countries.

So-called parliamentary elections were called in the Baltic countries by local Communists loyal to the Soviet Union after all non-Communist candidates were disqualified. The three Baltic parliaments "unanimously" petitioned the Soviet government to accept them as members of the USSR. On August 4, 1940, the Supreme Council of the Soviet Union generously approved the petition and the three states ceased to exist as independent nations. To the south, Soviet Russia annexed the Romanian provinces of Bessarabia and northern Bukovina on June 26, 1940, after a Soviet ultimatum to Romania demanded their surrender within twenty-four hours.

With the occupation of western Poland by the Germans additional 2 million Polish Jews fell under German domination. On the Soviet side, the Jewish population increased by 1.3 million people. When in 1940 the Soviet Union swallowed the Baltic countries and the Romanian provinces of Bukovina and Bessarabia, an additional 900,000 Jews came under Soviet domination. Around 300,000 of them were refugees fleeing from the German side.

Under Soviet domination the Jewish population went through difficult times during the 1939-1941 transition period, although in no way comparable to the situation on the German side. Jewish religious institutional and educational activities were banned. The Soviet Secret Police arrested as "unreliable elements" many hundreds of thousands of Polish and Jewish residents in Eastern Poland, including great numbers of Jewish refugees from German-occupied Poland, who had refused to accept Soviet citizenship before the deadline of January 1941 as required by a Soviet decree. They were deported to Siberia during 1940 and 1941, sharing the fate already suffered by political deportees. Of the approximately 1.25 million to 1.6 million Polish citizens deported to Siberia and Kazakhstan between 1939 and 1941, around 300,000 were Jews, a proportion more than double the 10 percent of Jews in the Polish population. The Siberia exiles were subject to hard labor and suffered hunger and cold. Many of them died, but they were not gassed or mass murdered as under the Germans. They were soon envied by the Jews who stayed behind.[25]

When the Germans attacked their Soviet partners on June 22, 1941, few Jews in the Soviet-occupied territories were able to flee deeper into the Soviet Union. The great majority of those who tried to flee to the Soviets in the early days of the invasion from annexed countries were turned back by the Soviet guards at the old prewar Soviet border. Neither the Soviet citizenship forced upon them by the Soviet annexation nor their desperate pleas were to any avail. They were ordered to go back to German occupied-areas to face a mortal enemy. Armed Soviet border guards had one stern response to their desperate pleas:

> Nobody is allowed to cross. These are orders. Move back twenty steps. We will shoot if you do not. Get moving! One, two . . . fire![26]

During the two years of the Ribbentrop-Molotov Pact (1939-1941), Jews in Soviet Russia proper, were held in complete ignorance about the atrocities being committed on the German side. Any information on Nazi atrocities was suppressed on purpose by the tightly controlled Soviet press so as not to disturb friendly relations with the Germans. As a result, the Jews inside the Soviet Union were caught totally unprepared to face the new deadly situation. Even after the invasion, the Soviets allowed no mention in the tightly controlled Communist media of the specific Jewish plight under the Germans, as if the Jews had not been singled out in particular as the main target for total extinction.

With the doors of the West closed, only 40,000 Jewish refugees managed to get out from Poland at the last moment. More than half of them fled to the neighboring countries of Romania, Hungary, and Lithuania. An estimated 15,000 fled to independent Lithuania during the fall and winter of 1939 when news on the transfer of Vilna from Soviet to Lithuanian control spread over Poland. Among the refugees fleeing to short-lived independent Lithuania there were approximately 1,500 students of the Polish elite yeshivas and their mentors.

Their hopes that Lithuania would survive as a neutral country throughout the war were short lived when the Soviet Union occupied the Baltic countries in 1940. Fortunately, many of the yeshiva students were able to obtain Japanese and Soviet transit visas to Curaçao that allowed them to leave almost at the last moment. Two righteous consular officials in Kovno, the acting Dutch consul Jan Zwartendijk (1896-1976) and the Japanese vice consul Chiune Sugihara (1900-1986), deviating from the rules of their respective governments, extended visas to them. Although visas to Curaçao were practically meaningless because only the governor of Curaçao had the authority to issue landing permits to foreigners, a power he rarely exercised, Zwartendijk extended these visas as a life-saving ruse to get them out of the USSR. He made clear to them that the visas would not allow them entry to the island.

On the basis of the Curaçao visas, Sugihara was able to issue Japanese transit visas. The Soviets allowed them to cross the USSR on their way to Japan. About half of the roughly 2,200 refugees who reached Japan with Zwartendijk's and Sugihara's visas succeeded in moving on to the United States, Palestine, and other final destinations. None of them went to Curaçao. Those less fortunate, which included the almost totality of the Mir Yeshiva, were shipped by the Japanese government to Shanghai, the only place just prior to the Holocaust where one could land without any documentation. There the entire Mir Yeshiva survived the war.[27]

## Ghettos and Labor Camps in Occupied Poland (1939-1941)

While the military campaign in Poland was still in full swing, Reinhard Hey-drich (1904-1942), SS chief of the Reich Central Security Police, forwarded what he called a housecleaning plan to the Army High Command and to the chiefs of all einsatzgruppen on September 21, 1939. "No General who read the confidential memorandum could have doubted that it meant extermination," points out William L. Shirer. [28] "The plan," Heydrich warned, "would take some time to achieve and must be kept strictly secret." It contained the preliminary steps required for the subsequent annihilation of the Jews that Hitler had announced in his 1939 Reichstag speech. It ordered the concentration of the Jews from the countryside in the larger cities located near railway lines in preparation of their deportation:

> I refer to the conference held in Berlin today . . . Distinction must be made between: the final aim (which will require extended periods of time) and the stages leading to the fulfillment of this final aim (which will be carried out in short periods) . . . For the time being, the first prerequisite for the final aim is the concentration of the Jews from the countryside into the larger cities. [29]

Normal life ceased to exist for Jews. Even before being enclosed in ghettos, Jews were required to wear identifying armbands and were forbidden access to certain sections of the cities. They were ordered to declare their valuables and their houses. Factories, shops, and personal property of all kinds were confiscated. Very soon began the concentration of Jews into walled ghettoes and expulsion of all the Jews of the Warthegau to the Generalgouvernement (with the exception of Lodz).

The Germans regarded the establishment of Jewish ghettos as a provisional measure to control, isolate, and segregate Jews. The ghettos were created gradually. About 400 ghettos were established in occupied Poland from 1939 to 1941. The first Holocaust ghetto was established at Piotrków Trybunalski not far from Lodz in October 1939. The Lodz ghetto followed in April 1940. The Warsaw ghetto was sealed off in November 1940; then the Kraków ghetto in March 1941, and the Lublin and Radom ghettoes in April 1941. The small ghettos were liquidated and their dwellers transferred to the larger ghettos in 1941.

The establishment of the Warsaw ghetto was preceded by a bloody pogrom carried out by the Poles in February 1940 that lasted for three days. The Germans used the pogrom as an excuse, to issue, on August 20, the ghetto decree. On November 15, the Warsaw ghetto was sealed off. The Lodz ghetto with 160,000 Jews was sealed off earlier on May 1, 1940. Slave factories were organized in the ghettos of Warsaw, Lodz and Kraków among others.

Seen in retrospect it is now well understood, that the identification, concentration, and enclosure of the Jews in ghettos was a crucial step in the Final Solution. Jews were reduced to helpless prisoners that could be easily dispatched to the concentration camps or murdered by the Einsatzgruppen in the forests.[30] The ghettos were only a transition to the physical destruction of the Jews. Their liquidation started with the beginning of the Final Solution in early 1942. By the time the advancing Soviet forces began liberating the Eastern occupied territories in 1944, not a single ghetto had survived the liquidation.

On October 26, 1939, Governor Frank published in the *Warschauer Zeitung* an edict ordering compulsory labor for all Jewish males between the ages of fourteen and sixty.[31] A total of 437 forced-labor camps were put in operation beginning in the spring of 1940. The aim was not so much to squeeze the last ounce of work out of the Jews as it was to kill them by overwork, starvation, physical torture, and sickness. The death toll in these labor camps was extremely high because of the prevailing inhuman conditions and the harsh regime. Plaszow, near Kraków, Poniatow and Trawniki in the province of Lublin, Janow near Lvov, and Szebnie near Jaslo are the more famous of these centers of slave labor. The largest such labor camp was Belzec (later transformed into a death camp after the attack on the Soviet Union), where thousands of Jews constructed fortifications and antitank ditches along the new German-Soviet border.

Heydrich thought of using the Jews themselves to implement the evil designs of the German administration. On November 28, 1939, Governor Hans Frank issued an order that every municipality in the Generalgouvernement had to establish a Judenrat and a Jewish police force that were responsible for carrying out Nazi orders. The chairman of the Judenrat was required to receive the orders of the German administration and was held responsible for the conscientious fulfillment of the orders. In smaller communities of up to 10,000 inhabitants the Judenrat consisted of twelve members and in larger communities there were twenty-four members.

Initially the Judenrat were in charge of the organization of the ghettos, the registration and identification of the Jews, and their transfer to the ghettos. Soon they were also assigned the collection of ransom payments, the recruitment of labor brigades, the elaboration of the lists of names for deportation, and the roundups that preceded aktionen. With threats, lies, and false promises the Germans would often turn the Judenrat into their pawns. In December 1939 they were ordered to carry out a Jewish census.

The ghettos as the labor camps were not only used as a means to isolate the Jews, use them as slave laborers for war production, or gather them for deportation but also as instruments of annihilation. Ghetto dwellers were cut off from the world and external work opportunities and confined in cramped conditions under the most severe restrictions. Overcrowding, starvation, inadequate sanitation, heavy work, and lack of medicines and medical care took a terrible toll on the imprisoned population. Typhus, dysentery, and tuberculosis, brought death to many inhabitants. Starvation reached the borderline of death. After the critically meager ghetto rations were cut in half, Hans Frank said in August 1942 to his officials:

It must be done in cold blood and without pity; the fact that in this way we condemn 1,200,000 Jews to death by hunger is only of indirect importance. If the Jews should not starve I sincerely hope that it will inspire further anti-Jewish regulations.[32]

In the Warsaw ghetto approximately 25 percent of its population (100,000) died from starvation and epidemics, while in the Lodz ghetto, 34.7 percent of its population died within its walls from what the Germans called natural causes. Unable to keep pace with the high mortality, piles of decomposing corpses lay unburied in the cemeteries of the larger ghettos. But "natural" deaths by starvation and disease in the ghettos were too slow for German executioners. Faster and more efficient methods of killing were in store.

Although the death camps were not put in operation before the attack on the Soviet Union, murderous actions to reduce the Jewish population were constantly carried out by the Germans. Death marches to the Soviet border to force the Jews out were common. Anyone unable to keep up with the marches was liquidated. The Soviet guards on the other side of the border had strict orders not to accept the Jews and to force them back to the German side. Testimony of such an early death march from the towns of Chelm and Hrubieszow, to the Soviet border was presented on May 1, 1961, at the Eichmann trial by survivor Zvi Pachter. From two thousand Jews who began the death march on the Sabbath of May 2, 1940, only around one hundred reached the Soviet border alive. That small remnant was turned back by the Soviets with callous cruelty.

The brutal herding of more than 2 million Jews in the ghettos took place without the slightest act of protest or opposition by the bishops and the population, and in Warsaw with their collaboration, as described by the martyr historian Emmanuel Ringelblum.[33] Gerald Reitlinger stated after the war that the forced separation of Jews in ghettos could not have been possible had the Polish Church or the population objected to the action. By 1941, almost all the Jews in the Generalgouvernement were already hermetically closed in more than four hundred ghettos at the complete mercy of the German overlords. A report sent by the Catholic Church in Poland to the Polish government in exile in summer 1941 has most significant praise for the Germans with regard to their handling of the Jewish question. It states that in spite of the evil the Germans had perpetrated they had been proven to possess a realistic attitude in "liberating Polish society from the Jewish plague."[34]

The hostility of the Poles to their Jewish neighbors made the plight of Polish Jewry immeasurably more difficult. The prospect of taking over the towns and Jewish homes, possessions, and businesses overnight was a major incentive that enticed the Poles to cooperate willingly with the Germans. The transition from elimination to extermination was seamless. The eyes of Polish neighbors were set on these assets which they hoped to inherit soon. Their greed and envy of the Jews turned many of them into willing informers and active Nazi collaborators. Although many of the movable possessions taken from the Jews were shipped to Germany, the homes and most of the goods ended up with local Poles who suddenly found themselves in possession of homes and stores they never dreamed of. These Poles became the direct beneficiaries of the Jewish tragedy who tried to make sure that Jews would never return to claim their properties.[35]

## The Nisko and Madagascar Reservation Plans

Between 1933 and 1939, the Nazis relied on forced emigration to make the Third Reich Judenfrei. Through the Central Office for Jewish Immigration (*Zentralstelle Fuer Juedische Auswanderung*), which opened offices in Vienna, Prague, and Berlin, Heydrich and Eichmann were able to expel in record time a substantial part of the Jewish population of the Greater Reich. However, with the war, forced emigration lost its effectiveness as a means to make the Reich Judenfrei. Deportation became the new Nazi formula to eliminate the Jews. On December 21, 1939, Eichmann was appointed head of Section IV of the *Reichssicherheitshauptamt* (RSHA, the Reich security main office) in charge of Jewish affairs and evacuation. He became the leading officer in the deportation of the Jews from all over Europe and the plunder of their property until the end of the war.

During the less than two years that transpired from the conquest of Poland to the invasion of the Soviet Union in June 1941, Nazi Germany created the fiction that it intended to "solve" the Jewish question in Europe by establishing territorial reservations for Jews outside of Germany. The Madagascar plan and the Nisko reservation are representative of these deceptive schemes. Although they were soon abandoned, they served long after being discarded as a cover to disguise the actual German genocide.

After the surrender of Poland, Eichmann came up with the idea to create a territorial reservation in Poland to resettle the Jews of Grossdeutschland and make the expanded Reich completely Judenfrei. Eichmann, at the time still director of the Central Office for Jewish Emigration in Prague, looked in haste for a geographic corner in occupied Poland for a *Judenreservat* for 400,000 Jews. Two weeks after the attack on Poland he chose the marshy area of Nisko inside the Generalgouvernement on the river San in the Lublin district for the so-called reservation. Seyss-Inquart, deputy governor of the Generalgouvernement found the area ideal to "bring about a severe decimation of the Jews":[36]

> This territory of Lublin with its extreme marshy nature can, in view of the district governor Schmidt, serve as a Jewish reservation, which could induce a severe decimation of the Jews.[37]

After the approval of Eichmann's plan to create a Judenreservat in the Lublin area, Gestapo Chief Müller signed the order to deport the Jews from the Czech Protectorate and the Warthegau to Nisko on October 6, 1939. On October 10, Hitler ordered that the "less-well-off Jews" of the Old Reich and Austria should also be included in the deportation order. On October 12, Eichmann dumped in Nisko without any means of survival the first transport of 1,672 Viennese Jews and a contingent of Jewish war prisoners of the Polish army.

By January 20, 1940, there were already in Nisko around 78,000 Jewish deportees from Czechoslovakia and Austria who were exposed to most harsh living conditions, leading to mass starvation, disease, and death.[38] Three weeks later, on February 13, 1940, Heydrich dumped in Nisko another group of around 1,300 German Jews from Stettin near Berlin in the old Reich. A month after they left their homes, a fifth of the transport (230 people) had already perished by what the Germans called "natural selection."

The German military advance in France in June 1940 brought another plan —the Madagascar plan—into focus. On June 8, 1940, not long before the surrender of France, Hans Frank, the governor of the Generalgouvernement, was informed by Hitler about the Madagascar plan. Instead of deporting the Jews from the German Reich to the Generalgouvernement they would be shipped directly to the French colony of Madagascar. Frank, who was opposed to accepting the additional burden of Jews from the Reich in his new dominions, was overjoyed. On June 12, Frank informed his underlings in Kraków:

> Very important is also the decision of the Führer which came from a proposal of mine that there be no further transports of Jews into the Generalgouvernement. In general political terms I would like to say that it is planned to transport the entire Jewish clan from the German Reich, the Generalgouvernement and the Protectorate to an African or American colony in the shortest conceivable time span following the peace settlement. Madagascar is being considered; it would be separated from France for this purpose.[39]

Expecting its immediate realization, Frank even provisionally interrupted ghetto construction and convinced Wartheland Gauleiter Arthur Greiser to postpone the expulsion of Jews from Lodz to the Generalgouvernement. Speaking before a large party meeting in Kraków, Frank told the audience:

> As soon as sea communications permit the shipment of the Jews (laughter in the audience), they shall be shipped, piece by piece, man by man, woman by woman, girl by girl. I hope, gentlemen, you will not complain on that account (merriment in the hall).[40]

Considering the key role the German navy was called to play in such a mass deportation movement to Madagascar, the German Navy Chief Admiral Raeder was briefed on the plan on June 20, 1940. When France surrendered on June 25, 1940, von Ribbentrop ordered Franz Rademacher, (1906-1973), the Judenreferat in the German Foreign Office, to draw up a plan for the "resettlement" of 4 million Jews to Madagascar after the end of the war, which they expected would come very soon. Rademacher in collaboration with Eichmann of the Reich Security Head Office, submitted on July 3, to von Ribbentrop, a paper under the title *The Jewish Question in the Peace Treaty* that proposed using Madagascar not merely to clear Europe from Jews but also to curtail the develop-

ment of a Jewish homeland in Palestine, a position that was shared at the time by
the Vatican as well:

> The approaching victory gives Germany the possibility and duty of solving the
> Jewish question in Europe. The desirable solution is: All Jews out of Europe.
> The task of the Foreign Ministry in this is: In the Peace Treaty France must
> make the island of Madagascar available for the solution of the Jewish question
> . . . This arrangement would prevent the possible establishment in Palestine by
> the Jews of a Vatican State of their own, and to exploit for their own purposes
> the symbolic importance which Jerusalem has for the Christian and Mohamme-
> dan parts of the world. Moreover, the Jews will remain in German hands as a
> pledge for the future good behavior of the members of their race in America . . .
> It can be emphasized at the same time that our German sense of responsibility
> towards the world forbids us to make the gift of a sovereign state to a race
> which has had no independent state for thousands of years.[41]

In a message Cardinal Maglione sent to the apostolic delegate in Washington, Msgr. Amleto Cicognani, on May 1943, the Madagascar plan still re-
sounded as a counterbalance to the development of Jewish Palestine:

> It would not seem difficult, in case there is a desire to create a "Jewish Home,"
> to find other territories that would be better suited for that purpose, while Pales-
> tine, under a Jewish majority, would give rise to new and grave international
> problems, would displease Catholics throughout the entire world, would pro-
> voke the justifiable protest of the Holy See.[42]

Hitler used the Madagascar plan in his bogus peace proposals of 1939 and
1940. In his talks with Swedish industrialist Birger Dahlerus, a personal friend
of Göhring, who visited him in an attempt to mediate peace between Great Britain and Nazi Germany after the attack on Poland in September 1939, he brought
up the Madagascar plan. The plan was also presented to Pope Pius XII by von
Ribbentrop in December 1939 as part of a German peace proposal. As France
was to surrender, Hitler and von Ribbentrop discussed the Madagascar proposal
with Italian Foreign Minister Galeazzo Ciano in Munich on June 17-18, 1940.

The Nisko plan came to an abrupt end when Hitler and his generals began
to secretly prepare the surprise attack on the Soviet Union in 1941. All the
movements of population from the annexed parts of Poland to the Generalgouvernement were provisionally stopped on March 15, 1941, due to military transportation needs.[43] The prospects of future war with the Soviet Union and the
realization that the Nisko reservation being near the new Soviet borders would
interfere with the war plans led soon after to its complete cancellation and the
dispersion of survivors.

The Madagascar plan actually never took off the ground for the simple reason that the Germans failed to secure a maritime route to Africa through the
Suez Canal, even while the island remained under the control of the collaborationist Vichy regime. Rommel's defeat in North Africa made it clear that the war
would not reestablish Germany as a colonial power in Africa. The British and

South African troops finally occupied Madagascar in 1942, and a year later handed over the island to the Gaullist French. On February 10, 1942, when much of the Soviet Union was already in German hands, Franz Rademacher of the Foreign Ministry informed his colleague Harald Bielfeld of the Africa and Colonial Affairs Department that the Madagascar plan was being definitively shelved because the Soviet east was now in German hands and that made it possible to carry out the Final Solution in their own backyard:

> The war against the Soviet Union has offered the possibility of putting other territories at our disposal for the final solution. Therefore the Führer has decided that the Jews shall not be deported to Madagascar but to the east. As a result it is no longer necessary that Madagascar be taken into consideration for the final solution.[44]

The Madagascar plan still served the Nazis as a cover for their genocide program in Eastern Europe long after it was shelved. Jewish victims were led to believe the German resettlement fabrications until the very final moment when they stood before the shooting guns of the Einsatzgruppen or entered the gas chambers. Dieter Wisliczeny, one of Eichmann's agents, testified in a written deposition in Nuremberg that the Madagascar plan was being used to deceive the Jews. While the Warsaw ghetto was reduced from 450,000 Jews to less than 35,000 from July 22, 1942, to October 3, 1942, Jewish leaders in the ghetto, such as Dr. Alfred Nossig (later tried and shot by the Jewish underground as a collaborator), still believed that the Germans were actually implementing the Madagascar plan.[45]

## The Surrender of France

Britain and France formally declared war on Germany on September 3, 1939, but did not undertake any military action to actually help the Poles. Instead of launching a counteroffensive in the Western front that could have changed the outcome of the war they dug themselves behind the Maginot Line. German Field Marshal Alfred Jodl (1890-1946) declared at the Nuremberg Trials that "if we did not collapse already in the year 1939 that was due only to the fact that during the Polish campaign, the approximately 110 French and British divisions in the West were held completely inactive against the twenty-three German divisions."

The seven months of military inactivity on the Western front ended on April 9, 1940, when Nazi Germany launched Operation Weserübung and invaded Norway and Denmark to ease the passage of German warships and submarines into the North Sea and the Atlantic and to facilitate the movement of Swedish iron ore to Germany. Denmark surrendered the same day, but Norway fought on heroically. From April 12 to April 15 Allied troops landed in Norway, but within two weeks most of Norway was in German hands and the Allied troops were evacuated from northern Norway. The Allied defeat in Norway brought down Chamberlain as prime minister. In Parliament, Leopold Amery turned to him paraphrasing Cromwell: "Depart I say, and let us have done with you. In the name of God, go!" On May 10, Chamberlain resigned and Churchill was asked to form a government by King George VI.

Despite repeated earlier statements by Hitler that he would not violate the neutrality of Belgium, Luxembourg, and the Netherlands, those three countries were treacherously attacked on May 10, 1940. Queen Wilhelmina and the Dutch government fled to London, while Belgian King Leopold III stayed behind. Belgian civil servants continued working with the German invaders to keep services running and prevent an economic breakdown. On May 13, 1940, Churchill spoke in London for the first time as premier before Parliament and told the British people that he had nothing to offer them at that moment but "blood, toil, tears, and sweat."

Pius XII expressed in a message his sympathy to the sovereigns of Holland, Belgium, and Luxemburg, but he abstained from explicitly naming the aggressor and condemning the unprovoked German attack against them. The French Ambassador Charles-Roux pointed out on May 13, 1940 to Msgr. Domenico Tardini that expressing compassion for the victims was quite different from condemning the aggressor.

On May 13, 1940, the Germans took the Allies by surprise when their panzer divisions completely outflanked the impregnable Maginot Line and broke through at the Ardennes—which until then had been considered impassable to tanks—and split the Allied forces in two at Sedan on May 15 and raced for the Channel coast. They encircled in the north the British Expeditionary Force (BEF), which was forced to evacuate hastily at Dunkirk. The evacuation of 335,000 British and French soldiers between May 26 and June 3, 1940, was nothing short of miraculous, especially after the Belgian Army surrendered on May 28, opening up a twenty mile gap, on the left flank. The day after the evacuation, Churchill delivered in the House of Commons his promise to "defend our Island, whatever the cost may be," even if it involved fighting on the beaches.

The German panzer divisions advanced unhindered to Paris, reaching its gates on June 10, 1940. The 300,000 Jews in Paris were gripped with fear not knowing what the Germans had in store for them. On that day Italy declared war against France and Great Britain, attacking France from the south. The Italian bishops enthusiastically blessed the troops going to the front and taught them that "obedience to the State in war is ordained by God as a religious duty."[46] As in the case of the invasion of Ethiopia, the Vatican remained silent on Italy's attack on France. Cardinal Eugene Tisserant, a Frenchman, had some bitter words for Pius XII. In a letter written from Rome on June 11, 1940, he addressed Cardinal Suhard of Paris:

> I urgently asked the Pope as early as December to issue an encyclical about the individual duty to obey the imperatives of conscience, as this is the most vital point of Christianity . . . I am afraid that history may be obliged in time to come to blame the Holy See for a policy accommodated to its own advantage and little more. And that is extremely sad—above all when one has lived under Pius XI. [47]

Nuncio Orsenigo in Berlin was jubilant at the news of the German advance on Paris. German Undersecretary of State Woermann described Orsenigo's mood:

> He hopes that when we march into Paris, we will do so through Versailles. He also seemed actually to look forward to Italy's entry into the war.[48]

Paris fell without a fight on June 14, 1940. The German panzer divisions marched through the Arc de Triumphe down the Champs Elysees to the Place de la Concorde. The French government retreated to Bordeaux. The defeatists led by Pierre Laval (1983-1945) prevailed and convinced President Lebrun to call Marshal Henri Phillippe Pétain (1856-1951), the World War I hero of Verdun, to lead the French government. Pétain became premier on June 16, 1940, and next day requested an armistice. Charles de Gaulle, then a young French general, left for London where he organized the French National Committee and vowed to continue fighting the Germans.

To avenge the German defeat of 1918, Hitler ordered that the armistice be signed in the same place and in the same railroad car where the Germans had signed the armistice in 1918. On June 22, 1940, Pétain signed a humiliating surrender in Compiegne in Marshal Foch's private railroad car, where he had dictated the armistice terms to Germany twenty-two years earlier. Hitler sat in Foch's seat at the signing of the armistice. He later ordered the car blown up so it would never be used again. Next day, Hitler, in the company of Albert Speer, celebrated his victory over France with a visit to the Arc de Triumphe and Napoleon's tomb. In Germany, Archbisop Schulte of Cologne issued a special proclamation to give thanks for the Blitzkrieg victory over France.

The surrender resulted in the division of France into two zones, a large one in the north occupied by the Germans covering two-thirds of the country, and the other in the south under French control with Vichy as its capital. The French National Assembly abolished the Third Republic on July 10, 1940, by 569 votes to 80 following a harangue by Pierre Laval in which he accused the French Republic of being the source of all the misfortunes of France. Pétain rewarded Laval appointing him prime minister.

On October 24, 1940, Pétain met Hitler at Montoire-sur-le-Loir and issued a call to France to follow him down the path of collaboration with Germany. De Gaulle reacted to Pétain's call, branding him and his collaborators as traitors to France. In sharp contrast, Primate of France Cardinal Gerlier declared:

> Pétain is France and France is Pétain! In one of the most tragic hours of our history, Providence has given France a leader around whom we can be proud to gather. Marshal! You gave yourself to France. And now France has replied by giving herself to you. We pray God to bless you and bestow wisdom on your ministers. [49]

Educated in Jesuit and Dominican schools before attending the military academy of St. Cyr, Pétain had the full trust of the French clergy. The archbishop of Paris, Emmanuel Suhard, and the cardinals and bishops of France offered Pétain their firm support. "The war generation still remembers the Vichy bishops giving the Nazi salute before Petain and Göring," recalls historian Braham. No other institution was so closely identified with the collaborationist Vichy regime and its National Revolution as the Catholic Church was, points out Fr. Morley:

> The closest relations existed between the Church and the Vichy regime . . . Pétain himself was also greatly respected and praised by various members of the hierarchy. Moreover, the Vatican gave every evidence of being favorable toward the marshal.[50]

Taking high moral ground, Pétain raised the banner of what he called a national revolution that he claimed would bring a moral renaissance to France. He traded the slogan of the French Revolution *Liberté, Egalité, Fraternité* (Liberty, Equality, and Fraternity) for *Travail, Patrie, and Famille* (Work, Fatherland, and Family). Pope Pius XII warmly praised the Pétain "miracle" when referring to the marshal's national revolution and his so-called moral renaissance. The measures taken by his government such as outlawing the Freemasons, making religious instruction compulsory in the public schools, returning Church property, and making divorce more difficult endeared him to the Church. The French bishops even used his speeches on moral renaissance as the basis of their own sermons.

Attempts were made by the Germans during the early initial period of the occupation of France to push over Jews from Germany to unoccupied France. All Jews of the district of Baden and the Saar Palatinate (Saarpfalz) were deported to unoccupied France in October 1940. Around 7,450 Jews, young and old, were taken out of their beds at dawn leaving all their possessions behind. After convincing the French station master at the border railway station that these were German military transports, the Jews were taken in sealed carriages to the dreadful French concentration camp at Gurs in the foot of the Pyrenees where unbearable living conditions prevailed.

In Belgium the Germans appointed a military governor, General Alexander von Falkenhausen (1878-1966), who remained on that post until 1944. The overall administration of the country remained in the hands of Belgium's chief ministry officials and the regular civil service. These Belgian high-level civil servants cooperated with the Germans and very often became collaborators and accomplices. On November 19, 1940, King Leopold met with Hitler in his retreat at the Obersalzberg. In a subsequent letter to Hitler, Leopold's wife Lilian wrote that her husband was "loyal to the Führer."[51]

After the surrender of France in June 1940, Hitler expected the British would accept his conditions for a separate peace, leaving him free to pursue his Lebensraum plans in the East. He threatened in the Reichstag to invade the British Isles if Great Britain did not follow France in accepting his "peace" offer, which obviously implied that the English recognize Hitler's territorial gains. British Ambassador to the Vatican Francis d'Arcy Osborne reported to His Majesty's government that Pius XII was convinced in a German victory in case of an invasion and that the Pope hoped England would accept Hitler's peace offer:

> The success of the threatened invasion of Great Britain is, I fear, taken for granted by His Holiness. For this reason, he hopes that England will accept the peace offer made by Hitler in his Reichstag speech.[52]

By direct instructions of Pius XII, Cardinal Maglione urged the English government through its apostolic delegate in London to accept Hitler's offer, exactly as he had advised in the case of Poland:

> Persons of authority, supporters of a just peace, have expressed the wish that the Holy See should approach the British government suggesting that it should not discard the offer of peace made by the German chancellor without examining carefully, but should rather ask the German government to specify a concrete basis for eventual negotiations. [53]

When the British government valiantly rejected the Nazi offer, Pius XII and his secretary of state expressed regret. They called in Ambassador Osborne and through him sent a new message to the British government "not to accept so lightheartedly responsibility for the continuation of the war." Lightheartedness was the last thing on earth that characterized the mood of the English people at that critical juncture of world history when they rejected Hitler's threats and the Pope's advice. England, led by Churchill, heroically stood its ground. Alone and isolated, in what looked the darkest hour of its history, Winston Churchill summoned the English people to stand up against Hitler no matter what the cost:

> The Battle of France is over. The Battle of Britain is about to begin. Hitler knows that he will have to break us in this island, or lose the war. If we can stand up to him, all Europe may be free . . . But if we fail then the all world will sink into the abyss of a new dark age. Let us therefore brace ourselves to our duty . . . So bear ourselves, that if the British Empire and Commonwealth lasts for a thousand years, men will say: "This was their finest hour!"[54]

In preparation of Operation Sea Lion, the German code name for the invasion of the British Isles, the Luftwaffe began a relentless air campaign to defeat the Royal Air Force and gain control over British air space. Despite being outnumbered four to one by the Luftwaffe, the British Royal Air Force was able to inflict enough damage to the Luftwaffe during the Battle of Britain to cause Hitler to suspend Operation Sea Lion by the end of September 1940. The Battle of Britain was over but the Luftwaffe turned to terror bombing London. This was indeed England's finest hour as Winston Churchill had told his courageous nation in his eloquent message. Neither Hitler's threats nor his bombs were able to break the spirit of the British people. On September 27, 1940, Hitler signed with Japan and Italy the Axis Pact. The members of that military alliance pledged "to assist one another with all political, economic and military means when one of the three contracting powers is attacked."

It took four years for Allied forces to return to French soil. On June 6, 1944, the Allied armies under the command of General Dwight Eisenhower disembarked in the beaches of Normandy in Northern France, opening the long-awaited Second Front. Two months later, on August 15, 1944, the Allies disembarked in Southern France between Toulon and Cannes. Paris became free again on August 25, 1944.

## The Balkan Countries Join the Axis

After the defeat of France, Hitler began to prepare for what had been his main goal of military rearmament: The conquest of new Lebensraum in the vast expanses of the Soviet Union. At a time that German-Soviet friendship looked solidly cemented by the Molotov-Ribbentrop Non-Aggression Pact, Hitler was preparing a new act of betrayal. To convince his top military commanders, who were reluctant to fight a war on two fronts at the same time, Hitler told them on July 31, 1940, that "the destruction of the Soviet Union would remove England's last hope." Army Chief of Staff General Franz Halder took note:

> The master of Europe and the Balkans is then Germany. Decision: In the course of this conflict Russia must be finished off, spring 1941.[55]

On December 5, 1940, Hitler was already discussing with his generals Operation Barbarossa—the attack on the Soviet Union. Two weeks later he ordered all preparations for the invasion be ready by mid-May 1941. On January 9, 1941, Hitler presented to his generals Operation Barbarrosa within the wider perspective of his global frenzied geopolitical vision:

> The smashing of the Soviet Union would cause the English to give up, enable Japan to attack the United States in the Pacific, engage the Soviet army while it was still weak in leadership and armaments, relieve Germany's economic dilemma by opening up Russia's immense riches while simultaneously allowing a reduction in the German army to the benefit of the air force and navy. Germany would then have the capacity to wage war against continents without fear of defeat. [56]

The success of Hitler's new adventure depended in great measure in blocking the access to the Soviet territory and cutting off the Soviets from its neighbors and their raw materials. Before attacking the Soviet Union, Hitler therefore sought to secure first his control over Finland in the north and the countries of the Danube basin to the south such as Hungary, Romania, Yugoslavia, and Bulgaria—whether as willing members of the Axis Pact or as conquered vassals.

Mussolini was a major player in the Balkan region long before Hitler stepped in there. He had long hoped of turning the Adriatic Sea into an Italian lake to challenge British supremacy in the Mediterranean. On April 7, 1939,

Mussolini ordered the Italian Army to invade Albania, which he promptly annexed to Italy. He also made demands on Greece to surrender parts of its territory and when Greece refused he ordered the Italian Army to invade it on October 28, 1940. Despite their numerical inferiority, the Greek forces were able to force the Italian Army into retreat to Albania. As soon as the Germans occupied Yugoslavia and their troops could cross friendly territory, they came to the rescue of their Italian partners.

To draw the Balkan countries into the German orbit, Hitler applied once again the technique that worked so well in the past with Poland and the Soviet Union; he promised the various Balkan dictators territorial gains if they joined the Axis. Impressed by Hitler's military growing power and territorial promises, it was relatively easy to convince the Fascist dictators of the Balkan countries to join the Axis. Important territorial changes sponsored by Hitler and Mussolini intended to nulify the accords of Versailles took place in the Balkans as a result of Hitler's promises even before the attack on the Soviet Union.

Romania was the great loser in these territorial changes. As a result of the signature of the Hitler-Stalin Pact, Hitler supported opportunistically the revisionist demands for Romanian territory made by the Soviet Union, Hungary, and Bulgaria. Romania was forced to surrender the provinces of Bukovina, Bessarabia, and Northern Moldavia to Soviet Russia on June 26, 1940. On August 30, Romania was again forced to sign away at the Second Vienna arbitration Northern Transylvania to Hungary and Southern Dobruja to Bulgaria. In total, Romania lost about 30 percent of its territory and population.

After these territorial losses, King Caroll II abdicated in favor of his son Michai on September 6, 1940. He appointed General Ion Antonescu (1882-1946) as prime minister and Mihai Antonescu (1904-1946) as deputy prime minister and foreign minister. To recover the territories lost to the Soviets, Antonescu sought to ally Romania with Nazi Germany. Romania's oil reserves, food production, and large army were very attractive resources to Hitler and he responded positively to Romanian advances. On November 23, 1940, Romania joined the Axis.

Hungary recovered all the territories it lost at the Treaty of Trianon in 1920 after World War I. At the First Vienna Arbitration sponsored by Hitler and Mussolini. It received back from Czechoslovakia on November 2, 1938, the southern edge of Carpatho-Ruthenia, At the Second Vienna Arbitration it recovered Northern Transylvania from Romania on August 30, 1940, and the Backa basin between the Danube and the Tisza from Yugoslavia on April 17, 1941. Romania was forced to sign away Southern Dobruja to Bulgaria at the Second Vienna Arbitration on August 30, 1940, and after the surrender of Yugoslavia, Bulgaria also received Serbian Macedonia. These territorial transfers had momentous consequences for Jewish communities that changed hands. They lost all their rights overnight and became pariahs exposed to robbery, deportation, and death. On November 20, 1940, Hungary joined the Axis. Romania and Slovakia followed on November 23 and 24, 1940, and Bulgaria on March 1, 1941. Yugoslavia joined the Axis on March 25, 1941 but shortly after backed out.

Information from reliable sources reached von Ribbentrop at the time that Pius XII expressed his conviction of a military victory of the Axis powers to important visitors of Italian nobility. Ribbentrop requested confirmation of these reports from Ambassador von Bergen on February 15, 1941:

> On a number of occasions in the recent past the Pope, surprisingly enough, has expressed extreme optimism about Germany's prospects of victory. In conversations with high ranking members of the Italian nobility, he has left no doubt that everyone in Italy must get used to the idea of certain victory for Germany. Request full report on this by return. [57]

Although in his lengthy answer to Ribbentrop, von Bergen tries to impress the point that Pius XII is generally reluctant to make pronouncements that could prejudice his role as a peacemaker, he nonetheless confirmed the Pope's inclination in favor of a German victory:

> This is evident from the utterances of personalities particularly close to Pius XII, who describe Germany as the presumptive victor in this struggle, as if this were a foregone conclusion . . . aside from the Italians there is no nation to which the Pope's inner feelings bring him closer than to the Germans, a people for whose great qualities his admiration is unconcealed; his objections are purely a matter of Church policy and religious in nature. [58]

## The Dismemberment of Yugoslavia

Yugoslavia, like its neighbors, joined the Axis on March 25, 1941, but a pro-Allied government coup by the Serbian army, seized power two days later in Belgrade, and switched the country to the Allied side. Enraged, Hitler postponed Operation Barbarossa and launched an attack on Yugoslavia and Greece on April 6, 1941, assisted by his Italian, Hungarian, Romanian, and Bulgarian allies who were promised parts of Yugoslavia. On April 17, 1941, Yugoslavia surrendered and King Peter and the remnants of the royal government fled to London. British Ambassador to the Vatican D'Arcy Osborne appealed to the Pope to condemn the attack on Yugoslavia, but Pius XII turned down the request.[59] On May 4, 1941, Hitler exulted in the Reichstag in his triumph in the Balkans, which were almost completely in his hands.

Yugoslavia like Czechoslovakia was established at the Versailles Peace Conference as a multiethnic state following the collapse of the Austro-Hungarian Empire in 1918. Four different religions and ethnic groups lived side by side in Yugoslavia: Serbian Greek Orthodox, Croat Catholics, Bosnian Moslems, and Jews. The Greek-Orthodox predominated in Serbia, the Catholics in Croatia, Moslems in parts of Bosnia, while the Jews were a small minority everywhere. After Yugoslavia's failed attempt to switch sides in 1941, Hitler could not miss the opportunity to liquidate another Versailles state by fanning its internal ethnic and religious rivalries as he did in Czechoslovakia.

Yugoslavia was dismembered like Czechoslovakia. Croatia was declared an independent Catholic state under the name Nezavisna Država Hrvatska, or NDH, very much following the model of Clero-Fascist Slovakia. Serbia became German-occupied territory under the rule of puppet collaborator General Milan Nedic. The Dalmatian coast of Yugoslavia, part of Slovenia, and the southeast of Fiume were annexed by Italy. Serbian Macedonia was ceded by the Germans to Bulgaria and the Backa basin between the Danube and the Tisza went to Hungary.

Croatia was given over in the hands of the Ustashi, a bloody terrorist secessionist group, long supported by Hitler and Mussolini, who wished to separate Croatia from Yugoslavia. They gave the Nazi salute, wore the Fascist black uniforms, marched with the goose step, and eagerly awaited the day when they would "cleanse" their country from the Greek-Orthodox Serbs and Jews. Their Führer or *Poglavnik*, Ante Pavelić (1889-1959) was a Zagreb lawyer educated in his youth in Jesuit schools. Sentenced in absentia to death in France for his part in the assassination in Marseilles of Yugoslav King Alexander and French Foreign Minister Barthou in 1934, he found ready asylum in Fascist Italy where he organized Ustashi guerrillas that were trained by the Italian Fascist militia.

The new state of Croatia came into being on April 10, 1941, and immediately joined the Axis. A week later, on April 17, Pavelić officially declared war against the Allies. On June 15, Croatia joined the Tripartite Pact. The Catholic Church favored the establishment of the state of Croatia as it had favored a separate Catholic Slovakia. Although the Vatican abstained from granting Croatia *de-jure* recognition in accordance with its principle of not granting recognition to territorial changes during a war, it gave Croatia the greatest measure of de facto recognition possible, while not severing its formal diplomatic relations with the Yugoslav government in exile.

The Catholic Church had long considered Croatia its outer bulwark in the Balkans against the Eastern Orthodox Church. The dismemberment of Yugoslavia was seen as a unique opportunity to boost the power of Catholicism in the region. The Ustashi's avowed Catholicism combined with their anti-Serbian and anti-Communist militancy made them very attractive to the Vatican. The Croatian Catholic clergy presided by the Primate of Croatia Archbishop Alojzije Stepinac (1898-1960) of Zagreb gave the new state its blessing and support. As head of the Council of Bishops, Archbishop Stepinac blessed the arriving Ustashi leadership in a public ceremony in the cathedral of Zagreb and on April 16, 1941, hosted a dinner in honor of Pavelić. Archbishop Stepinac issued a pastoral letter that was read over the radio and in every Catholic parish on April 28, 1941, calling Catholic clergy and laity to cooperate with the Poglavnic and his government:

Honorable brethren!
   I do not speak to you only as a son of the Croatian people but even more as a representative of the Holy Church . . . You should therefore readily answer my call to do elevated work for the safeguarding and progress of the Independent State of Croatia . . . In light of this we determine, that on Sunday May 4th

this year a solemn Te Deum should be performed in all parochial churches, to
which the parochial offices should invite the local authorities and the faithful.

Stepinac's diary reveals his enthusiasm for Pavelić:

If that man, [Pavelic] rules Croatia for ten years . . . Croatia will be a paradise
on earth.[60]

Within the political boundaries of Croatia lived 6.5 million people, of
whom only 3.3 million were Catholics, followed by 2.2 million Greek-Orthodox
Serbs, 350,000 Moslems, and 45,000 Jews. Bosnia and Herzegovina, which became part of the Croat state, contained a substantial Moslem population. For the
radical nationalists and racists who aimed at creating a pure racial or ethnic society, a multiethnic society represented a "problem" that called for a "solution."
The solution they envisioned contemplated expulsion, conversion, or death for
Eastern Orthodox Serbs and Jews. On August 14, 1941, Ante Pavelić himself
formulated the official policy of the NDH in a speech in Vukovar:

This is now the Ustashi and Independent State of Croatia; it must be cleansed
of Serbs and Jews. There is no room for any of them here. Not a stone upon a
stone will remain of what once belonged to them.[61]

The Catholic organ *Katolicki List* enthusiastically welcomed the entry of
German troops into Zagreb and the proclamation of the Croat state on April 21,
1941:

The Catholic Church, which has led the Croat nation spiritually through 1300
years of difficulty, accompanies with rejoicing and delight the whole Croat
people in this moment of its reconstruction and political independence.[62]

Within the political boundaries of Croatia lived 6.5 million people, of
whom only 3.3 million were Catholics, followed by 2.2 million Greek-Orthodox
Serbs, 350,000 Moslems, and 45,000 Jews. Bosnia and Herzegovina, which became part of the Croat state, contained a substantial Moslem population. For the
radical nationalists and racists who aimed at creating a pure racial or ethnic society, a multiethnic society represented a "problem" that called for a "solution."
The solution they envisioned contemplated expulsion, conversion, or death for
Eastern Orthodox Serbs and Jews. On August 14, 1941, Ante Pavelić himself
formulated the official policy of the NDH in a speech in Vukovar:

This is now the Ustashi and Independent State of Croatia; it must be cleansed
of Serbs and Jews. There is no room for any of them here. Not a stone upon a
stone will remain of what once belonged to them.[63]

Croatia truly became a clerico-fascist state in practice as well as in ideology. Many Croat priests and friars had joined the Ustashi long before the creation
of the state, including Archbishop of Sarajevo Dr. Ivan Saric. In the majority of

towns and villages throughout Croatia, Catholic priests became the official local Ustasha authority. Many priests were named members of the Great Council of the State, the *Sabor*, including Archbishops Stepinac and Saric. Other priests were appointed advisors to the ministerial cabinet.[64]

In return for Italian recognition of his regime, Pavelić signed the Pact of Rome on May 18, 1941, ceding to Italy nearly all the Croatian islands, most of Dalmatia, and a substantial part of Rijeka. On that day, Pavelić declared Croatia a monarchy, crowning an Italian prince, the Duke of Spoleto, as King Tomislav II. A day before the crowning, Pius XII received the future king and gave him his blessing. On the day of the crowning, the Pope granted an audience to the Poglavnic Pavelić and warmly addressed him as "a son of the Church." Pius XII told him about "his affection for the Croatian people, whose loyalty he knew so well" and gave him his Papal blessing. Pavelić on his part assured the Pope that "the Croatian people wanted all their conduct and legislation to be inspired by Catholicism." To keep diplomatic appearances, the two audiences were given a private character.[65]

Pius XII appointed Benedictin Abbot of Montevergine Giussepe Ramiro Marcone as apostolic visitor to Croatia in July 1941. Notwithstanding that as Apostolic Visitor Marcone held a lower diplomatic status than an apostolic delegate, he was recognized as the de facto nuncio and became the dean of the diplomatic corpus in Zagreb not long after his arrival.

Pavelić met with Hitler on June 6, 1941, at Hitler's retreat in the Berghof. The Poglavnik accepted Germany's unlimited right to Croatia's raw materials and special privileges for the Germans living in Croatia.[66] The tragic destiny of Croatian Jewry was sealed when a "common understanding on the Jewish Question" was established between them. Pavelić's aims like those of Hitler went far beyond isolation of the Jews through legislation—Jews were marked for extinction. After discussing the question of population transfers, Hitler offered advice to Pavelić on the Serbian question:

> After all, if the Croat state wishes to be strong, a nationally intolerant policy must be pursued for fifty years, because too much tolerance on such issues can only do harm.[67]

When Hitler invaded the Soviet Union, most of German and Italian divisions in Croatia left for the Soviet front. The most important Catholic organizations in Croatia such as Catholic Action and Crusaders Brotherhood mobilized many of its members in Ustashi military units that fought as part of the Waffen SS in Russia. Many Catholic priests joined these units. A Bosnian Muslim military unit named *Handjar*, the Sword, joined the Waffen SS in the front. The mufti of Jerusalem, Hajj Amin al-Husseini, came from Berlin to Sarajevo to give his blessing to the Muslim division.[68]

In January 1942, Msgr. Stepinac was appointed Supreme Military Vicar of the Ustashi by the Vatican, which meant that he also was the head of military chaplains. Priests and nuns marched with the Ustashi in a display of unity and celebrated the Poglavnic's birthday with high masses and tedeums in churches and cathedrals, at a time they were commiting the most heinous crimes, murdering Jews and Serbians. In 1941-1942 alone around 240,000 Serbs were converted by terror to Roman Catholicism. Jews, Orthodox priests, and Serbian teachers were not given the option to convert and were murdered, often after torture. On May 8, 1943, Archbishop Stepinac presented a report to the Pope in which he pointed out with pride as an accomplishment of the Ustashi regime that "up to this date, 244,000 Orthodox Serbs have been converted to the Church and that would be lost in the event Croatia would fall."[69]

## The Surprise Invasion of the Soviet Union

On Sunday, June 22, 1941, less than two years after the Soviet-German Pact was signed in Moscow, Hitler put into practice Operation Barbarossa and launched without warning a surprise attack on the Soviet Union. Already in full control of Central Europe and the Balkans, Hitler decided that the time had finally arrived to materialize Haushofer's predatory Lebensraum ideas and conquer the wide steppes of the Ukraine and Russia. He broke the Non-Aggression pact he signed, which turned out to be nothing but a Nazi maneuver to win time and avoid fighting on two fronts simultaneously while preparing for the conquest of the Soviet territories.

To mask his real intentions after the secret approval of Operation Barbarossa, Hitler feigned solid friendship with Russia and signed the Russo-German Frontier Treaty on January 10, 1941. Less than a month later, on February 3, Hitler held a conference attended by Generals Keitel and Jodl at which it was decided that Barbarossa should be camouflaged as if it were part of Operation Sea Lion, the plan for the invasion of England.[70]

On March 30, 1941, Hitler called together his commanding generals to a conference at which he told them that the upcoming war with Russia would be a race war in which Communist commissars and Jews would be exterminated by SS Einsatzgruppen, the special paramilitary groups, following on the heels of advancing armies. Putting his trust in Blietzkrieg warfare strategy that was so successful in Western Europe, Hitler expected that the Soviet military campaign would be over in a matter of weeks, long before the winter:

We have only to kick in the door and the whole rotten structure will come crashing down. [71]

Rudolph Hess's flight to Scotland on May 10, 1941, six weeks before the attack on the Soviet Union, was a last minute attempt to entice the British to sign a separate peace with Germany that would give the Third Reich free hands to attack the Soviets without having to fight on two fronts. Hess parachuted near Glasgow, Scotland, within thirty miles of the residence of the Duke of Hamilton, whom he had met briefly during the Berlin Olympics in 1936. He hoped to use the duke to convince the British government that Hitler had no ambitions to the West and only wanted Lebensraum in the East as he had written in *Mein Kampf*.

Too many times taken in by Hitler, the British ignored Hess's advances and locked him up. The prosecution at the Nuremberg Trial highlighted Hitler's tactics in violating his international commitments to deceive and take by surprise his chosen victims:

> Perhaps their guilt as murderers and robbers is of less importance and of less effect to future generations of mankind than their crime of fraud—the fraud by which they placed themselves in a position to do their murder and their robbery. That is the other aspect of their guilt. The story of their "diplomacy", founded upon cunning, hypocrisy and bad faith, is a story less gruesome but no less evil and deliberate.[72]

The German attack on June 22, 1941, took Stalin completely by surprise. Three army groups with more than 3 million German soldiers and 500,000 more from other Axis members, moved ahead with lightning speed conquering Eastern Poland, the Baltic countries, Byelorussia, and the Ukraine in only three weeks. German allies Italy, Hungary, Romania, Bulgaria, Croatia, and Slovakia joined and declared war against Soviet Russia immediately after. The combined forces attacked simultaneously on three fronts from the Baltic to the Black Sea.

Stalin had dismissed all warnings from his own intelligence services in the mistaken belief that they were part of a British disinformation campaign designed to push him into a war against Germany. He risked everything on the false assumption that Hitler would not start a war without first bringing the war with Britain to a close. He was in shock for days. Molotov had to take his place to address the Soviet people and tell them that Hitler had deceived them and that a horrible war between the two nations had begun.

The Baltic countries and Byelorussia were overrun by German forces in one week. Lithuania in its entirety fell within three days of the initial assault. German tanks swept through Byelorussia and occupied Minsk, its capital, on June 28, 1941. On June 30, the Germans entered Lvov and occupied southeastern Poland and made it part of the Generalgouvernement as Distrikt Galizien. Riga, the Latvian capital was taken on July 1, 1941; Kiev the capital of the Ukraine fell on September 19, 1941. German tanks reached the gates of Leningrad in the north in early September 1941 and the suburbs of Moscow on November 25.

The reaction of Pius XII to the invasion of Soviet Russia by the German armies was one of jubilation. Authors Murphy and Arlington refer to the Pope's houskeeper's version of events:

> As Hitler's armies crossed the Russian frontier in June 1941, the nun showed as much jubilation as the Pope. They both joined in joyful prayers. Even in defiance of world opinion, Pius and Pascalina said novenas for the Nazis and asked God to intercede for their total victory in Russia . . . Cardinal Secretary of State Maglione, in explaining the papacy's position to Myron C. Taylor, Roosevelt's personal envoy to the Vatican, said the Pope hoped that communism would be defeated by the Nazis.[73]

A week after Hitler attacked the Soviet Union, Pope Pius XII expressed in a wireless speech on June 29, 1941, in his characteristic ellyptic style his admiration for the daring and courage of the "defenders of the foundations of Christian culture." He did not name these defenders of Christianity, but it was obvious by elimination that he was referring to Axis soldiers, including the Italians, who were fighting in Russia. He expressed his trust in their final victory:

> Certainly in the midst of surrounding darkness and storm, signs of light appear which lift up our hearts with great and holy expectations—these are those magnanimous acts of valour which now defend the foundations of Christian culture, as well as confident hope in victory.[74]

The Italian bishops had no inhibitions to spell out in unambigious language their jubilation at the attack on the Soviet Union. The head of the congregation for the Propagation of the Faith, Archbishop Constantini, prayed for an Axis victory, and in his homily in the Basilica dela Concordia in Venice gave his blessing to the Italian military forces fighting against the Soviet Union:

> Yesterday on the soil of Spain, today in the Bolshevist land itself, in that inmeasurable land in which Satan appears to have his representative on earth, brave soldiers, many of our own land, are fighting the greatest of all fights. With all our heart we pray that this struggle may bring us final victory and the destruction of a system based on negation and subversion. Our blessing to the Italian soldiers who at this decisive hour defend our ideals of freedom against the Red Barbarism.[75]

Although the word "crusade" was generally avoided to describe the war against Soviet Russia, it was implied in the Catholic press in Italy. The Catholic newspaper *L'Italia* wrote:

> Italians can be proud that the spiritual weapons of the Church, too, are ranged in the struggle against Bolshevism.[76]

The call of war against Bolshevism resonated all over Catholic Europe. Nazi sympathizers who claimed that Christianity was being saved from Bolshevism responded to Hitler's exhortation to join the fight against Soviet Russia. Anti-Communist legions were formed in Spain, Portugal, Vichy France, and Belgium that enlisted in the Waffen SS. Countries that could not send soldiers sent money and organized meetings and nationwide propaganda against the Soviet Union.

To curry Hitler's favor, Romania supplied Nazi Germany and the Axis armies with oil, grain, and industrial products, mostly without monetary compensation. Its troops at the Soviet front exceeded in number that of all the other German allies combined.[77] Hitler agreed to return Bessarabia and Northern Bukovina to Romania and to allow Romania to annex Soviet territory in South Western Ukraine across the Dniester, including the important port city of Odessa. Romanian territorial claims against Hungary and Bulgaria concerning Northern Transylvania and Southern Dobruja were put on hold, although Antonescu did not give up hope to recover these provinces some day and even going eventually to war with Hungary for them.

When the Germans invaded the Baltic countries, the Lithuanians, Latvians, and Estonians greeted the Germans as liberators in hope that the Germans would restore their independence. They were glad to get rid of the Soviets and set up provisional governments in hopes that they would be officially recognized by the Germans. But Hitler had very different plans for them. The Baltic countries were considered part of the German Lebensraum and were to be incorporated into Germany's Ostland territory. Their hopes of national independence received a severe blow when the provisional governments they had established were ordered dissolved by the Germans on July 28, 1941.

The plans of the German masters for the occupied countries were vastly different than those that they themselves considered. The grand plan of Nazi conquest was to create four politic-administrative regions, or *Kommissariats* in the occupied lands for colonization by Aryans: the Baltic, Byelorussia, the Ukraine, and Moscovia. The Moscovia region was to stretch from Moscow, which would become an artificial lake, to the Urals. The ideologue of Aryan blood purity and Lebensraum, Alfred Rosenberg (1893-1946), was appointed Reichminister of the *Ostministerium* in charge of Eastern Occupied Territories. Three ruthless Nazis were put in charge of the three regions: Heinrich Lohse in the Baltic, Wilhelm Kube in Byelorussia, and Eric Koch in the Ukraine. The scope of Hitler's aims in Russia can be grasped from a later address that Himmler delivered to the members of SS and police leadership in his field headquarters in southwestern Russia on September 16, 1942:

> Thirdly, we must develop land and soil for our people! In the next twenty years we must colonize the present eastern German provinces from East Prussia down to Upper Silesia and the whole of Polish territory under German rule. We must Germanize and colonize White Russia, Estonia, Latvia, Lithuania, Karelia and the Crimea. We will proceed in other areas as we have begun here, building small cities of 15,000 to 20,000 inhabitants, along lines of communication where our super-highways, railways and airports are protected by our garrisons, and surrounded by a ten-kilometer radius of villages, so that the people are always immersed in German life and related to an urban cultural center.
>
> These nuclei of settlements which we are extending forward from here to the Don and the Volga—and I hope to the Urals—will some day, some year, in the course of a generation have to accumulate more and more layers of an eternally young succession of Germanic blood. This Germanic East up to the Urals must be the seedbed of Germanic population. Thus in four or five hundred years, if the fate of Europe gives us that much time before some intercontinental conflict, instead of one hundred twenty million, there will be five or six hundred million people of Germanic race.[78]

The swift German advance came to a halt at the gates of Moscow in the heavy Soviet winter. Hitler's hope of a rapid victory and end to the war vanished. Instead of weeks the war on the Eastern Front lasted four long years at an enormous cost of lives and indescribable suffering. Hitler's expectation that Japan would join him in declaring war against the Soviet Union was not fulfilled. Japan attacked instead the United States at Pearl Harbor on December 7, 1941. According to the Axis agreements, Germany, as member had to follow suit. Germany declared war against the United States on December 11, 1941. As in World War I Germany was now fighting on multiple fronts.

By the end of 1941, German generals realized that victory in the Soviet front would not come as easy as they planned. Deeply aware of the difficulties of fighting a war on two fronts, they looked with favor on the Vatican's interest of driving a wedge between the Western Allies and Soviet Russia. Given the difficult task ahead they again realized that "their best option," as pointed out by Rhodes, would be a "compromise peace that would leave Germany most of her acquisitions intact." They again tried to use the Vatican to seek a separate negotiated peace with Western powers hoping that the Vatican could influence them to accept a negotiated peace that would give them the freedom to continue their war against the Soviet Union.

Vatican diplomacy tried to influence the outcome of the war by persuading the Allies to give up their demand of unconditional surrender by Germany. Pius XII favored a separate negotiated peace agreement with Germany that would split apart the Allies and leave the Germans free to fight the Soviet Union. In the exact words of Anthony Rhodes:

> The Pope wanted peace so the world could form a united front against Bolshevism.[79]

On April 1942, von Papen, the German ambassador to Turkey, Hitler's political godfather and architect of Catholic-Nazi friendship, approached in Ankara Msgr. Roncalli, the future Pope John XXII, and used the Pope's five-point peace plan of 1939 to launch a new peace initiative. An unofficial German emissary, Baron von Lersner, appeared in the Vatican, with a request for Vatican mediation. Anthony Rhodes summarizes Msgr. Roncalli's report of his meeting with von Papen to the Vatican:

> Von Papen returned to the subject with an accent of lively solitude if not anxiety . . . Roncalli says he began to wonder if von Papen might not be expressing the views of his master—particularly as he knew that von Papen was the only German Ambassador whom Hitler received alone, without the presence of his Foreign Minister.[80]

Von Papen's intrigue to split the Allied-Soviet alliance did not prosper as the Allies stood united in their demand of unconditional surrender. In this context, argues Rhodes, one can understand the active pro-Axis strategy followed by many nuncios all over the world during the war, particularly in South America, to influence governments not to break their relations with the Axis powers. Rhodes quotes von Bergen's report to Berlin of March 21, 1942, concerning the lobbying activities of the nuncios at the Rio de Janeiro conference that took place January 15-28, 1942:

> I have secret information that the Holy See has used its diplomatic representatives to lobby the countries taking part in the Rio de Janeiro Conference with the object of keeping them neutral.[81]

On September 3, 1942, more than a year after Operation Barbarossa was launched, the German Sixth Army of Field Marshal von Paulus reached the outskirts of Stalingrad. The symbolic importance of the city bearing Stalin's name turned this battle into a life and death struggle. This battle became the turning point in the war on the Eastern Front and of World War II as a whole. The whole German Sixth Army was effectively destroyed in the most catastrophic military defeat suffered by the Germans in the war. Over 500,000 of the German-led troops were dead, including the majority of the Romanian soldiers fighting with them. Von Paulus surrendered on February 2, 1943, with what remained of his army—some 91,000 men. From that moment on, the Soviets began their relentless drive westward, which took them to Berlin in early 1945.

As a result of the battle of Stalingrad, Axis members reassessed their policy of cooperation with the Third Reich. Italy, Romania, Hungary, and Finland, were having second thoughts and began to look for ways to switch sides. Two weeks after the Allied Forces landed in Sicily, on July 25, 1943, the Fascist Grand Council in Italy ousted Mussolini from power and ordered his arrest. The new prime minister of Italy, Marshal Pietro Badoglio (1871-1956), capitulated secretly to the Allies on September 3, 1943. The enormous losses in men and equipment that the Romanian and German armies suffered at Stalingrad destroyed Romanian confidence in a Nazi victory and awakened great fear of future Allied retribution.

Nonetheless, even after Italy deserted the Axis in the aftermath of the Stalingrad debacle, wishful thinking of a German victory in Russia, and a separate German peace with the Western Allies prevailed in the Vatican. Cardinal Maglione, expressed to various people at the time his wish for the victory of the Third Reich in the Soviet front:

> The Fate of Europe depends on the victorious resistance by Germany on the Soviet front.[82]

As the Soviet forces were approaching the borders of Hungary, the Hungarian government attempted in March 1944 to establish secret contacts with the Soviets to defect to their side, but knowledge of these contacts reached the Germans and they frustrated these plans by sending in eight German divisions to ensure Hungary's continued cooperation. The Romanians were more successful. King Mihai decided to follow the Italian example and with support from opposition politicians and the army led a successful coup. After they deposed the government and ordered the arrest of Ion and Mihai Antonescu on August 23, 1944, they switched to the Allied side.[83]

By mid-April 1945 the Soviet forces reached Berlin. On April 30, 1945, Hitler committed suicide, designating naval commander Karl Dönitz as his successor. Hitler's thousand-year Reich and his dreams of Lebensraum and Aryan hegemony lay buried under the ruins of Berlin. On May 8, 1945, the Allies accepted Germany's surrender. For the 6 million Jews of Europe annihilated by the Einsatzgruppen in Russia and in the gas chambers of Poland, V-Day came too late.

# Notes

1. Maz Domarus, *The Speeches of Adolf Hitler Volume 4* (Mundelein, IL: Bolchazy-Carducci Publishers) 369-370.

2. Danzig was separated from Germany in 1920 when modern Poland was established. When the municipal administration of Danzig had come under Nazi rule, Poland retained the rights she held there under the Danzig statute.

3. Domarus, *The Speeches of Adolf Hitler*, 369-370. Max Domarus, *Hitler: Speeches and Proclamations* (Wurzburg, 1962).

4. Güenther Lewy, *The Catholic Church and Nazi Germany* (New York: Mc Graw Hill Book Company, 1964), 312.

5. Winston S. Churchill, *The Second World War. Vol. 1* (New York: Houghton Mifflin Company, 1948), 311.

6. John Cornwell, *Hitler's Pope: The Secret History of Pius XII* (New York: Viking, 2008, 229.

7. Anthony Rhodes, *The Vatican in the Age of Dictators 1922-1945* (London, UK: Hodder and Stoughton, 1973), 232.

8. Cornwell, *Hitler's Pope,* 229.

9. Cornwell, *Hitler's Pope,* 231. Rhodes, *The Vatican,* 233. J. Beck, *"Dernier Rapport"* (Politique Polonaise, 1926-1939).

10. Cornwell, *Hitler's Pope*, 229.

11. Strobel Ferdinand. *Erklarung der Deutschen Bischofe zum Kriegsausbruch*, (Munich: Verlag Otto Walter, 1946), 116. Gordon Zahn, *German Catholics and Hitler's Wars: A Study in Social Control* (New York: Sheed and Ward, 1962), 64.

12. Zahn, *German Catholics,* 185.

13. Rhodes, *The Vatican,* 239.

14. Friedrich Heer, *God's First Love* (New York: Weybright and Talley, 1967), 319-320.

15. Saul Friedlander. *Pius XII and the Third Reich* (New York: Alfred A. Knopf, 1966).

16. *1939 Reichsgesetzblatt, Part I,* 2042.

17. *"Nazi Conspiracy and Aggresion. Vol.1, chap. XIII",* Nizkor Project, 10023.

18. Michael Phayer, *The Catholic Church and the Holocaust, 1930-1965* (Indiana University Press, 2001), 6.

19. Rhodes, *The Vatican,* 238. *"A.A. Pol. III Besiehungen des heiligen Stuhls zu Polen, Vol. I"* (Dec. 23, 1939).

20. It proposed complete disarmament, the reconstruction of a League of Nations as a guarantee of security, the establishment of mechanisms for equitable treaty revision, and the need to satisfy the needs and demands of racial minorities.

21. Rhodes, *The Vatican,* 240.

22. Annual Register of 1940 drawing upon "Vatican sources".

23. Owen Chadwik, *Britain and the Vatican During the Second World War* (UK: Cambridge University Press, 1988). John S. Conway. The Meeting between Pope Pius XII and Ribbentrop (University of British Columbia CCHA Study Sessions, 35(1968)), 103-116.

24. Alberto Giovanetti, *Der Vatican und der Krieg* (Cologne, 1961).

25. Jan Tomasz Gross, *Revolution from Abroad: The Soviet Conquest of Poland's Western Ukraine and Western Byelorussia* (Princeton, NJ: Princeton University Press, 1988), 194.

26. Yakev Rasen, *Mir Viln Lebn* (New York: 1949), 22-25. William Perl, *The Holocaust Conspiracy* (New York: Shapolsky Publishers, 1989), 110. Similar testimonies are to be found in almost every Jewish Town memorial book published after the war.

27. David Kranzler, *Japanese, Nazis and Jews: the Jewish Refugee Community of Shanghai 1938-45* (New York: Yeshiva University Press, 1976).

28. William L. Shirer, *The Rise and Fall of the Third Reich* (New York: Simon and Schuster, 1959), 661.

29. Shirer, *The Rise and Fall,* 661.

30. Raul Hilberg, *The Destruction of the European Jews* (Teaneck, NJ: Holmes & Meier, 1985), 267.

31. The Warschauer Zeitung published details of the decree.

32. *Records of the Nuremberg Trial*, Frank Diary. D. No. 2233.

33. E. Ringelblum, *Polish–Jewish Relations in the Second World War* (Jerusalem: Yad Vashem, 1974).

34. Carol Rittner, S.D. Smith, Irene Steinfeldt. *The Holocaust and the Christian World* (Jerusalem: Yad Vashem, 1974-1978).

35. The Polish President, Daniel Kwasniewski, rejected the demand that the private properties taken from Jews be returned to their rightful heirs, which he argued at a meeting with Jewish representatives of WJRO, could only lead to a revolution in Poland. *Dos Yiddische Wort*, Nissan, 1997.

36. Eduard Wagner. *Der Generalquartiermeister: Briefe und Tagebuch Eduard Wagners*, 135. Ch. Browning, *The Origins of the Final Solution*, 45.

37. *Records of the Nuremberg Trial*, Frank Diary, D. No. 2233.

38. Peter Longerich, *"Policy of Destruction Nazi Anti–Jewish Policy and the Genesis of the Final Solution"*, 1999 Meyerhoff Lecture at the Holocaust Memorial Museum, Washington, DC. Henry L. Feingold, *The Politics of Rescue* (New York: Holocaust Library, 1970). Deborah Dwork and Robert Jan Van Pelt, *Holocaust: A History* (New York: W. W. Norton and Company, 2002) , 211.

39. Philip Friedman, *Roads to Extinction: Essays on the Holocaust* (New York: JPS, 1980).

40. Friedman, *Roads to Extinction.*

41. Yad Vashem documents 97 and 98.

42. John F. Morley, *Vatican Diplomacy and the Jews During the Holocaust 1939-1943* (New York: Ktav Publishing, 1980), 91-94.

43. Peter Longerich, *"Policy of Destruction"*. Feingold, *The Politics of Rescue,* 120. Dwork & Van Pelt, *Holocaust: A History,* 211.

44. *Akten zur Deutschen Auswatrtigen Politik, Serie E: 1941-1945.* Vol.1, 403.

45. Hillel Seidman *Warsaw Ghetto Diaries* (New York: Targum Press, 1997), 220.

46. Rhodes, *The Vatican,* 247-248.

47. Lewy, *The Catholic Church*, 307.

48. Rhodes, *The Vatican,* 246. A.A. Buro, *Des Staatssekretars, Vol. 2.*

49. Michael Curtis, *Verdict on Vichy: Power and Prejudice in the Vichy France Regime* (New York: Arcade Publishing, 2003).

50. Morley, *Vatican Diplomacy*, 84.

51. Albert De Jonghe, *De laatste boodschap van Kiewitz namens koning Leopold III voor Hitler*, 15 juni 1944; Belgisch Tijdschrift voor Filologie en Geschiedenis, LXV, 2 ,1987, p, 274-300, p, 299-300.

52. Actes. Vol. 1, No. 370. Rhodes, *The Vatican.*

53. Actes. Vol. 1, No. 370. Rhodes, *The Vatican.*

54. Winston S. Churchill, *The Second World War.*

55. Christopher R. Browning, The Origins of the Final Solution. The Evolution of Nazi Jewish Policy, September 1939-March 1942 (Nebraska: University of Nebraska Press, 2007). 215. Halder. Kriegstagebuch des Oberkommandos der Wermacht 1940–1941. 1:203-209, 1:237, 1:257-258, 2:49.

56. Browning, *The Origins of the Final Solution*, 215. Halder. *Kriegstagebuch des Oberkommandos der Wermacht 1940–1941.* 1:203-09, 1:237, 1:257-258, 2:49.

57. R. J. Sontag, Ed, *The private papers of Baron Diego von Bergen. Documents on German foreign policy, 1918-1945.* (Washington, D.C: U.S. Government Printing Office, 1949).

58. Sontag, *The private papers.*

59. Milan Bulajic. *The Role of the Vatican in the Break-Up of the Yugoslav State.* (Beograd: Struchna kniga, 1994), 10.

60. Bulajic, *The Role of the Vatican*), 74.

61. *Ustasha Hrvatski Narod* newspaper of August 15 and 16, 1941.

62. *Katolicki List*, April 21, 1941.

63. *Ustasha Hrvatski Narod* newspaper of August 15 and 16, 1941.

64. Vladimir Dedijer, *The Yugoslav Auschwitz and the Vatican* (Amherst, NY: Prometheus Books, 1992), 133.

65. Pierre SJ Blet, *Pius XII and the Second World War According to the Archives of the Vatican* (New York: Paulist Press, 1999), 108.

66. Srdja Trifkovic, *Ustasa: Croatian separatism and European Politics 1929-1945.* The Lord Byron Foundation for Balkan Studies, 1998, 323 pp (139, English ed.). Pavelic met with Hitler three times during the war.

67. Srdja Trifkovic. DGFP, D, 12, Minutes of Hitler's talks with Pavelic, 6 June 1941.

68. Enciclopedia Judaica. Ed. Staff. *Jewish History of Yugoslavia.*

69. Carlo Falconi, *The Silence of Pius XII* (Boston: Little, Brown, 1970), 315-316. Bulajic, *The Role of the Vatican,* 99.

70. The Trial of German Major War Criminals. Nuremberg, Day 12: December 4, 1945.

71 . Albert Speer. *Inside the Third Reich* (New York: Simon & Schuster. 1982).

72. The Trial of German Major War Criminals. Nuremberg, Day 12: December 4, 1945.

73. Paul I. Murphy and Rene R. Arlington, *La Popessa: The Controversial Biography of Sister Pascalina, the Most Powerful Woman in Vatican History* (New York: Warner Books, 1983). 199.

74. Rhodes, *The Vatican,* 258. A.A. Pol III Buro des Staatsekretars, Vol. 3. Menshausen report. Sep. 12, 1941.

75. Friedlander, *Pius XII,* 79.

76. Friedlander, *Pius XII,* 298.

77. Country Study by the U.S. Federal Research Division of the Library of Congress: Romania, 1990.

78. A. Jacobsen and W. Jochmann, eds., Zur Geschichte des Nationalsozialismus. Usgewahlte Dokumente (Bielefeld, 1961). Translation by the editor Source: Himmler Files (Washington, D.C.); microfilm at Institut fiir Zeitgeschichte, Munich. The conference was convened by the SS Police Führer of the Ukraine, Hans Prijtzmann.

79. Rhodes, *The Vatican,* 242.

80. Rhodes, *The Vatican,* 269.

81. Rhodes, *The Vatican,* 265, 298.

82. Braham Ed, 32.

83. Antonescu was tried and shot on June 1, 1946.

# Chapter 8
## The Einsatzgruppen

## The Einsatzgruppen in the Soviet Territories

The invasion of the Soviet Union provided the window of opportunity that Hitler and his henchmen were waiting to carry out the physical annihilation of European Jewry. It gave them the cover of secrecy they needed to put in practice the Final Solution in their own backyard. At the Wansee Conference Heydrich contrasted in his presentation on January 20, 1942, months after the Final Solution had begun, the limited options to make Europe Judenfrei that existed before the war, which mainly relied on forced immigration, with the possibilities that the global war opened in this respect.

The wider plan to annihilate the totality of European Jewry was taking shape as Hitler was preparing the attack on the Soviet Union. The SS under the command of Himmler and Heydrich were put in charge of the total European Final Solution. Eichmann testified at his trial in Jerusalem that Heydrich informed him around two to three months before the invasion of Russia that the Führer had ordered the physical annihilation of all the Jews in Europe.[1] Although great numbers of Jews were already dying from starvation, epidemics, and exhaustion in the ghettos and labor camps in Poland before the invasion of Soviet Russia, that was too slow to fulfill Hitler's plan in the short period he wished to make Europe Jüdenfrei. Even the instigated pogroms during the first days of the invasion in which many tens of thousands of Jews were killed by local mobs and militia, were only meant to condition the population for the plan of total annihilation.

Two mass-murder systems, the Einsatzgruppen, using firearms, and the death camps, using poison gas, were put in practice by the Germans to accelerate the Final Solution. In the territories taken from the Soviets, the Einsatzgruppen firing squads were assigned the task of wholesale murder of Jews in front of open mass graves, while in the rest of Europe the death camps with their gas chambers and crematoriums were considered better suited for the task. While in the first case the killing teams would go after the victims, in the second, the victims would be gathered from all over Europe to be murdered in strategically situated death camps.

In anticipation of the attack on the Soviet Union, Hitler called a conference with his commanding generals on March 30, 1941, at which he made clear to them that the conquest of new Lebensraum and the annihilation of the Jews were the two parallel aims of the invasion. The upcoming war with Russia would be a race-war totally different from the war in the West. He laid down the guidelines of that war: Jews and Communist commissars would be killed by firing squads of SS Einsatzgruppen, the special paramilitary groups following on the heels of the advancing armies.

The invasion of the Soviet Union also marks the beginning of the establishment of death camps to carry out the Final Solution in the rest of Europe. The plans for the establishment of death camps to rapidly destroy the Jews of Europe were also taking shape, although they actually began to operate a few months later. In the summer of 1941, Rudolf Höss, the commander of Auschwitz, at the time a camp for Polish prisoners, was summoned to Berlin and was told about the need to mobilize Auschwitz for the Final Solution. In his autobiographical notes, Höss refers to the total annihilation plan of the totality of European Jewry, which went beyond the more limited task assigned to the Einsatzgruppen:

> In the summer of 1941 Himmler summoned me to Berlin to give me the disastrous and harsh order for the annihilation of the Jews from all over Europe. This resulted in Auschwitz becoming the greatest killing institution in history. [2]

On July 17, 1941, five days before the attack on the Soviet Union, Heydrich issued in writing his Commissar Order in which he called for "the separation and further treatment of . . . all Jews." It meant that the Final Solution of the so-called Jewish Question would now be taken to a new level of radical mass murder in Europe as a whole. On July, 20, 1941, in Lublin, Himmler ordered Odilo Globocnik (1904-1945), one of the vilest individuals in the Nazi hierarchy, to expand what later became known as Operation Reinhard and establish death camps in the Generalgouvernement to annihilate the Jews of Poland and to administer property taken from them. [3] On July 31, 1941, as the German armies were advancing in the Soviet territories and the Einsatzgruppen were already mass murdering Jews in Russia, Heydrich was told by Göring to prepare "a general plan of the administrative, material and financial measures necessary for carrying out the desired Final Solution of the Jewish question."

On October 10, 1941, Heydrich and Eichmann attended a meeting in Prague where a program of action for the Final Solution was mapped out months before the 1942 Wansee Conference. Heydrich announced Hitler's immediate initial target of clearing Germany of Jews by the end of 1941. On October 23, 1941, Himmler sealed the last crack in the impregnable wall of the Nazi empire and issued an order to Heinrich Müller, the chief of the Reich's Security Office, that no Jew should be allowed to emigrate from anywhere in occupied Europe.

Massive deportations of Jews from the Reich and Western Europe were put in motion to the ghettoes in Poland, the Baltic countries and White Russia as a prelude to their annihilation by the Einsatzgruppen or in the death camps being established.

On November 18, 1941, Alfred Rosenberg (1893-1946), Reichminister of the Ostministerium in charge of the Eastern Occupied Territories, gave a confidential background report to the German press on the situation in the East after a four-hour conference with Himmler. He stated unequivocally that the Jewish question would only be considered solved for Europe when not a single Jew was left on the European continent up to the Urals.

> In the east some six million Jew still live, and this question can only be solved in a biological eradication of the entire Jewry of Europe. The Jewish question is only solved for Germany when the last Jew has left German territory, and for Europe when not a single Jew lives on the European continent up to the Urals.[4]

On December 12, 1941, one day after Germany declared war on the United States, Hitler told the top echelons of the Nazi Party that the Jews would in any case be annihilated. Goebbels made the following entry into his diary:

> With respect of the Jewish Question, the Führer decided to make a clean sweep. He prophesied to the Jews that if they again brought about a world war, they would live to see their annihilation in it. That was not just a catchword. The world war is here, and the annihilation of the Jews must be the necessary consequence.[5]

Hans Frank, who attended this meeting, returned to the Generalgouvernement and transmitted this message to his district governors and division leaders:

> In Berlin we were told: why all this trouble [with the Jews]; we cannot use them in the Ostland or the Reichskommissariat either; liquidate them yourselves! Gentlemen, I must ask you, arm yourselves against any thoughts of compassion. We must destroy the Jews, wherever we encounter them and wherever it is possible, in order to preserve the entire structure of the Reich.[6]

Most of the ghettoization process in the newly conquered areas of the Soviet Union was completed by August 1941. The ghettoes would obviously play an important role in the mass annihilation process. In the larger cities where the killing of all the Jews could not be achieved in one day or single action, the Germans would establish a priority order. First they would go after the intelligentsia in order to decapitate community leaders capable of organizing resistance. Those left behind would be exploited as slave workers until their turn to be liquidated arrived. Last, they would liquidate the slave workers that were used for the German war effort. These workers carried out forced labor inside and outside of the ghettoes in the vain hope that their work would make them indispensable to the Germans. But that was seldom the case and sooner or later they would also be liquidated.

# The Einsatzgruppen Organization

In preparation for the upcoming invasion of the Soviet Union, the SS began training candidates in early May 1941 for the SS Einsatzgruppen in Pretzsch near Leipzig.[7] The leaders of the murderous Einsatzgruppen belonged to the intellectual elite of the Nazi Party: Of the twenty-five Einsatzgruppen and Einsatzkommando leaders, fifteen of them had PhDs; most of them were doctors of jurisprudence or philosophy. One of the commanders of Einsatzgruppe C, Ernst Biberstein, was a Protestant pastor, theologian, and Church official. There was also a Catholic priest among them: ObersturmFührer Albert Hartl (1904-1982) who was consecrated by Cardinal Faulhaber in 1929, served initially in the Church Information Service in the Reich Security Main Office seeking support for the T4 euthanasia program among Catholic theologians. He was put in charge of the staffing section of Einsatzgruppe C.

Consisting initially of between 500 and 900 men each, some of the Einsatzgruppen were greatly enlarged over time. Each Einsatzgruppe was subdivided into smaller units called Einsatzkommandos and Sonderkommandos. Days before the opening of the Soviet campaign, the newly appointed chiefs of the Einsatzgruppen and the unit commanders were verbally informed at a conference in Pretzsch of Hitler's orders to kill Jews and Communist commisars in the conquered Soviet territories. Ohlendorf testified in Nuremberg, on January 3, 1946, concerning the original annihilation orders they received before the campaign from Himmler in Hitler's name:

> COL. AMEN: So that before you commenced to march into Soviet Russia you received orders at this conference to exterminate the Jews and Communist functionaries in addition to the regular professional work of the Security Police and SD; is that correct?
> OHLENDORF: Yes.[8]

Four Einsatzgruppen named A, B, C and D were attached to different army groups and deployed from north to south across the occupied Soviet territory. Group A, under the command of Walther Stahlecker, was assigned to the Baltic countries (Estonia, Latvia, and Lithuania), group B under the command of Arthur Nebe was assigned to Byelorussia, group C under the command of Otto Rasch was assigned to Northern and Mid Ukraine, and group D under the command of Otto Ohlendorf was assigned to Southern Ukraine, Crimea, and Caucasia.

The Einsatzgruppen were in constant movement along carefully planned routes, not leaving out even the smallest Jewish communities on their way as can be seen from the reports. The list of mass killings or aktionen of Einsatzgruppe A included all the Jewish communities in Northeastern Poland and the Baltic in the regions of Bialystok, Vilna, Kovno, and Riga. The Einsatzgruppe B list included all the Jewish communities in Belarus such as Grodno, Minsk, Brest-Litovsk, Baranovich, Slonim, Mogilev, and Bobruisk going beyond east to Gomel, Briansk, Kursk, Orel, and Tula. The Einsatzgruppe C list includes the communities of North and Center-Ukraine such as Lvov, Tarnopol, Zlochev, Kremenets, Kiev, Kharkov, Rovno, and Rostov-on-Don. The Einsatzgruppe D list included all the communities in the Southern Ukraine and Crimea around Czernowitz, Moghilew-Podolsk, Nikolayev, and Kherson, reaching as far as Simferopol, Sevastopol, and Feodosiya in the Crimea.

The Wehrmacht was required to provide logistical support to the Einsatzgruppen, including supplies, transportation, and housing. When needed, Wehrmacht commanders would reinforce the Einsatzgruppen with contingents of their own. The Einsatzgruppen operated in coordination with the Waffen SS, the Gestapo, regular police, and locally recruited police. In concert with them, they applied a highly sophisticated system of deception at every step to create false expectations and disorientation among Jewish victims.

At the arrival of the German troops, special SS Vorkommandos entered with them to incite behind the scenes through their contacts the local population to carry out bloody pogroms against their Jewish neighbors. The Germans enlisted great numbers of local people into special police battalions and local police forces. Given the anti-Semitic environment nurtured by Church and state it was not difficult to inflame the traditionally anti-Semitic population against the Jews, blaming them for the war and every other conceivable problem. Although the Jewish communities suffered at least as much as the Christian population from Soviet occupation, Jews were accused of being Bolshevik agents and partisans fighting against the German army. The initial pogroms conditioned the local population to accept favorably the Final Solution. The local police participated in the pogroms and later enthusiastically assisted the Einsatzgruppen in their killing campaign.

The Einsatzgruppen arrived on the heels of the Wehrmacht to the doorsteps of the Jewish communities to immediately begin their deadly mission in June 1941. They preceded the death camps in Poland by a number of months and continued to operate in the Soviet territories well into 1943 in parallel with the death camps. Before carrying out a Judenaktion in a town, the SS would typically post a deceptive proclamation instructing all the Jews with their families to gather on a certain day and place, allegedly for "resettlement." From there, selected victims would be brought to the killing sites either by foot or in trucks. People of all ages and conditions would be marched under the brutal surveillance of the Einsatzkommandos to an open isolated area 2.5 to 3 miles outside the towns:

> One step to the left—we shoot! One step to the right—we shoot! One word—we shoot! March![9]

Reaching the killing site, the assembled Jews would be ordered to hand over their valuables, undress, and line up in front of the mass grave. Whole families were arrayed, kneeling or standing in front of open pits to face a deadly hail of fire. Otto Ohlendorf, commander of Einsatzgruppe D, described at his trial in

Nuremberg, the routine procedure applied by the Einsatzgruppen in the Judenaktionen:

> The unit selected would enter a village or city and order the prominent Jewish
> citizens to call together all Jews for the purpose of resettlement. They were re-
> quested to hand over their valuables and shortly before execution, to surrender
> their outer clothing. The men, women, and children were led to a place of ex-
> ecution, which in most cases was located next to a more deeply excavated anti-
> tank ditch. Then they were shot, kneeling or standing, and the corpses thrown
> into the ditch. [10]

Ohlendorf noted that where antitank ditches or ravines were not available,
the SS forced the victims to dig their own collective graves:

> The men, women deeply excavated antitank ditches. Then they were shot,
> kneeling or standing, and the corpses thrown into the ditch . . . The kommandos
> filled the graves to efface the signs of execution, and then labor units of the
> population leveled them. [11]

Waffen SS units of many nationalities, Werhmacht personnel, military
chaplains, and German contractors were often eyewitnesses to the Judenaktionen
by the Einsatzgruppen in the outskirts of the towns in Soviet-occupied territories. The horror stories witnessed by so many people came back to their home
countries and reached all strata of society. The photos taken by them of the
shooting of Jews before open pits bear witness to these unspeakable crimes.
Hermann Graebe, a German building contractor in the Ukraine, witnessed such
an aktion on October 5, 1942 in the outskirts of Dubno in the Ukraine. He voluntarily presented his testimony before the International Military Tribunal in
Nuremberg: [12]

> I walked around the mound, and found myself confronted by a tremendous
> grave. People were closely wedged together and lying on top of each other so
> that their heads were visible. Nearly all had blood running over their shoulders
> from their heads. Some of the people shot were still moving. Some were lifting
> their arms and turning their heads to show that they were still alive. The pit was
> already 2/3 full. I estimated that it contained about 1,000 people.
> I looked for the man who did the shooting. He was an SS man, who sat at
> the edge of the narrow end of the pit, his feet dangling into the pit. He had a
> Tommy gun on his knees and was smoking a cigarette. The people, completely
> naked, went down some steps which were cut in the clay wall of the pit and
> clambered over the heads of the people lying there, to the place to which the SS
> man directed them. They lay down in front of the dead or injured people; some
> caressed those who were still alive and spoke to them in a low voice. Then I
> heard a series of shots. I looked into the pit and saw that the bodies were
> twitching or the heads lying already motionless on top of the bodies that lay be-
> fore them. Blood was running from their necks.
> I was surprised that I was not ordered away, but I saw that there were two
> or three postmen in uniform nearby. The next batch was approaching already.

They went down into the pit, lined themselves up against the previous victims and were shot. When I walked back around the mound, I noticed another truck-load of people which had just arrived. This time it included sick and infirm persons. An old, very thin woman with terribly thin legs was undressed by others who were already naked, while two people held her up. The woman appeared to be paralyzed. The naked people carried the woman around the mound. I left with Moennikes and drove in my car back to Dubno.

On the morning of the next day, when I again visited the site, I saw about thirty naked people lying near the pit, about thirty to fifty meters away from it. Some of them were still alive; they looked straight in front of them with a fixed stare and seemed to notice neither the chilliness of the morning nor the workers of my firm who stood around. A girl of about twenty spoke to me and asked me to give her clothes, and help her escape. At that moment we heard a fast car approach and I noticed that it was an SS detail. I moved away to my site. Ten minutes later we heard shots from the vicinity of the pit. The Jews still alive had been ordered to throw the corpses into the pit; then they had themselves to lie down in this to be shot in the neck.[13]

Although the modus operandi of the Einsatzgruppen differed in many respects from the death camps, they were able to rob the victims with no less efficiency. Their robbery began the moment they entered a town and culminated when the Jews were forced to surrender their clothing and jewelry at the execution site. Taking as a model the collective fine imposed on the Jews after Kristallnacht in the Third Reich, the Germans imposed astronomical ransom payments in the ghetto Judenrats in cash money, gold, silver, and jewelry. They made sure the Jews would come forward with the amounts requested by taking hostages they threatened to kill. Yitzhak Arad documented major collective ransom payments imposed by the Germans in countless towns in the ex-Soviet territories such as Vilna, Minsk, Lvov, Brest Litovsk, Pinsk, Kobryn, Lutsk, Baranowicze, Kharkhov, Dniepropetrovsk, Orsha, Borisov, and Drohoczyn.[14]

At the mass executions of the Einsatzgruppen, the SS kept an eye on every piece of property the victims brought along to the execution sites. All the goods were handed over to the Reich Finance Ministry, either through the RSHA or directly. Watches, clocks, and pens were distributed to troops in the front. To win the goodwill of the local population, the clothes were initially given to them, but in the winter of 1941-1942, they were collected and sent to the Third Reich for the National Socialist Welfare Agency. From the Einsatzgruppen killing aktionen in Kiev and Zhitomir, 137 truckloads of clothing went to the NS Welfare Agency in the Third Reich.

On August 1, 1941, Heinrich Müller, the head of the Gestapo, forwarded an order to the four Einsatzgruppen requiring them to keep the Führer continually well informed of their operations: Müller demanded "visual materials of special interest, such as photographs, via the speediest possible delivery."[15]

The Führer is to be kept informed continually from here about the work of the Einsatzgruppen in the East.[16]

The four Einsatzgruppen dutifully submitted periodic detailed reports of their Judenaktionen to their superiors, which reached to the top. Event reports were first sent by radio and then by written dispatch signed by the commander of the Einsatzgruppe or his deputy. The coded radio messages were picked up and deciphered in England at Bletchley Park through Enigma machines very early on. The British knew as early as July 18, 1941, a month after the attack on Russia, that the Jews and Soviet POWs were being massacred. These messages were read by Prime Minister Winston Churchill who informed the world of these mass executions without revealing the source of his information.[17]

The recovered written reports cover the period from June 1941 to May 1942. They quite specifically detail the number of people murdered and the property looted. It becomes clear from these reports that the overwhelming majority of the victims were Jews. The sequentially numbered written reports were found at the headquarters of the offices of the Berlin Reichssicherheitshauptamt by the U.S. Army. The originals are currently held by the German government in the archive at Coblentz where they are available to researchers and historians.[18] Considering the substantial number of copies of reports that were distributed to various government ministries there can be no doubt that the actions of the Einsatzgruppen and their helpers were widely known in the government offices of the Third Reich.

One report, known as the Jäger Report, written by SS StandartenFührer Jäger is one of the most terrifying documents of the Einsatzgruppen. It lists the numbers of Jews killed in mass-shooting actions town by town in Lithuania between July and November 1941. Jäger lists a total of 137,346 Jews liquidated in that small country during that short period. At the end of his report dated December 1, 1941 Jäger declared with pride:

> Today I can confirm that our objective, to solve the Jewish problem for Lithuania, has been achieved by EK 3. In Lithuania there are no more Jews, apart from Jewish workers and their families.[19]

To evoke the unspeakable tragedy of the many thousands of Jewish communities, large and small, now extinct as their citizens were executed by firearms at the edges of antitank ditches and pits in Eastern Poland, the Baltic countries, Byelorussiaand and the Ukraine is beyond human capacity. Every town and city in Soviet-occupied territories has a tragic story to tell. The names of the sites where these aktionen took place have become, like Auschwitz and Treblinka, symbols of the Holocaust: Babi Yar near Kiev, Ponary near Vilna, and the Ninth Fort near Kovno, Rumbula near Riga, just to mention a few of the best-known killing sites behind the Soviet borders where many hundreds of thousands of Jews were annihilated by the Einsatzgruppen. An enormous literature has grown around the Einsatzgruppen Judenaktionen, although few, very few Jews, survived to tell their stories to future generations. No more can be attempted here than to evoke that unfathomable tragedy than to sample a few aktionen among many thousands other.

The impossible task of describing the destruction of many hundreds of Jewish communities by the Einsatzgruppen was recognized in the final judgment at the trial of the Einsatzgruppen commanders held during 1947 and 1948 before the Nuremberg International Tribunal:

> Only the fact that the reports from which we have quoted came from the pens of men within the accused organizations can the human mind be assured that all this actually happened. The reports and the statements of the defendants themselves verify what otherwise would be dismissed as the product of a disordered imagination . . . A crime of such unprecedented brutality and of such inconceivable savagery that the mind rebels against its own thought image and the imagination staggers in the contemplation of a human degradation beyond the power of language to adequately portray . . . One cannot grasp the full cumulative terror of murder one million times repeated.[20]

## The Einsatzgruppen Campaign in Eastern Poland

The arrival of the Germans in Eastern Poland after the attack on the Soviet Union in June 1941 was greeted in many towns by the local Poles with pogroms on their Jewish neighbors. The Polish Institute for National Remembrance, recently created, identified twenty-three towns in Eastern Poland such as Jedwabne, Radzilow, Wasosz, Wizna, Stawiski, and many others where pogroms were carried out. The perpetrators who turned on the Jews in a wild orgy of blood were Polish Catholics who had lived side by side with their fellow Jewish townspeople for countless generations.

Lone survivors testified right after the war about some of these crimes carried out collectively by Polish townspeople, often with the knowledge of their priests, but their testimonies were ignored or buried in the enormity of German crimes. The Jedwabne massacre in Northeastern Poland in the Lomza region, which was brought to light recently by Tomasz Grosz in his book *Neighbors*, had been described more than fifty years ago by survivor Rivkah Fogel in a Yiddish article published in Australia by the Yivo Committee in Melbourne. The story was also chronicled in 1980 in a memorial book by survivors who had been rescued by a local Polish family. Testimony on the massacre in the nearby town of Radzilov was given by Menachem Finkelstein before the Historical Commission in Bialystok on June 27, 1945, and published in the Yizkor book of Radzilov in 1945.

Townspeople rounded up their Jewish neighbors, including visitors from nearby towns such as Wizna and Kolno, and took them to the square in the center of town, where they were bludgeoned to death and savagely butchered with nail-studded clubs, axes, poles, and knives during an eight-hour blood orgy on July 10, days after the German arrival. They forced the Jews, including the ninety-year-old rabbi of the town, to run down Cemetery Road to Bronislaw Sleszynski's barn where they closed every exit, poured kerosene, and burned some 1,600 people alive. Other smaller groups of forty Jews each were driven to the Jewish cemetery, ordered to dig deep ditches, and buried alive. All these actions were carried out under the direction of the town council of Jedwabne and its mayor Marian Karolak. Only a handful of fleeing Jews survived in a nearby village sheltered by a humanitarian Polish couple, Antonina and Aleksander Wyrzykowski. Leon Dziedzic, a Christian Pole from Przestrzele near Jedwabne, added recently some glimpses of the scene he witnessed two or three days after the massacre, as the remains of the martyred Jews lay still unburied:

> The German gendarmerie was afraid that an epidemic might break out because it was very hot and dogs were getting at the corpses. But this was an impossible job, for the piled-up bodies of Jewish victims were entwined with one another as roots of a tree. Somebody hit upon the idea that we should tear them into pieces and throw these pieces into the dugout. They brought pitchforks, and we tore the bodies as best we could: here a head, there a leg.[21]

Sixty years later the Polish Institute of National Remembrance undertook the task of reconstructing and reassessing these atrocities. Polish historian Tomasz Szarota wrote:

> The facts that Neighbors brought to light are so shattering that they force even me, a historian who has read much and written a good deal about various instances of disgraceful behavior by Poles under German occupation, to come to completely new conclusions . . . We did not realize that Poles were also perpetrators of the Holocaust. In Jedwabne, they were . . . And not only in Jedwabne, but in many other places as well. Grosz has forced us to change our views on the subject of the attitudes of the Poles during the Second World War. [22]

The Jedwabne pogrom was not exceptional but one that was repeated in many other towns. The townspeople in nearby Radzilov forcibly assembled in the marketplace 1,700 Jewish men, women, and children on July 7, 1941, surrounded them from all sides and drove them up against Mitkowski's barn near the village of Radivyesh where they were burned alive. During the next three days the Poles continued hunting down Jews and killing them in front of the barn. Menachem Finkelstein described how his mother pleaded with the Catholic local priest Aleksander Dolegovski, whom she knew well, to use his moral authority to stop his parishioners, but her pleas fell on deaf ears.

As the massacre of Radzilov became newsworthy sixty years later, the town was visited by the *New York Times* correspondent Steven Erlanger who interviewed local residents. One resident, Mariusz Gryczkowski told the correspondent that he and many others grew up knowing about the burning alive of the Jews. When asked about what brought about the massacre he said:

The Jews had money and the Poles were jealous.[23]

Grosz dealt in his book with the accusation that the collaboration of the Jews with the Soviet occupiers caused such reactions as the Jedwabne and Radzilov pogroms. He showed the falsity of that canard. The collaborators with the Soviets were not Jews, but Poles—the same who later collaborated with the

Germans most willingly. When the Soviets returned after the war, indicates Grosz, "the natural allies of the Communist Party on the local level, were people who had been compromised during the German occupation." He arrives at a conclusion well known to every survivor—the Poles coveted the houses and belongings of the Jews—a factor the Germans used to their utmost advantage to involve the Polish population in the elimination of the Jews.

On June 26, 1941, only four days after the invasion of Eastern Poland, Vilna was occupied by the Wehrmacht. Einsatzgruppe A, led by SS StandartenFührer Franz Walter Stahlecker arrived soon after. On July 4, 1941, the Germans ordered the establishment of a Judenrat. That day the Nazis began seizing Jewish males from the streets and homes of Vilna supposedly for forced labor, with the assistance of Lithuanian and Polish youths wearing white armbands. The abducted Jewish men were taken first to Lukiszki prison and then by foot and trucks to Ponary Forest around 6 miles from Vilna. After being shot by the Einsatzkommandos with the help of Lithuanian police units and "self-defense" militia, they were buried in ditches previously used by the Red Army to store petrol. The executions, which included women and children, continued periodically in the Ponary Forest. From the German occupation in late June to the creation of the ghetto on September 6, 1941, around 20,000 Jews were murdered in Ponary.

Abba Kovner, who later became a partisan leader, personally witnessed an aktion on August 31, 1941, in which 2,019 Jewish women, 864 men, and 817 children were taken in trucks to Ponary and murdered. Next day, according to SS StandartenFührer Karl Jäger's report, a column of more than 3,700 people was marched during the night through the streets of Vilna to the Ponary killing site. The aktion continued for four days, murdering a total of 8,000 victims. A wounded Jewish woman managed to escape alive and return from Ponary to Vilna to inform Dr. Mark M. Dworjetsky on September 3, 1941, that Ponary was not a labor camp but an extermination site. Dworjetsky repeated the alarming news at a gathering but no one believed him, accusing him of panic mongering.

Two contiguous ghettos separated by Niemiecka Street were established in Vilna on September 6, 1941. Approximately 29,000 people were enclosed in Ghetto 1, and around 11,000 in Ghetto 2. The lack of sanitation and extreme congestion created unbearable living conditions. The ghetto police published a notice on September 15, 1941, stating that those without work permits would have to move to Ghetto 2 to alleviate congestion. That night approximately 3,000 people started out toward the second ghetto but only 600 reached its gate. All the rest were taken to Lukiszki prison and from there to Ponary, where they were shot. During September 1941, Jews continued to be slaughtered day after day without interruption at Ponary by Einsatzkommando units. By the end of 1941, the Einsatzgruppen had executed more than 48,000 Jews by firearm, the majority of them from Vilna itself. During the total period from July 1941 to August 1944, Ponary became the collective grave of 100,000 Jews, 70,000 of them from Vilna proper, the rest from surrounding towns.[24]

Four days after the German army invaded Eastern Poland on June 26, 1941, the Germans took Bialystok where approximately 50,000 Jews lived there at the time. Next day, known as Red Friday, Order Police Battalion 309 spread over Jewish neighborhoods, throwing grenades into Jewish homes and wounding many people. They dragged Jewish men from their dwellings, beat them, and forced them into the Great Synagogue, the largest wooden synagogue in Eastern Europe, which they surrounded on all sides. Those resisting were shot in front of their wives and children. As the large synagogue filled with people, they spilled gasoline at the entrances and hurled grenades to the interior, which immediately went up in flames. The Nazis forced victims to push one another into the blazing building. The synagogue burned for twenty-four hours until Saturday morning when the Germans gave an order to extinguish the fire.[25]

The fire spread to contiguous streets. More than thirty Jewish streets, which accounted for a third of all Jewish homes in Bialystok, were burned down that day. Entire streets and buildings disappeared leaving mountains of ash. The burning houses were surrounded by cordons of heavily armed Nazis, but some Jews managed to escape. The death toll was tragic, 2,200 Jews were burned to death on Red Friday. Next day, Saturday, June 28, 1941, the German military commander summoned Bialystoks's official town rabbi, Dr. Gedaliah Rosenmann, and the chairman of the Jewish Community Council, Efraim Barasz, and ordered them to form a Judenrat.

On Thursday, July 3, 1941, at four o'clock in the morning, Einsatzkommando 9 closed off various streets and dragged from their homes around 1,000 men between the ages of sixteen and sixty to carry out a *selection*. Workmen and artisans were separated and eventually freed, but around 300 members of the intelligentsia and merchants were loaded onto a truck and taken to Pietrasze Field, approximately 1.2 miles outside the city which the Germans designated as the killing site for Bialystok Jewry, where they were shot.

On July 8, 1941, Heinrich Himmler and Adolf Eichmann visited Bialystok. Four days later, on Saturday, July 12, a second much larger aktion, remembered as the "Saturday Martyrs Aktion" took place. More than 3,000 Jewish men were rounded up, chased through the streets, ridiculed, beaten, and taken away in trucks to Petrasze and executed there by shooting, while claiming that they had sent these people to work. No one survived. Adding insult to injury, the treacherous Nazi commandant told the members of the Judenrat shortly after the Judenaktion, that for a ransom of 11 pounds of gold, 2 million Soviet rubles, 220 pounds of silver, and other valuables, the vanished men would be returned. This cruel hoax on helpless victims went beyond the one carried out in Rome in 1943 on the Jews there. The heartbroken wives, mothers, and children of the victims gave away their jewelry, large sums of money, and everything else they owned in order to help free their loved ones. After taking the ransom and making the Judenrat delegation wait for several hours, the German commander announced with a smirk on his face that the victims would not return—that they had been sent away to labor camps in Germany.

On July 28 and August 1, 1941, all the Jews of Bialystok (around 50,000) were driven into two small ghettoes divided by the Biala River where previously no more than 6,000 people had lived. Starved and exploited as slave laborers inside and outside of the two cramped ghettos, the ghetto population was thinned by periodic deportations to nearby Treblinka and to Majdanek, after these death camps began to operate in 1942. The final liquidation of the Bialystok ghetto took place on August 20, 1943, following the heroic week-long revolt led by Mordechai Tenenbaum-Tamaroff.

## The Einsatzgruppen Campaign in the Baltic Countries

In the Baltic countries of Lithuania, Latvia, and Estonia, the Germans armies were greeted at their arrival as liberators from Soviet domination. The highest Church authorities gave them a most enthusiastic welcome and held solemn mass ceremonies in the cathedrals. When Kovno, the capital of Lithuania, fell on June 24, 1941, only two days into the invasion, the Catholic metropolitan of Kovno, Archbishop Juosapas Skvireckas (1873-1959), and Bishop Vincentas Brizgys (1903-1992) welcomed publicly the German armies and expressed their gratitude to Hitler.

The bishops promised to fight together with the Germans against the Soviets and strongly supported the formation of Lithuanian Waffen SS divisions and SS police. The people's participation in the SS Einsatzgruppen could never have reached large-scale proportions without the pro-German message heard from their highest religious authorities.[26] As a result, many Catholics volunteered in these formations that helped the Germans to annihilate Jews, even in faraway places outside of their own countries. Catholic priests from the Baltics served in these death formations as documented by Yitzhak Arad.

The Lithuanians celebrated the German arrival, staging one of the most brutal pogroms in memory against the defenseless Jewish population of Kovno. Given the strong influence of the Catholic Church in Lithuania and its anti-Semitic tradition, the pro-German proclamations of the highest Church authorities were understood by the Lithuanians as a green light to join the Germans against the Jews. A special German SS Vorkommando incited the local Lithuanian militia of Kovno to carry out violent attacks against the peaceful Jewish population. During the pogrom, which lasted three days (June 26-29, 1941), 1,500 defenslessless Jewish men and women were dragged into the town square of Kovno and mercilessly beaten to death with clubs by the Lithuanians, while synagogues and many homes were put on fire.

In Slobodka, a suburb of Kovno, its venerable rabbi R. Zalman Osovsky was bound hand and foot to a chair and his head sawed off. His decapitated body was found still sitting at his desk before his open Talmud folio at page thirty-three of the treatise Niddah. His head was displayed at the window with a sign: "This is what we will do to all the Jews!"[27] Ten days later, on July 9, more than 2,300 Jews were again murdered in the cruelest manner by the Lithuanian militia in Kovno. In a report by Einsatzgruppe A of October 1941 there is an explicit reference to the Kovno pogrom and its origin:

> To our surprise it was not easy at first to set in motion an extensive pogrom against the Jews. Klimatis, the leader of the partisan unit mentioned above, who was used for this purpose primarily, succeeded in starting pogroms on the basis of advice given to him by a small Vorkommando operating in Kovno and in such a way that no German order or German instigation was noticed from the outside. During the first pogrom in the night from 26 to 29 June, the Lithuanian partisans did away with more than 1,500 Jews, set fire to several synagogues or destroyed them by other means, and burned down a Jewish dwelling district consisting of about sixty houses. During the following nights, approximately 2,300 Jews were rendered harmless in a similar way.[28]

The attitude of the bishops and priests at that crucial time in these strongly Christian countries could have made the difference between life and death for the Jews. They had the moral power to influence the majority of the population not to join the murderers in their crimes and extend help to the Jews, but instead they chose to give them their moral support. Not a single word was heard coming from the episcopate to their loyal flock in behalf of the Jews; their silence spoke louder than words. Friendly lifetime neighbors turned into merciless enemies that killed people whom they personally knew and with whom they had lived in close proximity for a lifetime. Most revealing is the following important quote from the 1941 report of Einsatzgruppe A concerning the refusal of Bishop Brisgys to help the Jews in any way and the instructions he issued as acting head of the Catholic Church in Lithuania:

> The attitude of the Church regarding the Jewish question is, in general, clear. In addition, Bishop Brisgys has forbidden all clergy-men to help Jews in any form whatsoever. He rejected several Jewish delegations that approached him personally and asked for his intervention with the German authorities. In the future he will not meet with any Jews at all. Conversion of Jews to the Catholic faith did not take place so far. The Church would also object to this type of conversion. It is convinced that the Jews would not come out of conviction but because of the possible advantages connected with it.[29]

When the Germans ordered the Jews to move out from their homes in Kovno to a ghetto in the suburb of Slobodka under the claim that the Lithuanian population was demanding the isolation of the Jews, a delegation headed by Rabbi Samuel Snieg turned to Bishop Brizgys, the acting head of the Catholic Church of Lithuania, to appeal to him to intervene with the German commander. Bishop Brizgys replied:[30]

> With all my regrets, I cannot do it. This may endanger the position of the Catholic Church in Lithuania. Such a responsibility I cannot take upon myself.[31]

More than 37,000 Jews were forced out from their homes and enclosed in two ghettoes on August 15, 1941, after the bloody pogrom carried out by the Lithuanians. The Einsatzgruppen immediately began thinning the ghetto population by periodically selecting groups of victims, which they executed with firearms at Ninth Fort. The total population of the small ghetto in Kovno of around 3,000 people was completely liquidated at Ninth Fort by the Einsatzgruppen shooting squads seven weeks later on October 4, 1941.

On October 28, a date rememberd by the Great Aktion carried out that day, the population of the large ghetto was ordered to assemble at Democrats Square for a selection. Over 9,200 people—half of them children—were declared unfit for work and marched off to Ninth Fort where large pits dug by Soviet POWs were prepared for them. Stripped of their clothes, the victims were ordered to wait in freezing cold before being taken in groups of 200 to the edge of the pits where they were mercilessly gunned down by the Einsatzkommandos and their Lithuanian assistants. By the end of December 1941, more than half of the Jews of the Kovno ghetto had already been liquidated by the Einsatzgruppen in periodic aktionen at the Ninth, Fourth, and Seventh Forts. The remaining 17,412 Jews were all eventually deported to the death camps where very few survived.

On Himmler's order SS Obergruppenfüehrer Friedrich Jeckeln, one of the bloodiest mass murderers serving Himmler and Heydrich, was dispatched from Kiev to Riga to liquidate Latvian Jewry. From their arrival in June 1941 to the end of September 1941, the Einsatzgruppen were able to murder in the smaller towns and villages of Latvia approximately 30,000 Jews, one-third of the total Jewish population, with the active participation of Latvian collaborators. The annihilation of Jews living in the larger cities such as Riga, Dünaburg, and Libau, followed not long after.

The mass shooting of around 27,000 Riga Jews and 1,000 Jewish deportees from Germany was carried out by Jeckeln in the Rumbula and Bikerniek forests in two massacres, one on November 30, 1941, and the second on December 8, 1941. The victims were forced to march ten kilometer from Riga to the execution site in a wooded area near the Rumbula train station. At their destination they stood in a waiting line a mile long to surrender their jewelry and suitcases before approaching the deep pits further down that Soviet POWs had dug earlier.

Jeckeln turned the Riga massacre into a public spectacle with special invited guests. In search of optimum efficiency and order (*ordenung über alles!*), SS General Jeckeln developed a original mass murder and burial system that became famous among the SS as the *Jeckeln Sardinenpackung method* (sardine-packing method), which he wanted to demonstrate to them. German Army Engineer Colonel Walter Bruns, who was there, described the method. The first group of victims was forced to undress, descend into the pit, and lie face down to be shot in the back of the head. Layer after layer, the victims were executed in the same fashion, until the pit was full. Normally there were five or six layers of bodies in the pits before they were covered over with earth. Dr. Andrew (Andrievs) Ezergailis, professor at Ithaca College in New York, recently described in an academic paper presented at a Riga conference on November 29, 2001, how Jeckeln gallantly played host to his guests at the bloody spectacle:

> Jeckeln himself stood on top of the sand bank with invited guests and observed the work of the killing team. Schnapps and zakuski for the guests and those working in the vicinity of the pits were laid out on tables. [32]

The shooting of approximately 27,000 people including the chief rabbi of Riga, M. M. Zak, and the elderly prominent historian Simon Dubnow, in full public view, rapidly reached the outer world. Two radio broadcasts, one in German from Moscow and the other a BBC broadcast from London, announced the killings at Rumbula and Bikerniek to the world at large.

The Riga ghetto was nearly emptied after the two aktionen and only 4,500 men and 300 women remained there. Deportation trains from the Third Reich filled with Jews were now directed to Riga. Einsatzgruppe A received from Berlin fifteen gas vans to liquidate them. The Jews deported from Germany eventually shared with the local Jews the same tragic fate as their predecessors at the killing grounds of Rumbula and Bikerniek or in the gas vans. Under Soviet rule after the war, the execution sites at Rumbula and Bikernieki Forests near Riga were off-limits to Jews for many years until the fall of Communism. Commemorative ceremonies at the site of the mass killing were strictly banned.

The last report of Einsatzgruppe A officially informed Berlin that they had executed a total of 229,052 Jews in the Baltic countries. This number is only a fraction of the totality of the victims. Not included are the many Jews that died from hunger and diseases in the ghettoes and those deported from the larger ghettoes to death camps after the Einsatzgruppen ceased their operations. It has been estimated that 254,000 Jews, 95 percent of the 265,000 Jews living in Lithuania in June 1941, were murdered during the German occupation. Historians have pointed out that no other Jewish community in Nazi-occupied Europe suffered such proportionally high losses as Lithuania.

## The Einsatzgruppen Campaign in Byelorussia

Minsk, the capital of Byelorussia, fell to German hands on June 28, 1941, six days after the beginning of the invasion. German terror began immediately upon their arrival to the city. Thirty Soviet prisoners who refused to bury alive a group of forty-five Jews were killed together with the Jews. Upon arrival, Einsatzgruppe B, under the command of Arthur Nebe, took hostage around 40,000 Jewish and non-Jewish men and boys and surrounded them in a field with machine guns and floodlights. On the fifth day, they issued an order that all Jewish members of the intelligentsia should step forward. Under the false impression that their skills were needed, 2,000 unsuspecting Jewish men moved forward. They were marched off immediately to a nearby forest and shot.[33]

The Minsk ghetto was established on July 20, 1941. Around 100,000 Jews were enclosed in its limited area. Under the false claim that they were taking people for work they took groups of Jews to nearby forests and executed them. Five thousand Jews were executed on August 14, 26, and 31, 1941. Himmler visited Minsk, accompanied by Karl Wulff and Erich von dem Bach-Zelewski on August 15-16. He requested from Arthur Nebe to arrange for him a Einsatz-kommando shooting demonstration.

A model mass execution of Jews was prepared for Himmler in a forest north of Minsk. Otto Bradfisch's Einsatzkommando 8 executed there a group of around 120 to 190 Jews at the edge of two excavated pits. When brain matter of one of the Jewish victims splashed on Himmler's cheek, the weak stomached arch murderer nearly fainted in the arms of his liaison man SS General Karl Wulff. [34] According to postwar claims of SS General Erich Bach-Zelewski, Higher SS and police leader in Central Russia, himself a hardened perpetrator, he turned to Himmler on that occasion with the following comment:

> I said to him: ReichsFührer that was only a hundred! What do you mean by that? I answered: look at the eyes of the men in this Kommando, how deeply shaken they are! These men are finished (fertig) for the rest of their lives. What kind of followers are we training here? Either neurotics or savages! [35]

As he became personally aware of the depressing effect of the mass shoot-ings on the SS executioners, Himmler saw the need to adopt murder methods less stressful to them, not for their victims.[36] He authorized Arthur Nebe to test dynamite on patients of a mental asylum in Novinki near Minsk. Nebe arranged to kill the patients using dynamite and fire bombs. He closed the patients inside two concrete pillboxes and detonated the dynamite. The results of the explosions were gruesome, destroying the victims together with the bunkers, leaving parts of bodies strewn all around and hanging from the trees. As a result, dynamite explosions were discarded as impractical.

Himmler and his advisors thought of using gassing vans for the Ein-satzgruppen similar to those that had been used in the Reich by the euthanasia program. Bottled carbon monoxide, however, was expensive and difficult to transport in wartime in large quantities from Germany to Russia. Seeking to go around the problem, Nebe fell on the idea of using the exhaust fumes of truck engines instead of pure bottled carbon monoxide. A few days after the Minsk experiment, Nebe introduced in Mogilev the exhaust fumes from two trucks into a sealed room with around thirty mental patients causing their death. The "suc-cessful" experiment gave birth to the production of *Gaswagens* (mobile gassing vans), in which lethal exhaust gases were redirected to the passenger compart-ment to poison the unsuspecting passengers.

By early September 1941, Heydrich gave instructions to Walter Rauff in Berlin, the head of Technical Affairs in the Reich Security Main Office whose office had jurisdiction over motor vehicles, to remodel heavy trucks as mobile gas chambers for the Einsatzgruppen in occupied Soviet territories.[37] About thir-ty gas vans were produced for the different Einsatzgruppen during early 1942 by the Gabschat Farengewerke GMBH, a private car manufacturer at Will-Walter Strasse 32-38 in Berlin.[38] Rauff explained the original purpose of the Gaswagens

in a voluntary deposition at the embassy of the Federal Republic of Germany in
Santiago de Chile in 1972:

> So far as the extermination of Jews in Russia is concerned, I know that gas vans
> were used . . . Whether at that time I had doubts against the use of gas vans I
> cannot say. The main issue for me at the time was that the shootings were a
> considerable burden for the men who were in charge thereof and that this bur-
> den was taken off of them through the use of the gas vans.[39]

A 1941 top secret memo under the title *The Solution of the Jewish Question* from the advisor for Jewish Affairs of the Reich Ministry for the Occupied
Eastern Territories has an explicit reference to the production of the gassing ap-
paratuses (*Vergasungsapparate*) to be used in Riga and Minsk:

> Please be informed that [Chief Executive Officer] Brack from the Führer's
> Chancellery has stated his readiness to assist in the construction of the neces-
> sary accommodations. At the present time we do not have on hand a sufficient
> quantity of the apparatuses, so they must first be constructed . . . I might further
> point out that Eichmann, the Advisor on Jewish Affairs in the Reich Security
> Main Office, is in complete accord with this procedure. According to informa-
> tion received here from [Major] Eichmann, camps for the Jews will be set up in
> Riga and Minsk . . . Given the present situation, Jews who are unfit for work
> can be eliminated without qualms through use of the Brack device.[40]

The unsuspecting victims boarded the gassing vans under the deception
that they were going to be transported to another locality. Before boarding they
were ordered to hand over their valuables and undress themselves to go through
a delousing procedure inside the vans. The two back doors were closed after the
victims were all inside and the driver started the motor in neutral gear for about
ten minutes. During this time the motor produced enough carbon monoxide to
poison the victims. When the screaming and pounding had stopped, the driver
drove to the burial or cremation site with the dead cargo. There, Jewish slave
workers would unload the corpses and dispose of them. Although the SS disguised the trucks by painting simulated windows on their sides, the local population began to identify the gassing trucks as *todeswagens* or death trucks.

The Einsatzgruppen operators were not too happy with the gas vans either.
The SS inspectors were complaining about the heavy emotional toll the gas vans
were taking on the delicate SS operators. On May 16, 1942, SS SturmFührer Dr.
August Becker submitted a secret report to Walter Rauff on the gas trucks in
which he expressed his concern that they were imposing great stress on the murderers:

> The men suffered "enormous emotional and health injuries" (ungeheure see-
> lische und gesundheitliche Schäden) and complained of headaches after each
> unloading. The gassing is without exception not undertaken properly. In order
> to finish the job as quickly as possible, the drivers without exception open full
> throttle. For this reason those to be executed suffer death from suffocation and

are not, as intended, put to sleep peacefully. The result was ghastly—horribly distorted faces and bodies covered with excrement and vomit (verzerrte Gesichter und Ausscheidungen).[41]

Einsatzgruppe D received gas vans in the spring of 1942 and used them in the Crimea and Caucasus. Otto Ohlendorf, their commander, testified in Nuremberg about the use of the Gaswagens and also confirmed that the Einsatzkommandos disliked them because burying the victims was a "great ordeal" for them:

These vans were in the future to be used for killing of women and children . . . The actual purpose of these vans could not be seen from the outside. They looked like closed trucks, and were so constructed that at the start of the motor, gas was conducted into the van causing death in ten to fifteen minutes . . . The vans were loaded with the victims and driven to the place of burial, which was usually the same as that used for the mass executions . . . They were told that they were to be transported to another locality . . . The time needed for transportation was sufficient to insure the death of the victims . . . I received the report that the Einsatzkommandos did not willingly use the vans because the burial of the victims was a great ordeal for the members of the Einsatzkommandos. [42]

Gassing vans did not displace firearm executions, which continued to be the main killing method of the Einsatzgruppen in the ex-Soviet-occupied territories, at least until late 1943. Gassing vans were also used in Chelmno, at Majdanek, Maly Trostinec near Minsk, and in the Riga ghetto.

On November 7, 1941, 12,000 Jews from Minsk were taken to be executed at Tuchinki and on November 20, another 7,000 Jews suffered the same tragic end. The immediate aim was to make room in Minsk for 25,000 Jewish deportees from Germany, Austria, and the Protectorate. A total of 45,467 Jews had already been executed in Minsk by November 1941 according to a report of Einsatzgruppe B. During the Purim holiday, on March 2, 1942, another 5,000 Jews were executed, including a group of children from the Shpalerna Street orphanage. The children were thrown alive into a deep pit at Ratomskaya Street. In one of the reports intercepted and decoded by Enigma in London, the massacre of 7,819 men, women, and children in a ravine at Ratomskaya was reported.[43]

On May 7 and 8, 1942, the Germans put in operation an extermination center in Maly Trostinec, 7.5 miles east of Minsk. Most of the victims in Maly Trostinec were killed by shooting in nearby forests such as Blagowshtchina, Shashkowa, and Dzerzhinsk-Koidanovo, and some by gas vans. An estimated 150,000 people were shot in Blagowshtchina and over 50,000 in Shashkova. Four gas vans belonging to Einsatzgruppe B, with a capacity of seventy-five people each, shuttled between Maly Trostinec and Minsk, gassing 500 victims each day. The last 2,000 Jews were taken from the Minsk ghetto to Maly Trostinec on October 21, 1943. According to Nazi statistics, 86,632 Jews—almost all of the prewar Jewish population of Minsk—were murdered between the occupation of the city in 1941 and February 1, 1943.

The largest Judenaktion began on July 28, 1942, during which 30,000 Jews of Minsk ghetto were executed in four days. The total ghetto population had been gathered at Yubileiny Square in great fear. There, Judenrat chairman Moshe Yaffe received an order from German authorities to address the crowd and allay their fears. At first Jaffe attempted to comply with that order, but when he saw the gas vans arriving at the square, he realized the deception and cried out bitterly to the people:

Jews! The bloody murderers have deceived you—flee for your lives! [44]

Yaffe and forty-eight physicians, the leading medical specialists of Belarus, were among the victims killed in the Judenaktion. The ghetto police chief was also among them. The Minsk Judenrat ceased to exist. Barely 8,794 Jews were left in the ghetto by August 1, 1942, according to German official figures.

Before the Maly Trostinec camp was burned down June 28-30, 1944, the last 6,500 prisoners held at the Wolodarski Street Prison and the Schirokaja Street Camp in Minsk were brought to Maly Trostinec. After being driven inside a barn they were shot. Arranged with firewood in ordered layers, their dead bodies reached the top of the barn. Another three funeral pyres were erected outside of the barn. Everything, including the camp structures were set on fire on June 30, 1944. When the Soviet troops arrived four days later on July 4, the charred remains were still there as witnesses of the unspeakable crime perpetrated by the Germans.

Since Maly Trostinec was only one of several places where Jews were murdered in the Minsk region, historians have found it difficult to arrive at an accurate figure of the number of Jews killed there until the war's end in June 1944. The total estimates vary from a minimum of 200,000 to as many as 500,000 Jews. Approximately 80 percent of the 400,000 Jews living in Eastern Byelorussia were annihilated in Maly Trostinec.

## The Einsatzgruppen Campaign in the Ukraine

The advance of the Germans in Eastern Ukraine took place with lightning speed. Countless large-scale Judenaktionen in Eastern Ukraine were detailed in the Einsatzgruppen reports or were intercepted by Enigma, in addition to the Kiev massacre such as the shooting of 35,782 in Nikolayev and Cherson (16-30 September 1941), 8,800 in Berdichev (September 7-October 5 1941), 28,000 in Vinnitza (September 22, 1941), 23,000 in Rovno (November 7-8 1941), 21,600 in Kharkov (late December 1941), 15,000 in Dnepropetrovsk, and 10,000 in Simferopol.[45] In their route the Einsatzgruppen annihilated the ancient Jewish communities of Zhitomir, Uman, Mogilev, and countless other smaller towns. During the initial three months of the invasion, from August to the end of October 1941, a total of 363,211 Jews had been liquidated in the Soviet occupied-territories according to Himmler's November 1941 report to Hitler.[46]

The reports of the Einsatzgruppen make explicit reference to the support they received from the Ukrainian clergy in particular to carry out their killing Aktionen against the Jews. In one of such reports SS SturmbannFührer Bruno Magill from the SS cavalry regiment informs his superiors:

> The Ukrainian clergy were very cooperative and made themselves available for every Aktion. It was also conspicuous that, in general, the population was on good terms with the Jewish sector of the population. Nevertheless they helped energetically in rounding up the Jews. The locally recruited guards, who consisted in part of Polish police and former Polish soldiers made a good impression. They operated energetically and took part in the fight against the looters [euphemism for the Jews used in the reports.] [47]

During the interwar period (1919-1939), Western Ukraine or Galitzia and its capital Lvov were part of Poland, but the Ukrainians considered it to be a historical part of the Ukraine and fought for its independence. After the Hitler-Stalin Pact it became part of the Soviet zone of occupation. The Ukrainians harbored dreams that Hitler would grant them statehood as he had given the Slovaks and the Croats. Their dream never materialized as Hitler considered the Ukraine to be part of the German Lebensraum. A week before the German arrival to Lvov, the Ukrainian nationalists, under the leadership of Stefan Bandera, rebelled against the Soviets and declared Ukrainian statehood. In retaliation, the NKVD executed in its jails around 3,000 Ukrainian nationalists.

At the arrival of the German troops to Lvov (Lemberg), the capital of Western Ukraine on June 30, 1941, Ukrainian crowds enthusiastically greeted Hitler's marching troops as liberators in the central square of Lvov—renamed Adolf Hitler Square. Andreas Alexander Szeptyckyj (1865-1944), metropolitan archbishop of Lvov, highest authority of the Greek-Catholic Uniat Church in the Ukraine that recognized the authority of the Pope in Rome, issued a proclamation welcoming the German troops. Like Cardinal Innitzer in Vienna and Archbishop Brysgis in Kovno, Szeptyckyj called for collaboration with the Germans.

Szeptyckyj, who was the political leader of the Ukrainian Nationalists in Poland, put all the weight of his great prestige and influence among the Ukrainian population in favor of the German invaders. He expressed the gratitude of the Ukrainian people to Hitler for their "liberation" and supported the creation of a Ukrainian division within the Waffen SS and ordered that a solemn mass be officiated in the Lvov cathedral to celebrate the formation of the division.[48] As late as 1943, Szeptyckyj, with several other Ukrainian leaders, signed a letter addressed to Hitler, pledging support for the Führer's "New Order" in Europe and giving his blessing to the Ukrainian Waffen-SS Galicia divisions as they set out to the front.

The German invasion was a sign for the Ukrainians to launch pogroms against the Jews. Even before the Germans arrived, Ukrainian police went on a three-day killing rampage of Jews in Lvov. On July 2, a day after their arrival, the Germans released most of the inmates held by the Soviets in the three prisons of Lvov. Jews were rounded up in great numbers and taken to the NKVD prisons to dig out the corpses of those killed by the Soviets. Every morning around 1,000 innocent Jews were brought in and forced to dig. The action was filmed to inflame the population against what they called the "Jewish Bolshe-viks." As a result, the Ukrainians began rioting against the Jewish population in Lvov and the surrounding towns.

In his desperation, chief rabbi of Lvov Rav Yehezkel Levin went to the residence of Archbishop Szeptyckyj on the Iura Hill on the morning of July 2 in the company of two representatives of the Jewish council to plead for his help in stopping the attacks on the Jews. The archbishop promised to issue a pastoral letter to his parish, in which he would warn the Ukrainians against murder and plundering, but refused to intervene with the Germans. He offered asylum in his home to the rabbi, which he declined. Upon his return home, Rabbi Levin was arrested at the doorstep of his home by two policemen and taken to the Lvov prison. There he was murdered together with more than 3,000 Jews including his brother, the eminent rabbi of Rzeszow, Seym deputy Rav Aaron Levin.[49]

On July 25, 1941, a second pogrom called "Petliura Days" named after Symon Petliura (1876-1926), the bloody Ukrainian nationalist leader during the Soviet revolution was let loose. Many Jews still remembered the terror that Pet-liura's bands spread all over the Ukraine during the Soviet revolution. Numerous groups of Ukrainian youth appeared in the streets of Lvov wearing his yellow and blue armbands or rosettes, dragging Jews from their homes. Around 2,000 Jews were murdered in the pogrom, mostly by civilian collaborators, after being marched in groups to the Jewish cemetery or to the Lunecki prison.

Szeptyckyj linked the future of his country to the Third Reich and its Führer, while his followers where annihilating Jews everywhere; they helped to round up Lvov's Jews and marched virtually every Jew in Lvov, around 140,000, to their death. Szeptyckyj's correspondence with Pius XII reveals two strands in his relationship to Jews. In an early letter he wrote in December 1939 to Pius XII, he complained about the mass of Jewish refugees that fled in great haste from the Germans to the Soviet side, swelling the Jewish population of Lvov to a record high of 135,000 souls. His remarks maligning the fleeing refu-gees in classical anti-Semitic terms as unethical and avaricious belong in the same class as the defamatory reports of Vatican representatives in Bolivia and Chile to Pius XII, intended to stop the small flow of Jewish refugees from Nazi Germany to South America.

In August 1942, Szeptyckyj wrote a letter to Pius XII, in which he makes reference to the atrocities carried out by the Germans, pointing out that the Jews are the primary targets of German bestiality. Pius XII on his part had no other advice to offer Szeptyckyj but to "bear adversity with serene patience," in other words, to stand aside quietly while the Jews were annihilated.[50] To Szeptyckyj's personal credit it must be pointed out, that regardless of his pro-German stand, a number of Jews to whom he provided asylum, owe their survival to him; He hid 21 Jewish children in his cathedral and 183 more in convents and monasteries. He is remembered by them with much gratitude as their saver.

Kiev, the capital of the Ukraine was occupied by the rapidly advancing German military forces on September 19, 1941. Approximately 100,000 Jews were able to flee before the Germans entered the city, but 60,000 nonetheless remained behind. There were few men of military age among them as they had been conscripted and retreated with the Soviet army. Most of those who remained were women, children, the elderly, and the sick. As in Odessa, the Soviet Secret Service was able to blow up the German military headquarters and part of the city center in two powerful explosions. The Germans used the sabotage act as a pretext to begin their genocide campaign against the Jews in Kiev. On September 26, SS Colonel Paul Blobel posted 2,000 proclamations all over the city and its suburbs, ordering the Jews to appear at the corner of Melnikovskaya and Dukhtorovskaya on the morning of September 29, 1941:

> All the Jews of Kiev and the vicinity are to appear on Monday, September 29, 1941, at 8:00 a.m. on the corner of Melnikovskaya and Dukhtorovskaya (near the cemeteries). They are to bring their documents, money, other valuables and warm clothes, linen, etc. Any Jew found disobeying these orders will be shot. Citizens breaking into flats left by the Jews and taking possession of their belongings will be shot.[51]

The rumor was intentionally spread by the Germans that the Jews were going to be relocated to a ghetto or a labor camp. Deceived by German promises and afraid to be shot for disobeying German orders, 33,771 Jews, mostly women, children, and the elderly, showed up at the point of concentration on September 29, 1941. In his report the commander rejoices in the fact that more than 30,000 Jews arrived voluntarily when they only expected 5,000-6,000 at most:

> Although at the start, one could count on the participation of about 5,000-6,000 Jews, more than 30,000 Jews turned up who, due to extraordinarily skillful organization, believed in the transfer, right up to the moment of their execution.[52]

The scene was described by a SS officer at his trial in Darmstadt in 1967: "It was like a mass migration . . . the Jews sang religious songs on the way."[53] When the Jews arrived in great numbers to the cemetery in the Syrets suburb, they were herded into a closed area bounded by barbed wire to prevent their escape at the last moment; from there, they were marched down to a ravine situated nearby, whose name has become a symbol of Nazi evil—Babi Yar:

> Then the Germans began shoving the Jews into new, narrower lines. They moved very slowly. After a long walk, they came to a passageway formed by German soldiers with truncheons and police dogs. The Jews were whipped through. The dogs went at those who fell but the pressure of the surging lines behind was irresistible, and the weak and injured were trod underfoot. Bruised and bloodied, numbed by the incomprehensibility of their fate, the Jews emerged onto a grassy clearing. They had arrived at Babi Yar; ahead of them lay the ravine.[54]

Their terrible agony was just beginning. The Jews were led in groups down the side of the ravine and ordered to put down their bundles and to strip naked. To expedite the final entrance to the deep ravine, Dina Pronicheva, a survivor, noticed that when mothers with children tried to hold back, the Germans grabbed the children and threw them over the edge into the ravine:

> The ground was strewn with clothing. Ukrainian militiamen, supervised by Germans, ordered the Jews to undress. Those who balked, who resisted, were assaulted, their clothes ripped off. Naked bleeding people were everywhere. Screams and hysterical laughter filled the air. [55]

Sonderkommando 4a, under the direct command of GruppenFührer Dr. Otto Rasch (1891-1948), supported by German police units and Ukrainian auxiliaries carried out the shooting. The fire squads were placed strategically on the other side of the ravine. Pushed to the edge of the ravine or into it, the Jews were machine-gunned by the fire squads from the other side. More than half of the Jewish population of Kiev was murdered at Babi Yar on September 29 and 30. According to official SS reports to headquarters, 33,771 Jews were massacred in these two days. It was one of the largest single Einsatzgruppen aktion during World War II. In the months ahead, many more Jews were murdered at the same site. It is estimated that until Kiev was recovered by the Soviets on November 6, 1943, some 100,000 people, 90 percent of them Jews, were massacred at Babi Yar. The rest were Soviet POWs and Gypsies. Paul Blobel, in charge of the operation, was decorated for his "heroic action" in Babi Yar with the Iron Cross, Germany's highest award for valor. Under him was Dr. Rasch, who was in charge of the shooting operation. Ben Ferencz, a member of the prosecution team in Nuremberg, made the following meaningful comment on Dr. Rasch, who held two doctoral degrees:

> Dr. Rasch. I being an ignorant little guy from Transylvania, I never heard of people Doctor Doctor, I thought somebody was stuttering: Two doctorates! And Dr. Dr. Rasch was the biggest mass murderer I ever heard of. He did the Babi Yar job. 33,771 Jews killed in two days. Imagine that . . . What does it take for your machine gunners dropping them into a ditch outside of Kiev and covering up the whole mound? He did that job. And his commander there was Blobel.[56]

On March or April 1942, five to six months after Blobel commanded the Babi Yar action, Blobel passed by the killing site on his way to a dinner reception in the company of Albert Hartl (1904-1982), a SS Catholic priest who was a commanding officer of the Einsatzgruppen. After the German occupation in Rome in September 1943, Hartl was transferred to Rome where he was close to Bishop Hudal.[57] Gita Sereny transcribed verbatim what Hartl told her about his fleeting visit to Babi Yar in the company of Blobel:

> At one moment—we were driving down past a long ravine. I noticed strange movements of the earth: clumps of air rose into the air as if by their own pro-

pulsion—and there was smoke: it was like a low-toned volcano; as if there was burning lava just beneath the earth. Blobel laughed, made a gesture with his arm, pointing back along the road and ahead of us, all along the ravine—the ravine of Babi Yar—and said, "Here lie my thirty thousand Jews. Corpse gases were bubbling up through the thawing earth.[58]

Blobel was sentenced to death by the U.S. Nuremberg Military Tribunal in the Einsatzgruppen Trial and hanged at Landsberg prison on June 8, 1951. Dr. Dr. Rasch died during the trial. However, not one of the many members of Sonderkommando 4a was tried there. It took more than twenty-six years to bring eleven members of Sonderkommando 4a to trial in Darmstadt during 1967-1968. Only seven of these mass murderers were convicted, receiving a total of sixty-one years in prison.[59]

In the postwar years, some intellectuals in the Soviet Union tried in vain to get a monument built at Babi Yar. The Communist government under Nikita Khrushchev had very different plans in mind. In a display of callous contempt, he was prepared to build a football stadium on the killing grounds. For many years, Jews who tried to gather at Babi Yar on the anniversary of the massacre to recite Kaddish and eulogize their martyred dead were harassed, removed by force from the site by the Soviet police, and jailed. On September 19, 1961, a young gentile Soviet poet, Yevgeny Yevtushenco, now a professor in Oklahoma, published in *Literaturnaya Gazeta* a poem *Babii Yar* that shook the very foundations of the Soviet system:

No monument stands over Babii Yar . . .
Today I am as old in years as all the Jewish people.
Now I seem to be a Jew . . .
I am each old man here shot dead. I am every child here shot dead.
Nothing in me shall ever forget! [60]

When the Soviets finally agreed under pressure to erect a memorial at Babi Yar, they eliminated any reference to the Jewish identity of the victims.[61] The ashes of the men, women, and children that were murdered at Babi Yar for no other reason than their being Jews were denied that posthumous distinction. In the selective memory of Soviet "history" there was no room for Jews. It took sixty years for an official commemoration to take place for the first time in Babi Yar on September 29, 2006.

Even a cursory overview of the major crimes committed by the Einsatzgruppen in the Ukraine cannot go over in silence the shattering episode of the annihilation of over ninety Jewish orphans in Byela Tzerkow, not far from Kiev, on August 1941. Its uniqueness is derived not from its numbers, but from the extremes of inhumanity reached there. The facts of this gruesome crime are most carefully documented by German authors Ernst Klee, Willi Dressen and Volker Riess in their memorable book *The Good Old Days*. Catholic chaplain Ernst Tewes C.O. (1908-1998), later principal co-consecrator of the present Pope Benedict XVI on May 28, 1977 as archbishop of München, was an impor-

tant protagonist in this drama together with three other chaplains of the Wehr-
macht: Reuss (Catholic), Wilczeck (Protestant), and Kormann (Protestant).
Their reports provide testimony to the agony of the young orphans in Byela
Tzerkov.[62]

A month before the fall of Kiev, the entire Jewish population of Byela
Tserkow, several hundred Jewish men and women, were shot by a platoon of
Einsatzgruppe C during August 8-19, 1941, under the command of SS OberscharFührer Jäger with the help of the Ukrainian militia. Their orphaned children were separated in a building at the edge of the town. On the evening of August 19, half of the children were taken out in three trucks to the rifle range and
killed. Around ninety children, many of them babies, were left behind in the
closed house without food or water with practically no one to care for them. A
Wehrmacht officer living nearby informed the chaplains the next day about their
tragic situation. Together, the four chaplains visited the site and reported the
facts to the Generalstabsoffizier of the division, Lieutenant-Colonel Helmuth
Groscurth. Dr. Reuss, who after the war became the Catholic bishop of Mainz,
wrote:

> In the courtyard in front of the house the crying and whimpering of children
> could be heard very loudly . . . We immediately entered the house unobstructed
> and in two rooms found some ninety (I counted them) children aged from a few
> months to five, six or seven years old . . . The children lay or sat on the floor
> which was covered in their feces. There were flies on the legs and abdomens of
> most of the children, some of whom were only half dressed. Some of the bigger
> children (two, three, four years old) were scratching the mortar from the wall
> and eating it . . . The stench was terrible. The small children, especially those
> that were only a few months old, were crying and whimpering continuously. [63]

Protestant chaplain Kormann only found fault in the fact that such a thing
was happening in full public view:

> As I consider it highly undesirable that such things should take place in full
> view of the public eye, I hereby submit this report. [64]

After a visit to the children, Lieutenant-Colonel Groscurth sent a lengthy
report on August 21, 1941, to Field Marshal von Reichenau (1884-1942):

> The execution could have been carried out without any sensation if the Feld-
> kommandantur and the Ortskommandantur had taken the necessary steps to
> keep the troops away . . . Following the execution of all the Jews in the town it
> became necessary to eliminate the Jewish children, particularly the infants.
> Both infants and children should have been eliminated immediately in order to
> have avoided this inhuman agony.[65]

In his answer of August 26, 1941, von Reichenau found no reason for
complaint. Following von Reichenau's orders, SS Colonel Paul Blobel and a
representative of the Wehrmacht headquarters arrived and ordered the execution

of the children. The Wehrmacht had already dug a grave. SS ObersturmFührer August Hafner, in charge of the operation, reported back describing the final act:

> I went out to the woods alone. The Wehrmacht had already dug a grave. The children were brought along in a tractor . . . The Ukrainians were standing round trembling. The children were taken down from the tractor. They were lined up along the top of the grave and shot so that they fell into it. The Ukrainians did not aim at any particular part of the body. They fell into the grave. The wailing was indescribable. I shall never forget the scene throughout my life. I find it very hard to bear. I particularly remember a small fair-haired girl who took me by the hand. She too was shot later . . . The grave was near some woods. It was not near the rifle-range. The execution must have taken place in the afternoon at about 3:30 or 4:00. It took place the day after the discussions at the Feldkommandanten . . . Many children were hit four or five times before they died.[66]

Different estimates have been produced on the total number of victims killed by the Einsatzgruppen but the numbers reached at Nuremberg on the basis of the Einsatzgruppen reports themselves remain a solid reference point. The International Military Tribunal at Nuremberg stated in its decision of October 1, 1946, that the total number of people killed by the Einsatzgruppen stood around 2 million people.

Only twenty-four Einsatzgruppen commanders, a small fraction of the Einsatzgruppen perpetrators were indicted for their participation in the murder of 1 million people in Nuremberg between September 29, 1947, and April 9, 1948. In the verdict, all twenty-four defendants were found guilty on one or more charges. Fourteen of them were sentenced to death, but only four commanders were actually executed while ten had their sentences reduced. The Nuremberg judges made clear that their victims were only a fraction of the 2 million victims annihilated by the Einsatzgruppen as a whole:

> The International Military Tribunal in its decision of October 1, 1946 declared that the Einsatzgruppen and the Security Police, to which the defendants belonged, were responsible for the murder of two million defenseless human beings, and the evidence presented in this case has in no way shaken this finding. No human mind can grasp the enormity of two million deaths because life, the supreme essence of consciousness and being, does not lend itself to material or even spiritual appraisement . . . The number of deaths resulting from the activities with which these defendants have been connected and which the Prosecution has set at one million, is but an abstract number. [67]

Michael Phayer has pointed out that Pius XII intervened in favor of some Einsatzgruppen and death camp commanders as stated in the private diaries of his personal representative in occupied Germany, Bishop Aloysius Muench (1889-1962. He sought pardons for such major Einsatzgruppen mass murderers as Otto Ohlendorf and Franz Six[68] Rauff, the producer and manager of the gas vans, was helped after the war by the Vatican ratline to flee from Europe and settle in Chile where he was located by Simon Wiesenthal. Taking cover in court decisions, Presidents Frei, Allende, and Pinochet protected Rauff and declined to extradite this major perpetrator to West Germany to stand trial. He died in Santiago de Chile in May 1984.

## The Romanian Genocide in Transnistria

The Romanian army joined the German eleventh army in the attack against the Soviet Union in June 23, 1941. The two armies crossed the Prut River and recaptured the provinces of Bessarabia, Bukovina, and Northern Moldavia that Romania had lost to the Soviets in 1940 and rapidly reached the Dniester, the border with the Ukraine, on July 10, 1941. They crossed the river and moved forward into Southwestern Ukraine (renamed Transnistria by the Romanians), on their way to Oddesa, Crimea, and the Caucasus.

While Ohlendorf and his Einsatzgruppen were murdering in the Ukraine, the Romanians took the lead in the annihilation of the Jews in Southwestern Ukraine and spared the Einsatzgruppen much of the work. The brutality and greed displayed by the Romanian gendarmes and military was in no way inferior to those of their German counterparts, although they lacked their planning and coordination skills. They carried out killings leaving unburied bodies everywhere. While the German military praised their killing, they were critical of the lack of organization, as attested in military correspondence.

As soon as Bukovina and Bessarabia came under Romanian control, the Romanians readied themselves to eliminate Jews from the recovered provinces. Based on his meeting with Hitler on June 12, 1941, Antonescu brought up at the cabinet meeting of July 8, 1941 his immediate plans of clearing Bukovina and Bessarabia from its approximately 180,000 Jews by deporting them to the Ukraine, followed later by the deportation of all the Jews from Old Romania (the Regat). In his plan Jews were to be deprived of their property and livelihood, in preparation of their deportation and murder. [69]

Major pogroms followed immediately after the invasion in the recovered provinces of Bessarabia and Bukovina in such places such as Chernovitz (July 5-6, 1941), Edinets (July 6, 1941), Beltz (July 11, 1941), Kishinev (August 1, 1941), and many others. The pogrom in Iaşi organized by the Romanian Secret Service and the German Foreign Affairs Office of Counter-Intelligence during June 27-30, 1941 in Old Romania, stands out with its unspeakable brutality. The official toll given by the Romanian government indicates a total of 13,266 dead, but according to the Jewish community of Iaşi the figure surpassed 15,000. Around 6,000 Jews were rounded up and brought to the police headquarters courtyard in Iaşi on Saturday June 28, 1941, while others were forced to dig large ditches in the Jewish cemetery. More than 8,000 Jews were executed next day in cold blood by the Romanian police while another 5,000 Jews were rounded up for deportation. Robbed and beaten with rifle butts they were herded into closed freight cars and sent off in the scorching sun of July without any water or food.

People died or went mad during the trip. A train with 2,500 people aboard arrived after traveling for seven days to Călăraşi with only 1,011 people alive; another train going to Podul Iloaiei with 1,900 people arrived with 700 people alive. The official police report of the trip to Podul Iloaiei expressed regret that 1,900 Jews boarded the train and "only 1,194 died." [70] Italian war correspondent Curzio Malaparte (1898-1957) refers in his famous wartime book *Kapputt* to the pogrom in Iaşi, which he personally witnessed:

> Squads of soldiers and policemen, groups of men and women, bands of gypsies with their hair in long ringlets were gaily and noisily chattering with one another, as they despoiled the corpses, lifting them, rolling them over, turning them on their sides to draw off their coats, their trousers and their underclothes; feet were rammed against dead bellies to help pull off the shoes; people came running to share in the loot; others made off with arms piled high with clothing. It was a gay bustle, a merry occasion, a feast and a marketplace all in one.
>
> I flew at a group of policemen busily stripping dead bodies and hurled myself screaming against them, "Dirty cowards," I shouted, "get away, you lousy bastards!" One of them looked at me in amazement, picked up some suits and two or three pairs of shoes from a pile of clothing on the ground and pushed them toward me saying, "Don't get angry, Domnule Capitan [Mister Captain] there's enough for everybody." [71]

Without consulting with the Wehrmacht, Antonescu attempted to deport the Jews of Bukovina, Bessarabia, and Dorohoi across the Dniester to the Ukraine. The Wehrmacht drove back 27,500 deportees and killed many of them. Some drowned in the river and others were shot by the Romanian gendarmerie while trying to reach back to the western bank. On their march back to the camps inside Bukovina and Bessarabia, Jews died in great numbers from weakness and starvation or were murdered by Romanian guards.

The suspension of deportation plans was only momentary. Antonescu ordered the concentration of all the Jews of Bukovina and Bessarabia in ghettos and camps in wait of their future deportation east. Jews who lived in the countryside and townlets were interned in concentration camps. By late August 1941 around 80,000 Jews already were concentrated in ghettoes in Bessarabia and enclosed in seven large concentration camps. German killing squads or Romanian gendarmes entered the ghettos and camps, removing Jews and murdering them. In that short period of two to three months before deportations formally began, at least 25,000 Jews died whether by killing or "natural" death in the recaptured provinces.

The Tighina Agreement of August 30, 1941, placed under Romanian rule the newly conquered area between the Dniester, the Bug, and the Black Sea in Southwestern Ukraine in reward for Romania's participation in the war and authorized the deportation of the Jews to Transnistria up to, but not beyond, the Bug River, until military operations would make it possible to drive them further east. The Tighina agreement made it possible for Antonescu to carry out his plans to expel the Jews of Bukovina, Bessarabia, and Dorohoi over the Dniester. Deportations began with the Jews in the Vertujeni camp on September 16, 1941.

Jews were deported without any legal formalities. All their personal documents of identification were systematically destroyed at the crossing of the Dniester to erase their identity. An order was given to prepare graves along deportation routes every 6 miles for one hundred people, for those unable to keep pace. Antonescu also deported Jews from the Dorohoi district, which was part of the Regat, violating his promise to spare the Jews from Old Romania. The Jews of Bukovina were packed in cattle trains without food, water, and sanitary facilities. Many went insane or died aboard.

Even worse was the fate of the Bessarabian Jews who were forced to walk on foot to Transnistria, guarded by the Romanian gendarmes and their helpers. The cruelty and greediness of the Romanian guards knew no bounds. Peasants would approach the gendarmes in the escort, single out a Jew wearing good clothing or footwear, and offer a price, usually between 1,000 and 2,000 lei. After briefly bargaining, the gendarme would shoot the victim, and the peasant would pay the agreed price and strip the body. In the march to the camps, great numbers of deportees died of exhaustion, cold, hunger, and illnesses. Bodies were abandoned on the roadsides by the Romanian guards. In two months of deportations from Besarabia, 22,000 Jews died underway, mostly murdered by the gendarmes that accompanied them on their journey.

By December 1941 a total of 157,000 Jews had been deported to Transnistria: 91,845 from Bukovina, 55,867 from Bessarabia, and 9,367 from Dorohoi. Transnistria became a vast concentration and death camp, a "Romanian Auschwitz." About 200 different labor and concentration camps throughout the 118 counties of Transnistria were set up by the Romanians for Jews. Most of the Jews from Bessarabia and Bukovina were herded into ghettos and camps in northern and central Transnistria. They died from hard labor, disease, starvation, cold, and executions. Antonescu authorized the National Bank of Romania to expropriate the money and jewelry of deported Jews. Their money and valuables were looted by representatives of the Romanian national bank. On October 6, 1941, Ion Antonescu addressed the cabinet on the deportations, explaining that these were only the first step to future "deportation over the Ural mountain."

After the invasion, the Germans and Romanians immediately victimized the local Jewish population in every town and village in Transnistria. On August 4, 1941, the Romanian army ordered the immediate registration and enclosure of all local Ukrainian Jews into ghettos and used them for forced labor. Of the 331,000 Jews in the region limited by the Dniester, the Bug, and the Black Sea counted by the Soviet census of 1939, there were still around 200,000 Jews living in 120 localities when the Germans and Romanian armies arrived, including 90,000 Jews in Odessa, the major Jewish center in the region.

The German ambassador to Romania, Manfred von Killinger informed Berlin on September 1, 1941, that Antonescu was ready to deport 60,000 Jews from Old Romania (the Regat) for forced labor in the areas just occupied.[72] Concerned that deportations from Old Romania might have a negative impact on the fulfillment of the Romanian commitment to provide food, the plan was postponed by German instructions. The delay proved to be the salvation for the majority of the Jews of Old Romania when the military-political situation in Romania underwent changes after the Stalingrad debacle.

The German and Romanian armies reached Odessa, the important port city on the shore of the Black Sea, on August 5, 1941. The city held against a siege of seventy-three days and was taken on October 16, 1941, after the Soviets evacuated their troops by sea. Although men of military age had been called up to the Red Army and many other residents fled during the two months' siege of the city, many Jews from Bukovina, Bessarabia, and western Ukraine had sought refuge in Odessa while it was still in Soviet hands. In addition, the Romanians forced all Jews out from the surrounding villages to Odessa. There were between 90,000 and 120,000 Jews in the city when the German and Romanian armies arrived.

Six days after the occupation of Odessa, a powerful delayed-action landmine prepared by the Soviet military exploded at 5:35 p.m. in the NKVD building on October 22, 1941, in Romanian headquarters killing General Glogojeau, head of the Romanian Occupation Command, along with many officers and soldiers. As could be expected, the Romanians chose the defenseless Jews to retaliate. Order no. 302.826 demanded "immediate retaliatory action, including the liquidation of 18,000 Jews in the ghettos and the hanging in the town-squares of at least one hundread Jews for every regimental sector." Antonescu ordered from Bucharest by telephone that 300 Jews should be executed for every officer killed, and 100 for every soldier. One hostage was to be taken from every Jewish family. By noon of next day, 5,000 innocent people, most of them Jews, were hanged at crossings and public squares of Odessa. The horror that followed is described by historian Sir Martin Gilbert:

> That same morning, October 23, 19,000 Jews were assembled into a square near the port, which was surrounded by a wooden fence; they were sprayed with gasoline and burned alive. In the afternoon, the Gendarmerie and the Police rounded up over 20,000 persons in the streets—most of them Jews—and squeezed them into the municipal gaol [jail]. The next day, October 24, they removed 16,000 Jews from the gaol and led them out of the city in long convoys. They were marched in the direction of Dalnik, a nearby village.
>
> When the first Jews reached Dalnik, they were bound to one another's arms in groups of between forty and fifty, thrown into an anti-tank ditch and shot dead. When this method proved too slow, they were pressed into four large warehouses, which had holes in the walls. Machine gun nozzles were pushed into the holes, and in this manner, mass murder was committed in one warehouse after the other . . . The fourth warehouse, which was filled with men, was shelled in the afternoon of October 25, at 5:35, exactly three days after the bombing of command headquarters.[73]

Two memorials were built after the war near the port to mark the site where more than 25,000 people, 19,000 of them Jews, were burned alive. In 1996 the Jewish community in Odessa was involved in a struggle to stop construction on Lyusdorfskaya Street at the site were the massacre occurred.

Around 48,000 Jews who survived the initial Odessa massacres were deported from Odessa to the concentration camps along the banks of the Bug in the Golta district such as Bogdanovka, Domanovka, and Acmechetca.[74] Their possessions were looted by the local Odessa inhabitants and occupying forces. Odessa was declared Judenfrei on February 23, 1942, when the last deportation convoy left the city. Very few, if any, Jews survived in Odessa and lived to see the liberation of Odessa by General Malinovsky on April 10, 1944. A report of the SKR to the RSHA in Berlin on deportations from Odessa to German settlements states: [75]

> As of early May, the 28,000 Jews (of Odessa) transported to German villages in Transnistria have been exterminated. Not one Jew in the German settlement area survived.[76]

Besides the Jews deported from Oddesa, many tens of thousands of Jews from Southern Bessarabia and Southern Transnistria were brought by the Romanians to these camps. Weakened by hunger, cold, brutal exploitation, lack of sanitation, and medical assistance, lice infestation set in and a deadly typhus epidemic followed during the winter of 1941 in the Golta camps. At least 50,000 deportees died from typhus during the winter of 1941-1942, the harshest winter on record in the twentieth century. When Ion Antonescu learned about the raging typhus epidemic, which threatened German and Romanian troops and the Volksdeutsche in the area, he gave the order to kill more than 70,000 Jews at Bogdanovka and Domanovka on December 16, 1941, to stem the spread of the epidemic: "Let them die," he said.[77]

According to some historians, the massacre at Bogdanovca surpassed even the savagery of Babi Yar. Col. Modest Isopesco, the governor (prefect) of the Golta district, began mass executions in Bogdanovka on December 21, 1941. Some 5,000 sick and disabled prisoners were enclosed in two cowsheds that were set on fire. Other Jews were arranged in rows of 300 to 400, led to a ravine near the camp, and shot in the neck. Grenades were tossed into the ravine. Jews waiting for their turn in bitter cold dug pits with their bare hands and packed them with frozen corpses. The killing was interrupted during the evening hours of December 24, 1941, so the murderers could celebrate Christmas.

Prefect Isopescu, accompanied by invited friends and relatives from Bucharest, went on an inspection ride in sleighs to the killing sites on Christmas Eve. The Aktion was resumed on December 28 to be interrupted on December 31, for the New Year's celebrations and again resumed on January 3, 1942, to be finished on January 8. The slave workers who helped cover the bodies with earth were shot after they did their job. The burning of the bodies extended well into the spring, producing an acrid smell in the region. A total of 48,000 Jews of all ages and conditions were executed in Bogdanovka.

After the liquidation of the camp at Bogdanovca, the same team liquidated the camp at Domanovka. At Acmechetca the camp was fenced off with barbed wire, and the Jewish prisoners were left to die of hunger. Prefect Isopescu would be visiting every few days to check the "progress" and to take photographs of the dying Jews. By May 1942, two-thirds of all the Jews in Transnistria had been liquidated.[78] The following figures of the number of Jews killed according to the reports speak for themselves:

> In Bogdanovka, 48,000; in Domanovka, 18,000; in Acmechetka, 5,000; in Vertujeni-23,000; Thousands more were shot along the River Bug. [79]

Romania is directly responsible for the murder of a total of 280,000-380,000 Jews in Bessarabia, Bukovina, and Transnistria. Between 45,000 and 60,000 Jews were murdered locally in Bessarabia, Bukovina, and Dorohoi during the early months of the war and 105,000-120,000 were murdered in Transnistria, after the deportations. The count does not include the 115,000-180,000 local Ukrainian Jews killed. There were no more than 485 Ukrainian Jews alive by March 1943 in all of southern Transnistria!

The Germans had still important unfinished business to take care of—the Jews of Old Romania. Eichmann conducted negotiations through his representative in Bucharest, Gustav Richter, with Romanian Vice Premier Mihai Antonescu, to deport them to the Belzec death camp. They reached an agreement on July 22, 1942, to begin in September the deportation to Belzec of the entire Jewish population of the Regat, a total of 292,149 Jews. German embassy journal *Bukarester Tageblatt* announced the deportation of the Jews from Old Romania as part of "an overall European solution to the Jewish problem." A time table of the deportations was presented in August 1942 to Antonescu.

Miraculously, more than 290,000 Jews of Old Romania avoided the tragic fate of the Jews of Bessarabia, Bukovina, and Transnistria.[80] On October 13, 1942, Michai Antonescu announced in Bucharest that deportation transports over the Dniester were being discontinued. The deportation of the Jews from Old Romania to Belzec was put on hold. Antonescu was able to navigate the new course since Hitler was seeking the mobilization of additional divisions of the Romanian army to the Soviet front. On August 23, 1944, King Mihai, with the support from opposition politicians and the army, deposed the government of Ion and Mihai Antonescu and switched to the Allied side.[81]

After sixty-five long years of official denial and distortion of the Romanian Holocaust following World War II, the president of Romania, Ion Ilescu finally agreed in the summer of 2003 to convene an International Commission on the Holocaust in Romania, to examine the country's record. Chaired by Elie Wiesel, the commission was formed with the most recognized experts on the subject from Romania and the outside world. It released its report on November 11, 2004, and for the first time the world heard clearly that the Romanian state was indeed the main perpetrator of the Holocaust in Romania and Transnistria. The report states:

> Of all the allies of Nazi Germany, Romania bears responsibility for the deaths of more Jews than any country other than Germany itself. The murders committed in Iasi, Odessa, Bogdanovka, Domanovka, and Peciora, for example,

were among the most hideous murders committed against Jews anywhere during the Holocaust. Romania committed genocide against the Jews. The survival of Jews in some parts of the country does not alter this reality.[82]

## Erasing the Traces of the Einsatzgruppen Mass Graves

As long as the German armies were victorious on the eastern front and it looked as the totality of Europe would be dominated by them, the Germans worried little about the possibility that the mass graves left behind by the Einsatzgruppen could be used against them as proof of their crimes. However, when the expectations of a rapid victory on the Soviet front did not materialize, they began to worry that the mass graves would someday be used against them. On April 30, 1942, Himmler issued a secret order that all the mass graves should be identified and obliterated.

On Himmler's orders *Sonderaktion 1005* (Special Commando 1005), under the command of Paul Blobel, was formed in June 1942 to eliminate one by one the mass graves left by the Eisatzgruppen. Blobel was instructed to abstain from any written correspondence on the subject. The district commissars in occupied territories received instructions to immediately submit the information concerning the location of mass graves in their jurisdictions to the RSHA in Berlin.

To determine the most efficient clearing method, Blobel carried out experiments at the site of the Chelmno mass graves in the Rzuchow Forest. The graves measuring 286 x 30 x 20 feet, held the decaying bodies that the Chelmno gas vans brought there daily from the main Schlosslager. Blobel experimented initially with explosives and incendiary bombs to clear the mass graves, but failed, starting fires in the forest. He then began to experiment with open pyres to incinerate the bodies, trying different mixtures of fuel. At the conclusion of these experiments in late 1942, open-air burning of the corpses was adopted by Sonderaktion 100 as the standard method of body disposal and grave clearing. Although Blobel and his Einsatzkommando 1005 did not have any jurisdiction in the death camps, his methods were also adopted and used by them to eliminate their mass graves. Höss, the commander of Auschwitz, made personally a special journey to Rzuchow in September 1942 to observe directly Blobel's open-air cremation technique.

A special school to train German camp personnel to clear mass graves was set up in the Janowska Labor camp near Lvov. Twelve officers from each area of occupation where mass graves were located attended the course during a period of five months. Ten different groups went through the course at Janowska in these five months. The participants were taught how to exhume and burn the corpses, grind the bones, dispose of the ashes, and landscape the sites with trees and shrubbery.[83]

Hundreds of mass graves in Eastern Europe left behind by the Einsatzgruppen were opened and the bodies exhumed and burned in pyres. The ashes were scattered, thrown into rivers, or reburied. Jewish camp inmates were forced into *Verbrennungskommandos* (burning commandos), to exhume the bodies and burn them on pyres in shallow ditches. After a Verbrennungskommando finished its harrowing assignment, all its members would be killed. As witnesses of the gruesome operation they were to disappear with the evidence. Nevertheless, here and there, a few individuals miraculously survived to tell their tragic story to the world.

Retracing his steps in occupied territories, Paul Blobel returned to Kiev in July 1943 to clear Babi Yar. On August 18, he began opening the mass graves in Babi Yar with bulldozers. Under the command of eight to ten SD men and thirty German policemen, 327 inmates, 100 of them Jews from the nearby concentration camp Syretsk, dragged the bodies to cremation pyres. The cremation went on for six weeks ending on September 19. The ashes were sifted to retrieve any gold or silver while the unburned bones were crushed on tombstones from the Jewish cemetery. No traces were left behind. The prisoners were forced to carry out the gruesome task with bolted chains on their feet. Those who fell ill or lagged behind were shot on the spot. Only fourteen prisoners survived of the original team after an attempted escape.[84]

In Maly Trostinec clearance operations began on October 27, 1943. One hundred Jewish camp inmates who refused to carry out the grisly task were immediately killed in gas vans. In their place, a group of Jews from the Minsk prison was brought in and promised freedom on completion of the clearance. Thirty-four mass graves were opened in Blagovshchina Forest. Some graves, 164 feet long, contained as many as 5,000 corpses each. After the cremation of around 100,000 corpses, a team of Soviet POWs were made to sift the ashes in search of gold. The ashes were used as fertilizer for the camp fields. When the team finished the clearance they were all gassed using the gas vans. A cremation facility, still visible in 1960, was also built in Shaskowa Forest (1640 feet away from the camp) in the autumn of 1943. The thirty workers who built the cremation facility were shot and burned in the pit.[85]

In Kovno and Bialystok teams of around eighty people were left alive for a while as Verbrennungskommandos. At Ponary, near Vilna, detachments of Jewish slave laborers opened the mass graves in September 1943, and burned the corpses. They were all put to death when they finished their gruesome task. Mr. Jenton, one of very few survivors from the Bialystok ghetto who was part of a Verbrennungskommando at Petrasze Forest and other sites in the Bialystok region, told his tragic story in Mexico City years later.

Despite Blobel's effort to obliterate the traces of all mass graves, the Soviet advance took them by surprise in some places. Soviet investigation committees began finding and exhuming mass graves as the war was still raging. Blobel made the following sworn statement in Nuremberg on June 18, 1947:

> According to the order, my duties were to have covered the entire territory of the Einsatzgruppen; however, because of the retreat from Russia, I could not carry out my orders completely.[86]

# Notes

1. Yad Vashem Archives: Eichmann Trial: Transcript. Interrogation notes by Captain Avner Less (Israeli Police), 30 May 1960, tape No. 5, 172.

2. Rudolf Höss, *Commandant of Auschwitz: The Autobiography of Rudolf Hoess* (New York: Phoenix Press, 2000), 286.

3. Yitzhak Arad. *Belzec, Sobibor, Treblinka: The Operation Reinhard Camps*, (Bloomington, In: Indiana University Press, 1987). Raul Hilberg, *Sonderzüge nach Auschwitz: The Role of the German Railroads in the Destruction of the Jews* (Germany, 1981). Gitta Sereny, *Into that Darkness* (New York: McGraw Hill Book Co., 1974). Alexander Donat, ed., *Willenberg: Surviving The Death Camp Treblinka*. (New York: Holocaust Library, 1979).

4. Christopher R. Browning, *The Origins of the Final Solution. The Evolution of Nazi Jewish Policy, September 1939-March 1942* (Nebraska: University of Nebraska Press, 2007). 404.

5. Louis Lochner, Ed. *The Goebbels Diaries* (New York: Doubleday & Company, 1948).

6. Browning. *The Origins of the Final Solution,* 409.

7. Richard Rhodes, *Masters of Death* (New York: Alfred Knopf, 2002).

8. Nuremberg Trial Proceedings, Volume 4. Thursday 3 January 1946. Harris, 241. TMWC IV 258–9.

9. Ruta Puisyte, *Holocaust in Jurbarkas (Yurburg)* (University of Vilna).

10. *"The Avalon Project"* at Yale Law School: Nuremberg Trial Proceedings, Volume 4, 26th day, Thursday January 3, 1946.

11. *"The Avalon Project."*

12. Trials of War Criminals Before the Nuremberg Military Tribunals Under Control Council Law No. 10, Volume IV, Washington, D.C.: U.S. Government Printing Office. 38-42. (*2992-PS, Pros. Ex. 33*).

13. *"The Avalon Project."*

14. Yitzhak Arad, *Plunder of Jewish Property in the Nazi-Occupied Areas of the Soviet Union* (Jerursalem: Yad Vashem).

15. Rhodes, *Masters of Death,* 122.

16. *"The Avalon Project."*

17. Robert J. Hanyok, *Eavesdropping on Hell* (July, 2005).

18. There are copies at Yad Vashem and at the Holocaust Museum in Washington.

19. E. Klee, W. Dressen, V. Riess, Report to the Commander of the security police in Kaunas during the period July to November 1941, 46-58.

20. Trials of War Criminals Before the Nuremberg Military Tribunals Under Control Council Law No. 10, Volume IV, Washington, D.C.: U.S. Government Printing Office. 23-29.

21. Jan T. Gross. *Neighbors: The Destruction of the Jewish Community in Jedwabne, Poland.* (Princeton, NJ: Princeton University Press, 2001).

22. Tomasz Szarota interviewed by Jacek Żakowski. *The Devil is in the Details.* Gazeta Wyborcza, November 18-19, 2000

23. *New York Times,* April 19, 2001.

24. E. Klee, W. Dressen, V. Riess, and Trevor-Roper. The Free Press, NY, 1988. Dos Naje Lebn Nr. 9, Sz. Kaczerginski: "Ponary," Archives of the Central Jewish Historical Committee.

25. Sources: Bialystoker Memorial Book. Empire Press. Brooklyn, NY. Dr. Szymon Datner, (Nov-Dec 1946 issue of the Bialystoker Stimme). Oral eyewitness account by the late Bialystock survivor Mr. Jenton in Mexico City at Bialystock commemoration gathering.

26. Carol Rittner, Stephen D. Smith, and Irena Steinfeldt, *The Holocaust and the Christian World - Reflections on the Past Challenges for the Future*, (London: Kuperard Publication, 2000). Arad, *Plunder of Jewish Property*, 108-111.

27. Rabbi Ephraim Oshry, *Annihilation of Lithuanian Jewry* (New York: Judaica Press, 1995).

28. Oshry, *Annihilation of Lithuanian Jewry*, 38-42.

29. Operational Situation Report USSR No. 54. 1941. Einsatzgruppe A. Location: Riga.

30. Arad, *Plunder of Jewish Property*, 108-111. Rabbi Samuel Snieg survived and published in the DP camps in Germany the first full edition of the Talmud in Europe after the Holocaust.

31. Operational Situation Report USSR No. 54. 1941. Einsatzgruppe A. Location: Riga.

32. Andrew Ezergailis, *The Holocaust in Latvia, 1941-1944* (Riga and Washington: The Historical Institute of Latvia, in association with the United States Holocaust Memorial Museum, 1996).

33. ARC Group (Aktion Reinhard Camps): Peter Laponder, Michael Peters, and Chris Webb. Hilberg, Raul, *The Destruction of the European Jews* (New Haven, CT: Yale University Press, 2003). Gilbert, Martin, *The Holocaust* (London, UK: Collins, 1986). Israel Gutman, ed. *Encyclopedia of the Holocaust* (New York: Macmillan Publishing Company, 1990). Frank Buscher, *Investigating Nazi Crimes in Byelorussia*.

34. Van Pelt Report.

35. Deposition by Karl Wolff, StA Muenchen, Az.10a Js 39/60, Anklageschrift [bill of indictment] [ZSL, Az.Sammelakte 137, Bl.140ff]. Deposition by Back-Zelewski in: Aufbau (New York), 23.8.46, p.2. Willi Frischauer, *Himmler: Evil Genius of the Third Reich* (London, 1953), 148. Rhodes, *Masters of Death*, 151-154.

36. Richard Breitman, *Official Secrets: What the Nazis Planned, What the British and Americans Knew* (New York: Hill and Wang, 1998), 61.

37. Browning. *The Origins of the Final Solution*, 355.

38. Yitzhak Arad, *Belzec, Sobibor, Treblinka-The Operation Reinhard Death Camps*. (Indiana University Press, 1987), 10-11.

39. In a criminal procedure against SS officer Bruno Streckenbach.

40. The later-day Holocaust denier D. Irving discovered in 1977 the document.

41. Nürnberg Document 501-PS, Becker to Rauff, 16.5.42, printed in: IMT, vol. 26, 103-105.

42. Gerald Reitlinger, *The Final Solution* (London: Vallentine Mitchell, 1953).

43. Sir Martin Gilbert, *The Holocaust* (New York: Henry Holt and Company, 1987).

44. Sir Martin Gilbert, *The Holocaust*. Hilberg, *The Destruction of the European Jews*.

45. DEJ, 298, 373. Rhodes, *Masters of Death*, 141-146.

46. Trials of War Criminals Before the Nurenberg Military Tribunals Under Control Council Law No. 10, Volume IV, Washington, D.C.: U.S. Gov. P.O. pp. 23–29. The Einsatzgruppen Case: Military Tribunal II. Case No.9. William L. Shirer, *The Rise and Fall of the Third Reich A History of Nazi German* ( New York: Simon and Schuster. 1960), 962.

47. Rhodes. *Masters of Death,* 116.

48. Carol Rittner, Stephen D. Smith, and Irena Steinfeldt, *The Holocaust and the Christian World* (New York: Continuum Press, 2000), 108-111.

49. Zvi Gittelman, *Bitter Legacy: Confronting the Holocaust in the USSR* (Bloomington, In: Indiana University Press. 1997) 278-280

50. ADDS. Vol. 3.2, No. 406, 625-629. Hilberg, *Perpetrators Victims Bystanders*, 267. Szeptyckyj was praying for a German victory until his death in 1944.

51. Reitlinger, *Final Solution,* 223-225. Rhodes, *Masters of Death,* 177.

52. Operational Situation Report USSR No. 126, October 27, 1941.

53. Lucy S. Dawidowicz, *What is the Use of Jewish History?* (New York: Random House, 1994). 73, 103-107.

54. Rhodes, *Masters of Death,* 177.

55. Rhodes, *Masters of Death,* 177.

56. Holocaust Museum. Benjamin Ferencz in Conversation with Joan Ringelheim. Thursday, October 5, 2000.

57. Rhodes, *Masters of Death*, 163, 258, 276.

58. Sereny, *Into That Darkness,* 97-98. Rhodes, *Masters of Death*, 258.

59. Vera Mironovna Pronicheva, one of the very few survivors testified in April 1968 as a witness at the Darmstadt trial (October 1967-November 1968). She had described the massacre to the Soviet author Anatoli Kuznetsov after her miraculous survival.

60. Yevgeny Yevtushenko, *The Collected Poems 1952-1990* (New York: Henry Holt and Company, 1991), 102-104.

61. William Perl, *The Holocaust Conspiracy* (New York: Shapolsky Publishers, 1989).

62. Bishop Ernst Tewes (1908-1998), C.O. Titular Bishop of Villamagna in Proconsulari, Auxiliary Bishop Emeritus of München und Freising {Munich}, Principal Co-Consecrator of Pope Joseph Ratzinger as Deacon and Archbishop.

63. Ernst Klee, Willi Dressen and Volker Riess, Ed., *The Good Old Days: The Holocaust as seen by its perpetrators and bystanders* (New York: The Free Press, 1988).

64. Klee, *The Good Old Days.*

65. Klee, *The Good Old Days.*

66. Klee, *The Good Old Days.*

67. Gilbert, *The Holocaust.* Raul Hilberg, *Perpetrators Victims Bystanders: Jewish Catastrophe 1933-1945* (New York: Harper Collins, 1993). Gerald Reitlinger, *The SS: Alibi of a Nation* (New York: Viking Press, 1957).

68. The diaries that are kept at the Catholic University of America became known through M. Phayer.

69. Dr. Jean Ancel, *Documents, vol. 6: no. 15*, 199-201.

70. Memorandum from the Iaşi Inspectorate of Gendarmes.

71. Curzio Malaparte, *Kaputt* (New York: E. P. Dutton and Company, 1946).

72. Ancel. Nuremberg Documents NG–3989, Sept. 1, 1941. Vol. 3, no. 51, 102.

73. Gilbert, *The Holocaust,* 218. See The Nizkor Project, 1991-2005: Transnistria The Giant Forgotten Cemetery.

74. Bogdanovka, Acmechetca, Domanovka, Berczovka, Vaselinovono, Peciora, Mostovoi, Slivina and Vapniarka.

75. The US Holocaust Museum estimates that "Romanian and German forces killed almost 100,000 Jews in Odessa during the occupation of the city."

76. Gilbert, *The Holocaust,* 218. See The Nizkor Project, 1991-2005: Transnistria The Giant Forgotten Cemetery.

77. Final Report of the International Commission on the Holocaust in Romania. . Includes a related October 12, 2004 speech by Ion Iliescu and a message from Elie Wiesel. 55.

78. Dr. Jean Ancel, *"Antonescu and the Jews,"* Yad Vashem Studies, Vol. XXIII, 255-260.

79. Ancel, *"Antonescu and the Jews,"* 255-260.

80. The Jews of Northern Transylvania are not included in the count.

81. Antonescu was tried and shot on June 1, 1946.

82. Final Report of the Commission on the Holocaust in Romania, presented to President Ion Iliescu, Bucharest, November 11, 2004. Yad Vashem.

83. Leon W. Wells, *The Death Brigade: The Janowska Road* (New York: Macmillan Publishing Company, 1963).

84. Gilbert, *The Holocaust,* 202-205, 612-613, 742, 820-821. Shmuel Spector, *Encyclopedia of the Holocaust*, (New York: Macmillan Publishing Company, 1990).

85. ARC. Maly Trostinec.

86. Blobel was condemned to death in 1948 and executed in Landsberg in 1951.

## Chapter 9
## The Death Camps

### The Establishment of the of the Death Camps

Shortly after the invasion of the Soviet territories, Himmler and his henchmen reached the conclusion that the mobile Einsatzgruppen killing system was not well suited for the rest of Europe. It lacked secrecy, did not allow for easy removal of hidden valuables, body disposal was difficult and left behind incriminating traces, and as already mentioned, was too stressful for the delicate SS mass executioners. Instead of going after the victims from town to town, they decided to bring them together in mass extermination centers, *Vernichtungslagern*, in a few strategically located sites well hidden from the prying eyes of outsiders, where the victims could be brought from all over Europe to be killed.

The Vernichtungslager was conceived as an industrial plant run under principles of modern industrial organization capable of turning great numbers of live people into dead bodies in assembly-line fashion in a very short period after their arrival by train or truck. By reducing the waiting time between the arrival of the victims and their killing, the death camps, unlike the concentration and labor camps, would eliminate the need of feeding and housing the victims and would minimize personnel needed to run the camp. The only inmates kept alive for a time would be those disposing of the bodies of victims. With minimal housing needs these killing centers could be accomodated in reduced areas.

By means of the death camps, the Nazis intended to turn the Final Solution into a perfect crime with no incriminating evidence left behind. Confident that they could get away with murder and that no one would be around after the war to prove what happened to the Jews, they introduced a sanitized code language in their official communications and reports related to the Final Solution. They used such code words as resettlement, disinfections, special actions, and so forth in order not to leave behind a paper trail of the Final Solution.

# The Euthanasia Program—Training Ground
# Of the Final Solution

The euthanasia program in Germany and Austria that was undertaken to alleged-ly improve the Aryan race was the forerunner of the Final Solution. Death camps commanders that later carried out the Final Solution in Poland were orig-inally trained and prepared in that program. Long before he came to power, Hit-ler incorporated euthanasia, an idea that violated the most sacred moral and reli-gious principles, into Nazi ideology. In 1926 he stated in *Mein Kampf*: "The achievement of that task will one day appear as a deed greater than the most victorious wars of our present bourgeois era." The elimination of the mentally retarded and the physically disabled people was explained by Hitler as a way to improve the Aryan race but it was really meant to do away with the burden of maintaining medical institutions that diverted human and economic resources needed for rearmament and the German Lebensraum struggle.

Shortly after he came to power, Hitler approved in July 1933 the Law for the Prevention of Hereditarily Diseased Offspring, which mandated compulsory sterilization for people with a long list of hereditary illnesses, including various forms of social deviance such as alcoholism. It is estimated that 360,000 people were sterilized by the Reich Interior Ministry under this law by 1939. This was one of the earliest products of the Frankenstein that the Church in Germany helped to bring to power.

Hitler wished to go beyond sterilization and legalize the actual killing of newborns with mental retardation or physical deformities and the incurably ill. In 1933 he told Dr. Karl Brandt, his personal physician, and to Hans Lammers, the head of the Reich chancellery, that he was in favor of killing the incurably ill, but he realized that public opinion was not yet ready for it. In 1935, Hitler told Dr. Gerhard Wagner, the leader of the Reich doctors that the killing of adults with mental or physical disabilities would be difficult in peacetime but "could be more smoothly and easily carried out in war." He intended, in the event of war, "to radically solve the problem of the mental asylums."[1]

As he was preparing for war, Hitler also began to mature his murder plan against the mentally and physically disabled people. Bühler, the head of the Fuehrer's chancellery, commissioned Albert Hartl (1904-1982), a Catholic priest who headed the Church Information Service in Heydrich's *Reichssicherheit-shauptamt* (Reich Security Main Office), to look for support for euthanasia among Catholic theologians.[2] Dr Joseph Mayer (1886-1967), a professor of moral theology at the Catholic University of Paderborn, a longstanding defender within the Catholic Church of sterilization and abortion of the mentally ill, was consulted by Hartl in early 1939. After six months, Professor Mayer presented his conclusions to the chancellery. He suggested that in his opinion, the Church would not oppose such a program if it was seen to be in the national interest.

Beginning August 1939, midwives and doctors were required to report to the Reich Health Ministry any children up to age three that showed symptoms of mental retardation or physical deformity. Solely based on these paper reports, without requiring any additional medical examination, three medical experts were authorized to issue a death warrant. The child would be transferred to the Children's Specialty Department to be killed by lethal injection or gradual starvation. The program was soon expanded to include adults as well.

As soon as the war broke out, Hitler signed at the beginning of October 1939 a letter, which was backdated to September 1, authorizing officials of his chancellery to prepare plans for the killing of incurably ill adult mental patients. The plans to eliminate "life unworthy of life" were developed and administered from the Führer's chancellery at Tiergartenstrasse 4 under the code name Aktion T4 by the president of the German Red Cross and SS head surgeon Dr. Ernst Robert Grawitz, in cooperation with Hitler's chancellery chief Philipp Bühler, his deputy director Victor Brack, and Hitler's personal physician Dr. Karl Brandt.

The euthanasia program was first implemented in the Wartheland, the part of Poland annexed to the Reich, before it was applied in the old Reich. Initially, the victims were murdered by lethal injection, but that method was considered too slow and problematic. Then, experimental gassings were tested in the Brandenburg prison in a gas chamber prepared for that purpose by Dr. Albert Widmann, chief chemist of the the Kripo, the German criminal police. Pure carbon monoxide bottled in steel cylinders provided by the I.G. Farben factory in Ludwigshafen was used as the killing agent. Himmler personally came to witness one of these gassings in December 1939.[3]

Six euthanasia centers, with their gas chambers camouflaged as shower rooms, were established at Bernburg, Brandenburg, Grafeneck, Hadamar, Hartheim, and Sonnenstein. The Kriminaltechnisches Institut of the Reichssicherheitshauptamt (KTI, RSHA), under the supervision of Albert Widmann and Christian Wirth, began to murder defenseless patients in January 1940. From their hospitals and asylums, the patients were taken to transit institutions to cover the traces of their movements. They were then transported in buses to killing centers by teams of SS men wearing white robes to create the impression of medical legitimacy. Relatives would receive an urn with the ashes and a false certificate of natural death.

When Bishop Clemens August von Galen of Münster learned that a large group of so-called unproductive mental patients in his diocese were being transported from the Marienthal Provincial Asylum near Münster to the Eichberg asylum to be killed, he protested in his sermons on July 13 and August 3, 1941, in the cathedral of Münster.

> These unfortunate patients must die because, in the opinion of some department, on the testimony of some commission, they have become "worthless life" because according to this testimony they are "unproductive national comrades."
> The argument goes: they can no longer produce commodities, they are like an old machine that no longer works, they are like an old horse which has become incurably lame, they are like a cow which no longer gives milk.
> But have they for that reason forfeited the right to life? Have you, have I the right to live only so long as we are productive, so long as we are recognized

by others as productive? . . . Once admit the right to kill unproductive persons, then none of us can be sure of his life. A curse on men and on the German people if we break the holy commandment "Thou shalt not kill" . . . Woe to us German people if we not only license this heinous offence but allow it to be committed with impunity. [4]

Von Galen's sermon was pronounced at a time that the hospitals and asylums in Germany began to fill up with maimed and disabled German soldiers brought back from the Soviet front. Rumors began to spread among the German population that these soldiers too would be subject to euthanasia. Their relatives and friends had ears for von Galen's message and could not be ignored by the government. It is in this context that Hitler decided to allegedly interrupt for a while Aktion T4 inside Germany until after the war.

While von Galen's outspoken protest against the killing of helpless German mental patients was a courageous act, he stopped short when it came to condemn the mass murder of Jews in the East by the Einsatzgruppen or in the gas chambers at the hands of the same T4 executioners that introduced the euthanasia program. Never did he call the German Catholics to stand up to protect their Jewish neighbors who were being deported to their death. Fr. Ludwig Volk, a German Jesuit historian bemoans the fact in an article in the Catholic journal, *Stimmen der Zeit*:

> It was a genuine and deplorable difference that the Jews, unlike the racially unfit, mentally retarded, and handicapped, found no champion the likes of Bishop von Galen to attempt to stop their murder through a calculated appeal to the public.[5]

Like almost all of his colleagues in the German episcopate, Galen, a German Nationalist, supported the German war effort and preached against disobedience to the Nazi state and the Führer. Before and after the euthanasia episode, von Galens relationship with the Nazi state was one of conformity and accommodation. He was the first bishop to swear the oath of allegiance prescribed by the concordat on October 23, 1933. He never wavered in his loyalty to Hitler and the Nazi regime. Trying to exculpate the Führer of any responsibility or even knowledge of the crime, he laid the blame on "some department or commission." After asking rhetorically in his sermon, "Does the Führer know?" he responded, "Ich kann es kaum glaubem!" (I can hardly believe it!) :

> We Christians make no revolution. We will continue to do our duty in obedience to G-d, out of love of people and fatherland. Our soldiers will fight and die for Germany.[6]

After the war, Galen made a scathing attack on the Nuremberg Trials, claiming that their aim was to defame Germany, not to seek justice.

On August 24, 1941, two months after the invasion of the Soviet territories, the T4 euthanasia program was put on hold and postponed for after the war. According to most authorized historians, to speak of the "suspension" of the euthanasia program is misleading, it merely went underground. Actually, children continued to be murdered and euthanasia centers continued to be used to kill concentration camp inmates. Until August 24, 1941, when the program went underground, approximately 100,000 patients had already been murdered, 70,273 using pure bottled carbon monoxide and 20,000 by lethal injection. Chancellery deputy director Victor Brack testified in Nuremberg about the transfer of the T4 euthanasia personnel to Poland:

> In 1941, I received an oral order to discontinue the euthanasia program. I received this order either from Boühler or from Dr. (Karl) Brandt. In order to reserve the personnel relieved of these duties and to have the opportunity of starting a new euthanasia program after the war, at the beginning of September 1941, within two weeks of the termination of the T4 gassings requested, I think after a conference with Himmler, that I send these personnel to Lublin and put them at the disposal of SS BrigadeFührer Globocnik. I then had the impression that these people were to be used in the extensive Jewish labor camps run by Globocnik. Later, however, at the end of 1942 or the beginning of 1943, I found out that they were used to assist in the mass extermination of the Jews, which was then already common knowledge in the higher Party circles.[7]

The euthanasia program was the dress rehearsal of the Final Solution. The entire personnel, including its physicians, were ordered to relocate to the Generalgouvernement under the command of Odilo Globocnik to organize and run Operation Reinhard. Among the personnel transferred were Christian Wirth, Franz Stangl, Herbert Lange, Lorenz Hackenholt, Erich Bauer, Kurt Franz, Dr. Irmfried Eberl, Dr. Friedrich Mennecke, Gerhard Bohne, Dr. Helmuth Kallmeyer, and many other well-known perpetrators who became the murderers of millions of innocent people. They selected the sites for the Operation Reinhard death camps, managed the construction teams, provided ideas, trained personnel, and ran the mass murder operations.

Christian Wirth and Franz Stangl, who were in charge of the euthanasia center in Hartheim, became the commanders of Belzec, Sobibor, and Treblinka. Dr. Imfried Eberl, the superintendent of the Brandenburg Psychiatry Hospital became Treblinka's first commandant. They and their colleagues previously mentioned received their early basic training as professional mass murderers in the T4 euthanasia program. Expert chemist Albert Widman from the Criminal Technology Institute in Berlin was called in when needed. He helped Nebe in Minsk, Höss in Auschwitz, and all the other perpetrators who required his expertise to murder people more efficiently.

## Poland, the Site of the Final Solution

Holocaust historians have wondered why occupied Poland, rather than any other country in Europe, was chosen as the site of the death camps to carry out the Final Solution in Europe. The decision was not only made based on Poland's geographic position as the center of gravity of European Jewry, but also in consideration of the fierce eliminationist anti-Semitism that prevailed there. The decision was made on the well-founded assumption that the war of annihilation against the Jews would best be received in Poland and could serve to create a common bond with them. The enthusiastic promise given to Hitler by the Polish ambassador in Germany, Joszef Lipski, on September 20, 1938, to build him a "beautiful monument in Warsaw" if he carried out his plan of eliminating the Jews from Poland, was not forgotten by the Führer.[8] This was well understood by the courageous Polish courier Ian Karski (1914-2000), who wrote in a report from occupied Poland to France in 1940:[9]

> Nazi Jewish policy posed a grave danger to the Polish resistance because a large proportion of Polish society appreciated Nazi anti-Jewish policies and a narrow bridge was thus created between Germans and Poles.[10]

Darius Libionka, a Polish scholar at the Historical Institute in Warsaw, points out that none of the three councils held by the Polish bishops during the German occupation mentioned the mass murder of the Jews, much less expressed any protest about it. Even during the synod that took place on June 1, 1943, days after the bloody liquidation of the Warsaw ghetto, the bishops were silent. He comments on the fact that in their correspondence with Rome, the Polish bishops passed over in total silence the annihilation of the Jews to which they were first-hand witnesses.[11]

Six main death camps well linked to the railroad network of Europe were strategically placed in Poland to facilitate the transportation of the victims. Chelmno and Auschwitz were established in Western Poland while four, Belzec, Sobibor, Treblinka, and Majdanek were established in the *Generalgouvernement* under the umbrella of Operation Reinhard. The implementation of that decision began in late 1941, some months before the Wansee Conference, which was held in January 1942. Auschwitz-Birkenau and Majdanek were part of vast labor and concentration camp complexes while the four others were exclusively death camps.

Chelmno, in the vicinity of Lodz, was the first death camp to be put in operation on Polish territory on December 9, 1941, under the command of Herbert Lange, the perpetrator of the Konin quicklime experiment. A large part of the Jews of the Lodz ghetto and the surrounding region found their deaths in Chelmno. Lange had begun his killing career poisoning psychiatric patients in Pozen in the euthanasia program using gas vans. He also introduced in Chelmno gas vans provided from Berlin. With three converted gas trucks, a large one for 150 people and two smaller ones for between eighty and 100 each, he gassed as many as 340,000 victims there. Höss described Chelmno (renamed Kulmhof by the Germans), which he visited on September 16, 1942:

> During my visit to Kulmhof I also saw the extermination installation, with the lorry which had been set up for killing by means of motor exhaust fumes. The head of the Kommando told me that this method, however, was very unreliable, as the gas build-up was very irregular and was often insufficient for killing. [12]

Auschwitz (Oswiecim in Polish, Oshpitzin in Yiddish), situated in Eastern Upper Silesia, a region of Poland near the prewar German-Polish border, was originally established by Himmler as a camp for Polish political prisoners on April 27, 1940. Himmler visited Auschwitz for the first time on March 1, 1941, and ordered its commander Rudolf Höss (1900-1947) to build in nearby Birkenau, 1.8 miles from the original camp, a new camp that could hold 100,000 prisoners. As a result of Himmler's plan to recolonize Upper Silesia with pure Aryans, Auschwitz was eventually turned into a vast network of forty-five satellite slave labor camps that provided slave workers to the large German industrial concerns of I. G. Farben, Krupp, Siemens, and Bayer. SS General Karl Wulff accompanied Himmler in his visits to Auschwitz as the SS liaison man with I. G. Farben.

In the summer of 1941, Himmler informed Höss about the forthcoming role of Auschwitz-Birkenau as the main death camp for the Final Solution. On October 8, 1941, began the actual construction of the death camp of Birkenau (Brzezinka). Höss writes:

> In the summer of 1941, I cannot remember the exact date, I was suddenly summoned to the Reichsfuehrer SS, directly by his adjutant's office. Contrary to the usual custom, Himmler received me without his adjutant being present and said in effect: "The Führer has ordered that the Jewish question be solved once and for all and that we, the SS, are to implement this order. The existing extermination centers in the East [referring to the Einsatzgruppen] are not in a position to carry out the large actions which are anticipated. I have therefore earmarked Auschwitz. [13]

In February 1942 the greatest factory of death ever conceived began to operate in Auschwitz-Birkenau under Höss. Höss's pious Catholic parents had planned for him to become a Catholic priest and had often taken him in his youth to pilgrimages to Lourdes and Einsedeleln. He later expressed regret of not having fulfilled his father's vows at the birth of his sister to devote him to the priesthood. His role in Auschwitz as the greatest perpetrator of murder in human history, Höss interprets in his memoirs as an act of obedience to the highest authorities of the Reich personified by Hitler and Himmler. [14]

On October 13, 1941, Himmler met in Lublin Odilo Globocnik, the head of Operation Reinhard, and gave him the order to start building the first of the Operation Reinhard camps in Belzec. The first camp commander of Belzec, Christian Wirth (December 1941-August 1942), arrived from Berlin shortly before the end of 1941 with Dr. Helmuth Kallmayer, a chemist who worked for the T4 euthanasia program.[15] At the end of February 1942, Belzec was ready to operate with three wooden gas chambers. Wirth and Hackenroth tried out their effectiveness by gassing three transports of Jews. At the end of the test they also gassed the Jewish prisoners that built the gas chambers. On the morning of March 17, 1942, 1,400 Jews from the Lublin ghetto arrived to Belzec in nineteen wagons. They were immediately gassed. A complex of six concrete gas chambers was built sometime later in which more than 1,000 victims could be gassed at a time. The daily toll of victims was much higher as multiple gassings were carried out every day.[16]

Sobibor was put in operation on April 10, 1942, under the command of SS ObersturmFührer Franz Stangl, an Austrian who was part of the euthanasia personnel in Berlin. The death camp located near the Chelm-Wlodawa railway line began with three gas chambers, with a total killing capacity of 600 people per gassing. Around 250 Jews from the Krychow labor camp were brought in mid-April 1942 to test their efficiency. Once their efficiency was demonstrated, Sobibor began to operate in the first days of May 1942. Six new gas chambers were built in Sobibor during the summer of 1942, which allowed them to murder 1,300 people per gassing. In February 1943 Heinrich Himmler inspected Sobibor and was given a special demonstration in which several hundred Jewish girls from a nearby work camp were gassed. After his capture in Brazil, Franz Stangl was asked during his interrogation in West Germany on how many people were normally murdered in Sobibor daily. Stangl answered:[17]

> Regarding the question of what was the optimum amount of people gassed in one day, I can state: according to my estimation a transport of thirty freight cars with 3,000 people was liquidated in three hours. When the work lasted for about fourteen hours, 12,000 to 15,000 people were annihilated. There were many days that the work lasted from the early morning until the evening.[18]

On July 19, 1942, Himmler issued an order that the annihilation of all the Jews of the Generalgouvernement must be completed by the end of the year. Only a reduced number of Jews were to be kept alive to work in *Sammellager*, assembly camps. As a result of Himmler's orders, the commanders of the Reinhard death camps expanded their gassing facilities and increased their extermination capacity during the summer of 1942. On July 28, 1942, Himmler wrote to SS GruppenFührer Gottlob Berger, the chief of the SS main office:

> The occupied eastern territories are to become free of Jews. The carrying out of this very difficult order has been placed on my shoulders by the Führer. No one can take this responsibility from me.[19]

Treblinka began to operate on July 22, 1942 with three gas chambers disguised as shower rooms. The majority of the Jews of Warsaw, the greatest Jewish community in Europe, were gassed in Treblinka. Yankiel Wiernik, a Treblinka survivor who escaped during the uprising in 1943, testified in 1945 that between 10,000 and 12,000 Jews were killed daily in Treblinka:

> Between ten and twelve thousand people were gassed each day. We built a narrow-gauge track and drove the corpses to the ditches on the rolling platform.[20]

The Warsaw ghetto was practically emptied during ten weeks from July 22 to October 3, 1942. As many as 310,322 Jews of the nearly 450,000 living in the Warsaw ghetto were deported from Warsaw to Treblinka, according to the official report of SS BrigadenFührer Stroop. He was later responsible for the destruction of the ghetto during the ghetto revolt (April 19-May 16, 1943). SS General Karl Wulff, Himmler's liaison man to Hitler, was in charge of the requisition and schedule of the trains carrying Jews to their deaths in the camps. On July 22, 1942, the day the first transports arrived to Treblinka from the Umschlags Platz in Warsaw, Globocnik, the head of Operation Reinhard, wrote to Wulff:

> The ReichsFührer SS . . . has given us so much new work that with it now all our most secret wishes are to be fulfilled. I am so very thankful to him for this, and he can be sure of one thing, that these things he wishes will be fulfilled in the shortest time.[21]

On July 28, 1942, Dr. Theodor Ganzenmüller, Nazi minister of transport, sent to Wulff a report on the trains going to the death camps of Treblinka and Belzec:[22]

> Since 22 July a train carrying 5,000 Jews has been traveling daily from Warsaw to Treblinka via Malkinia. In addition there is a biweekly train carrying 5,000 Jews from Przemysl to Belzec.[23]

Karl Wulff responded with delight on August 13, 1942, exulting over the fact "that 5,000 members of the chosen people are traveling every day from Warsaw to Treblinka":

> I should like to thank you personally and on behalf of the ReichsFührer very much indeed for your memorandum of 28 July 1942. I was particularly gratified to learn from your communication that for the past two weeks a train containing 5,000 members of the chosen people is traveling to Treblinka every day and as a result we are thus now in the position to carry out this population transfer at an accelerated pace.[24]

Majdanek in the outskirts of Lublin was initially established on October 1941 as a prisoners of war camp and began to operate as a death camp in April 1942 with two stationary gas chambers. Soon another six gas chambers were added that increased the total killing capacity to around 2,000 victims per gassing. On February 16, 1943, Majdanek was expanded by the Waffen SS as a slave labor camp for SS armament industries such as Steyr-Daimler-Puch. Majdanek was the first of the death camps to be liberated and was active until the arrival of Soviet forces on July 24, 1944. When the Soviet army entered Majdanek they found many of the mass murder installations intact, including gassing chambers and crematoria that the Germans did not manage to destroy. The photographs traveled the world over, but practically nothing was done to save the remnant of European Jewry that was being murdered by the Germans.

Since the end of the war until today, research on the number of victims in the death camps has continued. In the Reinhard operation camps the number of victims adds up to a total of 1.75 million, 600,000 in Belzec, 250,000 in Sobibor and 900,000 in Treblinka.[25] For Auschwitz-Birkenau the estimates vary between 1.1 million and 1.5 million victims, although some historians have produced much higher figures. For Chelmno the estimates vary between 152,000 and 320,000. The conclusion that at least 3 million Jews were murdered in death camps is a conservative estimate. The colosal magnitude of the killing in death camps can be appreciated from an intercepted telegram sent by SS-SturmbannFührer Hermann Höfle on January 11, 1943 to Adolf Eichmann in Berlin that lists 1,274,166 Jews killed in the four camps of Aktion Reinhardt during 1942 alone.[26]

## Carbon Monoxide versus Zyklon B

As they decided to build death camps to carry out the Final Solution, the masterminds of the plan were looking for the most efficient mass-murder technique that could kill the greatest number of people in the shortest time at the lowest cost. Lacking any moral inhibitions, they were ready to test out and apply any promising killing method. Thus, a series of different murder techniques were tested in a very short period of time in the second half of 1941. Besides firearms the list includes poison injections, fire bombs, dynamite, quicklime pits, and gassing.

At the Nuremberg Trials the original proposal to use poison gas in death camps as the mass-murder agent was traced to the president of the German Red Cross and SS head surgeon, Dr. Ernst Robert Grawitz (1899-1945). When consulted by Himmler in the summer of 1941, he proposed poison gas. Not only was it possible to kill great numbers of people in one operation taking only a few minutes, it was also much more impersonal and indirect than shooting them face to face with firearms. Grawitz had earlier used poison gas in the T4 euthanasia program, according to the testimony in Nuremberg of SS Judge and legal investigator for the *Kriminal Polizei* in the Reich Dr. Konrad Morgan. Grawitz, however, stopped short of recommending a specific gassing agent:

> By the late summer of 1941, when possible solutions to the Jewish Question were emerging, the Reichsarzt-SS und Polizei [Reich Doctor for the SS and Police], SS-GruppenFührer Dr. Grawitz, advised the HHE/KdF that gassing was the most appropriate means for carrying out sonderbehandlung [special treatment] of large numbers of people. The means Dr Grawitz favored were static chambers supplemented by mobile chambers (gas vans), as [later] used at

Chelmno and the former collective farm at Maly Trostenets ([Minsk]. Only the "gassing agent" had to be determined. [27]

At the Eichmann trial in Jerusalem, Dr. Servatius, Eichmann's defense lawyer, confirmed the role of Dr. Grawitz:

> Rather the description given by SS Judge Morgen would seem to be correct. According to this description, the method of using gas for killing was introduced by Brack of the Fuehrer's Chancellery. This method is said to have been used already by Brack's unit in the killing of mentally deficient persons, and these killings by gas are said to have been developed by the Reich Physician, Dr. Grawitz. [28]

Adolf Eichmann met with Victor Brack in the summer of 1941 to discuss which particular poison gas would be best for the death camps.[29] Bottled pure carbon monoxide (CO), the poison gas used in the T4 euthanasia program, required transportation in gas cylinders, was difficult to obtain and relatively costly, and involved plumbing installations and pumps to conduct the gas to the gas chambers. Eichmann decided to look for a more cost-effective alternative and invited the SS commanders to look for alternatives to bottled pure carbon monoxide. Höss in Auschwitz, Wirth in Poland, Lange in Pozen, Nebe in Russia and Rauff in Berlin, to mention a few, were trying to outdo each other. Soon various gassing alternatives were available: 1) stationary gas chambers using carbon monoxide; 2) stationary gas chambers using Zyklon-B; 3) mobile gassing vans that reinjected their exhaust carbon monoxide to the interior.

Rudolf Höss began searching in Auschwitz very early on for a gas other than carbon monoxide that could be obtained easily and did not require special installations, as he stated in a written declaration in 1946:

> In Widmann's option, extermination in bathrooms with carbon monoxide required complex installations, taking into account the masses of people who were going to be asphyxiated; besides, to obtain that gas was quite difficult . . . Eichmann was concerned with finding a gas that could be obtained easily and did not require special equipment . . . We reckoned together that by using the proper gas in the room we had at our disposal, 800 people could be exterminated simultaneously.[30]

One of Höss's deputies, Karl Fritzsch, tried out Zyklon-B (hydrogen cyanide), an insecticide used until then for pest control and disinfection, as a killing agent on humans, on September 3, 1941. In his first trial Fritzsch introduced 600 Soviet POWs and 250 Polish prisoners in a closed room improvised as a gas chamber, killing them all. Unlike carbon monoxide which required gas-pipe installations and mechanical pumps, Zyklon-B crystals (commonly known as crystallized Prussic acid) could simply be thrown in manually to the chamber after removing the pellets from their containers. When the temperature in the room rose sufficiently, the Zyklon-B crystals reacted chemically with the oxygen in the air releasing the deadly gas. Höss, camp commandant, felt exceedingly proud of the innovation to use Zyklon-B to kill people. In his autobiography, written before his execution, he describes his first observation of a gassing operation with Zyklon-B:

> The gassing was carried out in the detention cells of Block 11. Protected by a gas mask, I watched the killing myself. In the crowded cells, death came instantaneously the moment the Zyklon B was thrown in. A short, almost smothered cry and it was all over . . . I must even admit that this gassing set my mind at rest, for the mass extermination of the Jews was to start soon, and at that time neither Eichmann nor I was certain as to how these mass killings were to be carried out. It would be by gas, but we did not know which gas and how it was to be used. Now we had the gas, and we had established a procedure. [31]

The German companies, Tesch/Stabenow and Degesh, supplied to Auschwitz the Zyklon B crystals on a patent from I. G. Farben. Tesch supplied two tons per month and Degesch three-quarters of a ton per month. No more than two operators were needed to extinguish the lives of the thousands trapped inside the gas chamber:

> While the Jews were driven into the underground room, a van marked with a Red Cross sign parked along its side, which projected 1.5 feet above ground. Two disinfecting operators climbed the basement, carrying sealed tins manufactured by the Degesch Company. They chatted leisurely, smoking a cigarette. Then, on signal, each of them walked to a one foot high concrete shaft, donned a gas mask, took off the lid, opened the tin, and poured the pea-sized contents into the shaft. They closed the lids, took off their masks, and drove off. [32]

Fillip Müller, of the very few Jewish prisoners working in the gas chambers who survived, provides a description of the gassing installations in an underground gas chamber built in Auschwitz-Birkenau:

> The Zyklon-B gas crystals were inserted through openings into hollow pillars made of sheet metal. They were perforated at regular intervals and inside them a spiral ran from top to bottom in order to ensure as even a distribution of the granular crystals as possible. After they were crammed in, the doors closed, and the lights were turned off. [33]

In an interview on Swedish television in 1981, Dr. Hans Munch, an SS physician at the Hygienic Institute at Auschwitz who witnessed the gassings, was asked by the anchorman if doctors were present at the gassings. His answer opens another vista to the darkest chambers of the German mentality:

> They had to be present. According to strict regulations they had to be present, as in civilized states at every normal individual execution for legal reasons. In the same way there was a military order that at least one doctor had to be present at exterminations by gas in Auschwitz, for two reasons. Firstly, the whole thing had to be under medical supervision. And the gas wasn't thrown in by the regular camp personnel but by the camp doctors' medical orderlies. [34]

When Munch revisited Auschwitz in 1995 along with Eva Kor (a survivor who, as a child, was a subject of Josef Mengele's medical experiments) he declared:

> I saw thousands of people gassed here at Auschwitz. Children, old people, the sick and those unable to work were sent to the gas chambers . . . I, a former SS physician, witnessed the dropping of Zyklon B into simulated exhaust vents from outside the gas chambers . . . After three to five minutes, death could be certified, and the doors were opened as a sign that the corpses were cleared to be burned. [35]

In a public appearance in 2006, Oskar Groening, a Nazi guard in Auschwitz, described a gassing operation that he witnessed in 1943 in which the Zyklon-B pellets were thrown in from a side vent into the chamber:

> On one night in January 1943 I saw for the first time how the Jews were actually gassed . . . There were more than one hundred prisoners . . . In that moment the cries of the people inside rose to a crescendo, a choir of madness. These cries I have ringing in my ears to this day. [36]

After an attempt was made to use Zyklon-B in Belzec failed because the primitive wooden buildings were not airtight enough, the commanders decided to use bottled carbon monoxide, the poison gas with which they were familiar from the euthanasia program in Germany. In order not to delay killing operations, they decided to import the gas in cylinders from Germany, until they could figure out a way of producing the gas locally.[37]

Wirth and Kallmayer were able to produce carbon monoxide in sittu in February 1942 using the exhaust fumes of stationary high-power tanks or locomotive motors. By controlling the revs per minute of the engines and restricting the air intake they were able to raise the concentration of CO in the exhaust fumes to the levels necessary to produce lethal poisoning. Water pipes that conducted the poisonous gas to the shower heads ran along the ceiling creating the illusion of a shower as in the simulated shower rooms. In Sobibor and Treblinka they applied the same system to produce carbon monoxide using heavy gasoline engines from tanks or locomotives captured from the Soviets. Wirth, accompanied by chemist Dr. Karl Blaurock, arrived at Sobibor to witness the first experimental gassings. Erich Fuchs, an officer who served in Belzec, described the preparations for the first experimental gassing in Sobibor:

> On Wirth's instructions I traveled by truck to Lvov and collected a gassing engine there, which I transported to Sobibor . . . It was a heavy Soviet gasoline engine (probably a tank or train engine) with at least 200 hp (V-engine 8 cylinders, water cooled) . . . The chemist, whom I already knew from Belzec, entered the gas chamber with a measuring instrument in order to test the gas concentration.[38]

The system used in Treblinka was similar. Yankiel Wiernik, a Treblinka survivor who escaped during the uprising in 1943, described the system in 1945:

> A motor taken from a dismantled Soviet tank stood in the power plant. This motor was used to pump the gas, which was let into the chambers by connecting the motor with the inflow pipes. The speed with which death overcame the helpless victims depended on the quantity of combustion gas admitted into the chamber at one time.[39]

All the different killing methods were used in Majdanek: stationary gas chambers, gas vans, and firearms. The Committee of Technical and Chemical Experts of Lublin found after the war that some of the Majdanek gas chambers operated with carbon monoxide while others used Zyklon-B. Rolf Günther, Eichmann's deputy, delivered regularly during various years to Lublin large orders of potassium ferro cyanide through Kurt Gerstein.[40] Two witnesses, Stetdiener and Atrokhov, gave a detailed description of the gas vans in which the Germans poisoned their victims with the aid of the exhaust fumes of their engines.

In the middle of September 1942, Rudolf Höss visited Treblinka and Chelmno to observe their gassing operations. In his memoirs, Höss wrote that he saw at Treblinka large trucks and tanks that "were started up and the exhaust gases were fed by pipes into the gas chambers." The master killer was not impressed. He dismissed the Treblinka method as primitive and inferior to those of his own camp. Höss was very proud of all the "improvements" he made in Auschwitz-Birkenau, such as having introduced Zyklon B, which did not require gas pipes or pumps, and having built gas chambers with a tenfold capacity of those of Treblinka.[41]

Great numbers of Jews were exterminated in Majdanek by machine gun fire. The largest massacre occurred on November 3, 1943, when over 18,400 Jews were shot by SS firing squads. They were part of a greater group of 43,000 Jewish men, women, and children murdered as part of Erntefest Aktion. The SS men led them to the trenches behind the crematorium in groups of fifty and 100, forced them to lie with their face downward in the bottom of the trenches, and shot them with automatic rifles. Row upon row was shot until the trench was filled, and then it was covered with a thin layer of earth. Two or three days later the bodies were disinterred and burnt in the crematorium and on bonfires. Loudspeakers near the crematorium and in different parts of the camp blasted forth jazz music to drown out the sound of the firing and the shrieks of the victims. Polish Prince Radziwill, a POW in Majdanek, testified after the war how the Polish prisoners in Majdanek celebrated in the evening the killing of the Jews.

There were other experimental attempts to find alternative mass-murder methods. A diabolic experiment was carried out near Konin in Western Poland in mid-November 1941 by Obersturmführer Herbert Lange, who became commander of Chelmno. The experiment, which even according to the Nazi standards stands out with its unspeakable cruelty, was described in a deposition presented by an eyewitness, Dr. Mieczyslaw Sekiewicz, before a juridical Polish committee on October 27, 1945, and again in June 1968 before the Polish Committee Investigating the Nazi Crimes in Poznań.[42]

Herbert Lange wished to combine in one single operation the killing with the disposal of the bodies. He hit upon the idea of introducing the victims while alive into a pit containing dry quicklime (calcium oxide). Water would then be poured with hoses into the pits transforming the quicklime into calcium hydroxide, a powerful caustic substance that burns and dissolves when combined with water. The victims would be chemically burned and their bodies dissolved in the pits, which would serve as their mass graves after being covered with a layer of soil.

Two pits containing quicklime, fifty and sixty feet long, twenty feet wide and seven feet deep were prepared by the Gestapo in the forest near the village of Kazimierz Biskupi for a group of Jewish victims from Zagorow and Konin. This is a fragment of Dr. Sekiewicz' testimony:

> On the bottom of the larger pit I saw a layer of quicklime . . . The Jews already stripped naked were thrown by the Gestapo men onto the heads of those already crammed in the pit. Then the Germans set up a small motor connected it with hoses to one of the vats . . . and the two Gestapo men began to pour some liquid on the Jews . . . Apparently because of the slaking of the lime, people in the pit were burning alive. The cries were so terrible that we who were sitting by the piles of clothing began to tear pieces off to stop our ears. The crying of those boiling in the pit was joined by the wailing and lamentations of the Jews waiting for their perdition. All this lasted perhaps two hours, perhaps longer . . . The next morning the Gestapo men ordered us to cover the large pit with soil. The human mass inside it seemed to have collapsed and dropped to the bottom. [43]

The SS did not adopt the quicklime killing method in order not to expose their guards to excessive stress, although quicklime became very popular with them to facilitate the rapid decomposition of bodies killed by other methods. Blobel's kommando 1005 used it extensively in 1944 to erase the mass graves left behind by the Einsatzgruppen before their retreat from Russia.

## The Psychology of Deception

Deception was an essential component of the the Final Solution. A sophisticated system of deception to disorient the Jews and their leaders was instrumented. The claim was made that deportations were being done to engage the Jews in productive work to aid the war effort. By using psychological warfare, elaborate lies on the resettlement to the east of Europe were given credibility through multiple channels to disguise the true intentions behind the deportations. *Ausiedlung* and *umsiedlung* (deportation and resettlement) became Nazi code words to hide from the world the terrifying truth of the Final Solution.

Disinformation and rumors were systematically spread among the population to frustrate their efforts to save their live. When deported from the ghettos in Eastern Europe to the death camps, Jews were generally told that they were being transferred to work camps. In Poland they were told that they were being taken to Madagascar. Hoping to escape the terrible ghetto conditions some even went willingly. Others clung to the illusion that their lives would at least be spared in their new locations. The deportees were given detailed lists of what to take along, including their work tools. The deception made it possible for the Nazi death machine to lead the Jews to their deaths without physical resistance or large-scale efforts to escape and hide.

In a display of unparalleled Nazi deceitfulness and trickery, far-away Jewish communities such as those of Rhodes and Corfu were told they are being taken for a vacation trip to Europe; they were charged a vacation train ticket to be transported to their deaths. The ruse used with the Jews of Corfu was also played in some cases in Western Europe. The Germans sold the deportees first-class tickets and transported them a short distance in luxurious cars to be transferred to animal boxcars at later points. A survivor from Sobibor, Kalmen Wewryk (1906- ), living in Montreal, describes the voyage of Jewish deportees from Holland to the Sobibor death camp:

> Thousands and thousands of refined and educated Amsterdam Jews were shipped to Sobibor with First Class Round-Trip tickets . . . How do I know this? because a few of them were thrown into my shop to work. They had been transferred three times during their trip to Sobibor; from their First Class carriages to other less luxurious ones, and finally to the sealed cattle cars which brought them to Sobibor. On the Sobibor arrival ramp they still clutched their "Round Trip" tickets in their hands.[44]

When the cattle trains reached the death camps and the bolted doors were pried open by the guards, the passengers sighted the heavily armed SS guards with their dogs. No time was allowed for the tormented passengers to comprehend what was happening. Everything upon arrival to the death camps was carried out with so much speed and pressure not to give the deportees a opportunity to look around and reflect. Terrified Jews would be pushed and shoved out of the wagons amid a barrage of beatings and screaming from the guards. They were ordered to leave behind their suitcases and bundles and form two separate columns, one of men, the other of women and children. The dead bodies in the boxcars would then be thrown out from the cattle trains and carried away for incineration by the Jewish Sonderkommandos.

In her book *Into That Darkness*, Gitta Sereny quotes Franz Stangl, the commandant of Treblinka and Sobibor, who explained to her the essence of the death camp system:

> The killings were organized systematically to achieve the maximum humiliation and dehumanization of the victims before they died. This pattern was dictated by a distinct and careful purpose, not by "mere" cruelty or indifference:

the crammed airless freight trains without sanitary provisions, food or drink, far worse than any cattle transport; the whipped-up (literally so) hysteria of arrival; the immediate and always violent separation of men, women and children; the public undressing; the incredibly crude internal physical examinations for hidden valuables; the hair cutting and shaving of the women; and finally the naked run to the gas chambers, under the lash of the whips. [45]

To turn the march to the gas chambers into a smooth operation after the shock of the violent reception at the arrival platform, the Nazi masters applied elaborate deception schemes to mislead the victims. They were made to believe that they had merely stopped to take a disinfection bath or a shower before the final leg of their trip. The illusion that they were still in transit to a final destination was kept alive among the victims even at the doorstep of the gas chambers. That simple scam allowed the Nazi murderers to turn the death operation into a well-running industrial process and to lead millions of people to their death without arousing any resistance, although some suspected that they were being led to their deaths. Although each camp developed its own version of the deception, they were all based on similar make-believe techniques.

The thought that normal human beings were capable of gassing other human beings did not enter in the minds of most Jewish victims even at the threshold of death. The deeply ingrained belief in the ultimate decency of human beings did not allow Jews to accept the terrible truth. Jewish victims projected their own values of the sanctity of human life on their merciless persecutors. Even the sight of the black clouds rising from the open-air pyres and the smell of burning human flesh in the air did not shake that deeply ingrained belief of the arriving Jews:

But the imagination could not possibly envisage that the smoke clouding the sun, the huge fire raging behind the screen and the sickly smell polluting the air came from the burning of thousands of murdered human beings who, only a few hours earlier, had suffered the fate now awaiting them. [46]

Rudolf Höss refers in his memoirs to the central importance given in Auschwitz to maintaining the fluency of the final death-march by keeping the victims calm and unaware of what awaited them:

In the spring of 1942 the first transports of Jews, all earmarked for extermination, arrived from Upper Silesia. It was most important that the whole business of arriving and undressing should take place in an atmosphere of the greatest possible calm. People reluctant to take off their clothes had to be helped by those of their companions who had already undressed, or by men of the Special Detachment. [47]

SS doctors stood ready at the arrival platform in Auschwitz to carry out the split-second decision that separated the people going to gas chambers to the left, from those going to the right to become slaves or guinea pigs in medical experiments. [48] SS officers would make the deceptive announcement that those going to the left were being transported to other work camps, but they first had to bathe and be disinfected. They went instead directly to the gas chambers without being registered or tattooed. The elderly and pregnant woman would go to the left. Children would be "intentionally, systematically, unremittingly, and without exception murdered."[49] Families were split in a most tragic way. Höss describes the selection process that took place at the train platform:

> We had two SS doctors on duty at Auschwitz to examine the incoming transports of prisoners. These would be marched by one of the doctors, who would make spot decisions as they walked by. Those who were fit to work were sent into the camp. Others were sent immediately to the extermination plants. Children of tender years were invariably exterminated since by reason of their youth they were unable to work.[50]

In Chelmno, where the almost totality of the deportees was gassed, a member of the Sonderkommando, Franciszek Piekarski, dressed as the squire of the estate in a feather hat, jack boots, and pipe, welcomed the arriving victims. He told them that some of them would go to work to Austria or further east, while others would work at his estate where they would be fairly treated and receive good food; for sanitary reasons it was necessary that they take a shower first, and their clothes be disinfected. After the reassuring speech the Jews were led to the undressing room and from there in small groups of between 100 and 150 people to the gassing vans. The Central Commision for the Investigation of German Crimes in Poland published in 1946 and 1947 a report on Chelmno that describes the final stage of the killing operation:

> From the courtyard they were sent inside the house, to a heated room on the first floor, where they undressed. They then came downstairs to a corridor, on the walls of which were inscriptions: "to the doctor" or "to the bath", the latter with an arrow pointing to the front door. When they had gone out they were told that they were going in a closed car to the bath-house . . . Before the door of the country house stood a large lorry with a door in the rear, so placed that it could be entered directly with the help of a ladder. The time assigned for loading it was very short, gendarmes standing in the corridor and driving the wretched victims into the car as quickly as possible with shouts and blows.
>
> When the whole of one batch had been forced into the car, the door was locked, and the engine started, poisoning with its exhaust fumes those who were locked inside. After 5-10 minutes of horrible screaming, all of the people in the loading compartment had been suffocated. According to the witness Bruno Israel, a fourth van was used for disinfection of clothing.[51]

Höss makes reference to the desperate efforts of mothers who suspected the tragic truth to save their babies:

> Many of the women hid their babies among the piles of clothing. The men of the Special Detachment were particularly on the look-out for this, and would speak words of encouragement to the woman until they had persuaded her to take the child with her. I noticed that women who either guessed or knew what

awaited them nevertheless found the courage to joke with the children to encourage them, despite the mortal terror visible in their own eyes.[52]

Höss felt the need to apologize for having felt weak-kneed when pushing pleading children into the gas chambers:

I did, however, always feel ashamed of this weakness of mine after I talked to Adolf Eichmann. He explained to me that it was especially the children who have to be killed first, because where was the logic in killing a generation of older people and leaving alive a generation of young people who can be possible avengers of their parents and can constitute a new biological cell for the reemerging of this people.[53]

A gentile member of the French resistance, Marie Claude Vaillant-Couturier who was held for three years as a prisoner in Auschwitz, witnessed the selection process at a short distance of no more than 330 feet from the gas chambers during 1944. She testified in Nuremberg on January 28, 1946, before Deputy Prosecutor Charles Dubost.

Generally speaking, of a convoy of about 1,000 to 1,500, seldom more than 250—and this figure really was the maximum—actually reached the camp. The rest were immediately sent to the gas chamber. At this selection also, they picked out women in good health between the ages of twenty and thirty, who were sent to the experimental block; and young girls and slightly older women, or those who had not been selected for that purpose, were sent to the camp where, like ourselves, they were tattooed and shaved.[54]

Vaillant-Couturier described the orchestra of young girls that played music while those selected to the left marched to the gas chambers unaware of the destiny that awaited them:

All these people were unaware of the fate awaiting them. They were merely upset at being separated, but they did not know that they were going to their death. To render their welcome more pleasant at this time—June to July 1944—an orchestra composed of internees, all young and pretty girls dressed in little white blouses and navy blue skirts, played during the selection, at the arrival of the trains, gay tunes such as "The Merry Widow" the "Barcarolle" from "The Tales of Hoffman," and so forth.

They were then informed that this was a labor camp and since they were not brought into the camp they saw only the small platform surrounded by flowering plants. Naturally, they could not realize what was in store for them. Those selected for the gas chamber, that is, the old people, mothers, and children, were escorted to a red-brick building . . . Later on, at the time of the large convoys from Hungary, they had no more time left to play-act or to pretend; they were brutally undressed, and I know these details as I knew a little Jewess from France who lived with her family at the "Republique" district. [55]

The orchestra also played at roll call for those selected for work. It played for the exhausted women during their march back from work, at the periodic death selections of the debilitated or sick prisoners, during the addresses of camp commanders, and at hangings. When the doomed victims approached the gas chambers they noticed an ambulance marked with the Red Cross symbol parked in their vicinity. That ambulance brought the lethal Zyklon-B chemicals for the gassing. Rudolf Vrba, the famous escapee from Auschwitz, pointed out that this was not accidental; the Red Cross ambulance carrying the poison gas served to calm the victims and to reassure them that no harm could occur to them under the protection of that symbol:

> The Jews were somewhat calmed when they spotted an ambulance with the Red Cross on it; if they only knew that the ambulance was filled with chemicals that would kill them in another half hour in the gas chamber, they would certainly not have been so calm. [56]

Fillip Müller, one of the few Jewish sonderkommando who survived Auschwitz working in the crematoriums, gives a description of the deceptive setting in the basement at the entrance of the gassing chambers that made the victims believe that they were going to take a disinfection bath:

> At the entrance to the basement was a signboard, and written on it in several languages the direction: "To the baths and disinfecting rooms." The ceiling of the changing room was supported by concrete pillars to which many more notices were fixed, once again with the aim of making the unsuspecting people believe that the imminent process of disinfection was of vital importance to their health. Slogans like "Cleanliness brings freedom" or "One louse may kill you" were intended to hoodwink, as were numbered clothes hooks fixed at a height of 1.50 meters . . . There were other multilingual notices inviting them to hang up their clothes . . . and to remember the number of their hook . . . Every single detail was carefully aimed at allaying the victims' suspicions and calculated to take them quickly and without trouble into the gas chamber. [57]

Müller witnessed how the shower ruse was tested for the first time in Auschwitz to convince a few hundred frightened Jewish factory workers to undress voluntarily, in order to retrieve the clothes of the victims in the best possible condition and avoid both the difficult task of undressing dead bodies and damaging the clothes:

> One of the SS men must have had the bright idea that it was more expedient to send these people to their doom naked. For then the irksome task of undressing them after their death would be avoided. Besides, if they undressed while still alive, their clothes would not be torn because they would think that they need them again. Today this new procedure was to be tried out for the first time. [58]

SS officers Aumeier, Grabner, and Hössler would usually address the hapless victims with the following words:

You have come here to work in the same way as our soldiers who are fighting at the front. Anybody who is willing to work will be all right . . . Therefore everyone will have to take a shower. Now, when you've had your showers, there will be a bowl of soup waiting for you all . . . We need craftsmen of all kinds, fitters, electricians, motor mechanics, welders, bricklayers and cement mixers; you must all report. But we'll also need unskilled helpers. Everybody is going to get well-paid work here . . . Now get undressed quickly, otherwise your soup will get cold.[59]

The hoax had a magical effect on the victims; they undressed speedily to be first in the "shower." The hoax passed the test and became standard procedure in Auschwitz:

Afterwards this technique was used as a reliable method for the mass extermination of human beings without bloodshed, and it began to assume monstrous proportions. From the end of May 1942 one transport after another vanished in this way into the crematorium of Auschwitz.[60]

Not all the victims, however, fell for the trap and rightly suspected the worst. They realized the moral abyss into which Germany had descended. As their forefathers before them who sanctified God's name in bygone ages, they marched to death with heroic stoicism. Rudolf Höss's own words written before his execution are most significant:

One woman approached me as she walked past and, pointing to her four children who were manfully helping the smallest ones over the rough ground, whispered: "How can you bring yourself to kill such beautiful, darling children? Have you no heart at all?"
One old man, as he passed me, hissed: "Germany will pay a heavy penance for this mass murder of the Jews." His eyes glowed with hatred as he said this. Nevertheless he walked calmly into the gas-chamber.[61]

Oskar Groening, eighty-three-years-old, a member of the Nazi Party and one of the last surviving SS guards in Auschwitz, addressed the deniers of the Holocaust in the BBC documentary *Auschwitz: The Nazis and the Final Solution*, produced in 2005. He spoke about what he witnessed in Auschwitz where he spent two-and-a-half years after his arrival in October 1942: [62]

I see it as my task, now at my age, to face up to these things that I experienced and to oppose the Holocaust deniers who claim that Auschwitz never happened. And that's why I am here today. Because I want to tell those deniers: I have seen the gas chambers, I have seen the crematoria, I have seen the burning pits and I want you to believe me that these atrocities happened. I was there.
It was completely understood by all that the majority was going straight to the gas chamber, although some believed they were only going to be showered before going to work. Many Jews knew they were going to die . . . One time a drunken SS man discovered a crying baby on the platform. He grabbed the waif

by its legs and smashed its head against the side of a truck. My blood froze when I saw it. [63]

Few of the lucky ones selected for slave labor survived more than six months; they died from starvation, disease, hard work, beatings, torture, and summary execution. Periodically, the doctors of Auschwitz-Birkenau would visit the surrounding labor camps and select the weak and sick for the gas chambers. The periodic selections to the gas chambers rapidly diminished their numbers. Of the 405,000 prisoners recorded as slave laborers between 1940 and 1945 in the Auschwitz factories, 340,000 perished through executions, beatings, starvation, and sickness.

There were normally no selections for slave workers in the Operation Reinhard camps except where prisoners were needed to assist in the disposal of the bodies. They had no work camps as in Auschwitz. Belzec, the first of the Operation Reinhard death camps to be put into operation, was considered a laboratory were the procedures applied in other Reinhard camps were first tested. When the transports arrived, the doors were pried open by the Ukrainian guards and the Jews violently driven out from the wagons. The dead bodies inside the cars were thrown out into piles. At the high point of Belzec, three transports would arrive daily at the camp. In a typical transport many passengers died in transit. In a transport from Kolomyja that arrived on September 10, 1942, around 2,000 of the 8,205 passengers were already dead. Karl Alfred Schluch, who spent one month as a guard in Belzec, [64] described at the Belzec trial in 1963 the deceptive technique used to calm down the deportees after the initial violent reception at the train platform. Camp commander Christian Wirth or Fritz Jirmann would address the incoming deportees through a loud speaker:

> This is Belzec. Your stay is temporary—you will move onto work camps where your skills are needed. There is work for everyone. Even you housewives are needed to feed your families and to keep the houses clean. First I must have your co-operation so that we can get you on your way quickly . . . There was often a ripple of applause and shouts of "Thank you Mr. Commander". Then Wirth mentioned the crucial part of the deception: We must have order and cleanliness. Before we feed you, you must all have a bath and have your clothes disinfected. It is necessary for women to have their hair cut.[65]

According to the testimony of Kurt Franz, an SS officer under Wirth, the Jews believed what Wirth was telling them:

> Inside the undressing barrack was a counter for the deposit of valuables. It was made clear to the Jews that after the bath their valuables would be returned to them. I can still hear, until today, how the Jews applauded Wirth after his speech. This behavior of the Jews convinces me that the Jews believed Wirth.[66]

When Stangl was brought from Sobibor to put Treblinka in "order" in August 1942, the master killer ordered the construction of a fake railway station to make the deception more realistic. A clock with painted numerals, ticket windows, and various timetables and arrows of train connections that gave the impression of a town station were in place by December 1942. Signs with various inscriptions such as "refreshment room," "waiting room," or "booking office," and signs showing the passengers where to get in for Byalostok were strategically placed. When Eichmann visited Treblinka in the company of Höfle, he saw the simulated railroad station. "It resembled," said Eichmann in his interrogation in Jerusalem, "the type of station that might be seen anywhere in Germany."[67] A Jewish survivor of Treblinka Kalman Teigman recalls:

> There were flowers planted on the ground and of course people couldn't imagine where they were. He painted the huts and put up all sorts of signs as if it was a real railway station.[68]

To make sure that the march to the gas chambers would proceed fluently, the sick, elderly, and infirm were taken aside and executed in front of an open pit, while the camp orchestra was ordered to play such tunes as *Drei Lilien* or *Highlander Do You Have No regrets*. A Jew arriving at 10:00 a.m. to Belzec would be dead by midday, his body thrown into a deep pit while his personal property and dental gold fillings were being processed in an adjoining building. Schluch described in his testimony the march of people to the undressing barracks and from there to the gas chambers:

> Next the Jews were led to the undressing barracks. In one of the barracks the men and in the other the Jewish women and children had to undress. After undressing the male Jews and the women with children were led separately through the tube . . . My position in the tube was quite near the undressing barracks. Wirth had installed me there, because in his opinion I could have a pacifying effect on the Jews. I had to direct the Jews along the path to the gas chamber after they left the undressing barracks. I believe that I made the way to the gas chambers easier for the Jews, because they must have been convinced from my words or gestures that they were actually to be bathed.[69]

Alfred Schluch described the actual operation of the gas chambers in Belzec:

> After the Jews had entered the gas chambers, the doors were tightly closed by Hackenholt himself or by the Ukrainians assigned to him. Then Hackenholt started the motor that was used for the gassing. After about five to seven minutes—and I only estimate the length of time—the peephole into the gas chamber was looked through to establish whether everyone was dead. Only then were the outer doors opened and the gas chambers aired out.[70]

The earliest description of Belzec that reached the outer world was written by Waffen SS officer Kurt Gerstein (1905-1945), who supplied chemical materials for the gassings in the camps. Gerstein visited Belzec on August 17-18, 1942, in the company of Dr. Wilhelm Pfannenstiel (1890-1979), a professor of hygiene at the University of Marburg/Lahn. In Gerstein's testimony, which was forwarded secretly to Sweden in 1942 and which he again replicated in a French prison before he committed suicide on May 4, 1945, he described what he witnessed:

> Next morning, a few minutes before 7 o'clock, I was told that the first train would arrive in ten minutes. And in fact the first train from Lvov arrived a few minutes later. There were forty-five carriages with 6,700 persons, of whom 1,450 were already dead on arrival. Through small openings closed with barbed wire one could see yellow, frightened children, men, and women. The train stopped, and 200 Ukrainians, who were forced to perform this service, tore open the doors and chased the people from the carriages with whips. [71]

Gerstein describes the last march of the Jews to the gas chambers:

> Then the march starts: Barbed wire to the right and left and two dozen Ukrainians with rifles at the rear. They came on, led by an exceptionally pretty girl. I myself was standing with Police Captain Wirth in front of the death chambers. Men, women, children, infants, people with amputated legs, all naked, completely naked, moved past us. I see everything! The mothers, their babies at the breast, the little naked children, the men, and women, naked. They enter into the death chamber, pushed by the leather whips of the SS. Pack well! that is what the captain ordered. Seven to eight hundred persons on twenty-five square meters. More than half are children . . . In one corner there is a whimsical SS man who tells these poor people in an unctuous voice, "Nothing at all will happen to you. You must just breathe deeply, that strengthens the lungs; this inhalation is necessary because of the infectious diseases, it is good disinfection!" [72]

Operating by trial and error, the gas chamber operators would often open the doors too soon while the victims were still alive and then close them again. Breakdowns and interruptions were common in the operation of the engines that produced the toxic fumes. When such incidents occurred, the victims were left standing for hours inside the chambers in an unending agony until the equipment was repaired. Such an incident was witnessed by Kurt Gerstein:

> When the doors closed, the diesel engine broke down after pumping some gas into the chamber. In their agony the Jews cried and prayed inside, while mechanics worked for almost three hours to repair the diesel engine. SS officer, Professor Wilhelm Pfannenstiel, looking through a glass peep hole commented that the "Jews were weeping as they do in the synagogue." UnterscharFührer Hackenholt was making great efforts to get the engine running. But it doesn't go. Captain Wirth comes up. I can see he is afraid because I am present at a disaster. Yes, I see it all and I wait. My stopwatch showed it all, fifty minutes, seventy minutes, and the diesel did not start. The people wait inside the gas chambers in vain. They can be heard weeping, "like in the synagogue," says Professor Pfannenstiel, his eyes glued to a window in the wooden door.
> Furious, Captain Wirth lashes the Ukrainian assisting Hackenholt twelve, thirteen times, in the face. After 2 hours and 49 minutes—the stopwatch recorded it all—the diesel started. Up to that moment, the people shut up in those four crowded chambers were still alive. Four times 750 persons in four times

forty-five cubic meters. Another twenty-five minutes elapsed. Many were already dead, that could be seen through the small window because an electric lamp inside lit up the chamber for a few moments. Up till then people were alive in these chambers. Another twenty-five minutes went by. True, many were now dead. After 28 minutes, only a few were still alive. At last after 32 minutes, everyone was dead. Finally, all were dead like pillars of basalt, still erect, not having any place to fall . . . One could tell families even in death. They were still holding hands, stiffened in death so that it was difficult to tear them apart to clear the chamber for the next load. [73]

Wilhelm Pfannenstiel, alive and well after the war, confirmed on June 6, 1950, before the Darmstadt Court the essential points of Gerstein's testimony as accurate and true, although he denied having said that the Jews were "weeping as they do in a synagogue." He claimed that the gassing at Belzec had taken only eighteen minutes and not thirty-two minutes. He did indeed confirm that the Jews had to strip naked, the women had their hair cut before being driven into four of the six gas chambers. He confirmed that exhaust gas from an engine was then piped in, and that the gold teeth were extracted from the dead victims before the bodies were thrown in a trench by Jewish slave workers.[74]

From Belzec, Gerstein traveled in the company of Wirth to Treblinka where they arrived on August 19, 1942. On his return trip to Germany through Warsaw, Gerstein unexpectedly met on the train on August 21-22. Baron Göran von Otter, secretary of the Swedish Legation in Berlin. He told him about the gassing he had witnessed in Belzec in order that knowledge of the crime might reach the outer world. Von Otter filed a report to his government in which he described his encounter with Gerstein:

He sobbed and hid his face in his hands. From the very beginning as Gerstein described the atrocities, weeping and broken hearted I had no doubt to the sincerity of his humanitarian intentions. [75]

The testimonies that exist on Sobibor and Treblinka are consistently similar. In the Sobibor death camp, the convoys consisting of up to sixty freight wagons stopped first at Sobibor station. A locomotive pushed eighteen to twenty freight cars into the camp alongside the ramp where they were opened by the Ukrainian guards. SS OberscharFührer Hermann Michel, the deputy commander, received them disguised as a physician in a white robe. Ada Lichtmann, a survivor from Sobibor, remembered his exact words:

SS-OberscharFührer Michel, standing on a small table, convincingly calmed the people; he promised them that after the bath they would get back all their possessions, and said that the time had come for Jews to become productive members of society. They would presently all be sent to the Ukraine where they would be able to live and work. The speech inspired confidence and enthusiasm among the people. They applauded spontaneously and occasionally they even danced and sang.[76]

SS OberscharFührer Kurt Bolender, a Sobibor guard, described at his trial the extermination process in Sobibor:

> After undressing, the Jews were taken through the "Tube", by an SS man leading the way, with 5 or 6 Ukrainians at the back hastening the Jews along . . . After the Jews entered the gas chambers, the Ukrainians closed the doors. The motor was switched on by the Ukrainian Emil Kostenko and by the German driver Erich Bauer from Berlin. After the gassing, the doors were opened and the corpses were removed by a group of Jewish workers.[77]

Erich Bauer, the Sobibor gas chamber operator (April 1942-November 1943), tried to present the march to death in the best possible colors to favor his defense at his trial: "It may sound astonishing that the Jews went unsuspecting to their death. Resistance occurred extremely seldom." The victims did not always go to their death as passively as Bauer pretended. The head of the SS administration in Sobibor, Hans-Heinz Schütt presented a different picture:

> Getting the detainees into the gas chambers did not always proceed smoothly. The detainees would shout and weep and they often refused to get inside. The guards helped them on by violence. These guards were Ukrainian volunteers under the authority of members of the SS.[78]

Kalmen Wewryk, a Jewish Sobibor survivor who was spared due to his skill as a carpenter, witnessed from a distance the gassing of an arriving group of Jewish children from Holland. One of the few who managed to escape from Sobibor, he described the unfathomable tragedy after the war:

> I remember a certain transport from Holland-ach, this was horrible! There were too many Jewish children to be "processed" rapidly so they were in a long, steadily shrinking circular line from morning to night. Such beautiful children, gorgeous little blonde girls with pigtails, decently dressed. These poor unfortunates were well-fed, with pretty, round little faces. Their parents must have loved them so, must have lavished such care on them, and now.[79]

Treblinka, where the Jews of Warsaw were annihilated was the latest of the Operation Reinhard death camps to begin operations on July 22, 1942. One of the very few survivors of Treblinka, Oscar Strawczynski, describes the violent reception they received at Treblinka when descending from the trains. SS Officer Willi Mentz, one of the defendants at the Treblinka trial, recalled the deceptive words SS officers Stadie or Maetzig addressed to the arriving Jews, telling them that they would continue their journey the following day:

> When the Jews had got off, Stadie or Maetzig would have a short word with them. They were told something to the effect that they were a resettlement transport, that they would be given a bath and that they would receive new clothes. They were also instructed to maintain quiet and disciplined. They would continue their journey the following day. [80]

To convince the passengers that they would soon continue their journey, a large placard in Polish and German informed them as soon as they crossed the inner gate that they had arrived to a transit camp:

> Attention Warsaw Jews! You are in a transit camp from which the transport will continue to labor camps. To prevent epidemics, clothing as well as pieces of baggage are to be handed over for disinfection. Gold, money, foreign currency, and jewelry are to be deposited at the "Cash Office" against a receipt. They will be returned later on presentation of the receipt. For physical cleanliness, all arrivals must have a bath before traveling on.[81]

The passengers were handed out picture postcards to send home. Mentz would take aside the ill, frail, and wounded deportees to a secluded area and personally shoot them in the neck with a 9 mm pistol, very much as it was done in Sobibor. The rest were ordered to take along a zloty in their hands to pay for the "bath" that waited for them. A Ukrainian guard would pick up the fee on the way. Mentz continued:

> Then the transports were taken off to the so-called "transfer" area. The women had to undress in huts and the men out in the open. The women were than led through a passageway, known as the "tube" to the gas chambers. On the way they had to pass a hut where they had to hand in their jewelry and valuables.[82]

When they reached the doors of the gas chambers they had to face Ukrainian guards "Ivan the Terrible" and Nicholas who reigned supreme in this kingdom of hell:[83]

> Suddenly, the entrance door flew open and out came Ivan, holding a heavy gas pipe, and Nicholas, brandishing a saber. At a given signal, they would begin admitting the victims, beating them savagely as they moved into the chamber. The screams of the women, the weeping of the children, cries of despair and misery, the pleas for mercy, for God's vengeance ring in my ears to this day, making it impossible for me to forget the misery I saw.
>   As soon as the gassing was over, Ivan and Nicholas inspected the results, moved over to the other side, opened the door leading to the platform, and proceeded to heave out the corpses. It was our task to carry the corpses to the ditches. We were dead tired from working all day at the construction site, but we had no recourse and had no choice but to obey. We could have refused, but that would have meant a whipping or death in the same manner or even worse; so we obeyed without grumbling.[84]

Yankiel Wiernik, a survivor of Treblinka who witnessed the actual gassings there described them in his short book *A Year in Treblinka*:[85]

> Between 450 and 500 persons were crowded into a chamber measuring twenty-five square meters. Parents carried their children in their arms in the vain hope that this would save their children from death. On the way to their doom, they were pushed and beaten with rifle butts and with Ivan's gas pipe. Dogs were set

upon them, barking, biting and tearing at them. To escape the blows and the dogs, the crowd rushed to its death, pushing into the chamber, the stronger ones shoving the weaker ones ahead of them. The bedlam lasted only a short while, for soon the doors were slammed shut. The chamber was filled, the motor turned on and connected with the inflow pipes and, within twenty-five minutes at the most, all lay stretched out dead or, to be more accurate, were standing up dead. Since there was not an inch of free space, they just leaned against each other.

## Body-Disposal in the Death Camps

Disposal of the bodies of tens of thousands of victims gassed daily in the death camps was a problem that the masterminds of the Final Solution found difficult to tackle. Initially, the prisoners used straps to drag the dead bodies from the gas chambers and transported them on rolling platforms to dump them into excavated shallow pits.

Before being thrown into the ditches, the bodies were inspected for gold and valuables. While the gas chambers were being cleaned by one brigade to prepare for the next gassing, another brigade collected and sorted the clothing, suitcases, and goods left behind by the victims. This procedure, with some variations, was typical of all the death camps at their beginning. The death brigades themselves were granted a very short life and gassed periodically. In Belzec, a death brigade of approximately 500 Jews worked initially in shifts digging graves and dragging the corpses on rolling platforms to the pits. New arrivals took their place as the earlier members were killed. After a while camp commanders realized that it was more expedient to keep alive the death brigades for longer periods of time to make sure that the entire process would function smoothly with experienced workers.

As the mass graves filled up, they became a source of serious environmental effects. The unbearable smell of putrefying bodies was felt far and wide in the surrounding region. In the town of Ostrow, thirteen miles away from Treblinka, the stench was unbearable. An entry in the war diary dated October 10, 1942, of the oberquartiermeister of the military commander in Poland reports:

> OK Ostrow reports that the Jews in Treblinka are not adequately buried and as a result an unbearable smell of cadavers pollutes the air. [86]

When Stangl visited Belzec for the first time to meet its commander, Christian Wirth, who intended to appoint him commander of Sobibor, he was overwhelmed by the smell and was shocked by the sight of countless unburied corpses that had rolled down the hill from an overflowing mass grave:

> I remember they took me to him . . . he was standing on a hill by to the pits . . . they were full. I cannot tell you; not hundreds, thousands, thousands, thousands of corpses . . . that's where Wirth said that was what Sobibor was for. Wirth told me I should definitely become the commander of Sobibor. And that he was putting me officially in charge. [87]

The shallow mass graves in the death camps not only had serious negative environmental effects, but they constituted the most potentially revealing sign of the crimes committed. As in the case of the Einstazgruppen it was decided to cease burial in mass graves and to obliterate existing mass graves in the death camps. Camp commanders looked to Blobel for guidance and adopted the method he developed in Chelmno of open-air cremation on external pyres using wood and oil in shallow pits. For the SS, this was the ideal and most simple method to dispose of the bodies: its capacity was practically unlimited. Death camp commanders were ordered by Himmler to exhume and burn the bodies in the existing mass graves. Open-air cremation became the method to dispose of the newly arriving victims gassed after the mass graves were discontinued in the spring of 1942.

Exhumation and burning of the corpses in mass graves began in Belzec in November 1942 and was completed by March 1943. Heinrich Gley, who arrived in Belzec in the summer of 1942, described in his trial the exhumation and burning process in Belzec:

> This incineration of disinterred corpses was such a horrific procedure from the human, aesthetic, and olfactory aspects that it is impossible for people who are now used to living like ordinary citizens to be able to imagine this horror.
>
> As I remember the gassing was stopped at the end of 1942 . . . Then the general exhumation and cremation of the corpses began; it might have lasted from November 1942 until March 1943 . . . It was possible to cremate some 2000 corpses at one fire site within twenty-four hours. About four weeks after . . . the second fire site was constructed. On average, therefore, some 300,000 corpses were cremated at the first site over five months, at the second site some 240,000 over four months. Naturally this is a matter of estimates based on averages. To figure the total number of corpses at 500,000 could be correct.
>
> When all the bodies had been removed from the graves, a special search commando sifted through the earth and extracted all the leftovers—bone, clumps of hair, etc. and threw these remains on the fire. An additional mechanical excavator was brought to accelerate the work. One mechanical excavator came from Sobibór and the other from the Warsaw district, which were operated by Hackenholt.[88]

When Himmler visited Treblinka in February 1943 he ordered to obliterate all incriminating evidence and carry out the exhumation of the bodies from mass graves. That order was carried out between February and July 1943.[89] When the Verbrennungskommando finished its work, all its members were killed like their fellow Jews that worked at the gas chambers. No witnesses dead or alive were left to tell.

Hundreds of thousands of corpses, including those of the newly arrived deportees, were dug up and burned in batches of 2,000 or 2,500 on large grids made of railway ties using brush wood drenched with gasoline. Mechanical excavators were used for moving the bodies from mass graves to the pyres. There are photos taken by SS Deputy Camp Commandant Kurt Franz of the mechanical excavators operating in Treblinka.[90] SS OberscharFührer Heinrich Matthes, who was responsible for the extermination sector in Treblinka, described the open-air burning system at his trial in Düsseldorf in 1964:

> When the fire had died down, whole skeletons or single bones remained behind on the grating. Mounds of ash had accumulated underneath it. A different prisoner commando, the "Ashes Gang," had to sweep up the ashes, place the remaining bones on thin metal sheets, pound them with round wooden dowels, and then shake them through a narrow-mesh metal sieve; whatever remained in the sieve was crushed once more. Bones not burnt and which could not easily be split, were again thrown into the fire. [91]

In Auschwitz-Birkenau the gassed victims were buried in large graves not far from the bunkers transformed into gas chambers until the summer of 1942.[92] The situation became unbearable when the bodies in the graves started to putrefy with the heat of the summer and the earth's crust burst open, contaminating the air and ground water. Slovak Jewish slave laborer Otto Pressburger describes the situation:

> When summer came everything started to rot. It was terrible, the majority of the people working here were from my home city of Trnava, I knew all of them and every day there were less and less of them. They must still be buried around here somewhere. My brother and my father are buried here as well, you know. [93]

After Höss's journey to Rzuchow forest in September 1942 to personally observe Blobel's open-air cremation technique, he began, on orders from Himmler and Eichmann, to exhume the mass graves and to burn the bodies together with those of the newly arriving victims in open-air pyres. The pyres, which held around 2,000 corpses, were burning day and night until the end of November 1942. Otto Pressburger describes the horrendous experience of opening graves and burning the bodies. He said "The SS men were constantly drinking vodka or cognac or something else from their bottles—they couldn't cope with it either, it was terrible." Eichmann recalls in his prison memoirs the burning activity he witnessed in 1942 in Auschwitz-Birkenau:

> Höss, the Kommandant, burned the corpses on an iron grill, in the open-air. He led me to a shallow ditch where a large number of corpses had just been burned.[94]

A major expansion effort was undertaken in Auschwitz between March and June 1943 to accelerate the Final Solution in Europe; new gas chambers with a capacity of 2,000 people per gassing were built and forty-six crematoria ovens of coke and wood were constructed by Hoch und Tiefbau AG Kattowitz and delivered by the Erfurt firm J.A. Topf & Sons. A conveyor belt moved the bodies from the gas chambers to the crematoriums. A female Polish guard at Auschwitz during the summer of 1944, Seweryna Szmaglewska, testified at the

Nuremberg Trials that when the gas chambers were working beyond capacity the children were thrown alive to the ovens:

> When the extermination of the Jews in the gas chambers was at its height, or-
> ders were issued that children were to be thrown straight into the crematorium
> furnaces, or into a pit near the crematorium, without being gassed first . . . They
> threw them in alive. Their screams could be heard at the camp.[95]

In the beginning of 1944 special preparations were made in Auschwitz-Birkenau to annihilate Hungarian Jewry. Himmler sent back Höss from Orianenburg to Auschwitz to supervise the operation. Between May and July 1944, as many as 148 transports carrying 437,402 Jews arrived from Hungary. The railway ramp was extended right to the door of the gas chambers. To keep up with the heavy cremation load the pyres near the White Bunker were reactivated on a full-time basis at the same time that the crematoria ovens were working to full capacity. Different burning materials were supplied for the pyres such as old wooden railway sleepers and beams, rags, barrels of waste lubricating oil, conifer branches, wood alcohol. The beams arrived in open wagons coupled to the de-portation trains. The Verbrenungskommando was increased from 450 to 900 members. Müller writes:

> It was the job of another twenty-five bearers to stack the corpses in three layers
> on top of the fuel in the pits. About fifteen stokers had to place the fuel in the
> pit and to light and maintain the fire by constantly stoking in between the
> corpses and pouring oil, wood alcohol and liquid human fat over them. There
> were approximately 35 men in the ash team. Some had to dig the ashes from
> the pits and remove them to the ash depot. The others were busy pulverizing
> the ashes. Smaller group loaded clothing, shoes and other of the victim's be-
> longings, on trucks to be taken to Canada.[96]

The ashes were moved from the burning pits to ash depots, where limbs and bones were separated and burned again while the rest went through a process of pulverization and sifting. Originally the sifted ashes were buried in pits and covered over, but later they were transported in trucks to the Vistula River where the current would carry them away. While 100 railroad cars were needed to bring 10,000 victims to Auschwitz, no more than a few trucks were required to carry away their ashes to the Vistula River. The murder process had been perfected to leave no trace behind.[97]

## The Economics of the Final Solution

Michael A. Musmanno, the respected American judge in Nuremberg who pre-sided over the trial of Oswald Pohl, the chief of the Economic and Administra-tive Department of the SS in charge of the concentration and extermination camps, pointed out how murder and greed were intertwined at every step of the Final Solution. The robbery, just as the killing, was organized and systematized to the smallest detail as in a well-run major industrial enterprise:

> Throughout the whole program of Jewish persecution in Nazi Germany that has disgraced mankind you find that robbery and pillage accompanied every step. There was first the humiliation of the wearing of the badge, the yellow badge, accompanied of course, by robbery. Then there was the deportation, accompanied by robbery. Then there was commitment to the concentration camps, accompanied by robbery. And then finally there was murder, accompanied by robbery . . .
>
> The story of the robbery of the Jews under the Nazi rulers is something that staggers the imagination . . . If I had not seen those documents, if I had not heard the witnesses who described how every item of possession was taken from factories, railroads, automobiles, household furniture, and every piece of wearing apparel down to little, tiny baby shoes all listed, businesslike. Had I not seen that documentation, I could never believe that so gigantic a program of thievery could be worked out and carried into fulfillment. [98]

Most of their belongings had been already taken from the Jews at the time of the evacuation of the ghettos, but many valuables and gold were taken from them in the camps. The harvest of their robbery contained enormous quantities of every conceivable type of articles from every country of Europe: suitcases, footwear, clothes, eyeglasses, artificial limbs, baby carriages, children's toys, rubber teats, watches, combs, scissors, knives, pots and pans, and a vast quantity of other household utensils. After being sorted, the goods were packed and sent back in the empty trains to the *Heimat* to compensate for wartime scarcities and prevent dissatisfaction in the home front.

Wedding rings and jewelry were melted down and transferred to the Reichsbank together with currency of every denomination that was found. Gold teeth were melted down to be herded as a lower class of gold metal in the vaults of the Reichsbank. All this wealth was transferred to Swiss banks and used to buy vital goods from neutral countries. Oskar Groening, who was in charge in Auschwitz of securing the possessions of Jews for the Third Reich coffers, said in a recent interview:[99]

> The Jews had diamonds and gold worth millions and it was my duty to make sure all of it got to Berlin.[100]

Every camp had accountants subordinate to the Economic and Administrative Department of the SS run by Oswald Pohl that administered the loot. Meticulous bookkeeping was kept of every item shipped to Germany. Large warehouses were established in the death camps where the baggage and clothing of the deportees was gathered, searched for valuables, disinfected, and sorted by Jewish slave workers. In Auschwitz-Birkenau the warehouses were in a block called *Canada*, seemingly called so because it was a place of abundance. The Reinhard Aktion camps had a central gigantic warehouse facility in Lublin in the disused hangars of the Lublin Airfield at Chopin Street, where all the loot was stored and classified. The enormous magnitude of the robbery system in Auschwitz and its operation receives much attention in the memoirs of its commander, Höss. The description given by Rudolf Vrba, the escapee who was a slave worker in the Canada section at Birkenau, is relevant here:

> I was in a factory of death. A center of annihilation in which many thousands of men, women and children were killed with gas and burned, not so much because they were Jews—although that was the original idea that came up in the Führer's sick mind—but because through their death they contributed to the German war effort.
>
> Every day I saw the freight trains arrive empty. I saw how they would load shirts of high quality on Monday; Mink coats on Tuesday; Children's linen's on Wednesday; Coats or textiles according to Wiglef's command; I understood that the commodities were sent to a Germany under siege to improve the morale of its citizens who were required to tighten their belts. For that they needed Auschwitz . . . I saw the Marks, Franks, Liras and dollars of the Black market, the Pounds Sterling, the diamonds and the gold taken from the Jews.[101]

RottenFührer SS Vogel, a German prisoner of war, testified before the Special Commission to Investigate the German Crimes in Majdanek:

> I was Deputy Chief of the clothing warehouse at the Majdanek Camp. The clothing and footwear of exterminated prisoners was sorted and the best was shipped to Germany. In 1944 alone, I myself shipped to Germany over eighteen carloads of clothing and footwear. I cannot say exactly how many pairs of boots and shoes and sets of clothing were dispatched, but I assert that it was a very large quantity. What I sent off was only a part of what was shipped to Germany. Everything was shipped to the address: Ploetzensee-Berlin, Strafanstalt.[102]

The commission found large stocks of various kinds of men's, women's and children's underclothing, tens of thousands of men's neckties bearing the labels of shops from different cities such as Paris and Prague, tens of thousands of women's belts, bath robes, pajamas, bedroom slippers, and a large variety of other personal belongings.

Gerstein's description of the robbery system in Belzec, which he observed in August 1942, is typical of all the Operation Reinhard death camps:

> Then instructions were given through a large loudspeaker: The people are to take off all their clothes out of doors and a few of them in the barracks, including artificial limbs and glasses. Shoes must be tied in pairs with a little piece of string handed out by a small four-year-old Jewish boy. All valuables and money are to be handed in at the window marked "Valuables," without any document or receipt being given. The women and girls must then go to the barber, who cuts off their hair with one or two snips. The hair disappears into large potato sacks, "to make something special for the submarines, to seal them and so on," the duty SS Unterscharfuehrer explained to me.[103]

Alfred Schluch, a Belzec guard, described in the Belzec Trial in Munich, (August 1963-June 1964) how the death brigade would retrieve the golden teeth and wedding rings for the Reichsbank in Berlin after every gassing:

> The corpses were pulled out of the chambers and immediately examined by one of the dentists. The dentist removed rings from the fingers and pulled out gold teeth. The valuables recovered in this way were tossed into a box that had been provided. After this procedure the corpses were thrown into the large graves nearby. [104]

Gerstein's description referes to Wirth's insatiable greed:

> Before the corpses were tossed into large trenches, they were searched for valuables in the form of gold teeth or gems or gold hidden in the vagina or rectum: With gold to the left—without gold to the right. Dentists hammered out gold teeth, bridges, and crowns. In the midst of them stood Captain Wirth and showing me a large can full of teeth, he said: "See for yourself the weight of that gold! It's only from yesterday and the day before. You can't imagine what we find every day—dollars, diamonds, gold. You'll see for yourself!" [105]

SS OberscharFührer Kurt Bolender testified in his trial to the robbery operated in Sobibor:

> After the first few weeks of undressing in the open-air square of Camp II, an undressing barrack was erected. Inside this barrack were signs indicating directions "To the Cashier" and "To the Baths." The Jews handed over their money and valuables through the window of the cashier's room. The cashier was SS-OberscharFührer Alfred Ittner, who was the camp accountant. Later he was replaced by SS-ScharFührer Herbert Floss. [106]

In Treblinka, as passengers descended from the boxcars, they were ordered to leave their baggage behind on the platform. When they were marched to the showers they had to hand in for safekeeping valuables and money that they would supposedly receive back after they had showered. Further down, their hair was cut and the golden fillings in their mouth were extracted. At the showers they were ordered to undress and tie together their shoes and clothing. To make sure that they were not hiding valuables, they went through a body search even in the private parts of their bodies before entering the "showers." After their dead bodies were dragged out from the gas chambers, a posthumous inspection made sure no valuables escaped detection. Finally, when the decaying bodies were exhumed and burned on pyres, the ashes were sifted for undetected hidden gold and silver.

Müller describes the division of labor at crematoria 4 and 5 where around 140 prisoners covered a shift:[107]

Some twenty-five bearers were employed in clearing the gas chambers and removing the corpses to the pits. Ten dental mechanics and barbers had to wrench out golden teeth, search the bodies for valuables and cut off the women's hair.[108]

In Chelmno, the 1946-1947 report of the Central Commission for the Investigation of German Crimes in Poland makes reference to the magnitude of the robbery of Jewish property that took place there:

A further important factor inspiring the destruction of the Jews by the Nazi authorities was economic. The value of the property owned by 340,000 people amounted to a large sum . . . It was stated for instance, that on September 9, 1944, 775 wristwatches and 550 pocket watches were sent from Chelmno to the Ghettoverwaltung at Lodz . . . The value of Jewish property robbed in Chelmno has been assessed at 178,045,960 GRM, today's value around US$760,000,000. [109]

Personal enrichment by the SS at every level was part and parcel of the robbery system. SS ObersturmFührer Ternes, former camp auditor of Majdanek testified before the special commission that great amounts of money and valuables were diverted by German camp officers for their own personal gain. Their excesses reached such magnitude that it gave occasion to investigation and prosecution by Konrad Morgan, SS Judge and legal investigator for the Kriminal Polizei. Those found guilty of stealing faced the death penalty. Ternes testified:

I know personally that the money and valuables taken from the prisoners were sent to Berlin . . . I know all about this because I worked as an auditor at the camp. I must emphasize that a great deal of the money and valuables that was taken from prisoners was not entered in the books, as they were appropriated by the Germans who took them from the prisoners. [110]

The 1946-1947 report on Chelmno of the Central Commission for the Investigation of German Crimes in Poland makes reference to the high-level robbery of the Gauleiter of the Warthegau Arthur Greiser (1897-1946) and his officers:

It was found that Greiser and the higher functionaries of the German administration who were in contact with the camp had received valuables which had belonged to murdered Jews. But the gendarmerie and police were very severely punished if they appropriated such things. [111]

The robbery carried out on the Jews of Europe was not obviously the only source of enrichment of the Third Reich. Looting the wealth of conquered people became part of its mission. A special unit named *Sonderkommando Jankuhn* was created by Himmler to plunder the cultural treasures of the conquered countries. Entire contents of museums, scientific collections, libraries, and archaeological finds were looted and shipped to Berlin or to the headquarters of *Ahnenerbe* in the Wewelsburg castle.

## Recycling the Bodies of the Victims

One of the most terrifying aspects of the death camps, without precedent in human history, is the attempt to recycle human bodies industrially to draw economic benefit from them. The incredible extent of that ultimate desecration of man by the Nazis has not yet been fully disclosed nor fully understood. Neither denial nor feigned ignorance will ever prevail against the awesome facts. The tons of human hair and gold teeth fillings are still there in Auschwitz and in the Reichsbank for anyone to see. But they are merely the tip of the iceberg of a far wider attempt to use every body part and component of the gassed victims as an industrial by-product: Not only hair, but also human skeletons, ashes, organs, fat, and flesh.

In their concern for economic benefit, the Nazi death industry recovered the hair of the victims. The German military found a use for human hair as weaving and insulating material in the war industry. It proved to be a good insulating material for submarines. Fillip Müller describes the industrial operation of preparing the human hair that Jewish slave workers were carrying out under SS supervision in Auschwitz in the building of crematorium 3, for export to Germany:

> Spread all over the brick floor warmed from the crematorium ovens below, was women's hair of every color and hew, from black to chestnut brown and blonde to grey. The hair was cut after the women had been gassed. Washing lines were strung across the room. Pegged on these lines like wet washing were further batches of hair which had been first been washed in a solution of ammonium chloride. When the hair was nearly dry, it was spread on the warm floor to finish off. Finally it was combed by prisoners and put into paper bags . . . From the thoroughness and care with which SS men checked that the hair was absolutely dry it was obvious that this was important material for their industry. It was only after the war that this was confirmed. The hair was used in the manufacture of felts and threads.[112]

Müller provides an exact description of the special workshop that was established toward the end of the summer of 1943 for melting the gold fillings retrieved from the mouths of the victims in the Birkenau crematorium 3 for the Reichsbank in Berlin:

> Two Jewish dental technicians were transferred to Birkenau from the dental hospital in Auschwitz . . . A board outside their door announced "No Admission" to prisoners and SS men alike. For it was behind this door that the boxes of gold teeth were opened. These were teeth pulled from the jaws of Jews murdered in the gas chamber before their cremation. The teeth were soaked for a few hours in hydrochloric acid in order to clean all remnants of flesh and bone. Then they were melted in graphite moulds with the help of a blow-lamp and

formed in bars. At intervals of about a fortnight the gold was collected by ambulance and taken to Auschwitz. I was told by the technicians that frequently
they melted down between five and ten kilogram's a day. After the war it was
learned that this gold went into the strong rooms of the Reichsbank.[113]

The body fat of the victims themselves was used as fuel for the crematoriums and open pyres in Auschwitz. In the summer of 1944, at the time of the
mass killing of Hungarian Jewry, they began to collect the human fat during the
open pyre cremations and reusing it to save fuel. On the two sides of the open
rectangular pits, canals collected the dripping fat of the burning bodies and conducted them by gravity into pans in the corners. From there the fat was scooped
up with buckets and poured at regular intervals over the bodies by the Sonderkommando.[114] Höss was very proud with the fuel-saving schemes he introduced
in the autumn 1943 for the crematoria ovens in Auschwitz-Birkenau:

> In the course of these experiments corpses were selected according to different
> criteria and then cremated. Thus, the corpses of two Mussulmans [emaciated
> prisoners] were cremated together with those of two children or the bodies of
> two well nourished men together with that of an emaciated woman, each load
> consisting of three, or sometimes four, bodies. Members of these groups were
> especially interested in the amount of coke required to burn corpses of any par-
> ticular category, and in the time it took to cremate them. During these macabre
> experiments different kinds of coke were used and the results carefully record-
> ed.[115]

A use was found for the great quantities of human ashes produced in the
death camps. The disposal of the ashes posed a problem. Initially the ashes were
buried in pits. After a time, dumping the ashes in flowing rivers took the place
of pit burial. Then they found that human ashes were an excellent fertilizer and
they began mixing the ashes with dung to produced fertilizer. In some camps,
such as Majdanek, Maly Trostenec, and Dachau, the Nazis used the human
ashes as fertilizer in the neighboring crop fields and in the vegetable and flower
plots in the camps. In Majdanek alone, over 47,700 ft³ of compost made with
ashes of incinerated victims were found after the war stored within the area of
the death camp.[116]

The death camps became providers of human skeletons and specimens to
German anatomy institutes. Institutes working on the scientific substantiation of
the race theory knocked at the doors of the death camps requesting skeletons and
specimens. Himmler established these institutes within the framework of the
Ahnenerbe Foundation to demonstrate the superiority of the Nordic race. The
Kaiser Wilhelm Institute of Anthropology in Berlin-Dahlem, the Anatomic Institute at the Reich University in Strasburg, the Anatomical Institute of Danzig,
and the Medical Academy in Graz housed them. Through Josef Mengele,
Auschwitz became the provider of specimen skeletons and organs to Professor
Otmar von Verschuer at the Kaiser Wilhelm Institute at Dahlem in Berlin and to
other medical institutions such as the Medical Academy in Graz.

The representatives of the anatomy institutes carefully selected their specimens among the camp inmates while there were still alive, murdered them and defleshed them on order. The chairman of the Anatomic Institute at the Reich University in Strasburg, SS HauptsturmFührer Prof. Dr. August Hirt (1898-1945) made a specific request in 1942 to Dr. Wolfram Sievers, the head of Ahnende for specimens of the Jewish race:

> Extensive skull collections from nearly all races and people are in existence. It is only of Jews that so few skulls are available to science that work on them admits of no secure findings. The war in the East now offers us an opportunity to make good this deficiency. In the Jewish-Bolshevistic commissars, who embody a repulsive and characteristic type of subhuman, we have the possibility of acquiring a reliable scientific document by acquiring their skulls . . . The person charged with securing this material is to prepare a previously specified series of photographs and anthropological measurements. After the subsequently induced death of the Jew, whose head must not be injured, he will separate the head from the trunk and send it, immersed in a preserving fluid, in well-sealed lead containers made especially for this purpose, to the designated address.[117]

Rudolf Brandt, deputy of General Karl Wulff in the command chain of the SS, informed Eichmann on November 6, 1942, that Himmler had ordered that Hirt should be supplied with everything he required for his research. Hirt's assistant, the Nazi anthropologist Dr. Bruno Beger (1911-2004) arrived to Auschwitz to select 115 living inmates; he took their photographs and anthropological measurements and did comparison tests on their anatomical and pathological features, form and size of the brain, and other characteristics. After Beger finished his work on June 15, 1943, the prisoners were quarantined and sent off in July and early August 1943 to Natzweiler-Struthof concentration camp, where they were gassed and their bodies sent to Hirt to deflesh them in his laboratory and add them to his collection.

A French inmate, who had to assist the project's director, described how "preservation began immediately" with the arrival of bodies that were "still warm, the eyes wide open and shining." There were two subsequent shipments of men, from whom their left testicle had been removed and sent to Hirt's anatomy lab. Although Hirt received orders to destroy his laboratories in the summer of 1944, "many wholly unprocessed corpses, others partly processed, and a few that had been defleshed [were found] . . . late in 1944." Hirt was captured at Strasbourg by French troops. He vanished and was last reported seen in Chile or Paraguay. His assistant, Dr. Beger, who is also known to have worked in Dachau, continued undisturbed his career in the German academic underworld. In 2004, he celebrated his ninety-third birthday.[118]

Producing skeletons and specimens on order and making fertilizer from human ashes was not the ultimate frontier of Nazi technology. At the laboratories of the SS Institute of Hygiene at Rajsko, a satellite of Auschwitz, they came upon the idea of using human flesh instead of animal flesh for the growth of bacterial cultures. SS doctors Kitt and Weber appeared periodically in Auschwitz to select, among the living victims, those whose flesh they found most appropriate for bacterial cultures. Prisoner Müller described their visits:

> From time to time SS doctors visited the crematorium, above all Kitt and Weber. During their visits it was just like working in a slaughterhouse. Like cattle dealers they felt the thighs and calves of men and women who were still alive and selected what they called the best pieces before the victims were executed. After their execution the chosen bodies were laid on a table. The doctors proceeded to cut pieces of still warm flesh from thighs and calves and threw them into waiting receptacles. At first we thought the Nazis planned to use human flesh for plastic operations on wounded soldiers. Only later we learned that these buckets of living flesh were taken to the Institute of Hygiene at Rajsko where they were used in the laboratories for the growing of bacterial cultures. Once I heard from OberscharFührer Quackernack remark: Horseflesh would do, but in war-time it is too valuable for that sort of thing.[119]

An experimental attempt to develop a technology to produce soap from human corpses and the tanning of human skin for industrial purposes was undertaken by Dr. Rudolf Spanner in the Anatomical Institute of Danzig, although it seems that these attempts did not go beyond the experimental stage. Originally established to prepare human skeletons from murdered psychiatric patients and prison inmates to satisfy the demand of German race theorists, the institute's director Spanner and his assistants Wollman, von Bargen, Reichert, and Borckmann became interested in 1943 in the use of the by-products of the defleshing process to manufacture soap from human body fat.

Uncontested testimony of three first-hand witnesses who took part in these experiments was accepted at the Nuremberg Trial. The testimony of the 3 witnesses and the judgment of the Nuremberg Tribunal are part of the historical literature on the Holocaust.[120] One of the witnesses was a salaried Polish laboratory assistant Sigmund Yuzefovich Mazur of Danzig who was employed from January 1941 until April 1945 by the Danzig Institute.[121] The other two witnesses were the British POWs William Anderson Neely and John Henry Witton who were held captive in Danzig by the Germans for four years. Neely and Wilton rendered their testimony after they returned home from German captivity before the British Judge Advocate General's Office in the City of Westminster on January 3, 1946 and on January 7, 1946. Their testimony was given in England totally independent of Mazur's deposition. It fully corroborated Mazur's testimony on the soap production experiments at the Danzig Anatomical Institute. The signed affidavits of the 3 witnesses Mazur, Witton and Neely were presented at the International Military Tribunal at Nuremberg. In his affidavit, William Anderson Neely stated:

> I myself was employed in taking the corpses down to the cellar and laying them on the tables in the dissecting room and also in clearing them away at the end of the day.[122]

John Henry Witton witnessed the daily arrival of new corpses:

Corpses arrived at an average of 7 to 8 per day, with sometimes 5 to 6 in a Red
Cross wagon and sometimes 3 to 4 in a small truck. [123]

They described the soap experiments:

Owing to the preservative mixture in which they were stored, the tissue came
away from the bones very easily. The tissue was then put into a boiler about the
size of a small kitchen table. After boiling the liquid it was put into white trays
about twice the size of a sheet of foolscap and about 3 centimeters deep . . .
Approximately 3 to 4 trays per day were obtained from the machine. [124]

Sigmund Mazur's testimony was given in a completely independent manner before the Committee for the Investigation of German Crimes in Poland on
May 12, 1945 and before a Soviet prosecution team days later. Mazur stated that
Spanner corresponded with prisons and camps to obtain as many corpses as
possible:

The production of soap in our institute was of an experimental nature, but I do
not know when it was suggested that corpses should be used for soap production on a large scale. Professor Spanner was trying to obtain as many corpses as
possible, and was corresponding with prisons and camps, with which he was
negotiating for corpses in these places to be reserved for the Danzig Anatomical Institute.
    They initially came from the psychiatric hospital of Konradstein; apart
from this, there were about 400 corpses in the Anatomical Institute which had
been guillotined in the Königsberg prison. When a guillotine was set up in the
Danzig prison in 1944 we began to receive corpses which were still warm. On
each corpse there was a label giving the surname and year of birth, and these
names were noted down in a special book in the Anatomical Institute. I do not
know where that book is now. I went to the prison in Danzig for corpses 4-5
times. From the Stutthof Camp, Borkner brought 4 corpses of Soviet people
men. [125]

Mazur described in detail the experimental production process in which he
was a participant:

In the summer of 1943, a one-storey stone building with three rooms was built
inside the yard next to the Anatomical Institute. The building was constructed
for processing human corpses and boiling bones; this was the official laboratory of Professor Spanner. This laboratory was designated as a laboratory for
preparing human skeletons and incinerating flesh and superfluous bones. But as
early as the winter of 1943-1944, Professor Spanner gave me the order to collect human fat and not to throw it away. This order was given to Reichert and
Borckman . . . Borkner and Reichert collected fat from human bodies.
    After I received Professor Spanner's instructions to start boiling human fat
into soap, Professor Spanner at once, on that same day, personally handed me

the recipe for making this soap, in written form; that is to say, the recipe had been typed out on the letterhead of the Anatomical Institute . . . This happened on 15 February 1944 in the presence of Secretary Horn and four students. This recipe gave instructions to take 5 kilograms of human fat, with 10 liters of water and 500 or 1,000 grams of caustic soda, boil all this for 2-3 hours, then leave to cool. The soap floats to the surface, and the residues and water remain at the bottom, in buckets. Common salt and a further handful of soda were added to the mixture. Then fresh water was added and the mixture was again boiled for 2-3 hours. After cooling, the finished soap was poured out into moulds. The soap produced has an unpleasant smell. To eliminate this unpleasant smell, benzaldehyde was added.

On that same day, we prepared soap from human fat. The recipe shown to me, dated 15 February 1944, is the same recipe about which I have just testified. This recipe was stuck to a plywood board which hung in the building where the soap was prepared. The senior laboratory assistant von Bargen was the immediate head of the soap factory. All the equipment was taken from the Anatomical Institute. [126]

Mazur makes reference in his testimony to the interest shown in the experiments by high level officials of the Hitler government outside of the SS circles, such as the ministers of health and education and by German medical scientists:

The Hitler government was, I know, interested in the work on production of soap from human bodies. The Minister of Education Rust, the Minister of Health Koschti [Conti], the Gauleiter of Danzig Albert Forster, and also many professors from other medical institutes, came to the Anatomical Institute . . . Conferences of a scientific nature took place in the Anatomical Institute, and I know of about 3 such conferences, but I cannot say what was discussed, since I did not attend them. [127]

Mazur also testified about Spanner's experiments to turn human skin into leather:

In exactly the same way as human fat, Professor Spanner ordered that human skin should be collected; after degreasing, it was treated with certain chemicals. The senior assistant von Bargen and Professor Spanner himself attended to the production of human leather. The processed skin was stored in a box, and went for special purposes; what special purposes these were, I do not know. [128]

The well-known British author Alexander Werth, who was attached to the Soviet army as a war correspondent of the *London Sunday Times* and the BBC during the war, visited the Danzig Anatomy Institute just days after the Germans fled in 1945. In his book he quotes his conversation with one of the German technicians in the Institute who assured him that they had no shortage of human bodies for future soap production. [129]

William Shirer wrote in his history of the Third Reich:

There was testimony at the Nuremberg Trials that the ashes were sometimes sold as fertilizer. One Danzig firm, according to a document offered by the Soviet prosecution, constructed an electrically-heated tank for making soap out of human fat . . . The document mentioned (IMT document, USSR-272) was the written testimony of a British corporal and POW William Anderson Neely . . . Its recipe called for "12 pounds of human fat, 10 quarts of water, and 8 ounces to a pound of caustic soda . . . all boiled for two or three days and then cooled".[130]

In their final summation, the Nuremberg Tribunal judges concluded:

After cremation the ashes were used for fertilizer, and in some instances attempts were made to utilize the fat from the bodies of the victims in the commercial manufacture of soap.[131]

After quoting extensively from the Mazur affidavit, L. N. Smirnov, Chief Counselor of Justice for the USSR, said on Feb. 19, 1946 at the Trial of the Major War Criminals:

The same base, rationalized SS technical minds which created gas chambers and murder vans, began devising such methods of complete annihilation of human bodies, which would not only conceal the traces of their crimes, but also to serve in the manufacturing of certain products. In the Danzig Anatomical Institute, semi-industrial experiments in the production of soap from human bodies and the tanning of human skin for industrial purposes were carried out.[132]

The Ludwisburg Central Authority for the Investigation into Nazi Crimes which opened its doors on December 1, 1958, reached the conclusion that the Nazis definitely made an attempt to produce soap and fertilizer from the bodies but seem to have abandoned the idea when it proved impractical. Gitta Sereny cites their conclusions:

The Authority has found after considerable research that only one experiment was made, with a few corpses from a concentration camp. When it proved impractical the idea was apparently abandoned.[133]

A plaque placed after the war on the wall of the laboratory of the old Danzig Institute of Anatomy, today part of the Gdansk Medical Academy, reminds the world that experiments to produce soap from human fat were indeed conducted there by the scientists of the Third Reich. The idea that Jews would be turned into soap was so popular among the Nazis and their local helpers that German civilians taunted Auschwitz inmates that they would be turned into soap. It was common for Poles when they came across deportation trains loaded with Jews on their way to the death camps to gleefully shout "Jews to soap!" It is easy to understand how it came about that German soap bars that bore the impressed initials RIF were erroneously believed to stand for *Rein Jüdisches Fett*, pure Jewish soap.

## The Camp Inmates as Guinea Pigs

With an unlimited supply of people destined for death arriving at the camps, the Ubermenschen decided to use some of the victims as guinea pigs for medical experiments before murdering them. The experiments were undertaken in Auschwitz-Birkenau, Dachau, Ravensbruck, Sachsenhausen, Natzweiler, and Buchenwald, among other sites. From 1939 to 1945, about 200 German medical doctors were involved in more than seventy medical research projects using human as guinea pigs. At least 7,000 specific cases of human subjects are documented from existing records and personal testimonies, although it is certain that there were countless more cases of which no documentation or personal testimony survived.

The quest for Lebensraum for the Third Reich was not only fought by the military at the war front but also by the German scientific establishment at home. Hitler's medical advisors convinced him that mass sterilization could provide a powerful weapon to destroy Germany's enemies; the eastern territories could be emptied in one generation of German colonization, while using the sterilized population as cheap labor during the transition. Researchers looked for an inexpensive, inconspicuous, and rapid method to sterilize millions of people that would allow them to wipe out Soviets, Poles, and other so-called inferior people while using them as slave workers. At the same time they were looking for effective fertility methods to multiply the German population at a much faster rate than the conquered population.

This was not an individual enterprise but a major organized effort of institutional science in Germany spearheaded by the SS Ahnenerbe Society to advance so-called racial research. Himmler's interest in racial research went way back to his early career. In 1935 he founded *Das Ahnenerbe Forschungs und Lehrgemeinschaft* (the Society for Ancestral Heritage Research and Teaching) to prove the Nazi theories of racial superiority through historical, anthropological, and archaeological research. The society maintained close professional ties with the German medical establishment and used the universities and research institutes of Germany and Austria for its work.

The role played by Ahnenerbe became far more sinister when Himmler incorporated the society into the SS in 1940 and made biological military research part of its agenda. The Institute for Functional Research in Military Science (Institut für Wehrwissenschaftliche Zweckforschung) was set up within the Ahnenerbe Society to respond to the research requests of the three branches of the German armed forces and to further the implementation of race and Lebensraum policies of the Third Reich. The institute promoted barbaric experiments on innocent human beings who were subjected to untold suffering, mutilation, and death. The elite institution of German science, the Kaiser Wilhelm Institute, readily cooperated with Ahnenerbe in these criminal programs.[134]

Himmler took enormous personal interest in the human experiments and often got involved with them. The requests for authorizations to perform experiments in the camps went first to SS Chief Medical Officer Dr. Ernst Robert Grawitz. After obtaining the opinions of Dr. Karl Gebhardt (1897-1948), Himmler's medical attendant and president of the German Red Cross, and other two SS officers, Grawitz passed them on to Himmler with his recommendation. Not only Jews but also Poles, Soviets, and Gypsies were selected for the murderous experiments. The helpless subjects were frozen, drowned, burned, infected, mutilated, and poisoned in senseless experiments. Most of them died a terrible death or were permanently crippled as a result, suffering severe pain and intense agony before death or permanent disability.

Experiments on sterilization and fertility were performed on Hitler's initiative in Auschwitz and Ravensbrück from March 1941 to January 1945. Dr. Adolf Pokorny, a specialist in skin and venereal diseases, drew Himmler's attention in 1941 to a claim made by Dr. Madaus that caladium seguinum, a drug obtained from a North American plant, if taken orally or by injection produced sterilization, and he suggested that it should be developed and used against 3 million Soviet prisoners of war. As a result of Pokorny's suggestion, efforts were made to grow the plant in hothouses. Experiments were conducted on camp inmates to test the effectiveness of the drug:

> If, on the basis of this research, it were possible to produce a drug which after a relatively short time, effects an imperceptible sterilization on human beings, then we would have a powerful new weapon at our disposal. The thought alone that the three million Bolsheviks, who are at present German prisoners, could be sterilized so that they could be used as laborers but be prevented from reproduction, opens the most far-reaching perspectives.[135]

Viktor Brack, who was in charge of the euthanasia program of the chancellery, submitted to Himmler a proposal on March 1941, in which he suggested that x-rays could be used for mass sterilization of non-Aryans. Lined up against a counter for such an innocuous task as answering a questionnaire, the unsuspecting victims could be irradiated from the back without their knowledge from two simultaneous sources to make them infertile:

> With one such installation with two tubes about 150 to 200 persons could be sterilized daily, while twenty installations would take care of 3,000 to 4,000 persons daily. In my opinion the number of daily deportations will not exceed this figure.[136]

Brack suggested that the sterilization of a fraction of the Jewish deportees destined for death could alleviate the critical scarcity of manpower that German war production began to face in 1942. In a letter to Himmler dated June 1942, Brack wrote:

> Among ten millions of Jews in Europe there are, I figure, at least two to three millions of men and women who are fit enough to work. Considering the ex-

traordinary difficulties the labor problem presents us with, I hold the view that these two to three millions should be specially selected and preserved. This can, however, only be done if at the same time they are rendered incapable to propagate. [137]

Dr. Horst Schumann (1906-1983), the director of the Euthanasia-Institute Grafeneck in Wurttemberg set up an x-ray station for sterilization purposes in 1942 in the Auschwitz woman's camp. Men and women were forcibly positioned for several minutes between two x-ray machines aiming at their sexual organs. The testicles of males were then removed surgically by Polish prisoner Dr. Wladyslav Dering and sent to Breslau for histopathological examination. Most subjects died because of inner injuries and radiation burns after great suffering. Those who survived were unfit for work and gassed immediately. Schumann had to admit in his report to Himmler in April 1944 that x-ray sterilization was a failure. He recommended surgical castration instead:

Using x-rays castration of males is almost impossible or requires an effort which does not pay. As I have convinced myself, operative castration requires not more than six to seven minutes, and therefore can be performed more reliably and quicker than castration by x-rays. [138]

This was merely the beginning. Other research projects by the highest representatives of the German medical establishment followed in Auschwitz to develop sterilization methods with the cooperation of the elite scientific institutes of the Third Reich. Dr. Carl Clauberg (1898-1957), doctor-in-chief at the university gynecological clinic in Kiel and professor for gynecology at Konigsberg University, came to Auschwitz in December 1942 after being recommended on May 29, 1941. He received part of women's block 10 for his medical experiments on sterilization and fertilization. Clauberg experimented with injecting chemical substances such as Formalin into the wombs of his subjects to sterilize them. These chemicals caused inflammation and scarring that totally destroyed the lining membrane and seriously damaged the ovaries of the victims, which were removed and sent to Berlin. The sterilization experiments were carried out on unsuspecting Jewish women during routine gynecological examinations. Höss described Clauberg's technique as "injections to paste together the Fallopian tubes and thereby prevent offspring from Jewish women."

The women of cell block 10 lived in constant terror of being gassed, sterilized, or forcibly inseminated. Several thousand Jewish and Gypsy women were sterilized, going through terrible pain and bleeding. A Orthodox Jewish woman who heard that Clauberg selected her for forced insemination decided to poison herself. When Himmler inquired how long it would take to sterilize 1,000 women with his method, Clauberg informed Himmler in June 1943 that a staff of one doctor and ten assistants could do it in a single day.

Nazi evil reached new summits in Auschwitz with the arrival of Dr. Josef Mengele (1911-1979) on May 30, 1943, as the senior doctor of the women's camp in Auschwitz-Birkenau. Josef Mengele grew up in a devoutly Catholic

home in Gunzburg, Bavaria. His mother Walburga, a devout Catholic, saw to it
that her sons strictly practiced her faith. For the early part of his life, a nanny
called Monika fulfilled the dominant maternal role, coaxing and at times intimi-
dating Josef into holding fast to the Catholic faith. In his autobiography he expressed pride for the Christian significance of his name Joseph. [139]

In 1937, Mengele became an assistant to Professor Verschuer at the Frankfurt University Institute for Hereditary Biology and Racial Purity and a visiting
scientist at his Kaiser Wilhelm Institute of Anthropology, Human Genetics, and
Eugenics at Dahlem in Berlin. An old Hitler admirer, Verschuer greeted the efforts of the Nazi regime to realize a race utopia with great enthusiasm and paid
tribute to Hitler publicly for "being the first statesman to recognize hereditary
biological and race hygiene." He recommended as early as 1927 the forced sterilization of the "mentally and morally subnormal." As he was involved with anti-
Semitic organizations, the Nazi government appointed him as an expert and re-
searcher of world Jewry (*Weltjudentum*). In a letter to well-known eugenicist,
Eugen Fischer, von Verschuer wrote on November 11, 1937:

> It is however important that our racial politics in the Jewish question as well-
> develop a scientific context so that it is recognized in wider circles. [140]

Mengele became interested in the genetic key that would make it possible
to engineer an Aryan master race and to double its fertility to repopulate the
expanding German Lebensraum. He believed that twins held the key to the secret. In close collaboration with the Kaiser Wilhelm Institute for Anthropology,
Genetics, and Eugenics, he studied the phenomena of twins, as well as the phy-
siology and pathology of dwarfism.

Mengele enlisted with the Waffen-SS and was wounded in the Soviet front.
When he returned to Berlin in 1942, Verschuer had began a project on twins
research at Berlin's Kaiser Wilhelm Institute.[141] Verschuer encouraged Mengele
to apply for a position in Auschwitz where no humane or moral restrictions
would interfere with his work. As director of the Kaiser Wilhelm Institute of
Anthropology, Verschuer assigned funds from the German Research Council for
Mengele's experiments in Auschwitz in exchange of interesting specimens dis-
playing genetic abnormalities for further study. Mengele was given in Auschwitz his own laboratory block, independent financing, and a medical staff. In a
proposal for new research written in 1944 at the Kayser Wilhelm Institute, Verschuer clearly underlined his close collaboration with Mengele:

> My assistant Dr. Mengele has joined me in this branch of research. He is pre-
> sently employed as HauptsturmFührer and concentration camp physician in the
> concentration camp at Auschwitz. Anthropological investigations on the most
> diverse racial groups of this concentration camp are being carried out with
> permission of the SS ReichsFührer [Himmler]; the blood samples are being
> sent to my laboratory for analysis. [142]

When he arrived to Auschwitz, Mengele initially began studying "noma," a disease previously almost unknown in Europe that became widespread among Gypsy children due to the terrible camp conditions.[143] On Mengele's orders Gypsy children suffering from noma were put to death for pathology investigations to be carried out in his laboratory at the Gypsy Family Camp. Organs and even complete heads of these children were preserved and sent in jars to scientific institutions including the Medical Academy in Graz, Austria.[144]

Soon Mengele concentrated on his race project. He removed limbs and organs in gruesome surgical procedures without an anesthetic; he carried out twin-to-twin transfusions, stitched twins together, castrated or sterilized them. Eva Mozes, a surviving twin, describes how Mengele attempted to create a Siamese twin by connecting the blood vessels and organs of Gypsy twins. The twins screamed day and night until gangrene set in; after three days in agony, they died. Of about 1,500 pairs of twins he experimented upon, only about 200 survived. They bear witness to the unparalleled depravity of the Master Race and its scientists.[145]

Mengele made sure that every arriving convoy was inspected for twins and for people with genetic abnormalities such as dwarfs, giants, or unique hereditary traits such as a club foot or eyes of two different colors. With twins he carried out controlled experiments using one member of each pair as a control. He attempted to change the color of eyes to blue with the injection of chemicals directed into the eyeballs of his subjects in accordance with the Nazi claim that blue eyes were part of the Aryan archetype.

To select his specimens among the arriving Jewish prisoners as they marched by, Mengele took rotations with other SS doctors at the unloading ramps. Known as the "Angel of Death" (Malach Hamoves) among Jewish prisoners, Auschwitz survivors remember Mengele as he signaled with his hand who is to go left to the gas chambers, or right to slave labor or medical experiments:

Prisoners would march before him with their arms in the air, while he continued to whistle his Wagner—or it might be Verdi or Johann Straus.[146]

When Mengele decided that the usefulness of a twin pair had come to an end, he, or his collaborators, would proceed to take all body measurements and data before injecting chloroform into their hearts. A post-mortem dissection to prepare his specimens for the Kayser Wilhelm Institute would follow. In one instance, seven sets of twins with eyes of different colors were killed with phenol injections and after dissection, their eyes were sent to the Kaiser Wilhelm Institute. Mengele's assistant, POW Miklos Nyiszli, an Hungarian pathologist carried out the task of dissection and preparation for the Third Reich Museum:

I would bathe the corpses of cripples and dwarfs in calcium chloride and cook them in large pots so that their skeletons could be preserved in the Museum of the Third Reich.[147]

Nyiszli regularly shipped "fresh research materials" from Auschwitz to von Verschuer at the Kaiser Wilhelm Institute in packages marked *kriegswichtig* (essential to the war effort). When the Soviets approached Auschwitz, Mengele sent all his materials and findings in two trucks to Verschuer in Berlin. The full extent of what Mengele did at Auschwitz may never be known because Verschuer destroyed the materials. Mengele left Auschwitz on January 17, 1945, days before the arrival of Soviet troops. He did not stand trial and was able to obtain from the International Committee of the Red Cross in Italy travel papers that allowed him to flee to Argentina and Brazil in 1949 (see chapter 12). As for Verschuer, a denazification tribunal considered that his activities were merely misdemeanors, and fined him 600 Marks, the equivalent of $140 US dollars. In 1951, Verschuer was offered a position at the University of Münster where he established one of West Germany's largest genetic research centers. He retired as chairman of the Department of Genetics in 1965 and died in 1969.[148]

To describe the gruesome medical experiments is beyond the scope of this book. A year-and-a-half after the end of the war, from December 9, 1946, to August 20, 1947, an American military tribunal opened criminal proceedings in Nuremberg against twenty-three leading German physicians and administrators for their willing participation in war crimes and crimes against humanity. The defendants had either been involved in the euthanasia program, or in the medical experiments in the death and labor camps. The cruel experiments produced no worthwhile results.[149] In his memorable words at the opening of the trial, the Chief Prosecutor Telford Taylor said at Nuremberg on December 9, 1946, the following:

> As a result of all of these senseless and barbaric experiments, the defendants are responsible for manifold murders and untold cruelty and torture . . . These experiments revealed nothing which civilized medicine can use . . . Apart from these deadly fruits, the experiments were not only criminal but a scientific failure. It is indeed as if a just deity had shrouded the solutions which they attempted to reach with murderous means . . . I fervently hope that none of us here in the courtroom will have to suffer in silence while it is said on the part of these defendants that the wretched and helpless people whom they froze and drowned and burned and poisoned were volunteers.
>
> The utter brutality of the crimes committed in conducting this series of experiments is reflected in all the documents . . . The victims who did not die in the course of such experiments, surely wished that they had.[150]

After the testimony of eighty-five witnesses and the submission of almost 1,500 documents, American judges pronounced their verdict on August 20, 1947. Sixteen of the doctors were found guilty of war crimes and crimes against humanity; seven were sentenced to death and executed on June 2, 1948. Dr. Wolfram Sievers, the leader of Ahnenerbe, was sentenced to death and executed on June 2, 1948—the only member of the wartime Ahnenerbe to suffer this punishment—while all the other members of that criminal gang became prominent members of the postwar German academic world. Like Mengele, many other major medical perpetrators escaped the hand of justice.

## Notes

1. Ian Kershaw, *Hitler, 1889-1936 Hubris*, (New York: W. W. Norton and Company, 2000), 256.

2. Hartl later joined the SS Einsatzgruppe C in Russia that carried out the greatest massacres.

3. Christopher Browning, *Fateful Months: Essays on the Emergence of the Final Solution*.(Teaneck, NJ: Holmes & Meier, 1991), 188.

4. Beth A. Griech-Polelle, *Bishop von Galen German Catholicism and National Socialism.* (New Haven, CT: Yale University Press, 2002).

5. Volk Ludwig, *Episkopat und Kirchenkampf im Zweiten Weltkrieg* (Germany: Stimmen der Zeit Verlag, 1980), 687-702.

6. Güenther Lewy, *The Catholic Church and Nazi Germany* (New York: Mc Graw Hill Book Co., 1964), 311.

7. Philippe Burrin and Arnold Edward, *Hitler and the Jews: The Path to Genocide* (New York: Oxford University Press, 1994), 127.

8. Lipski, Columbia University. Doc. 99.

9. David Engel, *Jewish Social Studies 45.* 1983, 12–13.

10. Philippe Burrin, *Hitler and the Jews*, 127.

11. Carol Rittner, Stephen D. Smith, and Irena Steinfeldt, *The Holocaust and the Christian World* (New York: Continuum Press, 2000), 75-76.

12 . Rudolf Höss, *Commandant of Auschwitz: The Autobiography of Rudolf Hoess* (New York: Phoenix Press, 2000). Gerald Reitlinger, *The Final Solution* (London: Vallentine Mitchell, 1953).

13. Höss, *Death Dealer*.

14. Höss, *Death Dealer*, 153.

15. Wirth was replaced by SS HauptsturmFührer Gottlieb Hering when he became general inspector of the 3 camps.

16. Yitzhak Arad. *Belzec, Sobibor, Treblinka. The Operation Reinhard Death Camps* (Bloomington In: Indiana University Press, 1987). Raul Hilberg. The *Destruction of the European Jews* (New Haven, CT: Yale University Press, 2003). Adalbert Rückerl (Ed.): *NS–Vernichtungslager im Spiegel deutscher Strafprozesse. Belzec, Sobibor, Treblinka, Chelmno,* dtv dokumente (München, 1977).

17. Arad, *Belzec.*

18. Arad, *Belzec.*

19. Christopher R Browning. *Evidence for the Implementation of the Final Solution.* Nürnberg Document NO–626, 28/7/42: Himmler to Gottlob Berger: Die besetzten Ostgebiete werden judenfrei. Die Durchführung dieses sehr schweren Befahls [sic] hat der Führer auf meine Schultern gelegt. Die Verantwortung kann mir ohnedies niemand abnehmen.

20. Yankel Wiernik. *A Year in Treblinka.* Published by the American representation of the General Jewish Workers' Union of Poland. 175 East Broadway, New York, New York, 1945. Alexander Donat. *The Death Camp Treblinka* (New York: Holocaust Library, 1979).

21. Arad, *Belzec,* 60-61, 392. Globocnik SS file, Berlin Document Center. (Breitman), 238.

22. Willi Dressen, Volker Riess, and Ernst Klee, *The Good Old Days* (New York: The Free Press, 1988), 233.

23. Arad, *Belzec,* 60-61, 392. Globocnik SS file, 238.

24. Dressen Riess and Klee, *The Good Old Days*, 233.

25. W. Benz ed. *Dimension der Volkermords. Die Zahl der Judischen Opfer das Nationalsozialismus* (Munich, 1991).

26. Kept in the Public Record Office at Kew in England.

27. Robin O'Neil. *Belzec - Stepping Stone to Genocide.* Chap. 2. PRO File No. WO/208/4209: Statement of Konrad Morgan, 13 July 1946.

28. Record of Proceedings in the Supreme Court of Israel. Appeal Session.

29. Martin Gilbert. *The Holocaust.* New York, 1985, 219.

30. Oliver Lustig, Concentration Camp Dictionary. (Eichman 4).

31. Höss, Rudolf, *Commandant of Auschwitz: The Autobiography of Rudolf Hoess* (New York: Phoenix Press, 2000).

32. Filip Muller. *Eyewitness Auschwitz: Three Years in the Gas Chambers* (1999), 115.

33. Muller. *Eyewitness Auschwitz,* 60.

34. Hans Münch, *Swedish Television Interview*, The Nizkor Project.

35. Hans Münch. *The Auschwitz Declaration*, January 27, 1995. Nizkor Project.

36. BBC documentary: *Auschwitz: the Nazis and the Final Solution.*

37. Franz Suchomel, a SS guard at Belzec, characterized the camp in his testimony included in the documentary film *Shoah* as a laboratory where the methods used in the Reinhard camps were tried out first.

38. StA Dortmund AZ: 45 Js 27-61.

39. Wiernik. *A Year in Treblinka.* Donat, *The Death Camp Treblinka.*

40. Potassium ferro cyanide releases Zyklon–B when heated to a very high temperature or when adding acid. Günther's orders begin on June 8, 1942. Orders from February to May 1944 show more than 2,000 kilogram's were delivered.

41. Shirer, *The Rise and Fall of the Third Reich,* (New York: Simon and Schuster, 1959), 968-969.

42. Shmuel Krakowski, *A Small Village in Europe Chelmno (Kulmhof), The First Nazi Mass Extermination Camp*, (Jerusalem: Yad Vashem, 2001), 19-21. Rhodes, *Masters of Death*, 200-203.

43. Rhodes, *Masters of Death,,* 200-203. Lawrence Langer, *Preempting the Holocaust* (New Haven, CT: Yale University Press, 1998).

44. Kalmen Wewryk, Howard Roiter. Ed., *To Sobibor and Back: An Eyewitness Account.* Published by Concordia University Chair in Canadian Jewish Studies. 1999.

45. Gitta Sereny, *Into that Darkness* (New York: McGraw Hill Book Co., 1974). Franz Stangl, commandant of Treblinka, was arrested in Brazil in 1967, extradited to Germany and sentenced to life imprisonment for his part in the murder of 400,000 people in December, 1970, died in prison the following June.

46. Müller, *Eyewitness Auschwitz*, 134.

47. Höss, *Death Dealer.*

48. Professor Rita Thalman. Eugenics in Western Countries (Except France) Before 1945. January 29, 2007. UNESCO, Dec. 2005.

49. Olga Lengyel, *Five Chimney: The Story of Auschwitz* (Chicago, Il: Academy Chicago Publishers, 1995), 110-111. Robert S. Wistrich, *Anti-Semitism* (New York: Pantheon Books, 1991).

50. Höss, *Death Dealer*.

51. The report of the Commission created immediately after the war by the Polish Provisional Government to prepare the evidence for the Nuremberg trial bears the title *German Crimes in Poland*.

52. Höss, *Death Dealer*.

53. Höss, *Death Dealer*.

54. Vaillant-Couturier was arrested by the Germans in 1942 and deported to Auschwitz in 1943. After the war she became a deputy of the French Constituent Assembly and Knight in the Legion of Honor.

55. Nuremberg Trial Proceedings Vol. 6. Forty-Fourth Day Monday, 28 January 1946. *"The Avalon Project."*

56. Rudolf Vrba, *I Cannot Forgive*, (Toronto, ON: Bantam Publishers, 1964).

57. Müller, *Eyewitness Auschwitz*, 61.

58. Müller, *Eyewitness Auschwitz*, 31-32.

59. Müller, *Eyewitness Auschwitz*, 37-38.

60. Müller, *Eyewitness Auschwitz*, 39.

61. Höss, *Death Dealer*.

62. Mathias Geyer, *Der Spiegel, The Bookkeeper From Auschwitz* (May 9, 2005).

63. Geyer, *Der Spiegel*.

64. After having worked at the euthanasia institutes of Grafeneck and Hadamar.

65. Arad, *Belzec*, 70. Robin O'Neil, *Belzec: Prototype for the Final Solution*. Rudolf Reder, *Belzec* (Krakow: Fundacja Judaica w Krakowie, 1999).

66. Arad. *Belzec*, 70.

67. Jochen von Lang. *Eichmann Interrogated* (Cambridge, MA: Da Capo Press, 1999). Arad, *Belzec*. Christopher Browning. *Fateful Months*.

68. Laurence Rees: Auschwitz: Inside the Nazi State.

69. Arad, *Belzec*.

70. Arad, *Belzec*. The Belzec trial took place in Munich between August 1963 and January 1964.

71. Saul Friedlander, *Counterfeit Nazi* (New York: Knopf, 1969), 116-120.

72. Friedlander, *Counterfeit Nazi*, 116-120.

73. Saul Friedlander, *Pius XII and the Third Reich* (New York: Alfred A. Knopf, 1966). *Kurt Gerstein*, New York, 1970.

74. Gerstein was arrested after the war in France. He was found dead in his call in 1945, 20 days after his arrest.

75. Friedlander, *Pius XII and the Third Reich*. Gerstein, New York, 1970.

76. Yad Vashem Archives 0-3/1291, 18.

77. StA Dortmund AZ: 45Js 7/61.

78. Klee, Dressen, and Riess, *The Good Old Days*, 240.

79. Wewryk. *To Sobibor and Back*.

80. Willi Dressen, Volker Riess, and Ernst Klee *Those were the Days* (New York: The Free Press, 1988), 245-247.

81. Verdict of LG Dusseldorf AZ 81 Ks 2/64, 81.

82 . Dressen, Riess and Klee, *Those were the Days*, 245-247.

83. Dressen, Riess and Klee, *The Good Old Days*, 245-247.

84. Verdict of LG Dusseldorf AZ 81 Ks 2/64, 81.

85. Wiernik. *A Year in Treblinka*. Donat, *The Death Camp Treblinka*.

86. War Diary of the Oberquartiermeister, Mbfh Polen, 1.5..41-31.12.43, in National Archives, T-501/219/461. Christopher Browning in Irving vs. Lipstadt trial.

87. Gita Sereny, *Into the Darkness*, 109-111.

88. Arad, *Belzec.*

89. Testimony of Franz Stangl at his trial in Düsseldorf (Sep. 1969–Dec. 1970).

90. The Kurt Franz photo album. Bundesarchiv No. 183-F0918-0201-011. ARC archives.

91. Adalbert Rüerl, NS-Vernichtungslager im Spiegel deutscher Strafprozesse: Belzec, Sobibor, Treblinka, Chelmno (Munich, 1977). Operation Reinhard.

92. Höss. *Death Dealer, 32.*

*93 . PBS, Auschwitz Inside the Nazi State. (2004-2005).*

94. Interrogation of Hoess on April 30, 1946. Dr Grawitz also witnessed the burning, once.

95. The *Nuremberg Trial*, Macmillan Publishers Limited, London, 1984. Raul Hilberg, *Documents of Destruction*: Germany and Jewry 1933-1945, (Chicago Il: Quadrangle Books, 1971), 50-51.

96. Müller, *Eyewitness Auschwitz*, 132-133, 143.

97. Müller, *Eyewitness Auschwitz*, 139.

98. Interview of Judge M. M. Musmanno. Heritage and Hope: Dialogues in Judaism. Thomas Yoseloff, 1965.

99. Interview published in the tabloid *Bild* in 2005.

100. Interview of Judge M. M. Musmanno. Heritage and Hope: Dialogues in Judaism. Thomas Yoseloff, 1965.

101. Rudolf Vrba, Alan Bestic *Escape from Auschwitz: I Cannot Forgive*, (New York: Grove Press, 1968) 158-59, 165-166.

102. Communique of the Polish-Soviet Extraordinary Commission for Investigating the Crimes Committed by the Germans In the Majdanek Extermination Camp In Lublin. (Moscow: Foreign Langauges Publishing House, 1944).

103. Saul Friedlander, *Kurt Gerstein*, (New York: Albert Knopf, 1969). Jennifer Rosenberg, *Kurt Gerstein - A German Spy in the SS,* Article in About.Com.

104. Christopher Browning, *Evidence for the Implementation of the Final Solution* (Report Produced at the Pacific Lutheran University, Tacoma, Washington, 2000).

105 . Browning, *Evidence for the Implementation.* Arad, *Belzec.*

106. Arad *Belzec.*

107. Müller, *Eyewitness Auschwitz*, 136.

108. Müller, *Eyewitness Auschwitz*, 136. Glowna Komisja Badania Zbrodni Niemieckich w Polsce.

109. Glowna Komisja Badania Zbrodni Niemieckich w Polsce.

110. *Communique of the Polish-Soviet Extraordinary Commission For Investigating the Crimes Committed by the Germans In the Majdanek Extermination Camp In Lublin..* Foreign Langauges Publishing House Moscow 1944.

111. Report of the Central Commission for Investigation of German Crimes in Poland. (Warsaw, 1946, 1947) Extermination Camp Chelmno (Kulmhof) Part I.

112. Müller, *Eyewitness Auschwitz*, 65.

113. Müller, *Eyewitness Auschwitz*, 68.

114. Müller, *Eyewitness Auschwitz*, 136.

115. Müller, *Eyewitness Auschwitz*, 99. Hoss, 45. Mendelsohn. *The Holocaust*, 114.

116. Jozef Marszalek, *Majdanek: The Concentration Camp of Lublin* (Warsaw, 1986), 142-143.

117. Robert Lewis Koehl, *The Black Corps: The Structure and Power Struggles of the Nazi SS* (University of Wisconsin Press, 1983), 113, 119-120. Brandt coordinated the different branches of the SS. Beger participated under Ernst Schäffer in the famous Nazi expedition to Tibet (1938-1939).

118. Michael Kater, *Das "Ahnenerbe" der SS 1935–1945. Ein Beitrag zur Kultur–politik des Dritten Reiches*, (Munich 1997).

119. Müller, *Eyewitness Auschwitz*, 46-47.

120. Norman Davies, *God's Playground: A History of Poland* (New York: Columbia Univ., 1982), vol. 2, 457; Max Weinreich, *Hitler's Professors* (New York: Yivo, 1946), 200; Leon Poliakov and J. Wulff, *Das Dritte Reich und seine Diener* (East Berlin: Volk und Welt, 1975), 165 (photo caption).

121. He was a native of Danzig who lived at no. 2, Betschergasse, Danzig; His mother lived in Danzig at no. 10, Neuschottland Street.

122. Avalon Project, The Nuremberg Trial Proceedings, Vol. 7, 19 February 1946 IMT USSR-272.

123. Avalon Project, 19 February 1946. IMT USSR-272.

124. Avalon Project, 19 February 1946. IMT USSR-272.

125. Avalon Project, 19 February 1946. IMT USSR-272 Document USSR-197.

126. Nizkor Project. The Trial of German Major War Criminals Sitting at Nuremberg, Germany 14th February to 26th February, 1946. The text of the original formula is kept among the proceedings of the Special State Commission in Moscow.

127. Nizkor Project. The Trial of German Major War Criminals Sitting at Nuremberg, Germany 14th February to 26th February, 1946.

128. Document USSR-197.

129. Alexander Werth. *Russia at War 1941-1945*. (New York: Avon, 1965), 918. Republished by Carroll and Graf Publishers, NY.

130. Shirer, *Rise and Fall*, 1264.

131. IMT, Blue Series, vol. 1, 252.

132. IMT, Blue Series; Nuremberg: 1947-1949, vol. 7, pp. 597-600.

133. Sereny, *Into That Darkness*, 141.

134. Dr. Susanne Heim. The Contribution of Nazi Scientists to Nazi Rule in Germany. Confession of Historical Responsibility by President Hubert Markl in Max Planck Society's declaration on the symposium "Biomedical Sciences and Human Experimentation at Kaiser Wilhelm Institutes–The Auschwitz Connection" on June 7–8, 2001 in Berlin, Germany.

135. United States of America vs. Karl Brandt et al. The "Medical Case" IV. Opening Statement of the Prosecution by brigadier General Telford Taylor, 9 December 1946. Part 2, (NO–035).

136. United States of America vs. Karl Brandt.

137. Gerald Reitlinger *The Final Solution* (London, Sphere Books, 1971). Ulf Schmidt. *Karl Brandt, The Nazi Doctor: Medicine and Power in the Third Reich*.

138.Stanislau Klodzinski, *Sterilisation und Kastration durch Röntgenstrahlen im Auschwitz-Lager. Verbrechen Horst Schumann" in Internationales Auschwitz-Komitee (Hrsg.) "Unmenschliche Medizin" Anthologie, Bd. 1, Teil 2*, (Warschau 1969). Vera

Laska, Ed., *Women in the Resistance and in the Holocaust: The Voices of Eyewitnesses.* (Westport, CT: Greenwood Press, 1983).

139. Gerald L. Posner and John Ware, *Mengele: The Complete Story* (New York: Dell, 1987). Gerald Astor, *The 'Last' Nazi: The Life and Times of Dr. Joseph Mengele* (Toronto: Paperjacks, 1986).

140. Holocaust and Genocide Studies. Volume 21, Number 1. 55-72.

141. Holocaust and Genocide Studies. Volume 21, Number 1. 55-72.

142. Paul Weindling, Doris Kaufmann, Ed. *Tales from Nuremberg: The Kaiser Wilhelm Institute for Anthropology and Allied medical war crimes policy. Geschichte der Kaiser-Wilhelm-Gesellschaft im Nationalsozialismus v.2* (Goettingen: Wallstein, 2000), 635-652.

143. United States of America vs. Karl Brandt et al. The "Medical Case" IV. Opening Statement of the Prosecution by brigadier General Telford Taylor, 9 December 1946. Auschwitz-Birkenau State Museum Publications.

144. Auschwitz-Birkenau State Museum Publications.

145. Eva Moses Kor and Mary Wright. *Echoes from Auschwitz: Dr. Mengele's Twins: The story of Eva and Miriam Mozes* (Terre Haute, In.: C.A.N.D.L.E.S Holocaust Museum, 1995).

146. Robert Jay Lifton, *The Nazi Doctors: Medical Killing and the Psychology of Genocide* (New York: Basic Books, 1986), 344.

147. Miklos Nyisli, *Auschwitz: A Doctor's Eyewitness Account,* (New York: Arcade Paperbacks, 1960). Gisella Perl, *I Was a Doctor in Auschwitz,* I.U.P. (1948).

148. Lifton, *The Nazi Doctors,* 23-45, 337-383. Benno Muller-Hill, *Todliche Wissenschaft: Die Ausorderung von Juden, Zigeunern und Geisteskraken,* 1933-1945, (Hamburg, 1985), pp. 71-85, 120-130, 157-164. Barry Mehler, *A History of the American Eugenics Society* (University of Illinois, 1988), The Nazi Experiments by Ruth Guttmann.

149. Vivien Spitz. *Doctors from Hell: The Horrific Account of Nazi Experiments on Humans.* (Boulder Co.: Sentient Publications, 2005). United States of America vs. Karl Brandt et al. The "Medical Case" IV. Opening Statement of the Prosecution by brigadier General Telford Taylor, 9 December 1946.

150. United States of America vs. Karl Brandt et al. The "Medical Case."

# Chapter 10
## The Final Solution in Christian Europe

### The Wansee Conference

On December 1941, Göhring instructed Reinhard Heydrich (1904-1942) to call together a conference of the representatives of the Nazi Party, the SS, and fifteen government ministries to coordinate the Final Solution in Europe. The Wansee Conference was not called together to decide the Final Solution. At that time, it was already underway for many months. Hundreds of thousands of Jews had already been slaughtered in the occupied Soviet territories by the Einsatzgruppen and the death camps were already being put into operation. The conference was called to formally introduce the Master Plan of the annihilation of European Jewry to the representatives of these bodies to better coordinate and accelerate its implementation. Set initially for December 9, 1941, the Wansee Conference took place more than a month later, on January 20, 1942, in a villa at the shores of the Wansee Lake confiscated from, the famous German Jewish Impressionist painter Max Liebermann (1847-1935).

The minutes of the conference discovered among the files of the German Foreign Office in 1947, were written in a veiled coded language well understood by Nazi leaders. Eichmann who edited them, later testified at his trial in Israel in 1961 that the talk was all about killing and liquidation, disguised in the protocol by euphemisms such as evacuation and special treatment. In his introductory address, Heydrich informed the participants of the Wansee Conference that the Final Solution of the Jewish question in the totality of Europe had been entrusted to ReichsFührer SS Heinrich Himmler to coordinate all offices concerned:

> The final solution of the Jewish question in Europe makes necessary an initial common action of all central offices immediately concerned with these questions in order to bring their general activities into line. The ReichsFührer-SS (Heinrich Himmler) and the Chief of the German Police (Chief of the Security

Police and the SD) was entrusted with the official central handling of the final
solution of the Jewish question without regard to geographic borders.[1]

Heydrich stated that Europe was to be combed through from west to east
for Jews to be "evacuated group by group into transit ghettos and transported
from there to the East":

> Another possible solution of the problem has now taken the place of emigra-
> tion, i.e. the evacuation of the Jews to the East . . . In the course of the practical
> execution of the final solution, Europe will be combed through from west to
> east . . . The evacuated Jews will first be sent, group by group, to so-called
> transit ghettos, from which they will be transported to the East . . . The possible
> final remnant will, since it will undoubtedly consist of the most resistant por-
> tion, have to be treated accordingly, because it is the product of natural selec-
> tion and would, if released, act as the seed of a new Jewish revival (see the ex-
> perience of history).[2]

Assured at the height of their military successes that all of Europe including Great Britain would shortly be under Nazi domination or control, Heydrich
presented a master plan of the Final Solution covering all of Europe. Making a
distinction between the countries already under the control of the Third Reich at
the moment (marked A in the list) and those that would eventually come under
its control (marked B), which included England, Ireland, Sweden, Switzerland,
Turkey, Spain, and Portugal. Heydrich presented a detailed list with the number
of Jews in each of these countries to be disposed of in the Final Solution, which
came to a total of approximately 11 million Jews. He made clear that the list did
not include baptized Jews although they should also be included according to
Nazi racial definition:

### THE FINAL SOLUTION OF THE JEWISH QUESTION IN EUROPE

| Country | Number |
| --- | --- |
| A | |
| Germany proper | 131,800 |
| Austria | 43,700 |
| Eastern territories | 420,000 |
| Generalgouvernement | 2,284,000 |
| Bialystok | 400,000 |
| Protectorate Bohemia and Moravia | 74,200 |
| Estonia | free of Jews |
| Latvia | 3,500 |
| Lithuania | 34,000 |
| Belgium | 43,000 |
| Denmark | 5,600 |
| France / occupied territory | 165,000 |
| Unoccupied territory | 700,000 |

| | |
|---|---|
| Greece | 69,600 |
| Netherlands | 160,800 |
| Norway | 1,300 |
| B | |
| Bulgaria | 48,000 |
| England | 330,000 |
| Finland | 2,300 |
| Ireland | 4,000 |
| Italy, including Sardinia | 58,000 |
| Albania | 200 |
| Croatia | 40,000 |
| Portugal | 3,000 |
| Romania, including Bessarabia | 342,000 |
| Sweden | 8,000 |
| Switzerland | 18,000 |
| Serbia | 10,000 |
| Slovakia | 88,000 |
| Spain | 6,000 |
| Turkey (European portion) | 55,500 |
| Hungary | 742,800 |
| USSR | 5,000,000 |
| Ukraine | 2,994,684 |
| White Russia (excluding Bialystok ) | 446,484 |
| | |
| Total | ≥ 11,000,000 |

The participants at the conference were Josef Bühler, Adolf Eichmann, Roland Freisler, Reinhard Heydrich, Otto Hofmann, Gerhard Klopfer, Friedrich Wilhelm Kritzinger, Rudolf Lange, Georg Leibbrandt, Martin Luther, Heinrich Müller, Erich Neumann, Karl Eberhard Schöngarth, Wilhelm Stuckar. They discussed the degree of cooperation they might expect in the different European countries to deliver their Jews for deportation to the east. They felt assured that with the exception of the Scandinavian countries they would find no opposition. They expressed satisfaction that in the two Catholic clero-Fascist states of Slovakia and Croatia "the matter is no longer so difficult, since the most substantial problems in this respect have already been brought near a solution." No one at the conference was even concerned about the possibility of any opposition from the Catholic Church.

Phillip Bühler (1899-1945), the former head of the euthanasia program in Hitler's chancellery and now state secretary of the Generalgouvernement, urged that the Final Solution should begin as quickly as possible in the Generalgouvernement "since on the one hand transportation does not play such a large role here nor would problems of labor supply hamper this action considering that of the approximately 2.5 million Jews concerned, the majority is unfit for work."

He recommended that "certain preparatory activities for the final solution should be carried out immediately, but alarming the populace must be avoided."

The participants agreed that "persons of mixed blood of the first degree should be treated as Jews," in accordance with the racial principles of the Nuremberg Laws. Sterilization of those exempt from evacuation was agreed upon "to prevent any offspring and to eliminate the problem of persons of mixed blood once and for all." They agreed that even individuals of mixed blood of the second degree should not be exempt from evacuation if they had "a racially undesirable appearance that marks them outwardly as a Jew."[3]

Ten days after the Wansee Conference, Hitler declared in a speech at the Sports Palace in Berlin recorded by the Allied monitoring service:

> The result of this war will be the complete annihilation of the Jews . . . the hour will come when the most evil universal enemy of all time will be finished, at least for a thousand years.[4]

When the prospects of serving the German people a quick military victory vanished in 1942, the Final Solution gained greater urgency in the eyes of Hitler and his henchmen. Even if he lost in the battlefields he could still appear in the eyes of the Germans as victor handing them a surrogate victory—the annihilation of the defenseless Jews of Europe. On June 23, 1942, Victor Brack[5] wrote to Himmler from the Führer's chancellery warning him that "unforeseen circumstances" might stop the Final Solution and urging him to accelerate its completion:

> BrigadeFührer Globocnik has stated that the campaign against the Jews should be carried out as quickly as possible, as unforeseen difficulties might stop the campaign altogether and then we should be stuck in the middle of the road. You yourself, ReichsFührer, some time ago drew my attention to the necessity of finishing this work quickly, if for no other reason than the necessity to mask it. In view of my own experience I now regard both attitudes, which after all have one and the same end in view, as all the more justified.[6]

With the opening of the death camps in Poland, the Final Solution entered its ultimate decisive stage. Deportation transports from all over Europe traveled directly to the camps where the deportees were gassed immediately upon arrival. The ghettos in Poland were emptied and liquidated with incredible speed. By the end of 1943 all of Europe was practically Judenfrei with the exception of Hungary. It only took a few months for Hungarian Jewry to be annihilated in 1944 in Auschwitz.

Before the death camps were put in operation, the victims deported from Western Europe were sent to the ghettoes of Minsk, Kovno, and Riga to be liquidated by the Einsatzgruppen in the nearby forests. They shared with the local Jews the same tragic end in front of the execution squads of the Einsatzgruppen. As soon as the death camps started to operate in early 1942, trains began to bring the deportees directly to their doorstep. On March 27, 1942, began the deportation of 75,721 French Jews from Drancy; on July 16, 1942, the deportation of 100,000 Dutch Jews from Westerbork and of 25,631 Belgian Jews from Mechelen (Malines); on October 25, 1942 the deportation of 767 Norwegian Jews from Oslo. Hungary was the last country to deport its Jews to death camps. From May 15 to July 1944, over 450,000 Hungarian Jews were deported and gassed in Auschwitz-Birkenau in the short period of only ten weeks.

Most Jews from Western Europe were deported to Auschwitz-Birkenau to be gassed, but some were also shipped to Reinhard Operation camps whose main mission was to annihilate the 3 million Polish Jews. Sobibor received 34,313 Jews from the Netherlands in addition to 6,000 deportees from Slovakia and 4,000 from France. Majdanek received around 130,000 Jews from the Third Reich, France, Belgium, Italy, the Netherlands, Czechoslovakia, Greece, Yugoslavia, Denmark, Norway, and others. Personal documents found in Majdanek represent every country in Europe. Treblinka received 7,000 deportees from the Third Reich, 8,000 from Slovakia, 4,000 from Theresienstadt, and 7,000 from Macedonia. Mali Trostinec, near Minsk, which served as a killing site for the Jews of Byelorussia, also received Jews from Western Europe who were exterminated hours or days after their arrival. Chelmno received around 15,000 Jews from Germany, Austria, Czechoslovakia, and Luxemburg.

The Nazi ultimate goal was to exterminate 11 million European Jews. They managed to murder around 6 million Jews, the most dynamic and lively part of the Jewish people. The rest survived only because the Third Reich was defeated and could not put its hand on them.

## The Balance Sheet of the Final Solution

Many have undertaken the task of estimating the number of victims of the Final Solution. Notwithstanding the differences in the methods used, there is a remarkable consistence in the estimates of different assessments that confirm the magnitude of that cataclysmic event. The conclusion that Hitler annihilated at least 6 million Jews in Europe between 1939 and 1945 is well substantiated. The following summary of death toll estimates and their numerical range reveal the order of magnitude of the Holocaust in different countries, and their relative place in the total balance. Poland and Russia alone account for two-thirds of the victims of the Holocaust and occupy the first places on the list. Nonetheless, it is important to keep in mind that even in those countries where the Jewish communities were small, such as Lithuania, almost all the Jewish population was annihilated (95 percent).

STATISTICS OF THE FINAL SOLUTION [7]

| COUNTRY | N° OF VICTIMS |
|---|---|
| Poland (1939) | 2,900,000 - 3,271,000 |
| - Western Poland | 1,600,000 |

| | |
|---|---|
| - Eastern Poland | 1,210,000 |
| USSR (1939) | 1,050,000 - 1,316,500 |
| - Belarus | 250,000 |
| - Ukraine | 656,000 |
| Hungary (1940) | 410,000 - 569,000 |
| - Transylvania | 105,000 |
| Romania | 271,000 - 287,000 |
| - Bessarabia | 200,000 |
| - Bucovina | 124,600 |
| Baltic Countries | 220,000 |
| - Lithuania (1939) | 140,000 |
| - Latvia (1939) | 70,000 - 77,000 |
| - Estonia (1939) | 1,000 - 1,500 |
| Czechoslovakia (1940) | 203,000 - 217,000 |
| - Protectorate | 77,297 |
| - Slovakia | 66,000 |
| - Ruthenia | 60,000 |
| Germany | 150,000 - 195,000 |
| Netherlands | 100,000 - 120,000 |
| France | 76,134 - 140,000 |
| Greece | 59,000 - 67,000 |
| Yugoslavia | 56,000 - 65,000 |
| Austria | 49,000 - 53,000 |
| Belgium | 28,518 - 57,000 |
| Italy | 7,680 - 20,000 |
| Luxemburg | 1,950 - 3,000 |
| Macedonia | 7,122 |
| Denmark | 1,500 |
| Norway | 1,000 |
| Albania | 591 |

At the end of the war, General Dwight D. Eisenhower (1890-1969) antic-ipated with rare foresight the possibility that the Nazis and their heirs would eventually deny the facts of the Final Solution. He therefore requested that Con-gress, the media, and the film industry should send representatives to witness with their own eyes the remnants of the camps. When he toured on April 12, 1945, the Ohrdruf-Nord camp in the company of Generals George Patton and Omar Bradley he came face to face for the first time with Nazi inhumanity. The dead bodies of the camp inmates had been left just as they had been found by the American soldiers on April 4, 1945, in the abandoned camp. Eisenhower de-scribed in his book *Crusade in Europe* the day he visited the Ohrdruf-Nord camp and the salt mines that held treasures looted by the Nazis:

I have never felt able to describe my emotional reactions when I first came face to face with indisputable evidence of Nazi brutality and ruthless diisregard of every shred of decency . . . I am certain, however, that I have never at any other time experienced an equal sense of shock.

I visited every nook and cranny of the camp because I felt it my duty to be in a position from then on to testify at first hand about these things in case there ever grew up at home the belief or assumption that the stories of Nazi brutality were just propaganda . . . I not only did so but as soon as I returned to Patton's headquarters that evening, I sent communications to both Washington and London, urging the two governments to send instantly to Germany a random group of newspaper editors and representative groups from the national legislatures. [8]

# The Deportations

The emigration office created before the war by Heydrich and Eichmann to expel the Jews from the Third Reich was transformed into a far more sinister organization when the Russian campaign began. In a communication from Göring to Heydrich in July 1941, he ordered him to update the function of the Reich Central Office for Emigration of Jews and make preparations to an overall solution of the Jewish Question in the German sphere of influence. Under the pretense that the Jews were being taken to be "resettled in the east" the emigration office now delivered them to the doorsteps of the death camps and transit ghettoes.[9]

The implementation of the Final Solution depended on the readiness of the governments of Europe to deliver their Jewish citizens into German hands. The governments of Slovakia, Croatia, Vichy France, Belgium, the Italian Salo Republic, and Hungary did not need any prodding to go along with the Führer's wishes. The anti-Semitic laws and decrees adopted by these Catholic countries opened the way for the deportations to the ghettoes in the ex-Soviet territories and to the death camps in Poland. With necessary anti-Semitic legislation already in place, the client governments would typically organize a public campaign well supported by the Nazi and Catholic press demanding that the Jews in their midst be deported "to defend Christian society from the Jews."

Eichmann negotiated with European governments to deliver to him their Jewish population for deportation to the east. His gang of ruthless SS villains of the Reich Main Security Office (RSHA) such as Rolf Günther, Alois Brunner, Theodor Dannecker, Dieter Wisliceny, Otto Hunsche, Hermann Krumey, Frank Novak, Friedrich Suhr, Heinz Röthke, and others, did not overlook a single corner in Europe in search of Jews for deportation, always making sure that their office would benefit from their confiscated assets. With the assistance of *Evakuierungsgruppen* (evacuation teams) and the help of local police and military forces they would lay their hands on every Jew and Jewess, wherever he/she could be found, whether in their homes, workplaces, or streets and taken to detention centers and deportation stations where they were deported. Jews of every age, gender, and condition were rounded up, insuring a steady stream of trains and trucks to the east.[10] These deportation officials were as much a part of the Final Solution as the operators of the gas chambers or the Einsatzgruppen.[11]

The German Reichsbahn and the Ostbahn played a key role in the deportation process transporting the Jews Eichmann's teams rounded up. They profited from the deportations, receiving from the government one-third of a third-class ticket for every Jew transported in their boxcars. Endless convoys of trains tightly packed with thirsty, hungry, dying Jews were moving from all over Europe to the death camps. As transportation administrator of the trains carrying Jews to their death, Eichmann made sure that the necessary vehicles were always available, although they were badly needed for the war-effort. "No Jew was left alive for lack of transport," said Hilberg. "The machinery of death worked like clockwork," said Eichmann in Jerusalem.

With the prospect of acquiring the properties, left behind by the Jews, Nazi satellites such as Slovakia were even willing to pay the Germans for every Jew deported. "They offered us their Jews as discarded beer cans," said Eichmann in Jerusalem. Their German overlords would then reciprocate and declare themselves ready to assist them in the task of "solving their Jewish problem." At departure points local police forces working for the SS evacuation teams would rob the deportees even of their most essential personal belongings, brutally forcing them into the boxcars that would transport them to their death.

To facilitate the killing processs, the deportation trips themselves were converted into mass murder operations. The Jews were packed into hermetically closed boxcars whose floors were covered with burning lime. The number of passengers crammed in each car far exceeded their normal capacity, with the result that there barely was space to stand or even breathe. The deportees traveled for days on end without water or food. A single bucket was all that an average of 200 people had available for their physical needs. The unbearable stench would add another terrible dimension to the trip that often took many days and even weeks depending on where it originated. On occasions, roofless cargo cars were used in the severest winter conditions.

Denying water to the deportees along the journey was a calculated method to break their resistance. Fillip Müller describes the suffering inflicted on a transport of desperately thirsty Jews traveling from Hungary to Auschwitz:

> Moll explained to the waiting crowd that now it would really not be long before they were given a drink. Several of the people were so desperately thirsty that they crouched on the ground licking the dew-wet grass. When the long-promised drink failed to materialize the people began to grow restless, distressed above all by the piteous cries and entreaties of their children who were begging their mothers for just a few drops of water . . . This pre-programmed suffering was deliberately aimed at paralyzing the ability to notice things and the will to resist in order to allow the giant machinery of murder to run smoothly and at full speed . . . In Moll's strategy of extermination the reduction of vital energies by producing thirst played a carefully planned and psychologically important part.[12]

The number of dead often exceeded the number of survivors at the arrival. The train that brought the deportees from the Island of Corfu for a "vacation trip" to Europe arrived at Auschwitz after a trip of twenty-seven days without one live passenger aboard![13] Even in short trips the results were devastating. A report by German Police Reserve Lieutenant Westermann on the deportation of 8,205 Jews from Kolomyja to Belzec arrived with 2,000 dead passangers, one-fourth of the total.[14]

The barbaric round-up actions and deportation of Jews in cattle trains headed to the East was a daily public spectacle witnessed by the population all over Europe. The deportation was a public spectacle not a secret operation. Hundreds of thousands of Jews from every European country, Slovakia, the Netherlands, France, Belgium, Luxembourg, Norway, Italy, Yugoslavia, Romania, Hungary, Greece, even as far as Rhodes and Corfu offshore, were deported to extermination centers.

It goes without saying that the Vatican was well informed of the deportations by its own representatives all over Europe and by the desperate calls of help from the Jewish communities that turned to them to intervene on their behalf. Church authorities in every country were spectators and often actors involved in a variety of ways in the cruel drama that led directly to the killing sites in the East and were deaf to these tragic calls of help. The deportation of Jews from Rome to Auschwitz, later reviewed, is a paradigm of that callous attitude. Nevertheless, there still are those who maintain that these mass deportations took place without the clergy or the Vatican knowing about them.

## The Final Solution in the Greater Reich

After the invasion of the Soviet Union in June 1941, a decree ordering the deportation of the Jews from the Reich for "resettlement in the east" was issued. Every Jew in the Third Reich above the age of six was required to wear the Yellow Star in public. On September 18, 1941, Himmler informed the gauleiter of the Warthegau, Arthur Greiser, that the Jews in the Reich would be sent to the Lodz ghetto in the Warthegau, in accordance with Hitler's wish:

> The Führer wishes that the Old Reich and Protectorate be emptied and freed of Jews from west to east as quickly as possible. [15]

On October 10, 1941, Heydrich announced in Prague Hitler's immediate objective of clearing Germany of Jews by the end of the year. Jews of the Greater Reich would be sent to the ghettoes of Lodz, Riga, Minsk, and Kovno for "resettlement." The deportations to the Lodz ghetto took place between October 15 and October 31, with 25,000 Jews, mostly elderly people from Berlin, Prague, Vienna, Frankfurt, Cologne, Luxembourg, and Düsseldorf. They were all gassed in the following weeks in the nearby Chelmno death camp.

According to the balance sheet presented by Heydrich at the Wansee Conference, up to October 30, 1941, a total of 537,000 Jews had been cleared from the Greater Reich: 360,000 from Germany; 147,000 from Austria, and 30,000 from the Protectorate. There were still 163,000 Jews living in Germany at that moment.[16] The deportations from the Reich to the ghettoes were a prelude to their annihilation by the Einsatzgruppen or in the death camps. On October 23, Himmler issued an order to Heinrich Müller, the chief of the Reich's Security Office that no Jew should be allowed to leave from occupied Europe.

Around 20,057 Jews from Berlin, Wien, Munich, and other German cities were deported to the Riga ghetto between November 27, 1941, and February 21, 1942, in twenty-two convoys. Many of them were killed upon arrival by the Einsatzgruppen either by shooting or with gas vans. No more than 3 percent of them survived. One transport that left for Riga on November 28, 1941, carrying approximately 1,000 Jews from Berlin was liquidated hours after its arrival on November 30, 1941 in Rumbula, together with about 4,000 local Jews. In Kovno the Einsatzgruppen executed more than 30,000 Jews from Austria, Germany, and France at the Ninth Fort. Abraham Wechsler, a French Jew of Limoges, inscribed before his death on a wall of the Ninth Fort: "We are 900 Frenchmen."

Another 35,442 Jews from Greater Germany were deported to the Minsk ghetto. They were separated from local Jews in a Sonderghetto known as Ghetto Hamburg adjoined to the main ghetto. Every night seventy to eighty Jews of Ghetto Hamburg would be taken to be liquidated either by shooting or gas vans. The Commissioner General of White Russia, Gauleiter Wilhelm Kube, who felt no regrets with annihilating local Jews, had some misgivings with regard to the German Jews. He wrote to his superior Reich Commissioner Heinrich Lohse on December 16, 1941:

> I beg you to send me instructions . . . These Jews include war veterans, holders
> of the Iron Cross, those wounded in war, half-Aryans, and even three-quarter
> Aryans . . . I do not lack hardness and I am ready to contribute to the solution
> of the Jewish problem, but people who come from the same cultural circles as
> ourselves are different from the bestial, aboriginal hordes. [17]

A "showcase ghetto" was established in Theresienstadt, in northwest Czechoslovakia, on November 24, 1941, for the deportation of special categories of Jews from the Greater Reich such as decorated World War I veterans, prominent personalities, and people over sixty. Actually, Theresienstadt was only a stopover to the death camps and Einsatzgruppen killing sites. At least 139,654 Jews were deported to Theresienstadt: 42,104 from Germany, 15,253 from Austria, and 75,666 from Czechoslovakia.[18] Of them, 86,934 were taken to Auschwitz and other death camps, while 33,430 died from disease and starvation in Theresienstadt ghetto itself.[19] Only 16,832 of the original deportees survived the war in the ghetto, which existed until the end of the war.

During November 1941 at the height of the deportations, Cardinal Faulhaber wrote to Cardinal Bertram, president of the Fulda Bishops conference, that he was being asked by lay people whether the bishops could not do something about the "brutal deportation of non-Aryans to Poland under inhuman conditions paralleled only in the African slave trade." Bertram's answer is a replica of the answer given ten years earlier by Faulhaber himself when Oskar Wasserman appealed to him for beleaguered German Jewry and he answered that "for the higher ecclesiastical authorities there are immediate issues of much greater *importance.*" Now, Bertram responded exactly the same words:

> The Bishops must concentrate on other concerns which are more important for the Church and more far reaching; in particular, the ever more urgent question of how best to prevent anti-Christian and anti-Church influences on the education of Catholic youth. [20]

The German bishops, including those who had protested against the euthanasia program, remained silent on the deportation and annihilation of Jews. Their attitude on the Jewish question during the war is aptly described by the late German Church historian Klaus Scholder:

> Active attempts to oppose the mass murder of the Jews and those unfit for labor in the occupied zone, in the East, are so few as to be hardly worth mentioning, measured by the extent of the crime.[21]

The German Bishops had direct information on what was happening on the eastern front through the Catholic chaplains serving in the German army. They were the eyes and ears of their ecclesiastic superiors back home. They witnessed the extermination of the Jews carried out by the Einsatzgruppen. Their reports, oral and written, reached the highest Church authorities. In one letter quoted by historian Klaus Scholder, a Catholic chaplain of the Second Panzer Division, describes the mass execution of the whole Jewish population of Berditchev, men, women, and children, which he witnessed in 1941 after they were forced to undress and dig their own collective grave.[22] Historian Doris Bergen gathered more recently conclusive evidence that the military chaplains were not only eye-witnesses to genocidal crimes, but often important participants.[23] They "normalized," says Bergen, the brutality in which the men in their care were involved and provided group absolution to them.

> The great majority of German military chaplains, Catholics and Protestants, weighed in on the side of the perpetrators, condoning and blessing their crimes through words, actions, and silence. One of the most obvious manifestations of this function was the provision of group absolution for soldiers. [24]

The bishops also had other high-placed informants. Dr. Joseph Muller, an officer in Canaris's Military Intelligence Service who was a confidant of Cardinal Faulhaber kept the cardinal well informed of the annihilation campaign. Another high source of information of Cardinal Faulhaber was Dr. Hans Globke, a Catholic and a high official in the Ministry of the Interior in charge of racial matters. On August 18, 1942, SS Officer Kurt Gerstein (1905-1945) visited Majdanek, Belzec, and Treblinka and witnessed the gassing of Jewish men, women and children. After Papal Nuncio Orsenigo refused to see him, he contacted Dr. Winter, the coadjutor of the Catholic Bishop of Berlin Msgr. Preysing

who received the report in order to forward it to Bishop Preysing and to the
Pope in Rome. In his notes written in 1945 Gerstein writes:

> Taking my life in my hands every moment, I continued to inform hundreds of
> people of these horrible massacres. Among them was . . . Dr. Winter, the coad-
> jutor of the Catholic Bishop of Berlin—so that he could transmit my informa-
> tion to the Bishop and to the Pope. [25]

May 7-8, 1942, the Germans put in operation the extermination center at
Maly Trostinec, near Minsk. Jews arrived at Maly Trostinec from as far as the
Third Reich and France. Many of the deportees were taken directly to the killing
site without stopping in Minsk. When the convoys arrived at the freight terminal
in Minsk, the deportees were told that they were being transferred to houses and
estates around Minsk and that their suitcases would follow them later in trucks.
They had to leave their identification cards, money, and valuables for which
they were given receipts. They were taken directly to the execution sites in the
forests on trucks. Pits 200 feet long and 10 feet deep excavated by Soviet slave
laborers were prepared for them. After undressing and handing over their last
valuables they marched in their underwear to the open pits. They were shot in
the neck by squads of up to 100 Sipo and SD men. Music from a loudspeaker
covered the shots and screams. After the first major aktion of July 31, 1942,
Kube reported to Lohse:

> At Minsk approximately 10,000 Jews were liquidated on July 28 and 29, 1942.
> . . . Most of them had been deported to Minsk last November from Vienna,
> Brunn, Bremen, and Berlin by order of the Fuehrer. [26]

The last Jews from the Reich deported to the Minsk ghetto were liquidated
on March 8, 1943, and autumn 1943 at the time the Minsk ghetto came to its
final end. Only ten Jews from the Reich were still alive in Minsk when the city
was liberated on July 4, 1944, by the Soviet army. From the 9,000 Austrian Jews
deported directly to Maly Trostinec beginning May 6, 1942, only seventeen are
known to have survived.

By the beginning of 1943 the total number of Jews left in the Greater Reich
stood around 75,000 souls. Around 25,000 among them were baptized and married to Aryan women, while 15,000 were married to non-Jewish spouses or were
racially classified as mischlinge. Even when participating in Church services
they were required to wear the Jewish patch. The verbal promise given at the
end of concordat negotiations in 1933 to spare non-Aryans Christians was applied only to those converted before the approval of the Nuremberg Laws on
September 15, 1935. Those baptized afterward were not immune. [27]

Nuncio Cesare Orsenigo who had strong sympathies for the Nazis was
completely indifferent to the tragedy of the Jews but showed some interest in
baptized converts and mixed marriages. When the *Raphaelsverein*, the Catholic
organization to aid the emigration of baptized non-Aryans from Germany, was
closed down by the Gestapo in July 1941 and exit permits were no longer

granted to them, Orsenigo informed the Vatican in January 1942. On July 28, 1942, he again wrote to the Vatican:

> Every intervention even if only in favor of the Catholic non-Aryans was till now rejected with the habitual response that baptismal water does not change Jewish blood and that the German Reich is defending itself from the non-Aryan race, not from the religious confession of baptized Jews. [28]

In November 1942, the Nazis decided to legally annul the mixed marriages of Aryans with non-Aryans, including those carried out prior to the Nuremberg Laws, in order to deport non-Aryan spouses to the east. Orsenigo informed Rome on November 7, 1942. Bishop Konrad von Preysing in a letter to Pius XII in connection with the annulment decree dated February 26, 1943, had some strong words on "the total uselessness of the nuncio;" Orsenigo had told him: "Charity is well and good but the greatest charity is not to make problems for the Church."[29] Concerned for the 5,000 Catholic racially mixed couples in Vienna, Cardinal Innitzer wrote to the Pope on April 3, 1943, criticizing Orsenigo who "is too frightened and is not interested in things as serious as these."

On November 11, 1942, Cardinal Bertram requested in a letter to various ministries of the Reich that the planned annulment ordinance be withdrawn because it infringed on the religious rights of Catholic Christians. The cardinal was only objecting to the deportation of converts but not the deportation of Jews. Bertram reaffirmed in the letter the bishops' patriotic feelings and their awareness of the harmful Jewish influence on German society. It is clear that for men like Bertram and Orsenigo the fate of the Jews meant nothing. Fr. Morley characterizes the role of Orsenigo during his long tenure in Germany (1930-1946) as the nuncio replacing Pacelli:

> His acts of defense, however, were never extended to the Jews . . . It could hardly be expected that he would have acted more forcefully, if indeed he would have acted at all, to defend the rights of German Jews . . . Except during the period when Jews married to Christians were being threatened with the dissolution of their marriages and being deported themselves, he said nothing . . . he apparently felt no similar sympathy for the 100,000 Jews deported. [30]

From February 27 to March 3, 1943, a major roundup campaign was launched by the Gestapo and SS in Berlin. Around 12,000 skilled Jewish workers from 100 weapon factories in Berlin were rounded up for deportation to the death camps. Among them there were thousands of non-Aryan baptized converts and mixed marriages. They were separated from the rest and taken to the Jewish Community Center at Rosenstraße 2-4 to await their deportation to the east. On March 6, 1943 Bishop Preysing wrote to Pius XII about the Berlin roundups informing him that many baptized converts were seized directly from their workplaces to be deported. He appealed to the Pope to intercede for them:

Among the deportees are also many Catholics. Is it not possible for Your Holiness again to intervene for the many unfortunate innocents? It is the last hope for many and the profound wish of all decent people.[31]

Pius XII was not moved to action. He returned the ball to Preysing's court telling him in a much delayed answer dated April 30, 1943, that this was a matter that should be dealt by the local bishops—Preysing should in any case be the one to intervene, if he considered it appropriate:

In the present situation we can unfortunately not offer them any effective help outside Our prayers. We are, however, determined to raise Our voice anew on their behalf as circumstances indicate and permit.[32]

What the Pope, the nuncio and the bishops refused to do was achieved by the German spouses of the men to be deported. In an unprecedented act of daring they staged a protest demonstration in front of the detention center for various days. The Gestapo decided it was preferable to release non-Aryan husbands than to jeopardize the secrecy of the Final Solution. The Jews, however, were sent directly to Auschwitz, while a minority was deported to Theresienstadt.[33] In May 1943 the Third Reich was officially declared Judenfrei. The miraculous survival of the Jewish Hospital in Berlin until the end of the war is still waiting for an explanation.

At the last Fulda Conference that German bishops called together during the war in August 1943, Msgr. Preysing from Berlin failed to convince his colleagues to approve a petition on behalf of baptized non-Aryan deportees. The petition that he had asked Dr. Margarete Sommer to draft, referred to the "crescendo of rumors regarding the mass death of the deported non-Aryans" and the Bishop's duty to take "a protective stance on behalf of many thousands of non-Aryans who have become members of our holy Catholic Church." The statement that "we would stand guilty before G-d and man because of our silence" did not move the bishops and the draft was rejected.

Despite the verbal assurances given by the Nazi government to Bishop Bernning that non-Aryan Catholics would not be deported, around 8,000 non-Aryan converts were rounded up in the Reich and deported in the last stage of the war. The bishops went along with the resettlement hoax and limited their interventions exclusively to enquire whether Catholic pastoral care was being denied to them in their new locations. In January 1944, Cardinal Bertram wrote to the Nazi Minister of the Interior in reference to deportations of non-Aryan Christians. While pleading for them he was expressing his acquiescence to the murder of the Jews:

The German Catholics would feel deeply hurt if these fellow Christians now would have to meet a fate similar to the Jews.[34]

Johann Neumann, a German emeritus professor of sociology of law and religion at the University of Tübingen addressed the issue of the appalling record of the German Church with regard to the Jews in a memorable lecture at the university in 1995. He eloquently put forward the rhetorical question: "Where was the obedience to the word of God that the churches normally swore to uphold? Was the commandment 'Thou shall not kill' no longer the word of God in the Third Reich?"

> Not only did the Christians as believers fail morally, but above all the churches as institutions did so, too . . . Like so many others in the Nazi period, the churches didn't set any standard for moral behavior. On the contrary, with their directives about the authority sanctioned by God they soothed the troubled consciences of many Germans, and indeed they discredited and often criminalized the voice of individual conscience. The churches were mirrors of their society, but in no way models of moral behavior. [35]

The affinity between the churches and the Nazis, and the failure of the churches to oppose them is rooted, contended Neumann, not only in their latent anti-Semitism but in the Christian fondness for authority that the Nazis inherited from the Church, making them undistinguishable on many issues. Their millennial anti-Semitism could understand and even accept Hitler's genocidal "logic." Church leaders were silent contends Neumann, not due to fear but rather, as Lutheran Bishop Heinrich Rendtorff stated at the height of the Hitler era, "from considerations of principle."

## The Final Solution in Slovakia

Slovakia promulgated its harsher and more demanding second anti-Semitic *Codex Judaicus* on September 9, 1941. Every Jew was required to wear a yellow armband with a Star of David, and was banned from traveling in the same trains with non-Jews. They were required to surrender all gold and bank deposits to the government and transfer their factories to Aryan ownership. Jews were to serve in forced labor battalions. In preparation of the confiscation of Jewish property, Jews were required to register all their real estate property and identify their enterprises as Jewish. Slovak custodians were appointed to carry out the process of Aryanization. Implementation of the second Codex Judaicum followed without delay. During October 1941, 15,000 Jews were expelled from Bratislava and taken to concentration camps in rural towns such as Sered, Novaky, and Vyhne. Forced labor was imposed on able-bodied Jews in the camps.[36]

The second codex annuled the exemptions that baptized converts had been granted in the first. In line with the Nazi approach established in the Nuremberg Laws, they were subjected to the same anti-Semitic regulations as the Jews. Mixed racial marriages were outlawed, which meant that Jews converted to Catholicism could not marry Aryan Catholics.

Slovak Catholic bishops assembled in full in Bratislava on October 7, 1941, to discuss the second Codex Judaicus. Although the bishops did not object to its harsh measures against the Jews, they objected to the use of race as a criterion of identification of Jews and to the inclusion of baptized converts in anti-

Jewish legislation. The restriction of marriages between non-Aryan Catholics (Jews in Nazi terms) and Aryan Catholics was seen by them as an invasion of Church rights. Their implied support for anti-Jewish legislation and their objections were expressed in a joint statement addressed to Tiso in which they requested that the state rely upon the clergy to establish the identity of converts and their religious and nationalistic sincerity.

Apostolic Delegate Msgr. Burzio forwarded the text of the second Codex Judaicum to the Vatican secretariat of state for study. As elsewhere, the Vatican did not object to the exclusion of the Jews from civil society but expressed its opposition to the infringement of Church rights and the measures taken against non-Aryan Catholics. Cardinal Maglione expressed disappointment that a country honored with the "best Catholic tradition" should adopt an ordinance that diminished Church rights by prohibiting marriages between Catholics due to racial differences, excluding the children of baptized converts from general schools, in contravention to canon law.[37] He was concerned that many of these children would end up attending Jewish schools where they would lose their contact with the Church, requiring "heroic actions to remain faithful subjects of the Church."

Following Vatican instructions, Msgr. Burzio visited President Tiso, a loyal son of the Church, and pointed out to him that by including Catholic converts of Jewish ancestry in the category of Jews, around 3,000 Catholic converts would have to wear the Star of David "like the rest of the Jews." Burzio was appeased when Tiso told him that the requirement would be waved for converts that were baptized before September 9, 1941, the date at which the law was promulgated. This case, as many others, has been used to misrepresent the position of the Church, as if it stood up in defense of the Jews, when in truth it was agreeing to the anti-Jewish legislation as long as it did not affect the rights of the Church and of baptized Catholic converts in this most Christian of lands. Fr. John Morley states:

> Maglione's letter of protest to Sidor on November 12, 1941, did not deal with, nor did it intend to, the injustices committed against the Jews. Maglione made it very clear he was defending the rights of Catholics of "Jewish origin." [38]

Negotiations to deport Jews from Slovakia to Poland to clear the country from Jews began near the end of 1941 before the Wansee Conference. President Tiso and Interior Minister Alexander (Sano) Mach were summoned to Hitler and also met with Himmler to discuss deportation. The Codex Judaicus provided the legal base for such an action, which was looked upon with favor by the secular and clerical Catholic leadership. The plan, which was finalized by the German and Slovak governments in November 1941, began under the guise of an operation to provide 20,000 Jewish workers for the Axis war industries.

After the Master Plan for the annihilation of European Jewry was announced at the Wansee Conference on January 20, 1942, the Slovak government and the German ambassador signed officially in Bratislava on February 16, 1942, the agreement of deportation of 20,000 "strong and suitable" young Jewish men and women between the ages of sixteen and thirty-five. Slovak Prime Minister Voytech Tuka and Interior Minister Sano Mach personally took charge of the deportations. Martin Luther, a senior official of the German Foreign Office who participated in the Wansee Conference, cabled the German legation in Bratislava:

> As part of the measures for the Final Solution of the European Jewish Question, the German Government is prepared to take over 20,000 young, strong Slovak Jews immediately and to transport them to the east, where there is a need for labor.[39]

The date for the beginning of the deportations was set for March 26, 1942. President Tiso had already received at the time direct information from his chief army general at the Soviet front that 18,000 Jews from Slovak Ruthenia deported by the Hungarians to Kamenetz Podolsk had been mass murdered in September 1941 by the Einsatzgruppen and the Hungarian military.[40] The apostolic delegate in Bratislava Msgr. Burzio was equally well-informed of the massacre. The Slovak chief military chaplain, who was an eyewitness to the Kamenetz Podolsk massacre, personally described to Burzio the terrible crime. Burzio already knew the real meaning of "resettlement" and "labor mobilization." He received first-hand testimony that the Jewish population in the Ukraine was being mass murdered by machine-gun fire in the outskirts of the towns and that Jewish POWs were being executed as soon as they were taken prisoner, while Ukrainian and White Soviet POWs were allowed to return free to their homes. Msgr. Burzio transmitted that information to the Vatican on October 27, 1941; the news, however, did not make a ripple in the tranquil waters of the Vatican. In his response of December 20, 1941, Cardinal Maglione's only problem was whether any Slovak military personnel were involved in the mass executions.[41]

Eichmann personally visited Slovakia several times to make sure the deportations would run smoothly. He appointed one of his trusted lieutenants, Dieter Wiesliceny, to supervise the process. The Jewish Council was called in by the chairman of the Central Economic Office Moráveck and by Wisliceny and informed officially of the upcoming deportations to Poland. The deportees, often the sole providers of their families, left behind children, the elderly, and people unfit for work. Using the ploy of resettlement to deceive them, Wisliceny told the members of the Jewish Council:

> Slovakia does not need Jews; therefore it is going to transfer them to a new habitat, which the great German Reich has made available to them . . . It is important that artisans take the tools and machines they still have with them.[42]

Eager to put their hands on the possessions of deported Jews, the Slovak government agreed to pay 500 RM to the Germans for every deported Jew. The Slovaks considered this to be a highly beneficial deal in economic terms. On March 3, 1942, Slovak Prime Minister Tuka made the announcement in the Slovak State Council that the Germans had agreed to take the remaining 70,000

Jews of Slovakia. The Germans were doing Slovakia a favor and were to be compensated at the rate of 500 RM (US$200) for every Jew deported. For this sum they guaranteed that the deportees would never return to Slovakia and the state would be free to seize Jewish property left behind: [43]

> The Jews accepted as part of the de-Judaization of Slovakia will remain permanently in the Eastern territories and will not be offered any possibility of re-immigrating into Slovakia.[44]

Eichmann at his trial in Jerusalem described the eagerness with which the Slovak leaders pursued the offer:

> The Slovak officials offered their Jews to us like someone throwing away sour beer. [45]

According to the testimony of an official of the German embassy in Bratislava, Msgr. Burzio wrote to Prime Minister Tuka on February 1942, after the announcement of the deportations was made, that the Jews sent to eastern Poland would be taken to be killed and not to work. Burzio informed the Vatican about it in his reports of March 9 and March 11, 1942, and warned that the deportation meant certain death for most of the deportees, but the warning made no impression on the Vatican. This report among many others demolishes the apologetic claim which for decades attempted to derail historical research that the Vatican was unaware of the German annihilation campaign. Burzio's report, which is included in the published Vatican *Acts*, is clear in its warning:

> The deportation of 80,000 persons to Poland at the mercy of the Germans is the equivalent of condemning a great part of them to certain death. [46]

When the Jewish community learned the tragic news about their upcoming deportation to Poland, the leaders of the three religious groups of Slovak Jewry, the Orthodox, Status Quo, and Neologues, gathered in Bratislava on March 5, 1942, in a desperate attempt to decide what course of action to take. An underground cell known by the name Bratislava Working Group was formed in 1942 within the Bratislava Jewish Council to explore possible rescue avenues. Led by Rabbi Michael Dov Weissmandl (1903-1957), a pious rabbinical scholar of great courage and initiative, the group included various brave and spirited individuals such as Gisi Fleischman, engineer Ondrej Steiner, Oskar Neumann, Dr. Tibor Kovacs, and Rabbi Abraham (Armin) Frieder.

The fact that much information on the tragedy of Slovak Jewry reached the outer world is due mainly to the efforts of the Bratislava Working Group. They established effective communication links to the outside world, particularly to Switzerland and Turkey. Resolved to save Jewish lives by any means, they negotiated with the SS and their Slovak partners and paid bribes to stop the killings. They assisted the escape of Jews from Poland to Slovakia and from Slovakia to Hungary. When tragedy struck at Hungarian Jewry in 1944, the rescue efforts of that singular group were also directed at them.

Under the assumption that a Catholic state led by a Catholic priest loyal to the Pope would not ignore the will of its supreme spiritual leader, the group decided to appeal directly to the Pope in Rome and to the Slovak bishops to influence Tiso to stop the deportations. They hoped that the Pope would issue a warning of excommunication to the president-priest and his Catholic collaborators. Two appeals were addressed to the Pope, one was written in German and was signed by the lay leaders of the three religious denominations, while the other was written in Hebrew by Rabbi Weissmandl and was signed by the rabbis of Slovakia. The Slovak ambassador to the Holy See, Karol Sidor, visiting Slovakia at the time, was paid the hefty sum of 30,000 Kronen to see to it that the two appeals to the Pope reached him.[47] Copies of the appeals were also received by the nuncio in Budapest Angelo Rotta who forwarded them on March 13, 1942, to the Pope in Rome. They wrote:

Most Holy Father! The Jewry of all Slovakia, 90,000 souls have recourse to Your Holiness for help and salvation. We are condemned to destruction. As we surely know, we are to be shipped out to Lublin, Poland. Everything has already been taken away from us (money, linen, clothing, businesses, houses, funds, gold, bank accounts, and all household appliances) and now they want to banish us as Slovak citizens to Poland and send each one, without money or material goods to certain destruction and starvation. No one can help us. We place all our hope and confidence in Your Holiness as the safest refuge of all the persecuted. Since the nuncio here is away and we do not know when he will be back, we turn to Your Holiness, through the Nuncio in Budapest, whom we can reach easily. Would Your Holiness kindly influence the President of Slovakia, so that he, in the name of mankind and neighborly love, will receive us and not permit our banishment? [48]

On March 10, 1942, an appeal to the Pope from the World Agudath Israel Organization was forwarded through Cardinal Bernardini from Berne. But the hopes Jewish leaders pinned on Pius XII were in vain. On March 14, 1942, Vatican State Secretary Maglione handed a note to Ambassador Karol Sidor for the Slovak government:

According to information, which has now reached the State Secretariat, all the Jewish citizens are to be immediately expelled from Slovakia without regard to their religion, sex, or age. These people who number nearly 80,000, and according to some as many as 135,000, will be expelled to Galicia and to the Lublin area and that this expulsion will be executed separating men, women and children. [49]

The note was carefully studied at the ministerial meeting presided by Tiso. The subtle message did not escape the attention of Tiso. Slovak Minister of Education Josef Sivak later revealed to Rabbi Abraham Frieder the gist of the deliberations. Tiso, an experienced reader of scholastic jargon, inferred from the sentence that "all the Jewish citizens were about to be expelled without regard to their religion," that if religious affiliations were taken into account excluding the baptized converts from the deportations, the Vatican would not object. The critical words against "separating men, woman, and children" similarly meant that the Jewish families should not be broken up when deported. In other words, deportation of the Jews was acceptable to the Holy See as long as converts were excluded and complete families were deported together with their children. Fr. Morley comments:

> Maglione protested the deportation of Jews but seemed equally concerned that the deportations made no allowance for differences of religion among the Jews. It might be argued that the Cardinal would have said even less, or perhaps nothing, if the baptized Jews were not included in the expulsions. [50]

Tiso was right on target with his reading of the message. When the Slovak parliament approved on May 15, 1942, an amendment to the Codex Judaicus that exempted converts from deportation, full harmony was reestablished between the Vatican and the Slovak government. [51] Josef Sivak also revealed to Rabbi Friedler that at the ministerial meeting, Bishop Pecheni of Tyrnau raised a hypothetical question: "What if the allies win the war and the deported Jews return?" Tiso responded reassuringly: "I assure you they will not return!"

Five assembly points were set up in Slovakia for deportations: Poprad, Sered, Zilina, Patronka, and Novaky where deportation trains left with regularity to the Polish border. The Jews were packed in cattle trains and under the custody of Slovak *Hlinka* guards and taken to the Polish border where they were handed over to the Germans. Deportations began as scheduled on March 26, 1942. When the first deportation transport of 999 young Jewish girls left from Proprad to Auschwitz on March 26, 1942, news reached Rome that the girls were earmarked for prostitution for the front-line troops in Russia. A cable from Burzio stated that a total of 10,000 Jewish girls between the ages of sixteen and twenty-five had been rounded up near Bratislava and separated from their families to be deported for prostitution. The news was particularly disturbing to the Vatican because baptized Jewish girls were also included in the transport. The brutality of the roundup and deportation of the girls is described sparingly by Msgr. Burzio in his report to the Vatican of March 31, 1942:

> They are subject to a search, deprived of every object which they have taken along with them (suitcases, purses, rings, earrings, pens, foodstuffs, in sum everything), deprived of personal documents and assigned a simple registration number; if anyone protests or complains or begs that at least some small remembrance of their families be left, she is beaten with kicks and blows . . . These poor children are destined for prostitution or simply for massacre. [52]

When the report was confirmed by other sources, including by Msgr. Angelo Rotta, the nuncio in Hungary, Pius XII reacted with a reprimand to the Slovak government for "contradicting the responsibilities of a Catholic state to uphold morality," and in particular if some of the deported girls were baptized converts.[53] However, as soon as Slovak Ambassador Charles Sidor brought assurances to Cardinal Maglione on April 11, 1942, that the girls were not being deported for prostitution but for work and that baptized girls were exempted from deportation altogether, complete harmony was reestablished with Vatican authorities.

After a personal meeting with Interior Minister Sano Mach, Msgr. Burzio informed the Vatican secretary of state on March 31, 1942, that several convoys had already left for the German border. Mach denied that they were acting under pressure from Germany and declared that Slovak leadership was taking full responsibility for the deportations. He insisted that the Slovakian Church hierarchy was in full agreement with the government on the deportations. Msgr. Burzio expressed his concern in his report that these actions could eventually compromise the Church due to the involvement of a priest-president and many other priests in high office.

Following a calendar established by Wislizeny, transports would leave for Poland twice a week with 3,000 deportees each. In a short period of only three months, between March 26 and the end of June 1942, 52,000 Slovakian Jews were deported to Sobibor and Auschwitz to their death. Msgr. Burzio describes in his report the brutality with which the Jews were loaded into the trains. They were kicked and beaten, while families were torn apart "in the cruelest manner." From April onwards separation by age ceased. Entire families would be deported to their death, putting to rest the Vatican's concerns that families were being thorn apart. Now they were sent to their deaths together with their children.

Rabbi Michael D. Weissmandel's (1903-1957) description in *Min Hamezar* of the deportations he personally witnessed is heart-rending: Every Tuesday and Friday convoys of forty wagons each, with seventy-five deportees packed in each car would leave for the East amid indescribable misery and sorrow, while their Slovak neighbors would rejoice in the expectation that the property left behind would soon be theirs. The first Slovak Jews that arrived in Auschwitz from Nitra and Tyrnau were employed in building the crematoria which subsequently turned them into ashes.[54]

On April 26, 1942, the bishops of Slovakia issued a pastoral letter approving the deportations. Mach was indeed true to the facts when he claimed in his meeting with Burzio that the Slovak bishops fully supported the government in the way it was "excluding the Jews from Slovak life" and carrying out deportations. That pastoral letter bears testimony for all times to come to the villainous role of the Slovak bishops as full accomplices to the genocide of Slovak Jewry:

> The greatest tragedy of the Jewish nation lies in the fact of not having recognized the redeemer and of having prepared a terrible and ignominious death for him on the cross . . . Also in our eyes has the influence of the Jews been pernicious. In a short time they have taken control of almost all the economic and financial life of the country to the detriment of our people. Not only economically, but also in the cultural and moral spheres, they have harmed our people. The

Church cannot be opposed, therefore, if the state with legal regulations hinders the dangerous influence of the Jews. [55]

The pastoral letter of the bishops conference approving the deportations dovetails with the fierce animosity manifested by most dignitaries of the Slovak Church when appeals were directed to them personally on behalf of the persecuted community. Rabbi Weissmandl describes such a sad experience with the senior archbishop of Nitra, Dr. Karol Kmetko (1875-1948), whom Tiso served as secretary for many years. In hope that the octogenarian archbishop would be moved to intervene with Tiso once informed of the suffering of innocent women and children, his peaceful neighbors whose roots in Nitra went back 1,000 years, R. Weissmandel used all his powers of persuasion to convince his father-in-law and mentor, the elderly Rav and Rosh Yeshiva of Nitra, R. Shmuel David Unger to go and plead the cause of his people before the archbishop.

Rav Unger was adamant in the sure knowledge that he would find only humiliation, not help or sympathy. He nonetheless acceded. Sooner than he thought, Rabbi Weissmandel had to admit how much wiser his father-in-law had been when he saw him return downcast and dejected in the company of two respected Jewish citizens of Nitra from the humiliating visit. Unaware yet that gas chambers awaited the Jews at the end point of the deportations, Rabbi Unger tried to awaken the archbishop's humane feelings to the predicament of a people being uprooted from their homes and sent into exile. The archbishop, far ahead of him on the real facts, brusquely interrupted him and with base cruelty responded:

These are not expulsions, there you will not die from hunger and epidemics, there you will be slaughtered all together, old and young, children and women, all at once. This is the punishment you deserve for the death of our savior. Your only salvation is to accept our religion, only then will I intervene for the decree to be repealed.[56]

In such a prevalent evil environment, there were a few exceptional priests who had the moral courage to rise above the moral abyss that surrounded them. One of them was Vicar of Bratislava Agustin Pozdech, followed by Bishop of Presov Jozef Carsky and Greek Catholic Bishop of Presov Petro Gojdic, who protested the deportations. They were the lonely exceptions whose voices was drowned among a clergy and a people dominated by anti-Semitic passions and greed for Jewish wealth.

After the majority of the Jews of Slovakia had already been brutally deported and robbed, the Slovak parliament retroactively approved an amendment to anti-Jewish legislation on May 15, 1942, to provide a legal basis for deportations. The amendment deprived the Jews of their citizenship, confiscated their property, and authorized their deportation from Slovakia. Discretionary power was granted to the president to exclude individual Jews from deportation if he considered them vital for the national economy. That power became a source for personal enrichment for the corrupt highest echelons of power in Slovakia.

To avoid objections from the Church, the decree excluded from deportation those converts who had been baptized before March 13, 1939, and those who had married Christians in Church ceremonies before September 10, 1941. The Catholic priests in the parliament voted in favor of the amendment according to a report by Msgr. Burzio to Cardinal Maglione dated May 23, 1942. After the official exemption of the converts, the Vatican ceased until February 1943 from any further interventions in Slovakia, satisfied that there were no threats against its baptized proteges. In the words of Fr. Morley:

> The Slovak law of May 1942 had exempted Jews baptized before March 14, 1939 and those married to Christians from anti-Jewish measures. As long as these Jews, officially members of the Church or married to Catholics in cere- monies presumably sanctioned by the Church, were protected, the Vatican ap- peared content not to intervene. The Italian embassy note of late September 1942 could also have confirmed the Vatican's view that these baptized Jews were relatively secure.[57]

When nothing was heard of the deportees, and no word came back from them, enquiries were made on their whereabouts. Frightening reports on the fate of the recent Slovak deportees began to arrive not only to the Jews in Slovakia but also to Msgr. Burzio and the Vatican. The Working Group and outside Jew- ish organizations had already received reliable information at the time that the Slovak deportees were being annihilated in the Lublin region. With the excep- tion of around 600-800 Jews, all the Jews deported from Slovakia until Septem- ber 1942 were murdered. The nuncio in Germany, Orsenigo, wrote from Berlin to Undersecretary Montini on July 28, 1942, that terrible stories were circulating of disastrous journeys and massacres of Jews.

On May 23, 1942, the Vatican received a letter from Slovak Prime Minis- ter Mach in which he presents what amounts to a summary of the Wansee Con- ference Master Plan for West European Jewry and explains the Slovak actions within its context. Fr. Blet's summary of the letter is here quoted:

> The deportation from Slovakia is part of a general plan and had been put into effect with the concurrence of the German authorities. A half a million Jews are going to be transported to Eastern Europe. Slovakia would be the first country from which Germany would accept inhabitants of Jewish descent. At the same time, the process had begun for other deportations of Jews in France, Holland, Belgium, in the protectorate, and in the Reich. Hungary would have to transfer 800,000; these would be settled in various places near Lublin, where they would be ultimately placed "under the protection of the Reich." The Germans have promised the Slovak government that Christians of Jewish descent would be grouped in a separate area.[58]

President Tiso, still serving as the priest of Banovce, spoke from the pulpit in Holic on August 15, 1942, that to expel the Jews was a good Christian deed since the Slovak nation had a right to free itself from what he called "its eternal enemies":

> As regards the Jewish question, people ask if what we do is Christian and humane. I ask that too: is it Christian if the Slovaks want to rid themselves of their eternal enemies the Jews? Love for oneself is God's command, and this love makes it imperative for me to remove anything harming me.

Tiso invoked the authority of his deceased predecessor and mentor Fr. Andrej Hlinka who loathed converts no less than loyal Jews:

> A Jew remains a Jew even if his baptized by a hundred bishops.

The discretionary powers to exclude individual Jews from deportation granted to Tiso in the May 15, 1942 amendment, became a source of personal enrichment for Tiso and his henchmen—a veritable gold mine that allowed them to extort great ransom payments from wealthy Jews for the exemptions. When the Working Group learned that individual Jews had been able to buy back their lives by bribery, they sought to open a back-door channel of communication to the highest Slovak government officials and to Eichmann's man in Bratislava, Wisliceny, to save the remnants of the community. Hochberg, a Jew from Vienna, who represented Wisliceny in his dealings with the Judenrat, was approached at great risk by Rabbi Weissmandl about a possible deal to stop the deportations by paying ransom money. Wisliceny agreed to stop the deportations for a ransom payment of $50,000 payable in two installments. He stipulated that the money must be given in U.S. dollars provided by Jewish world organizations abroad, seemingly with the aim of establishing a surreptitious link with world Jewry organizations

The Jewish representatives in Zurich, constrained by Allied government regulations for dealing with the enemy and distrusting Nazi promises, were unwilling to provide the ransom money. The Working Group turned to local help within Slovakia. The first installment was paid with dollars that were locally collected under a fictitious scheme that made it look as if it had been paid by a representative of world Jewry in Zurich. After he received the first installment, Wisliceny stopped the transports temporarily at the end of June 1942.

When the Working Group was unable to come up with the second payment for lack of American currency, Wisliceny renewed the deportations on Yom Kippur, September 10, 1942. Three thousand Jews were rounded up by order of Wisliceny and sent to their death on that holiest day. After desperate telegraphic appeals sent on Yom Kippur by Rabbi Weissmandl to the leaders of the Orthodox Jewish Community in Hungary, Kahn-Frankel and Rabbi Strasser, the amount in U.S. dollars finally arrived from Budapest through a special envoy by the name of Traitel. The transports were interrupted after 57,628 Jews, 75 percent of Slovakian Jewry, had already been deported. Wisliceny reprimanded the tormented Jewish representatives in typical Nazi manner:

> That's the way you Jews are. Without pressure one can not get anything from you. The delay had cost you 3,000 lives.[59]

Some have tried with baseless claims to credit the Church with the deportation interruption. Fr. Morley recognizes the emptiness of these claims:

> Some authors attribute the cessation of the expulsions to Vatican or ecclesiastical influence. It seems more likely that they ended because they had been so effective in ridding the country of the overwhelming majority of its Jewish residents.

Not to incriminate himself, Wisliceny avoided completely the subject of the bribery payments at his trial in Nuremberg. When interrogated during his trial on January 3, 1946, how it came about that the deportations were stopped in September 1942, he cleverly ascribed it to the discretionary powers used by Tiso in granting individual exemptions or to German refusal to allow Slovak representatives to inspect the deportation camps:

> I mentioned before that these first 17,000 laborers were followed by about 35,000 Jews, including entire families. In August or the beginning of September, 1942 an end was put to this action in Slovakia. The reasons for this were that a large number of Jews still in Slovakia had been granted—either by the President or by various Ministries—special permission to remain in the country. A further reason might have been the unsatisfactory answer I gave the Slovakian Government in reply to their request for the inspection of the Jewish camps in Poland. This state of affairs lasted until September, 1944; from August, 1942, until September, 1944, no Jews were removed from Slovakia. From 25,000 to 30,000 Jews still remained in the country. [60]

The lull in deportations lasted for full two years until Yom Kippur 1944, although there were repeated threats during that period that deportations would be renewed.[61] The relative calm that prevailed in Slovakia even brought in a trickle of Jews who managed to flee from the Polish inferno. The two-year reprieve in Slovakia stands in sharp contrast to the Rome ransom where the payment of 210 pounds of gold was nothing but an infamous extorsion that did not delay deportations.

Seeking to extort as much ransom money as possible from the Jews, Minister of the Interior Alexander Mach suddenly threatened in a speech on February 17, 1943, that deportations would resume in March or April 1943.[62] The Slovak newspapers announced that the new deportations would include converts. There were at the time around 10,000 baptized converts among the 20,000-25,000 remaining Jews.

The Slovak bishops wrote to the government on February 17, 1943, requesting that converts be exempted from deportations. They argued that the converts were members of the Catholic Church who had broken with their Jewish past and proven their sincerity as Catholics. From Budapest, Nuncio Rotta transmitted an appeal to the Vatican on February 26, 1943, from an association of baptized Hungarian Jews that 2,000 baptized converts were in imminent danger of being deported from Slovakia. Rotta indicated that among the 20,000 Jews remaining in Slovakia, 10,000 were baptized converts.

The Vatican instructed Msgr. Burzio on March 6, 1943, to confirm the truth of the information on the renewal of deportations. In his two reports to Rome, Msgr. Burzio stated he could not confirm the information, although he considered the renewal "very probable." He made reference to the corruption in which Tiso was involved in granting exemptions for large sums of money and criticized Tiso for not exempting converts from the upcoming deportations. Msgr. Burzio enclosed a letter from a parish priest together with a confirmation by a Nazi official that the Jews were being killed by gas or machine guns in Poland and that their bodies were being used to make soap.

Karol Kmetko, the rabidly anti-Semitic archbishop of Nitra who wanted the Jews out of Slovakia, requested in the name of Slovak bishops that the converts should be spared:

> The bishops of Slovakia see it as their duty to defend the Jews who have converted to Christianity and to repeat their request not to expel Jews who have converted to Christianity. It will be foreign to the Catholic Slovakian people, whose spirit is truly Catholic, if the Christian Slovakian government expels Christian Catholics from a Christian country.[63]

On March 8, 1943, the bishops issued a pastoral letter to be read in churches on March 21 in Latin—a language not understood by the lay people. Criticizing those Catholics that refused to attend services together with converts they stated that "the attitude to people should not be influenced by their linguistic, legal, national or racial connection."[64] Fr. Pierre Blet summarizes its contents:[65]

> Three weeks later the bishops published a pastoral on behalf of the Jews (?) especially the Jews who had become Catholics, and they criticized those elderly Catholics who refused to attend church with the new converts.[66]

On March 13, 1943, the Pope received in a personal audience Hungarian nun Margit Slachta, who came to tell him that the last 20,000 Jews of Slovakia were in imminent danger of being deported to their death. Slachta left Rome empty-handed and was not able to elicit any verbal comment from Pius XII on the terrible crime that a Catholic government led by a Catholic priest was on its way to bring to its final conclusion:

> Pius listened to me all the way through [and] expressed his shock . . . He listened to me but said very little.[67]

An internal memorandum written by Msgr. Federico Tardini on April 7, 1943, at a time that doubts on the victory of the Third Reich began to gain ground in the Vatican, opens another window to the opportunistic character of Vatican policy making:

Since, especially recently, leaders of the Jews have turned to the Holy See to appeal for aid, it would not be out of place to discreetly make known to the public this diplomatic note of the Holy See (the fact of its being sent, the content rather than the text). This will make known to the world that the Holy See fulfills its duty of charity rather than attracting the sympathy of the Jews in case they are among the victors (given the fact that the Jews—as much as can be foreseen—will never be friendly to the Holy See and the Catholic religion). [68]

On May 5, 1943, the Vatican secretariat of state sent a note through the Slovak legation to the government in Bratislava expressing its concern with the possibility that deportations might be renewed "without excluding even those who have entered the Catholic religion." The Slovak Council of Ministers officially responded to the Vatican on May 28, 1943, stating that converts would not be deported regardless of their date of conversion, but those Jews considered a danger to the state would be deported and the rest would be placed in concentration camps within Slovakia. To prove their high-minded Christian concern for converts, the council assured the Vatican that they would be held in separate camps from the Jews and given every opportunity to fulfill their Christian religious duties. On June 4, 1943, Burzio confirmed that deportations had been halted.

In December 1943, Tiso reached an agreement with the German Foreign Office to place all surviving Slovak Jews in concentration camps. When an order was issued in January 1944 that all Jews were to register with the police, the news created panic among them. Even converts panicked and saw this as a prelude to deportation. Nonetheless, Burzio informed the Vatican that the police registration was not meant for deportation purposes.

The Red Army reached the Czech border on April 8, 1944, but did not move forward for several months. Following the increasing partisan activity in the central and northern areas of Slovakia, the German army occupied Slovakia on August 29, 1944. A partisan uprising launched in September was crushed by the Germans at the end of October. The fate of the last remnant of Slovak Jewry was sealed. The number of Jews was calculated in early 1944 as between 16,000 and 18,000 and that of converts as 10,000.

The arrests in Bratislava began on September 29, 1944. The Hlinka guards and the Germans began to round up the terrified Jews. On October 26, 1944, Burzio reported that deportations are taking place and the search for Jews in hiding was continuing without foreseeable relief. Around 13,500 Jews were rounded up and taken to the Sered labor camp between October 1944 and March 1945. From there they were deported. The first five transports went to Auschwitz, the rest to Bergen Belsen and other German concentration camps. When the U.S. and Latin American passports held by 400 Jews sent to Bergen Belsen were declared forgeries, they were all deported to their death. Most members of the Working Group were deported. In the tragic final balance, at least 65,000 of the 70,000 Jews deported from Slovakia since 1941 were annihilated.

As in the past, Burzio shuttled back and forth to Tiso to intervene for baptized Jews. On November 4, Burzio went to convey in the name of the Pope his sorrow for the suffering inflicted on so many people because of their "nationality or race" and to remind Tiso that "his opinions and decisions are to conform to his dignity and his sacerdotal integrity." The Vatican worried, says Michael Phayer, that its loyal servants in Slovakia should not implicate the Church and the Pope in mass murder because, "in Slovakia the Church's fingerprints were undeniably on the trigger."

Five days later, Tiso summoned the papal delegate and gave him a letter, handwritten in Latin, which arrived in Rome on December 19, 1944. Taking high-moral ground, this major perpetrator justified his collaboration with the Germans, which, he said, recognized and protected Slovakia's independence. He defended his actions against the Czechs and the Jews, which were designed to eliminate their noxious influence. "The dignity of the priesthood was always before my eyes," he wrote, "it was pharisaic on the part of Slovakia's enemies to express concern for the reputation of the clergy." He had not acted on the basis of his own judgments, but "had consulted the best advisors within the Church."[69] Vatican historian Fr. P. Blet seems to agree, when he calls this perpetrator "a man of undeniable loyalty to the Church."[70]

"At no time," points out Phayer, "had the Holy See publicly protested the murder of the Jews of Catholic Slovakia who were the first and the last victims of the Holocaust." The conclusions drawn by Fr. Morley, on the nefarious role played by the Vatican in the Catholic model state Slovakia are irrefutable:

> The Vatican's options were more extensive in Slovakia than in other countries. It was a heavily Catholic country with a priest as president and a prime minister who prided himself of being a practicing Catholic. That anti-Semitism was rampant is evident from the bishops' own statement on the Jews. It was also a country proud of its dedication and loyalty to the Pope . . . Yet the Vatican did not act. It issued no threats of excommunication or interdict against the president, the prime minister, or the people . . . The failure of Vatican diplomacy in Slovakia must be attributed as much to its own indifference to the deportation of the Jews as to any other factor. German influence was a factor . . . The unique conditions presented to the Vatican in the case of this truly Vatican nation were not exploited . . . Nonetheless, the nation was independent. An unambiguous statement from the Vatican condemning the deportation of the Jews would more than likely have affected the nation's leaders.[71]

## The Final Solution in Croatia

When the Germans arrived in April 1941, there were more than 80,000 Jews living in Yugoslavia: 45,000 in Croatia, 16,000 in Serbia, 14,000 in Bosnia-Herzegovina, and 8,000 in Macedonia, in addition to over 4,000 Jewish refugees from Germany, Austria, and other countries. By the end of the war, 80 percent of Yugoslavian Jewry had been annihilated. At least 26,000 Croatian Jews died in the Ustashi death camps and 7,000 in Auschwitz-Birkenau. Only twenty-four

Croatian Jewish deportees returned alive from Auschwitz-Birkenau after the war! In Bosnia-Hercegovina about 12,000 Jews perished. The Jewish community in Sarajevo of 10,500 souls was reduced to 800 survivors.

On the evening of the arrival of German troops to Zagreb on April 10, 1941, local Croat newspapers began to incite the population against Jews. Signs were placed in the shop windows: "Jews, entrance forbidden!" Next day, the eve of Passover, a Gestapo man arrived at the Jewish community offices in Zagreb where matzoth and charity were distributed. He confiscated all the community's funds, about 700,000 Dinars, and declared that the buildings, as well as the Chevra Kadisha building next door, were being seized. All the people present were placed under arrest and interrogated for hours. The Germans arrested the wealthy Jews of Zagreb and kept them hostage demanding a ransom price of 100 million gold dinars, which they soon raised to 150 million gold dinars ($2,500,000). They arrested all Jewish lawyers and took them to a camp in Kerestinetz.[72]

When the German troops took Sarajevo on April 17, 1941, one of their first criminal acts was to set on fire the central Sephardic synagogue in the city, the most precious architectural jewel in the Balkan countries. They were assisted by local Muslims, who willingly collaborated with them. In Osijek, the Germans seized Jewish hostages, demanding a ransom of 20 million dinars ($333,000). Synagogues and Serbian Orthodox churches were pillaged and burned down by the Ustashas in many regions of Croatia.

Only a week after the declaration of Croatian independence, Croatia enacted the Law on the Protection of the People and the State, which granted the government the power to cancel the national and citizens' rights of anyone it considered unworthy.[73] Capital punishment was made mandatory for all those who "offended the honor and vital interests of the Croat people" and who "in whatever way" threatened the Croat state. It allowed them to kill anybody they wished to eliminate on the most ludicrous charges. The law was retroactive, so a person could be found guilty of "offending" the state even before it came into being. Special popular courts and mobile martial courts were immediately established. There was no appeal, and each sentence had to be carried out within two hours.

The first specifically anti-Semitic law was issued by the Ustashi on April 18, 1941, under the title Law on the Aryanization of Jewish Property. It authorized the regime to expropriate Jewish businesses and real estate, and to distribute the spoils among its followers. On April 30, 1941, a second law followed under the title Law on the Protection of Aryan Blood and the Honor of the Croatian People. It was an elaborate copy of the Nuremberg Laws which also applied to baptized Jewish converts. It stripped Jews of citizenship that had been granted them at their emancipation in 1873 and dissolved and banned marriages between non-Aryan Catholics (converted Jews) and Aryan Catholics. The civil service and professions were declared off limits to Jews. Jews were required to identify their stores as Jewish and were forbidden to change their Jewish surnames, raise the Croatian flag, or employ Aryan servants below forty-five years of age.[74]

Jews, including baptized converts, were required to wear the Star of David and the letter Z (*Zidov*, Jew) on their garments, while the Serbs had to wear blue sleeve bands with the letter P (*Pravoslavni*, Orthodox) beginning May 11, 1941. The official Catholic Croat press welcomed the racist anti-Semitic decrees. The Catholic weekly *Hrvastka Strazha* wrote on May 11, 1941:

> The laws are vital for the survival and development of the Croatian nation . . . the protection of our blood and honor . . . with it the Poglavnik wants to prevent the dangerous worm from eating away at the tree of our Croatian national identity.[75]

In accordance with Vatican policy, the decree that banned and dissolved the marriages of non-Aryan converts with Aryan Catholics was seen by Archbishop Stepinac as an unacceptable interference of the state in the area of marriages and he expressed his objection in a letter to Pavelic in May 1941. With regard to the laws against the Jews, however, Stepinac expressed no complaint at all. He objected that baptized converts were included in the anti-Jewish laws which required them to wear the Star of David like the Jews:

> As a representative of the Catholic Church, and following my holiest duty, I raise my voice against interference of the state into questions of lawful marriages that are insolvable, regardless of racial affiliation. There is no state authority having the right to dissolve these marriages. [76]

Committed to the idea of a homogeneous Croat Catholic state, Ustashi leaders declared that there was no room in Croatia for Eastern Orthodox Serbs, Jews, and Gypsies. The clero-Fascist Ustashi were resolved to carry out a merciless ethnic cleansing campaign in Croatia against the 1.9 million Serbs, 50,000 Jews, and 30,000 Gypsies living inside its borders. As soon as they proclaimed their own state on April 10, 1941, the Ustashi did not wait for the Germans to implement the Final Solution, but immediately on their own started a brutal campaign of ethnic cleansing, as if to prove to the Germans that they had little to learn from them. Minister of Justice Milovan Zanic spoke at Nova Gradiška on June 2, 1941:

> This state, our country, is only for Croats and for no one else. There are no methods and means which we, Croats, will not use to make our country truly ours, and to clean it of all Orthodox Serbs. All those who came into our country 300 years ago must disappear . . . It is the policy of our state, and during its realization we shall do nothing else than follow the principles of the Ustashas. [77]

On July 22, 1941, Mile Budak, Pavelic's minister of education, spelled out clearly in a well-publicized speech in Gospic the means the Ustashi would use to reach their objective of a pure Croatian society:

For the rest—Serbs, Jews, and Gypsies—we have three million bullets. We shall kill one third of all Serbs. We shall deport another third, and the rest of them will be forced to become Roman Catholic. [78]

Anti-Semitic decrees followed in rapid succession in the following weeks. On June 26, 1941, all Jewish bank accounts were blocked, all safes were confiscated and all storage depots were sequestered, prohibiting the release of anything to their Jewish owners. On June 27, 1941, a curfew was declared forbidding Jews and Serbs to be in the streets from 7 p.m. to 7 a.m. On August 27, 1941, a decree was issued confiscating Jewish-owned real estate. By the end of August most Jewish enterprises below $2,500 were already Aryanized. On October 9, 1941, a law declaring the nationalization of Jewish enterprises and possessions was issued, requiring Jews to hand over all their properties:

Art. 1) The State Direction for reconstruction is authorized, in view of reconstruction and national economy, to nationalize all Jewish enterprises and possessions whatsoever for the benefit of the Independent State of Croatia. [79]

A terrifying ethnic mass-murder campaign was launched by means of mobile punitive expeditions and concentration camps. Large-scale massacres began first in Bosnia and Herzegovina, and then in Croatia and Dalmatia in July and August 1941. Punitive expeditions, similar in many respects to the German Einsatzgruppen, went out in May 1941 and continued during the following months. At the same time, Jews began to be rounded up and sent to detention and extermination camps. Although Pavelić needed no encouragement from the Nazis to proceed with his ethnic-cleansing program, the violent campaign of mass murder reached its climax in the months after his meeting with Hitler in June 1941.

Bands of Ustasha killers organized so-called punitive expeditions in the Croatian countryside against defenseless civilians, paralleling the Einzatsgruppen mass killings in Poland and Russia. While Eastern Orthodox Serbs were given the option to convert to Catholicism, such a choice was not available to Jews. Thus, Orthodox Serbs could save their lives by conversion while Jews could not.[80] The leading role of Catholic clergy and their personal participation in mass murder in both programs singles out the Holocaust in Croatia from the rest of Europe. Carlo Falconi highlights the uniqueness of Croatia in this respect:

Ustasha massacres—as opposed to exterminations in other countries during the Second World War—in that it is almost impossible to imagine an Ustasha punitive expedition without a priest in its head or spurring it on, and usually a Franciscan.[81]

Historians register the names and terrible deeds of many of the Franciscan friars commanding the punitive expeditions who personally participated in mass murders and conversions. Their names turn up constantly in the horror descriptions of these massacres. They incited the Catholic population, killed, sacked villages, and set fire to houses as they roamed through the countryside. The terror unleashed by them instilled fear in the hearts of Jews and Serbs. Where the Ustashi decided to spare their lives, conversion was a preliminary condition. Entire villages of Serbs converted to Catholicism to avoid death. The description of Cambridge Professor Jonathan Steinberg of the brutal crimes of the Ustasha is shocking:

> Serbian and Jewish men, women and children were literally hacked to death. Whole villages were razed to the ground and the people driven into barns to which the Ustashi set fire. There is in Italian Foreign Ministry archive a collection of photographs of the butcher knives, hooks, and axes used to chop up Serbian victims. There are photographs of Serb women with breasts hacked off by pocket knives, men with eyes gouged out, emasculated and mutilated.[82]

A British emissary to Yugoslav guerillas, Fitzroy MacLean, describes the Ustashi expeditions:

> Bands of Ustashi roamed the countryside with knives, bludgeons and machine guns, slaughtering Serbian and Jewish men, women and little children . . . torturing, raping, burning, drowning and killing. Killing became a cult, an obsession. The Ustashi vied to outdo each other, boasting of the number of victims and of their own particular methods of dispatching them. Some Ustashi collected the eyes of Serbs they killed sending them to the Poglavnik for his inspection or proudly displaying them and other organs in the cafes of Zagreb.[83]

Even Heydrich, the master killer, marveled at the cruelty of the expeditions and expressed his opinion that it derived from the struggle of the Catholic Church against the Orthodox Church. In a report to Himmler of February 17, 1942, he wrote:

> The number of Slavs massacred by the Croats with the most sadistic of methods must be estimated at a count of 300,000 . . . The fact is that in Croatia, living Serbs who have converted to the Catholic Church are able to remain residing unharrassed . . . From this it is clear that the Croat-Serbian state of tension is not least of all a struggle of the Catholic Church against the Orthodox Church. [84]

Although many detention camps were already in operation since the declaration of Croat independence in April, they became officially authorized in a decree on September 25, 1941.[85] Minister of the Interior Andrija Artukovic and his chief of police, Eugen Kvaternik, son of one of the main Ustashi leaders, Marshall Slavko Kvaternik, created an extensive net of twenty-six detention and extermination camps within Croatia.[86] Some of the camps only existed during short periods, but others, like Jasenovac, operated until the end of the war. A total of 26,000 Jews, more than half of Croatian Jewry, were taken during the summer of 1941 to detention camps were they were brutally murdered, worked to death, or deported to the killing ghettoes of Lithuania.

Many Catholic priests were appointed as commanders and staff officers of concentration camps. The list of these priests is extensive. The Franciscan priest Miroslav Filipovic-Majstorovic, known as "Brother Satan" was the commander of Jasenovic in its worst period. He was assisted by other Catholic priests and friars such as Zvanko Brekalo, Pero Brzica, Anselmo Chulina, Zvanko Lipovac, Cvitan, and Brkljania. Ante Djuric was commander of all the camps in the Dvar district, Dragan Petronovic was the commander in Ogulin, and Stepan Lukic was camp adjutant of the Zepce concentration camp.

More than 6,000 Jews were rounded up from Zagreb and other places and taken to the salt mines of Karlovac and Yudovo in Bosnia for forced labor in the summer of 1941. Lionello Alatri, the president of the Union of Italian Jewish Communities, appealed in vain to the Vatican on August 21, 1941, to use its influence with Pavelić and the Italian government:

> Without means, without clothing, because required to leave carrying only as much as can be contained in a mountain sack, they are forced to live in the open in rocky areas bereft of vegetation, scorched land, with a hot climate, without sufficient water, deprived of every agricultural resource, without a roof in the literal sense of the word. [87]

The most important camp was Jasenovac, known as the Croat Auschwitz. Located on the Zagreb-Belgrade line, Jasenovac began to operate in August 1941. Around 18,000 Jews died in Janesovac from December 1942 to October 1944, as testified at the trial of Dinko Sakic, the commander of Jasenovac, by Ivo Goldstein, a history professor at the Zagreb Faculty of Philosophy.[88] Only twenty Jews survived there at the end of the war. In two days alone, on November 15-16, 1941, the Germans rounded up more than 3,000 Jews and took them to Jasenovac. No fewer than 6,000-7,000 Jewish children were put to death in Stara Gradizka, a subsidiary camp of Jasenovac for woman and children. Jews from Zagreb were taken early in May 1941 to Jadovno and Danica, two of the earliest extermination camps. The Jews taken to Danica were already dead by July 1941, and those to Jadovno by August 1941.

In an account of the crimes committed against Jews published by the Jewish communities of Yugoslavia there is a terrifying description of the "ritual killings" in Jasenovic of Ljubo Miloš (1919-1948), one of the senior officials in the camp. Dressed in a white robe, Miloš would line up arriving prisoners who applied to be hospitalized, put them along the wall, and with a slaughtering knife slit their throats. Helped after the war by the Vatican representative to the Allied prison camps, Msgr. Draganovic, who provided him with substantial monetary assistance and documents, Miloš escaped. The Janesovac commander Sakic lived unmolested for fifty years in Argentina, and only in 1999 was he extradicted and sentenced in Zagreb to twenty years, the maximum punishment in contemporary Croatia.

Susan Zuccotti quotes an official report of the Italian army of September 1941 after they arrived at two Croatian detention camps for Jews on the island of Pag. The army unearthed the bodies of 791 Jewish men, women, and children murdered by the Ustashi with knives and hatchets. Many of the women had been raped and other victims had been buried alive. The king of Italy, the Pope, and many prelates received the report, which did not produce a ripple in the tranquil waters of the Vatican.[89] Dr. Milan Polak, vice president of the Jewish community in Zagreb, recalled in recent times the murder of 170 Jewish youngsters, from sixteen to nineteen years old, commited in Jadovno in May 1941, for which Andrija Artukovic (1899–1988), an Ustashi minister who fled to the United States, bears direct responsibility:

> In May, 1941 I myself was interned in that camp when those 170 young men were brought from Zagreb, Dr. Polak related . . . These youths were isolated, completely despoiled, tortured with hunger, ultimately being taken to Jadovno and Lika, and killed, every last one of them. For this, too, Artukovic bears responsibility because, as in the case of so many other crimes, these youngsters as well were liquidated on his orders and instructions. [90]

Apostolic Visitor Giussepe Ramiro Marcone, who was designated to represent the Vatican in Croatia, arrived in early August 1941 as the terrible blood orgy was at its highest point. He and his secretary Guiseppe Masucci, who spoke Serbo-Croatian fluently, moved freely within Croatia and were even allowed to visit the concentration camps, including Jasenovac. They interacted directly with those Croatian officials and priests responsible for the genocide. Through them, the Vatican was better informed of the situation inside Yugoslavia than about any other area of Europe. "Marcone had," says Fr. Morley, "far more contacts with the government and greater accessibility to it than many apostolic delegates would have."[91]

Marcone found great spiritual uplift in the fact that there were Jews who were rushing to convert. There is no trace in his reports at that time of the enormous suffering, but much gloating over the fact that some unfortunate Jews rushed to convert in a desperate attempt to save their lives. Marcone saw in this a manifestation of "divine grace." His first report to Maglione dated August 23, 1941, and Maglione's answer of September 3, open a window to the abyss in which the Catholic Church had descended in Catholic Croatia:

> This badly tolerated badge (the yellow star) and the hatred of the Croats toward them, as well as the economic disadvantages to which they are subject, often brings about in the mind of the Jews the desire to convert to the Catholic Church. Supernatural motives and the silent action of divine grace cannot be a priori excluded from this. Our clergy facilitates their conversion, thinking that at least their children will be educated in Catholic schools and therefore will be more sincerely Christian. [92]

In his response Cardinal Maglione's instructed Marcone to invariably preserve the impression of loyalty to the regime and avoid any official actions on behalf of the Jews:

If you can find a suitable occasion you should recommend in a discreet manner that would not be interpreted as an official appeal, that moderation be employed with regard to Jews residing in Croat territory, confidentially and always in a way so that an official character cannot be attributed to your step . . . The impression of loyal cooperation with the civil authorities must always be preserved. [93]

Marcone was a regular visitor to Croatia, shuttling back and forth on military planes between Rome and Zagreb. After his assessment of the interventions of Marcone in Croatia Fr. John Morley reaches the following conclusion:

In all of these contacts, however, with one possible exception, there is no evidence of a protest against or condemnation of the actions taken by the authorities against the Jews . . . Moreover there is an underriding current in all of Marcone's efforts that appears to limit his interest and activities to those Jews who had been baptized Catholic or who had married Catholics in ecclesiastically approved ceremonies. [94]

A synod of Croat bishops was called by Archbishop Stepinac between November 17 and November 20, 1941, with the participation of Apostolic Visitor Marcone, to discuss the conversions of the Serbians. The bishops conference addressed a letter to Pavelić recommending that the "converts of Jewish origin" be treated as humanely as possible. As customary in the apologetic literature their request in behalf of the converts, the so-called citizens of Jewish origin as they are called in Maglione's response (December 3, 1941), has been deliberately misrepresented as an expression of concern for the Jews. Morley points out:

It must be concluded that Marcone's activity in Croatia was only minimally concerned with the Jews. . . . He could, and did, claim success in aiding only those who had been baptized Catholics or were married to Catholics . . . Marcone made few efforts to defend the Jews and failed to use his personal and ecclesiastical prestige to aid them.[95]

By the end of 1941, no more than 12,000 Jews were left alive in the German zone of Croatia, as can be gathered from a memorandum of December 16, 1941, by Pavelić to Italian Foreign Minister Ciano.[96.] At the Wansee Conference on January 20, 1942, Eichmann declared that Croatia had no longer a "Jewish Problem" to solve. On February 26, 1942, Artukovic gave a speech in Zagreb before the Croat Parliament, the *Sabor*, in which he stated the Jewish question had been solved in Croatia:

The Croatian people, having re-established their independent state of Croatia, could not do otherwise but to clean off the poisonous damagers and insatiable parasites—Jews, Communists, Freemasons. The independent state of Croatia, as an Ustashi state settled the so-called Jewish question with a decisive and healthy grasp. [97]

The Vatican, vitally interested in expanding Catholic power in the Balkans, saw in the Ustashi regime a guarantee of Catholic permanence and expansion and never dissociated itself from Croatia and its leaders. Although it was better informed than with regard to any other country of Europe of the terrible crimes they were committing, the Vatican would abstain as a matter of policy from any public criticism of the Croatian government or the Ustashi. Susan Zuccotti points to the deeper moral implications of such a policy: "The Ustashi were, after all, not Germans, but loyal Catholics who pledged their fidelity to the Pope."[98] The Church became an accomplice in the Croatian Holocaust to an extent unequaled anywhere else in Europe. Michael Phayer pointedly asks:

> In the case of Poland, Vatican knowledge of the murder of people was limited and sketchy in comparison to the Croatian case, in which both the nuncio and the head of the Church, Bishop Aloijzije Stepinac, were in continuous contact with the Holy See while Genocide was being committed. Would these circumstances matter? Would the Holy See condemn the genocide by an avowedly Catholic country? [99]

Fr. Morley rightly points out:

> The record of Croatia on the Jews was particularly shameful, not because of the number of Jews killed, but because it was a state that proudly proclaimed its Catholic tradition and whose leaders depicted themselves as loyal to the Church and the Pope. [100]

After the Wansee Conference, the Germans proposed through the SS police attaché, Hans Helm, that Croatia should deport the remaining Jews from the Croatian camps to Eastern Europe. Eugen Dido Kvaternik, chief of the NDH security services, agreed to pay the Germans thirty RM ($12.00) for each deportee, to cover the cost of transport—a most profitable transaction in proportion to the wealth left behind by the Jews. By May 1942, arrangements were finalized to deport the last remnant of Croatian Jewry to Auschwitz. HauptsturmFührer Franz Abromeit was delegated by Eichmann to work with the German police attaché in Zagreb to supervise the deportations, which were carried out by the Croats. Finance Minister Kosak paid out for every Jew deported the agreed sum.

On July 17, 1942, Fr. Marcone informed the Vatican in a memorandum that Chief of Croat Police Eugene Kvaternik told him that as many as 2 million Jews had already been killed in Europe and the same fate awaited the Jews of Croatia who would be deported in the coming months. He also makes reference to the visits of Chief Rabbi Miroslav Shalom Freiberger seeking to rescue his community:

> The German government has ruled that within a period of six months all the Jews residing in the Croat State must be transferred to Germany, where, according to what Eugene (Dido) Kvaternik [chief of the Croat police] himself told me, two million Jews have been recently killed. It appears that the same fate awaits the Croat Jews particularly if old and incapable of work . . . He also

will be pleased if the Holy See can intervene for the repeal of this ordinance, or at least to propose that all Croatian Jews be concentrated on an island . . . Since this news has also spread among the Jews, I am continually beseeched to do something for their salvation. Also the Chief Rabbi himself of Zagreb comes to see me and to inform me of new misfortunes. [101]

In spite of Marcone's warning that deportation meant certain death, no papal action to prevent the deportation of the last Jewish remnant in Croatia was undertaken. Not even when the respected chief rabbi appealed on August 4, 1942, in a personal letter to Pius XII to save the last remnant of Croatian Jewry:

Now at the moment when the last remnants of our community find themselves in a most critical situation—at a moment when decisions are being made about their lives—our eyes are fixed upon Your Holiness. We beseech Your Holiness in the name of several thousand women and abandoned children, whose supporters are in concentration camps, in the name of widows and orphans, in the name of the elderly and the feeble, to help them so that they may remain in their homes and spend their days there, even if necessary, in the most humble circumstances. [102]

Between August 13 and August 20, 1942, approximately 5,500 Jews from the Croatian concentration camps at Tenje and Loborgrad and from Zagreb and Sarajevo were taken in five convoys to Auschwitz-Birkenau. They were all gassed. [103] Marcone received instructions from Maglione to answer the appeal of Rabbi Freiberger with the usual protocol formula: "The Holy See always desirous of bringing help to the suffering has not neglected to involve itself on several occasions in favor of the recommended persons." Msgrs. Tardini, and Montini, who were in charge of Croatian affairs, abstained even privately from censuring Croatia in their meetings with the Croatian ambassador. Instead, Pius XII would impart his blessing to Pavelić through the Croatian cabinet ministers at the personal audiences he granted them. [104]

As the German military situation was deteriorating, the Germans were in a hurry to finish their murderous work and frantically searched for any living Jew left. Between 6,000 and 7,000 Jews were rounded up during the early months of 1943 in the German zone of Croatia and Slovenia and deported to their deaths. In March 1943 they managed to round up and deport 2,000 Jews more. On March 30, 1943, Cardinal Maglione learned that as many as 80 percent of the last remnant of Jews in the German zone of Croatia were really baptized converts and that the Germans started to deport converts who had been baptized long ago. He wrote to Marcone:

If that is true . . . take whatever steps that are possible and opportune to impede such grave measures. [105]

In his response, Marcone assured Cardinal Maglione that baptized Jews or those married to Catholics had nothing to fear. He made reference to an earlier March report in which he stated among other things:

Repeatedly, both orally and in writing, I have insisted to Pavelić that above all families resulting from mixed marriages and, in general, all the baptized Jews, not be molested. Pavelić has always promised me to respect the Jews who had become Catholics or were married to Catholics.[106]

Fr. John Morley comments:

There is an underriding current in all of Marcone's efforts that appears to limit his interest and activities to those Jews who had been baptized Catholic or who had married Catholics in ecclesiastically approved ceremonies . . . There is little doubt, however, that the interest of the Vatican in the Jews of Croatia was directed primarily toward those who had become a Catholic or who had been married according to Church rule. It was only in the spring of 1943 that these Jews were in jeopardy, occasioning the directive of Maglione to intervene.[107]

During Himmler's official state visit to Zagreb, two trains left on May 5 and May 10, 1943, with 1,150 Jews aboard to Auschwitz-Birkenau. The last deportation convoy of 600 Jews to leave Croatia carried Chief Rabbi Freiberger and Ugo Kon, the president of the Jewish community.[108] When the train reached Auschwitz and Rabbi Freiberger saw his people being manhandled and treated with brutality, he pleaded with the Nazi officers to treat the people like human beings. The commanding Nazi officer responded by shooting the noble rabbi point-blank in front of his community.[109]

During May 1943, at a time Croatian Jewry had already been practically wiped out, Archbishop Stepinac visited the Pope in Rome. According to the report of the Croat ambassador in the Vatican, Erwin Lobkowicz, Stepinac presented the Ustashi government in the "best possible light" and preposterously justified the persecution of the Jews on grounds that they were allegedly pro-abortion:

He [Stepinac] revealed that he had kept quiet about some things, which he is not at all in agreement in order to be able to show Croatia in the best light possible. He mentioned our laws against abortion, a point very well received in the Vatican. Basing his arguments on these laws, the Archbishop justified in part the methods used against the Jews, who are in our country the greatest defenders of crimes of this kind and the most frequent perpetrators.[110]

In April 1944, German Minister to Croatia Siegfried Kasche and SS police attaché Hans Helm sent their final report to Berlin in which they informed that the Jewish question in Croatia had been solved: There were no Jews anymore in Croatia.

The only Jews to survive were those who fled to or had lived previously in the Dalmatian coastal zone annexed to Italy. Approximately 7,000 Jews, around 20 percent of Croatian Jewry, survived in the zones controlled by the Italians or by the Partisan resistance.[111] The Germans wanted back for deportation 5,000 Jews who escaped in 1942 from the German to the Italian zone of Croatia, putting pressure on the Italians to return them. Prince Otto von Bismarck, minister of state at the German Embassy in Rome, officially requested on August 18, 1942, their deportation. At the same time he quietly confided to his Italian counterpart, Marchese Blasco Lanza d'Ajeta, that their deportation meant certain death for them.

When Himmler personally pressured Mussolini to sign the deportation order, 4,000 Jews were rounded up in the Italian zone of Croatia and confined along the Dalmatian coast where they lived in constant fear of deportation. When fifty Jews were actually delivered to the Germans, the rest began to fear for their lives, and some even committed suicide.[112] The Germans requested that these Jews be transferred to Trieste, from where it would be easy to deport them to Poland or to kill them in local installations. When Italian General Giuseppe Pièche, who did not initially object to the deportation, learned that the 5,500 Jews deported in August 1942 by the Germans from Croatia had been gassed, he advised Mussolini not to go along with German deportation demands. Some other Italian army officers and generals, who had looked the other way when the Jews were massacred by the Ustashi in 1941, also had second thoughts and persuaded Mussolini to refuse.

In March 1943, Mussolini decided to move the Jews off the Dalmatian coast to a single camp in the island of Rab, where they remained under Italian custody until Italian surrender in September 1943. The Germans occupied the Italian zone after the Italian surrender, but the Italian military command delayed handing over the area to the Germans until Yugoslav partisans arrived in Rab and freed the Jews. The Jews took refuge among Tito's partisans who had already liberated a considerable portion of Yugoslav territory.

The fate of the Jews in Serbia and Macedonia was no less tragic than in Croatia. After the adult male Jewish population in Serbia had been shot in the fall of 1941 by the German military administration under the command of Harald Turner, surviving women and children were interned in a special camp near Belgrade. Emanuel Schäfer, the head of security police in Belgrade requested a gas van from Berlin. A Saurer gassing truck was promptly sent from Rauff's Berlin headquarters to Semlin in early 1942. In a letter to Karl Wolff in Berlin of April 11, 1942, Harald Turner makes reference to the preparations to gas the women and children in a matter of days:

> Already some months ago I had everything that could be got hold of in the way of Jews in this land shot, and had all the Jewish women and children concentrated in a camp and at the same time, with the help of the SD, procured a delousing vehicle that will now finally have carried out the clearing of the camp in some fourteen days to four weeks.[113]

Shortly after, Emanuel Schäfer reported back to Berlin that he had no need anymore of the gas van, which he was sending back to Berlin with its two drivers Goetz and Meyer, "who had carried out their special task." On June 9, 1942, Schäfer informed his commanding general in Serbia, Paul Bader, that there was no longer a Jewish question in Serbia, its prewar population of 80,000 Jews had been exterminated.[114]

## The Final Solution in France

At the time of the surrender of France in June 1940, 330,000 Jews were living inside its borders. More than one-third of them were either stateless refugees or holding foreign passports. Among them were 17,000 stateless German and Austrian Jewish refugees who had lost their nationality as well as many Polish Jewish immigrants who had arrived between the two world wars. After the invasion of Belgium another 8,000 German Jewish refugees arrived in France and a few thousand from Luxembourg. After the surrender tens of thousands of Jews fled to the unoccupied zone in the south.

Like the other clero-Fascist regimes of Europe, Vichy France initiated a brutal anti-Jewish campaign immediately after the armistice. On July 22, 1940, it took away citizenship from all immigrants naturalized after 1927. On August 27, it lifted the ban on anti-Semitic publications. On October 3, Jews were ordered to register at local police stations. Employees were to denounce anyone in their workplace suspected of being a Jew. A person was considered Jewish if two grandparents and his/her spouse were Jewish. On October 7, citizenship was taken away from the Algerian Jews who held French citizenship since 1871.

Three weeks before Petain met with Hitler at Montoire, on October 3, 1940, Vichy France, without any request from the Germans, approved its first Statut des Juifs. The first Statut excluded Jews from the army, the government, the judiciary, and journalism. Teaching, medicine, and law were declared off-limits to Jews as well as every position influencing the culture of the country, such as entertainment in all forms, the cinema in particular. Even veterans that had fought in World War I or distinguished themselves in battle in 1939-1940 were excluded from higher-level public-service jobs.

Seeking to identify and segregate Jews, the Statut mandated a Jewish census. Around 150,000 Jews presented themselves voluntarily to police offices to comply with the registration decree, unaware of the upcoming danger. The French police, under the direction of Inspector Tulard, created a central alphabetically classified filing system, which identified nationality, profession, and address. That filing system was later instrumental in the internment and subsequent deportation of foreign Jews.

A day after the publication of the first Statut des Juifs, Nuncio Valerio Valeri (1883-1963), in a report to Cardinal Maglione, echoed anti-Semitic propaganda and laid on the Jews the responsibility for the outbreak of the war:

> The regime was preparing additional anti-Jewish legislation out of a desire to imitate the totalitarian countries also because without a doubt, unfortunately, the Jews have contributed as much as they could to the outbreak of the war. [115]

The armistice gave Vichy legal authority in both the occupied zone and in the unoccupied south. The French police operated in both zones, although they were subordinate to the German s in the occupied zone. In the unoccupied zone, local authorities were given the power to arrest foreign Jews on October 4, 1940, on the sole basis of a police order, and to hold them in internment camps. A Commissariat-General for Jewish Affairs (CGQJ, Commissariat Général aux Questions Juives), was created on March 29, 1941, under the direction of Xavier Vallat, which worked with German authorities to Aryanize Jewish businesses in the occupied zone.

Internment camps were established by the French police in Les Milles and Le Vernet, Rivesaltes and St. Cyprien, Compiègne, Pithiviers, and Beaune-la-Rolande, Gurs, and Drancy. The Drancy internment camp eventually became the central transit camp for detainees on their way to Auschwitz and other camps. Designed to hold 700 people, it held more than 7,000 at its peak. In total, around 100,000 Jews languished in French internment camps suffering hunger and dying from epidemics.

The first group of 3,700 foreign Jews were arrested in Paris on May 10, 1941, and brought to the Pithiviers and Beaune-la-Rolande camps. In August 1941 a raid was carried out in the XI arrondissement of Paris, during which 3,200 foreign Jews and 1,000 French Jews were interned in various camps, including Drancy. At least 2,000-3000 Jews died in local camps and more than 1,000 were executed. Transit camps became the waiting rooms of death from where the Jews were later delivered to the Germans to be deported to extermination camps in the east.

A second, much harsher and stricter, Statut des Juifs was approved on June 2, 1941. It legalized the seizure of Jewish property and further restricted the civil and human rights of the Jews. Many more professions and occupations were declared off-limits to Jews. Highly restrictive quotas were established for those few professional activities in which they could still be employed. Forced labor was decreed a few months later. To identify and locate every single Jew, a census of Jews and their property was taken using an elaborate card-file system that had been tried out by the special French anti-Jewish police squad one year earlier in the occupied zone. Jewish files were handed over to Theodor Dannecker, head of the Gestapo in France, and used to carry out raids.

Petain, as a loyal Catholic, sought the approval of the Holy See for the second Statut des Juifs. He instructed his ambassador to the Vatican, Léon Bérard (1870-1956), on August 7, 1941, to consult the Vatican on the legislation. The reply published in recent years is one of the most explicit and important documents that throws light on Vatican policy during World War II. The text of Bérard's extensive reply informs Petain that Vatican experts found no objections against the legislation from a doctrinal viewpoint. Referring to historical precedent, the Vatican specialists found justified that "appropriate measures be taken to limit the action of the Jews and to restrict their influence." Even the requirement to wear the yellow star, Bérard was told, was well established in ecclesiastical law. Ambassador Bérard was given the strongest assurances that, unlike the case of Italy, no conflict, censure, or even objections from the Church to the Statut des Juifs would follow.

When false rumors appeared in the foreign press that the Pope had sent a handwritten letter to Petain expressing his disapproval of the anti-Jewish Vichy legislation, Vichy Commissar for Jewish Affairs Xavier Vallat issued without delay a public denial on October 14, 1941:

> From information obtained from the most authoritative sources, there is nothing in the legislation worked out for the protection of France from Jewish influence which is in opposition to Church doctrine. [116]

Vallat was obviously referring to the Bérard report in which the highest authorities in the Vatican had given the green light to anti-Semitic legislation in August 1941. The text of the Bérard report is also included in a coded message intercepted by the British Intelligence Service concerning a conversation that the Ecuadorian ambassador had with Pétain in a Vichy hotel on July 1942. Pétain told the ambassador that he was at peace that the Pope approved his policy of deporting Jews. [117]

Typical of the support that the French episcopate gave to the anti-Jewish legislation are the words of the bishop of Marseilles, Jean Delay (1879-1976). He justified the anti-Jewish legislation as an act of "self-defense against those who abused the hospitality that had so liberally been extended to them":

> We do not ignore the fact that the Jewish question poses difficult national and international problems. We are all aware that our country has the right to take all appropriate steps to defend itself against those who, especially in recent years, have done her so much harm and to punish those who abuse the hospitality that has so liberally been extended to them. [118]

Catholic historian Renée Bedarida seems to forget these declarations in his apology for the French bishops of their complacent attitude toward anti-Jewish legislation:

> In offering full support to the National Revolution regime installed by Marshal Petain, and for fear of endangering the Vichy program of restoration of the country, the Catholic hierarchy refrained from protesting against the unjust decree punishing the French Jews and kept silent. They maintained the same silence when foreign Jews were shamefully confined in special camps of evil character. [119]

Xavier Vallat, the commissioner of Jewish affairs who was tried after the war as a war criminal, claimed before the tribunal that had the Church hierarchy approached him as commissioner with a protest expressing their disapproval of the Statut, he would have modified it. One can of course doubt the sincerity of his claim, but the fact that the Vatican gave its explicit approval to the Statut des Juifs, which inflicted indescribable misery on French Jewry and laid the basis for the deportations of Jews in France to the death camps in Poland, is a fact beyond dispute.

Beginning February 1942, Jews were forbidden to use telephones, elevators, or bicycles and to enter cafes, hotels, cinemas, theaters, museums, and children's playgrounds. The French police oversaw the confiscation of telephones and radios from Jewish homes. Jews were subject to a curfew. They were only allowed to travel in the last carriage of Metro trains and their shopping was restricted to one hour in the afternoon when most rationed food supplies were gone. Regulations were strictly enforced by the French police. Violators ran the risk of detention and deportation. A flood of denunciations by common Frenchmen overwhelmed the French Police and the Gestapo. Three million letters denouncing and betraying Jews to the German authorities were received during the occupation.[120] On May 29, 1942, the decree that Jews had to wear the yellow star came into effect and on December 12, 1942, it was decreed that the word "Juif" had to be stamped on identity documents and ration cards of Jews.

Anti-Semitic legislation and the census prepared the ground for the implementation of the last stage of the Final Solution—the deportation of Jews to the death camps. Pierre Laval, the second most important figure in the Vichy regime, a fervent Catholic, was directly in charge of deportations. He fully cooperated with Dannecker and Eichmann's team to hunt down Jews. The French police rounded up foreign Jews whereas the French Jews were hunted down by the Gestapo, who did not trust the French authorities enough.

Deportations to the death camps began in March 1942. The first deportation trains left to the east with 5,000 stateless Jews seized in the occupied zone on March 27, 1942. Loaded onto cattle cars they were brought to the Drancy transit camp northeast of Paris, the last stop before the journey to Auschwitz or Sobibor where they arrived a week later.

The largest deportation action known as La Grande Rafle took place on July 15 and 16, 1942, in Paris. Around 13,300 Jewish men, women, and children were rounded up by French police and marched in groups through the streets of Paris to the Velodrome d'Hiver, where they were held without food or water until their deportation to Auschwitz. On what became known as as Black Thursday more than 100 desperate deportees committed suicide in that Dante inferno in the heart of Paris. From the Velodrome they were taken to Drancy, the antechamber of death, and deported to Sobibor.

On June 29, 1942, the Nuncio Valeri informed Cardinal Maglione about La Grande Rafle. Although the deportations were carried out in the heart of Paris in full public view by the French police, the French Church hierarchy decided to remain passive. Cardinal Celestin Suhard (1874-1949) of Paris sent a private letter to Petain, expressing his displeasure with the manner of the deportations. With that the French episcopate felt that they had discharged their moral duty. At the annual assembly of the French episcopate on July 22, 1942, the cardinals and bishops voted to abstain from any public protest against the deportations on grounds that their protest might bring about the banning of *Catholic Action*. The nuncio dutifully informed Cardinal Maglione about the decision.

Another major roundup occurred on August 15, 1942, when 7,000 foreign Jews were arrested by the French police and handed over to the Germans. Even Bishop Delay of Marseilles was shocked by the cruelty displayed by the French police. Nuncio Valeri informed Cardinal Maglione on August 7, about the August deportations, adding that the sick and old were also being deported, a fact which he correctly interpreted as disproving the claim that the Jews were being sent to work. A month later, on September 8, 1942, Monsignor Alfredo Pacini, the counselor of the nunciature, informed Cardinal Maglioni that deportations from France were continuing.

Maglione, who himself had been nuncio to France in the past, was mainly interested in maintaining excellent relations with the Vichy regime. He remained undisturbed by the reports and gave no suggestions or orders to Valeri to protest to the government: "On the contrary, the secretary of state would probably have forbidden any such actions because of the favor which the Vichy government enjoyed at the Vatican," states Fr. Morley. Nuncio Valeri did not protest the deportations of Jews to the east, where they disappeared without a trace. Neither did he stand up to Petain to let him know the moral abyss in which he was descending. In the words of Fr. Morley:

> Valeri, as far as it can be ascertained, never made known to Petain the moral horror involved in the 1942 and 1943 actions taken against the Jews. [121]

The Vatican remained silent at the sight of these crimes committed by a Catholic government in the heart of Europe. Nuncio Valeri justified the Pope's lack of response as a result of his inclination "toward prudent delay and enlightened reserve." When Cardinal Maglione was asked by the nuncio in London, Archbishop William Godfrey, at the request of the English press, if he could officially confirm the rumors that the Pope had protested to Vichy the deportations through the nuncio, Maglione responded on August 11, 1942, that his office had no knowledge of such a protest.

After the war, General Charles de Gaulle requested the removal of the Nuncio Valerio Valeri and of at least twenty-seven of the wartime bishops as Vichy collaborators.[122] Within a general climate of passive complicity, only six bishops out of 100 took a different stand. While reaffirming their loyalty to Petain, they expressed their disapproval of the harsh treatment inflicted on the Jews by the French police. Cardinal Pierre-Marie Gerlier of Lyons, Archbishop Jules-Géraud Saliège of Toulouse, Bishop Pierre Marie Théas of Montauban, Msgr. Vansterberghe of Bayonne, and Msgr. Moussaron of Albi issued pastoral letters in August 1942.[123] Appalled by the deportations, Saliege ordered that a pastoral letter be read in every parish of his diocese on August 23, 1942:

> That children, women, men, fathers and mothers, should be treated like a vile herd; that family members should be deported to an unknown destination—it has fallen to our times to witness such a sad sight . . .

Here in our diocese, terribly moving scenes have taken place in the camps of Noe and Recebedou. Jews are men, Jews are women. Foreigners are men, foreigners are women. It is forbidden to harm them, to harm these men, to harm these women, to harm these fathers and mothers of families. They are part of the human race; they are our brothers like all others. A Christian may not forget this.

To erase any impression that his letter was intended as a personal attack on Petain, Archbishop Saliege promptly issued a statement reiterating his loyalty to the marshal.[124] At a time that deportation trains were rolling to the east, Cardinals Gerlier of Lyons and Suhard of Paris even went personally to express their loyalty to Petain on October 29, 1942, and to discuss government subsidies for religious education, Petain showed his generosity and increased the subsidies for the Catholic schools.[125] No more protests were heard again.

Angered by the pastoral letters of the six bishops, Pierre Laval told Monsignor Carmine Rocco, the secretary of the nunciature, that Catholic bishops were certainly in no position to admonish the French government:

Anti-Jewish measures were after all no novelty for the Church either, since it had been the Popes who had first introduced the yellow hat to distinguish people as Jews.

Fr. Morley draws the following conclusions after researching the correspondence between the nuncio and Cardinal Maglione:

The Jews of France were of little concern to the nuncio. Those stateless Jews who died, and those French Jews who survived, did so without any intervention on his part. He was well informed, and even suspicious, but his orientation was totally diplomatic and his interest in human suffering minimal . . . It does not appear from the report made to the Vatican of the discussion or from the remarks of Abetz that Rocco made any defense of Saliège let alone a protest of the government's attitude.[126]

When the Allies landed in North Africa in November 1942, the Wehrmacht invaded the unoccupied zone in the south of France. The Italians, still allies of the Germans at the time, invaded the southeastern corner of France, east of the Rhone River. Thousands of Jews flocked to the Italian zone, particularly to Nice, in hope to escape the roundups, many of them with the assistance of the Italian Jewish rescue activist Angelo Donati and the noble Capuchin priest Fr. Marie Benoit. As long as the Italian military held control there, they refused to allow the French police to arrest the Jews for deportation.

The Reich Security Main Office had set a goal to deport 125,000 Jews from France in 1942, but due to transportation difficulties "only" 42,000 were actually deported to the death camps during that year. A short providential four-month reprieve in deportations took place from November 1942 to February 1943 due to the North African Allied invasion. Soon, however, the deportations were renewed. The leadership of the manhunt passed from French to German hands throughout the country. The Jews were now required to wear the yellow star everywhere. Deportations were reinitiated on February 9, 1943, with a transport of 1,000 Jews from Drancy to Auschwitz.

When Italy surrendered to the Allies on September 8, 1943, and the Germans invaded the Italian zone they went after the Jews in the Cote d'Azur. A few thousand Jews managed to hide or escape to Switzerland. The individual voices of protest among the Church hierarchy that were heard in the summer of 1942 were this time silent. The Allied Forces landed in Normandy, in northwestern France, on June 6, 1944, but deportations to Auschwitz via Drancy continued until August 1944, claiming the lives of another 33,000 victims.

From March 27, 1941, to July 31, 1944, seventy-six deportation convoys left France for Auschwitz and Sobibor carrying 75,721 Jews, around 25 percent of the approximately 330,000 Jews living in France.[127] At least sixty of those convoys with 62,000 Jews aboard originated in Drancy. Only 2,570 Jews, 3 percent of those deported, survived. At the request of Laval, deportations included women and children. Among the the deportees were 11,400 children of which 6,000 were under thirteen years of age. Twenty-three thousand of the deportees had French nationality, while the rest were foreigners that sought refuge in France at one time or another.[128]

On July 16, 1995, fifty-three years after La Grande Rafle, French President, Jacques Chirac spoke at the commemoration site about the moral burden that rests on the shoulders of France:

> These black hours will stain our history forever and are an injury to our past and our traditions . . . France, home of the Enlightenment and the Rights of Man, land of welcome and asylum, France committed that day the irreparable. Breaking its word, it delivered those it protected to their executioners."[129]

On September 30, 1997, the French Catholic bishops issued at Drancy, a declaration of Repentance:

> The anti-Semitic legislation enacted by the French government—beginning with the October 1940 law on Jews and that of June 1941, which deprived a whole sector of the French people of their rights as citizens, which hounded them out and treated them as inferior beings within the nation—and given the decision to put into internment camps foreign Jews who thought they could rely on the rights of asylum and hospitality in France, we are obliged to admit that the bishops of France made no public statements, thereby acquiescing by their silence in the flagrant violation of human rights and leaving the way open to a death-bearing chain of events . . . we must recognize that silence was the rule in face of the multifarious laws enacted by the Vichy government, whereas speaking out in favor of the victims was the exception.[130]

## The Final Solution in Belgium

It is estimated that around 90,000 Jews lived in Belgium at the time of the German invasion in 1940, including 30,000 refugees from Germany. During the early months following the invasion, many thousands of Jews fled the country. As a result, by late 1940 the Jewish community was reduced to 52,000-55,000 Jews.[131] Only 5 percent of the Jews living in Belgium had Belgian citizenship, all the rest had immigrated in the interwar period. Upon arrival, the Germans ordered the Jewish community to set up a so-called Association of Jews of Belgium (AJB). Their intention was to use the organization to facilitate their implementation, of the Final Solution.

The first anti-Jewish ordinance was issued by the Belgian authorities on October 28, 1940, followed by a chain of decrees that aimed at identifying and isolating the Jews in preparation for their deportation. In November 1940, the German overlords required Belgian authorities to register Jews. The order violated the Belgian Constitution, but after legal consultations the government decided to allow the registration. Around 42,000 Jews complied but even among them many went underground once the deportations began.

Jews were forced to concentrate in the major cities such as Antwerp and Brussels. A curfew was imposed on the Jews. They were not allowed to use many public places, sites of entertainment, and social establishments. In December 1940, employment of Jews in the government was outlawed and all Jews holding official positions were fired. On April 14, 1941, a pogrom was carried out by the Flemish SS and the Belgian Anti-Jewish League. Windows of Jewish-owned shops were smashed and two synagogues were burned down.

In July 1941, the Belgian Internal Affairs secretary-general ordered that identity cards of Jews had to be stamped "Juif-Jood" (Jew). Jewish assets were blocked and their businesses confiscated. In October 1941, Belgian authorities outlawed textbooks that were edited by Jews and in December 1941 Jewish children were expelled from public schools. On May 27, 1942, Jews were mandated to wear the yellow star. Their isolation was now complete. They became social pariahs who were barred from a normal existence. Deportation to the death camps of Poland was soon to begin camouflaged as labor mobilization. On July 25, 1942, the delegate of the Association of Jews of Belgium received 10,000 labor mobilization summonses from the SS officer responsible for Jewish Affairs, to be distributed among the Jews. Two days later, the Dossin barracks in Mechelen were opened as an assembly camp to receive the first arriving group of Jews summoned for so-called labor mobilization.

Upon their arrival to the Mechelen transit camp, Jews of all ages were subject to a humiliating search and stripped of all their belongings. Each person received a number as his new identity. The length of stay in the Dossin barracks of Mechelen before being dispatched to Poland was generally only a few days. Some stayed longer until a sufficient contingent for the transport of at least 1,000 persons was gathered. Inside the borders of Belgium, Belgian locomotives and personnel operated the trains going to the death camps.

The first convoy of deportees was programmed to leave for the east on August 4, 1942. Most of the first 10,000 Jews summoned did not present themselves voluntarily. Until September 3, 1942, only 3,900 of them came on their own. Belgian authorities decided to round up the Jews from Antwerp and Brussels in night raids. From August 4, 1942, when the Mechelen transit camp began to operate, to July 31, 1944, Belgian authorities deported 25,631 Jews from Mechelen to the death camps, including 1,000 Jews holding Belgian citizenship. Most of the deportees were sent to Auschwitz, others to the ghettos of Riga, Lodz, and Theresienstadt, and to the Bergen-Belsen camp. According to wartime reports, Belgian Jews were also deported to occupied Soviet territories to be killed by the Einsatzgruppen. More than 60 percent of the arrivals to Auschwitz-Birkenau from Mechelen were not even registered but gassed immediately. Practically all of the children, the old and sick people, and the majority of the women automatically fell into this category. The official count of Belgian Jews killed in Auschwitz-Birkenau totals 28,518, including 5,430 children. Among those selected for work only 1,207 survived the war.

Belgian Queen Mother Elizabeth and Cardinal Van Roey intervened successfully with German Military Governor Alexander von Falkenhausen (1878-1966) to exempt from deportation the small minority of Belgian Jews (5 percent) who held citizenship. But even that group was not inmune, and 800 among them who had refused to wear the Jewish star or had violated other anti-Jewish decree were deported to their death.

At the end of the war, Belgium was afraid to open the Pandora's box of their wartime collaboration with the Germans in the Final Solution. The Belgian government decided it was best to keep silent and forget. Aware that a trial of the police officers who participated in the deportation of Jews would incriminate the total chain of command and the government as a whole, they decided not to try any of them. The tragic fate suffered by the 50,000 deported Jewish men, women, and children was not allowed to disturb the peace of mind of postwar Belgium.

It took sixty-two years for Belgium to look back at its role of collaborators in the Final Solution. It was not until 2002 that the Belgian Senate appointed a committee of historians to investigate the extent of the Belgian collaboration with Nazi Germany in the persecution and deportation of Jews. The product was a comprehensive report under the title *La Belgique Docile* (Obedient Belgium). The Belgian Senate report identified three crucial moments that marked Belgian cooperation in the Final Solution. The first was when the Germans ordered the Belgian authorities to register all the Jews in the country, the second when the Belgian Internal Affairs secretary-general ordered that identity cards of Jews had to be stamped "Juif-Jood," and the third when Belgians helped the Germans to gather the Jews to Mechelen to deport them to the death centers. The study points out that even the exile government in London never issued a call to the Belgian population or to the resistance to oppose the persecution of the Jews:

> They never let it be known that policies had to be adapted and that behavior of leading civil servants and magistrates was unconstitutional and democratically reprehensible.[132]

In its conclusions, the report states that although much power was left in the hands of the local Belgian authorities and the Germans needed their collaboration, they mostly used that power against the Jews not in their favor. Belgian authorities, tainted with xenophobia and anti-Semitism, acted as though the Jews, not the Germans, were their enemies and carried out the Germans' instructions. In Antwerp the police helped the German forces close off streets to seize the Jews. The Antwerp police alone, without German assistance, carried out one of the three roundups that took place on August 28-29, 1942, detaining 1,243 Jews that were sent to the death camps. The editor of the report, historian Rudi Van Doorslaer, wrote:

> In general, it can be said that the Belgians sacrificed the Jewish community to try to preserve "normality" and the orderly functioning of the economy. [133]

The bishops of Belgium were silent while the Jews without citizenship were being hunted down and dispatched to death camps by the Belgian authorities and police. Cardinal Joseph-Ernest van Roey, archbishop of Mechelen, never issued a public protest against the persecution and deportation of the Jews.[134] In a Catholic country like Belgium, where the clergy had a strong influence on the people, exhortations by the bishops to help the Jews could have made a difference. Cardinal van Roey disbanded the *Katholiek Bureau voor Israel*, an Antwerp Catholic organization that tried to help Jewish refugees.[135]

After the war, German Governor Baron von Falkenhausen was brought back to Belgium to stand trial as a war criminal. Sentenced to twelve years in March 1951 for deporting Jews to the death camps and executing hostages, he was freed after three weeks.

## The Final Solution in Hungary:
## The Grand Finale of the Holocaust

It was already pointed out that Hungary was the first country in Europe, after the Third Reich, to adopt anti-Jewish legislation. In 1938, two years before it joined the Axis, it began to adopt legislation against its Jewish citizens. Approval in 1938 of the anti-Semitic Bill for a More Effective Guarantee of a Balanced Social and Economic Life, and the Law to Limit the Expansion of Jews in the Public and Economic Domain in 1939 was merely a beginning. Harder days still awaited them.[136]

On December 2, 1940, the Hungarian army expelled all the Jewish soldiers from its ranks. Compulsory Jewish labor battalions under military command were created by a special decree, the Labor Battalions Act, promulgated on April 1941, with the full support of the Church representatives in the parliament. When Germany invaded Soviet Russia on June 22, 1941, and Hungary joined with an army of 250,000 soldiers, the Jewish labor battalions were dragged to the front as slave laborers. Life in these units was made so unbearable that in many of them it was not very different from the death camps. Between 50,000 and 60,000 Jewish members of the labor battalions died.

It is often assumed incorrectly that the Holocaust in Hungary began on April 1944 when the first deportation train departed from Hungary to Auschwitz. It actually began almost four years earlier when Hungary received through Hitler's grace various contested provinces. Approximately 300,000 Jews living in these provinces fell overnight under Hungarian domination. Admiral Horthy declared them "aliens" and denied them citizenship rights.

When Carpatho-Ruthenia was annexed to Hungary after the dismemberment of Czekoslovakia, the Hungarians decided to make the area Judenfrei. The Hungarian Alien Control Office proposed a plan to Admiral Horthy to banish from Carpatho-Ruthenia all persons of dubious citizenship (meaning the Jews) and to hand them over to German authorities in the Ukraine (East Galizia). A law issued on June 27, 1941, took away citizenship and residency rights from those unable to prove that their ancestors resided without interruption in Hungary for the previous ninety years and were listed as Hungarian taxpayers.

Three weeks after the attack on Soviet Russia, Horthy and his council of ministers approved the expulsion plan on July 12, 1941. Under the deception of "resettlement to the east," around 30,000 Jewish men, women, and children were brought in trucks from all over Carpatho-Ruthenia to Iasin for deportation and transported in cattle trains to the ghettos of Kamenetz-Podolsk, Stanislaw, Kolomea, Horodenka, and Tarnopol in east Galitzia.[137] Very often the Hungarian gendarmes in the smaller towns of Carpatho-Ruthenia ignored the documents that proved Hungarian citizenship and placed the people on deportation trucks to Iasin. Many of the smaller Jewish communities in Carpatho-Ruthenia disappeared completely.

The late rabbi of Munkacs, Baruch Rabinowitz, was among the deportees; he described in a Yad Vashem deposition the collective tragedy of the Carpatho-Ruthenian Jews and spoke with pain about the readiness of the Ruthenians to betray their Jewish neighbors "for a quart of liquor."[138] The deportees did not suspect the tragic fate that awaited them in East Galitzia when they boarded the trucks that were to take them to their new "homes." Kamenetz Podolsk ghetto was one of them.

The German and Hungarian military chiefs of staff at the military HQ in Vinnitza set up a time table for the liquidation of the Kamenetz Podolsk ghetto on August 25, 1941. Commanded by Friedrich Jeckeln, this was his first major mass murder operation in the Ukraine which preceded his massacres of Kiev and Riga. He committed himself to complete the liquidation of Kamenetz Podolsk no later than September 1, 1941. Under deception, 23,600 defenseless Jews were notified that they were being "relocated" further east. They were marched on foot fifteen miles outside Kamenetz-Podolsk under a Hungarian sapper platoon and Einsatzgruppe D units to an area filled with bomb craters.[139] After being ordered to undress, the Jews were gunned down into the pits on August 27 and 28, 1941. Many wounded were buried alive. On September 11, 1941, Jeckeln forwarded his official report to Berlin with business-like casualness:

In Kamenetz Podolsk 23,600 Jews were shot in three days by a commando of the Higher SS and Police Leader. [140]

It is estimated that between 14,000 and 18,000 of the victims were Hungarian deportees from Carpatho-Ruthenia, the rest were native Jews of Kamenetz Podolsk.[141] Another 2,000 deportees from Carpatho-Ruthenia held in the Stanislaw ghetto were killed on October 11, 1941, on the night of Hoshana Raba, together with many thousands of local Jews.

When the shattering news that the deportees from Carpatho-Ruthenia were being executed by shooting in the Ukraine reached Budapest, the Jewish leadership there desperately intervened with Minister of the Interior Ferenc Keresztes-Fischer. They were able to rescue in the last minute seven transports that were on their way to the Ukraine. The deportations from Carpatho-Ruthenia to the Ukraine were suspended by Keresztes-Fischer and were not renewed until 1944 when the Germans invaded Hungary.

The Jews of Carpatho-Ruthenia were not the only victims of the early Hungarian Holocaust. Those in other annexed Hungarian territories suffered the same fate. In April 1941 the Hungarians began to mass murder the 25,000 Jews in the Backa basin annexed from Yugoslavia. At least 3,000 Jews were massacred in January 1942 in Novi Sad, Stari Becej, and Titel.[142] On January 21-23, 1942, in the middle of a bitterly cold winter, the Hungarian military rounded up hundreds of families at Novi Sad, took them to an area of the Danube known as the Strand, and mowed them down with machine guns at the shore. After breaking open the icy sheet of the Danube with artillery fire, the bodies were dumped into the icy waters.

According to a somewhat different version, the Jews were first driven over the ice sheet while alive and then drowned by shelling the ice sheet. The memories of the crime committed sixty-four years earlier by the Hungarian military were still alive in the minds of the elderly people in Novi Sad. The memorial at the river site where the Jews were killed and drowned bears an inscription: "Memory is a monument harder than stone."[143]

A third round of harsher anti-Jewish legislation was approved by the Hungarian Parliament on August 8, 1941. As in Italy and other Catholic countries, differences between the Nazis and Catholics surfaced with respect to the prohibition of mixed marriages between Hungarian Christians and baptized Jewish converts in the legislation. Cardinal Serédi, the primate of Hungary, while giving his full support to the main body of the new anti-Jewish law, expressed his objections on this particular point to the prime minister. He assured the prime minister that his objections did not stem from any interest in the welfare of the Jews:

Had this bill prohibited marriages between Jews and Christians, I too would have supported it. But the bill does not distinguish between real Jews and those Jews who had already become Christians. This bill harms mainly Christians of Jewish origin. This bill will drive them back to Judaism forever—them, their children and their posterity—and in so doing will increase to a considerable degree the number of Jews in our midst . . . My opposition to the proposed bill does not stem from my interest in Jewish welfare. [144]

There were in Hungary 725,000 Jews and approximately 100,000 converts according to the census of 1941. United in the common aim of eliminating the Jews from Hungarian life, the dividing issues were pushed aside, and the bill— the Hungarian equivalent of the Nuremberg Laws—was approved with the support of the Church. As a result of the third anti-Semitic law, baptized converts were also expelled from the army and forced to join the Jews in the Labor Battalions. When the Labor Battalions Law was updated on July 31, 1942, the Synod of Bishops focused their concerns on the inclusion of baptized converts in the same labor units with the Jews. Finding no fault with the labor battalions per se except that converts were grouped together with the Jews, Bishop Glattfelder spoke in parliament: [145]

He who classifies converts to Christianity as Jews insults them. [146]

When Miklos Kállay became prime minister on March 3, 1942, his first legislative act was to propose the expropriation of estates and forests owned by Jews. The law was approved by both houses of parliament and issued on June 15, 1942. The Church, one of the major landowners in the country, which traditionally opposed land expropriation, was in this csae pleased with the confiscation of Jewish landholdings. While deportations did not take place as long as Kállay was prime minister, he nonetheless expressed his wishes of removing the Jews from every important position in preparation of the final solution:

I know there is no final solution to this problem other than the removal of the Jews who number 800,000 people . . . In the meantime the Jews must be removed from each and every socially and nationally important position—until such time as the final solution becomes feasible.[147]

Amid a torrent of unrepressed slander and defamation of Judaism, the Hungarian Parliament abolished on July 29, 1942, the law that had granted equal rights to the Jewish religion in 1895, and eliminated the meager subsidies that the impoverished Jewish communities were receiving. The Church, which had fiercely opposed the law of religious equality in 1895, could claim another victory in its struggle of "protecting" Hungary from the Jews. Nevertheless, compared to the infernal conditions that the Jews were subject to in the rest of Europe, their life in Hungary at the time was relatively calm.

In April 1943, Hitler summoned Admiral Horthy to Klessheim Castle near Salzburg to demand his cooperation in the deportation of Hungarian Jewry. As the military situation in the Eastern front began to deteriorate for the Axis forces, and the Soviets were approaching the borders of Hungary, Kállay and his government was secretly trying to extricate itself from the war, as Italy had done in September 1943, and attempted to establish contacts with the Soviets in March 1944. When knowledge of the contacts reached the Germans, Admiral

Horthy was summoned to Hitler on March 17, 1944. He agreed to dismiss Kállay as prime minister and to deport the Jews of Hungary.

On March 19, 1944, Horthy appointed Lt. General Döme Sztójay, the pro-Nazi Ambassador to Berlin, as prime minister. Eight German divisions moved swiftly into Hungary to ensure Hungary's cooperation. Former Prime Minister Kállay took refuge in the Turkish Embassy and Interior Minister Keresztes-Fischer was sent to a concentration camp. The new government's first action was to decree on March 31, 1944, that all Jews without exception, including converts, were to wear the yellow star on their clothing. Cardinal Jusztinián Serédi (1884-1945) only objected that the decree included converts:

> The six-pointed star is not the emblem of the Jewish race but of the Jewish religion. Consequently, the display of it is, in the case of Christians, a contradiction, and constitutes a renunciation of faith.[148]

As German divisions entered Hungary in March 1944, the Germans marked for immediate extinction the last great reservoir of Jews in Europe, a community of 767,000 souls. Aware that they had lost the war, the Germans were doing everything in their power to wipe out the last remnants of European Jewry in the short time left to them, and raised their death machinery to new unprecedented levels of efficiency. They readied themselves to kill as many as 1 million Jews and Auschwitz-Birkenau was expanded to handle efficiently the increasing volume. The rail lines were extended into the center of the camp to facilitate access to the gas chambers.

Adolf Eichmann and his SS team came in to Hungary to carry out the deportation of Jews to Auschwitz. The new Hungarian government of Sztójay responded most cooperatively and put the rabid anti-Semites, Laszlo Endre and Laszlo Baky, in charge of deportations. Four trains of forty-five wagons each carrying 4,000 Jews instead of their normal capacity of between 1,600 and 1,800 were assigned to leave daily from Hungary to Auschwitz. As a preparatory step to deportations, all the Jews in the rural towns and villages of Hungary were enclosed in ghettos by the Hungarian gendarmerie with the full collaboration of the Hungarian population who were eager to take possession of the properties of the Jews. After inspecting a total of forty-four towns in which the enclosure of the Jews in ghettos was carried out, State Secretary Laszlo Endre described before the Hungarian press on May 12, 1944, the enthusiastic cooperation he received from the population in his expulsion of the Jews from their homes:

> In every town and in every village the local population accepted the steps taken for the de-Judification of their settlement with open support and undisguised rejoicing . . . Everywhere the local population assisted in furthering the actions taken by the authorities. In most places the people placed at the disposal of the authorities, and at no cost whatever, vehicles to speed up the removal of those, who, by their very presence in the immediate vicinity, detracted from the ability of the Christians to survive.[149]

The tragedy of the Jews was played out in Hungary on an immeasurably larger scale than in Italy or France. Deportations advanced geographically from east to west, leaving Budapest to the end. The first Jews to be sent to Auschwitz on April 24, 1944, were taken from a detention camp where they had been arrested as a result of libel and informers. The Jews of Northern Transylvania and Carpathian-Ruthenia were next. Helpless men, women and children were beaten and loaded in cattle cars, invalids were taken out of hospitals together with the insane and handicapped. As many as 100,000 Jews were deported from Northern Transylvania alone. Upon arrival, the deportees were marched directly from the cattle trains to the gas chambers. The deportations also included many baptized converts, which were made to share the same destiny as the Jews. Within three weeks, the majority of the deportees had been gassed in Auschwitz.

In the town of Paks, State Minister Endre personally ordered the passengers to stand in the train cars with raised hands to push in an additional twenty Jews in each wagon. In his written and oral reports, Endre prided himself that in separating and transporting the Jews he was carrying out his mission humanely in accordance with the "Spirit of Christianity." He made abundantly clear what the "Spirit of Christianity" meant to him at the dedication ceremony of the newly founded so-called Hungarian Institute of Jewish Studies on May 15, 1944, the day the first deportation train from Hungary proper left for Auschwitz:

> The Popes, as well as our own ancient and saintly kings, legislated draconian laws and imposed severe decrees upon this parasitic race. Thus, no one can complain that we are not acting with the spirit of Christianity when we enact draconian regulations against the Jews so as to protect our nation. [150]

M. Herczl comments:

> Thus the voice of Christianity reached the ears of the Hungarians from the mouths of such government ministers as Endre and his colleagues. They spoke in the name of Christianity, and no priest voiced other opinions. [151]

A campaign of systematic robbery seldom witnessed was put into action by the Hungarian government as they prepared deportations. A moratorium was declared on all debts owed to Jews by Christians. Every Jew was required to declare all his properties and to immediately hand over to the banks their jewelry and gold. Jewish bank accounts were frozen and Jews could not open their safes in the banks. Not only was the robbery carried out to fill the government coffers but to win the goodwill of the Hungarian population. They were allowed to take possession overnight of Jewish properties. When the deportation trains reached the borders, the Hungarian border police would rob the Jews of the food they were taking along for the journey to Auschwitz. The last act of robbery took place in the death camps themselves with the confiscation of the clothing and the golden fillings taken from the mouths of the deportees. Interior Minister Jaross spoke to the Hungarian people on May 18, 1944, three days after the deportations had begun:

I make it clear that all property and valuables which Jewish greed managed to accumulate during the liberal period has ceased to be their property. All this belongs to the Hungarian nation . . . This property must benefit the entire Hungarian nation. We must inject it into the economic bloodstream, so that every honest and fair working Hungarian will receive his portion.[152]

The German overlords obviously did not miss the opportunity to enrich themselves and confiscate priceless Jewish art treasures and major industries. The acquisition of the powerful Manfred Weiss industrial consortium, whose owners were Jewish, in exchange for their lives, is an eloquent example of German industrial empire building through the plunder of Jewish wealth.[153]

Rudolf Vrba and Alfred Wetzler had learned before their escape from Auschwitz-Birkenau that the death installations were being expanded and the railway tracks extended for the upcoming annihilation of Hungarian Jewry.[154] The Auschwitz protocol they put together on April 25-27, 1944, was forwarded to Jewish organizations in Hungary and Switzerland, to the primate of Hungary Cardinal Justinian Serédi, to the nuncio in Budapest Angelo Rotta, and to the Vatican. It was received by the nuncio in Budapest around May 10, 1944, five days before the deportations were to begin, as testified by Pinhas Freudiger at the Eichmann trial. The escapees also met personally with the apostolic delegate in Slovakia, Msgr. Burzio, who forwarded the protocol to the Vatican on May 22, 1944.[155]

The Church hierarchy, who strongly supported anti-Jewish legislation as long as it excluded converts from its rulings, adopted exactly the same policy with regard to deportations. On May 10, 1944, Cardinal Serédi wrote to the prime minister:

I must again repeat my demand for discrimination between converted Jews and Jews adhering to the Israelite faith . . . Most of all, it must be prevented that they, as a consequence of indiscriminate deportation, suffer loss of life . . . Therefore I respectfully request the Royal Hungarian Government that bearing in mind its historical responsibility, it should cause steps to be taken by Hungarian and non-Hungarian authorities alike to prevent such deportations.[156]

Even Msgr. Rotta, a far more humane person than Serédi, who as nuncio had transmitted the SOS messages from Slovak and Croat Jewry to the Pope, was essentially concerned with baptized converts as can be seen from his meetings with Prime Minister Sztojay and Deputy Foreign Minister Jungerth in the critical period of April and May 1944 when deportations began. He complained to them that by treating baptized converts like Jews, Church rights were being violated. In a memorandum delivered to the Hungarian government on May 15, 1944, Rotta stated:

I regard it my duty to present this note of protest and again to demand that the rights of the Church and its flock be respected . . . to pass anti-Jewish laws without taking into consideration that many Jews have, through baptism, become Christians, is a serious offense against the Church . . . On many previous occasions the Apostolic Nunciate has brought to the notice of the Hungarian government those provisions of the new anti-Jewish decrees that it considers unjust, especially the failure to discriminate between baptized and Israelite Jews.[157]

From the moment on that Rabbi Weissmandl and the Working Group in Slovakia learned the truth about Auschwitz from Vrba and Wetzler they began to send requests that the Allies bomb strategically the railway lines, tunnels, and bridges leading from Hungary to Auschwitz and the crematoriums to stop or a least slow down the tempo of the killings. On July 4, 1944, J. J. McCloy, assistant secretary of the U.S. War Department responded to John Pehle of the War Refugee Board turning down the request. The task, he contended, did not merit "the diversion of considerable air support essential to the success of our forces."[158] It is one of the great tragedies of the Holocaust that the warnings and appeals of these two heroic escapees were ignored at the last stage of the Holocaust and the aim of halting deportations was missed. The terrible asymmetry between the Nazis and the Allies with regard to the Jews played itself out once more: while for the Nazis the destruction of the Jews had the highest priority, for the Allies the rescue of the Jews carried a low priority, if any at all.

On May 24, 1944, only nine days after deportations began in Hungary proper, the counselor of the German Legation in Budapest, Eberhard von Thadden, informed Berlin that 116,000 Jews had already been deported. The gas chambers and crematoriums in Auschwitz were working day and night. "I witnessed the gruesome workings of the machinery of death; gear meshed with gear, like clockwork" are the words with which Eichmann described the death machinery he was feeding with train loads of Jewish men, women, and children from Hungary and every corner of Europe. The last great Jewish community of Europe was annihilated in only seven weeks from May 15 to the end of June 1944: with the full complicity and cooperation of the Hungarian gendarmerie and people, 437,000 Hungarian Jews were deported to Auschwitz-Birkenau and turned into ashes hours after their arrival. A crime that Winston Churchill described in the summer of 1944 in the following words:

> Perhaps the greatest and most horrible crime ever committed in the whole history of the world. [159]

On May 25, 1944, Msgr. Rotta, in a note to the Hungarian Ministry of Foreign Affairs, for the first time protested the deportations, "which the whole world knows what the deportation in fact means." He raised the possibility that "the Holy See would feel obliged to protest, if the deportations continued":

> The Hungarian Government is preparing to deport 100,000 people. The whole world knows what this deportation in fact means. The office of the Apostolic Nuncio regards it as its duty to protest against such measures . . . it requests the

Hungarian government . . . to avoid any action against which the Holy See and the conscience of the entire Christian world would feel obliged to protest. [160]

That the nuncio only mentions 100,000 deportees, instead of the much higher number of Jews in Hungary, can only be explained by the fact that this was the number of baptized converts in Hungary. The Germans were not impressed with the protest. They knew that the gassing of the Jews was not an issue that would come between them and the Vatican. Edmund Veesenmayer, the Reich Plenipotentiary in Budapest, had made this point in his correspondence with the German Foreign Office when it came up with a plan on May 27, 1944, to launch a diversionary campaign that would create the impression that the Budapest Jews were organizing military actions against German forces in order to justify the upcoming deportations. Veesenmayer responded on June 8, 1944 that such diversionary action was unnecessary, because it was unlikely that the deportation of the Jews would produce any protest:

So far as is known here, the evacuation measures carried out in Hungary up to now have not produced any major reaction abroad. No such reaction is likely to occur in the case of the operation against the Budapest Jews either, as it has been known for a long time that the ghettoization process in Budapest, as elsewhere, is being pushed through to the end. [161]

The subsequent notes by Nuncio Rotta confirmed Veesenmayer's unconcerned attitude. The nuncio limited his defense to converts who he complained were being treated like Jews. In a memorandum on June 5, 1944, to the Hungarian government, the nuncio again demanded that converts that were above suspicion of having converted for convenience be exempted from the anti-Jewish measures:

Baptized Jews are to be exempted from anti-Jewish legislation, at least those Jews who, with regard to the date of their conversion, are above of reasonable suspicion (of having converted to escape persecution). [162]

In his personal visit to Prime Minister Sztojay on June 6, 1944 Rotta said:

You yourself see what the theory of racism leads to. People born as Christians and those who have been living Christian lives for the last thirty to forty years are now being subjected to the same unfair treatment accorded to the other Jews. [163]

In July 1944 Cardinal Serédi again wrote to Prime Minister Sztojay objecting to the inclusion of converts in the anti-Jewish decrees:

I have in mind those decrees, which without the legal basis cause injury to Hungarian citizens, my Catholic brethren . . . I herewith insistently request the Royal Government to consider the baptized Christians and distinguish them from the Jews. [164]

There is also clear confirmation from the German side that the interest of both the cardinal and the nuncio was limited to the converts. The report of SS General Winkelman to Himmler of July 13, 1944, makes this abundantly clear:

> Last week such incidents occurred here as would elsewhere have given rise to much anxiety. The Nuncio and Cardinal Seredi registered constant protests with the regent concerning the Jews of Budapest. The fact that in this context all their anxiety was for the converts alone stems undoubtedly from the very nature of the church. [165]

Hungarian Minister of the Interior Andor Jaross declared after the war:

> The leaders of the priesthood made declarations on behalf of the converts only. Cardinal Serédi requested that they be exempted from the obligations of the anti-Jewish legislation. [166]

After all the provinces to the east of the Danube were made Judenfrei, the deportations advanced to the doorstep of Budapest in June 1944. All Jews from the suburbs of Budapest were deported. In a telegram of July 11, 1944, the German ambassador to Budapest informed the Foreign Ministry in Berlin, that a total of 437,402 Jews had already been deported until that date in 148 transports to Auschwitz. Of them, 25,000 were *Durchgangs-Juden* (transit Jews) that were sent to Auschwitz in transit to other concentration camps in the Reich.

The Allied Forces liberated Rome (June 4, 1944) at the time that deportations from Hungary reached their culmination point. Chief Rabbi of the Holy Land, Y. I. Herzog traveled to Cairo to request a personal audience with the Pope in Rome through Apostolic Delegate Hughes, to plead at the last hour for the rescue of the remnants of Hungarian Jewry. His request for an audience was flatly denied. His plea that the Pope make a public appeal to the Hungarian people to place obstacles in the way of deportations and declare that any person doing so would receive the blessing of the Church, whereas those aiding the Germans would be censured was rejected off-handedly from Rome under the excuse that it may drive the Germans to liquidate the rest of the Hungarian Jews, as if the Germans were not already doing exactly that. [167] A prominent Hungarian clergyman Jozsef Elias pointed out in later years the tragic repercusions of this refusal:

> The gendarmerie and the police in Hungary were trained in a religious spirit to view obedience to the Church as an obligation. Had all these people that took a direct part in the deportations of the Jews been informed that neither they nor their families would be permitted to partake of any sacred ceremony, their transgressions would not be forgiven, they would not be eligible to receive the final sacraments, and their newborn children would not be baptized . . . I am sure that many people who assisted in the Jewish expulsion, officials and train workers would have announced that they were unwilling to take upon them-

selves the dispatch of their neighbors to their deaths . . . they would be unwilling to act on the same moral level as Cain.[168]

A heart-rending appeal to the Christians of Hungary was issued by Jews in the shadow of death when the turn came for the Jews of Budapest to be deported. The appeal circulated illegally in thousands of copies in the summer of 1944 in Budapest:

> In this final hour of their tragic destiny, the Jews of Hungary turn imploringly to the Christians of Hungary. They address their words to those whose existence they have shared for a thousand years, in good times and bad, on soil in which their ancestors are at rest.
>
> We kept silent when we were robbed of our possessions, when we lost our human dignity, and our status of citizens. We did not decide upon this extreme step even when we were driven from our homes. But now our very lives are at stake. And this we write in pain: that the lives involved are, those, alas, of but a fraction of Hungary's Jews.
>
> In the name of our children, our aged, and our defenseless women, in the name of us all as we face certain death, a frightful death, we address this prayer to the Christian community of Hungary.[169]

The response to the SOS call of their Jewish neighbors came on June 29, 1944, in the form of a pastoral letter by Primate of Hungary Cardinal Serédi scheduled to be read on July 16. Defaming Hungarian Jewry in their most tragic moment and expressing his support for anti-Jewish laws the letter will forever remain a stain on Christian Hungary. While he deplores the persecution of the converts "our Hungarian compatriots and devout members of our Catholic Church," as far as the Jews is concerned, he expresses his agreement to the measures taken against them and his wish that their "noxious influence" should disappear. The document is a sad reminder of what made the Holocaust of Hungarian Jewry possible:

> We do not deny that many Jews had a wicked, destructive influence on the economic, social and moral life of Hungary. It is also true that the others did not protest against the actions of their coreligionists. We do not doubt that the Jewish question must be settled in a legal and just manner. And so, we do not voice any opposition to the measures taken against them until now in the economic field in the interests of the state. We do not protest either against the elimination of their noxious influence. On the contrary, we wish it to disappear. But it would be neglect of our and Episcopal duty if we did not raise a warning voice against suffering inflicted on our Hungarian compatriots and devout members of our Catholic Church, who are being harmed only because of their racial origin . . . We therefore solemnly reject all responsibility for the consequences . . . Pray and work for our Catholic brethren, our Catholic Church and our beloved Hungary.[170]

In anticipation to Serédi's epistle, Gyula Czapik, the second-highest-ranking clergyman of Hungary wrote to him advising him against helping the Jews in any manner:

> While it is true that everyone is aware of the horrors, and everyone knows what happens to them at their final station, it would not be right to put this before the public in writing; what is happening to the Jews at the present time is nothing but appropriate punishment for their misdeeds in the past. We at any rate are not permitted to do so . . . We will be criticized because the epistle presents the Jews only as persecuted beings who are suffering, without mentioning the fact that many of them sinned against Hungarian Christianity while none of the community reprimanded them . . . I am opposed to the suggestion that we criticize the government publicly and we break off all contact with them.[171]

The reading of the epistle was postponed a few times and finally cancelled when the government satisfied the cardinal's demand to exempt converts from most of the decrees against the Jews. On July 8, 1944, Prime Minister Dome Sztojay in the company of three of his cabinet ministers paid a visit to Cardinal Serédi at his summer home in Gerecse. He informed him that the converts would be spared from deportation, would be exempt from wearing the Star of David, and would not be anymore under the tutelage of the Jewish Council. Serédi was appeased and cancelled the reading of the epistle scheduled for July 16.[172] On July 18, the government informed officially the foreign delegations in Budapest of the new regulations approved for the converts.

Serédi's unpublished epistle provides an answer to the question of how it was possible for Eichmann and his small team to send more than half a million Hungarian Jews to their death in Auschwitz in a smooth operation of a few weeks. The loyal assistance of the Hungarian gendarmerie, the local bishops, and the Hungarian people in general was made possible by the blessings of almost all the Hungarian episcopate following Cardinal Jusztinian Serédi.[173] Clergymen such as Ignác László and András Kun rejoiced in the deportations and publicly called for the annihilation of the Jews.[174] When all the Jews of Veszprem, including converts, were deported, a Tedeum was officiated on June 25, 1944, at the Franciscan Church of Veszprem, overflowing with people to celebrate that the town was Judenfrei. Adding insult to injury, Cardinal Serédi and the Hungarian episcopate, the main champions of the anti-Jewish laws in Hungary, are presented as charitable Samaritans who stood up in defense of Hungarian Jewry in their most tragic hour.

Before the Germans had time to destroy the gas chambers, crematoriums, and piles of dead in Majdanek, the advancing Red Army captured the camp. On July 24, 1944, photographic visual images of the Majdanek death camp near Lublin taken by advancing Soviet troops were made public in two English publications, the *London Illustrated News* and the *Sphere*. Hitler was incensed at his clean-up teams, which failed to fulfill his orders to timely erase the traces of his death machine.[175]

When the Auschwitz Protocol arrived in Switzerland it came in the hands of leading Protestant theologians Karl Barth and Visser t'Hooft who reacted publicly to the unprecedented crime. The Swiss daily press displayed prominently the Hungarian tragedy and the news spread far and wide.[176] Appeals were again issued by Jewish organizations to the Pope, the king of Sweden, and to President Roosevelt to use their influence to stop the annihilation of Hungarian Jewry. President Roosevelt warned Horthy and the Hungarian perpetrators they would be tried as war criminals if the deportations continued.

Placed in an embarrassing situation by the reaction of the main Protestant theologians and the Swiss press, Pius XII sent an open cable to Admiral Horthy, the regent of Hungary, on June 25, 1944, in which he avoided identifying the Jewish victims by name and requested in his typical elliptic style that the suffering borne by "numerous unfortunate people" in Hungary not be prolonged. Overlooking that the victims had to be saved from death and not merely from pain and sorrow, Pius XII wrote:

We have been requested from several sides to do everything possible to ensure that the suffering that had to be borne for so long by numerous unfortunate people in the bosom of this noble and chivalrous (Hungarian) nation because of the nationality or racial origin not be prolonged and made worse. [177]

Instead of issuing a warning of excommunication against the Catholic perpetrators of genocide, Pius XII showered praise on the "chivalrous and noble Hungarian nation" that was sending them to death. His reaction stands in stark contrast to his excommunication of Italian Catholics who voted for the Communist Party in 1948 and those joining that party in 1949.

As the deportations were advancing with lightning speed, Eichmann, acting under Himmler's direct orders, still continued to hatch extortion schemes to trade Jewish lives for valuable commodities and foreign currency. In December 1943 Himmler devised an extortion scheme with Hitler's approval after the German military situation suffered a serious setback at Stalingrad. Himmler wrote at that time:

I have asked the Führer about releasing Jews in return for foreign currency. He gave me full authority to approve such cases that really bring in considerable foreign currency from abroad.[178]

A major extortion deal was presented by Eichmann in the summer of 1944 to the Vaada in Budapest that was intended to drive a wedge between the Western Allies and Soviet Russia. He offered to trade the lives of 1 million Jews in exchange for 10,000 winterized trucks to be used on the Soviet front. Eichmann dispatched two Jewish emissaries Joel Brand and Bundy Grosz (the British suspected Grosz of being a Gestapo agent) from Budapest to Istanbul to contact the representatives of the Jewish agency. To prove his good faith, Eichmann promised to suspend provisionally for a few days deportation convoys until the prompt return of the representatives. Unwilling to even consider the idea of transferring a million Jews to Allied territory or to allow any commodities to reach the Germans, the British imprisoned the two emissaries and did not allow them to return, while the Germans renewed the daily deportations of Hungarian Jews to Auschwitz.

To gain credibility for his offer, Himmler traded with the Vaada in Budapest, represented by Dr. Reszo Kastner, the lives of a group of 1,685 Jews for $1.6 million. Kastner included the Satmar Rebbe R' Joel Teitlbaum and R' M. D. Weissmandl among them. The group was taken to Bergen Belsen in July 1944 and transferred in December to Switzerland. The circumstances leading to this last deal have been the subject of highly charged, still-unresolved controversial claims such as those made by the accusers of Dr. Reszo Kastner, among them Rudolf Vrba, the famous escapee of Auschwitz.[179]

Under the assumption that the presence of Jews all over Budapest acted as a protection against allied bombings of the city, the Hungarians abstained from segregating them in a separate walled Ghetto, and decided instead to isolate them in specific buildings scattered all over the city. All the Jews of Budapest occupying a total of 21,250 apartments were squeezed into 2,681 apartments, (12 percent of their previous accomodations) in a period of eight days until June 21, 1944. Their food rations were reduced to a minimum in accordance with the Nazi starvation technique applied in the ghettos. A curfew was imposed, which only allowed them to be in the streets for shopping purposes during three hours, from 2-5 p.m.

As the Germans were retreating on all fronts Allied messages announcing the upcoming bombardment of Budapest were intercepted. Horthy interrupted for a while the deportations from Budapest on July 7, 1944, saving the lives of the quarter of a million Jews residing in the capital. The lull in the deportations lasted until November 1944. Nonetheless, even during the short period of calm, Eichmann was able to deport on July 19, 1,220 important Jews of Budapest held in the Kistarcsa camp.

On August 25, 1944, Romania switched sides and joined the Allies against Germany. Horthy wished to follow the example of Italy and Romania and leave the sinking ship before it capsized, dragging Hungary along. He dismissed Sztójay as prime minister on August 29, 1944, appointed Col. General Geza Lakatos, and initiated secret peace talks with the Soviets. In a radio message to the Hungarian people, Lakatos addressed the Jewish question and said that the task of removing the foreign race living among them—although they speak Hungarian—had not yet been completed. He reached an agreement with the Germans to remove all the Jews from Budapest to forced labor camps outside the city.[180]

The temporary interruption from July to early November 1944 was crucial in the rescue of many Budapest Jews who managed to obtain consular protection papers from the Swedish envoy Raoul Wallenberg (1912-?) and the Swiss consul Carl Lutz (1895-1975). Wallenberg housed the Jews in safe houses that he placed under Swedish diplomatic protection. The nuncio in Budapest, Msgr. Angelo Rotta, helped save converts by issuing letters of protection for them. In their desperation, as centuries ago in the days of the Spanish massacres, lines of Jews stood outside the Church offices in Budapest seeking to convert, in the belief that conversion would save their lives. [181] A contemporary statement quoted by Herczl is a sad testimony to Hungarian Catholic anti-Semitism:

> Why must we suffer, in that by virtue of the invasion of all these new Christians our churches will turn into inferior, stinking synagogues? . . . The priests must not allow these bloodsucking peddlers to manage their business at the expense of the priests in the sacred temples of God. [182]

On September 12, 1944, the Red Army entered Hungarian territory and advanced to positions only fifty miles from Budapest. The Soviet siege of Budapest began in October and lasted for three months. On October 11, Horthy secretly sent a delegation to Moscow and signed a provisional cease fire by which Hungary committed itself to switch sides and to declare war on Germany, giving up all annexed territories. When the Germans learned about these negotiations, they stormed the Royal Palace in Budapest and abducted Horthy's son Nicholas. Horthy reversed himself and revoked the armistice and appointed the Arrow Cross leader Ferenc Szálasi as prime minister on October 16, 1944.

Jews were again in deadly danger under the Arrow Cross who let loose a campaign of deadly terror in Budapest. Between October 17, 1944, and January 1945 approximately 100,000 Hungarian Jews were murdered by the German and Hungarian Nazis. Adolf Eichmann returned to Budapest on October 17, 1944, and ordered the deportation of the city's Jews. Since the railway lines were too close to the front, Eichmann ordered a death march to the camps in Austria on November 8, 1944. Approximately 20,000 Jews, (some put the number much higher)—men, women, and children—were concentrated in the Ujlaki brickyards in Obuda, and forced to march on foot to the Austrian border. Thousands died as a result of starvation or exposure to bitter cold, and many more were shot during the march. Those who survived reached Austria in late December 1944, where they were taken to various concentration camps, such as Mauthausen in northern Austria, Dachau in Southern Germany, and Vienna where they were employed in the construction of fortifications. Following the marching Jews in his car, Wallenberg was able to rescue a number of them, claiming that they were under his diplomatic protection.

In November 1944, the Arrow Cross ordered that Jews without diplomatic protection papers had to move to a closed ghetto not later than early December. Between December 1944 and the end of January 1945, the Arrow Cross seized around 20,000 Jews from the ghetto, took them to the banks of the Danube and shot them along the shore. Their bodies were thrown into the river. "The Budapest orgy of blood has no equal in the black pages of Nazidom," says Philip Friedman. He quotes the Christian scholar Istvan Bibo and the Jewish Hungarian writer Robert Major on the callous indifference of the Christian population:

> Both agree that the attitude of the Christian populace at large toward the ordeal of the Jews was one of complete indifference. Among officialdom and the of-

ficer corps many participated in the anti-Jewish excesses. However, the crude savagery displayed by the Arrow Cross horrified and alienated many of those who, up until then, had passively condoned the harsh anti-Semitic decrees.[183]

Soviet forces entered Budapest January 1945. They liberated the ghetto and safe houses on February 13, 1945. Between 100,000 and 120,000 Jews were still alive in the city at the time of liberation; many of them owed their lives to Wallenberg and the Swiss consul Lutz who remained in the city during the siege. When the Soviets entered Budapest, Wallenberg was summoned in January 17, 1945 by Soviet officers to meet the Soviet Commander General Rodion Malinovsky (1898-1967). He never returned.

# Notes

1. John Mendelsohn, ed., *The Holocaust: Selected Documents in Eighteen Volumes. Vol. 11: The Wansee Protocol and a 1944 Report on Auschwitz by the Office of Strategic Services* (New York: Garland, 1982), 18–32.

2. Mendelsohn, *The Holocaust: Selected Documents,* 18-32. Gerald Fleming. *Hitler and the Final Solution*, 1984.

3. Gerald Fleming, *Hitler and the Final Solution* (Los Angeles, CA: University of California Press, 1984).

4. Gilbert, Martin, *The Holocaust* (New York, Henry Holt and Company, 1987).

5. Victor Brack was sentenced to death by hanging at the Doctor's trial in Nuremberg 1946. He committed suicide.

6. Robin O'Neil, *Belzec - Stepping Stone to Genocide* (New York: Museum of Jewish Heritage).

7. Martin Gilbert, Raul Hilberg, Guttman and Rozett etc. The year in parenthesis defines the boundaries of the country considered in the estimate.

8. Dwight D. Eisenhower, *Crusade in Europe* (New York: Doubleday, 1948), 408-409.

9. Exhibit T/179, document No. 461. The Trial of Adolf Eichmann. Session 78, (June 23, 1961).

10. Bulgaria did deliver the Jews of Macedonia, an area acquired during the war, to the Germans for their annihilation in Auschwitz.

11. Christopher Browning, *Evidence for the Implementation of the Final Solution* (Report Produced at the Pacific Lutheran University, Tacoma, Washington, 2000), 354. Philip Friedman, *Roads to Extinction: Essays on the Holocaust* (New York: JPS, 1980), 170.

12. Filip Muller. *Eyewitness Auschwitz: Three Years in the Gas Chambers* (1999).

13. Friedrich Otto, *The Kingdom of Auschwitz* (New York: Harper Perennial, 1982), 30.

14. Browning, *Evidence for the Implementation.*

15. M. Broszat, *Hitler und die Genesis der Endlösung. Vierteljahreshefte für Zeitgeschichte* (1977), 750.

16. Protocol of the Wansee Conference.

17. Leon Poliakov, *Harvest of Hate: The Nazi Program for the Destruction of the Jews of Europe* (Syracuse University Press, 1956).

18. Ludmila Chladkova, *The Terezin Ghetto* (Pub. House of Nase vojsko Terezin Monument, 1991).

19. Richard Glazar, *Trap with a Green Fence* (Northwestern University Press, 1995). He arrived to Treblinka on October 10, 1942.

20. Martin Rhonheimer, *The Holocaust: What Was Not Said.* (November 2003), 18-28.

21. Klaus Scholder, *A Requiem for Hitler and Other Perspectives on the German Church Struggle* (Philadelphia, PA: Trinity Press International, 1989).

22. Scholder, *A Requiem for Hitler* 31.

23. Doris L. Bergen, *The Sword of the Lord: Military Chaplains from the First to the Twenty-First Century* (University of Notre Dame Press, 2004).

24. Doris L. Bergen, Article in Bartov Omer and Mack Phyllis, Eds. *In God's Name: Genocide and Religion in the Twentieth Century.* (New York, Berghahn Books, 2000), 128-132. A CC H. Annual Scholars Conference on the Holocaust and the Churches, March 3-6, 1996.

25. Saul Friedlander, *Counterfeit Nazi* (New York: Knopf, 1969), 116-120.

26. Poliakov, *Harvest of Hate,* 146-149.

27. Güenther Lewy, *The Catholic Church and Nazi Germany* (New York: Mc Graw Hill Book Co., 1964), 285.

28. John F. Morley, *Vatican Diplomacy and the Jews During the Holocaust 1939-1943* (New York: Ktav Publishing, 1980), 114.

29. Preysing makes reference to Orsenigo's words in a letter to Pius XII. Freiburger Rundbrief 28 (1976), 93. Michael Phayer, *The Catholic Church and the Holocaust, 1930-1965* (Indiana University Press, 2001), 76.

30. Morley, *Vatican Diplomacy.*

31. ADSS, 9, No. 82, 170, ADSS, 2, No. 105, 323).

32. ADSS, 2, No. 105, 318–327. Gitta Sereny, *Into That Darkness* (New York: McGraw Hill Book Company, 1974), 297-299. Phayer, *The Catholic Church,* 49, 148.

33. Morley, *Vatican Diplomacy,* 124.

34. Lewy, *The Catholic Church,* 291. Bertram to Thierack, January 29, 1944 Bundesarchiv Koblenz.

35. Johann Neumann. Emeritus professor for the sociology of law and the sociology of religion, lecture at the University of Tübingen, 1995. http://www.ibka.org/artikel/ag98/1945.html

36. Abraham Fuchs, *The Unheeded Cry* (New York: Mesorah Publications, 1984.

37. In his note of November 12, 1941 to the Slovak ambassador Charles Sidor,

38. Morley, *Vatican Diplomacy,* 90.

39. Deborah Dwork and Robert Jan Van Pelt, *Auschwitz: 1270 To the Present* (New York: W.W. Norton and Company, 1997), 299-300.

40. Livia Rothkirchen, Article in *The Holocaust and the Christian World,* 105.

41. Rotkirchen, *The Holocaust,* 12-19. Morley, *Vatican Diplomacy,* 79. Raul Hilberg, *The Destruction of the European Jews* (Teaneck, NJ: Holmes & Meier, 1985), 458-465. Fuchs, *The Unheeded Cry,* 50.

42. Fuchs, *The Unheeded Cry,* 53, Neumann, B'Zel Hamavet 61-64.

43. Dwork and Van Pelt, *Auschwitz,* 303-304.

44. Dwork and Van Pelt, *Auschwitz*, 303-304.

45. Livia Rotkirchen, *Churban Yahadut Slovakia* (Jerusalem: Yad Vashem 1961), xx-xxi.

46. Rotkirchen, *Churban Yahadut*, 12-19. Morley, *Vatican Diplomacy*, 79. Hilberg, 458–465. Fuchs, *The Unheeded Cry*, 50. Van Pelt, 303–304

47. D. B. Weissmandel, *Min Hameizar* (Brooklyn, NY: Emunah 1960), 20. Fuchs, *The Unheeded Cry*, 141.

48. Morley, *Vatican Diplomacy*, 80.

49. Kevin Madigan, *What the Vatican Knew About the Holocaust and When*, Commentary, 10/1/2001.

50. Morley, *Vatican Diplomacy*, 99.

51. Weissmandel . *Min Hameizar*, 20–22. Fuchs A, 141–143.

52 . Morley, *Vatican Diplomacy*. Jonathan Steinberg, *All or Nothing: The Axis and the Holocaust, 1941-1943* (Florence, KY: Routledge, 1990).

53. Morley, *Vatican Diplomacy*, 84.

54. Fuchs *The Unheeded Cry*, 30.

55. John Vidmar, *O. P. The Catholic Church through the ages: A history* (New York: Paulist Press, 2005).

56. Weissmandel, *Min Hameizar*, 23

57. Morley, *Vatican Diplomacy*, 89.

58. Pierre SJ Blet, *Pius XII and the Second World War According to the Archives of the Vatican* (New York: Paulist Press, 1999), 172.

59. Interview by M. Praguer with R. Weissmandl at Mt. Kisco on March 7, 1953. Reprinted in Dos Yiddishe Vort. July–August, 2006.

60. Avalon Project. Nuremberg Trial Proceedings Volume 4, Thursday 3 January 1946. 361.

61. See Rabbi Weissmandl's Min Hamezar and Abraham Fuch's The Unheeded Cry

62. Rotkirchen Livia, Article in The Holocaust and the Christian World, 106.

63. Rotkirchen Livia, Doc 55, 133–135. Fuchs, 144.

64. Morley, *Vatican Diplomacy*, 90.

65. Blet, *Pius XII and the Second World War*, 183

66. Rotkirchen Livia. Doc 55, 133–135. Fuchs, 144.

67. Morley, *Vatican Diplomacy*, 91-93. Phayer, *The Catholic Church*, 91. Maria Schmidt, *Remembering for the Future* (Oxford: Pergamon), 209.

68. Daniel Goldhagen, *Jonah: A Moral Reckoning* (New York: Alfred A. Knopf, 2002), 169.

69. *Le Saint Siege et Les Victimes de la Guerre, 1944-1945*, (Actes et Documents), (Vatican City, 1980), 54-55 and 475-477. Dennis Barton. Fr. Tiso, Slovakia and Hitler. Pierre SJ Blet, *Pius XII and the Second World War*, 178.

70. Blet, *Pius XII*, 168.

71. Morley, *Vatican Diplomacy*.

72. Testimony of Alexander Arnon, secretary of the Jewish Community in Zagreb at Eichmann Trial.

73. 32 Narodne novine (Zagreb), 18 April 1941; Zakoni NDH: Zakonske odredbe i naredbe, vol. 12 (Zagreb, 1942), 86.

74. Enciclopedia Judaica. Ed. Staff. *Jewish History of Yugoslavia.* In the European Law Division of the US Library of Congress in Washington anyone can consult these laws.

75. Hrvatska Straza. May 11, 1941.

76. Carol Rittner, Stephen D. Smith, and Irena Steinfeldt, *The Holocaust and the Christian World* (New York: Continuum Press, 2000), 106, 113. Jonathan Steinberg, *All or Nothing: The Axis and the Holocaust, 1941-1943* (Florence, KY: Routledge, 1990).

77. Novi List (Zagreb), 3 June 1941.

78 . Srdja Trifkovic. Ustaše: Croatian Separatism and European Politics, 1929-1945. London 1998. 141.

79 . Zbornik Zakona I Naredba NDH Zagreb 1941. 126.

80. Historian Ivo Goldstein of Zagreb University.

81. Carlo Falconi, *The Silence of Pius XII* (Boston, MA: Little Brown and Company, 1970).

82. Steinberg professor of modern European history at the University of Pennsylvania and Trinity Hall Cambridge, 30.

83. Alexander Kimel, *Holocaust: Understanding and Prevention.* Vol 1, Issue 2, Sep. 1997.

84. Karlheinz Deschner, *With God and Fürher* (Germany), 282.

85. Decree-law, No. 1528-2101-Z-1941.

86. There were camps in Đakovo, Lobor Grad, Gornja Rijeka, Krušcica, Kupari, Danica, Jadovno, the Island of Pag, Stara Grad, Karlovac, Yudovo, Sisak, Gradiska, Lepoglava, Kereslinek, Caprag, Tenj, Jastrebarsko.

87. ADSS, Document 132, Alatri to Maglione, August 14, 1941. 250-252. Susan Zucotti, *The Italians and the Holocaust* (New York: Basic Books, 1987), 114.

88. Other most reliable estimates, arrived at a figure of 20,000 Jews.

89. Zuccotti, *The Italians,* 115.

90. The Pavelic Papers. Private Collection. As the Surviving Jews Remember Artukovic. March 9, 1958. Added: October, 2002

91. Morley, *Vatican Diplomacy,* 163.

92. Morley, *Vatican Diplomacy,* 163-167.

93 Morley, *Vatican Diplomacy,* 163-167.

94. L. Rotkirchen. *The Churches and the Deportation and Persecution of Jews in Slovakia.* Rittner, Smith, Steinfeldt, *The Holocaust and the Christian World,* 106.

95. Morley, *Vatican Diplomacy,* 164-165.

96. Ciano's Diplomatic Papers. Zuccotti, *The Italians,* 356, note 2.

97. Carl K. Savich. *The Holocaust in Bosnia-Hercegovina, 1941-1945.*

98. Zuccotti Susan: *Under His Very Window: The Vatican and the Holocaust.* (New Haven, CT: Yale University Press, 2000), 115.

99. Phayer, *The Catholic Church.*

100. Morley, *Vatican Diplomacy,* 165.

101. Zuccotti, *Under his Very Window,* 102. Actes et documents, vol. 7. Anthony Rhodes, *The Vatican in the Age of Dictators 1922-1945* (London, UK: Hodder and Stoughton, 1973).

102. Morley, *Vatican Diplomacy,* 154.

103. Yahil, *The Holocaust,* 351. Phayer, *The Catholic Church,* 33.

104. Falconi, *The Silence of Pius XII,* 344, 350, 351.

105. Morley, *Vatican Diplomacy,* 158-159.

106. Morley, *Vatican Diplomacy,* 158–159.

107. Morley, *Vatican Diplomacy,* 158–159.

108. Phayer, *The Catholic Church,* 38.

109. Rabbi Dovid Goldwasser, *Pearls of Wisdom* (The Jewish Press, June 17, 2005).

110. Falconi, *The Silence of Pius XII,* 315-316.

111. Zuccotti, *Under His Very Window,* 121-123.

112. Morley, *Vatican Diplomacy,* 155.

113. Christopher R Browning, *Evidence for the Implementation of the Final Solution, Part III* (Tacoma, WA: Pacific Lutheran University, 2000).

114. Only 20,000 Jews survived mostly among the partisans.

115. Actes et documents du Saint-Siège relatifs a la Seconde Guerre Mondiale.

116. Michael Marrus and Robert Paxton, *Vichy France and the Jews.*

117. Robert J. Hanyok, *Eavesdropping on Hell* (July, 2005). Hanyok is a historian working with the National Security Agency's Center for Cryptologic History in Maryland.

118. Marrus and Paxton, *Vichy France and the Jews,* 272.

119. Rittner, Smith, and Steinfeld, *The Holocaust and the Christian World,* 83-86.

120. Paul Webster, *Petain's Crime* (Chicago, IL: Ivan R. Dee, 1991), 96-97.

121. Morley, *Vatican Diplomacy.*

122. E. Klausener, *Von Pius XII to Johannes XXIII,* (Berlin: Morus Verlag, 1958), 75. Phayer, *The Catholic Church,* 94.

123. Rittner, Smith & Steinfeldt. *The Holocaust and the Christian World,* 85.

124. Webster, *Petain's Crime,* 123.

125. Webster, *Petain's Crime,* 132.

126. Morley, *Vatican Diplomacy.*

127. Data by Serge Klarsfeld..

128. Webster, *Petain's Crime,* 93.

129. Allocution de M. Jacques CHIRAC, Président de la République, prononcée lors des cérémonies commémorant la grande rafle des 16 et 17 juillet 1942. Présidence de la République.

130. Rittner, Smith & Steinfeldt, *The Holocaust and the Christian World,* 253.

131. Peter Longerich, ed., Die Ermordung der europäischen Juden: Eine umfassende Dokumentation des Holocaust, 1941–1945 (Munich and Zurich: Piper, 1990), 265; Raul Hilberg, *The Destruction of the European Jews* (Teaneck, NJ: Holmes & Meier, 1985), 601. (doc. NG-219).

132. Rudi Van Doorslaer, La Belgique Docile: *Les autorités belges et la persécution des juifs en Belgique durant la Seconde guerre mondiale* (Brussel, Luc Pire/Ceges, 2007).

133. Rudi Van Doorslaer, La Belgique Docile.

134. Gevers Lieve: Bisschoppen en bezetting: De Kerk in de Lage Landen tijdens de Tweede Wereldoorlog.

135. Max Vanden Berg to Mgr. Kerkhofs, 21 Sept. 1942, in Maxim Steinberg, L'Etoile et le fusil: La traque des juifs, 1942-1944, Brussels, 1986. Vol. II, 201.

136. The Jews represented 4.2 percent of a population of eighteen million people in 1940.

137. Randolph Braham (ed.), *Hungarian Jewish Studies, Vol. 1, NY: The Destruction of the Jews of Carpatho–Ruthenia* (World Federation of Hungarian Jews, 1966),

223–233. Randolph Braham, *The Politics of Genocide: The Holocaust in Hungary*, *Vol. 1*. (New York: Columbia University Press, 1994). Richard Rhodes. *Masters of Death*. (New York: Alfred Knopf, 2002). Martin Gilbert. *The Holocaust: A History of the Jews of Europe during the Second War* (New York: Holt, Rinehart and Wilson, 1985).

138. Yad Vashem Archives (03/3822).

139. Braham. Collected Research of Yad Vashem, 9, (1973), 111-118.

140 . Rhodes, *Masters of Death*. 128-130.

141. Operational Report USSR No. 80.

142. On January 26–28, the Hungarian military murdered one hundred Jews at Stari Becej. At Titel, they murdered 35 of the 36 Jews living in the village.

143. Martin Gilbert. *The Holocaust: A history of the Jews of Europe during the Second War* (New York: Holt, Rinehart and Wilson, 1985), 487.

144 . Moshe Y. Herczl, *Christianity and the Holocaust of Hungarian Jewry* (New York University Press, 1993), 136.

145. Herczl, *Christianity and the Holocaust*, 140–143.

146. Herczl, *Christianity and the Holocaust*. 142.

147. Herczl, *Christianity and the Holocaust*. 152.

148. Friedman, *Roads to Extinction*, 85.

149. Herczl, *Christianity and the Holocaust*. 230.

150. Herczl, *Christianity and the Holocaust*. 180–181.

151. Herczl, *Christianity and the Holocaust*, 183.

152. Herczl, *Christianity and the Holocaust*, 235–236.

153. Fischer, 273–274, 287. Herczl, *Christianity and the Holocaust*, 177, 230.

154. Another pair of inmates escaped Auschwitz in May 44, Arnost Rosin and Czeslaw Mordowicz. David Kranzler, *The Man Who Stopped the Trains to Auschwitz* (Syracuse University Press, 2000).

155. Jerusalem Post, December 4, 2006.

156. Herczl, *Christianity and the Holocaust*, 196.

157. Herczl, *Christianity and the Holocaust*, 191, 200-201.

158. See Copy of Document in Fuchs, 195. See air photograph of Auschwitz taken by the American Air Force on August 23, 1944.

159. Richard Langworth, *Churchill by Himself: The Definitive Collection of Quotations* (New York: Perseus Books, 2008).

160. Raul Hilberg, *The Destruction of the European Jews. 3 Vols* (Chicago, IL: Quadrangle Press, 1961), 838.

161. Braham, *The Politics of Genocide*. Docs I, documents 172, 397, 78. Kranzler, *The Man who Stopped the Trains*, 58.

162. Acts and Documents of the Holy See Relative to the Second World War. Volume 10.

163. Herczl, *Christianity and the Holocaust*, 200-201.

164. Friedman, *Roads to Extinction*, 86.

165. Herczl, *Christianity and the Holocaust*, 204.

166. Herczl, *Christianity and the Holocaust*, 204-205.

167. Friedlander Saul. *Pius XII and the Third Reich*.

168. Herczl, *Christianity and the Holocaust*, 189.

169. Braham, *The Politics of Genocide*.

170. Herczl, *Christianity and the Holocaust*, 207

171. Herczl, *Christianity and the Holocaust*, 206. Phayer, *The Catholic Church*, 106.

172. Herczl, *Christianity and the Holocaust*.

173. Herczl, *Christianity and the Holocaust*.

174. Herczl, *Christianity and the Holocaust*, 215.

175. Rolf Hochhuth, *The Deputy. Sidelights on History* (New York: Grove Press, 1964).

176. Kranzler, *The Man Who Stopped the Trains*.

177. Kranzler, *The Man who Stopped the Trains*, 116.

178. Steinberg, *All or Nothing*, 54. Dwork and Van Pelt, *Auschwitz: 1270 To the Present*, 328.

179. Rudolf Vrba, Alan Bestic *Escape from Auschwitz: I Cannot Forgive* (New York: Grove Press, 1968), 268-275.

180. Herczl, *Christianity and the Holocaust*, 223.

181. Kranzler,*The Man Who Stopped the Trains*, 202.

182. Herczl, *Christianity and the Holocaust*, 223-229.

183. Friedman, *Roads to Extinction*, 82, 83.

# Chapter 11
## Vatican Response to the Final Solution

## Vatican Support for Anti-Semitic Legislation

The Catholic press in Europe conducted before the war a relentless campaign against an alleged Jewish "enemy" menacing Christian Europe, whom they accused of being responsible for every problem and malfeasance in the world. Competing with the Nazis for popularity, the Catholic press tried to convince the public that as far as anti-Semitism was concerned, they were at least as trustworthy as their competitors.

The Catholic clergy and Catholic political parties stood behind a campaign that aimed at turning back the clock to pre-emancipation society by actively promoting the adoption of anti-Semitic laws to strip the Jews from their hardly gained civic and political rights. These laws actually prepared the ground for the Final Solution by identifying and isolating the Jews. The Church found a common language with the Nazis in adopting legislation that followed the pattern set by the Nuremberg Laws. The official Catholic organ in Germany, the *Klerusblatt*, welcomed the Nuremberg Laws in January 1936 as an "indispensable safeguard for the qualitative make-up of the German people."

Country after country in Catholic Europe approved a Codex Judaicus that reduced Jews to the status of pariahs and conditioned the population to accept willingly the persecution of Jews, which culminated in the deportations to death camps. Although differences between the Catholics and the Nazis surfaced with regard to the inclusion of converted Jews in the anti-Semitic legislation, these differences did not stand in the way of lending their enthusiastic support to that legislation.

The anti-Semitic legislation in the clero-Fascist countries of Europe such as Slovakia, Croatia, Hungary, Italy, and Vichy France, was issued between 1938 and 1942 in rounds of increasing severity. The first round excluded Jewish children from public schools, banned Jews from the armed forces, the civil service, and institutions of higher education, and prohibited Jewish professionals from practicing their professions among the general population. Jews were forbidden to employ Aryan domestic servants.

The second round required that Jewish enterprises be identified and transferred to Aryan (Christian) ownership. Jews were prohibited from owning land or other forms of real estate. Properties owned by Jews above a minimum value were to be confiscated. In the third stage, Jews were required to concentrate in ghettos and forced to serve in labor battalions, wear the yellow star, and have their passports and rationing cards stamped as Jews. They could only shop at certain hours, were forbidden to own radios, be listed in telephone directories, visit public parks, and place any type of advertisements, including death notices in the newspapers.

Each of the clero-Fascist governments allied with Hitler consulted their own Church authorities and the Vatican concerning these laws. Skillfully, both would invariably give recognition, to the "right" of these Christian states to take, what they euphemistically called defensive measures against the Jews. At the same time they would object to the inclusion of baptized converts in anti-Semitic legislation and to those provisions that affected Church rights in the area of marriages, which it considered the exclusive domain of the Church. Professor David Kerzer points out that the Pope accepted the legislation because it embodied the same principles that the Church championed throughout the ages:

> Anyone should not find it surprising that in response to these measures against the Jews neither the Pope nor the Vatican hierarchy uttered a single word of protest. The explanation for this fact is simple: Mussolini's new laws embodied measures and views long championed by the Church itself.[1]

The 1939 declaration of the cardinal of Florence, Elia Dalla Costa (1872-1961) in support of anti-Semitic legislation is representative of the ecclesiastic approach all over Catholic Europe:

> Above all, however, the Church has in every epoch judged living together with the Jews to be dangerous to the Faith and to the tranquility of the Christian people. Hence the laws promulgated by the Church for centuries aimed at isolating the Jews. The Church has never changed its policy of forbidding Christians from working in Jewish homes, or forbidding Christian children from being taught by Jews.[2]

Even when these laws were amplified to include forced labor, ghettoization, and deportation the Church accepted them as justified. Rome itself provides an eloquent example. Every Italian Jewish male between the ages of eighteen and fifty-five was conscripted for forced labor by means of an administrative decree issued on May 6, 1942. More than 15,000 Jewish men were registered, of which 2,038 were put to work in heavy labor along the banks of the Tiber to reinforce its earthworks. Bare-chested Jewish slave workers could be seen from the windows of the Vatican doing their back-breaking work. The American Charge d'Affairs Harold H. Tittman expressed his shock to the

Vatican in June 1942 that Roman Jews were being coerced to do forced labor in the very shadow of St. Peter's, "the fountain of Christian charity" as he put it.

But the Vatican was not disturbed by the sight of the forced labor imposed on the Jews. They only expressed concern that baptized converts were being put to work together with Jews. For the Vatican secretary of state "it was humiliating for the converts to be mixed with the Jews."[3] Cardinal Maglione instructed the nuncio to the Italian government, Msgr. Francesco Borgonini Duca, to intervene for the separation of the two groups. "Borgonini Duca never protested the use of Jewish forced laborers in Rome, much less the principle of compulsory labor itself," comments Susan Zuccotti. Nonetheless, the self-serving legend about the Vatican secretariat of state's untiring concern for the well-being of Jews is still being repeated.[4]

## What Pius XII and the Vatican Knew about the Final Solution

To justify the silence of the Vatican on the mass annihilation of European Jewry, the excuse is often given that the Vatican knew little during the war of what was happening with the Jews. Even Holocaust deniers such as Butz, who intended to use Vatican denial in support of their own twisted contention that the Holocaust never happened, find the argument to be a "ridiculous claim that cannot be entertained from more than a few seconds." The deportation of Jews to the east was carried out for all to see all over Europe. Pius XII himself witnessed the deportation of the Jews of Rome to Auschwitz taking place under his own windows, so to speak. Gassed in Auschwitz a few days later, the Vatican preferred to forget about them. German historian Peter Longerich addressed these claims of ignorance at a recent lecture in the U.S. Holocaust Memorial Museum:

> Rather, we are dealing with an unimaginable massacre lasting several years, in which hundreds of thousands of perpetrators and helpers tortured and killed millions of victims under the eyes of millions of observers in large parts of Europe.[5]

Catholic priests in every town and city of Europe were the eyes and ears of the Vatican. The military chaplains that accompanied the armies of the Axis were observers and often even participants in the crimes. In Poland, a Catholic country where the death camps were located, the priests of every town and village were direct witnesses to the unfathomable tragedy of the more than 3 million Polish Jews, their close neighbors, who were taken to these camps, disappearing forever together with the many more Jews coming in from all over Europe. Historian Michael Marrus speaks for many in his conclusions on the question of Vatican knowledge:

> When mass killings began, the Vatican was extremely well informed through its own diplomatic channels and through a variety of other contacts. Church officials may have been the first to pass on to the Holy See sinister reports about

the significance of deportation convoys in 1942 and they continued to receive the most detailed information about mass murder in the east. [6]

The Vatican had no need to rely on Jewish reports and appeals to ascertain the truth that "resettlement to the East" was a Nazi euphemism for death by shooting or gassing. Their own reliable sources were telling them what awaited the Jews at the end of the deportation journeys. The Vatican was advised by its nuncios and bishops in Germany, Slovakia, Croatia, and Switzerland that the Nazis were literally annihilating day-by-day the Jews of Europe. Much of that information comes to the surface in written reports to the Vatican that have been published. Much more might be available in the unpublished reports in the inaccessible Vatican archives.

The correspondence between Msgr. Konrad von Preysing from Berlin and the Pope in Rome shows full knowledge of the unprecedented crime that was being committed against the Jews. In January 1941, six months before the invasion of Russia, Preysing transmitted a direct appeal to the Pope on the desperate situation of Jews in Germany and its neighbors:

> Your Holiness is certainly informed about the situation of the Jews in Germany and the neighboring countries. I wish to mention that I have been asked both from the Catholic and Protestant side if the Holy See could not do something on this subject . . . in favor of these unfortunates. [7]

On February 4, 1941, Cardinal Theodor Innitzer, who had so enthusiastically welcomed Hitler to Vienna and supported the Anschluss, informed Pius XII that 60,000 Jews had already been deported from Vienna to the east. He alerted the Pope about the "terrible fate awaiting them."[8] Concerned about the converts among the deportees in whose behalf he conducted welfare activities, Innitzer complained to the Pope that "no consideration is given to age or religion" in organizing the deportations, and that 11,000 baptized converts were included in them.

Soon after the invasion of the Soviet territories on October 27, 1941, Msgr. Giuseppe Burzio, the charge d'affaires of the Vatican in Slovakia, informed Cardinal Luigi Maglione, Pius XII's secretary of state, that the Einsatzgruppen in the Soviet territories were not only killing in a systematic way Jewish prisoners behind the lines but the Jewish civilian population as well:

> Jewish civilians are systematically executed without any distinction of age or gender.[9]

An unimpeachable eyewitness beyond suspicion in the eyes of the Vatican was Fr. Pirro Scavizzi (1884-1964), who began to present his reports personally to Pius XII on the Einsatzgruppen mass murders beginning early 1942. Some of Scavizzi's reports are included in volume 8 of the eleven-volume *Actes et Documents*. Scavizzi was a close, trusted friend of Pius XII who shuttled back and forth between Italy and the Ukraine as a chaplain of Italian military hospital trains and as a courier to the high-ranking prelates in Eastern Europe, Germany and Austria. The late Vatican historian Fr. Robert A. Graham SJ (1912-1997), one of the editors of the *Actes*, acknowledged in a lecture delivered on October 10, 1989, at the Catholic University of America the role that Fr. Scavizzi played in keeping Pius XII informed on the Einsatzgruppen genocide in the Soviet occupied territories since 1942:

> As far as the Vatican is concerned, one key is found in the audience that Pope Pius XII had with his old friend Don Pirro Scavizzi, a parish priest of Rome, war veteran, and chaplain on the hospital train sent by the Order of Malta to pick up wounded Italian soldiers on the Eastern front in 1942. The priest was able to tell the Pope about the mass slaughter of Jews by the Nazi police. This no doubt helped to establish in the Pope's mind the inhuman character of the Nazi occupation of Russia.[10]

It has been suggested that Scavizzi had four audiences with the Pope, two of which go unmentioned in the *Actes*. At least twice he reported to the Pope about the "systematic slaughter of Jews."[11] After returning from a trip to the Ukraine to Bologna on May 12, 1942, Fr. Pirro Scavizzi not only informed Pope Pius XII that the Germans had already completed their Einzatsgruppen campaign in the Ukraine, but also they were annihilating the Jews of Germany and Poland with a "system of mass-killing," seemingly referring to the death camps and their gas chambers:

> The massacre of the Jews in the Ukraine is already complete. In Poland and Germany they also intend to carry it to completion, with a system of mass-killing the next candidates in line for death.[12]

The chaplains that accompanied the Axis armed forces were near or on the scene of Einsatzgruppen actions in many towns and villages of the Soviet-occupied territories. They were often direct eyewitnesses to the massacres or knew about them from the officers and soldiers that were there. The Byela Tserkow episode (August 8-19, 1941), documented by Klee, Dressen, and Riess in *The Good Old Days* is an eloquent example of the chaplains' closeness to these shattering crimes committed by the Einsatzgruppen and their helpers. The gruesome facts of systematic mass murder of Jewish men, women, and children not only got to their ecclesiastic superiors back home, but also eventually reached to the top in Rome.[13] Once in Rome, however, the information reached a dead end not being allowed to go further to alarm the world. One can understand why Heinrich Himmler personally praised the "discretion" of the Vatican in his visit to Count Ciano in Rome in October 1942.[14]

The reports of Fr. Scavizzi confirmed in essence the information that the Vatican was receiving from its delegate in Slovakia. Msgr. Burzio forwarded to the Vatican a report from the Catholic head chaplain of the Slovak army who personally witnessed the execution of the near 24,000 Ruthenian Jews outside of Kamenetz Podolsk on August 27-29, 1941, by the Hungarian forces and the Einsatzgruppen. The chaplain personally informed Msgr. Burzio about the mass murder. The apostolic delegate in turn forwarded the information to Rome on October 27, 1941.

Burzio also informed that the entire Jewish population in the Ukraine was being mass murdered by the SS Einsatgruppen in the outskirts of the towns and that the Jewish prisoners of war were being executed as soon as they were taken prisoner, while the Ukrainian and White Soviet prisoners were allowed to return free to their homes.[15] In spite of the exceptional gravity of the reports, no action or protest whatsoever came forward from the Vatican to Admiral Horthy and the Hungarian government much less to the Germans. In its response to Burzio on December 20, 1941, the Vatican secretariat of state only cared to find out if the Slovak military had also participated in the massacre.

When the Slovak government announced the upcoming deportation of Slovak Jewry to the east, Msgr. Burzio informed the Vatican about it in his reports of March 9 and March 11, 1942, and made clear that the deportation meant certain death for most of the deportees:

> The deportation of 80,000 persons to Poland at the mercy of the Germans is the equivalent of condemning a great part of them to death.[16]

Even more alarming was the information forwarded by Croatian apostolic delegate Fr. Abbé Marcone on July 17, 1942, from the well-informed Chief of Police of Croatia Eugene Kvaternik that as many as 2 million Jews had already been killed in Europe. Kvaternik's estimate was very close to the real numbers. The same estimate is mentioned in the second report of Fr. Pirro Scavizzi to Pius XII of October 7, 1942, at a time the German death machinery had already managed to annihilate most of the Jews of Poland and Russia.

> The German government has ruled that within a period of six months all the Jews residing in the Croat State must be transferred to Germany, where, according to what Eugene (Dido) Kvaternik [chief of the Croat police] himself told me, 2 million Jews have been recently killed. It appears that the same fate awaits the Croat Jews particularly if old and incapable of work.[17]

On September 30, 1942, Marcone already informed Cardinal Maglione that with the exception of converts and mixed marriages, all the Jews of Croatia had been deported to Auschwitz.[18] In response to an inquiry from Msgr. Giovanni Montini concerning the fate of the converts deported from Germany, the pro-Nazi nuncio in Berlin Orsenigo responded on July 28, 1942, that the worst-case-scenario of mass destruction (eccidi in massa) can be assumed, because for the Nazis "baptismal water does not change Jewish blood":

> Also every intervention in favor only of the non-Aryan Catholics has thus far been rejected with the customary reply that baptismal water does not change Jewish blood and that the German Reich is defending itself from the non-Aryan race, not from the religion of the baptized Jews.[19]

According to the account given by the Pope's housekeeper, Pascalina Lehnert, Pius XII personally telephoned his good friend Archbishop Francis Spellman in New York in the late summer of 1942 to confirm directly with President Roosvelt the veracty of the reports on the Nazi atrocities. Spellman reported back:

> Your Holiness, President Roosevelt has given me every assurance that the vicious Nazi war crimes are entirely true . . . Thousands of Jews are being gassed to death in concentration camps and other thousands are being burned alive in ovens.[20]

The Gerstein report of Waffen SS Officer Kurt Gerstein's (1905-1945) of his visit to Lublin, Belzec, Sobibor, and Treblinka during August 17-19, 1942, already mentioned, is one of the most terrifying eyewitness descriptions of the German death factories forwarded to the Vatican through various channels. When Nuncio Orsenigo refused to receive Gerstein, he went to see Bishop Winter, the secretary of the bishop of Berlin Msgr. Preysing, with the urgent request to forward it to the Pope in Rome. Gerstein also met with personalities of other denominations such as Dr. Dibelius, bishop of the Confessing Church, who stated after the war that he forwarded the information to intermediate levels of the Roman Catholic hierarchy in Switzerland and Sweden.

The facts of the report were fully verified before the Land Court of Darmstadt in the Federal Republic of Germany on June 6, 1950, by SS ObersturmbannFührer Dr. W. Pfannenstiel, who was present in Belzec with Gerstein. The different personalities who were informed by Gerstein in Berlin, such as Baron von Otter of the Swedish Embassy, Dr. Hochstrasser, and Dr. Dibelius, among others, all confirmed Gerstein's alarm attempts. Nonetheless, the Vatican chose to leave out the report completely from the *Actes*.[21]

In a message written on December 9, 1942, by Msgr. Giuseppe Di Meglio, a staff member of Orsenigo's office in Berlin, there is a description of the deadly conditions of the deportation trains and of the camps at the end of the journey:

> Generally, they are forced to leave in the middle of the night; they are permitted to take little clothing with them and only a small sum of money . . . An Italian journalist, returned from Romania . . . related to me that a train was completely filled with Jews; every opening was then closed, so that no air could enter. When the train arrived at its destination, there were only a few survivors.[22]

## The Vatican, a Dead End to Information on Nazi Genocide

One of the most appalling aspects of the Vatican's record is its systematic refusal to transmit further the alarming reports it received on the annihilation of the Jews, or even to confirm the gravity of the situation when approached by third parties. The dead-end policy that earned Himmler's praise played into the hands of Germany and helped mantain the cover of secrecy of the Final Solution.[23]

The few internal Vatican documents that have been allowed to come to light on the information that the Vatican possessed on the situation in Poland, reveal the advanced knowledge it had, which it strictly kept to itself. In one such memorandum of the Vatican secretariat of state of May 5, 1943, it is stated that of the 4.5 million Jews of Poland no more than 100,000 were still alive and that the Jews were being gassed:

> In Poland there were, before the war 4.5 million Jews; it is calculated that now there remain only 100,000 (with the others who came from other countries occupied by the Germans). At Warsaw a ghetto was formed which contained around 65,000, now there are 20,000-25,000.
> [They are] carried off in cattle wagons, hermetically sealed, with quicklime floors . . . Naturally some Jews have escaped; but it cannot be doubted that the greater part has been suppressed. After months and months of transports of thousands and thousands of persons nothing more is known: this can be explained in no other way than death, considering above all the enterprising character of the Jews, who in some way, if alive, show up . . . Special death camps near Lublin [Majdanek] and near Brest Litovsk. It is told that they are locked up several hundred at a time in chambers where they are finished off with gas.[24]

On July 8, 1943, Msgr. Angelo Roncalli, then the apostolic delegate in Turkey and later Pope John XXIII, in a report written about a meeting he had with von Papen in Ankara refers to "the millions of Jews sent to Poland to be annihilated there" as a well known fact:

> I saw von Papen [German Ambassador to Turkey] only once in six months, and only hastily and in passing on the occasion of my Easter visit to Ankara. At the time there was much talk of the Katyn affair which, according to von Papen, should have made the Poles reflect on the advantage of their turning to the Germans. I replied with a sad smile that it was necessary first of all to make them overlook the millions of Jews sent to Poland to be annihilated there.[25]

On September 26, 1942, Myron Taylor, the personal representative of President F. D. Roosevelt visited Rome and presented in the name of the President a memorandum to Cardinal Maglione on the reports concerning the annihilation of the Jews in Poland. Myron Taylor made an official request to Cardinal Maglione for a confirmation of the truth of the reports and if Pius XII had some suggestions to make to prevent the continuation of this barbarism:

> I would be very grateful to Your Eminence if it were possible to tell me if the Vatican has any information which tends to confirm the report contained in this memorandum. If so, I would like to know if the Holy Father has some suggestions touching on some practical means of using the forces of public opinion of the civilized world in order to prevent the continuation of this barbarism. [26]

Although in the two weeks before an answer was given, alarming reports arrived to the Vatican confirming the seriousness of the situation, in his answer of October 10, 1942, Cardinal Maglione raised doubts on the accuracy of the alarming reports. These reports came from sources the Vatican trusted such as Count Malvezzi who had returned from Poland on September 18, from the Polish ambassador to the Holy See, and from Abbot Pirro Scavizzi who arrived with his hospital train of the Knights of Malta from Poland on October 7, Cardinal Maglione blunted the sense of urgency of the situation, ignoring completely the possibility of undertaking any action to stop the genocide, doing irreparable damage to the rescue initiatives in the making:

> The reports on severe measures adopted against non-Aryans have also come to the Holy See from other sources, but at present it has not been possible to verify their accuracy. [27]

When Myron Taylor personally asked Pius XII at that time about the extermination reports, the Pope responded that "he felt there had been some exaggeration for the purposes of propaganda."[28] On March 1943, Msgr. Burzio wrote to Maglione from Slovakia:

> What Matters is that the pope and his diplomatic officials knew enough about the Jewish genocide to believe and understand that it was a disaster of immense, unprecedented proportions. Given what they knew they should have acted differently.

When the turn came in May 1944 for Hungarian Jewry to be annihilated, little changed in the Vatican. The Nazi death machine made the necessary preparations in Auschwitz for the mass murder of the last remaining Jewish community in Europe. The Auschwitz Protocol by the two courageous Slovakian Jewish inmates, Rudolf Vrba (Rosenberg) and Alfred Wetzler, who escaped from Auschwitz-Birkenau on April 7, 1944, warned of these preparations. It was forwarded by the Bratislava Working Group to Nuncios Rotta and Bernardini in Budapest and Bern with a request to forward it to the Vatican. Vrba and Wetzler also met personally with Msgr. Burzio in Slovakia in the middle of May 1944 with a request to transmit the document to the Vatican. He actually did so on May 22, 1944.

It is now known, due to correspondence discovered in 2006 by Dina Porat that the Auschwitz Protocol was also forwarded by Msgr. Giuseppe Roncalli, the apostolic delegate in Turkey and future Pope John XXIII from Ankara to Rome in June 1944 after the emissary of the Jewish Agency in Turkey, Haim Barlas, brought it to him.[29] Nonetheless, the fate of this life-and-death report was not much different than that of the Gerstein report, which the Vatican never acknowledged. In this case the claim is made that the report allegedly only made it to Rome for the first time in October 1944, months after most of Hungarian Jewry had already been annihilated. The Vatican did its best to prove that it was indeed worthy of the praise of discretion that Himmler so gratefully bestowed upon it.

# Pius XII Reaction to the Holocaust

The Church's stubborn silence on the annihilation of the Jews was a subject of burning concern very early on during the war, decades before the Hochuth drama. The Pope himself was of course aware of the far-reaching significance of his silence with regard to the Nazi annihilation program as becomes clear from his words to Cardinal Roncalli, the future Pope John XXIII, on October 11, 1941, that he registered in his diary:

> [The Pope] continued to tell me of his generosity toward the Germans who visit him. He asked me if his silence regarding Nazism was not judged badly.[30]

The Pope was not simply another important public figure with influence at the time; he was the supreme spiritual leader of the Catholics in the world, who followed his guidance. Among them were the Catholic heads of state of Europe. The diplomatic correspondence of the foreign envoys to the Vatican show that he was impervious to the appeals to make his voice heard against the Nazi campaign to annihilate the Jews. Even when the appeals came from men of the Church close to him, Pius XII could not be swayed to change his policy.

Brazilian Ambassador to the Vatican Ildebrando Accioly took the initiative in August 1942 to summon the Allied ambassadors to isssue in concert separate appeals to Pius XII to condemn the Nazi atrocities in occupied Europe. Harold H. Tittmann, U.S. representative to the Vatican, wrote to the State Department on August 3, 1942:

> In recent reports to the State Department, I have called attention to the opinion that the failure of the Holy See to protest publicly against Nazi atrocities is endangering its moral prestige and is undermining faith both in the Church and in the Holy Father himself . . . Yesterday the Brazilian Ambassador to the Holy See called on me to inquire whether I would be prepared to join in a concerted (not collective but rather simultaneous) démarche to persuade the Pope to condemn publicly and in specific terms the Nazi atrocities in German-occupied areas.[31]

As a result, the diplomatic representatives to the Vatican of Brazil, Poland, Yugoslavia, Uruguay, Belgium, Great Britain, and the United States presented in concert separate diplomatic notes to the Pope around the middle of September 1942, urging him to issue publicly a moral condemnation of the Nazi atrocities. On December 19, 1942, the Polish ambassador in the Vatican, Casimir Papée, reported that the Jews of the Warsaw ghetto, including the children, the elderly, and the sick, were being deported to their deaths:

> The deportees are being sent to death inflicted by various methods in places specifically prepared for this purpose.

When Pius XII finally decided to respond to the exhortations of the Western diplomats, the reference took the form of an elliptic, almost meaningless paragraph at the end of his 1942 Christmas radio message, formulated in an ambiguous way which that leave him in good standing with both sides:

> This wish humanity owes to the hundreds of thousands of persons who, without any personal guilt, and sometimes because of their nationality or race alone, have been doomed to death or to progressive extermination.[32]

The single paragraph did not identify Jews or Poles or any particular people as victims nor the Germans as the perpetrators. By completely eliminating any reference, even implicitly, to a specific earthly power responsible for the suffering of these anonymous unidentified war victims, the Pope made sure that no one would take insult from his words. These ambiguous three lines were the only public statement ever made during the war by the Pope, allegedly intended to convey his displeasure with the wasting away of some unidentified victims.

Carlo Falconi, a former Roman Catholic priest and journalist, very perceptively pointed out in 1965 in his book *The Silence of Pius XII* that the greatest genocide ever known in human history was practically ignored by Pius XII: [33]

> All this notwithstanding, this scientifically organized genocide, which outdistanced all previous cruelty known to man in its scope and savagery . . . is never mentioned even once explicitly, and the allusions to it that do exist are too cryptic and vague to constitute any strong body of opinion . . . We look in vain among the hundreds of pages of Pius XII's allocutions, messages and writings for some evidence of anger, of fury, of condemnation of atrocities . . . It is this silence that has caused the most scandal.[34]

The British, Belgian, Polish, and Brazilian governments joined afterward in a diplomatic note to the Vatican secretariat of state indicating that the Pope should have stigmatized Germany by name. The Pope justified his position to the American envoy on grounds that he could not have condemned the crimes committed by one side without condemning the crimes of the other side as well, as if there could be any moral equivalence between the Nazi genocide of the Jews with conventional warfare. He also added that "certain things were being exaggerated by Allied Propaganda":

> He [said he] had spoken therein clearly enough to satisfy all those who had been insisting in the past that he utter some word of condemnation of the Nazi atrocities, and he seemed surprised when I told him that I thought there were some who did not share his belief . . .
>
> He explained that when talking of atrocities he could not name the Nazis without at the same time mentioning the Bolsheviks and this he thought might not be wholly pleasing to the Allies. He stated that he "feared" that there was foundation for the atrocity reports of the Allies but led me to believe that he felt that there had been some exaggeration for purposes of propaganda.[35]

The Christmas message went by, as expected, almost unnoticed in Germany. German Ambassador to the Vatican Weiszäcker offhandedly dismissed any German susceptibilities to the Pope's words in his communication to his superiors in the Wilhemstrasse:

> Only very few people will recognize it as having anything to do with the Jewish problem.[36]

Firmly sticking to his policy not to allow the Jewish question to come between him and the Third Reich, the Pope systematically avoided mentioning Jews by name in written or spoken communications; neither did he ever identify the Germans as their victimizers. An array of scholars that includes David I. Kertzer, Michael R. Marrus, Daniel J. Goldhagen, and Susan Zuccotti have all pointed out the significant fact that at the time of their greatest need, Pius XII did not even mention once the word "Jews" in any of his public statements.[37] Quoting Marrus: "The Vatican relentlessly refrained even from pronouncing the word 'Jews' throughout the entire war." David I. Kertzer writes: "As millions of Jews were being murdered, Pius could never bring himself to publicly utter the word Jew." Daniel J. Goldhagen says: In public statements by Pius XII . . . any mention of the Jews is conspicuously absent . . . Pius XII chose again and again not to mention the Jews publicly. Fr. Peter Gumpel, the Vatican's relator in the Pius beatification proceedings, admits this to be true.

> It is true that in his public protests Pius XII never used the word "Jew." [38]

That statement is not completely accurate. He did refer once to the contemporary Jews at the International Eucharistic Congress in Budapest on May 27, 1938. He spoke on that occasion about the Jews of this day and age as a people "whose lips curse him and whose hearts reject him even today." [39]

A statement made in good faith after the war to Gitta Sereny by the Polish ambassador to the Vatican, Kazimierz Papée, a loyal Catholic, tells much about the Pope's priorities. Papée witnessed the Pope's annoyance when the catastrophe unfolding in Poland was brought to his attention. These are the exact words of the ambassador as he told them to Gitta Sereny:

> I remember, when I came to see the Holy Father for perhaps . . . the tenth time in 1944; he was angry. When he saw me as I entered the room and stood at the door awaiting permission to approach, he raised both his arms in a gesture of exasperation: "I have listened again and again to your representations about Our unhappy children in Poland. Must I be given the same story yet again?" I knelt before him and I said, "Holy Father, however often I have come, I will come again and again to beg you to do more and yet again more for the Poles." With which, M. Papée added to me [Sereny], "I meant of course all the Poles, including the Jews, most of whom, of course, by this time, were dead." [40]

Michael Phayer points out:

Even though ambassador Papée and western diplomats repeatedly pressed Pius about the Holocaust, the Pope omitted time and again to discuss it with Germany's ambassador Weizsäcker, who would later be found guilty of war crimes against Jews at the Nuremberg trials . . . A condemnation of these atrocities by the Holy Father would have a helpful effect in bringing about some check on the unbridled and uncalled-for actions of the forces of the Nazi regime.[41]

The Pope's policy to look away and ignore the Holocaust had the most serious consequences for the Jews. The Nazis, counting on the Vatican "discretion," were able to carry out their annihilation of the Jews without interference. His silence was interpreted by the Catholic population as a tacit approval to the annihilation of the Jewish people, in accordance with the principle accepted by Catholic moral theology that silence presumes consent.[42] Pius XII refused to provide moral guidance to the Catholic population concerning the annihilation of European Jewry, as if the sixth commandment "You Shall Not Kill" was not applicable to them at all. Had Pius XII addressed the believers on the subject of the unprecedented crime being carried out against the Jews and the terrible implications of cooperating with their persecutors, the number of Christian perpetrators might have been much smaller. Had he spoken out about the duty to help a defenseless people marked for extinction, the number of Catholics extending a helping hand would have been enormously greater. But he did not and remained silent throughout the totality of the Hitler era, at the most critical and tragic period of history.

## The Rome Deportations, a Paradigm of Vatican Policy

The response of the Vatican to the deportation of the Jews of Rome on October 16, 1943, can be considered a true paradigm of the policy that it followed with respect to the annihilation of European Jewry. Hochhuth's choice of the Rome episode as a model of Pius XII's policy was on target. The tragic drama witnessed in Rome was a replica of many thousands of similar scenes taking place in every city, town, and village in Europe, at which the Church stood calmy at the sidelines. "No other event," points out Phayer, "placed Pius XII in greater physical proximity to the Holocaust than the deportation of the Roman Jews."[43] The crime took place at a distance of 885 feet from the Vatican in the *Collegio Militare*, literally "under the very windows of the Pope" as Weiszaker pointed out in his message to Berlin, at a time that the Vatican was already fully aware that deportation meant death.

It could have been expected that the Pope's reaction in Rome would have been different—it was after all the seat of the papacy. The Pope was forewarned of this action one week before it occurred by German Ambassador Weiszaker himself, as will be explained, but he failed to take any action. He did not warn the Jews of the forthcoming catastrophe. Neither did he condemn the crime after it occurred. If silent complicity was the response of Pius XII in his own city, then what could have been expected of him with respect to the genocide on the Jews in the rest of Europe?

The Allied military forces landed in Sicily on July 10, 1943. Two weeks later, on July 25, the Fascist Grand Council ousted Mussolini from power and ordered his arrest. In a rapid countermove, the next day Hitler ordered Field Marshall Albert von Kesselring (1885-1960) to occupy Rome and Northern Italy. SS General Karl Wulff, Himmler's liaison man with Hitler who was permanently attached to Hitler's headquarters, became the German military governor of north Italy and plenipotentiary to Mussolini's Salo government. Kesselring took control of Rome on September 10, 1943, and held it until June 4, 1944, when the American-British forces conquered Rome. The king and Marshal Badoglio fled the Germans to the south and established their government in Brindisi. In Rome, Kesselring appointed General Ranier Stahel, military Statskomendant of the city. Two days later, on September 12, 1943, a German commando led by Skorzeny rescued Mussolini from captivity. Soon after, Il Duce established his puppet Salo Republic in Northern Italy.

The Germans were interested in keeping their good relations with the Vatican intact. Through Ambassador Weiszacker, Hitler personally offered assurances on September 13, 1943, that the Germans would respect the sovereignty of Vatican territory and properties and protect Vatican City from the fighting.[44] In a telegram of September 24, 1943, after a meeting with the Vatican secretary of state, Weizsacker informed the Foreign Ministry in Berlin of the strong pro-German feelings of the Vatican:

> Maglione regarded the fate of Europe dependent upon the victorious resistance of Germany at the Soviet front. In case the German armies collapsed there the only bulwark against Bolshevism would fall and European civilization would be lost . . . The essence of the Vatican's dream is that the Western Powers will realize in time where their real interest lies and will join the German effort to help save European culture from Bolshevism.[45]

The occupation of Rome by the Germans gave rise to the accusation by the Allies that the Pope was being held hostage inside the Vatican walls. As a result, Weizsacker delivered a diplomatic note from Ribbentrop on October 9, 1943, requesting an official statement from the Vatican acknowledging that German military conduct toward the Vatican had been correct and respectful of its sovereignty.

After the occupation of Rome and Northern Italy, Himmler's SS murder team considered that their moment to carry out the Final Solution in Italy had finally arrived. The Allied advance made their murder designs more urgent. On September 10, Herbert Kappler (1907-1978), the senior security officer in the German Embassy in Rome who participated in the rescue of Mussolini, received orders from SS General Karl Wulff (1900-1975), supreme commander of the SS in Italy, to put himself under the command of the Gestapo chief of Italy, General Wilhelm Harster, who earlier had deported Dutch Jewry. A radiogram followed, instructing him to assure the secrecy and surprise of the operation:

The recent Italian events impose a final solution to the Jewish question . . . The ReichsFührer [Himmler] therefore requests SS ObersturmbannFührer Kappler to actuate without delay all necessary preliminary measures to assure the suddenness and secrecy of the operation to be carried out in the city of Rome. Immediate orders will follow.[46]

On September 25, 1943, a second communication followed from Himmler's office to Herbert Kappler to round up and deport the Jews of Rome to Auschwitz for *sonderbehandlung* (special treatment), but no specific date was yet assigned for the Judenaktion to take place:

The success of this undertaking is to be assured by means of a surprise action and for this reason it is absolutely necessary to suspend the application of any anti-Jewish measures in the nature of individual acts in order not to arouse any suspicion among the population of an imminent Judenaktion. [47]

Some Jews had managed to flee from Rome to the liberated south after the German invasion but around 150 non-Italian Jews in constant danger of being arrested by the Germans living temporarily in a Jewish school in Rome were in no condition to escape to the south because they spoke no Italian. Ugo Foá, president of the Jewish community in Rome, turned to the Vatican secretariat of state on September 17, 1943, pleading that they be granted asylum in one of the religious houses in Rome, but his request was turned down.

Busy with locating and arresting the cabinieri loyal to the king, Kappler put temporarily on hold the deportation action and decided to meanwhile blackmail the Roman Jewish community and extract from them a substantial ransom in gold. He summoned the two official leaders of the Jewish community, Ugo Foá and Dante Almansi, to appear on September 26 and demanded a ransom payment of 110 pounds of gold, within thirty-six hours to avoid the deportation of Roman Jews. According to the testimony of the Jewish leaders, he threatened them with the immediate deportation of 200 Jews if they failed to comply:

It is not your lives or the lives of your children that we will take—if you will fulfill our demands. It is your gold we want, in order to provide new arms for our country. Within thirty-six hours you will have to pay fifty kilograms of gold. If you pay, no harm will come to you. In any other event, 200 of you Jews will be taken and deported to Germany, where they will be sent to the Soviet frontier, or otherwise rendered innocuous.[48]

According to Kappler's own version of the events as cited by Robert Katz, his threat was far more ominous and included the deportation of all the Jews of Rome. To reinforce his words Kappler added:

Mind you, I have already carried out several operations of this type and it has always ended well. Only once did I fail, but that time a few hundred of your brothers paid with their lives. [49]

When Jewish community leaders asked Kappler whether converts to Catholicism and descendents of mixed marriages were also included in the order, Kappler in true Nazi fashion responded without hesitation:

> I don't make any distinction between a Jew and a Jew, inscribed in the community or disassociated, baptized or mixed, they are all the enemy.[50]

The ominous news of the threat and the call to every Jew in Rome to bring their contributions in gold to community offices went from mouth to mouth. The initial response on September 27, 1943, was slow for fear that this was a trap to round up the Jews. Concerned that time would run out on them and considering that baptized non-Aryans were also included in the Kappler blackmail, the leaders of the Jewish community turned to the Vatican, asking if it would be ready to lend them a fraction of the gold. When it became clear later in the day that the Germans were not arresting the Jews coming to the community offices, the impoverished Jews of the ghetto and Trastevere rushed and stood in line to bring their gold wedding rings and earrings. The target of fifty kilograms of gold had almost been met before the 8 p.m. evening curfew. The request of a gold loan was recalled, but for many years it served to sustain the false legend that the Vatican had provided the gold.

Next day at 4:00 p.m, community leaders brought to Kappler's underlings the full ransom of 110 pounds plus an additional 300 grams. In characteristic Nazi fashion, Kappler's men had initially tried to accuse the Jewish messengers of trying to deceive them with the weight. After delivering the ransom, the Jewish community regained a false sense of security, thinking that the danger was averted. Jewish community leaders failed to realize that the gold ransom was only a maneuver, an act of deception in preparation for the ultimate act of deportation. This false sense of security was obviously the state of mind that their cruel tormentors wished to maintain for the Judenaktion to come as a surprise.[51]

The arrival in Rome at the beginning of October of Eichmann's representative Theodor Dannecker and forty-four of his henchmen was an ominous sign that the Judenaktion was imminent. Dannecker had proven his skills as a merciless Jew hunter in *La Grande Rafle* in Paris on July 22, 1942. Upon his arrival, he presented his orders signed by Heinrich Müller to Kappler to conduct the roundup. Kappler's men carried out a search in the temple on September 29 and took the index cards with the names and addresses of all the Jews of Rome in addition to two million lire. The Italian Interior Ministry on its part provided Dannecker with the registration lists of the Italian Racial Census with names and addresses of Jews. Using the combined lists, Dannecker defined the geographic borders of twenty-six Judenaktionbezirken (action precincts), with the ancient ghetto and Trastevere across the Tiber as his center of operations.

Alfred Rosenberg's agents, who were systematically looting Jewish historical treasures all over Europe, also came down like vultures from Berlin and Frankfurt to plunder the archives of the Roman Jewish community. Priceless historical documents of 2,000 years of continuous history going back in time to imperial Rome before Christianity was born were robbed from the community archives on October 14, 1943, together with invaluable collections of manuscripts and books.

The order from Berlin to round up and deport the Jews of Rome also reached Kappler's former chief, General Stahel, the military Statskomendant of Rome. The military Statskomandant General Stahel, a Catholic, established excellent relations with the Vatican through two German prelates, Bishop Allois Hudal, the head of the German Church in Rome, and Fr. Pancratius Pfeiffer, Pius XII's personal liaison with German authorities. He passed on the information on September 25, 1943, to the German charge d'affaires to Mussolini's government, Eitel Friedrich Möllhausen. Möllhausen in turn informed Ernst von Weizsacker and Albrecht von Kessel, the German ambassador and consul general in the Vatican, respectively.

Weizsacker knew well from his own previous role as undersecretary of state under Ribbentrop (1938-1943) what deportation meant. Before he became ambassador, he played a central role in the deportation of French Jews to Auschwitz. He was tried after the war in Nuremberg in 1947 and sentenced to seven years in prison for "signing papers in France dooming people to resettlement."[52] Robert Katz provides a short summary of Weizsacker's links to the Final Solution before becoming German ambassador to the Vatican:

> While still in Berlin, as early as 1941, he had received the daily reports of the Einsatzgruppen describing the mass murders of Polish and Soviet Jews. He had read and initialed number sixteen of the thirty copies of the minutes taken at the secret Wansee Conference preparing the "Final Solution" to the Jewish question. He knew of the constant deportations, to the Polish town of Auschwitz, and the fate of the Jews who had already been sent there.[53]

Möllhausen and Weizsacker were concerned that relations with the Vatican might suffer irreparable damage by the Judenaktion and that it might trigger violent partisan reaction. Weizsacker communicated his concern to his superiors in Berlin that the Pope could not fail to react considering that the Judenaktion was to take place before his eyes, "under his very window," as he phrased it in a memorandum to Berlin. Consul Möllhausen, in a telegram to von Ribbentrop, expressed the same concern. He inquired telegraphically on October 6 and 7, 1943, whether it would not be better to put the Jews to forced labor fortifying Rome against the Allied invasion than to liquidate them. Ribbentrop rejected the idea in a telegram on October 9 and reprimanded Möllhausen for openly using the word "liquidation" and ordered him not to meddle and to leave matters to the SS":

> As directed by Führer's instruction, the 8,000 Jews living in Rome are to be taken to Mauthausen as hostages. Minister for Foreign Affairs requests you not interfere in affair in any circumstances, but to leave it to the S.S.[54]

Kaltenbrunner was not impressed with Kappler's gold ransom forwarded to Berlin on September 28, 1943 nor with Möllhausen's suggestion of forced labor and he ordered Kappler to proceed without any further delay with the roundup and deportation of the Jews:

> To postpone the expulsion of the Jews until the Carabinieri and the Italian army officers have been removed can no more be considered than the idea mentioned of calling up the Jews in Italy for what would probably be very unproductive labor under responsible direction by Italian authorities . . . [name missing] has been instructed in executing the ReichsFührer SS orders to proceed with the evacuation of the Jews without delay.[55]

The timing of the upcoming roundup at a time they were trying to discredit Radio London's allegations that the Pope was held hostage by the Third Reich, was particularly problematic for the two German diplomats in Rome. Weizsaker delivered a diplomatic note to the Vatican on October 9, 1943, from von Ribbentrop in which he made every effort that the Vatican issue a declaration acknowledging that the German military conduct toward the Vatican had been respectful of its sovereignty.[56]

After his suggestion was turned down from Berlin, Möllhausen decided that it would be wiser to inform the Vatican about the upcoming roundup to prevent the deterioration of good relations if the Pope were taken by surprise. He made sure that the information on the imminent roundup should reach the Vatican through Weizsaker approximately one week before it actually took place. Ernst von Weizsacker informed the Vatican secretariat of state about the upcoming roundup, although he did not reveal the exact date when it was scheduled.[57] Cardinal Maglione also received notice on October 11 from an independent source, an Italian military agent, that the Germans were planning a major roundup in Rome for October 18, 1943.[58]

The information provided by Weizsacker and the Italian agent failed to awaken the Vatican to action, exactly as the other communications related to the genocide of the Jews of Europe. Although informed timely by the most authoritative and credible sources about the upcoming deportation of the Roman Jews, the Vatican once again showed its "discretion" and did not alert the Jews of the impending catastrophe. Neither did the Vatican undertake any other action on their behalf, although they were fully aware at the time (October 1943) that deportation and resettlement meant certain death.[59] Susan Zuccotti's words go the heart of the matter:

> Möllhausen's testimony constitutes a terrible indictment of the Vatican. Neither he nor Weizsacker nor the Vatican officials whom Weizsacker informed knew the exact day of the planned roundup, but specific knowledge of Nazi intentions should have been enough . . . A quiet warning from the Pope to Jewish Community leaders would have been passed along and believed, and hundreds of lives would have been spared.[60]

The rainy day chosen for the Judenaktion, known as Black Sabbath, is forever engraved in the collective memory of Italian Jewry. Two weeks after the gold ransom was paid and one day after the American Fifth Army crossed the Volturno River, 365 German SS police and Wafen SS armed with machine guns under the command of Dannecker fell by surprise in the early morning of October 16, 1943, upon the old ghetto and the other twenty-six city districts were Jews lived. General Ranier Stahel, the devout Catholic Wehrmacht officer who allegedly opposed the Judenaktion, not only authorized the roundup as Statskomendant of Rome, but also provided three companies of German troops to join Dannecker's men. The Germans forced their way to the unsuspecting Jewish homes between 5:30 a.m. and 2:00 p.m. and rounded up 1,259 victims for deportation to Auschwitz.[61]

Believing in the German word of honor, the Jews of Rome were taken by surprise. When they saw the Germans, many Jews wrongly assumed that they were after able-bodied men for forced labor. As a result older people, women, and children did not try to hide. By contrast, many younger men fled through the roofs or momentarily hid somewhere, saving their lives. The result was that the overwhelming majority of the victims, 896 of them, were older men, women, and children. They were taken in army trucks to the barracks of the Collegio Millitare on the Lungotevere, 885 feet from the Vatican.

Among the 1,259 detainees caught, there were more than 250 baptized converts and spouses in mixed marriages. Exactly as Kappler had told the two Jewish leaders, their baptism seemed to make no difference. However, unexpectedly Dannecker released in the evening 236 of the detainees after a thorough revision of their documents that proved they were baptized or married to Christians. In his evening report to Himmler, Kappler, as organizer of the Judenaktion, wrote that the operation had been concluded successfully with the arrest of 1,259 persons and the release of those in mixed marriages or baptized, which left 1,007 in detention. He indicated the deportation date of the Jews was set for Monday, October 18.

> After the release of those of mixed blood, of foreigners including a Vatican citizen, of the families in mixed marriages including the Jewish partner, and of the Aryan servants and lodgers, there remain 1007.[62]

The explanation for the surprising release of baptized Jews should be sought in the meeting between Secretary of State Maglione and German Ambassador Weizsacker after the Pope learned the news about the roundup early that morning from Princess Enza Pignatelli Aragona Cortes, and he instructed Cardinal Luigi Maglione to meet with Weizsacker. Pignatelli, his former student at the Cenacolo, a private Catholic school for girls where she attended his class in religion, was alerted about the Judenaktion by a friend living near the ghetto. In the company of German diplomat Karl Gustav Wollenweber, she personally went to the ghetto in his car to confirm the fact. She then rushed to the Vatican and without any previous appointment managed through the maestro di camera to approach the Pope in his chapel where she personally told him that the Jews

were being taken away. An American journalist who interviewed her after the
liberation, noted what she witnessed in the ghetto:

> People, many still in their pajamas, being marched down the street in the rain
> and thrown into black-canvassed trucks . . . Frightened children clinging to
> their mothers' skirts and old women begging for mercy . . . Screams, pathetic
> wails of prayer, and the slap of leather on cobblestones as some Jews tried to
> flee.[63]

Following the instructions of the Pope, Cardinal Maglione invited von
Weizsacker to a friendly meeting. Concerned that the Vatican was thinking to
undertake actions damaging to German interests, such as a public protest, Weizsacker inquired from the cardinal if the Vatican was considering a public protest
by the Pope. Maglione assured him that for the time being the Vatican would *not*
utter a word of disapproval that the German people might interpret as a hostile
act, but in the event that such actions continue in the future a "word of disapproval" might be uttered:

> The Holy See would not want to be put into the necessity of uttering a word of
> disapproval if these things continued . . . For now the Holy See hopes not to say
> anything that the German people might consider an act of hostility during a ter-
> rible war, but there are limits.[64]

From the conditional phrase "if these things continue," Weiszacker understood that the Vatican had given up on the Jews already seized by Dannecker.
Weizsacker, according to Maglione's notes, then emphasized how important it
was for the Vatican not to turn away from the policy of noninterference that the
Vatican had followed so strictly in the past, and the risks involved in deviating
from that policy:

> For more than four years I have admired the attitude of the Holy See. It has
> succeeded in guiding the boat between rocks of all types and sizes without col-
> lisions and, even if it has greater confidence in the Allies, it has known how to
> maintain a perfect equilibrium. I ask myself if, now that the boat is about to
> reach the port, it is appropriate to put everything at risk. I am thinking of the
> consequences that a step by the Holy See would provoke . . . The order came
> from the highest source.

Cardinal Maglione commented in his notes:

> I wanted to remind him [Weizsacker] that the Holy See, as he himself has per-
> ceived, had shown the greatest prudence in not giving the German people the
> least impression of having done or wished to do the least thing against the in-
> terest of Germany during this terrible war.

Maglione's comment is most revealing of the Vatican's motivation. The
Vatican's main concern was not the more than 1,100 innocent Jews being sent to

their deaths, but how to avoid that the wrong impression of any action or words from the Vatican harmful to the Third Reich should ever emerge as a result of the incident. Before taking leave, Weizsaker inquired whether he could keep the conversation to himself and not report it to Berlin, to eliminate even the semblance of a protest. Maglione agreed and Weizsaker promised Maglione "to do something for the poor Jews":

> Your Excellency has told me he will do something for the poor Jews. I thank you. If you think it more opportune not to make any mention of our conversation that had been so friendly so be it.

The obvious question to be asked is what action did Weizsacker undertake to keep his promise "to do something for the poor Jews"? The confidential account given by Cardinal Maglione to English Ambassador Francis d'Arcy Osborne of his meeting with Weizsacker and a note from the secretariat of state holds the answer. According to Osborne's report to the Foreign Office in London cited textually by Fr. Pierre Blett SJ and other authors, the surprising release by Dannecker of the 236 baptized mischlingen, or spouses, in mixed marriages was the direct result of the Maglione-Weiszacker meeting:

> As soon as the cardinal secretary of state was informed of the arrests of the Jews in Rome, he called in the German ambassador and expressed some type of protest. The ambassador immediately intervened with the result that a good number was released.[65]

Weizsacker's promise to Maglione "to do something for the poor Jews" now becomes clear as referring to the non-Aryan Christians and mischlinge released by Dannecker that evening.[66] This piece of the puzzle would not only explain the release of the baptized detainees and mischlinge by Dannecker in the evening, but also Maglione's readiness not to pursue the matter any further, and his authorization given in such an easy-going manner not to inform Berlin of the meeting. It would also explain the compliant state of mind of the Vatican, which issued without delay on October 19, 1943, the morning after the trains left for Auschwitz, the statement so eagerly sought by Ribbentrop that the German behavior toward the Vatican in Rome had been civil and fully respectful of its sovereignty![67]

The Jews were held in the Collegio Millitare until Monday, October 18, 1943. The morning after the roundup, on Sunday October 17, the Vatican secretariat of state sent Fr. Igino Quadraroli to make sure that there weren't any other baptized non-Aryans among the detainees. Quadraroli found out that there were still twenty-nine baptized detainees there. He had seen, he declared, "Jews who had been baptized, confirmed, and married in the Church." A note of the Vatican secretariat of state confirms explicitly that the Vatican efforts were exclusively for the baptized converts still left behind with the Jews:

The Vatican efforts had been especially for cases of baptized non-Aryans, who were not liberated, like others in their condition, after their arrest.[68]

The suggestion of the Swedish minister to Msgr. Montini to issue a public statement condemning the deportation was ignored. Fr. Morley comments:

> It is regrettable that, during the two days that the Jews were sequestered in Rome before being transported north, there was no word of protest or sign of solidarity with them.[69]

History came full circle in Rome that day. The verbal accords reached ten years earlier in 1933 by Pius XII as Vatican secretary of state when he ratified the concordat in Rome, provided the basis for the Church to intervene for the converts, while ignoring the Jews. The lack of response to the seizure of the Jews in Rome, although there still was an opportunity to save them by a determined intervention to reroute the trains, falls in line with the policy followed consistently by the Vatican until the very end of the Third Reich in every country in Europe where the Nazis carried out the Final Solution. The systematic nonintervention was an expression of the Vatican's strict adherence to the terms of the concordat.

After being held for two days in the Collegio Millitare, robbed of their valuables without providing them with food, water, or a place to sleep, the 1,023 Jewish prisoners were taken to the Tiburtina train station in Rome on Monday, October 18, and packed into sealed cattle trains, sixty people in every car, without food, water, or toilet facilities. After waiting endlessly for long eight hours in the station, the train began a five-day deadly journey to Auschwitz. Fr. Tacchi-Venturi, the liaison of the Vatican to the Italian government, describes the brutality of the operation in a report to the Vatican secretary of state dated October 25, 1943:

> Men and women, young and old, children and babies were transported barbarously like beasts for slaughter last week from the Collegio Militare.[70]

On the morning after the deportation train left (October 19, 1943) Pius XII received English Ambassador Osborne in an audience. Osborne, still under the impression left by the deportation, told Pius XII not to underestimate his moral authority. He asked the Pope directly what more was necessary to happen to convince him to act and even to leave Rome. The Pope responded that he would never leave Rome and that "he had no complaint against General Stahel or the German police; they were indeed respecting Vatican neutrality and had even helped some Jews," obviously referring to the mischlinge and mixed marriages that had been released. For Pius XII everything was in perfect order.[71]

Weizsacker's fear that deportation of Jews to Auschwitz might get in the way of the statement eagerly sought by Ribbentrop, attesting that the Vatican was satisfied with the treatment received from the German military and their respect of Vatican sovereignty, turned out to be unfounded. That very day the

Vatican released the statement and on October 30, the official Vatican daily *L'Osservatore Romano* published it prominently.[72] Clearly, sending more than 1,000 Jews to their deaths was not a valid reason to scar the Vatican's excellent relations with the Third Reich. The Pope even made a request through Weizsacker for additional German military forces in Rome to control the Communists, a request that eventually led to the Ardeatine Caves massacre.[73]

During the journey to Auschwitz there still was hope among the desperate deportees in the train that the Pope would intervene to reroute the train to Mauthausen or Theresienstadt, but the rescue of Jews was not on Pius XII's agenda. Reports of the train passing different cities, such as Padua and Vienna, have survived in the Vatican archives. The train reached Auschwitz-Birkenau on Friday night, October 23, 1943, five days after leaving Rome. It was held at the platform overnight with its human cargo, including those that died on the way. Saturday morning, as the Jews descended from the cattle cars, Dr. Joseph Mengele selected immediately 811 of them for the gas chambers and 196 for slave labor. The Auschwitz logbook of October 23, 1943, has the following entry:

> RSHA transport Jews from Rome. After the selection of 149 men registered with numbers 158451-158639 and forty seven women registered with numbers 66172-66218 have been admitted to the detention camp. The rest was gassed.[74]

Among those sent to the gas chambers were some very prominent figures: Augusto Capon, a semi-paralyzed retired admiral of the Italian navy and the Jewish father in law of 1938 Physics Noble Laureate Enrico Fermi; Alina Cavalieri, a well-known philanthropist and benefactress of the Red Cross, Lionello Alatri, the owner of one of Rome's largest department store and member of the Jewish Council.[75]

From the 196 Jews and Jewesses sent to slave labor, only fourteen men and one woman survived to tell the world the story of German depravity. The numbers tattooed on their arms remain registered for posterity in the Auschwitz log. The lonely surviving woman Settimia Spizzichino, who Mengele used for medical experiments, was found barely alive at the time of the liberation among the dead bodies strewn in Bergen Belsen. She spoke in a BBC interview in 1995:

> I came back from Auschwitz on my own. I lost my mother, two sisters and one brother. Pius XII could have warned us about what was going to happen. We might have escaped from Rome and joined the partisans. He played right into the Germans' hands. It all happened right under his nose. But he was an anti-Semitic Pope, a Pro-German Pope. He didn't take a single risk . . . He did not save a single child.[76]

Maglione's inquiries about the whereabouts of the twenty-seven non-Aryan Christians in the transport received no answer. When prominent Italian Senator Ricardo Motta inquired with General Stahel about the fate of the deportees, Stahel sent an envoy to tell him that "these Jews will never return to their homes again." Motta forwarded the message to Msgr. Montini.[77]

On October 27, 1943, three days after the Roman Jews had been gassed, Rabbi David Panzieri, the acting chief rabbi who replaced Israel Zolli after he went into hiding, sent to the Pope a most moving cry for help, which went unanswered.[78] Neither did the Pope heed the plea of the Swedish minister to Rome who asked for a public statement by the Pope condemning the deportations.[79] The attempt by leaders of the Jewish community, Dante Almansi and Settimio Sorani (head of *Delasem*), to address an appeal to the Pope through the Yugoslav legation ended with the arrest of Sorani by the Gestapo, who somehow was miraculously freed after two weeks.[80]

The possibility of a protest by the Pope died down so quickly that by October 28, 1943, Weizsaker was able to inform the Wilhelmstrasse in Berlin that there was no reason for any concern—the Pope would definitely keep his peace. In a self-congratulatory message, Weizsacker proudly informed Berlin that Germany was winning the propaganda war against the Allies in the Vatican:

> By all accounts, the Pope, although harassed from various quarters, has not allowed himself to be stampeded into making any demonstrative pronouncement against the removal of the Jews from Rome. Although he must count on the likelihood that this attitude will be held against him by our opponents and will be exploited by Protestant quarters in the Anglo-Saxon countries for purposes of anti-Catholic propaganda, he has done everything he could, even in this delicate matter as in other matters, not to injure the relationship between the Vatican and the German Government or the German authorities in Rome . . . We can consider that a question so disturbing to German-Vatican relations has been liquidated. [81]

Phayer points out that Pius XII's role in the tragic Rome episode is considered by many historians as the Litmus test of his role during the Shoah:

> Having known in advance what would befall the Roman Jews, the Pope said nothing to forestall it. Afterward, he said nothing to condemn it . . . Not surprisingly, the judgment of many historians against the pontiff has revolved around the drama of the Roman Jews. There are three reasons for this: well before the roundup of the Jews, the Pope knew that they were going to be seized but failed to warn them; the incident occurred in the vicinity of Vatican City; and after the Jews had been deported, the Pope failed to condemn Germany for its barbarity.[82]

Goldhagen has contrasted the Pope's response with that of the Lutheran Church in Denmark which was published two weeks before the Germans began deporting the Jews of Rome. The letter moved ordinary Danes to act on the Jews' behalf, rescuing them to safety in neutral Sweden. Bishop Hans Fuglsang-Damgaard of Copenhagen, the head of the Danish Lutheran State Church, sent a letter of protest with the full support of his bishops to the German authorities before the Danish deportations began. The pastors read the letter from every pulpit in Denmark on October 3, 1943:

Whenever persecutions are undertaken for racial or religious reasons against the Jews, it is the duty of the Christian Church to raise a protest against it . . . race and religion can never be in themselves a reason for depriving a man of his rights, freedom, or property . . . We shall therefore struggle to ensure the continued guarantee to our Jewish brothers and sisters [of] the same freedom which we ourselves treasure more than life.[83]

The 500 Danish Jews whom the Germans did manage to lay their hands on were sent to Theresienstadt and not to Auschwitz because the Danes did not give up on them. There, Danish and Red Cross officials were allowed to monitor their well-being saving their lives. As a result, 90 percent of Denmark's deported Jews survived the war, while only 1.5 percent of the one thousand Roman Jews deported survived.

The claim that Maglione's warning to Weizsacker of a possible future Vatican protest "if these things continued" stopped the roundups of Jews in Rome and Italy is nothing but a myth. Jews continued to be hunted down in Rome and in the rest of Italy by the Gestapo and their Fascist helpers wherever they could be found after Black Sabbath. Mass roundups were not feasible anymore because Roman Jews fled from their homes and scattered to the four winds, hiding wherever they could. Those who dared to return to their former homes were captured, taken to the Regina Coeli Prison and sent to the Fossoli concentration camp in Northern Italy on their way to Auschwitz. Until June 4, 1944, when Rome was liberated by the American Fifth Army, the Gestapo with the help of the Italian Fascists and militia was able to round up another 1,087 Jews in Rome without any protest whatsoever from the Vatican.[84]

Hochhuth's statement about the Pope's silence while Jews were being rounded during all these crucial months when Rome was occupied by the Germans (September 1943-June 1944) is fully true to the facts:

For nearly nine long months (between September 8, 1943 when Rome was occupied by the Germans and June 1944 when it was liberated by the allies) he, (Pius XII) looked on in silence while the victims were being loaded on trucks in front of the very door of the Vatican.[85]

Pius XII continued to show his deference to the Third Reich. Thousands of members of the German armed forces were granted audiences by the Pope and received his blessing until the very end of the occupation of Rome.

Friedrich Robert Bosshammer, Eichmann's Italian affairs expert, replaced Dannecker on January 5, 1944. Jews were hunted down not only in Rome but also in Milan, Florence, Genoa, Turin, and Venice, and even in small remote mountain villages of Northern Italy where they sought to hide. Their properties were confiscated and looted. Pius XII was informed almost instantaneously of the arrests and deportations in Northern Italy as they were taking place, but he never used his moral authority with Mussolini and the Salo government on behalf of endangered Jews, even after the Allied military forces liberated Rome on June 4, 1944. Zuccotti states categorically:

No efforts were made to dissuade Italian police and carabinieri leaders from zealously carrying out the order to arrest Jews . . . Pius XII personally seems to have made no contacts and no appeal to the Italians for the Jews. Likewise, he seems never to have appealed personally to any German officials . . . During the second half of 1943 and the first half of 1944, for example, he met several times with German Ambassador to the Holy See, Ernst von Weizsacker. There is no evidence in the available papers of either the Holy See or Weizsacker himself that the subject of the Jews ever came up in their discussions.[86]

In regard to the claims that Jews were given asylum in the Vatican, Sam Waagenaar (1903-1976) quotes Mademoiselle Solange Pinzauti-Five of the French consulate, the most active diplomat to help Jews in Rome, who categorically denied that. She told Waagenaar:

I never, never, knew of Italian Jews who were in the Vatican during the war, and I can assure you that I have known a few. Yet I have never even met one.[87]

Zuccotti and Phayer seem to be in agreement on this point as well:[88]

Although it is possible that a small number of Jews found refuge within Vatican City itself, recent scholarship has not been able to verify this.

Zuccotti points out that most of those who were given shelter in Catholic institutions outside of Vatican walls were in fact "converts, relatives of converts, or the spouses and children of mixed marriages." For Jews seeking shelter in Catholic institutions after Black Sabbath, conversion would often be the prize demanded. Zuccotti describes the plight of the Ascarelli family:

Ana Ascarelli and her siblings were taken by their parents to a particular convent arranged before October 16. When they arrived the nuns said they could not enter unless they converted. They left.[89]

## Reflexions in the Literature on Pius XII's Jewish Policy

The Church as an institution, remained silent on the persecution of the Jews when Hitler consolidated his power in 1933, in 1935 when the Nuremberg Laws were adopted, and in 1938 during Kristallnacht when Nazi brutality against Jews was displayed all over Germany for all the world to see. It again kept silent, with far more tragic consequences, during the war, when millions of Jews were uprooted from their homes, confined in ghettos, starved to death, deceived, and deported to be gassed and cremated in death camps or mass murdered by the Einsatzgruppen.

Various explanations have been put forward in legitimate literature on Pius XII's unbending policy to not allow the plight of the Jews to come between the Catholic Church and the Third Reich. These different insights are not mutually exclusive nor do they necessarily contradict each other. They may well find their rightful place in a more general encompassing view.

Rolf Hochhuth, Gitta Sereny, and John Cornwell favor the thesis that old-vintage anti-Semitism was the reason for the Church's silence during the Holocaust. Sereny suggest that the Pope's "instinctive" anti-Semitism determined his silence:

> Anyone who has read Pius XII's letters to the German bishops (and in the original German the phraseology is even more significant) must find it difficult to doubt that the Pope was anti-Semitic.[90]

The aim of eliminating the Jews, or, in any case, of shunting them aside—be it through baptism or expulsion—has its roots in Christian history throughout the ages as argued by Hitler before the Church leaders of Germany in 1933. There is, of course, no lack of proof of extreme anti-Semitism or anti-Judaism of the worst kind in the Church in modern times as well that can be mustered in support of that thesis.[91] The fact that the Church conducted a virulent anti-Semitic campaign in the media and supported far-reaching anti-Semitic legislation all over Europe prior to the Shoah that made possible the deportations to death centers is the best proof. The question of the Church's silence almost becomes meaningless in that context: How could anyone expect a protest from the Church against something that it supported and made possible?

Although there are substantial differences in their formulation, Klaus Scholder, Saul Friedlander, and John Cornwell, among others, advocate the thesis that Pius XII's strong pro-German sympathies and orientation determined his policy of silence on the Nazi persecution of the Jews, Pius XII was convinced that Germany was the dam protecting so-called Western civilization from Communism. Pius XII was, therefore, unwilling to weaken Germany by condemning its crimes. Even as late as 1943 when Italy deserted the Axis after the Stalingrad debacle, wishful thinking of a German victory in Russia and a separate peace with Western Allies still prevailed in the Vatican. Cardinal Maglione, the Vatican secretary of state, expressed to various people at the time his wish for the victory of the Third Reich in the Soviet front in clear words:

> The Fate of Europe depends on the victorious resistance by Germany on the Soviet front.[92]

Von Weizsacker, German ambassador to the Vatican, expounded in these terms the essence of Vatican policy in a telegram to the Foreign Ministry in Berlin on September 24, 1943, after a meeting with Cardinal Maglione:

> Maglione regarded the fate of Europe dependent upon the victorious resistance of Germany at the Soviet front. In case the German armies collapsed there the only bulwark against Bolshevism would fall and European civilization would be lost . . . The essence of the Vatican's dream is that the Western Powers will realize in time where their real interest lies and will join the German effort to help save European culture from Bolshevism.[93]

Others authors, such as Phayer, have suggested that the Pope's policy of silence was motivated by his vital interest in maintainig before the Germans an image of being an unconditional friend. When Harold H. Tittman, the American charge de affairs in the Vatican, pointed out to Pius XII on August 3, 1942, that "the failure to protest publicly against Nazi atrocities was endangering the Church's moral prestige and undermining faith both in the Church and in the Pope himself," Pius XII responded that he could not speak out against the murder of European Jewry because he did not wish to alienate the Germans, the "German people, in the bitterness of their defeat, will reproach him later on for having contributed, if only indirectly to their defeat." In his communiqué to the State Department in Washington dated October 6, 1943, Tittman provides a clear account of the Pope's argument:

> Another motive, possibly the controlling one, behind the Pope's disinclination to denounce Nazi atrocities is his fear that if he does so now, the German people, in the bitterness of their defeat, will reproach him later on for having contributed, if only indirectly, to this defeat. It has been pointed out to me that such an accusation was directed against the Holy See by the Germans after the last war, because of certain phrases spoken by Benedict XV while hostilities were in progress. When it is borne in mind that Pius XII had many years of conditioning in Germany, it will not seem unnatural that he should be particularly sensible to this particular argument.[94]

After the Allies liberated Rome on June 4, 1944, and the Germans, at the brink of defeat, were destroying the last remnants of European Jewry, his concern for his future image in the eyes of the Germans took precedence over the most elementary principles of humanity. Michael Phayer finds the Pope's approach deeply disconcerting "because of the warped standard that is implied—German possible disappointment with the Pope as opposed to millions of innocently murdered Jews."

Fr. John Morley argued that Pius XII was silent because Jews and the Jewish situation had a very low priority in Pius XII's agenda, particularly when compared with the unique place that Germany occupied in the Pope's vision of world affairs. Jews were therefore not "really" important in his overall perspective. While in the Catholic press as well as in Nazi propaganda, Jews were presented as a superpower controlling the world, the Church knew better that Jews were powerless and helpless against their enemies, hence they counted little except as a convenient scapegoat or as a source of wealth to be easily taken. For someone like Pius XII who considered Nazi Germany to be the retaining wall protecting Christianity and Western civilization from the onslaught of Communism, the annihilation of the Jews by Nazi Germany was at most a distraction that counted very little in global Church politics:

> Jews and Judaism, therefore, had no great importance for Pope Pius XII. This is not to be interpreted as disdain for them, but as a realistic appreciation of their role in his worldview.[95]

Vatican Secretary of State Cardinal Luigi Maglione (1877-1944) and the nuncios followed the policy set by Pius XII and assigned minimal importance to the Jewish situation, argues Morley:

> The conclusion, therefore, is that the needs and sufferings of the Jews were of little importance to Maglione in the face of the overriding concern for other priorities. Chief among them was the desire to maintain relations with all other nations of Europe. Maglione himself admitted that this was the case with Germany, and a fortiori, it would be true for the other states . . . The link between the Pope and Maglione is evident. There is no doubt that the decisions of Maglione and the instructions he gave to the nuncios were the result of the leadership and orders of the Pope. [96]

Fr. Leiber, secretary and confidant of Pius XII, made the suggestion to Dutch historian Ger van Roon that Pius XII's strong interest in maintaining his potential as a neutral mediator between Germany and the Allies determined his silence. Pius XII looked forward eagerly to the breakup of the Soviet alliance with the Allies and to the development of a new power constellation that would unite the Allies with Germany against Soviet Russia. He resented the unconditional surrender demand the Allies made on Germany and advocated a negotiated peace between Nazi-Germany and the Western Allies.

There are actually known instances in which Pius XII tried to play the role of a mediator. When General Ludwig Beck (1880-1944) delegated in early February 1940 Dr. Josef Müller to inform him that they were ready for peace and to remove Hitler from power if Germany would be left in possession of the lands it annexed since 1933, the Pope secretely transmitted the proposal to British envoy Francis Osborne.

At a time it was becoming increasingly clear that Germany had lost the war, Msgr. Pankratius Pfeiffer, the father superior of the Order of the Salvatorians, arranged a secret audience on May 10, 1944, for Himmler's former liaison man with Hitler, SS General Karl Wulff, the highest-ranking officer in the SS after Himmler and Kaltenbrunner. [97] The high-placed genocide perpetrator received a most cordial welcome and the apostolic blessing of Pius XII. According to the restricted information published about this meeting, the Pope was greatly heartened by Wulff's readiness to accept a negotiated peace. In a contemporary letter by the Pope to Cardinal Faulhaber the Pope wrote that in a negotiated peace Germany should be allowed to keep Austria and the Sudetenland. [98] When taking leave Wulff made the Nazi salute, breaking protocol. Msgr. Pfeiffer rapidly put him at ease reassuring him that the Pope would understand. Wulff described his impression of the audience:

> From the Pope's own words I could sense the sincerity of his sympathy and how much he loved the German people. [99]

Guenter Lewy made the point that Pius XII was afraid that German Catholics, particularly those serving in the armed forces, would abandon the Catholic

Church altogether if a conflict should arise between the Church and the Third Reich. Placed in a situation of having to choose between their allegiance to the Third Reich and their Catholic faith, Pius XII feared that the Germans would choose the Third Reich. To prevent such a conflict he was ready to overlook the unspeakable crimes being committed by the Third Reich. When a correspondent for the Vatican newspaper brought up with him the possibility of speaking up against the Final Solution, Pius XII responded:

> Dear friend, do not forget that millions of Catholics serve in the German armies. Shall I bring them into conflicts of conscience?[100]

One must of course consider the crucial role that the concordat played in Pius XII's decision never to allow the Jewish question to come between the Catholic Church and the Third Reich, even to the degree of never referring publically by name to the Jews. Using the concordat as bait, Hitler was able with great cunning to successfully bring over the Church to his side and neutralize its opposition. The substantial monetary support the concordat provided for the Church and the rights it granted were powerful enough to keep the Church meekly subordinated. Hitler himself expressed in a cabinet meeting on July 14, 1933, his reason for pushing the treaty:

> He [Hitler] expressed the opinion that one should consider the concordat a great achievement because the concordat gave Germany an opportunity and created an area of trust that was particularly significant in the developing struggle against international Jewry. [101]

At the ratification of the concordat in Rome on September 10, 1933, Secretary of State Pacelli accepted the principle of noninterference, particularly with regard to the Jewish question and gave the Nazi government free hands to deal with the Jews in exchange of a verbal promise not to harm baptized converts of Jewish descent. John Cornwell rightly points out:

> The very fact of making such distinctions [between converts and Jews] betrayed, of course, Pacelli's diplomatic collusion with the overall anti-Semitic policy of the Reich [102]

A background of milenial anti-Semitism, pro-German bias, and the alluring benefits of the concordat reinforced each other to entice the Vatican to enter into a Faustian pact with Hitler by which the Church was turned into an accomplice of the Nazi crimes against the Jewish people. The Vatican responded positively to a deal in which the lives of the Jews of Europe were the prize requested by Hitler.

The extreme importance that the Vatican ascribed to the concordat explains why Pius XII was so scrupulous in fulfilling its strictures, in order not to provide Hitler with even a minimal excuse for breaking the treaty. From the moment Cardinal Pacelli signed the concordat he considered himself bound to remain silent with regard to any action of the Third Reich related to Jews. The Vatican only stood up to the Nazis when the concordat was violated by them. The policy of silence followed consistently by the Church can thus be understood in the light of the agreement as an expression of Pius XII's strict adherence to the concordat and its verbal accords in 1933. Against this historical backdrop, we can hardly be surprised by the remarks of Vatican secretary of State Maglione to the German ambassador at the time that Roman Jews were being herded into cattle trains for Auschwitz in October 1943:

> The Vatican had been quite prudent in all respects, so as not to provoke the slightest impression that she was prejudiced with regard to Germany during this terrible war. [103]

It is most unfortunate that the same man who signed the concordat, Pacelli, became its guardian during the twelve years of the Nazi regime and even after it breakdown, until his death in 1958. He made extensive the non interference commitment he accepted for the German concordat to all of Europe. As a result, what was established in Rome in 1933 became part of Church policy everywhere in Europe. The Jewish question was not allowed from that moment on to come between the Church and the Third Reich anywhere in Europe during the long twelve years of the Third Reich.

> The concordat had conditioned the Bishops to refrain from speaking about issues not directly related to Church matters. In their minds this stricture blocked them from commenting on what was happening to Mosaic Jews. [104]

The late 1990s witnessed a surprising twist in the attempts made to justify Pius XII's silence. The Vatican's "discretion" on the Shoah that Himmler commended so strongly was suddenly transmuted by Emilia Paola Pacelli into what she called a "martyrdom of silence." At the time that the cause of his beatification and canonization was being actively advanced in the Vatican, his failure to speak out was transformed into a heroic deed:

> Political and diplomatic ability aside, wisdom, strength and far-sightedness, concrete realism that comes only from a correct view of human events precisely that of faith—are needed to choose silence and impose it on oneself, when supreme and very serious reasons demand it, when the destiny of thousands of men and women is at stake and that silence seems the only way out. [105]

Pacelli argued on the pages of L'Osservatore Romano that Pius XII was silent because he feared that by speaking out he would worsen the situation of the Jews—as if anything could have made their march to the gas chambers worse. [106] Pius XII himself had used this alibi in his Consistorial Address of June 2, 1943, to justify his silence, seemingly in reference to the baptized non-Aryans, "because we must be careful not to harm those who we want to save." If Emilia Paola Pacelli meant to say that by his silence Pius XII was trying to protect the non-Aryan Catholics she should have said so explicitly without hiding behind semantic ambiguity. By labeling non-Aryan Catholics as Jews as the Nazis did, Pacelli turned Pius XII's deal with the Third Reich in 1933 that doomed the Jews in exchange for the non-Aryan Catholics into a spirited effort to save what she calls the "Jews" (read non-Aryan Catholics).

# Notes

1. David I Kertzer, *The Popes against the Jews: The Vatican's Role in the Rise of Modern Anti-Semitism* (New York: Alfred A. Knopf, 2001), 287.

2. Kertzer, *The Popes against the Jews,* 285. Published in the bulletin of the archdiocese.

3. John F. Morley, *Vatican Diplomacy and the Jews During the Holocaust 1939-1943* (New York: Ktav Publishing, 1980), 168, 174, 177.

4. Morley, *Vatican Diplomacy,* 168, 174, 177.

5. Peter Longerich, *Policy of Destruction Nazi Anti-Jewish Policy and the Genesis of the "Final Solution.",* Mayerhoff Lecture at the. US Holocaust Memorial Museum, Washington DC.

6. Carol Rittner, Stephen D. Smith, and Irena Steinfeldt, *The Holocaust and the Christian World* (New York: Continuum Press, 2000), 127.

7. *Actes et documents du Saint-Siège relatifs a la Seconde Guerre Mondiale* (ADSS) vol. 9, nr. 82, p. 170.

8. Pierre SJ Blet, *Pius XII and the Second World War According to the Archives of the Vatican* (New York: Paulist Press,1999), 144.

9. *Actes et Documents du Saint Siège relatifs à la seconde guerre mondiale* (ADSS). Vol. 8, 534.

10. Father Graham was a former editor of *America* magazine.

11. Sergio Minerbi, "Pius XII: A Reappraisal," at the symposium, "Memories, Intertwined and Divergent: Pius XII and the Holocaust", Kings College, Wilkes Barre, Pennsylvania, April 9–11, 2000.

12. *Actes et Documents du Saint Siège relatifs à la seconde guerre mondiale* (ADSS). Vol. 8, 534.

13. Willi Dressen, Volker Riess, and Ernst Klee, *The Good Old Days* (New York: The Free Press, 1988), 233.

14. Güenther Lewy, *The Catholic Church and Nazi Germany* (New York: Mc Graw Hill Book Co., 1964), 300. Hugh Gibson, *The Ciano Diaries: 1939–1943* (New York, Doubleday, 1946).

15. Livia Rothkirchen, Article in *The Holocaust and the Christian World*, 105. Livia Rotkirchen, *Churban Yahadut Slovakia* (Jerusalem: Yad Vashem 1961), 12–19. John F. Morley, *Vatican Diplomacy and the Jews During the Holocaust 1939-1943* (New York: Ktav Publishing, 1980), 79. Raul Hilberg, *The Destruction of the European Jews* (Teaneck, NJ: Holmes & Meier, 1985), 458-465. Abraham Fuchs, *The Unheeded Cry* (New York: Mesorah Publications, 1984), 50.

16. Rotkirchen, *Churban Yahadut,* 12-19. Morley, *Vatican Diplomacy,* 79. Hilberg, *The Destruction of the European Jews,* 458-465. Fuchs, *The Unheeded Cry,* 50. Deborah Dwork and Robert Jan Van Pelt, *Holocaust: A History* (New York: W. W. Norton and Company, 2002), 303–304.

17. Susan Zucotti, *The Italians and the Holocaust* (New York: Basic Books, 1987), 281. Zuccotti comments: "Maglione and Marcone . . . never protested the fact of the deportations themselves."

18. Five months after his May 1942 report.

19. *Actes et documents*, vol. 8, 607f.

20. Paul I. Murphy and Rene R. Arlington, *La Popessa: The Controversial Biography of Sister Pascalina, the Most Powerful Woman in Vatican History* (New York: Warner Books, 1983), 200, 201.

21. William Perl, *The Holocaust Conspiracy* (New York: Shapolsky Publishers, 1989), 202.

22. *Actes et documents*, vol. 8, 534, 738-742.

23. Lewy, *The Catholic Church,* 300. Gibson, *The Ciano Diaries*, 530.

24. Morley, *Vatican Diplomacy,* 142.

25. *Actes et documents*, vol. 7, 473f. Morley, *Vatican Diplomacy,* 142.

26 . Foreign Relations of the United States, 1942. 7 vols; III (Europe). Washington D, C. Gov. Print. Office 1961. 136, 177. Zucotti, *The Italians and the Holocaust* 104-105. Morley, *Vatican Diplomacy,* 87.

27 . Foreign Relations of the United States, 1942. 775-776.

28. Martin Gilbert, *Auschwitz and the Allies* (San Mateo, CA: Joseph, 1981), 104-105. Pierre SJ Blet, *Pius XII and the Second World War According to the Archives of the Vatican,* (New York: Paulist Press 1999) 166.

29. Jerusalem Post, December 4, 2006.

30. Alberto Melloni, *Fra Istanbul, Atene e la guerra. La missione di A.G. Roncalli (1935-1944)*, 240.

31. ADSS vol. 5, only reproduces the response to Myron Taylor, the American representative to the Pope. Saul Friedlander, *Pius XII and the Third Reich: A Documentation*, translated by Charles Fullman (New York: Alfred A. Knopf, 1966).

32. Blet, *Pius XII and the Second World War,* 161.

33. Carlo Falconi, *The Silence Of Pius XII* (Boston, MA: Little, Brown and Company, 1978).

34. Blet, *Pius XII and the Second World War,* 161.

35. Blet, *Pius XII and the Second World War,* 161.

36. Morley, *Vatican Diplomacy,* 123.

37. Mark Riebling. Article on Pius XII.

38. Werner Gumpel, *Cornwell's Pope: A Nasty Caricature of a Noble and Saintly Man* (New Zealand: Zenith Publishing Group, 1999).

39. Moshe Y. Herczl, *Christianity and the Holocaust of Hungarian Jewry* (New York University Press, 1993).

40. Gitta Sereny, *Into That Darkness* (New York: Vintage Press, 1983), 333.

41. Michael Phayer, *The Catholic Church and the Holocaust, 1930-1965* (Indiana University Press, 2001), 61.

42. Fr. Andrew Greeley q. by Richard Z. Chesnoff, *Pack of Thieves: How Hitler and Europe Plundered the Jews and Committed the Greatest Theft in History* (New York: Doubleday, 1999), 249.

43. Robert Katz, *Black Sabbath: A Journey Through a Crime Against Humanity* (New York: Macmillan, 1969). Phayer, *The Catholic Church and the Holocaust*, 97-102. John Cornwell, *Hitler's Pope: The Secret History of Pius XII* (New York: Viking, 2008), 301-312.

44. Robert Katz, *The Battle of Rome* (New York: Simon an Schuster, 2004), 52, 348.

45. Weizsacker to Foreign Ministry, Sep. 23, 1943. *PA Bonn, Staatssekretar Vatikan, Bd. 4.* Lewy, *The Catholic Church*, 249–250. Friedlander. *Pius XII and the Third Reich*, 193.

46. Katz, *Black Sabbath*, 44

47. Katz, *Black Sabbath*, 54.

48. Katz, *Black Sabbath*, 65.

49. Katz, *Black Sabbath*, 65.

50. Katz, *Black Sabbath*, 65.

51. Katz, *Black Sabbath*. Morley, *Vatican Diplomacy*, 179.

52. Phayer, *The Catholic Church and the Holocaust*, 102.

53. Katz, *Black Sabbath*, 25.

54. Friedlander, *Pius XII and the Third Reich*, 204–205.

55. Katz, *The Battle for Rome*, 77.

56. Blet, *Pius XII and the Second World War*, 211–218.

57. Susan Zuccotti, *Under His Very Window: The Vatican and the Holocaust* (New Haven CT: Yale University Press, 2000), 156-157. Phayer, *The Catholic Church and the Holocaust*, 98. Morley, *Vatican Diplomacy and the Jews*.

58. Katz, *The Battle of Rome*, 83–84. *Acts* 9:501, doc. 363.

59. Eitel Friedrich Möllhausen, *La Carta Perdente*, Rome 1948.

60. Zuccotti, *Under his very Window*, 157. Phayer, *The Catholic Church and the Holocaust*, 97-104. Robert Katz, *Death in Rome*.

61. Katz, *Death in Rome*.

62. Katz, *Death in Rome*, 222–223.

63. Katz. *The Battle for Rome*, 103. Fr. Graham R (1970) and Kurzman D. (1975).

64. Morley, *Vatican Diplomacy and the Jews*, 181.

65. Blett, Pierre SJ. *Pius XII and the Second World War*, 216. Foreign Office, 371/3725/19; *Acts* 9:506fn

66. Katz, *Death in Rome*. Cornwell, *Hitler's Pope*, 308. James Carroll, *Constantine's Sword: The Church and the Jews* (Boston, MA: Houghton Mifflin Company, 2001), 527.

67. Phayer, *The Catholic Church and the Holocaust*, 101.

68. Morley, *Vatican Diplomacy and the Jews*, 182.

69. Morley, *Vatican Diplomacy and the Jews*, 182, 184.

70. Morley, *Vatican Diplomacy and the Jews*, 182.

71. Katz, *The Battle of Rome*, 113.

72. Phayer, *The Catholic Church and the Holocaust*, 101.

73. Zuccotti, *Under his very Window*, 133. Phayer, *The Catholic Church and the Holocaust*, 101.

74. Perl, *The Holocaust Conspiracy*, 201.

75. Katz, *Black Sabbath*, 190. G. Battimelli & G. Paoloni, Ed. *20th Century Physics. Vol. 3*, (World Scientific), 112.

76. Morley, *Vatican Diplomacy and the Jews*, 180, 182. Phayer, *The Catholic Church and the Holocaust*, 97. Zuccotti, *Under his very Window*, 120-125.

77. Zuccotti, *Under his very Window*, 167.

78. Morley, *Vatican Diplomacy and the Jews*, 184.

79. Morley, *Vatican Diplomacy and the Jews*, 182, 184.

80. Morley, *Vatican Diplomacy and the Jews*, 182, 184.

81. Saul Friedlander, *Pius XII and the Third Reich* (New York: Octagon Books, 1980), 207-208. Zuccotti, *Under his very Window*, 164.

82. Phayer, *The Catholic Church and the Holocaust*, 97-98.

83. Daniel Goldhagen, *Jonah: A Moral Reckoning* (New York: Alfred A. Knopf, 2002), 50-51.

84. Katz, *Encyclopedia of the Holocaust*. Dannecker was captured by the American forces in Germany and hanged himself in his cell in 1945.

85. Rolf Hochhuth, *The Deputy. Sidelights on History* (New York, Grove Press, 1964) 324.

86. Zuccotti, *Under his Window*, 292–294.

87. Sam Waagenaar, *The Pope's Jews*, (La Salle, IL: Open Court Publishers, 1974).

88. Phayer, *The Catholic Church and the Holocaust*, 102. This refers to correspondence on the question with Zuccotti.

89. Zuccotti, *Under his very Window*, 195, 197.

90. Gitta Sereny, *Into That Darkness* (New York: McGraw Hill Book Co. 1974), 282-283.

91. Hochhuth, *The Deputy: Sidelights of History*, 317–18.

92. Randolph Braham, *The Politics of Genocide: The Holocaust in Hungary*, Vol. 1. (New York: Columbia University Press, 1994), 32.

93. Weizsacker to Foreign Ministry, Sep. 23, 1943. *PA Bonn, Staatssekretar Vatikan, Bd. 4.* Lewy, *The Catholic Church*, 249-250. Friedlander, *Pius XII and the Third Reich*, 193.

94. Phayer, *The Catholic Church and the Holocaust*.

95. Morley, *Vatican Diplomacy and the Jews*.

96. Morley, *Vatican Diplomacy and the Jews*, 207-208.

97. Mark Boatner III, *The Biographical Dictionary of World War II* (New York: Presidio Press, 1996), 617.

98. Friedlander, *Pius XII and the Third Reich*. Phayer, *The Catholic Church and the Holocaust*, 58-59.

99. Katz, *The Battle For Rome*, 290–293.

100. Lewy, *The Catholic Church*, 303-304.

101. Der Nationalsozialismus: Dokumente 1933-1945, Frankfurt am Main, 1957, 130.

102. Ernst Christian Helmreich, *The German Churches Under Hitler* (Detroit: Wayne University Press, 1979), 253-255. Cornwell, *Hitler's Pope*.

103. Phayer, *The Catholic Church and the Holocaust*, 97-98.

104. Phayer, *The Catholic Church and the Holocaust*, 44.

105. Dr Emilia Paola Pacelli, *Pius XII: The Martyrdom of Silence* ( L'Osservatore Romano, English edition, 15 November 2000), 10.

106. Lewy, *The Catholic Church*, 300. Gibson, *The Ciano Diaries*, 530.

## Chapter 12
## Pius XII in the Postwar Period (1945-1958)

### The Collapse of the One-Thousand-Year Reich

Hitler committed suicide in his bunker in Berlin on April 30, 1945, dragging along with him the thousand-year Reich he had promised to the German people. Before commiting suicide, Hitler appointed Admiral Karl Dönitz as Reichspräsident and Joseph Goebbels as Reichskanzler. Next day on May 1, 1945, Goebbels committed suicide leaving Dönitz to sign the unconditional surrender as representative of the German government. On May 7, 1945, General Alfred Jodl, chief-of-staff of the German Armed Forces signed in Rheims, France, the unconditional surrender of all the German forces. The Allied powers refused to recognize Karl Dönitz and his government and arrested them on May 23, 1945, at Flensburg. In their place, the Allies created the Allied Control Council to govern Germany.

The senior cardinal of Germany and life-long president of the bishops conference, Cardinal Adolf Bertram, received the news of Hitler's suicide on May 1-2, 1945. As he had always done during the twelve years of the Nazi Reich, Cardinal Bertram paid homage to Hitler in the name of the Catholic Church and called the German people to raise prayers for him. He ordered the parish priests of his diocese to hold a solemn requiem, a religious service that can only be held for a Catholic for a higher cause, for the man that was the supreme embodiment of evil in human history. In his own handwriting the cardinal issued the following order:

> To hold a solemn requiem in memory of the Führer and all those members of the Wehrmacht who have fallen in the struggle for our German Fatherland, along with the sincerest prayers for Volk and Fatherland and for the future of the Catholic Church in Germany.[1]

The collapse of the Third Reich and the disclosure of Nazi crimes did not bring about a reassessment in the Vatican. The sight of the piles of dead skeletons in the liberated camps, the ruins of the crematoriums, and the emaciated skeletal live shadows that miraculously survived death marches did not move Pius XII. He maintained his icy silence on the annihilation of 6 million Jews in Christian Europe.

One of Pius XII defenders justified the Pope's wartime record by claiming that to judge retrospectively was unreasonable because "no one can be accused of really knowing what the Holocaust was until the slave, labor, and death camps were liberated." Another argued: "It must be remembered that the Pope was not operating with a post-World War II vantage point on history. His decisions were reached prior to the liberation of the Nazi concentration camps by the Allied forces." These authors seem oblivious to the fact that when the camps and the Holocaust became exposed in their full horror after the war, Pius XII did not want to know what happened in the death factories and he refused to look back on his own earlier attitude and actions. The English envoy to the Vatican, Sir D'Arcy Osborne (1984-1964), proposed to Pius XII after the liberation that he visit the liberated Nazi concentration camps in order to "judge the breath of German guilt firsthand" and to come forward with a public condemnation of the unprecedented crimes—Pius XII declined both requests.

Jacques Maritain, the Catholic French ambassador to the Vatican from 1945 to 1948, understood that without disclosure of the responsibility that Germany bore for the Holocaust and full condemnation of the Final Solution, there was no hope for a new beginning in Europe. Convinced that anti-Semitism was at the core of the contemporary moral crisis of Europe, Maritain urged Pius XII to issue a declaration against anti-Semitism, particularly after the infamous Kielce Pogrom of July 4-5, 1946, that marked postwar Poland with the Cain sign on its forehead. Maritain's attempts on various occasions to impress upon Pius XII the importance of addressing the issue of anti-Semitism and the specific responsibility that the German nation bears for the Holocaust were futile.

In his first important appearance before the College of Cardinals shortly after World War II, on June 2, 1945, his reference to National Socialism was reduced to one single sentence expressed, as always, in his elliptic style. Although he refered to the hundreds of Catholic priests and religious who died in Nazi concentration camps, he avoided at the same time any mention of the Final Solution and the fact that 6 million Jews were mass-murdered and gassed by the Nazis and their collaborators in Christian Europe for no other crime than having been born Jewish. As during the war, Pius abstained in the postwar period from identifying the Jewish people by name as the main victims of National Socialism. His words about unspecified victims of National Socialism "who were often innocent," implied that many of these victims were somehow guilty.

Pius XII wished to deny to himself and to the world the recognition that an unprecedented crime had been committed that destroyed the moral order of the world for which not only the Nazis and their helpers had to answer, but Christian Europe as a whole. Obsessed by his fear of Communist expansion he still considered that Germany and the vanquished Nazis were the most reliable partners that could be trusted to stop its advance. To keeping his good relations with

Germany continued to be his first priority: "Neither the war nor the Holocaust," points out Michael Phayer, "diminished Pius esteem for the land where he had once lived." The Holocaust and anti-Semitism were to him nothing more than side notes, distractions to be pushed aside in the struggle against Communism and the Cold War. Phayer has this to say:

> Pius XII's failure to emphasize the moral issues that affected survivors, such as anti-Semitism and restitution and his reliance on Fascist opponents to Marxism, even if they were Holocaust perpetrators, attests to the ethical shallowness of his pontificate."[2]

Pius XII excommunicated in July 1, 1949 "all Catholics who voluntarily became members, promoters, and popularizers of communist parties and their ideology" and decreed that anyone supporting Communism should be denied the sacraments. With regard to the Nazis nothing of that sort happened during or after the war. Not a single Nazi perpetrator was excommunicated during or after the war by the Catholic Church anywhere. Mass was celebrated in their memory and church bells were tolled. Pascalina Lehnert, the Pope's housekeeper, described to Paul I. Murphy how she joined Pius XII in the papal chapel to pray for the repose of the souls of Hitler and Mussolini when the news of their deaths reached the Pope:

> When His Holiness was told of their demise, he said nothing, holding to the Catholic teaching that one does not speak unkindly of the deceased . . . Yet, he went to the to the Papal Chapel on both occasions and said silent prayers for the repose of the souls of Mussolini and Hitler. I joined him in those prayers.[3]

The Catholics that joined SS murder units that committed crimes against humanity were accepted back in good standing after the war by going to confession, receiving absolution, and taking communion. Gitta Sereny describes the welcome-back ceremony of Gustav Münzberger, the SS officer in direct personal command of the operation of the gas chambers in Treblinka, where 900,000 Jews were gassed, that took place at the Catholic Church in Unterammergau in Austria, when this perpetrator rejoined the flock in a festive ceremony after the war:

> There was a ceremony. After being a Gottgläubiger he was officially received back into the Church . . . Ordinarily, all a Catholic who had become a Gottgläubiger would have to do would be go to confession, receive absolution and then take communion. It is a matter of choice whether or not it is also made into a festive occasion.[4]

Pius XII's attitude in the postwar spoke much louder than words sending a dangerous message to Christian Europe that crimes against Jews did not really count. Postwar Poland, the main scene of the Holocaust, understood that silent message well. When the last survivors of Polish Jewry began to return after the war from German death camps and Soviet Gulags to their previous homes in

Catholic Poland, they found that the "new" Poland was actively engaged in finishing Hitler's work. While involved in a bitter power struggle between them, the Church and the Communists shared the common aim of eliminating the last remnants of Jews from Poland. The deeper unity of purpose of the two rivals as far the Jews was concerned is highlighted by the British historian Norman Davies:

> In a deeply Catholic country, the similarity between the conduct of the party and that of the militant Catholic orders cannot be overlooked . . . The new comrade is but the old patriot writ large . . . The exclusive, intolerant approach to the problem of national identity, which among other things had distinguished the postwar communist party from the pre-war Polish communist party, marks the ultimate victory of the basic ideas of Dmowski's National Democracy.[5]

When the lonely survivors crawled out from their underground hiding or returned from the Nazi camps physically and spiritually broken and began to knock at the doors of their previous homes in Poland, they not only found that their dearest had perished and their communities were gone but also that their own lives were in immediate danger.[6] Afraid that the survivors might come to claim the properties of their families the Polish beneficiaries were out to finish off the survivors. A pogrom climate was stirred in Poland after the liberation. NSZ leaflets called upon the Poles to "kill Jews and save Poland." Lucjan Dobroszycki describes the "welcome" given to the surviving human shadows in the towns of Poland at the end of the war:

> Jews were killed when they came to ask for return of their houses, workshops, farms, and other property. They were assaulted when they tried to open stores or workshops. Bombs were placed in orphanages and other Jewish public buildings. Jews were shot by unknown snipers in full view of witnesses. Jews were attacked in their homes and forcibly removed from buses and trains.[7]

Jan T. Gross points out that the Poles were so implicated in Nazi crimes against their Jewish neighbors, aiding and abetting and expropriating, that the mere sight of the living ghosts returning was too much to bear. These ghosts knew the Poles' dirty secrets and held title to their property. So they murdered or brutally chased them away.[8] When Mirka Cohen, to mention one case, an eighteen-year-old camp survivor came back to Lodsz to cry at her parents grave she was murdered.[9]

According to a report of the Polish Ministry of Defense, which greatly underestimated the situation, there were 350 known individual murders of survivors in Poland in 1945 and more than 400 during 1946. Unofficial estimates arrive at a higher figure of between 1,500 and 2,000 Jewish victims. The prewar Polish national project to eliminate forever the Jewish presence in Poland was being brought to its ultimate culmination. Anti-Semitic riots broke out in Kraków, Sosnowiec, and Lublin in August 1945. Another twenty-six pogroms of varying sizes took place in different towns during the last four months of 1945.

The implementation of the repatriation accord of exiled Polish citizens in Russia in 1946 brought back approximately 150,000 Jews from Siberia and the Gulags, the last remnant of the 3.5 million prewar-Poland Jewish community. Encouraged by leaders of the Catholic Church, Polish anti-Semites found it most easy to use the Jews as a scapegoat. Zypora Frank, who as a child returned from Tajikistan in a cattle train with her parents, recalls how they were surrounded by a mob of rioting Poles:

> It was May 23, 1946, I remember because it was my birthday, and I was wearing a nice dress. They threw stones, they were yelling "you are taking our coal and giving us the Jews," and somebody threw a grenade. Two people were killed, one next to me whose blood splattered my birthday dress. [10]

The Kielce pogrom was the culmination of a well-planned campaign against the presence of Jews in Poland. Out of a prewar community of 27,000 Jews, only 200 returned to Kielce in the hope of finding some of their kin alive, but found there their own deaths instead. When the first Jews returned they were welcomed in November 1945 by a grenade thrown at the community center. Rumors began circulating in town that the Jews were coming back to claim the properties that the Germans took away from them and gave to the Poles.

On July 1, 1946, a Christian nine-year-old child in Kielce, Henryk Blaszczyck, went away for three days without the permission of his parents to a distant village to visit his relatives. To justify his absence, Henryk made up a story about being abducted by a Jew and held in the cellar of the hostel for Jewish survivors in Kielce. A blood libel was fabricated that the Jews were abducting and killing Christian children in the basement of the hostel to draw their blood to knead matzos. On July 3, 1946, the father, accompanied by the boy, filed a complaint with the police claiming that somebody had given the child a package to deliver to the Jewish hostel at Planty 7, where he was abducted and tortured in the cellar. There he allegedly saw the corpses of murdered Christian children, but he somehow managed to escape. The fact that the hostel did not have a basement at all, that the child was safe and sound, and that there still were nine months to Passover meant nothing to a mob conditioned for generations from the pulpits by their priests to believe that Jews used Christian blood to bake their Passover Matzos.

The signal for the terrible blood orgy that lasted for 5 hours was given on July 4, 1946, by the police when 14 officers entered the office and shot to death the Jewish chairman who tried in vain to contact civil and Church authorities. A police patrol began spreading the blood libel on Scenkewisa Street. The mob then entered the hostel and massacred forty-two innocent and defenseless Jewish Holocaust survivors, children among them, wounding fifty others. Girls were thrown down from the second floor and finished off by the mob. Two survivors, Eisenberg and Yechiel Alpert, somehow managed to get away and reach the bishop of Kielce, Czeslaw Kaczmarek (1895-1965). They pleaded with him to intervene and stop the Christian mob. The Bishop's response to their pleas was venomous:

> You were good merchants and doctors before the war, but now Jews took to politics; in the ministries they relate badly to Poles and to priests in particular.[11]

The bishop pretended that he would go to the hostel in the company of another priest to calm the mob, but he never went there.[12] For one full week the Church in Poland kept ominously silent on the crime. Then several bishops came forward calling the massacre a Jewish provocation.[13] The primate of the Church in Poland, Cardinal Hlond (1881-1948), who was approached after the massacre by the leadership of Jewish survivors in Poland, with a plea to issue a call to Polish Catholics to desist from finishing Hitler's work, made declarations on July 11, 1946, whose evil significance time has not erased. As in the good old days, he again made vile accusations against the survivors of the Holocaust and the victims of Polish barbarity. The modern libel that the Jewish survivors were allegedly imposing Communism on Poland he regurgitated to "justify" the Kielce mass murder.

> The course taken by the unfortunate and grievous events in Kielce shows that racism cannot be attributed to them . . . They developed against a wholly different background, a painful and tragic one . . . Many are the Jews who owe their lives to Poles and Polish priests . . . Blame for the breakdown in these good relations is borne to a great extent by the Jews. In Poland they occupy positions in the first line of the nation's political existence, and their attempt to impose forms of government completely rejected by the majority of people is a pernicious game, for it is the cause of dangerous tensions. Unfortunately, in the fateful armed clashes taking place in the frontline of the political struggle in Poland, not merely Jews but incomparably more Poles are losing their lives.[14]

Their communities gone, their relatives killed, and their property confiscated or stolen by their Polish neighbors, the survivors understood that there was no future for Jews in Poland. A desperate exodus from Poland to the DP camps in Germany began. Within three months, 100,000 Jewish returnees fled to the DP camps in Germany. There, a new desperate struggle to find new havens awaited them. The population of the survivor camps swelled and reached the number of 250,000 people.

The Kielce pogrom prompted American Jewish organizations and their representatives in Europe into action. After the Kielce pogrom, Jacques Maritain, the French ambassador to the Vatican, received an appeal from the American Jewish Labor Committee on July 7, 1946, to intercede with the Pope to use his moral and religious authority with Catholics to prevent that the survivors of the Holocaust continued to be murdered. On July 12, 1946, Maritain addressed Msgr. Montini:

> When I think of the part that Catholicism has played in the development of an-
> ti-Semitism in Germany, in Europe and in places like Argentina, I see how ap-
> propriate a word from the Pope would be.[15]

Jewish sensibilities were deeply wounded by Maritain's appeal, when he justified his plea with missionary intention in mind trying to impress on the Pope not to waste the unique opportunity to draw new Jewish converts to the Church at the time of their tragic predicament:

> It seems to me that this is a particularly opportune moment for such a sovereign
> declaration . . . On the one hand the conscience of Israel is particularly
> troubled, many Jews feel deeply within them the attraction of the grace of Chr-
> ist, and the word of the Pope would surely awaken in them echoes of excep-
> tional importance. [16]

After a personal visit to Kielce, the adviser on Jewish Affairs to the U.S. Army Command in Germany, Chaplain Philip S. Bernstein (1946-1947) and Chaplain Herbert Friedman realized the gravity of the situation and the urgency of the survivors drive to leave Poland. At the behest of General Joseph T. McNarney, commander-in-chief of the U.S. Forces of Occupation in Germany, they traveled to Rome to plead with Pius XII to intervene with Polish Catholics to stop violent persecution against the survivors. In a private audience in Castel Gandolfo on September 11, 1946, Bernstein pleaded with the Pope to use his moral authority with the Polish episcopate and people and condemn publicly the Kielce pogrom.

Although Pius XII characterized the pogrom as "dreadful" he ignored the chaplains' plea to issue a public condemnation. Using as an excuse the conflict of the Catholic Church with the Communist regime in Poland, he refused to is-sue directives to the Polish episcopate to act. When Jacob L. Trobe, the head of the Joint Distribution Committee operations in the D.P. camps in Germany learned about the refusal, he expressed his regret at Bernstein's useless trip to Rome, which he termed an "act of futile servility in petitioning his people's his-torical arch-enemy."[17]

## Protecting the Holocaust Perpetrators

When the German resistance in Northern Italy began falling apart in 1944, the Vatican moved swiftly to provide help to German prisoners in the Allied POW camps. Pius XII, who refused at the end of the war to send his representatives to German death camps, was extraordinarily swift in extending a helping hand to the German and Axis prisoners in the Allied POW camps even before the end of the war. An urgent request was presented by the Vatican secretariat of state to the Allied powers in August 1944 to allow personal representatives of Pope Pius XII to enter POW camps to provide them with charitable assistance and reli-gious guidance:

The Holy See cannot fail to interest itself now in these German prisoners.

The personal representative of the American president conveyed to the Vatican Allied approval on November 10, 1944. Pius XII delegated Austrian Bishop Allois Hudal (1885-1963) and Croat priest Krunoslav Draganović (1903-1983), as his representatives in the POW camps.[18] They received the necessary travel permits to move freely in Allied military and civil internment camps. With the support of Msgr. Montini, Hudal and Draganović received full institutional backing of religious orders and Church organizations, including the Pontifical Commissione de Assistenza and Caritas, as well as from independent organizations cooperating closely with the Vatican, such as the International Red Cross.

After Hitler's suicide on April 30, 1945, Himmler set up a provisional government in Flensburg at the German-Danish border and many SS commanders joined him there. Rudolph Höss, Commandant of Auschwitz, was one of them. Following Himmler's directives, the fleeing perpetrators threw away their SS uniforms and appeared in regular Wehrmacht or navy uniforms taken from prisoners. Höss initially disguised himself as a sailor and then as a farm laborer at Gottrupel near Flensburg. The POW camps became a gathering and hiding place for the German war criminals and thousands of East European collaborators who found in the Vatican representatives ready helpers.[19]

The investigations of Mark Aarons and John Loftus, Gitta Sereny, Robert Katz, Isabel Gurevich, Holger M. Meding, and Uki Goñi, among others, have produced reliable documentary evidence on the involvement of the Church in the protection of the war criminals on both sides of the Atlantic and their evasion from justice. In spite of Vatican records being inaccessible, recently opened CIA and British intelligence secret postwar reports, International Red Cross, records and Argentinean immigration and shipping records that survived periodic shredding made it possible for them to confirm the protagonist role played by the Catholic Church in the mass escapes of Nazi war criminals from Europe to Argentina.

The essential facts of the protection the Church extended to perpetrators are confirmed by Bishop Alois Hudal, the papal representative in the POW camps, in his *Römische Tagebücher*, which he published in Insbruck in 1962 before his death, long before the subject became popular in fictional and historical literature:

> I thank God that He allowed me to visit and comfort many victims in their
> prisons and concentration camps and help them escape with false identity papers . . . The Allies war against Germany was not a crusade, but the rivalry
> economic complexes for whose victory they have been fighting. This so-called
> business . . . used catchwords like democracy, race, religious liberty, and Christianity as bait for the masses. All these experiences were the reason why I felt
> bound after 1945 to devote all my charitable work mainly to former National
> Socialists and Fascists, especially the so called "war criminals."[20]

Helping the perpetrators, writes Hudal, is what should have been expected from a "true Christian," which he obviously considered himself to be. Taking high moral ground, Hudal barefacedly contrasted his "Christian charity" with Jewish "an eye for an eye" revengefulness:

> To help people without thinking of the consequences, working selflessly and with determination, was naturally what should have been expected of a true Christian. We do not believe in the eye for an eye of the Jew.[21]

With great pride Hudal wrote about the help to evade justice that religious orders extended to such major perpetrators as Otto Gustav von Wachter, Hans Frank's deputy in the Generalgouverment, who was in charge of the Galician Ukrainian Nazi SS Division that were responsible, among other crimes of the murder of 100,000 Jews in the ghetto of Lvov.[22] Wachter died allegedly from poisoning in Hudal's arms in a Roman hospital in 1949:

> In Rome's Spital Santo Spirito, the vice-military governor of Poland, Lieutenant General and SS-Lieutenant Colonel Baron Otto von Wächter, who was wanted by the Allies and Jewish groups everywhere, died in my arms, loyal to me until his end. Although his boss Hans Frank was hanged at Nürnberg, Wächter succeeded, not least of all thanks to the stirring selfless aid of Italian members of the Orders, in living under an assumed name, until his death by poisoning.[23]

Hudal helped Franz Stangl, the commander of Sobibor and Treblinka, responsible for the death of more than a million Jews, to flee to Brazil where he found work at a Volkswagen factory in Sao Paulo. The Austrian government issued an arrest warrant for Stangl in 1961, but it was not until 1967 that he was arrested and extradited due to Wiesenthal's efforts. Sentenced in Düsseldorf to life imprisonment on December 22, 1970, he died in prison of a heart attack on June 28, 1971. He confirmed in his trial the role that Hudal played in his escape:

> During the time we were in the internment camps we knew that we should go to Rome . . . Catholics should go to Bishop Hudal who would give us an International Red Cross Identity card and then a visa.[24]

Some have tried to place all the blame for the help to the war criminals exclusively on the shoulders of Hudal and Draganović to clear Pius XII, Msgr. Montini, and the Vatican in general of any responsibility for their activities. The historical truth is very different as various authors have convincingly proven. Their activities were institutional under the supervision of Msgr. Montini within the framework and boundaries of the mission that Pius XII assigned to them officially in 1944-1945. Phayer has this to say:

> The documentary evidence now available (but not available in 1992, when Father Lapomarda, S.J., wrote or when Father Graham spoke) demonstrates the close collaboration between the Vatican and fascists Draganovic and Hudal.

Establishing this connection, however, carries somewhat less importance currently, because we know now that Pius XII himself was directly engaged in rat-line activity. [25]

Contrary to the myth that Hudal had little to do with Pius XII, there was a life-long close relationship between the two. Hudal's rise in the Church hierarchy followed closely that of Msgr. Pacelli. As nuncio, Pacelli officiated at Hudal's consecration as bishop; when Pacelli became secretary of state, Hudal was appointed rector of the Pontificio Santa Maria dell'Anima in Rome for the theological education of German priests; and when Pacelli became Pope, Hudal was called to serve in the Holy Office. [26] Again it was Pius XII who appointed Hudal to lead the assistance of the Vatican in the POW camps. "By allowing the Vatican," says Phayer, "to become engaged in providing refuge for Holocaust perpetrators, Pius XII committed the greatest impropriety of his pontificate." [27] The Sylesian priest Karl Bayer, who worked closely with Hudal, told Gitta Sereny: [28]

The Pope did provide money for Hudal's work; in driblets sometimes but it did come. [29]

The Pontifical Commissione de Assistenza and the International Red Cross became part of worldwide net helping wanted Nazi perpetrators to escape justice. The net sheltered perpetrators, resisted their extradition, provided them with false documents, found them safe havens and helped them escape. The two organizations issued the fugitives valid identification papers and passports under false names that enabled them to slip through Allied controls. Their passport applications were signed by such priests as Draganović in Rome, Fr. Dömöter in Genoa, and Msgr. Heinemann, the German representative at Hudal's Santa Maria dell'Anima church in Rome. [30] As early as 1946, U.S. intelligence stated conclusively that the International Red Cross was issuing temporary identity documents and passports to persons operating under the protection of the Vatican, often using false names. In a press release more than fifty years after the events, on February 17, 1999, the International Red Cross candidly admitted to its role and opened its archives to investigators.

With the help of the producer of the mobile gas trucks Walter Rauff, Hudal established communication with the most wanted SS criminals. Rauff was serving since 1943 as SS chief security in northwest Italy, and became after the surrender a protégé of Msgr. Guiseppe Bicchieri, secretary to Milan's Cardinal Schuster, one of the Vatican's intermediaries in Operation Sunrise, the secret Nazi surrender negotiations in Italy. Bicchieri went to work for Msgr. Hudal, becoming Hudal's most important contact to SS fugitives in the camps. The port of Genoa in Northern Italy became the gathering and departure point of the perpetrators fleeing to Argentina and other countries overseas.

A line of communication was opened to perpetrators hiding as civilians in Germany and Austria outside of POW camps. Vatican representatives provided them with the assistance necessary to escape justice, including provisional hiding places, false identity papers, visas, and ship tickets. It was circulated that the perpetrators should find their way to Rome or to the Port of Genoa where Hudal and Draganović would assist them to escape. They directed them to Spain, Switzerland, and Italy on their way to Argentina.

The archbishop of Genoa, Cardinal Giuseppe Siri (1906-1989), a protégé of Pius XII and close rival contender at the conclave that elevated John XXIII to the papacy in 1958, helped Hudal and Bicchieri to establish the ratline escape door in Genoa. In close cooperation with Hudal and Draganović, Cardinal Siri established there the National Committee for Emigration to Argentina and the Diocesan Committee Auxilium to render assistance to the fugitives. The Pontifical Commissione and Caritas Croata opened offices at Genoa's railway station.

Argentina became the center piece in the flight from justice of the war criminals. The once most liberal country of Latin America became the main haven for Axis collaborators and perpetrators under President Juan Domingo Peron (1895-1974). His great interest in them was not so much due to his sympathies for Hitler and Mussolini from his years as military attache in Fascist Italy (1938), but to his expectations to put their looted wealth and technical skills in service of Argentina's armament and aeronautical industry. In their anti-Communism and Catholicism he saw an additional advantage that could counter the liberal and leftist tendencies in Argentina's political life.

The Church-state alliance that held steady until Eva Peron's death in 1953 was a crucial factor in turning Argentina into a haven for fleeing war criminals. The top figures of the Catholic hierarchy in Argentina, Cardinal Antonio Caggiano (1889-1979), Cardinal Santiago Luis Copello (1880-1967), and Msgr. Agustin Barrére (1865-1952) gave their full support to the transfer of Europe's wanted war criminals to Argentina. The Nazi sympathies of the prelates were of old. Cardinal Copello, archbishop of Buenos Aires and primate of the Church in Argentina, was a regular visitor to the German embassy during the war. He personally conducted a solemn mass for Petain after he died in 1951.

As the Cold War gained momentum in 1947, fleeing Catholic clero-Fascist collaborators and war criminals became valued pawns in the war against Communism: Croatian Ustashis, Slovak Hlinkas, French Vichyites, Belgian Rexists, Italian Fascists, Hungarian Arrow Cross members, and Romanian Iron Cross militants were helped to flee to Argentina. Peron opened a special migratory agency in Europe, the Delegación Argentina de Inmigración en Europa (DAIE) with offices in Rome and Genoa, under the direction of Salesian Army Chaplain Fr. José Clemente Silva. Once in Argentina, Franciscan priests led by Fr. Blas Stefanic of the Bari Basilica in Buenos Aires, helped the fugitives establish themselves in the new country.

When Msgr. Caggiano's was invested as Cardinal by Pius XII in Rome in 1946 his return was followed by the admission to Argentina of high-level French and Belgian collaborators sentenced to death in absentia in their countries during 1946-1947. Among them were Pierre Daye, Charles Lesca, Rene Lagrou, George Guilbaud, and Emile Dewoitine. Their anti-Communism and ostensible Catholicism appealed both to Peron and the high Church hierarchy. The timing, contends Goñi, was not accidental at all, but the result of an invitation extended to them in the name of the Argentine government through the Vatican by Cardinal Cagiano and Msgr. Agustin Barrére, who accompanied him to Rome.[31]

More than 30,000 Catholic Croatian Ustashis and a similar number of Slovak Hlinkas were brought over to Argentina.[32] The entire Croatian wartime government ended up in Argentina with part of the loot they brought out from Croatia. The mass exodus of the Croatians was organized by Fr. Krunoslav Draganovic from the Pontifical Croat College of San Girolamo degli Illirici in Rome under the umbrella of Caritas Croata. A close collaborator of Pavelić, Draganovic arrived in Rome from Croatia in 1943 and turned San Girolamo into the center of Ustashi activities in Rome.

After the defeat of Hitler the most notorious Ustashi war criminals, many of them priests and friars, found refuge at the Croat College of San Girolamo. The wealth they robbed from the murdered Jews of Croatia was hoarded there. There, they were given assistance to escape the hand of justice. Ante Pavelić, among many others, was sheltered for two years there, and he made his way to Argentina with false documents and means provided by the Holy See. He died in Spain in 1959, receiving the papal benediction. Others, like Artukovic, were able to postpone for many years the day of reckoning until they were brought back to justice.[33] An American intelligence report of September 12, 1947, explains why Pavelić was never detained and brought to justice:

> Pavelić's contacts are so high and his present position so compromising to the Vatican that any extradition of Subject will deal a staggering blow to the Roman Catholic Church.[34]

Although Cardinal Tisserant declared that the Vatican possessed a list of all the "clergymen who participated in atrocities and we shall punish them at the right time to cleanse our conscience of the stain with which they spotted us," none of the Franciscan Croat mass murderers was ever punished or excommunicated by the Vatican, points out Phayer.[35]

The wave of Axis Nazi collaborators to Argentina paved the way for the wanted German war criminals, who came in their track at the beginning of the Cold War in 1947. On June 6, 1947, Argentina's First Lady Eva Peron began a grand tour over Europe, including a visit to Pius XII in Rome, to promote Peron's immigration project to bring German fugitives. Soon after Evita's state visit, high-ranking German Nazi war criminals began to move to Argentina. Most of them arrived between 1948 and 1950 after Hudal requested 5,000 visas from Peron on August 31, 1948, for what he called German and Austrian "soldiers" who were anti-Communist fighters. Goñi comments:

> This is perhaps the clearest example of the Church's central role . . . These were not refugees, Hudal explained, they were anti-Communist fighters whose wartime sacrifice had saved Europe from Soviet domination. In other words, in Hudal's shorthand they were German and Austrian Nazis. The bishop's letter

was drafted while Peron's special agent Carlos Fuldner was wrapping up his Nazi rescue mission in Italy.[36]

Mercedarian Friar Jose Pratto, Peron's Ecclesiastic adjutant was sent by him as his personal representative to the Pope in a top-secret mission to bring the most wanted Nazi perpetrators and European collaborators to Argentina and to recruit German scientists and technicians to develop Argentina's armament industry. Pratto was received by Pius XII. He was accompanied by a recruiting team and toured Italy, France, Belgium, Germany, and Switzerland. The recruiting agents not only brought back scientists and technicians but also many perpetrators such as Eichmann, Mengele, Priebke, and Schwammberger, among others, whose hands were stained with Jewish blood. In his office situated next to Peron's in the presidential palace, Pratto personally welcomed them. The immigration files to Argentina of major war criminals such as Eichmann were all opened within a very short period after the Argentinean Nazi rescue and recruiting teams began their work in Europe in 1948.

The reconstruction of the total list of war criminals that fled to Argentina and neighboring countries is a task that still lies ahead. However, a number of the many helped by the Vatican ratline has been identified with their visa numbers and Red Cross passports endorsed by the Pontifical Commission of Assistance. The list includes Adolph Eichmann, Josef Mengele, Franz Stangl, Gustav Wagner, Walter Rauff, Edward Roschmann, Josef Schwammberger, Ante Pavelić, Dinko Sakic (last commandant of Jasenovac), Klaus Barbie, Gerhard Bohne, (a leader of the euthanasia program), Erich Priebke (perpetrator of the Adreatine Caves massacre), and Ferdinand Durcansky, the slovak foreign and interior minister sentenced in absentia to death in Prague for crimes against Slovak Jewry.[37]

Simon Wiesenthal, who made it his life mission to seek out war criminals, soon found out that their traces led to Rome. Following clues in his search for Eichmann in 1951-1952, Wiesenthal was led to Anton Weber, a Pallottini Father, to Benedikt de Bourg d'Iré, a Capuchin friar, and ultimately to the head of the organization—Allois Hudal himself. A report of the German Agency Nord Press on December 6, 1949, indicates that by the end of 1949 Hudal was receiving from sixty to 100 Germans daily in Rome who were helped with tickets and visas to Latin America.[38]

Alfred Jarschel (alias Werner Brockdorff), a leader of the Hitlerjugend, described in his book *Flucht vor Nürnberg* published in the late 1960s how Catholic priests helped former SS members by taking them to Rome, disguising them as Catholic priests, and finally providing them passports and money to reach Latin America.[39] Hans Ulrich Rudel, the Luftwaffe ace and friend of Peron who arrived in Argentina in 1948 as advisor to Argentina's air force, gave recognition in his memoirs to Hudal and the Vatican for their role in opening a "path to freedom" from Rome for the Nazi fugitives of justice after the war:

Rome became a sanctuary and salvation for many victims of persecution after the "liberation." More than a few of our comrades found the path to freedom through Rome, because Rome is full of men of goodwill.[40]

The manner in which the Vatican ratline helped Eichmann as described by Uki Goñi in his book the *The Real Odessa* is a good example of its modus operandi. One of Eichmann's main underlings Dieter Wisliceny, who saw Eichmann for the last time in February 1945 in Berlin, testified on January 3, 1946, in Nuremberg that he told him he would jump laughing into the grave knowing he liquidated 5 million Jews:

Question: When did you last see Eichmann?
Answer: I last saw Eichmann towards the end of February, 1945, in Berlin. At that time he said that if the war were lost he would commit suicide.
Question: Did he say anything at that time as to the number of Jews that had been killed?
Answer: Yes, he expressed this in a particularly cynical manner. He said "he would leap laughing into the grave because the feeling that he had 5,000,000 people on his conscience would be, for him, a source of extraordinary satisfaction."

Adolph Eichmann (1906-1962) did not commit suicide as he had promised. He was arrested and held at the American internment camp of Oberdachstetten at the end of the war under the name Otto Eckmann. He escaped from the camp in 1946 and with the help of his SS comrades went into hiding in Germany, while his wife, Vera, declared him officially dead in a German court. When the mass exodus of Nazi war criminals to Argentina began in 1948, Eichmann became Riccardo Klement with the help of the Vatican ratline, which obtained for him new identity documents from the commune of Termeno in Northern Italy. At about the same time a new identity was also obtained there for Dr. Jozef Mengele under the name Helmut Gregor.

Under his new identity, Eichmann was issued an Argentinean visa in 1948 under file number 231489/48, but he waited until 1950 to begin his journey. He secretly made his way to Genoa where Fr. Edoardo Dömöter, the Hungarian priest in charge of the Franciscan parish of San Antonio, submitted to the International Red Cross a passport application (no. 100940) under his new name. The Catholic relief organization Caritas paid Eichmann's travel expenses to Argentina. He arrived on July 14, 1950, in Buenos Aires on the ship *Giovanna C.* After landing safely in Argentina, he decided to inscribe himself in his newly minted passport as a Catholic even though he was a Protestant. He explained:

I recall with deep gratitude the aid given to me by Catholic priests in my flight from Europe and decided to honor the Catholic faith by becoming an honorary member.[41]

The laughter that Eichmann promised would accompany him to his grave was not to be, after he was captured by Israel in Argentina and sentenced to death in Jerusalem and hanged on May 31, 1962. Eichmann's capture and trial clashed with the high-minded Christian sensibilities of Cardinal Antonio Caggiano. On December 23, 1960, he publicly condemned Eichmann's capture, declaring that Eichmann came to Argentina seeking forgiveness and oblivion and that it was a Christian duty to forgive him:

> He came to our fatherland seeking forgiveness and oblivion. It doesn't matter what is name is, Ricardo Klement or Adolf Eichmann, our obligation as Christians is to forgive him for what he has done.[42]

While Peron's agents were combing Europe to offer their visas to Nazi collaborators, visas were being denied to Jewish Holocaust survivors in the DP camps. Peron's immigration officers (1945-1947) Santiago Peralta and his successor Pablo Diana (1947-1949) saw to it that the anti-Semitic Directive 11 banning Jewish immigration should be strictly enforced. Directive 11 was issued at the time of Kristallnacht in 1938 by the Argentine Foreign Ministry to all its consulates in the world instructing them to deny visas to Jews fleeing the Nazis. Only illegally could a Jew enter Argentina, either by pretending to be a Catholic or by hefty payments to the Argentinean consular diplomats. Sixty-eight years had to pass until Directive 11 was repealed in a symbolic gesture by President Néstor Kirchner on June 8, 2005. Jews who entered Argentina posing as Catholics were granted the right to correct their original records. [43]

## Seeking Pardons for the Mass Murderers

On January 1942 the allied governments in exile issued in London the St. James Declaration that committed its signatories to "the punishment, through the channel of organized justice, of those guilty of or responsible for crimes committed against them." On October 26, 1943, the four main Allied powers, the United States, Great Britain, France, and the Soviet Union, established in London the United Nations War Crimes Commission to bring to justice war criminals after the war. The commission began to draw up lists with the names of war criminals more than a year before the end of the war.[44] Soon after the end of World War II on August 8, 1945, the four powers approved in London the charter of an International Military Tribunal (IMT) to try war criminals and established the rules and procedures that would govern the trials. Nuremberg, the cradle of the Nazi movement, was chosen as the site of the trials for its symbolic significance.

Aarons and Loftus estimate that at the end of the war there were as many as 150,000 war criminals registered in the lists of the War Crimes Commission, of which only 50,000 were apprehended. Many of the fugitives were directed by their protectors to Italy, Spain, and Switzerland and from there to Argentina and other countries. Thus, according to their assessment, 100,000 criminals who had on their hands the blood of millions of Jews completely evaded international justice in the postwar period. In a sad travesty of justice, the SS guards at Auschwitz were the ones to come out best. Of the 7,000 members of the SS in

Auschwitz who survived the war, fewer than 800 were ever put on trial. Nearly 90 percent of them were never prosecuted and ended up after the war in Peron's Argentina with the help of the Vatican ratline.

When the Nazi-occupied countries were liberated, they began to put to trial some of their collaborators and demanded the extradition of those foreign perpetrators that carried out war crimes in their territory. Rudolf Höss, the commander of Auschwitz, Dr. Ludwig Fischer, the German governor of Warsaw, and General Jürgen Stroop, who supressed the Warsaw ghetto revolt, were captured and extradicted to Poland by the Western Allies. Höss was captured by the British in Germany after his wife, Hedwig, revealed his whereabouts when she was threatened with being delivered with her son to the Soviets. Höss was executed in Poland on April 16, 1947. Stroop was one of the last to be extradicted to Poland and executed in 1951. When the Cold War set in and the war criminals became valued pawns in the hands of Western powers, the initial cooperation between East and West to bring war criminals to justice came to an end.

Twelve separate trials took place in Nuremberg from 1945 to 1949 involving more than 100 defendants. The first Nuremberg trial opened in the Palace of Justice in Nuremberg on November 20, 1945, and indicted twenty-four top figures in the Nazi hierarchy and six Nazi organizations. The accused were individually charged with the systematic murder of millions of people and with planning and carrying out the war in Europe. Robert H. Jackson, Maxwell Fyfe, Andre Gross, and I. T. Nikitchenko were appointed American, British, French, and Soviet chief prosecutors respectively. Prosecutors and judges pledged to act in accordance with international law as approved in The Hague Conventions of 1899 and 1907 and in the Geneva Conventions of 1864 and 1906.[45] In his opening address Justice Jackson spoke memorable words before the International Military Tribunal:

> That four great nations flushed with victory and stung with injury stay the hand of vengeance and voluntarily submit their captive enemies to the judgment of the law is one of the most significant tributes that Power has ever paid to Reason . . . What we propose is to punish acts which have been regarded as criminal since the time of Cain and have been so written in every civilized code.[46]

The eleven subsequent Nuremberg trials were of no lesser importance than the first one, although less publicized. They included the Einsatzgruppen trial, the doctor's trial, and the judge's trial. Also brought to trial in the former Dachau concentration camp between November 1945 and August 1948 were 1,672 former staff members of the Nazi concentration camps.

When the Holocaust came to light in all its horror after the war, it could have been expected that the Church would have welcomed or at least accepted the efforts made by the Allies to bring the genocide perpetrators to justice to reestablish in some measure the moral order that had been shattered. Things turned out differently. Although the German bishops issued a formal statement at the Fulda Conference in 1945 that perpetrators must be brought to justice, it very soon became clear what justice meant to them. No less an important figure of the German episcopate than Bishop von Galen published in Rome in March 1946 a slanderous attack on the Nuremberg Tribunals. As if he had never heard about the crimes committed by the Third Reich, he came forward with the accusation that the tribunal was not seeking justice but to defame Germany:

> The trials were not about justice but about the defamation of the German people.[47]

The German bishops issued in 1948 a collective statement denying the moral and legal grounds of the Nuremberg Trials and accusing the tribunal for putting on trial people for breaking "laws hitherto unknown in Germany." Michael Phayer asks pointedly:

> Did they really believe that there was no law against murdering Jews?[48]

Pope Pius XII became personally involved in seeking pardons for war criminals whose hands were drenched in Jewish blood in different European countries. He called upon President Harry Truman to show leniency toward war criminals and later pressed General Lucius Clay, the U.S. military governor of occupied Germany, to commute collectively all the death sentences handed out against them. The German bishops began to bombard General Clay and Commissioner John J. McCLoy, the two highest Allied authorities in occupied Germany, with requests for amnesty and sentence reductions for mass murderers convicted in the Allied tribunals. General Clay responded that there was no reason to pardon individuals who in just trials had been found guilty of heinous crimes.

The intervention that Pius XII undertook in favor of Einsatzgruppen and death camp commanders is one of the saddest chapters of his postwar activities. As can be learned from the private diaries of his personal representative in occupied Germany, Bishop Aloysius Muench (1889-1962), Pius XII sought pardons for some of the Einsatzgruppen commanders such as Otto Ohlendorf (1907-1951) that mass murdered the Jews of Southern Ukraine and Franz Six (1909-1975) who was responsible for the liquidation of the Smolensk ghetto.[49]

To fully appreciate the significance of Pius XII's intervention for such a mass murderer as Ohlendorf, it is relevant to quote here some excerpts of Ohlendorf's testimony given under oath in Nuremberg that were long available at the time of the Pope's appeal for Ohlendorf.[50] Ohlendorf and Himmler were close associates and, in fact, were traveling together when they were captured. When Ohlendorf was asked by the judge in his trial why he also killed the children, his answer was registered verbatim by Jack W. Robbins, legal aide to Telford Taylor, Chief of Counsel for War Crimes:

> I believe that it is very simple to explain if one starts from the fact this order did not only try to achieve security but also a permanent security; for that reason the children were people who would grow up and surely, being the children

of parents who had been killed, they would constitute a danger no smaller than that of the parents.[51]

His answer was very similar to what Himmler told a gathering of SS officers in Posen on October 6, 1943:

> We came to the question: what to do with the women and children? I decided to find a clear solution here as well. I did not consider myself justified to exterminate the men—that is, kill them or allow them to be killed—and allow the avengers of our sons and grandsons in the form of their children to grow up. The difficult resolve had to be taken to make this race disappear from the earth.[52]

In spite of Pius XII's appeal on behalf of Ohlendorf, he was hanged with three other Einsatzgruppen commanders in Landsberg prison on June 8, 1951.[53] He expressed no remorse for his actions, telling the prosecutor that the Jews of America would suffer for what the prosecutor had done The Pope was more successful with his appeals for other SS perpetrators such as BrigadeFührer Franz Six, who was actually released in 1952. The combined efforts of Pius XII and the German bishops were largely successful in commuting the sentences of many convicted genocide perpetrators, particularly after the beginning of the Cold War. As a result of the Pope's intervention, the members of the Ukrainian SS Galicia division who were held at the Rimini camp by the British Army never came to justice although they had committed unspeakable crimes in the Ukraine and Galicia. They were given the opportunity to migrate to Great Britain and from there to resettle in British Commonwealth countries such as Canada and Australia.[54]

Very special care and concern was shown by the Vatican for those Catholic collaborators who had helped to place the Catholic Church in a privileged position in their countries, such as Franz von Papen, Joszef Tiso, Ante Pavelić, Henri-Philippe Petain, Leon Degrelle, Pierre Laval, and their like. These collaborators became the object of the Vatican's solicitous defense efforts, concern, and even posthumous honors.

Weeks after the capitulation of the Third Reich, Tiso was captured by American military forces on June 8, 1945. Cardinal Faulhaber protested his arrest on June 9, 1945, on grounds that this was an attack on a good-standing member of the papal family:

> I feel duty bound to notify the Holy Father of your arrest of Dr. Tiso, since as a prelate in good standing he is a member of the papal family.[55]

Tiso stood trial for his crimes and was convicted on April 15, 1946. Unrepentant until the end, the genocide perpetrator whose venality only matched his anti-Semitism was hanged three days later. He declared before his death:

If God allowed me to carry out my policy again under similar circumstances, I would do exactly as I have done. [56]

When Tiso's death was announced, Church bells were tolled as a sign of mourning all over Slovakia by order of the bishops. The Slovak episcopate, anti-Semitic as ever, issued a letter on January 8, 1946, eulogizing the remorseless persecutor of Slovak Jewry:

> Dr. Tiso was always a zealous priest of exemplary life. In his extensive activity he worked and labored for the common good . . . The majority of the Slovak people agree with us that the intentions of Dr. Tiso in the execution of his public activity were always the best. [57]

The efforts for an acquittal were successful in the case of Franz von Papen who more than anyone in Germany was directly responsible for Hitler's coming to power in 1933. Acquitted in Nuremberg on October 1, 1946, the Vatican showed its great esteem to him by confirming on July 24, 1959, the honorary title of papal chamberlain that he received in 1923 for the first time. Always an honored guest in the Vatican, he was granted audiences with Pope Pius XII and Pope John XXIII in the years that followed.[58]

Pius XII intervened at least on four different occasions from August 1945 to April 26, 1947, with the British representative in the Vatican, Sir D'Arcy Osborne, to stop the extradition to Yugoslavia of fifteen Croat Nazi collaborators and war criminals, including Generals Vladimir Kren and Ante Moskov held in the POW camps in Italy and at Regina Elena military prison. Osborne was finally instructed by the Foreign Office in London to impress on the Vatican that it was creating in the world the impression of being the "deliberate protectors of Hitler's and Mussolini's minions":

> Though we do not for a moment wish to interfere in the Vatican's affairs . . . we should point out that the ministers of Nedic and Pavelić are not Thomas à Beckets.[59]

At the trials of brutal Nazi camp doctors accused of heinous crimes, the Vatican and the bishops worked behind the scene for their acquittal or pardon. What the Vatican denied to their victims during the war, it generously granted to their victimizers after the war in the name of Christian charity. The defense by the German bishops of such a vile death camp physician as Dr. Hans Kurt Eisele (1912-1967), an SS camp doctor at Natzweiler, Buchenwald, Mauthausen, and Dachau, is an eloquent example.

Eisele murdered an average of sixty Jewish "patients" per week, injecting evipan-natrium directly into their hearts to produce instantaneous death. He used Jews as guinea pigs performing on them criminal operations without anesthesia. Tried by an American Military Tribunal on May 29, 1946, in Dachau among forty other accused staff members, he was condemned to death. His execution was delayed because he still had to answer for crimes that he had committed in

Buchenwald. At the Buchenwald trial against thirty-one accused war criminals that began on April 11, 1947, Eisele was saved from the gallows by the director of Caritas Heinrich Auer. He mobilized the German bishops and the Pope's envoy in postwar Germany Aloysius Muench in favor of Eisele who had been a member of the Catholic St. Vincent de Paul Society in his youth. Using the testimony of non-Jewish inmates who Eisele treated in the normal medical manner, they obtained successive commutations of his sentences, and his complete release from the Landsberg prison on February 19, 1952. Eisele went back to a successful medical practice in Munich with funds provided by the German government.[60]

Eisele became again the focus of attention when the sadistic Buchenwald guard Martin Sommer, the "hangman of Buchenwald," was brought to trial. Jewish survivors testified about Eisele's killing of hundreds of Jews by means of injections of evipan-natrium. By the time a warrant for Eisele's arrest was issued on June 28, 1958, Eisele and his family was already aboard the *SS Esperia*, which had set sail from Genoa to Alexandria a day earlier. Under the name of Karl Debosch, Eisele went to work at Nasser's new aircraft and missile center at Helwan where more than 200 German and Austrian scientists and other personnel brought by Nasser to Egypt were deployed. He lived in the Cairo suburb of Maadi unmolested for ten years until his natural death on May 3, 1967.

In his diary Bishop Aloysius Muench (1889-1962),[61] Pius XII's representative in occupied Germany, made reference to efforts made by the Pope to obtain a pardon for such majors perpetrators as Oswald Pohl, the chief of the SS Main Office in charge of the Nazi death and labor camps, and Arthur Greisser the gauleiter of Western Poland who was convicted for the murder of 100,000 Jews. Pohl was responsible for securing that the wealth looted from the victims should reach the coffers of the Reich.[62] In an effort to save Greisser who was sentenced to death on July 15, 1946, the Vatican sent a special cable to the President of Poland. The interventions reached such a level that Bishop Muench, who himself helped to pardon various major war criminals such as Dr. Eisele, advised in a note to Msgr. Montini that the Holy See must desist from such interventions "especially if such interventions would eventually become public." Phayer comments:

> The Vatican's efforts in this regard became so blatant that Pope Pius's own envoy to postwar Germany, Bishop Muench, wrote to Monsignor Montini, Pius's trusted under-secretary of state, telling him that the Vatican must cease and desist. "I have not dared to advise the Holy See to intervene [for the atrocity perpetrators], especially if such interventions would eventually become public."[63]

The Americans caught SS General Karl Wulff after the war and handed him over to the British to try him for his role in the Ardeatina tunnel massacre, but let him go free for lack of direct evidence. Incriminated by his reports to Himmler and Luftwaffe Field Marshal Milch on the deadly "low-pressure, high altitude" experiments on Dachau-inmates carried out for the Luftwaffe by

Rascher, Wulff was sentenced to four years labor camp by a German court in 1946 for his part in them. Wulff, however, went free after one single week in jail.[64] At the Rademacher trial in February-March 1952, this major perpetrator cynically testified that even Hitler "did not know" about the murder of the Jews. His cynicism was only matched by the court's pronouncement that Wulff "only wanted to help Himmler carry out his task."

For sixteen years Liebes Wolfchen like Franz Six lived free as a prospering publicity agent in West Germany. It was only after the Eichmann trial in 1961 that the German Federal Supreme Court indicted Wulff for genocide crimes on January 18, 1962, but freed him again in 1971. He was characterized in his 1962 trial as "the eyes and ears of Himmler." It is this major perpetrator whom the Vatican considered worthy of being called before the Consistory and Metropolitan Court of Munich and Freising in 1972 as a witness in the beatification process of Pius XII. He testified to his many meetings with the Führer in 1943 and took credit for dissuading the Führer from his alleged plan to move the Pope and the Curia from Rome to Lichtenstein. Wulff lived comfortably his last years in Munich until his death in 1975.

The great majority of Nazi perpetrators included in the lists of the London War Crimes Commission never came to justice after World War II. After the Nuremberg Trials, the West-German government took responsibility for prosecuting war criminals and established the Zentrale Stelle der Landesjustizverwaltungen (Central Office of the Judicial Administrations of the Lander) at Ludwigsburg. No more than 100 indictments were handed down against Einsatzkommando commanders, officers, noncommissioned officers, and private perpetrators that figured in war criminals lists. No death sentences were handed down in these trials, since West Germany had abolished capital punishment.

## Pius XII Refusal to Return Holocaust Orphans

The loss of Jewish orphans entrusted in Christian homes and Church institutions during the war is one of the most tragic sequels of the Holocaust. A noble act of saving human lives was often turned into a vile act of abduction to "save" souls. The parents who made the decision to part from their children did it under extreme duress. They not only faced the enormous difficulty of finding Christian hosts ready to take the great risks involved in hiding Jewish children and of procuring the substantial sums demanded but also the possibility that their children might be baptized and torn away forever from their people and faith. They obviously did it to save their lives and not to convert them.

The martyred historian of the Warsaw ghetto, Dr. Emmanuel Ringelblum, makes reference in his ghetto chronicle to an agonizing discussion that took place among the Jewish leadership when a proposal to save a few hundred Jewish children by hiding them in Catholic convents came up for deliberation in the ghetto. It mainly failed, writes Ringelblum, because the "Polish clergy was not interested in the question of saving Jewish children":

For the sake of history, we mention a project to settle a few hundred Jewish children in convents in accordance with the following principles: the children would be aged ten and upwards; the annual charge of 8,000 zloty would be paid in advance; a card-register would be kept of the children, recording their distribution throughout the country, so that they could be taken back after the war.[65]

This project was discussed in Jewish social spheres, where it met with opposition from Orthodox Jews and certain national groups. The objection was raised that the children would be converted and would be lost to the Jewish people for good. It was argued that future generations would blame us for not rising to the necessary heights and not teaching our children Kiddush Ha-Shem (martyrdom for the faith), for which our ancestors died at the stake during the Spanish Inquisition. The discussion on the matter among social workers reached no agreed conclusions, no resolutions were accepted, and Jewish parents were left to decide for themselves.

The project was not carried out because of a variety of difficulties, but mainly because the Polish clergy was not very much interested in the question of saving Jewish children. [66]

In another section of his chronicle, Ringelblum states: "The Church was rather concerned with saving souls not lives." When Jewish children were accepted in the Catholic institutions the Church did it as part of its missionary activity to convert them to Christianity. These children were educated during the war years and after as Christians. Children saved in Christian institutions were generally not allowed by their rescuers to reassume their Jewish identity and return to their faith and people. Those children who were too young to remember were even denied the knowledge that they were Jews and that their parents had been killed in Auschwitz or Treblinka. At best, they learned about their real families only after they had grown up. Maritain refers to them when he states in his often quoted letter of July 12, 1946, to Msgr. Montini:

During the war six million Jews have been liquidated, thousands of Jewish children have been massacred, thousand of others torn from their families and stripped of their identity. [67]

Children were smuggled out from the Warsaw ghetto to the Aryan side by Irena Sendler (1910-2008), an employee of the Warsaw Welfare Department, with the cooperation of twenty-five women volunteers. Ten of the volunteers smugled the children out, another ten were in charge of finding families to shelter them, and five were in charge of obtaining false documents. Sendler personally smuggled out around 400 children, entering the ghetto with a pass from the Warsaw Epidemic Control Department.[68] The team is credited with having smuggled out around 2,500 children to the Aryan side. The hardest part was convincing parents to part with their children, surrendering them into Catholic homes or convents, where they might be baptized or taught Christian prayers. Many chose to die with their children instead. Sometimes, Sendler would finally convince the parents, only to be met with the grandparents' resolute refusal. She would be forced to leave empty-handed, returning the next day to find that the entire family had been sent to Treblinka. "Most of us came from secular homes," says Holocaust survivor Nechama Tec, "Jewish Orthodox children hardly ever made it to the Christian world."

By 1942, when the ghetto began to be rapidly emptied to Treblinka, Sendler's team in the city board joined forces with Żegota, the Council for Assistance to the Jews, which operated from 1942 to 1945. Żegota was subordinated to the Polish government delegation in the homeland. It included representatives of the various Polish parties, the Jewish National Committee, and of the Bund, the Jewish Workers' Party. Żegota obtained money for its activity from the Polish government in exile in London and about 10 percent of its budget from organizations representing Polish Jews.

Whenever possible, Sendler wrote down the child's Jewish name as well as the child's new Christian name and new address and buried them in jars in a friend's garden. Almost all the children's parents died in the Treblinka extermination camp where they were deported between September 1942 and April 1943. In January 1945, Sendler returned to the garden and dug up the jars. She turned over the names to Adolph Berman (1906-1978), a Jewish Żegota activist, and he and other members of the group tried to locate the children's foster families. Although the foster families had to promise to return the children to any surviving family members after the war, this promise was not always kept. Some 400 to 500 children were not accounted for at all. Many others chose to stay with their adopted parents as Christians. Some 400 orphans were taken to Israel after the war accompanied by Adolph Berman.

Jewish organizations and religious authorities demanded immediately after the war in the name of the most elementary principles of justice and human decency that surviving orphans all over Europe, the last precious remnant of their families, should not be torn away from their people and faith, increasing the toll of Holocaust victims. Chief Rabbi of the Holy Land Y. I. Herzog (1888-1959), with the assistance of Rabbi Y. H. Mishkowsky and the Sternbuch family of Switzerland, stood in the frontline of the effort to recover them. Against all odds, they undertook a rescue mission to Europe in 1946. Many obstacles stood in their way, not least the opposition of the Catholic Church to return children who had been baptized.

Rabbi Herzog was painfully aware that without the consent of the Pope the chances of recovering Jewish children all over Europe were minimal and he requested a personal audience with Pius XII. Unlike 1944 when a request for an audience was denied, now, after the collapse of the Third Reich, the Pope agreed to receive the chief rabbi. Rabbi Herzog personally appealed to Pius XII to give his consent to release the Jewish orphans entrusted during the Holocaust to Church institutions and homes. He also asked for his help to locate them in these institutions. The Pope asked him to put his request in writing for consideration.

The original letter has been located in the Vatican archives and was recently published by Andrea Tornielli. In his letter dated March 12, 1946, Rabbi Herzog began by expressing the deep gratitude of the Jewish people for the "refuge given in Catholic monasteries and private homes to thousands of Jewish children." In his letter, here shortened, he restated the oral request made to the Pope to allow the return of these children to their people and faith after 1.2 million Jewish children were murdered. At the same time he petitioned the Pope to condemn the virulent anti-Semitism that had not died with the Holocaust, obviously referring to Poland where the Jewish survivors were facing mortal danger at the time:

ISAAC HERZOG, M.A.D. Litt.
Chief Rabbi of the Holy Land,
Jerusalem

To His Holiness the Pope,
12 March 1946
Your Holiness,
In accordance with the wish . . . I have the honor to submit in writing my petition which I make on behalf of the entire people of Israel . . . Among, those who escaped extermination through obtaining refuge in Catholic monasteries and private homes were thousands of Jewish children. The parents of these children are no more and it falls to me, as the Jewish spiritual leader in Holy Land, to plead for them before Your Holiness . . . The required intimation on the part of Your Holiness to those who now have charge of these children would, we have no doubt, result in their immediate restoration . . . In Poland alone it is estimated that at least 3,000 Jewish children are still in Catholic monasteries and private homes of Catholics.

Need I stress how important these children are for Judaism and the Jewish people? We have lost in the late holocaust some million and two hundred thousand children . . . To the hundred of millions who adhere to the Catholic faith they would be but an insignificant accession. To sorely-diminished Israel every one of them is like to a thousand . . . May I also mention the matter of Your Holiness taking action against the attempts and reviving the poison of anti-Semitism in a number of countries . . . we venture to hope that Your Holiness will likewise use your massive influence to fight this criminal hatred-sowing movement. [69]

Pius XII forwarded the request of Rabbi Herzog to the Holy Office for a decision. Among its members were Msgr. Allois Hudal and Cardinal Giuseppe Pizzardo, secretary of the Holy Office, both well-known Nazi sympathizers. On March 27, 1946, "the most eminent Fathers" of the Holy Office had drawn up a document, which was submitted the following day for the approval of the Pope. They stated categorically that regardless of the way and circumstances in which a child was baptized, the Church could never allow his separation from the Church and his return to his Jewish roots. Furthermore, even nonbaptized Jewish children entrusted to the Church could not be released and "delivered to parties who have no right to them," referring to the Jewish organizations requesting the care of these children.

Although the original report of March 27, 1946, has never been published, its conclusions were made known to Rabbi Herzog and also served as a reference to subsequent official Church documents. Rabbi Berel Wein describes the broken-hearted journey of the chief rabbi to the United States after he verbally received in 1946 the denial that brought to an end the hope of recovering the orphans as a result of a humanitarian good will action. A group of Jewish school children and youngsters was gathered to welcome the highly respected chief rabbi of the Holy Land at the airport in Chicago. At the sight of the beautiful group of American Jewish youngsters he spoke to them heartfelt words with teary eyes:

> My dear children, I come not from Jerusalem, but from Rome where I spoke with the Pope. The Pope did not acquiesce to return the Jewish children hidden in Church institutions during the war; He said that once a child is baptized, he can never be returned. But we still have you![70]

Rabbi Herzog traveled through Europe trying to locate Holocaust orphans. Unlike Poland where such efforts involved the greatest measure of danger, Rabbi Herzog did find understanding in some places, such as the Netherlands where he received the support of Queen Wilhelmina and even of some clergymen. In France, where many of these children had been secretly baptized, the Church was in turmoil, torn between collaborationists and partisans of the Resistance. While the more liberal clergymen were hesitant to deviate from the official doctrine, the collaborationist pro-Vichy circles decided to keep the Jewish children at any cost.

On July 19, 1946, Rabbi Herzog had an audience in Paris with Nuncio Roncalli, the future Pope John XXIII, who had only recently been appointed to France. Although he provided Rabbi Herzog with a letter authorizing him "to use the Nuncio's authority with the relevant institutions so that whenever the case arises, these children may return to their original environment," a letter written by the Grand Rabbi of France Isaiah Schwartz and the head of the Jewish Central Consistory in July 1946 complains to the nuncio that Jewish children were not being released. The letter reminds the nuncio of his pledge to intervene to return Jewish-born children to their community and specifically makes reference to thirty Jewish children living in a Catholic charity that after two years of liberation have not been returned:

> Almost two years after the liberation of France, some Israelite children are still in non-Jewish institutions that refuse to give them back to Jewish charities. [71]

The members of the French episcopate responsible for the Church-run institutions turned to the nuncio and asked him to request from the Vatican clear guidelines on the question of the return of Jewish children. In his dispatch that arrived in the Vatican on September 5, 1946, the nuncio refers to the pleas of Chief Rabbi of France Isaiah Schwartz. He also makes reference to comments made by Cardinal Pierre-Marie Gerlier (1880-1965) of Lyons:

French Bishops originally issued orders that Jewish children who were given refuge in the convents should not be baptized, but some nuns in their excess of zeal had disobeyed the orders, baptizing the little guests and thereby creating a very difficult theological problem.

The gratitude which was often attested to us for the help given to these poor little ones would just as likely be thrown back in resentment, which could foment deplorable polemics.[72]

The reply of the secretariat of state signed by Msgr. Tardini on September 5, 1946, with the approval of Pius XII arrived on September 28, 1946, to the nuncio in Paris. It restates the rulings adopted on March 27, 1946, by the Holy Office, quoted earlier:

The Most Eminent Fathers decided that if possible, there should be no response to the request of the Grand Rabbi of Jerusalem. In any event, if it's necessary to say something, it should be done orally . . . Eventually, it will be necessary to explain . . . that children who were baptized cannot be entrusted to institutions that can't guarantee their Christian education. Furthermore, also those children who were not baptized and who no longer have living relatives, having been entrusted to the Church who received them, as long as they are not able to decide for themselves, they cannot be abandoned by the Church or delivered to parties who have no right to them. It would be something else if the children were requested by their relatives. The decision of the Eminent Fathers and the criteria here presented were referred to the Holy Father in an audience of March 28, and His Holiness deigned to provide his august approval." [73]

The doctrinal principle that considered converts under duress to be full-fledged Christians falling under the jurisdiction of the Holy Office stood behind the fierce persecution of the crypto-Jews that kept Judaism in secret. Even when they fled to other countries to return openly to the faith of their forefathers, the Holy Office would go after them. Vatican historian Fr. Pierre Blet correctly observes that the decision of Pius XII and the Holy Office did not represent a new policy but was in essence the same that his predecessor Pius IX applied a century earlier in the Mortara case.

The famous case of a Jewish child, Edgardo Mortara (1851-1940), abducted by the Church in Italy in 1858 under the "justification" that his Christian nurse baptized him as a six-year-old child when he became gravely ill stood as a precedent for the decision of the Holy Office on March 27, 1946. The Church considered baptism, even when performed illicitly, an irreversible fait-accompli that even stood above parental rights and the law of the land. Violating one of the most fundamental and sacred human rights of parents to their children, Edgardo was separated by force from his family. Pius IX (1792-1878) took personal charge of Edgardo's upbringing. He eventually became an Augustine monk. His devastated parents mourned him until the last day of their life and his aggrieved mother Marianna ended her tortured existence in a mental institution. Reaching old age he witnessed in Belgium the German invasion before his death in 1940.[74] Although Fr. Blet was candid enough to recognize the source of the decision, he failed to acknowledge that the Mortara case was a criminal act in which a six-year-old child was abducted from his parents, violating the Biblical injunction: "And he that stealth a man, and selleth him, or if he be found in his hand, shall surely be put to death" (Exodus 21:16).

The decisions of the Holy Office of March 27, 1946, had devastating consequences. The names and whereabouts of countless Holocaust orphans were maintained by the Church in the strictest secrecy and still remain unknown to the Jewish people to this day. A noble action of rescue was turned into a vile act of abduction. Treated like war booty, they were brought up as Christians and often as priests or nuns in violation of the last wishes of their martyred parents. Jews in Poland alone talk of several hundred contemporary priests—and a like number of nuns—who are Jewish.

The Holy Office decision provides the background of the sadly memorable Finaly Affair that agitated France for eight long years from 1945 to 1953. The Church in France refused to return two Jewish Holocaust orphans, illegally baptized three years after the end of the war, to their paternal aunts who were claiming them. After a protracted legal battle in the courts and a bitter fight in the media the Church was forced to return the orphans to their relatives. Moshe Keller, a Jew in France who literally devoted his life and livelihood to the return of the children, described in his book *L'Affair Finaly*, his extraordinary struggle with the Church.[75]

Dr. Fritz and Annie Finaly entrusted their little children Robert (Reuven) and Gerald (Gad) in February 1944 to the hands of a Christian neighbor before being deported to Auschwitz. Born in 1941 and 1942 respectively in La Tronche near Grenoble in the Vichy zone, the children were circumcised. Their parents left behind a letter in which they expressed their wish that the children should be given over, in case they were not to return, to Dr. Finaly's older sister Margaret Fischel living in New Zealand and be raised in the Jewish faith and tradition.[76] The Christian neighbor to whom the children were entrusted transfered them to the Notre Dame de Sion convent in Grenoble. Since the Finaly children were much younger than the children in the convent they were again transferred to the municipal child care center managed by a Catholic unmarried woman, Antoinette Brun.

As early as February 1945, as soon as France reestablished its prewar international postal communications, the aunt in New Zealand, Margarete Fischel, learned from the mayor of La Tronche about the tragic fate of the Finalys. The mayor added the good news that their little children, Robert and Gerald, had fortunately survived the war and were being cared for in the municipal day care center headed by Mlle. Brun. Mrs. Fischel obtained a New Zealand entrance visa for them and made all the traveling arrangement for the trip of the children to New Zealand by May 25, 1945. Antoinette Brun, in her missionary zeal, had other plans for the children and by different means blocked their return. A legal battle ensued for the custody of the orphaned children in the French courts. To assure the full support of the Church in her struggle, Mlle. Brun baptized the children illicitly in 1948 with the help of a priest, violating the last will of their parents.

Another paternal aunt, Yehudis Rozner, and her husband Moshe, living in Israel much nearer to France, took over in 1948 the legal battle to recover the children. They initiated a desperate court battle with the help of a Jewish resident of Grenoble, Moshe Keller, whom they granted power of attorney. Keller, a survivor who lost his parents and siblings at the hands of the Vichy government, saw the struggle as one more attempt of Vichy France and its Church supporters to destroy Jewish lives while allegedly "saving" souls. His attempt to initiate a civilized dialogue with Mlle Brun failed at the very beginning when he came to speak to her in 1948. Her venomous words made him turn back in shock:

> You coward ungrateful Jews, once under the slightest danger you run away like frightened mice, leaving your kids to the care of others, and now you have the nerve to ask them back? You don't know me yet, never ever are you going to see these kids . . . You will be pleased to know that I let them be baptized. I made them little Catholics.[77]

By himself, Moshe Keller took up the fight for six long years. Nobody had assisted him. The Government of Israel avoided getting involved into a fight with the Vatican. Keller paid a heavy personal price, being forced to give up his well-established chemical engineering firm in Grenoble. The verdicts of the civil French courts at the higher levels ordered the return of the children, but the Church claimed ignorance of their whereabouts. They were taken from Grenoble to a Catholic college in Bayonne in the Basque region. When Keller was tipped off and rushed to Bayonne, the Mother Superior of the Notre Dame de Sion of Grenoble preempted him the previous evening, taking the children away. Several senior nuns of the Notre Dame de Sion Order and Basque priests smuggled the children via the Pyrenees on foot to Spain.

In a public statement, the archbishop of Lyon countered the appeals of the children's relatives declaring that the "Church, being a mother too" cared about the well-being and the souls of the children. The Vatican decided to speak out publically. Cardinal Giuseppe Pizzardo, the secretary of the Holy Office, issued on January 23, 1953, a letter stating that the children belong to the Church:

> The Church has the indefeasible duty of defending the free choice of these children who belong to it by baptism. [78]

Msgr. Giuseppe Roncalli, the future John XXIII who was the nuncio to France during the Finaly affair (1946-1953), left his post some months before the end of the controversy. On his farewell visit to the French President Vincent Auriol on February 20, 1953, the president brought up the Finaly Affair, but the nuncio made nothing of it. He made a note in his diary:

Afternoon, farewell visit to President Auriol, who was most kind as always. He spoke to me about the Finaly matter, to which I showed I attached no importance.[79]

The final verdict was given a few months later on June 23, 1953. by the Cour de Cassation, the highest French Appeals Court, in favor of the relatives of the children. Overwhelmed by a growing negative reaction among the French public at large, the highest Church authorities finally decided to put an end to the nasty controversy. Two days later, the children were "found" in Spain and, with an escort of motorcycled police and reporters driven, from the Spanish border to an estate near Paris belonging to a prominent Jewish family. There, Yehudis Rozner embraced in tears the orphaned sons of her late brother and sister-in-law for the first time.

After a struggle of eight years that were taken away from their lives, the Finaly children, eleven and twelve years old at the time, joined their aunt, uncle and two cousins at their home in Gedera, Israel. Their hearts and souls had been abducted during the crucial years of their upbringing. It took a long time of family love and warmth to break through the wall that the keepers of the children had built around their tender souls against the evil Jews who wanted to harm them. Fifty years later, Robert, the older of the Finaly brothers, today a senior physician at the Soroka Teaching Hospital in Beersheva and not a priest as his keepers intended, spoke to D. Tzaftman in a recent interview:

Q: Do you actually remember the baptism ceremony?
A: Yes. I was six years old at the time. Obviously, we did not object, since we had faith in the education we had received as Christians. We just viewed it as part and parcel of the whole scene.
Q: How did you reach the point where you knew about the efforts being taken to rescue you?
A: By 1948, we had already been warned. We were never left long in one school. We were told that the Jews wanted to take us to Eretz Yisroel, and put us to work paving the streets like common workers. We were told, "You will be put in an orphanage" "you will break stones on the roads, and so on . . .
Q: Can you remember at what stage you became aware of what was happening?
A: Definitely. I remember very well being in the urban kindergarten of the convent Notre Dame du Sion, which was under the management of Miss Brun, we—my brother and I—and four other children, some of whom are still alive.
Q: Did other Jewish children go back to Judaism?
A: No, we were actually the only children who managed to return to Judaism after being brought up as Christians. This was of course thanks to the intensive efforts of our family. It is almost certain that if I would have remained there, I would have been ordained as a young priest.[80]

The autobiography *When Memory Comes* of Holocaust historian Saul Friedlander opens a window into the world of another Holocaust orphan in Church institutions who in a providential manner came back to his people. Friedlander was placed by his parents in a Catholic boarding school in France to save his life at a substantially older age than the Finaly children. Friedlander describes his entrance into the Catholic boarding school:

> As I entered the portals of Saint Beranger, the boarding school of the Sodality where I was to live from now on, I became someone else: Paul-Henri Ferland, an unequivocally Catholic name, to which Marie was added at my baptism, so as to make it even more authentic . . . a new world of the strictest Catholicism . . . almost Royalist, ferociously pro-Petain, anti-Semitic France, including the ladies of the Sodality, who were going to save a soul, but who were also taking serious risks, because the soul they were saving was that of a Jewish child.[81]

When Friedlander's parents brought him to the boarding school, placed before them was the decision to agree to his baptism. They signed the agreement. Friedlander reflects on his father's decision:

> I understand my father's letter: in the same circumstance, in the face of the same drama, would not I, too have written the same lines, given the same authorization, made the same promises? I never knew whether these promises had been explicitly demanded: this is not impossible . . . but what, I wonder would a religious Jew have done confronted with such a terrible dilemma? [82]

As in the case of the Finalys, Friedlander's parents' attempt to escape to Switzerland ended in failure. Turned back to France they were moved from one concentration camp to another until they were finally shipped to Auschwitz. Before his parents were deported, they made sporadic contacts with him. A few pictures and a few letters from them is all that remained. He oscillated "between hatred of Jews, and a vague sense of pride, when he learned one day, that Henri Bergson, almost a Catholic, was in fact a Jew."[83]

Strongly influenced by the Catholic environment in which he was growing up, Friedlander decided to become a priest. On the night before he was to take his vows, the Jesuit priest to whom he was sent for instruction and guidance, revealed to him that he was a Jew whose parents had perished in Auschwitz. As they walked and talked the priest began telling him about Auschwitz, about the extermination of the Jews, about himself. Friedlander recalls:

> I knew nothing of the extermination, [it was all] enveloped in vague images . . . that bore no relation to the real course of events . . . I listened: Auschwitz, the trains, the gas chambers, the cemetery, the ovens, the millions of dead.[84]

It took some time but young Friedlander came back to his people. The rest is history, the history of other survivors like him who from the DP camps longed to reach blockaded Palestine to procure historic justice for their persecuted people.

# Notes

1. Klaus Scholder, *A Requiem for Hitler* (Philadelphia, PA: Trinity Press Int., 1989), 166.

2. Phayer, *The Catholic Church and the Holocaust,* 221.

3. Paul I. Murphy and Rene R. Arlington, *La Popessa: The Controversial Biography of Sister Pascalina, the Most Powerful Woman in Vatican History* (New York: Warner Books, 1983), 228.

4. Gitta Sereny, *Into That Darkness* (New York: McGraw Hill Book Company, 1974), 164, 226.

5. Norman Davies, *God's Playground, A History of Poland* (New York: Columbia University Press, 1982), 551.

6. Paul Johnson, *A History of the Jewish People* (New York, Harper and Row, 1987). Martin Gilbert, *The Holocaust* (New York: Henry Holt and Company, 1987).

7. Lucjan Dobroszycki, "Restoring Jewish Life in Post War Poland", 1972, Soviet Jewish Affairs *3*, pg. 66.

8. Jan Gross, *Fear: Anti-Semitism in Poland After Auschwitz. An Essay in Historical Interpretation* (New York: Random House, 2006).

9. Yehoshua Eibishitz, *Ein Polin Leohr Haner* (New York: Algemeiner Journal, June 27, 1977)

10. *New York Times,* July 10, 1998.

11. Robert S. Wistrich, *Anti-Semitism* (New York: Pantheon Books, 1991). Gershon Chanachovits, *The Forward,* July 3, 1998.

12. Michael C. Steinlauf, *Bondage to the Dead,* (Syracuse University Press, 1997) Chanachovits Gershon. *The Forward*, July 3, 1998.

13. Kersten, *Polacy, Zydzy, Komunism,* 102-103. Steinlauf, *Bondage to the Dead.*

14. Israel Gutman, ed., *Encyclopedia of the Holocaust* (New York: Macmillan Publishing Company, 1990), 373-374.

15. Phayer, *The Catholic Church and the Holocaust,* 181-182, 265 notes 106, 107. M. Marrus, *The Ecumenist.* Vol. 39, Sprong 2002, 1-3.

16. Phayer, *The Catholic Church and the Holocaust,* 181–182, 265 notes 106, 107. M. Marrus, *The Ecumenist.* Vol. 39, Sprong 2002, 1-3.

17. Haim Genizi, *Philip S. Bernstein: Adviser on Jewish Affairs, May 1946-August 1947,* Simon Wiesenthal Center.

18. Draganović who in the past had been professor of the theological faculty of Zagreb was at the time the secretary of the Croat College of San Girolamo, the main center of the Ustashi in Rome.

19. Steven Paskuly, *Death Dealer: the Memoirs of the SS Commandant at Auschwitz,* (Buffalo, NY: Prometheus, 1992), 178.

20. Alois C. Hudal, *Römische Tagebücher, Lebensbeichte eines alten Bischofs.* (Germany: Stocker, Graz, 1976), 298. Aarons & Loftus, 35-39.

21. Hudal, *Römische Tagebücher.*

22. Simon Wiesenthal, *Murderers Among Us the Wiesenthal Memoir* (New York: McGraw Hill Company, 1968). Wiesenthal saw him on August 15, 1942 in Lvov ghetto leading the roundup of 4,000 elderly Jews, including his mother, for the death camps.

23. Hudal, *Römische Tagebücher,* 21

24. Sereny, *Into That Darkness*, 289, 357. Mark Aarons and John Loftus, *Unholy Trinity: The Vatican, The Nazis, and The Swiss Banks* (New York: St. Martin's Griffin, 1998), 26-27. Yitzchak Arad, *Belzec, Sobibor, Treblinka: Operation Reinhard Death Camps* (Bloomington: Indiana University Press, 1987).

25. Commonweal, June 6, 2003.

26. Sereny, *Into That Darkness,* 306.

27. Phayer, *The Catholic Church and the Holocaust*, 159.

28. Sereny. *Into That Darkness*, 315. Phayer, *The Catholic Church and the Holocaust*, 166.

29. Commonwealth, June 6, 2003.

30. Uki Goñi, *The Real Odessa: How Peron Brought the Nazi War Criminals to Argentina* (London, UK: Granta Books, 2003), 205. Fr. Draganovic's own brother Kresimir fled to Argentina on a Red Cross passport in 1948. 248. Note 338.

31. Uki Goñi, *The Real Odessa,* 93-99, 163-179.

32. Aarons and Loftus, *Unholy Trinity,* 198. Goñi, *The Real Odessa*, 39-44.

33. Phayer, *The Catholic Church and the Holocaust*, 170-174.

34. Goñi, *The Real Odessa,* 219. Note 379: Pavelic CIC File, September 12, 1947.

35. Phayer, *The Catholic Church and the Holocaust*, 38.

36. Goñi, *The Real Odessa.*

37. Goñi, *The Real Odessa,* 118, 250, 380, 195-199. Goñi provides the Argentinean immigration file numbers of each of the perpetrators in the list.

38. Matteo Sanfilippo, professor of the University of Viterbo, member of CEANA. *Ratlines and Unholy Trinities: A Review–essay on (Recent) Literature Concerning Nazi and Collaborators Smuggling Operations out of Italy.*

39. Werner Brockdorff, *Flucht vor Nürnberg. Plane und Organisation der Fluchtwege der NS–Priminenz in "Römischen Weg"*, (Munchen: Wels-München, Welsermüuhl Verlag, 1969).

40. Hans Ulrich Rudel, *Zwischen Deutschland und Argentinien. Funf Jahre in Ubersee, Memoiren.* (Gottingen, 1954), Vol. 3, 200.

41. Goñi, *The Real Odessa,* xi–xii, 118, 284, 298.

42. *La Razon*, December 23, 1960. Goñi, *The Real Odessa,* 96.

43. Goñi, *The Real Odessa,* 213.

44. Established in London on October 26, 1943.

45. The first trial of war criminals took place in the Soviet Union in Krasnodar near the Black Sea from July 14 to 17, 1943; thirteen Soviet collaborators of *Sonderkommando* 10a of *Einsatzgruppe* D were tried for the murder of over 7,000 patients using gas vans. Their German commandant SS–*Sturmbannführer* Kurt Christmann escaped to Argentina after the war.

46. Douglas Linder, University of Missouri, Kansas City School of Law.

47. Graf von Galen, *Rechtsbewusstsein und Rechtsunsicherheit* (Rome, March 1946). Phayer, *The Catholic Church and the Holocaust*, 139.

48. Phayer, *The Catholic Church and the Holocaust,* 142.

49. The diaries that are kept at the Catholic University of America became known through M. Phayer.

50. Vol. 3. Published under the Authority H.M. Attorney General by His Majesty's Stationary Office, London 1946, 244-274. The Nizkor Project. Phayer, *The Catholic Church and the Holocaust*, 162-165.

51. Robert Jackson Center, A Prosecutor's Remembrance of Nuremberg. June 7, 2004.

52. Martin Gilbert, *The Holocaust*. Raul Hilberg *Perpetrators, Victims, Bystanders* (New York: Harper Collins, 1933). Gerald Reitlinger, *The SS: Alibi of a Nation* (New York, De Capo Press, 1989). Bradley F. Smith, Agnes F. Petersen, *Heinrich Himmler. Geheimreden 1933 – 1945* (Frankfurt am Main, Berlin/Wien: Propyläen Verlag, 1974), 267 (Edition notes), 273 (Nr. 85) and 300, Note 1.

53. Aarons and Loftus, *Unholy Trinity,* 246, 342 n. 44. Goñi, *The Real Odessa,* 346, 389. Phayer, *The Catholic Church and the Holocaust.* Leni Yahil, *The Holocaust The Fate of European Jewry* (Oxford University Press, 1969).

54. Christopher Simpson, *Blowback* (New York: Weidenfeld and Nicholson, 1988), 180. Goñi, *The Real Odessa,* 387, 553.

55. Faulhaber to the Military Administration , Munich, June 9, 1945, BAM File 7500. Phayer, *The Catholic Church and the Holocaust,* 46.

56. Anthony X. Sutherland, *Dr. Josef Tiso and Modern Slovakia, Cleveland*: First Catholic Slovak U. 1978. 96-97. Pedro Ramet, *Religion and Nationalism in Soviet and East European Politics*, Duke University Press. 274.

57. Frantisek Vnuk. *This is Josef Tiso*. 1977. Cambridge, ON: Friends of Good Books. 65-66.

58. Osservatore Romano, third week of March 1946.

59. Goñi, *The Real Odessa*, 329-333.

60. Phayer, *The Catholic Church and the Holocaust,* 138–144. Eugene Kogon, *The Theory and Practice of Hell* (Archives of the Wiener Library, London). Anonymous-member of the KZLagergemeinschaft Buchenwald. SS-Stuf. Dr. Hans Eisele's activities at Buchenwald. 1938-1941 Eyewitness Accounts: Doc. No. P.III.h. No.927. (Buchen-wald) 5 pages. Reel: 55.

61. The diaries that are kept at the Catholic University of America became known through M. Phayer.

62. Oswald Pohl was convicted of war crimes and executed in 1951.

63. Michael Phayer, *The Catholic Church and the Holocaust, Moment* magazine, 163-165.

64. Gerald Reitlinger, *The Final Solution* (New York: Barnes & Company 1963), 258.

65. Emmanuel Ringelblum. *Polish-Jewish Relations during the Second World War*, (Jerusalem: Yad Vashem 1974), 140-151.

66. Ringelblum, *Polish-Jewish Relations*, 140-151.

67. Michael R. Marrus. *The ambassador & the pope: Pius XII, Jacques Maritain & the Jews* (Pittsburgh, PA: Commonwealth Press, 2004).

68 Debórah Dwork, *Children with a Star* (New Haven, CT: Yale University Press, 1991).

69. Published in its entirety and commented by Andrea Tornielli in Il Giornale on 19 January 2005. The Vatican Files Network.

70 Michael R. Marrus, *The Vatican and the Custody of Jewish Child Survivors after the Holocaust* (Oxford University Journals Article, 2007).

71 . Professor Matteo Luigi Napolitano director of the www.vaticanfiles.net site published a meticulous reconstruction of the document in Avvenire on January 18, 2005. Gianni Valente, *Pius XII, Roncalli and the Jewish children. The facts and the prejudices.* (Journalistic Polemics, January 2005). 30 Days. February 2005. Yaakov Herzog. *Mas'a*

*ha-Hazalah* (Journey of Rescue) (Jerusalem 1947). Rabbi M. Kamenetsky, *Up from the Ashes Parshas Netzavim*, (Project Genesis, Inc. 2001). Rabbi Berel Wein, *Tending the Vineyard: The Life, Rewards and Vicissitudes of Being a Rabbi* (New York: Shaar Press, 2007). Elaine Sciolino and Jason Horio, *Saving Jewish Children, but at What Cost?* (The New York Times, January 9, 2005).

72. Il Giornale, February 11, 2005. Gianni Valente. *Pius XII, Roncalli.*

73. Giussepe Roncalli, Etienne Fouillox Ed, *The French years. Diaries of Nuncio Roncalli 1945-1948], Vol. II.*(2005). Document in the apparatus criticus, October 23, 1946.

74. David Kertzer, *The Kidnapping of Edgardo Mortara* (English Edition –New York, Albert I Knopf, 1997, Hebrew Edition - Kinnereth 2000).

75. Moshe (Moise) Keller, *L'Affair Finaly* (Paris, Librarie Fischbacher,1960).

76. A bag containing the father's medical instruments, some jewelry, pictures, documents, and the letter was recently recovered.

77. Keller, *L'Affair Finaly.*

78. Valente, *30 Days.*

79. Giuseppe Roncalli, *Pope John XXIII. The Journal of a Soul*, originally published in Italian, 4th ed., 1965.

80. D. Tzaftman, *The Children who were Rescued from the Convent. Fifty Years after the Case of the Finaly Children* (Dei'ah veDibur, http://chareidi.shemayisrael.com /archives5764/REI64features2.htm)

81. Saul Friedlander, *When Memory Comes* (New York: Farrar, Straus, Giroux, 1979), 79.

82. Friedlander, *When Memory Comes,* 79.

83. Friedlander, *When Memory Comes,* 79.

84. Friedlander, *When Memory Comes,* 137.

## Epilogue
## After Pope Pius XII's Death

## Nostra Aetate

After the death of Pius XII on October 9, 1958, and the rise to the papacy of John XXIII (1881-1963), the new Pope decided in January 1959 to call an ecumenical council. Petitions arrived in Rome asking that the upcoming council include in its agenda the relationship of the Church to the Jews. Jules Isaac, a French-Jewish historian, whose wife, son, daughter, and son-in-law were deported to the death camps, was invited to Rome for consultation. While in hiding during the war, Isaac was pondering the question of what made the Holocaust happen in Christian Europe. He reached the conclusion that the ultimate blame lay on the Christian Church whose centuries-old tradition of anti-Semitism had incubated the Nazi monstrosity:

> Christian anti-Semitism is the powerful, millennial tree, with many and strong roots, onto which all the other varieties of anti-Semitism—even the most antagonistic by nature, even anti-Christian—have come to be grafted in the Christian world. [1]

The book he published on the question of the relationship of the Church to the Jewish people disturbed the inner peace of many Christian readers, including influential bishops, who in sight of the Shoah began questioning the attitude of their Church to the Jews. While a small minority came to recognize in their hearts that the Christian teachings that singled out Jews among all the nations of the world for persecution were immoral and unjust, the great majority had no problem with accusing all the generations of Jews of such "crimes" as deicide and for refusing to accept Christianity. For these heirs of immemorial hate, a Church declaration on the Jews could at best mean a condescending call to them to abandon the Covenant of Sinai and join the Church. As late as 1961, an article in *L'Osservatore Romano* claimed that the Jewish people "had stained themselves with a horrible crime deserving of expiation." No such thoughts came to their minds concerning the Christians who throughout history victimized the Jews.

Jules Isaac was received in audience by John XXIII on June 13, 1960. He argued for a fundamental reform in Catholic teaching with regard to the Jews, in the name of historical truth and justice. On September 18, 1960, Cardinal Augustine Bea, president of the Secretariat for Promoting Christian Unity, was commissioned by John XXIII to draft a declaration on the Church's relations with the Jews. The struggle that developed within the Church around the declaration brought to the surface all the ancient and modern prejudices against Jews within the Church.

The Second Ecumenical Council of the Vatican, or Vatican II, opened under Pope John XXIII on October 11, 1962, and came to a close three years later on December 8, 1965, under his succesor Pope Paul VI (1897-1978). The news that the conclave was going to discuss Christian teachings concerning Jews was received by the Jewish world with apprehension. Jews were painfully aware of the nefarious anti-Semitic legacy left behind by Church councils during the centuries, as Judith Banki properly pointed out in a conference at the Holocaust Museum commemorating the declaration:

> Jews had good reasons for being apprehensive about church councils. Early councils had subjected them to humiliating and restrictive legislation: forbidden to appear on the streets during Easter, (Third Council of Orleans 538-545); forbidden to officiate as judges, (Council of Mâcon, 581); and the fourth Lateran Council beginning in 1215, gave church-wide endorsement to these and other degrading measures, including the order that Jews must wear a distinctive badge on their clothing; and later rulings outlawed the Talmud, authorized the ghetto, affirmed the validity of forced sermons intended to lead to baptism, and denied Jews admission to the universities. It might be noted that almost every ruling adopted by the Nazis to degrade and de-legitimatize Jews had a precedent in church legislation, except of course, the "Final Solution," and that is a very, very critical distinction and we must remember that it is. [2]

Jews entertained the most serious doubts on the motivation behind the gathering and its possible outcomes and suspected another missionary attempt. Some Jews still remembered the fiasco of Friends of Israel, the missionary Catholic movement in 1928 that wished to facilitate missionary activity among the Jews by removing blatant anti-Semitic expressions from the liturgy. The movement ended up being banned by the Holy Office.

Four different drafts of the declaration on the Jews were produced during the sessions of the council. The first draft, titled *Decretum de Judaeis* (Decree on the Jews), completed in November 1961, seemed to confirm the suspicions of the Jews. The Church's supersessionary belief and missionary zeal came unabashedly to the forefront in the draft:

> Furthermore, the Church believes in the union of the Jewish people with herself as an integral part of Christian hope. With unshaken faith and deep longing the Church awaits union with this people. At the time of Christ's coming, "a rem-

nant chosen by grace" (Rom 11:5), the very first fruits of the Church, accepted the Eternal Word. The Church believes, however, with the Apostle that at the appointed time, the fullness of the children of Abraham according to the flesh will embrace him who is salvation (see Rom 11:12, 26). Their acceptance will be life from the dead (see Rom 11:15). [3]

The second draft, under the title On the Attitude of Catholics toward Non-Christians and Especially toward Jews, was distributed on November 8, 1963, and the third draft, under the title On the Jews and Non-Christians, was presented to the Council on September 28, 1964. This draft also included a paragraph expressing the Church's conviction on the ultimate conversion of the Jewish people:

It is also worth remembering that the union of the Jewish people with the Church is a part of the Christian hope. Accordingly, and following the teaching of Apostle Paul (cf. Rom. 11, 25), the Church expects in unshakable faith and with ardent desire the entrance of that people into the fullness of the people of God established by Christ. [4]

Although the declaration was strictly a Catholic affair, it concerned the Jews, and feelers were sent out to Jewish organizations and personalities. The Jewish reaction to these drafts was not late in coming. At a conference of the RCA, the Rabbinical Council of America (February 3-5, 1964), Rabbi Joseph Dov Soloveitchik (1903-1993), one of the leading voices of Orthodox Jewry in the United States, dismissed the proposed declaration as a condescending absolution of the Jewish people of a mythical guilt while passing over in silence the Church's own real guilt of persecuting an innocent people over the ages. He pointed out the one-sided patronizing nature of so-called dialogues that question the permanent legitimacy of the Jewish faith, which they declare superseded, looking forward to its ultimate liquidation:

A democratic confrontation certainly does not demand that we submit to an attitude of self-righteousness taken by the community of the many which, while debating whether or not to "absolve" the community of the few of some mythical guilt, completely ignores its own historical responsibility for the suffering and martyrdom so frequently recorded in the annals of the history of the few, the weak, and the persecuted . . . The small community has as much right to profess its faith in the ultimate certitude concerning the doctrinal worth of its world formula and to behold its own eschatological vision as does the community of the many. [5]

While he ruled out the medieval theological "dialogues" the council declaration had in mind, Rabbi Soloveitchik welcomed an exchange of views and cooperation in the secular realm:

The relationship between two communities must be outer-directed and related to the secular orders with which men of faith come face to face. In the secular sphere, we may discuss positions to be taken, ideas to be evolved, and plans to be formulated. In these matters, religious communities may together recommend action to be developed and may seize the initiative to be implemented later by general society. However, our joint engagement in this kind of enterprise must not dull our sense of identity as a faith community. We must always remember that our singular commitment to God and our hope and indomitable will for survival are non-negotiable and non-rationalizable and are not subject to debate and argumentation. [6]

In their resolution the rabbis cited the words of the prophet Micah, which laid the foundation of religious tolerance long before liberalism proclaimed the legitimate right of the Jewish people to go their way while the others follow theirs:

It is the prayerful hope of the Rabbinical Council of America that all inter-religious discussion and activity will be confined to these dimensions and will be guided by the prophet, Micah (4:5) "Let all the people walk, each one in the name of his god, and we shall walk in the name of our Lord, our God, forever and ever." [7]

Professor Abraham Joshua Heschel (1907-1972), who maintained close communication with Cardinal Augustine Bea during the consultation process, criticized in the harshest terms the call to conversion contained in the drafts on September 3, 1964:

It must be stated that spiritual fratricide is hardly a means for the attainment of fraternal discussion or reciprocal understanding. A message that regards the Jews as candidates for conversion and proclaims that the destiny of Judaism is to disappear will be abhorred by Jews all over the world and is bound to foster reciprocal distrust as well as bitterness and resentment. As I have repeatedly stated to leading personalities at the Vatican, I am ready to go to Auschwitz if faced with the alternative of conversion or death. Jews throughout the world will be dismayed by a call from the Vatican to abandon their faith in a generation which has witnessed the massacre of six million Jews and the destruction of thousands of synagogues on a continent where the dominant religion was not Islam, Buddhism, or Shintoism. [8]

On the eve of Yom Kippur 1964, Professor Heschel met with Pope Paul VI, the successor of John XXIII, to suggest that the final document should leave out altogether its eschatological dreams of Jewish conversion. When the fourth and final draft was produced it left unmentioned the expectation of ultimate conversion of the Jews, although the belief that the Church superseded the Covenant of the Jewish people was reiterated. The most important issue dealt with by Nostra Aetate (In Our Time) was the question of the collective "guilt" of deicide that the Jewish people allegedly carried from generation to generation. The declaration rejected that belief and postulated that the passion could not be charged "against all Jews then alive nor against the Jews of today":

True, the Jewish authorities and those who followed their lead pressed for the death of Christ; what happened in His passion cannot be charged against all the Jews, without distinction, then alive, nor against the Jews of today. Although the Church is the new people of God, the Jews should not be presented as rejected or accursed by God, as if this followed from the Holy Scriptures.

The fourth draft under the title Nostra Aetate was approved by a vote of 2,221 to 88 on October 28, 1965, and promulgated by Pope Paul VI. Its text was the shortest of the conclave's three declarations. Considering the entrenched nature of the accusation of deicide in Christian teaching and the untold misery that it inflicted on Jewish people over the ages, Nostra Aetate was indeed a revolution. But the admission of Jewish "innocence" by the Church in the historic declaration was not taken to its obvious and logical conclusions: If the Jewish people over the ages were innocent of the accusation, as they were indeed, then the Church had to answer before the tribunal of history and ultimately before God Almighty himself for accusing and persecuting an innocent people. The condescending tone of the declaration as if Jews were finally absolved by a generous Church did not denote contrition at all for the untold misery and indignities inflicted on the children of Israel throughout the ages. The fundamental realization that it is the victimizer, not the victim, who should ask forgiveness for relentlessly persecuting the innocent, was conspicuously absent in the declaration.

## *We Remember:* **A Missed Opportunity**

After the Cain murder of European Jewry, the Church had some explaining to do on its role in the Holocaust, but it took more than fifty years for the Vatican to recognize its moral obligation to look back and examine its record during the Shoah. Pope John Paul II (1920-2005), the successor of Paul VI who had personally witnessed the horror of the Holocaust in his homeland, put the question on the agenda for the first time on August 31, 1987. He delegated Cardinal Johannes Willebrands, president of the Holy See Commission for Religious Relations with the Jews, to produce an official document on the question of Christian responsibility for the Shoah.

The bishops of Holland, France, and Switzerland undertook on their part the examination of their record during the Shoah. As a result of their scrutiny the Dutch Bishops Conference issued a statement in 1995 that acknowledged "a tradition of theological and ecclesiastical anti-Judaism which taught that the Jews were a rejected people contributed to the climate in which the Shoah could take place." They rejected that tradition and expressed their regret for the terrible outcomes of such teachings.

In Switzerland, the Catholic Bishops' Conference recognized in their 1997 declaration that "for centuries, Christians and ecclesiastical teachings were guilty of persecuting and marginalizing Jews, thus giving rise to anti-Semitic sentiments for which we proclaim ourselves culpable, and ask pardon from the descendants of the victims."

In France, the Catholic Bishops Conference issued in 1997 a Declaration of Repentance in which they recognized that silence during the Shoah was a sin and that the Church of France failed in its mission as teacher of consciences. It made responsible those "priests and leaders" of the Church who throughout the centuries allowed the teachings of contempt against the Jews to develop into a collective religious culture that culminated in silence and indifference to the Shoah:

> In the face of so great and utter a tragedy, too many of the Church's pastors committed an offense, by their silence, against the Church itself and its mission. Today we confess that such a silence was a sin. In so doing, we recognize that the Church of France failed in her mission as teacher of consciences.[9]

In Poland, the epicenter of the Holocaust, no such attempts of retrospection and introspection by the Catholic Church were even considered. Instead, the Polish Church became involved in a bitter confrontation with Holocaust survivors and Jews all over the world when it established in May 1985 a convent in Auschwitz-Birkenau. The convent was established in a building that once housed the Zyklon B containers by nuns of the Carmelite Order to "pray for the souls of the murdered and for their oppressors." It was to provide "a guarantee of the conversion of stray brothers." The very thought that prayers were to be elevated for their persecutors and that the Jewish martyrs needed Church prayers to atone for not having been "redeemed" during their lifetime was too much for Jews to bear.

When a big cross, followed by smaller ones, was erected in 1988, the defiant action furthered new resentment. Auschwitz-Birkenau was after all the largest Jewish cemetery in history where the ashes of 1.5 million Jewish victims lay scattered. A cross to mark the collective graves of Holocaust victims was out of place there. This act of deceptive misrepresentation was construed as an attempt to Christianize the Holocaust and erase the memory of Jewish suffering. Elie Wiesel, an Auschwitz survivor, raised his voice in moral indignation. It took more than nine years and the direct intervention of John Paul II who ordered the nuns to move the convent to finally bring the conflict to a close.

The long-awaited Vatican declaration on the Shoah was finally issued on March 16, 1998, by Cardinal Edward I. Cassidy under the name *We Remember: Reflections on the Shoah*. In its introduction, the document promised to examine the Church's historic attitude to Jews through the centuries and its connection to the Shoah and summoned the Jewish friends to listen with open hearts to its words:

> The fact that the Shoah took place in Europe, that is, in countries of long-standing Christian civilization, raises the question of the relation between the Nazi persecution and the attitudes down the centuries of Christians towards the Jews.[10]

*We Remember* acknowledged without any ambiguity the uniqueness and magnitude of the Shoah. It recognized that the Shoah was not fiction but fact:

> This century has witnessed an unspeakable tragedy, which can never be forgotten: the attempt by the Nazi regime to exterminate the Jewish people, with the consequent killing of millions of Jews. Women and men, old and young, children and infants, for the sole reason of their Jewish origin, were persecuted and deported. Some were killed immediately, while others were degraded, ill-treated, tortured and utterly robbed of their human dignity, and then murdered. Very few of those who entered the Camps survived, and those who did remained scarred for life. This was the Shoah. It is a major fact of the history of this century, a fact which still concerns us today. [11]

However when it examined the role of the Catholic Church during the Shoah, those who expected to hear courageous words that feared not truth, were deeply disappointed. The document absolved the Church as an institution of any historical responsibility for the persecution of Jewish people over the ages and refused to acknowledge its role in the events that culminated in the Shoah. *We Remember* rejected any connection between millenial Church anti-Semitism and Nazi anti-Semitism and denied the formidable role played by German Catholicism in the rise of Hitler to power. "Am I my brother's keeper? (Genesis 4:1-16) was given new meaning in the Church document:

> The Shoah was the work of a thoroughly modern neo-pagan regime. Its anti-Semitism had its roots outside of Christianity and, in pursuing its aims, it did not hesitate to oppose the Church and persecute her members also. [12]

The International Jewish Committee on Interreligious Consultations published a carefully-worded response to the document. While it tried to avoid any criticism of John Paul II, it spoke clearly about the failure of the declaration:

> Nobody can doubt the Pope's sincere abhorrence of anti-Semitism but his apparent absolution of the Church from historical responsibility was, at least, puzzling. Jewish reactions went into great detail concerning the misdeeds of the historical Church. [13]

Fr. John T. Pawlikowski, himself a respected Catholic cleric, allowed historical truth to come forward in his highly articulate comments on *We Remember*:

> *We Remember* leaves the strong impression that there was no inherent connection between Nazi ideology and classical Christian anti-Judaism and anti-Semitism. This is basically inaccurate. Among Europe's Christian population, Christian anti-Judaism and anti-Semitism had everything to do with widespread acquiescence and even collaboration with the Nazi policy devoted to the destruction of the Jews. I like to speak of classical Christian anti-Judaism and anti-Semitism as providing an indispensable "seedbed" for Nazism. [14]

Pawlikowski reminded his Church, as the Dutch, Swiss, and French bishops had done earlier, that the anti-Semitic teachings did not originate outside but inside the Church—from its teachers and theologians:

> Nonetheless *We Remember* could have, and should have, made it clearer that the "sons and daughters" of the church who fell into the sin of anti-Semitism did so because of what they had learned from teachers, theologians (including the very important patristic writings), and preachers sanctioned by the institutional church. Reading the document in its present form leaves the impression that the sinful "sons and daughters" of the church who espoused anti-Semitism were led on this path by teachings and teachers apart from the official church.
>
> The Nazi ideologues themselves recognized the connection by drawing upon classical church legislation against the Jews in developing their posture toward the Jewish community. [15]

Pawlikowski referred to most authorized historical studies showing that the original source from where the Nazis learned the methods to turn the Jews into pariahs was canon law.[16] No wonder that the modern canonical law specialists in the Vatican, who were well versed in these ancient decrees, responded approvingly when consulted by the clero-Fascist governments of Europe regarding their anti-Semitic legislative proposals, as already shown.

> Yet we know from many studies on anti-Semitism such as Fr. Edward Flannery's classic volume, "The Anguish of the Jews" as well as from more recent studies such as "The Jewish-Christian Controversy from the Earliest Times to 1789" (edited by William Horbury) and Heinz Schreckenberg's "The Jews in Christian Art" that anti-Semitism permeated Catholic catechesis and preaching and the popular culture it created.[17]

Pierre Savage, who as a child was saved from the Nazis by the Huguenot community of Le Chambon in France, reacted with pain to *We Remember*:

> *We remember: A Reflection on the Shoah* is not merely feeble or vague, as is being said of it. For all its politically correct references to "the unspeakable" and to the "Shoah" the document strikes me as contrived and insincere. It hurts rather than heals . . .
>
> Christians and non-Christians, believers and non-believers, we all live in the shadow of a great lesson: the truth will make you free. The greatest reproach against Pope Pius XII is that he did not speak out when humanity was at a moral crossroads. Why is the Church still so tongue-tied in addressing this monumental failure? Why is it again lagging behind some of its flock? When will it speak clearly and forcefully on the Christian share of responsibility for the Holocaust? All this verbiage and no recognition of the central fact: the Holocaust would not have been possible without the complicity of most Christians and without the virulent tradition of anti-Semitism that had long infested the very soul of Christianity . . . Most tellingly, this theological document completely avoids indicating what, precisely, "might have been expected from Christians. On this, yet again, the document is tongue-tied. If not now, when? if not here, where?"[18]

Author James Carroll branded the attempts of *We Remember* to exonerate the Church as immoral:

> That is why the attempts to exonerate "the Church as such," or even to reduce the Church's failure to what it did not do between 1933 and 1945, are so evasive and finally immoral.
>
> Nazism, by tapping into a deep, ever fresh reservoir of Christian hatred of Jews, was able to make an accomplice of the Catholic Church in history's worst crime even though by then, it was the last thing the Church consciously wanted to be. [19]

Dismayed by the claims advanced by *We Remember*, Professor David Kertzer published his book *The Popes against the Jews*, in which he showed that the Popes of the nineteenth and early twentieth centuries, and Pius XII in particular, paved the way for the Holocaust.

While *We Remember* pointed out correctly that the Nazis wanted to convert the Church into a docile instrument serving the interests of the Nazi totalitarian state, it ignored the far more significant fact of the accommodating response of the Church and its enthusiastic cooperation with the Nazis. While it is true that Nazism was in its very essence a "Godless ideology," the fact that the Church considered Hitler and the Nazis to be the defenders of "Christian Civilization" is passed over in silence. All the well-known momentous political decisions of the Vatican and the German Church hierarchy, beginning with the concordat that helped to consolidate the Hitler regime and legitimize the fledgling Hitler government before its people and the world are ignored.

Forgotten is Pius XII's oral commitment of noninterference with the German solution of the Jewish problem given at the ratification of the concordat; his zealous observance of this commitment throughout the existence of the Third Reich, never mentioning, not even once, the persecuted Jewish people in his messages and public addresses. Instead of invoking religious sanctions against the perpetrators that could have been a "formidable and effective weapon" in the hands of the Church to save lives, he remained silent, even when the Jews of his own city, Rome, were rounded up by the Germans and deported to Auschwitz.[20]

Sixty years after Pius XII refused to visit Auschwitz at the end of the war, his successor Pope Benedict XVI visited Auschwitz-Birkenau on May 28, 2006. There he asked—where was God in those days? Julio Maria Sanguinetti countered that the right question he should have asked is—where was the Catholic Church in those days that the tragedy was unfolding?

> Where was God? Asked the present Pope when he visited the Auschwitz concentration camp and many with unquestionable logic asked him, where was then the Catholic Church, keeping silent at a time that a tragedy of which it was well informed was unfolding?[21]

It was Almighty God who endowed man with free will, who asked Cain the terrifying question: "Where is Abel your brother? What have you done? The voice of your brother's blood cries to me from the ground" (Genesis 4:9-10). This is the question that should be asked to Christian Europe from the hallowed ground that contains the ashes of murdered Jews: Where are the six million Jews that lived among you? What have you done to them?

Even after the war, as survivors were being murdered in Poland, Pius XII refused to speak out and condemn such heinous crimes as the Kielce pogrom. The helping hand of the Vatican and its organizations was instead directed to fugitive Nazi criminals. Pius XII himself often intervened on behalf of perpetrators who were brought to justice. The unqualified exoneration and the empty claim of the declaration that Pius XII did everything in his power to save Jews during the Nazi period was editorially called by the *New York Times*, a whitewash, an attempt to rationalize the conduct of the Church during the Hitler period.

To bolster its claims on how much the Church allegedly did for the Jews during and after the war, *We Remember* referred to the desperate appeals of Jewish leaders in wartime as well as to condolences sent by Jewish leaders at the time of Pius XII's death as proof of the gratitude felt by Jews:

> During and after the war, Jewish communities and Jewish leaders expressed their thanks for all that had been done for them, including what Pope Pius XII did personally or through his representatives to save hundreds of thousands of Jewish lives. [22]

In their tragic helplessness, Jewish representatives were in no position to pronounce words of reproach and could only plead and appease. Aware of the unusual circumstances in which these expressions of unearned gratitude were given, Susan Zuccotti dismissed these testimonials, adding that they were at best "often rooted in benevolent ignorance" and were meant to encourage some measure of goodwill:

> They were anxious to protect and preserve the fragile good-will between Jews and non-Jews that seemed to be emerging from the rubble of the war in Italy. [23]

The real meaning of these alleged statements of gratitude expressed by Jewish representatives to the Vatican was correctly understood by the short-lived Joint Historical Commission of Christians and Jews (1999-2001) in its preliminary report presented to the Vatican on October 2000:

> Such statements of praise were actually desperate appeals for help couched in language of efusive praise. [24]

*We Remember* misrepresented the encyclical *Mit Brennender Sorge* issued in 1937 and the informal comments Pius XI made before a group of Belgian pilgrims in 1938 as if they were protesting the Nazi persecutions of the Jews:

Pope Pius XI too condemned Nazi racism in a solemn way in his Encyclical
Letter Mit Brennender Sorge, which was read in German churches on Passion
Sunday 1937, a step which resulted in attacks and sanctions against members of
the clergy. Addressing a group of Belgian pilgrims on 6 September 1938, Pius
XI asserted: "Anti-Semitism is unacceptable. Spiritually, we are all Semites."

For all its merits, *Mit Brennender Sorge* was a protest against the violations of the concordat by the Nazis and their harassment of Catholic schools and
youth organizations. The persecution of the Jews was not mentioned at all and
anti-Semitism was not condemned.[25] The informal words "spiritually we are all
Semites" Pius XI pronounced before a group of pilgrims of the Belgian radio in
1938 were meant, as already pointed out, to underline the influence of the Hebrew Bible on Christianity. When Pius XI spoke about the contemporary Jews
on that occasion, he explicitly justified taking "defensive actions" against them,
as the Nazis in cooperation with the clero-Fascists were doing:

> We recognize that anyone has the right to defend himself, to take steps to pro-
> tect himself against anything that threatens his legitimate interests. But anti-
> Semitism is inadmissible.

The fact that the Church missed the opportunity and failed to acknowledge
institutionally in *We Remember* the historic role it played in the Shoah and to
come to terms with its moral obligations is not to be taken lightly. It means that
not having found fault with its past actions and policies the Church may continue to consider them as a valid model to follow in the future. The millenial venomous seeds can sprout again anywhere in the world where anti-Semitism can
be put to use to further political, religious, or economic interests.

The failure of *We Remember* should not invalidate, however, the friendly
gestures toward Jews shown by John Paul II to further the goodwill process initiated with *Nostra Aetate*. On April 13, 1986, he visited the Great Synagogue in
Rome where he declared: "With Judaism, therefore, we have a relationship
which we do not have with any other religion. You are our brothers and, in a
certain way, our dearly beloved older brothers." Forty-seven years after the
Shoah, the Vatican extended diplomatic recognition to the state of Israel on December 29, 1993, formally bringing to an end its fierce historic opposition to the
return of the Jews to the land of their forefathers. At the Western Wall he placed
on March 26, 2000, in accordance with the Jewish costum a written prayer
which read:

> God of our fathers, you chose Abraham and his descendants to bring your name
> to the nations. We are deeply saddened by the behavior of those who, in the
> course of history, have caused these children of yours to suffer. Jerusalem 26
> March 2000, Joannes Paulus II. [26]

Although the Polish bishops, refused to look back and examine their record during the Shoah, when *Neighbors*, by Jan T. Grosz, on the Jedwabne massacre appeared, it was not completely lost on them. A group of about 100 Polish priests participated in a ceremony May 28, 2001, commemorating the victims of Jedwabne and other towns and expressed contrition on behalf of the country's Catholics for that specific episode. Bishop Stanislaw Gadecki, who chaired the Polish Bishops' Commission for Interreligious Dialogue spoke in their name:

> We want, as pastors of the Church in Poland, to stand in truth before God and people, but mainly before our Jewish brothers and sisters, referring with regret and repentance to the crime that in July 1941 took place in Jedwabne and in other places . . . Among the perpetrators were also Poles and Catholics, baptized people. We are in deep sorrow over the actions of those who over history, but particularly in Jedwabne and in other places have inflicted suffering on Jews, and even death. [27]

Their declaration stood in stark contrast to the words of nearby bishop of Lomza Stanislaw Stefanek, whose jurisdiction includes Jedwabne, who only one month earlier claimed in his sermon of March 11, 2001, that "Jewish financial interests were behind" what he called the "attack on Jedwabne."

## Denying the Jewish People the Right to Perpetuate their Existence

Although *We Remember* spoke in positive terms of the loyalty of Jews to the "Holy One of Israel and to the Torah," the ultimate aim of the conversion of the Jews was not renounced and was left intact as a part of Christian expectations. Such a belief on the ultimate absorption of the Jewish faith into Christianity is not an inoffensive vision of the end of the days but the perennial source of persecutions against the Jews. By persecuting Jews, the Church intended along the centuries to hasten the fulfillment of the Christian vision of the end of days. The persecutions were supposed to "convince" them to "see the light," and abjure their faith. When Jewish communities chose death or exile over conversion, their loyalty gave place to their vilification as a "stubborn and blindfolded people."

Three years after the publication of *We Remember*, Cardinal Walter Kasper, the successor of Cardinal Edward Idris Cassidy as president of the Pontifical Commission for Religious Relations with the Jews, seemed to be opening new ground at the seventeenth meeting of the International Catholic-Jewish Liaison Committee on May 1, 2001, in New York City. He declared that although the Church will continue to accept individual converts from Judaism out of respect for religious liberty, it will no longer aim at evangelizing the Jewish people who already dwell in a saving covenant, whose mission is to serve as a "distinctive witness to God in human history":

It also acknowledges that Jews who already dwell in a saving covenant with God. However, the evangelizing task no longer includes the wish to absorb the Jewish faith into Christianity and so end the distinctive witness of Jews to God in human history. [28]

Cardinal Kasper's intention to bring an end to Catholic proselytism among the Jews was echoed in a document issued on August 12, 2002, by the Catholic members of the Bishops' Committee for Ecumenical and Interreligious Affairs at a conference with the National Council of Synagogues (an organization of reform and conservative synagogues). The bishop's committee formulated their view in the following words:

A deepening Catholic appreciation of the eternal covenant between God and the Jewish people, together with a recognition of a divinely-given mission to Jews to witness to God's faithful love, lead to the conclusion that campaigns that target Jews for conversion to Christianity are no longer theologically acceptable in the Catholic Church.

The statement immediately aroused strong negative reactions among influential Catholic circles. One Catholic theologian declared it nothing less than apostasy signaling the end of times. A hasty retreat followed announcing that the document "does not represent a formal position taken by the US Conference of Catholic Bishops or the Bishops' Committee for Ecumenical and Interreligious Affairs but was simply intended to summarize the current state of the dialogue and to encourage further reflection among Jews and Catholic."[29] Cardinal Kasper rapidly distanced himself from his own former position.

After the retreat on the eternal validity of the Covenant of Sinai with the Jews, the Catholic theologic pendulum began moving in the reverse direction. When Benedict XVI reintroduced again on July 7, 2007, the Latin Mass to bring back to the Catholic fold the followers of Cardinal Lefebvre, that action aroused much concern inside and outside Catholic circles. An action that seemingly only concerned Catholics, awakened fear because it was perceived as an ominous sign of retreat from Vatican II—a return to the days of the Good Friday prayer that spoke about Jewish faithlessness and blindness that inspired Christians to visit unspeakable calamities on the Jews:

Let us pray also for the perfidious Jews: that Almighty God may remove the veil from their hearts . . . Almighty and eternal God, who dost not exclude from thy mercy even Jewish faithlessness: hear our prayers, which we offer for the blindness of that people; that they may be delivered from their darkness.[30]

Although Pope John XXIII removed in 1960 the word perfidis (faithless Jews) and Pope Benedict XVI deleted on February 4, 2008, the offensive expressions on the "blindness" of the Jews and the "the veil that covers their heart," the main problem with the prayer remained: Its denial of the right of Jewish people to perpetuate their existence until the end of days as servants of the God of Israel according to the covenant at Mount Sinai. Julio Maria Sanguinetti, former Uruguayan president, argued compellingly that at issue was not religious dogma and belief but the principles of tolerance and respect among religions that define a free democratic society:

> The issue goes beyond a religious debate. The prayer questions the principle of tolerance which rules the institutional and social life of modern democratic states . . . When an established religion singles out the believers of another specific religion and demands that whatever is necessary should be done to "save" them, we are already taking the path of intolerance.
>
> With what right are the members of another community that have the same right as they to believe in their God, put in the bench of the accused of living in error? We can not ignore that to do that with the Jews and with "Israel as a whole" which has to be saved, means to go back to those days in which they were accused from the Catholic pulpits of deicide and of being Christ killers.
>
> The prayer itself as an expression of a very serious civic setback is what we should be concerned about. We insist on the word civic because this is a subject that concerns us as citizens.[31]

To question the right of the Jewish people to perpetuate their existence constitutes an affront to the very foundation of human peaceful and just coexistence. No Jew needs to ask permission for himself or his faith to exist and nobody on earth has the authority to take away that God-given right from him. It is sad that after the Shoah there are men who dare to sit in judgment, questioning the right of the oldest faith and nation on earth to exist. They cast lots on the remnant of Israel, at a time that the innocent blood of Jewish men, women, and children continues to cry to heaven from the soil of Europe. As of old, the Jewish people take refuge in the Holy One of Israel to whom they elevate the ancient prayer of their forefathers:

> Guardian of Israel, safeguard the remnant of Israel, allow not Israel to be destroyed—your people who proclaim "Hear O Israel, Hashem is our G-d, Hashem is One!" [32]

# Notes

1. Jules Isaac, *Jesus and Israel* (Austin, TX: Holt, Rinehart and Winston, 1971).

2. Judith Banki, *The Interfaith Story Behind Nostra Aetate* (US Holocaust Museum).

3. *The Drafting of Nostra Aetate* (Boston College, Retrieved 2008-12-26), http://www.bc.edu/research/cjl/meta elements/texts/cjrelations/resources/education /NA_draft_history.htm.

4 . *The Drafting of Nostra Aetate.*

5. Joseph B. Soloveitchik, *Confrontation. Tradition: A Journal of Orthodox Thought, 1964 volume , #2,* ww.bc.edu/research/cjl/metaelements/texts/ cjrelations/resources/articles/soloveitchik.

6. Soloveitchik, *Confrontation,* volume 6, #2.

7 . Statement adopted by the Rabbinical Council of America at the mid-winter conference, February 3-5, 1964. Tradition: A Journal of Orthodox Thought, 1964 volume 6, #2.

8 . Beatrice Bruteau, *Judaism, Holiness in Words: Recognition, Repentance, and Renewal* (Louisville, KY: Fons Vitae, 2003), 223-224. *Time magazine*, Sept. 11, 1964.

9 . L. Gregory Jones, *True Confessions* (Christian Century, Nov. 19, 1997).

10. John T. Pawlikowski, *We Remember: A Reflection on the Shoah* (Vatican City: Libreria editrice Vaticana, 1998), II.

11. Pawlikowski, *We Remember: A Reflection on the Shoah.*

12. Pawlikowski, *We Remember: A Reflection on the Shoah.*

13. International Jewish Committee on Interreligious Consultations, Response to Vatican Document *We Remember: A Reflection on the Shoah* (1998-03-20, www .jcrelations .net/en/?item=1016).

14. Pawlikowski, *We Remember*. John Pawlikowski, *John Paul II and Interreligious Dialogue,* (Shofar: Vol. 20. N.2 2002), 156-158. Judith H. Banki and John T. Pawlikowski, *O.S.M. Ethics in the Shadow of the Holocaust: Christian and Jewish Perspectives* (Chicago IL: Sheed and Ward, 2002) 364.

15. Pawlikowski, *John Paul II and Interreligious Dialogue,* 156-158. Banki and Pawlikowski, *O.S.M. Ethics in the Shadow,* 364.

16. Raul Hilberg, *The Destruction of the European Jews* (Teaneck, NJ: Holmes & Meier, 1985). Carol Rittner, Stephen D. Smith, and Irena Steinfeldt, *The Holocaust and the Christian World: Reflections on the Past, Challenges for the Future* (Toronto, ON: Balfour Books, 2004) 37.

17. John Pawlikowski, *John Paul II and Interreligious Dialogue* (Shofar: Vol. 20. N.2, 2002), 156-158. Banki and Pawlikowski, *O.S.M. Ethics in the Shadow,* 364.

18. Harry James Cargas, *Holocaust Scholars Write to the Vatican* (Santa Barbara, CA: Praeger Publishers, 1998). Pierre Sauvage, *The Vatican Fails To Remember the Holocaust, Chambon Foundation,* (Santa Barbara, CA: Greenwood Press, 1998).

19 . James P. Carrol, *Constantine's Sword: The Church and the Jews*, (Boston, MA: Houghton Mifflin Company, 2001).

20. Saul Friedlander, *Nazi Germany and the Jews, Vol.1.* (New York: Harper Collins Publishers, 1997). On November 1943, Pius XII authorized a courier of the senior German Cardinal Bertram of Breslau to make public the statement. The courier, a double agent, also reported the Pope's statement to Kaltenbrunner on December 16, 1943.

21. *Catolicos, Judios y Ciudadanos*. Article published on 03/11/08 in El Pais, Uruguay.

22. Susan Zuccotti, *Under His Very Windows: The Vatican and the Holocaust in Italy* (New Haven: Yale University Press, 2000), 301.

23. Zuccotti, *Under His Very Windows.*

24. Question forty-five of the preliminary report of the Joint Christian–Jewish Commission of October 2000.

25. "The other part emasculated the terms of the treaty, distorted their meaning, and eventually considered its more or less official violation as a normal policy."

26. E. Fisher & L. Klenicki, Spiritual Pilgrimage: Pope John Paul II on Jews and Judaism 1979–1995 (1995); New Catholic Encyclopedia Jubilee Volume: The Wojtyla Years (2001).

27 . Monika Scislowska, *Polish bishops apologize for 1941 Jewish massacre* (2001 Athens Newspapers, Inc. Athens Online).

28. Center for Christian Jewish Understanding . Reflections on Covenant and Mission. Consultation of the National Council of Synagogues and the Delegates of Bishops Committee for Ecumenical and Interreligious Affairs. Sacred Heart University. August 12, 2002. http://www.sacredheart.edu

29. Deal Hudson, Carl Olson (Envoy Magazine); Fr. James V. Schall, SJ, Dr. Ronda Chervin, Fr. Francis Martin and others voiced their criticism of the document in a symposium for the National Catholic Register.

30. Rabbi David Rosen president of the International Jewish Committee commented: "Any liturgy, such as the 'Indult' Mass, that presents Jews as being doomed in their faith doesn't present a healthy attitude towards Judaism and the Jewish people."

31. *Catolicos, Judios y Ciudadanos*. Article published on 03/11/08 in El Pais, Uruguay.

32 . *The Complete Artscroll Siddur. Daily Morning Prayer* (New York: Artscroll Mesorah Publications, 90).

# BIBLIOGRAPHY

Aarons, Mark and Loftus, John. *Unholy Trinity: The Vatican, the Nazis and the Swiss Banks*, New York: St. Martin's Griffin, 1998

Albrecht, Dieter. *Der Notenwechsel zwischen dem Heilign Stuhl und der deutschen Reichsregierung*. Mainz: Matthias Grunewald Verlag, 1965.

Bentley, Eric, ed. *The Storm over the Deputy*. New York: Grove Press Inc., 1964.

Bergen, Doris. *In God's Name: Genocide and Religion in the Twentieth Century*. New York: Berghahn Books, 2000)

Bergen, Doris. *The Sword of the Lord: Military Chaplains from the First to the Twenty First Century*. Notre Dame, IN: Notre Dame University Press, 2004.

Blet, Pierre SJ. *Pius XII and the Second World War According to the Archives of the Vatican*. New York: Paulist Press, 1999.

Boatner, Mark. *The Biographical Dictionary of World War II,* Novato, CA: Presidio Press, 1996 .

Braham, Randolph L. *The Vatican and the Holocaust. The Catholic Church and the Jews during the Nazi Era*. New York: Columbia University Press, 2000.

Breitman, Richard. *Official Secrets: What the Nazis Planned, What the British and Americans Knew*. New York: Hill and Wang, 1998.

Browning, Christopher R. *The Origins of the Final Solution*. Lincoln, NE: University of Nebraska Press, and Jerusalem: Yad Vashem, 2004.

Bukey Burr, Evan. *Hitler's Austria*. Chapel Hill, NC: The University of North Carolina Press. 2000.

Bullock, Allan. *Hitler: A Study in Tyranny* London, UK: Odhams, 1952.

Carroll, James. *Constantine's Sword: The Church and the Jews. A History*. Boston, MA: Houghton Mifflin Company, 2001.

Cornwell, John. *Hitler's Pope: The Secret History of Pius XII*. New York: Viking, 1999.

Djilas, Aleksa. *The Contested Country: Yugoslav Unity and Communist Revolution, 1919-1953.* Cambridge, MA: Harvard University Press, 1991.

Domarus, Max ed. *Hitler: Reden und Proklamationen 1932-45*, Wurzburg: 1962.

Dwork, Deborah & Van Pelt, Robert J. *Holocaust, a History.* New York: W. W. Norton & Company, 2002.

Falconi, Carlo. *The Silence of Pius XII.* Boston, MA: Little Brown and Company. 1965.

Faulhaber, Michael. *Akten Kardinal Michael von Faulhabers 1917-1945.* Mainz , 1978.

Faulhaber, Michael von. *Judaism, Christianity, Germany.* New York: Macmillan, 1934.

Feingold, Henry L. *The Politics of Rescue.* New York: Holocaust Library, 1970.

Fischer, Klaus P. *The History of an Obsession: German Judeophobia and the Holocaust.* New York: Continuum Press, 1998.

Flannery, Edward. *The Anguish of the Jews. Twenty-Three Centuries of Anti-Semitism.* New York: Stimulus Books. 1965

Fleming, Gerald. *Hitler and the Final Solution.* Berkeley, CA: University of California Press, 1984.

Fremantle, Anne. *The Papal Encyclicals in their Historical Context.* New York: Mentor, 1956.

Friedlander, Saul. *Nazi Germany and the Jews. Vol. 1,* New York: Harper Collins Publishers, 1997.

Friedlander, Saul. *Pius XII and the Third Reich,* New York: Alfred A. Knopf, 1966.

Friedlander, Saul. *Kurt Gerstein.* New York: Alfred A. Knopf, 1969.

Friedman, Philip. *Their Brothers' Keepers.* New York: Holocaust Library, 1978.

Fromm, Bella. *Blood and Banquets: A Berlin Social Diary.* York: Kensington Publishing Corp, 2002.

Fuchs, Abraham. *The Unheeded Cry.* New York: Mesorah Publications 1984.

Godman, Peter. *Hitler and the Vatican.* New York: Free Press, 2004.

Goldhagen, Daniel J. *Hitler's Willing Executioners.* New York: Alfred A. Knopf, 1996.

Goldhagen, Daniel J. *A Moral Reckoning.* New York: Alfred A. Knopf, 2002.

Goñi, Uki. *The Real Odessa. Smuggling the Nazis to Peron's Argentina.* London, UK: Granta Books, 2002.

Grosz, Jan T. *Neighbors. The Destruction of the Jewish Community of Jedwabne, Poland.* Princeton, NJ: Princeton University Press, 2001.

Grunberger, Richard. *The 12-Year Reich.* New York: Holt, Reinhart and Winston, 1971.

Hamman, Brigitte. *Hitler's Vienna. A Dictator's Apprenticeship.* New York: Oxford University Press, 1999.

Heiden, Konrad. *The Führer.* New York, Carroll & Graf Publishers, Inc. 1999.

Helmreich, E. C. *The German Churches under Hitler.* Detroit, MI: Wayne University Press. 1979.

Herczl, Moshe Y. *Christianity and the Holocaust of Hungarian Jewry.* New York: New York University Press, 1993.

Hilberg, Raul. *The Destruction of the European Jews.* 3 Vols. Chicago, IL: Quadrangle Press, 1961.

Hitler, Adolf. *Mein Kampf* (Reissue edition). Boston, MA: Mariner Books, 1998.

Höss, Rudolf. *Commandant of Auschwitz: The Autobiography of Rudolf Höss.* New York: Phoenix Press, 2000.

Höss, Rudolf. *Death Dealer: The Memoirs of the Ss Kommandant at Auschwitz.* New York: Phoenix Press, 2000.

Katz, Robert. *Black Sabbath: A Journey Through a Crime Against Humanity.* New York: Macmillan Publishing Company, 1969.

Katz, Robert. *Death in Rome.* Macmillan Publishing Company, 1967.

Kertzer David, I. *The Popes against the Jews: the Vatican's Role in the Rise of Modern Anti-Semitism.* New York: Alfred A. Knopf, 2001.

Klee, Ernst, Dressen, Willi and Ries, Volker. *The Good Old Days. The Holocaust as Seen by its Perpetrators and Bystanders.* New York: Konecky, 1988.

Kogon, Eugen, *The Theory and Practice of Hell: The Concentration Camps and the System Behind Them.* New York, 1950.

Koonz Claudia, *The Nazi Conscience.* Cambridge, MA: BelknapPress of Harvard University Press, 2005

Kranzler, David. *Japanese, Nazis and Jews: the Jewish Refugee Community of Shanghai 1938-45.* New York: Yeshiva University Press, 1976.

Kranzler, David. *The Man who Stopped the Trains to Auschwitz.* Syracuse University Press, 2000.

Kühner, Hans. *Der Anti-Semitismus der Kirche.* Verlag Die Waage, Zurich 1976.

Lewy, Guenther. *The Catholic Church and Nazi Germany.* New York: Mc Graw Hill Companies, 1964.

Manhattan, Avro. *The Vatican in World Politics. Chap. 9.* Gaer Associations, Inc, 1949.

Marrus, Michael R. *The Holocaust in History.* University Press of New England, 1987.

Marrus, Michael R. *The Vatican on Racism and Anti-Semitism 1938-39: A New Look at a Might Have Been.*

Marrus, Michael and Paxton, Robert. *Vichy France and the Jews.* New York: Schoken Books, 1983.

Mc Donald, James G, *Advocate for the Doomed: The Diaries and Papers of James G. McDonald, 1932-1935*. Indiana University Press, 2007.

McKale, Donald M. *Hitler's Shadow War*. New York: Cooper Square Press, 2002.

Modras, Ronald. *The Catholic Church and Anti-Semitism*. Poland, 1933-1939. Newark NJ: Harwood Academic Publishers. 1994.

Michael, Robert. *A Concise History of American Anti-Semitism*. Lanham, MD: Rowman & Littlefield, 2005.

Michaelis, Meir. *Mussolini and the Jews*. Oxford: Clarendon Press. 1978.

Morley, John F. *Vatican Diplomacy and the Jews During the Holocaust 1939-1943*. New York: Ktav Publishing, 1980.

Morse, Arthur, *While Six Million Died: A Chronicle of American Apathy* New York : The Overlook Press, 1983.

Müller, Filip. *Eyewitness Auschwitz: Three Years in the Gas Chambers* (Unknown Binding, Paperback, 1999.

Murphy, Paul I. and Arlington, Rene, R. *La Popessa: The Controversial Biography of Sister Pascalina, the Most Powerful Woman in Vatican History*. New York: Warner Books, Viking, 1983.

Noakes, Jeremy and Pridham, Geoffrey. *Nazism 1919-1945*. New York: Schocken Books, 1983.

Nobécourt, Jacques. *Le Vicaire et l'Histoire*. Paris: Editions du Seuil, 1964.

Parker James and Dee, Ivan R., *Anti-Semitism*. London, UK: Valentine Mitchell & Company, 1965.

Passelecq, Georges and Suchecky, Bernard. *The Hidden Encyclical of Pius XI*. New York: Harcourt Brace & Company, 1997.

Pawlikowski, John. *The Legacy of Pius XII*. Catholic International, Oct. 1998.

Peck , Abraham L., *American Jewish Archives vol. 8.,* Cincinnati, Oh: Wayne State University Press, 1990.

Phayer, Michael. *The Catholic Church and the Holocaust 1930-1965*. Indiana University Press, 2000.

Rauschning, Hermann. *Hitler Speaks*. London, UK: Thornton Butterworth, 1939.

Reitlinger, Gerald. *The Final Solution*. New York: A. S. Barnes & Company, 1953.

Rhodes, Anthony. *The Vatican in the Age of Dictators, 1922-1945*.London, UK: Hodder & Stoughton, 1973.

Rhodes, Richard. *Masters of Death, the SS Einsatzgruppen and the Invention of the Holocaust*. New York: Alfred A. Knopf, 2002.

Rittner, Smith & Steinfeldt. *The Holocaust and the Christian World*. New York: Continuum, 2000.

Scholder, Klaus. *A Requiem for Hitler and Other Perspectives on the German Church Struggle*. London UK: Trinity Press International, 1989.

Scholder, Klaus. *A Requiem for Hitler and Other Perspectives on the German Church Struggle*. London UK: Trinity Press International, 1989.

Sereny, Gitta. *Into That Darkness*. New York, McGraw Hill Book Company. 1974.

Shirer, William L. *The Rise and Fall of the Third Reich*. New York: Simon and Schuster, 1959.

Spector, Robert Melvyn. *World without Civilization: Mass Murder and the Holocaust, History, and Analysis*. University Press of America, 2004.

Steinberg, Jonathan. *All or Nothing: The Axis and the Holocaust, 1941-1943*. New York: Rutledge, 1990.

Taylor, Telford, *Sword and Swastika: Generals and Nazis in the Third Reich*. New York: Barnes and Noble Books, 1995.

Tec, Nechama, *When Light Pierced the Darkness*. Oxford University Press 1986

Von Papen, Franz. *Memoirs*. New York: E. P. Dutton & Company, 1953.

Waagenaar, Sam. *The Pope's Jews*, La Salle, IL: Open Court Publishers, 1974.

Webster. *Petain's Crime*. Chicago IL: Ivan R. Dee, 1991.

Weissmandel, Michael Dov. *Min Hameizar*. Brooklyn NY: Emunah, 1960.

Wills, Garry. *Papal Sin: Structures of Deceit*. New York: Doubleday, 2000.

Zahn, Gordon. *German Catholics and Hitler's Wars: A Study in Social Control*. New York: Sheed and Ward, 1962.

Zuccotti, Susan. *Italians and the Holocaust*. New York: Basic Books, 1987.

Zuccotti, Susan. *Under His Very Window: The Vatican and the Holocaust*, New Haven, CT: Yale University Press, 2000.

# Index

# About the Author

Born and raised in Mexico City, David Cymet was one of the first two Latin American students in American Rabbinical schools. He spent four years as a student at Mesivta Torah Vodaath in Brooklyn, NY, where he arrived in 1944 during World War II. Subsequently, he graduated as an architect from the School of Architecture and Engineering (ESIA) of the Instituto Politecnico Nacional of Mexico and taught at his alma mater for a number of years. He was instrumental in introducing an innovative academic program that brought about positive change in the teaching of architecture. During the 1960s, upon the establishment of the Graduate Division of the Facultad de Architectura of the National University of Mexico (UNAM) he was appointed there as a professor. In 1983 he spent a year at MIT as a Spurs fellow and obtained a Masters degree (MCP). In 1991 he obtained his doctorate at the University of Delaware. His doctoral thesis was published by the American University Studies.

Dr. Cymet has held senior positions in various agencies of the Mexican government, such as the National Housing Institute (INV) during the 1950s and at the Ministry of Human Settlements (SAHOP) in the 1970s. His policy proposal to President Jose Lopez Portillo to create a Ministry of Energy led to the establishment of that ministry by his successors in the 1990s. After a distinguished career in the academic and public sectors in Mexico, he relocated to the United States in 1986 where he worked for the Department of Education in New York City.

As a student of the Holocaust since his earliest youth, Dr. Cymet devoted himself full time during the last eight years to research and produce this study. *History vs Apologetics* is the result of the commitment.